1994

After the
Trail of Tears

The

Cherokees'

Struggle for

Sovereignty,

After the

1839–1880

Trail of Tears

William G. McLoughlin

The University of

North Carolina Press

Chapel Hill and

London

© 1993 The University of
North Carolina Press

All rights reserved

Manufactured in the United States
of America

The paper in this book meets the guidelines
for permanence and durability of the
Committee on Production Guidelines for
Book Longevity of the Council on Library
Resources.

The publisher wishes to express its gratitude
to Walter H. Conser, Jr., for his generous
editorial assistance following the death of
William G. McLoughlin.

The publication of this work was made
possible in part through a grant from the
Division of Research Programs of the
National Endowment for the Humanities, an
independent federal agency whose mission is
to award grants to support education,
scholarship, media programming, libraries,
and museums, in order to bring the results of
cultural activities to a broad, general public.

Library of Congress
Cataloging-in-Publication Data

McLoughlin, William Gerald.
After the Trail of Tears : the Cherokees'
struggle for sovereignty, 1839–1880 /
William G. McLoughlin.
p. cm.
Includes bibliographical references and index.
—ISBN 0-8078-2111-X (cloth : alk. paper)
ISBN 0-8078-4433-0 (pbk.: alk. paper)
1. Cherokee Indians—History—19th
century. 2. Cherokee Removal, 1838.
3. Cherokee Indians—Politics and
government. 4. Cherokee Indians—
Government relations. I. Title.
E99.C5M388 1993
973'.04975—dc20   93-18532
  CIP

97 96 95 94 93   5 4 3 2 1

This book is

gratefully dedicated to

Virginia, Helen, Gail, and Martha—

"To tell you that you're wonderful,

Too wonderful for words."

Contents

Maps

Introduction

*Whereas, it being the anxious desire of the Government of
the United States to secure the Cherokee nation of Indians . . .
a permanent home, and which shall, under the most solemn
guarantees of the United States, be and remain theirs forever—a
home that shall never, in all future time, be embarrassed by
having extended around it lines, or placed over it the jurisdiction
of any of the limits of any existing Territory or States . . . the
parties hereto do hereby conclude the following Articles.*

—Treaty of 1828

In 1831 the U.S. Supreme Court, led by Chief Justice John Marshall, defined the Cherokees as "a domestic, dependent nation." The Cherokees put the emphasis on "nation"; the Bureau of Indian Affairs put the emphasis on "dependent." Congress preferred to define Indians as "wards of the government." This is a study of how these varying interpretations worked themselves out in the years 1839–80. However, more was at stake than legal definitions.

The United States went through a major reorientation in race relations during the first administration of Andrew Jackson. Historians have generally agreed that the rise of the Cotton Kingdom, the nullification crisis, and the launching of William Lloyd Garrison's abolition movement in the years 1828 to 1832 led the way to the sectionalism of the Civil War and the consequent emancipation of the slaves. As George Fredrickson, a preeminent historian of racism, has noted, the "apparently paradoxical fact that the abolitionists could thus gain support for their attack on slavery at the very time a newly systemized doctrine of black inferiority was also triumphing in American thought" deserves attention.[1] Somewhat less noted in the history of racism was the dramatic change that took place in racial attitudes toward and among Native Americans with the passage of Jackson's Indian Removal Act in 1830. Jackson was not only a southern slaveholder but also a western Indian fighter, and freeing the "West," then the eastern half of the Mississippi Valley, of

Indians so that it could be settled by white pioneers was his first goal as president.

However, beyond this lies another paradox. By 1830 the southeastern tribes (Cherokees, Creeks, Choctaws, Chickasaws, and Seminoles), who held millions of acres of land in the Cotton Belt, were known as "the most civilized tribes in America" and had adopted the agricultural system of their white neighbors, including the institution of black chattel slavery. Yet Jackson engineered their removal across the Mississippi on the grounds that they were too savage to compete with whites: "Established in the midst of another and a superior race and without appreciating the causes of their inferiority or seeking to control them, they must necessarily yield to the force of circumstances and ere long disappear." [2]

To assess the impact of racism on the Cherokee Nation, this book examines the role of slavery in Cherokee culture after removal and the crisis it brought to the Cherokees in 1861 when they were forced to decide whether to take part in the white man's Civil War. Central to that issue, and to all of the questions facing Native Americans in the years 1830 to 1887, was the deep-seated question of Indian sovereignty. Were the 300 or so Indian "nations" with whom the United States dealt through treaties (and whom the various missionary societies classified under "foreign" missions) sovereign, or were they simply ethnic enclaves subject to the same assimilation process as foreign-born immigrants? If they were not assimilable, then must they be relegated to reservations to eke out their few remaining years until, like the buffalo, they became extinct? They could hardly be treated like the "unassimilable" Chinese and Japanese, who were prevented from entering the United States. Paradoxically, although white Americans (whether they were Indian reformers or Indian haters) concluded after 1865 that the "Indian race" could not succeed in competition against the Aryan or Teutonic races, Indians were told that they must give up their primitive, "non-American" method of owning tribal land in common and become homesteaders; that is, they must be detribalized and become American citizens. Few expected them to survive for long, but it was considered their only chance; "survival of the fittest races" was as divinely ordained as survival of the fittest farmers or businesspeople.

By 1830 most Native Americans were well aware that deeply ingrained prejudice would reduce them to second-class citizens if they ever gave up their status as independent nations. The Cherokees had adopted a constitution modeled on that of the United States in 1827 and, in effect, declared their independence from any ties to the United States, except for those mutually agreed upon in treaty obligations. Other tribes also insisted on their independence, arguing that while treaties required their diplomatic alliance with the

United States, they also guaranteed their right to self-government under their own elected officials and according to their own laws and customs. Although there was a certain amount of dependence upon foreign aid and assistance from the United States implicit and explicit in their treaties, as one Cherokee chief noted in 1871, "Dependence does not destroy sovereignty."[3]

The tactics and arguments used by the Cherokees in the nineteenth century are still drawn upon by Native Americans presently struggling for sovereignty—a word that does not mean simply self-government or autonomy but something of far deeper cultural significance, in some respects equivalent to ethnic and political separatism. In her 1988 book *Sovereignty and Symbol*, a study of recent Mohawk conflicts in New York State, Gail H. Landsman quotes a Mohawk spokesperson who says in 1988, "We shall resist by every means any aggression, any violation of the treaties, any disturbance of our people in the free use and enjoyment of our land, any usurpation of our sovereignty, and encroachment and oppression."[4] Landsman writes that members of many tribes teach their children (as the Cherokees did in the nineteenth century): "Boys and girls, the sermon today is do not call yourselves 'tribes' and your land 'reservations.' Stand on your own two feet and insist that you are a NATION and that your land is your TERRITORY."[5]

The forty years after the Trail of Tears constitute an all-but-forgotten era in Cherokee history. Historians have focused after 1839 upon the Indians of the Great Plains, whose heroic defense of their homelands in the last of the Indian wars distracted attention from the equally—if not more—significant struggle of the southeastern nations to retain their sovereignty by diplomacy in Washington, D.C. Between 1839 and 1880, the Cherokees, having lost 4,000 of their 18,000 people on the Trail of Tears, rebuilt their homes and farms, roads and bridges, mills and shops, in the northeast corner of the Indian Territory (present-day Oklahoma). They reinstituted their bicameral legislature and judicial system (modeled on that of the United States but retaining crucial aspects of their traditions) and inaugurated their own public school system to replace that of the missionaries (which the United States subsidized prior to 1830). They survived a serious guerrilla campaign from 1839 to 1846 involving those whom they held responsible for the false treaty that enabled Jackson to remove them. By the 1850s their nation was thriving once again, a showcase for foreign visitors of the progress that Indians could make in "civilization" and "Christianization."

The Cherokees then faced the dilemma of the Civil War, during which everything they had rebuilt was destroyed. From 1865 to 1880, they reconstructed their social order once again, but this time under regimes led by the full-bloods (non-English-speaking Cherokees), who had fought with the

North against the mixed-blood slaveholding Cherokees, who had fought with the South. They also struggled, as did white Americans, with the problem of granting citizenship to their former slaves. However, Cherokee sovereignty was now under a new series of attacks by railroads demanding land and rights-of-way, business speculators seeking timber and mineral rights, cattle herders seeking the right to graze their cattle on Cherokee land and drive them through the nation to meet the railroads in Missouri and Kansas, and especially white homesteaders intruding onto their land, claiming that most of it was "vacant" and therefore available to all citizens. The last stages of their battle for cultural sovereignty were waged in the halls of the U.S. Congress, where the Cherokees spent thousands of dollars yearly lobbying (and sometimes bribing) congressmen to defeat dozens of bills that sought to denationalize them and transform the Indian Territory (despite treaty guarantees) into a federally administered territory and ultimately a state in which whites would become the dominant majority.

It is astonishing that the Cherokee Nation survived so long given the intense forces working against it from outside and the equally intense factionalism that wracked it from within. There were few better statesmen and diplomats than the Cherokee chiefs and delegates to Congress in these years. They had learned to use every tactic of the white politician to defend their rights, and, where points of law were at stake, they spent thousands of dollars each year to obtain the service of the best lawyers money could buy.

To provide context, this book examines the evolution of Cherokee society, economics, and politics—the sources of factionalism, the role of women, the nature of farming, shopkeeping, herding, electioneering, family life, and religion. By 1830 the Cherokees had become a nation of nuclear families living on their own farmsteads and locked into a free-market economy linking them to the surrounding states, with whom they bought and sold. This society developed the beginnings of a class system in which those with large enterprises (cattle herds, corn and wheat fields, cotton plantations, merchandise trading) became increasingly alienated from the small, subsistence farmers. With care, it is possible to note correlations between those who were wealthy or those who were poorer and their acculturation or adherence to traditionalism— those who spoke and wrote only English or those who spoke and wrote only Cherokee, those who were of mixed ancestry or those who tended to marry only other full-bloods, those who were slaveholders or those who were not, those who were Christians or those who adhered more closely to their old religion. One of the striking differences between the Cherokee and the white slaveholding cultures is that among the Cherokees the poor dirt farmers did not, as in the Deep South, fight side by side with the rich slaveholders in the

Civil War but against them. One of the striking similarities was the existence in the Cherokee Nation of a populist movement after 1865 in which the same Cherokee-speaking dirt farmers (the large majority) adopted the white political strategies of the United States to elect their own leaders to replace the wealthy mixed-bloods. Similar too was the loss of power (though not prestige) for most Cherokee women as acculturation confined their functions within the terms of "the cult of domesticity" and deprived them of the leadership roles they had previously held.

I also delineate those vital sources of Cherokee strength and endurance that enabled them to face and overcome one catastrophe after another. This inner strength, I believe, came essentially from what they called "the Keetoowah spirit" (variously spelled "Ketoowha," "Kituwha," etc.) of loyalty to each other, concern for the spiritual power in their way of life, and their insistence upon the fundamental importance of tribal unity and harmony. No one can study the Cherokees without coming away with deep respect for their dignity, their familial commitment, their intelligence, and their profound generosity of spirit.

This is the story of how the Cherokees twice rebuilt their nation between 1839 and 1880, defined themselves as a people, and fought a crucial episode in the long battle for tribal sovereignty. Though small in scale, it is epic in its significance for the history of the United States in its years of white supremacy, manifest destiny, and imperialist expansion. Along with the Cherokees, white Americans were defining themselves as a multiracial nation. The relationship between the two countries—the United States and the Cherokee Nation— was symbiotic; we cannot historically understand one without understanding the other. For better or worse, each brilliantly illuminates the significant features of the other.

The lands ceded to the Cherokee nation in [the Indian Territory] . . .
shall in no future time, without their consent, be included within the
territorial limits of jurisdiction of any State or Territory. But they shall
secure to the Cherokee nation the right, by their national councils, to make
and carry into effect all such laws as they may deem necessary for the
government . . . within their own country.
—*Cherokee Treaty of 1835*

Amid the decay of Indian Nations . . . the five nations [Cherokee,
Creek, Chickasaw, Choctaw, and Seminole] . . . have not only survived
but increased in numbers, accumulated property, [and] advanced in
civilization. . . . All this prosperity under God and His gospel, we
owe to our separate national existence and the protection and
security afforded by our treaties.
—*Chief Lewis Downing, 1870*

The policy of the United States liquidating the institutions of the
Five Tribes was a gigantic blunder that ended a hopeful experiment in
Indian development, destroyed a unique civilization, and degraded
thousands of individuals.
—*Angie Debo,* And Still the Waters Run *(1972)*

1

Removal and the
Politics of Reunion,
1838–1839

Resolved that . . . the inherent sovereignty of the Cherokee

Nation . . . shall continue to be in perpetuity.

—Resolution adopted at Aquohee Camp Council,

Tennessee, August 1, 1838

By 1838, when the Cherokees were about to be forcibly expelled from their homeland, they had acquired a strong sense of history. They made abundantly clear to the world their own perspective on this bleak moment in their experience. Ten years earlier they had begun their effort to oppose removal by asserting their right as a sovereign nation to adopt a constitution (based on that of the United States) and to govern their own land under their own laws and elected officials. At the same time, the sovereign state of Georgia had asserted its right to abolish the Cherokee Nation and incorporate its people under its laws. Andrew Jackson was elected in 1828 to resolve this dilemma. He sided with Georgia, supporting a state's right to supersede treaty rights. The question came before the U.S. Supreme Court twice: in 1831 in *Cherokee Nation v. Georgia*, Chief Justice John Marshall described the Cherokees as "a domestic, dependent nation"; a year later, in *Worcester v. Georgia*, he asserted the unconstitutionality of Georgia's laws, asserting the supremacy of federal authority over states' rights with regard to Indian treaties. However, Andrew Jackson had already persuaded Congress to pass a law in 1830 that made it virtually impossible for any eastern tribe to escape ceding its land and moving to what was called "Indian Territory" west of the Mississippi River. When a small group of Cherokees, with no official standing in their nation, signed a treaty at New Echota in 1835 agreeing to sell their homeland and move west, Jackson's party in the Senate ratified it, and he signed it.[1]

Chief John Ross was thunderstruck by Jackson's denial of Marshall's decision and the treachery of the U.S. Senate. He urged his people to resist by every means short of violence Jackson's efforts to carry out the terms of the fraudulent treaty. For a time public opinion in the United States, especially among churchgoers in the northeastern states, supported the Cherokees' resistance. Ralph Waldo Emerson (among many others) protested to President Martin Van Buren in April 1838, declaring, "You, sir, will bring down that renowned chair in which you sit into infamy if your seal is set to this instrument of perfidy, and the name of this nation, hitherto the sweet omen of religion and liberty, will stink to the world."[2]

Van Buren, like Jackson, paid no heed to these objections, and a month after Emerson's plea, he ordered the U.S. Army into the Cherokee Nation to round up at bayonet point every Cherokee man, woman, and child. The army placed them in stockades guarded by soldiers until such time as plans were completed for sending them 800 miles to their new homeland in what is now northeastern Oklahoma. The Cherokees did not resist. Throughout the summer, as they languished in their hastily built relocation camps, they suffered hundreds of deaths from epidemics of dysentery, "bilious fever," measles, and whooping cough. The only concession they won was the right to have their own leaders, not the army, conduct them over the "Trail of Tears" at the end of the summer.

On August 1, 1838, the eve of their departure, a great council of the people was held at Aquohee Camp in eastern Tennessee. Here they met to assert the injustice of their removal and their inalienable right to sovereignty and self-government under their treaties with the United States. Though only a handful of white soldiers and officials witnessed this historic event, it marked a critical point in the still unresolved history of Native American–white relations in the United States. The sick, bedraggled, and dispossessed Cherokees who, between 1794 and 1830 had undergone an astonishing transformation from hunters to farmers, from an illiterate to a literate people, asserted their determination to endure and to make no concessions to the false treaty that had cost them their ancient homeland. Andrew Jackson, and most white Americans, believed that the Indians were doomed to extinction because they were inherently incapable of competing with the Anglo-Saxon race. Jackson had explained his removal program as a benevolent effort to give the eastern Indians one last chance to assimilate and give up their Indian ways: "Surrounded by our settlements," he had told Congress in December 1833, these Indians "have neither the intelligence, the industry, the moral habits nor the desire of improvement which are essential to any favorable change in their condition. Established in the midst of another and a superior race, and without appreciating the causes of their inferiority or seeking to control them, they must necessarily yield to the force of circumstance and ere long disappear."[3] Across the Mississippi, he said, they might yet survive for a while.

John Ross, their popularly elected chief, was only one-eighth Cherokee by ancestry, but ever since being chosen to membership in the National Council in 1817, he had dedicated himself to sustaining Cherokee sovereignty.[4] A short, wiry man, called "Tsan Usdi" (Little John) and later "Cooweescoowee" by the traditionalists or "full-bloods" who were his chief supporters, Ross had learned much from his white father and grandfather (traders and businessmen married into the nation) about how to cope with white officials. In 1827 he had been elected principal chief, and for the next decade he led the Cherokees' determined efforts to hold onto the land of their ancestors. At Aquohee Camp in August 1838, he stood before the assembled men, women, and children of the nation and asked them to reaffirm their belief that the Cherokee Nation was not dead and would never die. For the next forty years, even through the bitter divisions of the Civil War, Ross never wavered in this belief. He led the nation to a miraculous revitalization in their new homeland after the Trail of Tears and started them on a new revitalization in 1865.

The resolutions presented and approved at this meeting asserted four fundamental conceptions that the Cherokees held of their status: first, that they retained their sovereignty despite Georgia's effort to denationalize them; second, that they retained the ownership of their homeland despite the false treaty ratified by the Senate; third, that this treaty had no validity and must eventually be repudiated by the United States and renegotiated in good faith with the official representatives of the Cherokee people; and fourth, that their duly elected leaders, as well as their constitution and written laws, remained in full effect and their duly elected officials continued to exercise their offices. In short, fraud and force might remove them to the West, but the rights, integrity, and institutions of the Cherokee Nation remained unchanged. For the conservative Cherokees, these resolutions also affirmed the continuity of the ancient traditions, customs, and values of their forefathers as well as those new laws adopted since their military defeat by the United States in 1794.

The first resolution at Aquohee began: "Whereas the title of the Cherokee people to their lands is the most ancient, pure and absolute known to man, its date is beyond the reach of human records, its validity confirmed and illustrated by possession and enjoyment antecedent to all pretense of claim by any other portion of the human race." It went on to state that this title could not, by Cherokee law, be alienated by the act of an illegal treaty, hence "it follows that the original title and ownership of the said lands rest in the Cherokee Nation unimpaired and absolute."[5]

The resolutions went on to hold the United States responsible for "all damages and losses, direct and indirect, resulting from the enforcement of the . . . pretended treaty of New Echota." Under this treaty, the United States had agreed to pay for any "improvements" the Cherokees had made to the land—cultivated fields, farmhouses, barns, stables, corncribs, orchards, fences, ferries, gristmills, sawmills, blacksmith shops, inns, and taverns—but the "indirect" damages from illness, deaths, and the hardships of starting over again from scratch in a new land and climate were not considered. The government had agreed to pay for the costs of removal, but the estimates were never reconciled. Inadequate Cherokee removal payments were still being supplemented by Congress in the 1890s.[6]

The most controversial resolutions, and those that were to cause the Cherokees the most trouble in the next seven years of readjustment, arose out of the confusion created by an already existing Cherokee government in the West established by previous emigrants known as "western Cherokees." Ever since 1794 small groups of Cherokees had moved across the Mississippi. At first they settled along the St. Francis, White, and Arkansas rivers in what is now Arkansas. Over 1,000 Cherokees moved to that area in 1810–11 and another 2,000 or more in 1819 as a result of encroaching whites and forced land cessions in the East. In 1828, the federal government made a treaty with these western Cherokees, and in 1832 it moved them to the northeastern corner of present-day Oklahoma with the hope that they could entice the whole tribe to join them. Over the years the western Cherokees had adopted their own chiefs and laws. After 1835, another 2,000 Cherokees of the Removal party had joined them. At the time of the Aquohee Camp Council, there were about 5,000 Cherokees in the West and 14,000 in the East. The Cherokees were thus divided into three factions by 1838: the western Cherokees (later called the Old Settlers), the Removal (or Treaty) party, and the Patriot (or Ross) party. In 1819, the eastern Cherokees had formally disowned as expatriates those Cherokees who moved west and refused to recognize them as a separate Cherokee Nation. Members of the Removal party, sometimes called the Ridge-Boudinot party (after the names of its leading figures, John Ridge, his father, Major Ridge, and his cousin, Elias Boudinot), were even more bitterly disowned as traitors by the Patriot party. In fact, under Cherokee law, those who willfully sold Cherokee land without obtaining the approval of the National Council were subject to execution for treason.

Those who wrote the false treaty in 1835 neglected to specify in any of its clauses just how these three factions were to unite and govern themselves in the West once they were all living within the same boundaries. Because the United States was willing to let the Cherokees choose their own leaders, make their own laws, create their own constitution, and manage their own affairs in their new homeland, it left the means of uniting these factions to the Cherokees themselves. Those in the West in 1838 constituted only one-third of the tribe; even assuming that the Removal party members were now allied with them, it would hardly do for their chiefs and laws and council to remain in power once the 14,000 emigrants from the ancient homeland arrived. Furthermore, the westerners had no constitution and had adopted very few written laws. Many of them had gone west specifically to avoid the kind of acculturation that took place in the East between 1794 and 1830. Consequently, to protect their own constitution, laws, and elected officials, the eastern Cherokees adopted the fourth resolution at Aquohee: "And whereas the natural, political and moral relations subsisting among the citizens of the Cherokee Nation toward each other and towards the body politic cannot, in reason and justice, be dissolved by the expulsion of the nation from its own territory . . . *Resolved*, therefore, that the inherent sovereignty of the Cherokee Nation [that is, the easterners], together with its constitution, laws and usages of the same are in full force and virtue and shall continue in perpetuity." In short, the Patriot party asserted that the eastern Cherokees (constituting "the Cherokee Nation") remained a coherent body politic and would continue to do so after they arrived in the West.[7] How exactly the body politic of the western Cherokees and that of the eastern Cherokees were to coexist remained to be worked out once the emigration was completed. It proved to be such an intractable, tendentious process that it led to seven years of internal guerrilla war. In fact, the removal crisis so divided the Cherokees that they did not find real unity until after the Civil War, if then. Nonetheless, it is hard to imagine what other stand the eastern Cherokees could have taken. The Aquohee resolutions were overwhelmingly endorsed by those at the council.

While the extent of acculturation among the eastern Cherokees between 1800 and 1830 was remarkable, it would not be accurate to say that those in the West were traditionalists while those in the East were assimilated. Most western Cherokees were farmers even though the presence of deer and buffalo allowed those who wished to sustain a hunting economy of sorts. The 2,000 who went west between 1835 and 1838 and who willingly accepted the leadership of the westerners were as acculturated as those who fought removal to the bitter end—perhaps more so, for the traditionalists or full-bloods were among the most strenuously opposed to removal and they constituted over three-fourths of the Cherokees in 1830.[8] The divisions that split the nation after 1832 were ideological and political, not the result of divisions between "civilized" and "traditional" or "Christian" and "pagan" Cherokees.

The term "nation" was first given to Indian peoples by the Europeans. Prior to the eighteenth century, the Cherokees, like most tribes, had a highly decentralized political system in which local or town chiefs and councils made most of the political decisions. For their own reasons, the Europeans tried to force the tribes into nationalist centralization under one chief ("king" or "emperor"), one council, one process of majority rule. While the Cherokees resisted this, they came to realize after 1794 the necessity of "speaking with one voice" in order to avoid the divide-and-conquer policies of the United States. The adoption of the Cherokee Constitution of 1827 represented recognition that centralization was as necessary in diplomacy as sovereignty was in self-government.

White frontier dwellers, who surrounded the Cherokees after 1794, displayed such animosity and prejudice toward Indians that the federal policy of assimilating them seemed impossible. Once detribalized, they would not be treated as equals by whites. The laws that Georgia passed after 1828 making Cherokees who lived in that state citizens against their will also denied them equal rights. Georgia's laws placed Indians in the same political category as freed slaves—without the right to vote, to hold office, to serve in the militia, to attend white schools, or to testify against whites in the courts. (However, they could own property and engage in trade and business, they could be taught to read and write, and they could be tried in white courts and were subject to the same penalties as whites.) In short, once they lost their sovereignty, they were doomed to become second-class citizens—a caste of "colored" people. By 1828, the same racist theory that ruled out equality for Africans in the young republic was also applied to Indians. Hence nationalism among the Cherokees, as well as the demand for sovereignty (self-government under their own laws and chiefs and with communal ownership of land guaranteed by the federal government), was in part an effort to use the European concept of nationhood to defend their freedom and their land base.

The revitalization of the Cherokee people after their defeat in 1794 was one of the great success stories of Indian reformers in the years prior to removal. No other tribe had become so rapidly acculturated, "Christianized," and "civilized." Far from displaying the lack of intelligence, industry, moral discipline, and desire for improvement that Jackson considered innate in the "inferior" red race, the Cherokees, within a single generation, had created a social, economic, and political order so prosperous, stable, and progressive that it rivaled those of most of the frontier regions on their borders. They had given up a hunting economy for a farming economy. They had adopted written laws and a constitution. They had divided their country into eight electoral districts; every two years they elected representatives to a bicameral legislature; every four years they elected a first and second principal chief. The elected council made laws, established a treasury and police force, and created a system of district and superior courts to adjudicate civil and criminal cases under Anglo-Saxon procedures. They encouraged their children to attend mission schools. Their remarkable linguist, Sequoyah, who neither spoke nor read English, had invented in 1821 a simple way to write the Cherokee language, and by 1828 they were publishing a bilingual tribal newspaper. Some Cherokees became successful merchants not only among their own people but also within the white communities nearby. The Cherokees had demonstrated their friendship with the United States by joining with the frontier militia under Andrew Jackson to fight against the British and their Indian allies in the War of 1812. While removal would destroy their economic prosperity, they were determined that it should not destroy their self-government and self-sufficiency. They were not going west to return to the lives of "wild Indians." Cherokee nationalism was integral to sustaining the fabric of Cherokee society and culture. They had no idea in August 1838 how difficult it would be to reestablish political unity and economic prosperity in their new home.

Six weeks after the Camp Aquohee Council, the first of thirteen contingents of the Patriot party left the stockades in which they had been penned up for four months and began their 800-mile trek westward. Though the trip was estimated to take eighty days, some of the contingents took almost twice that long. They encountered bitter winter weather, dangerous ice flows crossing the Mississippi, constant sickness, and severe exposure to the elements. Before they left, almost 1,500 had died from the epidemics in the camps; another 1,600 died on the journey.[9] As a result of their weakened condition and the absence of housing and adequate food, many more died soon after reaching their destination. The government had promised to supply the emigrants with rations for a year after their arrival—until their first crops were harvested in 1839—but the western rationing was hired out to private contractors who made extra profits by providing less than they had agreed to supply. Often what they did provide included rotting meat and moldy corn and flour.[10] Malnutrition, sickness, and exposure during the year after their arrival brought the total number of Cherokee deaths during the removal process to at least 4,000.

On April 23, 1839, several weeks after the last contingent of the emigrant

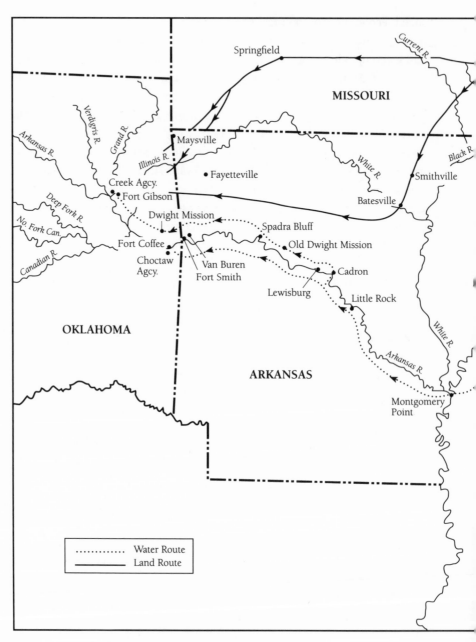

MAP 1. *Trail of Tears, 1838–1839*

Source: Grace Woodward, *The Cherokees*
(Norman: University of Oklahoma Press, 1963).

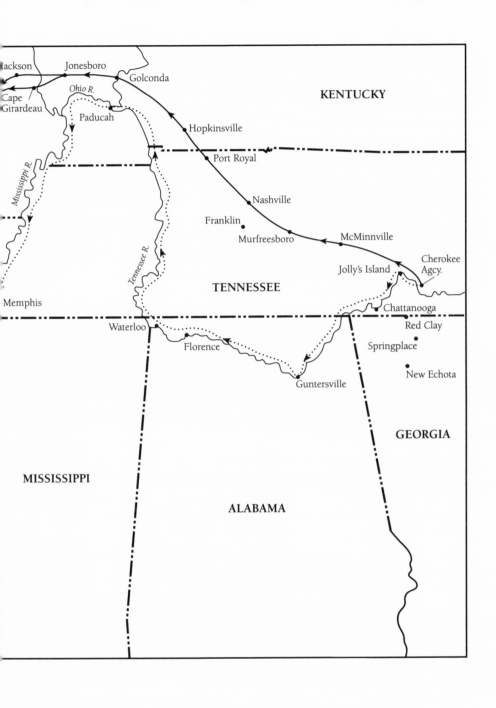

Jackson

Jonesboro

Golconda

KENTUCKY

Cape Girardeau

Ohio R.

Paducah

Hopkinsville

Mississippi R.

Port Royal

Nashville

Franklin

Murfreesboro

McMinnville

Tennessee R.

Cherokee Agcy.

Jolly's Island

TENNESSEE

Chattanooga

Memphis

Red Clay

Waterloo

Springplace

Florence

New Echota

Guntersville

GEORGIA

MISSISSIPPI

ALABAMA

Cherokees entered the western Cherokee territory, Chief John Ross wrote to the three chiefs of the 4,000 Old Settlers or western Cherokees—John Brown, John Rogers, and John Looney. Ross suggested that a joint council be held between the eastern and western Cherokees to discuss what kind of governmental structure was needed to reunite the Cherokee people. "We are all of the household of the Cherokee family and of one blood," Ross wrote; therefore, together they should "take measures for cementing our reunion as a nation by establishing the basis of a [unified] government." [11] The western chiefs agreed to meet with the Ross party. On June 3, 1839, over 6,000 Cherokees assembled at the Takatoka Camp Ground in the new homeland, four miles northeast of present-day Tahlequah. John Brown, principal chief of the Old Settlers, addressed the multitude: "We joyfully welcome you to our country. The whole land is before you. You may freely go wherever you choose and select any places for settlement which you may please. . . . You are fully entitled to the elective franchise . . . and eligible to any of the offices. . . . Next July will be an election . . . for members of both houses of our legislature. . . . At those elections you will be voters. . . . [Meanwhile] it is expected that you will be subject to our government and laws." [12] For the Ross party there were two jarring notes in this talk. First, Brown spoke of the area as "our country," the country of the Old Settlers; by implication the new emigrants were being admitted as a privilege not as a right. More disturbing was Brown's assumption that the emigrants had no country, no government, no constitution, no laws, no elected officials of their own. In effect, Brown was asking the eastern Cherokees to give up their government for his. What seemed generous to the western Cherokees left the majority to be governed by the minority.

Ross and the other elected leaders of the eastern Cherokee government were not willing to accept Brown's terms. If the government of the Old Settlers was to be the legitimate Cherokee government, then its officers would be the ones to enter into the final negotiations concerning removal. They might accept the terms of the Treaty of New Echota that the Ross party was dedicated to refusing. In addition, financial payments due from the United States would fall under the control of the western chiefs. All the eastern Cherokees' resistance and suffering from 1828 to 1839 would have been for nothing. Those who had been patriots fighting for their homeland would be expatriates in someone else's land.

On June 10, Ross explained to John Brown and the other chiefs of the Old Settlers why the new emigrants could not accept their terms: "The great body of the people who have recently been removed into this Country, emigrated in their National Character, with all the attributes, from time immemorial which belonged to them as a distinct Community and of which they have never surrendered." He assured the westerners that "notwithstanding the late emigrants removed in their National capacity and constitute a large majority, yet there is no intention nor desire . . . to propose or require anything but what may be strictly equitable and just. . . . I trust that the subject matter of this Council will be referred to the respective representatives [chiefs and councils] of the Eastern and Western people" for "joint deliberations . . . for the permanent reunion and welfare of our Nation," meaning the whole Cherokee people. Ross, a member of a Methodist mission church, concluded with a biblical text: "Let us never forget this self-evident truth, that a house divided against itself cannot stand" (Matthew 12:25). "We are all of the household of the Cherokee family and of one blood . . . embracing each other as Countrymen, friends and relatives." He hoped that the western Cherokees and their new Treaty party citizens—who had agreed to live under the Old Settler government—would not try to sustain the right of a minority to rule over a majority.[13]

Ross was surprised at Brown's ambiguous response. Brown said, "For the settlement of all matters growing out of your removal, . . . you are freely allowed your own Chiefs and Committee and Council . . . with the name and style of the Eastern Cherokee Nation."[14] That is, Brown now proposed not unity but two separate governments in the same territory. This plan had several difficulties. First, it was doubtful whether the federal government would enter into negotiations with the Ross government (which Jackson had declared null and void), especially inasmuch as Ross had so adamantly opposed removal and was determined not to accept the Treaty of New Echota. Second, Ross did not want to concede that his own government had only a temporary and contingent status in the West; to accept this would be to concede official recognition of the Old Settler government in the long run. Finally, two distinct Cherokee nations, living intermingled with each other even temporarily, would lead to civil confusion; it would certainly permit the federal government to play one party off against the other.

Ross suspected that the Old Settlers were reluctant to yield their control because they were hoping to obtain a large part of the money due under the Treaty of New Echota. That treaty had sold the eastern homeland for $5 million, and after the cost of removal was deducted, the remaining sum was to be divided on a per capita basis among all of the Cherokees. Ross took that to mean each and every Cherokee who had been forced to emigrate to the West. Other sums were due the Patriot party for remunerations and spoliations and unpaid removal costs. Ross explained: "Before the period subscribed for such an election" in July as John Brown had noted, "the western minority . . . would have possessed itself of all the moneys due to the [Eastern] Cherokee

Nation." [15] Not only did Ross have plans to renegotiate the sale of the home-land (at a much higher price), but he also wanted it clear that any treaty of removal concerned only the Eastern Cherokee Nation and not the western. Under Brown's plan, the United States might find it far easier to continue to deny the existence of Ross's government and insist on dealing only with the Old Settler government. Ross believed Brown expected that.

When Ross rejected Brown's proposal for a double government (for the time being), the Old Settlers concluded that he expected them to dissolve their government and submit to a reunion dictated by the Ross party. The eastern Cherokees had developed a far more complex and elaborate political structure than the western. The westerners lived a much simpler and more traditional way of life than the easterners; they were more isolated from the currents of the market economy and the pressures of whites on their borders. The westerners saw no need to abandon a system that had worked well for them for many years. In exasperation, Brown asked Ross to submit in writing precisely what political solution he expected in "plain and simple" terms.[16]

Ross consulted with his council, and on June 13 they sent a letter to the western chiefs saying that the best solution was for the westerners to elect three persons to represent them, for the easterners to elect three representatives, and then for those six to choose three others for a committee of nine. This committee, Ross suggested, should meet at once and start "revising and draft-ing a code of law for the [new] government of the Cherokee Nation." [17] When this committee had completed such a code, it was to submit it to a referen-dum at a council of all the Cherokees. If the whole Cherokee people assented, the new code of law drafted by the committee would become the basis for a unified Cherokee Nation. Then an election would be held under the terms of the new laws for new national officers and a new unified council. The two old nations, eastern and western, would cease to exist, being superseded by the newly elected council.

The western chiefs found this proposal totally unacceptable, unnecessary, and unreasonable; it would give the easterners majority control. Replying to Ross's plan on June 14, they said that the new emigrants (the Ross party), like the 2,000 members of the Treaty party before them, had been publicly welcomed into the Western Cherokee Nation, which was the only legitimate government in the West, and "thereby made partakers of all the existing laws in the country, enjoy all its benefits, and are in every respect as ourselves." As far as the Old Settlers were concerned, a reunion had already taken place. Nothing further was required. There was no need "to protract a debate when the uniting of the people has been already and satisfactorily accomplished." [18]

Up to this point in the discussion at Takatoka, the leaders and members of the Removal or Treaty party had taken no part. They were content to be as-similated into the Western Cherokee Nation. However, on the same day that Chief Brown rejected Ross's plan for reunification, Major Ridge, John Ridge, Elias Boudinot, Stand Watie (Boudinot's brother and John Ridge's cousin), and other leading signers of the Treaty of New Echota had appeared at the council grounds and began talking secretly with the chiefs of the Old Settlers. The Ross party, seeing these "traitors" on the grounds, assumed that they had urged the westerners to make no concessions to Ross and had promised to use their influence with the federal government to support the Old Settlers as the legitimate government. Knowing well the hostility felt toward them by the recent emigrants, the Treaty party leaders left the same day.[19] However, the damage was done. They were immediately branded by the Ross party as the chief roadblock to a reunited nation. Another black mark was placed against them; another betrayal of the majority will.

On that same day, unknown to Ross and probably at the instigation of the Ridge-Boudinot faction, the Old Settlers wrote a letter to the resident federal agent, Montfort Stokes, at Fort Gibson, requesting that he immediately pay to them all the annuities due to the Cherokee Nation from their trust fund. Ever since 1819, the income from the Cherokee trust fund (based on monies paid for ceded land) had been divided between eastern and western Cherokees—one-third to the westerners, two-thirds to the easterners. Both nations had used this annual income to support their governments. If Stokes acceded to this letter and now paid the total annuity to the western chiefs, he would in effect be granting them de facto recognition as the legitimate government of the whole Cherokee Nation.[20]

Having reached an impasse in these political discussions, Ross met with the members of his own council on June 15. He told them that if the deadlock continued, "it will become necessary to consult the feelings and sentiments of the people and take steps for ascertaining their will."[21] That same day, George Lowrey, the second principal chief (under Ross) of the eastern Cherokees, addressed a letter to the Ross council: "You will no doubt feel the regret and surprise that we do in relation to the singular views entertained" by the Old Settler chiefs. Lowrey said the failure of the chiefs of the two parties to achieve a mutually satisfactory reunion left only one remedy—an appeal to the Cherokee people as a whole, over the heads of both sets of chiefs and councils. "You, who are the immediate representatives of the people . . . as guardians of their rights" must turn to them for guidance. "It is your bounden duty to obey their will."[22] This appeal to "the people" was clearly self-serving. The easterners constituted two-thirds of the population and would dominate such a general council. However, an appeal to "the people in council" was a traditional way to settle complex issues concerning the whole tribe. Consensus and not majority rule was the Cherokee system of deciding major controversial issues. The appeal to a "people's council" or "national council" of all members of the tribe had been common in the past.[23] It also had a certain precedent in the formation of the United States, since in 1787 the framers of the U.S. Constitution had made an appeal to "We the people." However, to the western Cherokees and the Treaty party leaders Lowrey's proposal was nothing but an appeal to "mobocracy."

Heeding the advice of Ross and Lowrey, the council of "the Eastern Nation" voted on June 19 to express "their regret at the course pursued by their western brethren" and said they could not accept the Old Settlers' view "that the ancient integrity of the Eastern Nation should be dissolved and her existence annihilated without discussion."[24] This council therefore concluded "that the proceedings of the committee [their upper house] and council [their lower house] be forthwith laid before the people" at large for a decision regarding whether the process of reunion should move from the hands of their elected officials (eastern and western) to the hands of the assembled throng of 6,000 at Takatoka. The western chiefs and council did not acquiesce in this strategy, and on June 20, the Old Settler chiefs declared the council at Takatoka to be over as far as they were concerned. They then left the area. The 6,000 Cherokees were left in confusion.

At this point, two Cherokees whose fame and popularity transcended party lines—Sequoyah and Jesse Bushyhead—took the initiative. Sequoyah had lived in the Western Cherokee Nation since 1824, but he put unity over party spirit. Bushyhead, a leader among the eastern Cherokees noted for his absolute integrity, also considered himself above party matters when the good of the nation was at stake. Standing before the crowd, which was preparing to leave Takatoka, on June 20, Sequoyah and Bushyhead made a joint plea calling upon the Cherokees to assert the general will by agreeing to reassemble as a general or people's council on July 1 and take upon themselves the task of reuniting the nation.[25] In a *viva voce* vote, the response was positive. Ultimately, the result would depend on the willingness of the Cherokee people to give their support (over the long run) to whatever emerged from this popular council. For the moment, however, the Cherokees remained divided.

On June 21 the eastern Cherokee chiefs learned of the letter sent by the Old Settler chiefs to Montfort Stokes about the annuity. Fearful of the consequences, John Ross and Richard Taylor, leader of the upper house of the eastern council, wrote to Stokes explaining the failure of the effort at Takatoka to unite the nation and urging him not to take sides by paying any tribal funds to the western chiefs. After complaining that their "reasonable propositions" had been rejected, and deploring the "attempt of a small minority to enforce their will over a great majority," they concluded, "We feel it due to the interests of the late emigrants [the Ross party] . . . to request . . . that no disbursements of moneys due to those whom we represent, nor any other business of a public character . . . be made . . . until a reunion of the people shall be effected."[26] In this letter Ross and Taylor maintained that the Old Settlers had demanded "unconditional submission" of the majority to their domination.

Stokes, a veteran of the American Revolution in his nineties, was basically sympathetic toward the recent emigrants and to the concept of majority rule. He declined to make any payments to the Old Settler government. Instead, he wrote to the secretary of war asking his advice.[27] Stokes's influence might have been valuable had not a small group of angry men in the Patriot party allowed their hatred of the Ridge-Boudinot faction to push them to violence.

Angry and frustrated by the failure of the Takatoka Council, a group of 100 to 150 members of the Ross party met secretly on June 21 and decided to take vengeance against the signers of the Treaty of New Echota. They believed themselves to be acting within the laws of the nation, and they were aroused by their belief that these same men were now responsible for the intransigence of the Old Settlers. Several members of this group were closely related to the Ross family, including Ross's son Allen. Some were full-bloods who had served in the Cherokee light horse police; some were present as members of the same clans as the treaty signers and therefore directly involved in judging whether vengeance came within the traditional "law of blood" (a tradition of clan revenge) or lay outside it.[28] John Ross did not attend this meeting, and great care was taken to see that he was not aware of it.

Major Ridge, one of the signers of the false treaty, had been responsible for the passage of a law in 1829 calling for the death penalty against any who illegally sold tribal land. All the signers of the Treaty of New Echota knew they were breaking that law. When Major Ridge signed it, he said to his friends, "I have signed my death warrant."[29] His son, John Ridge, said after signing, "I may yet die some day by the hand of some poor, infatuated Indian deluded by the counsels of Ross and his minions. . . . I am resigned to my fate, whatever it may be."[30] The Reverend John Schermerhorn, a minister of the Dutch Reformed church who acted as President Jackson's chief commissioner in negotiating the treaty and who considered the Ridges, Waties, and Boudinots wiser and more enlightened than John Ross, wrote later, "These men, before they entered upon their business, knew they were running a dreadful risk, for it was death by their laws for any person to enter into a treaty with the United States" without authorization of the council.[31] Ross had held back those in his party who would have carried out the executions earlier because he knew such an action would only add to his difficulties in trying to overthrow the treaty. However, in June 1839, the anger could no longer be restrained.

Those who met to carry out the law on June 21 first drew up a list of a dozen or so leaders of the Treaty party whose actions warranted their execution. They presented this list to representatives of the clans to which these persons belonged and received their agreement that killing these "traitors" would not invoke the law of clan revenge.[32] At the head of the list were Major Ridge, John Ridge, Elias Boudinot, and Stand Watie. Others on the list probably included James Starr, John A. Bell, and George W. Adair, who had also signed the treaty. Lots were then drawn to decide who would perform the executions. Twelve names were drawn as executioners for each name on the list; others volunteered to be present at the executions in order to avoid easy detection of exactly who did the killing. It was probable that the U.S. government would feel obliged to arrest and try the executioners because it had promised protection to the signers of the treaty, and no one doubted that the relatives of those executed would try to avenge the murders. Decisions by the clan members present at this meeting could not prevent revenge by close relatives, for the clan system was no longer as powerful and binding as it had been in former times. Moreover, this was clearly an ex parte group whose political loyalties were at least as strong, if not stronger, than their clan loyalties.

The last decision of those at this secret meeting was to proceed at once to their task. The first four "traitors" on the list were to be executed the next day, June 22. Allen Ross was designated to remain close to his father to see that he received no intimation of the action.[33] The first four groups of executioners and witnesses (about twenty in each) set out in various directions to kill their victims at dawn. The group sent to kill Stand Watie did not find him at home, but the other three groups succeeded in executing Major Ridge, John Ridge, and Elias Boudinot.[34] The victims had no chance to fight back. Their deaths caused an immediate panic among all members of the Treaty party, a vehement reaction by the federal government, and general horror among the white American public. Some whites on the nearby frontier thought this might be the start of a general Indian uprising. However satisfying to the extremists in the Patriot party, these executions proved disastrous for Ross's effort to attain tribal unity and stability.

Stand Watie, suspecting that he was among those slated for death and not being a man to avoid danger, gathered a group of armed supporters, offered a $1,000 reward for the names of his brother's killers, and threatened retaliation against John Ross, whom the Treaty party considered responsible. Few believed that Ross was totally ignorant of the action. Some members of the

Treaty party fled immediately into Arkansas, where they were befriended by whites. Some accepted the protection offered by General Matthew Arbuckle at Fort Gibson. Fearing open warfare between the two parties, Arbuckle also offered protection to John Ross. However, several hundred armed members of the Ross party immediately gathered around Ross's home at Park Hill to fend off any attack by Watie's force. Ross agreed with Arbuckle that the first goal was to prevent further bloodshed. The secret executioners abandoned their plans to execute the other persons on their list. The Treaty party chose to appeal to the federal authorities rather than to take matters into their own hands. Watie made no attack, but from this point on he became the titular leader of the anti-Ross element in the Cherokee Nation—a leadership that he retained over the faction until his death in 1871. The Removal or Treaty party henceforth also became known as the Watie party.

From Ross's point of view, the timing of the Ridge and Boudinot executions could hardly have been worse. He told Agent Stokes and General Arbuckle that he did not know who the murderers were and expressed regret at the executions. Yet he hardly could have apprehended the murderers even if he had known who they were. They had only carried out tribal law and probably the majority will. Underneath he recognized that for many in his party, these actions had cleared the air and released their pent-up anger. However, the executions intensified tribal divisions to the breaking point. The best he could do now was to prevent any more executions. What he could not forestall was the ultimate vengeance that would be sought by the families and friends of the Treaty party.

Despite the widespread fear and confusion at the moment, Ross's priorities remained unchanged. He made no effort to call off or postpone the people's council scheduled to convene on July 1. The absence of telegraph lines in the Indian Territory meant that it would be weeks before the federal government in Washington, D.C., could take any action. Ross hoped that before then his efforts for unity would be achieved.

The people's council convened on July 1 at the Illinois Camp Ground near the place called Tahlequah, about a mile and a half from Park Hill. Attendance was smaller than Ross had hoped, partly because of the uneasiness over acts of vengeance and partly because the new emigrants were desperately trying to build homes, start farms, and get a crop in the ground. The Old Settler chiefs had no interest in this council and had written to Ross on June 28 stating that the people's council was "altogether irregular." Realizing that they would be outvoted by the Ross majority, these chiefs discouraged their followers from attending, though some Old Settlers went out of a higher loyalty to national unity. The Old Settler chiefs made a countersuggestion that a meeting should be held at Fort Gibson on July 25 "in which both parties should be equally represented" by a delegation of sixteen of each.[35] They said they recognized that some effort must be made to "harmonize and reunite the whole Cherokee people," but they had no faith in a popular convention. They may also have feared that Sequoyah's appeal might produce a schism in their own ranks.

General Arbuckle and Montfort Stokes, to whom the Old Settlers and Treaty party had appealed for military and political protection in the controversy, wrote a joint letter to Ross on June 28, endorsing the proposal of the Old Settler chiefs. They agreed that the nation could not exist with two separate governments: "Two governments cannot exist in the Cherokee nation without producing civil war," they wrote. Still, "We are of the opinion that the government that existed before the arrival of the later emigration should continue until it is changed in a regular and peaceable manner."[36]

Ross rejected the plan for a formal meeting at Fort Gibson. As structured, the Ross party delegates would have no official standing and would be suing for concessions. At such a conference, Ross said, the Eastern Cherokee Nation would appear as "private citizens" and be "denied recognition in the character of a political community." This was simply another effort to denationalize the majority and its government. He went on to say that the matter was now out of his control; the people "have taken the matter in hand," he wrote, and they were the proper body to act for the whole nation. He also told Stokes and Arbuckle that many of "their people"—the rank and file of Old Settlers— were in agreement with the plan for a people's council. Both his own leadership and that of the Old Settler chiefs must yield to the general will: "This convention has been called by the Cherokee People, not by the chiefs or people of the late emigrants alone."[37]

Only about 2,000 persons came to the Illinois Camp Ground on July 1, and some white observers claimed that only 35 to 150 of these were Old Settlers. There was no rule in law or tradition for deciding how large a general council of the tribe should be. Consensus must start somewhere and work its way through all the people by continuing debate and discussion. Time would tell whether this convention spoke for the nation. The convention began by electing, as its presiding officers, Sequoyah for the Old Settlers and George Lowrey for the recent emigrants. It then selected a steering committee of 17 to 27 persons. Ross served on this as one among equals, or so he claimed. On July 5, Sequoyah, speaking for the Old Settlers in attendance, sent a letter to the western chiefs at Fort Gibson urging them to put aside party feelings and attend the convention: "We, the old settlers, are here in council with the late emigrants, and we want you to come without delay that we may talk matters over like friends and brothers. . . . We have no doubt but we can have all things amicably and satisfactorily settled."[38] One of the three western chiefs, John Looney, changed his mind at this point and agreed to attend, but for some time he vacillated as to whether to join forces with Sequoyah and Ross or not.

In a report drafted by the steering committee of the convention, its agenda became clear: "We, the people of the Cherokee Nation in National Convention assembled," aware that the people were "dissatisfied with the failure of their representatives" to reach an agreement at Takatoka, "called a General Convention" in order to take matters into their own hands. The first problem was to clear the air with regard to the executions of the Ridges and Boudinot. On July 7 the convention granted a general pardon to everyone who had been accused of murder since the arrival of the eastern emigrants. Next, the convention declared to be "outlaws" all Cherokees who had expressed the desire to seek revenge for the murders. (The Treaty party later said that this made them all "outlaws" for trying to revenge the politically motivated murders of their leaders, but Ross argued that it merely sought to prevent Watie and others from gathering armed forces to wage vengeance on whomever it chose in a private—and equally politically motivated—civil war.)[39] To enforce civil order in the name of the people, the convention voted to create eight companies of provisional police. (Ross's enemies considered these little more than vigilante squads to support his self-imposed new government.) Another resolution granted amnesty to any members of the Treaty party who had threatened revenge for the murders, provided they appear within eight days (later extended to September 4), express public apologies for their threats, and agree to be law-abiding citizens. However, those receiving amnesty were denied the right to hold office for the next five years. (Stand Watie said he would die before accepting such humiliating terms.)[40] All these resolutions were designed to avoid a series of retaliations on both sides between the Ross and Treaty parties and to give legality to the police force, which could help prevent such actions.

The next resolutions were closer to Ross's goals. They declared that the Treaty of New Echota was invalid and asserted, as at Aquohee Camp, the continued ownership by the Cherokees of their eastern homeland.[41] This was to pave the way for future negotiations with the United States to replace the fraudulent treaty with a new one. The crowning achievement of the convention, if it could be made to stick, was the adoption on July 12 of the Act of Union, signed by Sequoyah and John Looney for the Old Settlers and by John Ross for the recent emigrants, stating, "We the people, composing the Eastern and Western Cherokee Nation[s], in National Convention assembled, by virtue of our original and inalienable rights, do hereby solemnly and mutually agree to form ourselves into one body politic under the style and title of the Cherokee Nation."[42] Ross wrote to the federal authorities, Arbuckle and Stokes, on July 19, explaining that by this important act the Cherokees had "agreed to unite and live as one people again." Ross noted that "a part of the Chiefs of the Old Settlers have now agreed to cooperate" in the new government—a reference to John Looney's presence at the convention.[43]

While the people's convention was still in session, the Old Settlers held their own council at Tahlontuskey on July 22. Many Treaty party leaders attended, making clear once again their preference for the Old Settler government over any government under Ross's aegis. This council invited Ross to send a delegation of eastern Cherokees to join them. He declined. However, the steering committee of the people's convention voted to send a delegation of observers to Tahlontuskey and to ask the Old Settlers to accept the Act of Union. When this delegation arrived at Tahlontuskey, they found the leaders of the Treaty party so hostile that they believed their lives were in danger and returned.[44]

The people's convention was still in session on August 20 when the Treaty party held its own separate convention at Price's Prairie. The Treaty party was so angry at the act that declared them "outlaws" that it resolved to fight rather than submit to Ross's leadership of the people's convention, which they described as "the mobocracy of John Ross." They then voted to send Stand Watie and John A. Bell to Washington to obtain federal protection against Ross's people. On their way east, Watie and Bell stopped at Andrew Jackson's home in Tennessee and obtained from him a letter to President Van Buren urging every possible protection and assistance to these loyal friends of the United States.[45] When Watie and Bell reached Washington, they received immediate attention and sympathy from Van Buren and his secretary of war, Joel Poinsett. They told Poinsett that all of the Treaty party members feared for their lives. They requested financial help for the widows and children of their martyred leaders and also asked the government to provide funds for those Treaty party refugees who had fled to Arkansas, seeking indemnities for the loss of their incomes or damage to their property in Cherokee territory while they were living in Arkansas. Watie and Bell reminded Poinsett that when they negotiated the Treaty of New Echota, they had expected trouble and had therefore written into it a clause requiring the federal government to protect their nation from "domestic strife." They now called on him to order the army troops at Fort Gibson to capture the murderers of their leaders and to provide full protection to the treaty signers. Poinsett readily agreed.

Late in August 1839, the people's council at Illinois Camp Ground adjourned temporarily while a committee drew up a constitution for the newly reunited nation. While the convention was in adjournment, Sequoyah, John Looney, Tobacco Will, John Drew, Young Wolf, and several other leading figures in the Old Settler party called a convention. They asked all the Old Settlers to attend to hear what the people's convention had done and to support its plan for national reunion. About 200 persons attended and voted to accept and sign the Act of Union. They then voted to depose their old chiefs, John Brown and John Rogers, for identifying themselves with "those individuals known as the Ridge Party" and for refusing to participate in the people's convention.[46] The drift toward reunion began to take hold, and in October one missionary reported that the majority of the Old Settlers (though not their chiefs) were now in favor of the new government.[47] He appears to have exaggerated.

The crisis was far from over. In October those Old Settlers who remained opposed to the reunion chose three chiefs committed to sustaining their government—John Rogers, John Smith, and Dutch. The people's convention meanwhile had reconvened at Tahlequah on September 6. The constitutional committee, headed by Ross's nephew, William Shorey Coodey, presented a draft of a constitution modeled closely on that adopted by the eastern Cherokees in 1827. This constitution was read and adopted by the convention. Its most significant change (apart from an indirect statement repudiating the Treaty of New Echota) was that the principal and second principal chiefs would now be elected by popular vote rather than by the legislature or council. It proclaimed: "We, the people of the Cherokee Nation, in National Covenant assembled, in order to establish justice, insure tranquility, promote the common welfare and secure to ourselves and our posterity the blessings of freedom—acknowledging, with humility and gratitude, the goodness of the Sovereign Ruler of the Universe in permitting us so to do, and imploring His aid and guidance in its accomplishment—do ordain and establish this Constitution for the government of the Cherokee Nation."[48] The convention then nominated and elected a full slate of officers under the new constitution, taking special care to include Old Settlers in at least one-third of the offices. For this purpose they defined as Old Settlers anyone who had come west prior to the Treaty of New Echota. Ross was chosen principal chief, and Joseph Vann, an influential and wealthy Old Settler, second principal chief. One-third of the upper house (or National Committee) were Old Settlers, and William Shorey Coodey (who had moved west in 1833) was named its presiding officer. One-third of the lower house (or National Council) were Old Settlers, and Old Settler Young Wolf was chosen Speaker of the House.[49] Lewis Ross, John's brother and one of the wealthiest merchants and largest slaveholders in the Cherokee Nation, was chosen treasurer. The convention also elected one of the new Old Settler chiefs, Dutch, to high office, but he resigned as soon as he learned of it.[50] Still, this new legislature demonstrated a decided commitment to be fair to the Old Settlers and to indicate that the Ross party intended to give them a strong proportionate voice in the new government. Nonetheless, Dutch, John Rogers, and John Smith, as the official chiefs of the westerners, protested against the new government, calling it a "usurpation."[51]

The newly elected council of the reunited Cherokee Nation assembled in Tahlequah on September 19, 1839, and took power as the official government.[52] It represented the will of the overwhelming majority, but the intransigence of its opponents and the refusal of the federal government to recognize its legitimacy made it, for the time being, only a de facto government. Ross believed that he had secured his objective and that gradually this government would win over all but the most recalcitrant opponents. Pursuant to the new constitution, this council increased the number of electoral districts from four (as the Western Cherokee Nation had adopted) to eight (as in the East). This allowed for broader representation by the greatly enlarged population. Each district elected three representatives to the lower house and two to the upper house every two years. This more than doubled the size of the council of the Old Settlers. As its final act of this session, on October 13 the reunited council chose nine leading figures (including both Ross and some Old Settlers sympathetic to the new government) to go to Washington as a delegation to negotiate a treaty with the secretary of war that would substitute for the treaty signed at New Echota and that Ross expected to include a much higher price than the $5 million the Ridge-Boudinot party had accepted for their homeland in 1835. In addition, the delegation was instructed to obtain a land patent in fee simple for the 7 million acres of the new homeland as promised by President Jackson, designed to prevent any future attempt to remove them on the grounds that Indians were only "tenants at will" in the United States. Beyond this, the delegation hoped to arrange payment of various sums due to the nation for remunerations and spoliations during the removal process, annuities, and a per capita sum for each Cherokee out of the money to be paid for their homeland under a new treaty.[53] Most of the Cherokees who had come along the Trail of Tears were virtually penniless and desperately needed funds to begin farms in the West. Ross also hoped to obtain sufficient money from a new treaty to establish a Cherokee National Bank that would provide loans at minimal interest to Cherokees who would engage in useful projects such as building roads, bridges, ferries, gristmills, sawmills, and cotton gins and developing the nation's mineral resources.[54] A considerable national debt had to be paid off for money borrowed to assist in emigration and resettlement.

The council wrote to Agent Stokes at its conclusion that the new government had reunified the Cherokees, and "henceforward there will exist no local cause to disquiet public feeling and . . . harmony will prevail uninterrupted throughout the country." It added the hope that "the [federal] Government will not permit the wanton fabrications" of the few still disaffected to inject itself into Cherokee affairs.[55] Nevertheless, the government was far from satisfied. Secretary of War Joel Poinsett was furious that Ross had done nothing to capture and try the "murderers" of the Ridges and Boudinot, and he was convinced that the new government had illegally seized power from the Old Settlers. On October 12, 1839, Poinsett sent orders to General Arbuckle that no further harm must come to any members of the Treaty party as a result of their being declared "outlaws" by the Ross government. He empowered Arbuckle to use his troops to maintain order. In effect Poinsett created a state of martial law and encouraged Ross's enemies to continue their opposition.

On November 9, Poinsett reminded Arbuckle that, under the clause of the Treaty of New Echota regarding protection of the Cherokees from internal "domestic strife," Arbuckle "had the right to arrest Ross" if necessary and take him "to be tried in the courts of the State of Arkansas" for promoting civil war against the duly constituted authority of the Old Settlers.[56] In addition, Poinsett suspended payment of all funds due the Cherokee Nation, including its annuity, until he was assured that peace and order prevailed. Presumably he believed good order would prevail only when the Treaty party refugees in Arkansas felt safe to return to the nation; this, in turn, meant that the law declaring them "outlaws" would have to be repealed. By this action, Poinsett gave the Treaty party the power to halt any federal negotiations with Ross until its demands were satisfied; its leaders had only to claim they were unsafe to sustain federal dominance over Cherokee affairs.

Arbuckle seriously considered arresting Ross in January 1840, just prior to his departure for Washington, but decided it might be best to have him out of the region, leaving Arbuckle free to enter into negotiations with the second principal chief of the new government, Joseph Vann. Vann, being an Old Settler, seemed more likely to cooperate in working out compromises that might lessen the tensions. Furthermore, because of what Arbuckle called "the blind attachment" of the eastern Cherokee masses to Ross, he did not think it would be wise to arrest Ross.[57]

The Old Settlers had decided at a council held on November 10, 1839, to deny any recognition of Ross's new government. They proclaimed their undying opposition to "the Ross Party" and declared all the laws passed by the new government—as well as the new constitution—"null and void."[58] John Brown, who had been principal chief of the western Cherokees when the Ross party arrived, became so discouraged about the future of his people that he left for Mexico with his family and some friends.[59] John Rogers, the new leader of those Old Settlers opposed to the Ross government, was implacable in his hatred of Ross. He had been an enemy of the easterners since he deserted the homeland for the West following the Treaty of 1817. He was also one of the signers of the hated Treaty of 1828, which President John Quincy Adams, hoping to be reelected, had engineered with the western Cherokees in the hope of encouraging the easterners to remove.[60] Rogers realized that a growing number of Old Settlers were inclined to accept the new government under Ross. Consequently he sought to strengthen his position by establishing a closer alliance with the Treaty party. This meant relying on the War Department to interpose in Cherokee affairs—an action with which few Cherokees were sympathetic no matter what they thought of Ross.

T. Hartley Crawford, Van Buren's commissioner of Indian affairs, wrote to Joel Poinsett, his immediate superior, on November 25, 1839, laying out Ross's claim for majority rule and explaining why it was impossible for the government to countenance it. He began by citing the resolutions adopted by the Ross party at Aquohee Camp in August 1838. Crawford told Poinsett that Ross's claim for Cherokee sovereignty "is remarkable for the pretensions it advances and utterly inconsistent with the acknowledged rights of the States and the just authority of the United States. It claims for the Cherokee tribe a title to the land ceded by the treaty of 1835 as paramount to that of 'any other portion of the human race' and that it is even now their property—[it] repudiates the treaty as void, and arrogates for the nation an existence 'as a distinct national community in the possession and exercise of the appropriate and essential attributes of sovereignty.' "[61] Crawford was astounded at "the arrogance of this" and told Poinsett that it was essential "to rebuke [it] at the threshold." Its arrogance rested on Ross's claim that "their rights are unchanged by the treaty of 1835" because it was fraudulent. "But the treaty must be considered valid," Crawford said; "it has been ratified by all the sanctions prescribed by the constitution and is now in a good measure executed." The fact that the treaty did not represent the will of the Cherokee people nor conform to Cherokee law was irrelevant. Because "the Government exerts control over all within the territorial limits of the United States," it had the right to do "what the Government may deem proper" for the general welfare. In short, government by the white majority (according to the majority's interpretation of the Constitution) could not be denied or thwarted by the minority. "The United States are, according to the highest judicial opinion [that is, the U.S. Supreme Court] the owners of the fee simple in the land" within the boundaries of the country. There could not be two sovereign powers under one government. The Aquohee resolutions were therefore denounced as absurd.

Yet when Crawford went on to examine Ross's claim for majority rule within the new territory assigned to the Cherokees by the Treaty of 1835, he reversed himself. Instead of supporting majority rule, he now defended minority rights. The Treaty party was a minority and so was the Old Settler party; the two of these united were less than half as large as the Ross party. Nonetheless Crawford took the view that the Old Settlers were the duly constituted national authority in the area. Ross had entered their jurisdiction and unlawfully employed the power of his majority to subvert the authority of the existing government. Though Ross complained of being denationalized, he had in Crawford's opinion denationalized the united government of the Old Settlers and the Treaty party. Moreover, Ross had branded the latter group as "outlaws" and forced them to flee for their lives. "It is impossible to look upon a denationalized minority, now struggling against, now flying from, the power in the hands of a majority that moves straight forward to its object regardless of the happiness or interests of the few, without feeling deep commiseration for their misfortunes." Ross was a tyrant; Andrew Jackson had been a true republican. The United States had no choice but to defend minority rights against Ross's tyranny: "The fifth article of the treaty of 1835 makes it incumbent on the Government to secure the Cherokee nation from domestic strife." The War Department must side with the Old Settlers and the Treaty party "by every consideration of humanity and duty." Any claims by Ross for Cherokee sovereignty were worthless, he insisted.

Crawford conceded that at the council of Takatoka in June 1839, Ross's effort to reunify the Cherokee Nation "was rejected" by "the Ridge party, uniting with the Old Settlers and being the effective opponents of Mr. Ross and his friends." Then when Major William Armstrong, the western superintendent, along with General Arbuckle had tried to arrange a new council at Fort Gibson, Ross had rejected that good office in order to assert the will of the majority at Illinois Camp Ground. Nevertheless, Crawford then undermined his own arguments. "The principle, however, is of general, as it ought to be of universal, adoption that the majority of any community shall prescribe rules for all." He added, however, that this general principle did not apply in the case because of "the qualifications necessarily arising out of their peculiar relations as Indians to the United States." Because the Treaty of New Echota granted the United States the right to prevent domestic strife in the Cherokee Nation, the War Department must defend the minority, not the majority. Ross was thus doubly condemned: he refused to accept the right of the United States to subvert the sovereignty of the Cherokees by making a treaty with an unofficial minority, and he refused to protect those who knowingly broke tribal laws that they themselves had helped to make. He was condemned a third time for "denationalizing" the Old Settler minority rather than giving up the "nationhood, constitution and laws" that (under the Aquohee declarations) the majority brought with them to the new territory.[62] Poinsett accepted this report as a full justification for placing Arbuckle in charge of reuniting the Cherokees.

Only the aging Montfort Stokes now showed any inclination to try to help the eastern Cherokees. He decided, after Ross had departed, that he would play the part of elder statesman and honest broker among the quarreling factions. He based his strategy on a reference in one of Crawford's letters regarding the importance of majority rule: "That the great and liberal principle of modern times is the only one in his [Poinsett's] opinion by which the Cherokee Nation can be made one in feeling, interest and government; and that the majority shall rule is an axiom in politics. . . . It is as applicable and its adoption as necessary to the Cherokees as to other Communities. . . . The minority . . . must eventually yield to the great mass."[63] Stokes, realizing that the Ross party was the majority and would remain so, tried his own hand at reconciliation.

After Ross had left for Washington, Stokes persuaded Joseph Vann, the acting chief, to call a joint council of all factions at Tahlequah on January 15, 1840. Vann being an Old Settler, Stokes hoped this council might find a compromise position that would create the kind of majority that Poinsett and Crawford had in mind.[64] Two thousand Cherokees attended this council, but few of them were Old Settlers or Treaty party members. Stokes persuaded the council to affirm the Act of Union and the new constitution. It also rescinded the act outlawing the Treaty party leaders. Stokes promised the Old Settlers (without authorization of the council) that they would share in any future payment of money paid for the old country.[65]

Elated by his success, Stokes wrote to Poinsett on January 28, 1840, explaining the compromise. He said that he had consulted General Arbuckle, who had reluctantly agreed to inform the western chiefs that their government was now dissolved and the new Ross government was the official one.[66] Majority rule had been achieved. Yet how Stokes came to believe that he had the power to work out such a compromise is hard to conceive. Nor were Ross, the Treaty party, or the Old Settlers as a whole likely to agree to it. Arbuckle wrote to Poinsett the day after this noting that while this council did not represent a large proportion of the Old Settlers, still he felt that the majority of all the Cherokees were in favor of a reunion under Ross.[67]

Stokes's solution and Arbuckle's acquiescence to it were short-lived. The Old Settlers at the council told Stokes that while they themselves agreed to this compromise, it lacked the power to bind the Western Cherokee Nation or its chiefs. The compromises would have to be approved by the Old Settler council before they became effective. John Rogers, however, remained strongly opposed to unification, and in the end the decisions of the compromise council were never even presented to the council of the Old Settlers.

Poinsett and Crawford were not pleased with Stokes's meddling while they were in the midst of diplomatic discussions in Washington. They believed that Stokes had been too sympathetic to the Ross party and were upset that he had ignored Arbuckle's responsibilities as the representative of the War Department. Poinsett was also angry that Stokes had made promises about the distribution of funds to the Cherokees; only the War Department could make those decisions.[68]

Arbuckle now considered that he had acted too hastily in endorsing Stokes's compromise. Once John Rogers and other chiefs expressed their opposition to it, he withdrew his support. He decided to continue to accept the Old Settler council as the legitimate government of the Cherokee Nation, concluding that any compromise was impossible.[69] Writing to Poinsett on January 28, Arbuckle said that the only solution was to dissolve both the Ross government and the western Old Settler government and to insist that a new government be drawn up that would require proportional representation elected from each faction. He did not believe the Ross government represented the Old Settlers because its representatives had not been chosen by the voters of that party.[70]

John Ross and his delegation had left for Washington late in November 1839. When they arrived, they found the delegations sent by the Old Settlers and the Treaty party already on hand. So low was Ross's standing in Washington that his delegation was forced to wait for an audience with Poinsett until after the other two delegations had presented their charges against him. Meeting with Poinsett on January 22 these two factions proposed their solution to the problem. They told Poinsett they believed that only a geographical and political division of the nation would end the difficulties. One-third of the 7 million acres should be given directly to their two groups, and within the boundaries of that part of the country they would form their own government, elect their own chiefs, and live by their own laws. The Ross party would be free to establish its own government in the remaining two-thirds of the Cherokees' territory. They argued that the Treaty party would never be free from fear under a Ross party government and that the Old Settlers would never truly receive their share of government offices and power; Ross party voters would elect their own members to all offices and majority tyranny would prevail.[71] In addition, the Old Settler and Treaty party delegates said that under a divided government, their part of the country would expect to receive one-third of all monies awarded from the treaty and one-third of the annuity.[72] T. Hartley Crawford expressed support for this division of the Cherokees into two separate nations. Poinsett however favored Arbuckle's plan for one nation with guaranteed proportional representation to be elected by each party.[73] Three weeks later, while Crawford and Poinsett were still debating the matter, the Treaty party and the Old Settlers called a council at Fort Gibson and formally united their two factions into one.[74]

When Ross's delegation finally met with Poinsett, they were told that he did not recognize them as legitimate representatives of the Cherokee people. Finding his way blocked in the executive branch of government, Ross decided to appeal to Congress and the American voters. He and his delegates wrote a long and detailed petition opposing division of the nation, which they presented to Congress on February 28, 1840. In response to the criticisms leveled by Old Settlers, the Treaty party, Arbuckle, Crawford, and Poinsett, Ross said that the present Cherokee government had the support of the great majority of Cherokees, treated all citizens equally, and had representatives of all parties in office.[75] The matter was referred to the Committee on Indian Affairs in the House of Representatives. John Bell of Tennessee, a Whig congressman on this committee, saw in this issue a means to embarrass the Van Buren Democrats and revive the Whig sympathy for the Cherokees. When he found that Bell's committee was friendly toward him, Ross submitted a second memorial to it on April 20. In this appeal, he denounced Poinsett's support of the Treaty party and the Old Settlers as part of "a deep-laid scheme . . . to denationalize us" and "to legislate us into non-entity."[76] (Ross always considered himself a Whig as far as American politics was concerned, and he shrewdly made the most of this opportunity.)

Bell's committee, after studying all of the official correspondence and examining a long counterpetition from the Treaty party, issued a report in July 1840, which concluded that the whole executive branch of government, from Poinsett to Arbuckle (and by implication Van Buren), had been prejudiced against Ross and unfair to the Cherokee majority. The report, in effect, upheld Ross's new government and censured the War Department for interfering improperly in Cherokee internal affairs. Bell based his criticism on the grounds that Poinsett himself had claimed to support majority rule for the Cherokees and then had upheld the minority. The report also noted that Poinsett's authorization of military control over Cherokee internal affairs infringed on the treaty pledges allowing the Cherokees self-government. The Democrats, however, had a majority in the House and concluded that Bell's report was politically motivated. The House therefore not only refused to consider the report but even refused to have it printed. The Whigs retaliated by crying "censorship." Describing it as "Bell's Suppressed Report," they then leaked the contents to the newspapers, where it received wider publicity than it otherwise might have. This did not, however, shake Van Buren or the War Department in their continued support for the Treaty party and the Old Settlers.[77]

Poinsett had suspended Montfort Stokes as federal agent in March 1840 for his meddling insubordination. Determined to defeat Ross, he told Arbuckle that it was now up to him to obtain a solution that would terminate "the tyrannical and oppressive conduct of the emigrating party toward the Old Settlers."[78] Arbuckle was also told that under no circumstances should he permit John Ross or William Shorey Coodey (Ross's nephew) to hold any office under any future government that he might work out with the contending parties.[79] Poinsett also expected Arbuckle to force Ross to assist in identifying and arresting the murderers of the Ridges and Boudinot. He seemed particularly outraged at Ross's failure to do this or even to condemn the executions. The plan to divide the Cherokees into two nations was suspended pending this final effort of Arbuckle to resolve the crisis.

While Ross was still in Washington working with Bell, Arbuckle asked Joseph Vann, the acting chief of Ross's government, to send delegates to Fort Gibson on April 20 to meet with delegates from the Old Settlers. He explained his proposal for proportional representation and Poinsett's demand that Ross and Coodey must be excluded from office. Vann was an ambitious man, not averse to becoming principal chief yet fully aware of Ross's popular support. Vann said the council would never agree to the latter restriction, which was a gross violation of the long-acknowledged right of the Cherokees to be governed by persons of their own choice.[80] Delegates from the two factions met briefly at Fort Gibson but adjourned without taking any action. Arbuckle requested another meeting in May, but the council declined. He then threatened that if Vann did not persuade his council to cooperate, he would himself constitute a new Cherokee government from among those who did agree to attend a meeting for reconciliation.[81] Failure to cooperate, Arbuckle said on June 2, would leave no option but a division of the nation into two groups. Ross would have ignored this threat, but Vann felt that Ross's power was weakening. He knew that the secretary of war had refused to meet with Ross in Washington. He knew that the Treaty party had proposed a division of the nation and that the commissioner of Indian affairs supported their plan. Consequently Vann finally agreed to send twelve delegates from the Ross government to meet with Arbuckle and with twelve delegates from the Old Settler government, now the combined government of the Old Settlers and the Treaty party.[82]

These twenty-four Cherokees met on June 10, 1840, at Fort Gibson. They struggled for two weeks to work out an effective compromise. On June 26 an agreement was signed by twenty-three of the twenty-four delegates—only John Rogers of the Old Settlers refused to sign.[83] Important concessions were made on both sides. Vann and his delegates agreed to let the westerners elect one-third of the members of the council for one term of office but made no guarantee that this would remain a permanent practice. The westerners agreed to sign the Act of Union (slightly reworded by Arbuckle) and to accept the constitution of September 6, 1839 (which Arbuckle considered fundamentally reasonable), as the basic law of the nation.[84] They also agreed that the Old Settlers would receive a share of any per capita money that might derive from the sale of the homeland, a provision that had been the chief object of many of the Old Settlers from the outset. Arbuckle promised the westerners that neither Ross nor Coodey would hold office, but Vann did not agree to this and it was not in the written document. As a result of these various concessions, the Old Settler party appeared to yield its claim of sovereignty and to accept merger into the Ross government (without Ross). Vann agreed to return to Tahlequah and request that one-third of the officers of the existing government resign so that the Old Settlers could elect their own representatives to replace them.[85] On June 26, 1840, Arbuckle proclaimed (for the second time) that the government of the Old Settlers was dissolved and the Cherokee Nation was reunited.[86] Determined to bring about the division of the Cherokees into two nations, John Rogers still held out.

The Ross delegation in Washington was aware of Arbuckle's negotiations with Vann, but neither Ross nor Coodey had any intention of resigning their own positions and they never acknowledged that any change had been made in the government organized by the people's convention. Several of the Old Settlers who signed the Arbuckle agreement at Fort Gibson later repudiated it on the ground that it was never ratified by their council.[87] The Ross delegation did not return to the nation until October 1840. When they did, Ross continued to act as chief and Coodey as president of the upper house. Arbuckle concluded that his plan was a failure. Thereafter he supported John Rogers's position that the Old Settler government still existed and exercised the only official authority in the nation.[88] However, Ross's stubborn pertinacity was about to be rewarded.

The elections in the United States in November 1840 brought the Whigs back to power after twelve years. The political climate in Washington now shifted toward the Ross party. President William H. Harrison and Vice President John Tyler would take office on March 4, 1841. Although Ross had returned empty-handed in October 1840, he now expected a much better reception when he visited Washington the next spring. Poinsett seemed to realize that he could no longer force his solutions on the Cherokees. Immediately after the elections, he rescinded his order denying the payment of the annuities to the Ross government.[89] The Cherokee council again chose Ross to lead a delegation to Washington with the same agenda as the preceding year. To Ross's great pleasure, Harrison appointed John Bell of Tennessee as his secretary of war. The westerners and the Treaty party could expect little help from Bell. Equally significant, Harrison relieved General Arbuckle from his post at Fort Gibson and dispatched him to Baton Rouge, Louisiana. However, Harrison did not replace T. Hartley Crawford as commissioner of Indian affairs, which meant continued difficulty for Ross.

President Harrison was cordial toward Ross and his delegates when he met briefly with them in March 1841, but he died a month later. In the confusing weeks ahead, President Tyler had little time for the Cherokee problem. However, Secretary of War Bell met the delegation and immediately authorized a payment of $100,000 in interest from the Cherokee trust fund—part of the annuity held back by Poinsett. Ross used this to pay off some of the nation's debt and thus improve its credit.[90] However, Bell did not resolve the more perplexing questions Ross raised about the payment of funds still due from the removal process and from spoliation claims. Nor was Bell ready to discuss making a new treaty. Ross remained in Washington throughout the summer trying to persuade Bell to speed up negotiations, but with little success.

Meanwhile the poorer Cherokees were finding it hard to get credit to develop their new farms and pay their debts. They desperately needed the promised per capita payments, which had been estimated at somewhere between $150 and $250 per person, at least as much as $750 for an average family of five. The Treaty party and the Old Settlers took advantage of the economic discontent during the Cherokee elections for new council members in August 1841. The election became a referendum on the per capita question.[91] Rumors spread that Ross was misappropriating tribal funds and depleting the money available for the per capita payments. Elijah Hicks, a key member of the Ross party, campaigned for office in the council by opposing Ross's plan to create a national bank with some of the funds due to the nation. The unrest was exacerbated by widespread sickness and a prolonged summer drought that reduced the harvest.[92] At the election on August 2, the voters elected Hicks and many other candidates to the council who had pledged to demand an immediate per capita payment of all the funds due to the nation at the earliest possible moment. While some Old Settlers were elected, most of the votes went to candidates loyal to the Ross party, even though many voters disagreed with Ross on the per capita issue.

This new council took office in October 1841 and amid rising discontent passed resolutions censuring Ross for the delays that had prevented a per capita payment. The council seemed to doubt that Ross would ever obtain a new treaty providing a higher price for their homeland and preferred to take what they could get under the Treaty of 1835. While these resolutions did not indicate a rejection of Ross's leadership, they were an attempt to change his priorities. One of the resolutions specifically prohibited Ross from using the funds due to the nation for any purpose other than a per capita payment.[93]

In September 1841, Ross finally persuaded Secretary Bell to pay $518,346 due to the Cherokees to cover the costs of removal—a sum Poinsett had admitted was due to the nation but that he had insisted must be subtracted from the per capita fund.[94] Ross's biggest success came when President Tyler agreed to give him a letter on September 20, 1841, stating that he would authorize treaty negotiations in the near future, "which shall give to the Cherokee Nation full indemnity for all wrong[,] . . . establish upon a permanent basis the political relations between them and the people of the United States [and] guaranty their lands [in the West] in absolute fee simple." [95]

On the strength of these achievements, Ross returned home to try to counteract the growing popular discontent with his policies. He applied the $518,346 to pay off more of the nation's debts, assuring the council that the new treaty promised by Tyler would soon provide a larger per capita fund. The council agreed to suspend its demand that this money must be used only for per capita payments. Ross was unable, however, to make good on his promises. Tyler replaced John Bell as secretary of war with John C. Spencer. Spencer came under the influence of T. Hartley Crawford and began to undermine Tyler's commitment to make a new treaty with Ross. Worse, he switched his support to the Treaty party and the Old Settlers. Spencer did not refuse to pay the annuity, but he held up other payments Ross believed were due for spoliations and removal expenses. Spencer apparently persuaded Tyler that for him to make a new treaty with Ross on the grounds that the Treaty of New Echota was fraudulent might cause countless other tribes to press for renegotiating old treaties. It would also cost the government more money if Ross persuaded the negotiators that the United States should pay more than the $5 million it had previously agreed to pay for the homeland.[96]

Under Spencer's administration, the Treaty party and the Old Settlers still loyal to John Rogers (who was now living in Arkansas because he claimed his life was in danger) renewed their complaints of persecution and usurpation. In order to give validity to their complaints, some of the more unruly members of Ross's opposition began to stir up trouble. They knew that border newspapers and politicians would play up any indications of disorder or violence in the nation and that this would lend credence to the claims of "refugees" like the Rogerses, the Boudinots, and the Ridges that it was unsafe for them to live in the nation. Ross paid no heed to these charges, but Spencer took them seriously. He considered Ross a stubborn, self-willed autocrat with a never-ending series of demands for more money and more concessions in the name of "justice to the Cherokees." Ross, on the other hand, insisted that his opponents were a handful of resentful die-hards who believed in rule or ruin.[97]

Two new U.S. officials living in the Cherokee Nation in the fall of 1841 came to know Ross well and developed a more positive estimate of his leadership than those in Washington. One of these, Colonel Ethan Allen Hitchcock, had been sent to the Indian Territory to investigate the frauds perpetrated by the private contractors who had provided beef, corn, and other rations for the emigrants from the East after their arrival in 1839. Hitchcock described Ross as "a man of strong passions and settled purposes which he pursues with untiring zeal." After careful observation and long conversations with him, Hitchcock reported to his superiors: "I am of opinion that John Ross is an honest man and a patriot laboring for the good of his people. . . . [Despite] unlimited opportunities, he has not enriched himself" at the expense of his people, as had many venal chiefs in other tribes.[98]

The Tyler administration had sent a new resident agent, Pierce M. Butler, to replace Montfort Stokes. In the fall of 1841, Butler reported that Ross seemed to him to be a "good man" who demonstrated "dignity and intelligence" in the conduct of tribal affairs. However, Butler added, "He is ambitious and stubborn and often tenacious of his own views to an extent that prejudices both himself and his cause." He also faulted Ross for unwisely "selecting at all times his own friends and partisans for public employment."[99] Butler did note, however, that tribal factionalism remained so bitter that it would have been difficult for Ross to trust officials not known to be personally loyal to him.

Despite these more favorable impressions of Ross and the acknowledgment that his new government was apparently functioning with general public support, Ross could make little headway with the Tyler administration. His enemies among the Old Settlers and the Treaty party, frustrated by the failure of their own agendas, began to adopt more desperate tactics. If a stable government strengthened Ross's position, they were determined to destabilize it. If Ross persisted in declaring his opponents to be "outlaws," some of them decided to act as outlaws. Within a short time, a large group of malcontents became marauders, horse thieves, robbers, barn burners, and murderers, bent on creating terrorism in the nation. The trauma of removal was about to be succeeded by the trauma of civil war.

2

Stalemate and Terrorism, 1841–1846

The Starrs and other outlaws kill at random in order

to arouse the United States army to enter the Nation and

depose John Ross.

—Agent Pierce M. Butler, 1845

From 1828 to 1838 the Cherokees' fight for sovereign control of their own nation and destiny was directed against the federal government and its removal policy. After 1839 they struggled chiefly against internal factions that were encouraged by the federal government and the frontier whites in Arkansas. Although the Ross party was dominant by force of numbers and support by 1841, its stability was constantly threatened by terrorism for another five years.

While Ross fought for Cherokee rights at the highest level of political ideology, the average Cherokee struggled desperately to survive from day to day. Though favorable to Ross's long-range goals, his supporters needed immediate assistance in the form of cash to purchase the essentials to establish small farms. Ross promised that patience would bring bigger rewards than compromising to meet immediate needs. However, Ross weakened his position both with his supporters and the federal government by his stubborn insistence on negotiating a new treaty to obtain a higher price for the old homeland. As the years passed with no resolution of this impasse, even his most loyal followers came to doubt the wisdom of his position.

After 1841 Ross continued to spend six months of each year in Washington, D.C., trying to obtain the agreements that would alleviate the nation's problems. Meanwhile the average Cherokee family did its best to clear some land, build a log cabin, and obtain a plow, a horse, seeds, tools, livestock, and the bare household necessities to sustain daily life. They had been able to bring precious little with them over the Trail of Tears and were in desperate straits during their first few years after arrival in the West. One Cherokee later remembered:

> Very few of the Indians had been able to bring any of their household effects or kitchen utensils with them, and the old people, who knew how, made what they called "dirt pots" and "dirt bowls." To make them they took clay and formed it in the shape desired and turned these bowls over the fire and smoked them, and when they were done, they would hold water and were very useful. We could cook in them and use them to hold food. In the same way they made dishes to eat out of, and then they made wooden spoons, and for a number of years after we arrived we had to use these crude utensils. . . . We had no shoes, and those that wore anything wore moccasins made out of deer hide, and the men wore leggins made of deer hide. . . . When it was cold, they made things out of coon skins and other kinds of hides.[1]

The older men tried to teach the young how to hunt and trap with bows and arrows and snares, for the government had taken their guns when they were removed. A people who had learned to live by the standards of white frontier families were suddenly thrown back upon skills that only the oldest members of the tribe remembered. They were pioneers with no resources except their own hands, their traditional craftsmanship, their native ingenuity, and the uncertain fertility of the soil beneath them. Even two years after reaching their new home, the great majority were living in dire poverty. A visitor from the East, Colonel Ethan Allen Hitchcock, noted in his travels around the nation in 1841 that most of the recent emigrants "are very poor and are obliged to work hard for a living. . . . Removal deprived them of what little property they had. . . . A great many Cherokees died for want of provisions in 1839. . . . The poorest Indians of the Cherokee nation . . . have sat down along the water course[s] and put up small huts, living miserably." Their "means of living are scanty. . . . They have often wanted an axe when they have been compelled hastily to construct a shelter from an approaching winter, and in the spring have wanted the common article of a hoe with which to put a little seed corn into the ground."[2]

The Cherokee lands in the West included 5 million acres in northeastern Oklahoma in addition to the Neutral Lands and the Cherokee Outlet. While the federal government argued that it had given the Cherokees a valuable and

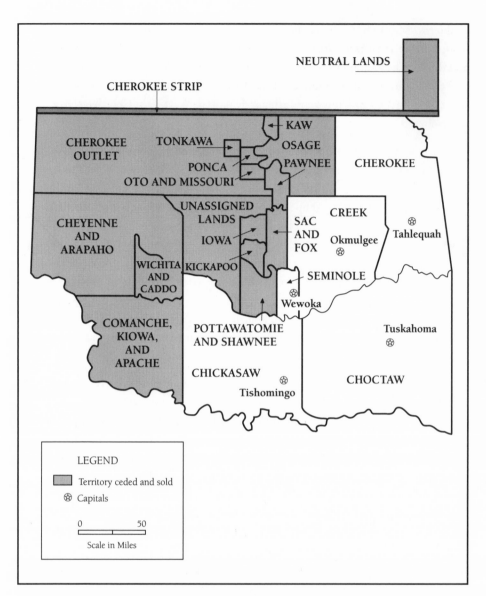

MAP 2. *Cherokee Lands in the West*

Source: Theda Perdue, *Nations Remembered*
(Westport, Conn.: Greenwood Press, 1980).

fertile new homeland equivalent in size to its old homeland, the areas that were capable of growing corn or wheat and that provided both the water and timber necessary to building farms were not extensive. Much of the best land was already occupied by the Old Settlers. An agent of the federal government described the area (excluding the Cherokee Outlet) as containing "something less than 5,000,000 acres. Of this at least two-thirds are entirely unfit for cultivation. A large share of the tillable land is of an inferior quality. Most of the untillable land is entirely worthless, even for timber, as it consists of stony ridges and valleys covered with a scrubby growth, mostly a scrubby oak called black jack. There are a few fine forests of very limited extent, also good timber of other kinds on the streams and in the south part of the nation. No country was ever less worthy of the high encomiums it has received" from those who justified the Cherokees' removal to it.[3]

White traders and merchants who came into Cherokee territory from Arkansas and Missouri brought badly needed manufactured goods and live-stock, but few Cherokees had the cash to pay for them. In despair, many had spent their last dollar for whiskey.[4] Most white traders knew, however, that the government would have to send hundreds of thousands of dollars to the Cherokees as soon as the treaty provisions were renegotiated. Eventually there would be a per capita distribution of perhaps a million dollars or more. Consequently some credit was available (at high prices and for a signed statement acknowledging the debt). However, no one knew exactly how much the per capita payment would be, so the credit was limited, and as long as Ross insisted on a new treaty to renegotiate the sale price of the Cherokee home-land, there would be no per capita payment. The Cherokees consequently had to rely on their tradition of family sharing and the hospitality ethic that had enabled them to survive disasters in the past. As on the white frontier, the Cherokee poor shared their food, helped each other raise their houses and barns, loaned each other horses or oxen for plowing, and shared their seeds, axes, plows, and wagons. Farm women gathered together to husk corn, make clothing, nurse the sick. The hospitality ethic spread more evenly what little they had. The poorer Cherokees felt justified in asking those who were better off to assist them, and such requests were always honored. Still, in those times there were few with much to spare; many of the well-to-do were themselves in debt and awaited federal compensation for losses as eagerly as the poor awaited the per capita payment.

Those best able to cope after removal were the members of the Treaty party. Arriving two years before the Ross emigrants, they obtained the best land not already occupied by the Old Settlers. They had already been handsomely remunerated before leaving the East for the homes, barns, stables, cultivated fields, and other "improvements" they had given up; they had sold their live-stock at good prices. Most of them spoke English and could deal shrewdly with traders from Arkansas. Comparatively few members of the Treaty party were poor; many of them owned black slaves. These slaves cleared their land in the West, built their new homes and barns, put up rail fences, plowed their fields, and cultivated their crops.[5] While those in the Treaty party helped their own relatives, they were not people to whom Ross party emigrants turned for help. Political antagonisms ran too deep; even clan relationships broke down as a result of the bitter feelings over the fraudulent treaty.

In addition to the lack of cash among the poor, many of the Ross emigrants who arrived in 1839 were sick or weak from their long and difficult journey. The food supplied by the contractors to help them through their first year was too little and of poor quality. Ross had to put the nation in debt to farmers and merchants in Arkansas to prevent a famine. What crops they planted after their arrival went into the ground late, and the crop that fall was so small that almost nothing was left for seed the next spring when the government rations ceased. By the end of 1840, thousands were near starvation.[6] Many discovered that the first places they chose to begin farming lacked good soil; others planted too close to streams that flooded in the spring, washing away what they had sown. Grasshoppers and other pests ate their crops. They were unacquainted with the amount of rainfall and the best times to plant in the new climate. It took years to become familiar with the rainfall, soil, and cli-mate in this new region. They also faced new epidemics of malaria, typhoid, smallpox, and other diseases, like "summer fever," that were prevalent in "sickly places." Herbal remedies they had learned to use in the East did not grow in the Southwest. Uncertain and restless, many Cherokees kept moving from place to place, searching for better soil, more rainfall, or less disease-producing conditions. Often whole neighborhoods left in a group, starting over again farther west in the new homeland with their meager resources. Droughts in the summers of 1841 and 1842 added to their difficulties.

Some Cherokees found solace in their old religious ceremonies. Others tried to reestablish ties with mission churches. Four missionary agencies came west to found new mission stations and schools: the Northern Baptists were the most popular; next were the Southern Methodists; the Moravians had the smallest following; and the American Board of Commissioners for For-eign Missions (chiefly Congregationalists from New England) appealed to the better educated and more acculturated.[7] The federal agent in 1842 estimated that there were "2,000 professors of the Christian religion" in the tribe—less than 12 percent. Missionaries were in low esteem because the Cherokees asso-ciated whites with their expulsion from their homeland and white Americans spoke of the United States as "a Christian country." Only the Baptist mission-ary superintendent had steadfastly supported the Ross party in its resistance to removal until 1838; only three missionaries walked with them over the Trail of Tears. Many Cherokees lost interest in religion of any sort. Some took up gambling or petty crime; some joined with renegade white outlaws stealing horses or robbing travelers. Many took to regular bouts of whiskey drinking that often resulted in brawls, stabbings, and shootings. Frontier whites were convinced that the Indians were peculiarly susceptible to whiskey and lacked the drive and self-discipline to survive as farmers.

Yet prior to removal the Cherokees had succeeded in adapting well to the white man's ways, both politically and economically. Their participation in the institution of slavery and the market economy had enabled some of them to become very well-off. In 1842 Agent Pierce M. Butler reported that these class distinctions remained in the West. "For intelligence and general integ-rity there are about 4,000 . . . who might be classed among the first [rank]."[8] Most of this class, Butler said, "are halfbreeds or what are known to be the middle class, who are ardent and enterprising." He found them "hospitable and well-disposed." Many of these were affiliated with the mission churches, and some were large farmers, traders, merchants, and slave owners. Those of mixed ancestry owned 90 percent of the slaves in the nation.

At the other end of the economic scale, Butler identified the "mountain Indians"—those who had formerly lived in the Great Smoky Mountains of North Carolina, remote from the more acculturated parts of the nation. These he described as "ignorant and but slightly progressed in moral and intellectual improvement, have few comforts and plant barely sufficient for subsistence." Among these, "the lowest class of whites" from Arkansas had the most success peddling whiskey, which, Butler said, was "the cause of all their troubles with citizens of the United States." Whenever a drunken brawl resulted in a shoot-ing, especially if a white were shot, the frontier newspapers and politicians raised the alarm of an imminent "Indian uprising."

By its treaty with the Old Settlers in 1828, the federal government was required to supply the Cherokees with 400 spinning wheels, eight public blacksmiths, and four public wheelwrights or wagonmakers, but as the fed-eral agents reported, these did not provide help to even one-third of the 3,500 Cherokee families.[9] The government was also to provide mills to grind corn, but it had not done so. The government provided no medical assistance, and only one or two missionaries had any medical training.

The missionaries, having been embarrassed by the removal policy, now adopted a policy of political neutrality and eschewed any part in the faction-alism that prevailed after 1839—with the notable exception of the Northern

Baptist Evan Jones, who was such an ardent Ross supporter that the secretary of war expelled him from the nation from 1839 to 1841 at the request of the Treaty party. The primary interests of the missionaries were in saving souls and promoting temperance. Eventually nine mission stations were founded in the new area, each with a school, but these served only a tiny proportion of the school-age children. The sermons of the missionaries, like their tracts and schoolbooks, inculcated an individualistic form of evangelical Protestantism emphasizing the ethic of economic and social success through hard work, self-discipline, piety, sobriety, and morality, measured by the standards of the American—and Victorian—middle class. Cleanliness, self-reliance, neatness, and good manners were the marks of a "civilized" person. Private inner strength through reliance on God's help was "respectable"; seeking charity or "hospitality" from those who were better off was "disgraceful." Missionaries were generally appalled at the lower moral standards of the "common Indian" and complained that they were inveterately "lazy" and "unreliable." Few Cherokees ever wanted to work for whites, so missionaries often hired black slaves instead.

While faith in John Ross's personal honesty remained strong, the continued poverty of the Cherokees rapidly eroded support for his long-range program to obtain a new treaty. Everyone knew that the cost of supporting a delegation of eight or nine Cherokees in Washington for six or seven months every year was a serious drain on limited tribal funds. Equally costly were the fees Ross paid to Washington lawyers who claimed to understand the complexities of politics, lobbying, and treaty making.[10] President Tyler's letter of 1841 promising to work out a new treaty and a new financial settlement raised false hopes. It led Ross to create a committee of Cherokees to gather documentary evidence and sworn statements for unpaid claims of spoliation connected with removal.[11] He expected these property losses to total hundreds of thousands of dollars, which the government would pay.

In the spring and summer of 1842, Ross and his fellow delegates in Washington continued to press Secretary of War John Spencer for the new treaty that Tyler had promised. Finally, in August, Spencer gave them a draft of what he considered the basis for negotiations. If Spencer intended to shock Ross, he succeeded.[12] Not only did it fail to increase the original price of $5 million for their homeland, but its chief purpose was to inaugurate a survey of the Cherokees' new territory in order to divide it up and "allocate" small tracts to each Cherokee family as private property, leaving the remainder open to be purchased by whites. In effect this meant denationalizing the Cherokees and incorporating them as citizens, each on his or her own farm, in an area that would be rapidly dominated by frontier whites. Holding their land in common was the chief bulwark of sovereignty for any tribe. Under Spencer's proposal, the Cherokees would have no tribal land, no tribal government, no sovereignty. Ross could scarcely believe the audacity of this proposal. He and the delegation immediately drafted a strong response explaining why it was totally unacceptable. They returned home in September 1842, stunned at the reversal of their fortunes.[13]

Spencer was well aware of the impact his proposals would have on Ross. He probably hoped to discourage Ross from continuing to seek a new treaty and wished to impress upon him that the War Department was unsympathetic to his leadership. The War Department continued to support the complaints of the Old Settlers and the Treaty party concerning Ross's "usurpation" of power and his failure to punish the murderers of the Ridges and Boudinot. It was embarrassing to federal officials that the United States was not able to protect those who had cooperated to effect Cherokee removal. Ross salvaged only one item from his agenda: Spencer did agree, prior to Ross's departure, to establish a new federal commission to examine all remaining Cherokee claims for spoliation against the federal government.[14]

This commission did not begin work until August 1844, when the commissioners traveled to the Cherokee Nation to meet with Ross and examine the claims his agents had been accumulating.[15] The commissioners were astounded to discover that Ross had gathered over 4,000 claims totaling over $4 million.[16] They refused to certify any claims for spoliation that had taken place after May 1838, the date specified in the Treaty of 1835 for termination of Cherokee residence in the East. Many of these claims were for damages sustained *after* the date when the U.S. Army ejected the 14,000 eastern Cherokees from their homes.[17] Spencer seems to have expected Ross to confine himself to the terms of the Treaty of 1835.

In the midst of this discouraging train of events, Ross and his supporters faced an even greater shock. The more violent and unruly members of the opposition—some members of the Treaty party and some Old Settlers loyal to John Rogers—concluded that their only hope of unseating Ross lay in the violent disruption of the Cherokee government. Some of these men were determined to find and kill those who had taken part in the murders of the Ridges and Boudinot (and some of the avengers may even have been family or clan relations). Others, however, appeared to be little more than renegades who wished to punish Ross's supporters indiscriminately. A third group of Ross opponents engaged in pillage and robbery simply to enrich themselves under the guise of rebellion against Ross. The most prominent among the terrorist avengers were James Starr and his six grown sons. Starr, a signer of the Treaty of New Echota, was probably one of those slated for execution in 1839.

Known as "the Starr gang" by the Ross supporters, James and his sons made every effort to drive Ross from office. Other families soon joined in the terrorism—notably the Wests, the Riders, and the McDanielses. Eventually, some of these gangs included fifty to sixty men. Claiming that if they were to be branded as "outlaws," they would act as outlaws, they began their activities in 1842 and continued for the next four years, until the Cherokee Nation was in such a turmoil that outsiders believed a genuine civil war was in progress. The terrorists became heroes to some members of the Treaty party and the Old Settlers, who gave them whatever aid they could, often hiding them in their homes and feeding them and their horses when they were pursued by Ross's police. They were also befriended by many whites in Arkansas who had been shocked by the Ridge and Boudinot murders and who gave shelter to those families of the Treaty party who fled to Arkansas in fear for their lives. As the terrorism mounted from 1842 to 1846, the downfall of Ross became a goal for many Arkansans who hoped to get rich off the Cherokees and thought they could benefit from befriending Ross's enemies.

The first incident in this bloody struggle for power took place on May 9, 1842, while Ross was still in Washington. A white man named Mitchell, who sympathized with the Treaty party, stabbed and killed Anderson Springston, a leading figure in the Ross party. The stabbing occurred in Arkansas and was thus outside the jurisdiction of the Cherokee authorities.[18] Because no attempt was made by the Arkansas authorities to apprehend and try the murderer, the members of the Ross party saw this as a symbol of frontier enmity to the Ross party and a typical example of the frontier view that the death of an Indian was too small a matter to warrant investigation and trial.

A week after the Springston murder, Stand Watie, the leader of the Treaty party, stabbed and killed James Foreman, another Ross supporter, also in Arkansas. Watie believed that Foreman was one of those responsible for shooting his uncle, Major Ridge. This time a trial was held, but the Arkansas jury let Watie off on the grounds of self-defense.[19] Foreman's relatives and other Ross supporters saw further evidence of collusion between the frontier whites in Arkansas and the Treaty party. Only with difficulty were the family and friends of Foreman restrained from seeking private revenge.

Governor Archibald Yell of Arkansas used the excitement generated by these two murders (kept heated by the frontier newspapers) to argue that the frontier was endangered by an imminent Cherokee civil war. He demanded military protection for white citizens on the border.[20] Ross was denounced as a tyrant. Although the War Department did not heed Yell's plea, this situation was to be repeated many times in the ensuing years. When news of these events traveled east, the sympathy that Ross had won during the removal crisis began to wane. The common theme in the eastern newspapers was that a tribe once called "the most civilized in America" was "reverting to barbarism" now that it had moved to the West. Ross was a shrewd politician who had for years played upon the sympathies of friends of the Indians in behalf of his cause, but the Treaty party now proved equally adept at this game.

Ross's failure in Washington produced a reaction in the Cherokee council in the fall of 1842. Once again the elected representatives responded to popular demands for a per capita payment—a policy that the Old Settlers and the Treaty party promoted for their own ends, namely the removal of Ross from office and a share of the per capita money. The council resolved that Ross must provide a full accounting for all of the funds that had been paid to the nation since 1839.[21] Rumors spread that Ross had used for other purposes money paid to the tribe by the government that should have been distributed per capita. Ross claimed that all monies received by him had been used to pay debts to creditors of the nation and that such payments were essential to keep up the nation's credit as it continued to need new loans. Nothing came of this investigation, for Ross's books were all in order. However, the council was so discouraged that in order to save money it voted not to send Ross back to Washington with a delegation in 1843.

To retrieve his reputation as a responsible leader and to demonstrate that the fears of an Indian uprising were ridiculous, Ross called a conference among all of the surrounding tribes that had been removed from the East—including the Choctaws, Creeks, Seminoles, and Chickasaws. He told Agent Pierce Butler that these tribes had many problems in common that they should discuss in a peaceable way (such as the marking of their exact boundaries, the extradition of wanted criminals, and reciprocal trade). Butler agreed that this would be useful, and invitations were sent to twenty-one tribes in the region. The convention was held at Tahlequah in June 1843.[22] It lasted a month, and the delegates worked hard to draw up a set of agreements, including a compact of peace, friendship, and mutual support. The most controversial clause in their agreement, and one that caught Butler by surprise, was a pledge by each tribe never to "cede to the United States any part of their present Territory."[23] However, many of the delegates said they did not have the power to bind their people to such a promise, and as a result, it was signed only by the Cherokees, Creeks, and Osages. Nevertheless, it served notice that no plan of "allocation" and "detribalization" would be acceptable. This intertribal convention provided new status for Ross among the various tribes in the area, but it also fueled the fears of an Indian uprising throughout the white frontier. Once again the frontier newspapers predicted a major onslaught. Governor Yell was among the most vociferous of the alarmists.[24]

Soon after the convention ended in July 1843, the Cherokees became involved in the biennial elections for council members and their quadrennial elections for a new chief and second principal chief. Joseph Vann, who had resigned from his position as second principal chief in 1840, decided to run against Ross, who stood for reelection. Vann chose another Old Settler, Walter S. Adair, as his running mate. George Lowrey ran as Ross's new running mate. The chief issue in the campaign was Ross's failure to obtain any financial settlement with the U.S. government (and hence any per capita money). Nevertheless, when the votes were tallied, Ross was reelected. Unfortunately, the election did not pass without violence.

On election day, August 8, while three election judges were counting the ballots in the Saline District, they were attacked by six armed men led by Jacob West, George West, and John West. One of the judges, Isaac Bushyhead, had been the prosecuting attorney at the trial of a Treaty party member, Archilla Smith, for murder. (Smith, a signer of the Treaty of New Echota, had been defended in this trial by Stand Watie, the leader of the Treaty party.) Smith, one of the leading figures among the extremist wing of the Treaty party, was convicted and hung. The Wests blamed Smith's hanging on the Ross party (and believed no jury in the nation would ever convict a Ross supporter). At the polling station, George West stabbed and killed Bushyhead. The assailants severely beat another election judge, David Vann, treasurer of the nation. They also attacked and beat Elijah Hicks, one of the leading figures in the Ross party and an associate justice of the Cherokee Supreme Court. The three assailants then destroyed the election ballots for the district. A crowd of spectators, at first held at bay by the gang, finally surged forward and captured some of them, but others escaped. A posse of 100 went after them. George West escaped, but his father, Jacob, was later tried and hung (although he tried to claim exemption from trial in a Cherokee court on the ground that he was a white man and, though married to a Cherokee, had the right to trial in the federal court in Arkansas—a view shared by many whites in Arkansas who disliked the idea that a white man, under any circumstances, could be tried in an Indian court). John West was captured, tried, and found guilty of assault; he was sentenced to 100 lashes and loss of his citizenship. No one doubted that the Wests' attack at the polling station was politically motivated, but it was never clear whether the assailants acted on their own or were part of a more general conspiracy among the extremist faction of the Treaty party. However, the victims were carefully chosen, and the overall purpose was to undermine confidence in the election and intimidate supporters of Ross.[25]

That the Treaty party was determined to keep the nation in turmoil became evident a month later when a group of men led by Thomas Starr, Bean Starr,

Ellis Starr, and Arch Sanders killed a white man named Kelly, who was a visitor in the nation, and Benjamin Vore, a white trader married to a Cherokee, and his wife.[26] After robbing Vore's house, they burned it. It was not clear whether the Starrs were after Vore for his money or for his supposed support of Ross. They may merely have wanted to intimidate travelers from visiting the nation and obtain negative press coverage for the nation. A company of U.S. troops under General Zachary Taylor went after the murderers, but they escaped into Arkansas. Arkansas law officers apprehended them but somehow let them escape. Ross supporters believed the law officers permitted them to escape because they backed the Treaty party's attacks on Ross. General Taylor held the frontier whites of Arkansas culpable. He wrote that there were "systematic efforts which are making by certain citizens of Arkansas to revive and keep up a political excitement in the Cherokee Nation in the internal affairs of which they have no legitimate interest whatever." [27] John Ross, on behalf of the nation, offered a reward of $1,000 each for the capture of these three Starr brothers.[28]

Despite the disruption, the newly elected council was still dominated by the Ross party. One of its first acts in October 1843 was to create a bodyguard for John Ross, fearing that he might be assassinated by some Treaty party extremists.[29] The council then voted to expropriate all of the saltworks within the nation and make them national property;[30] this would bring in handsome financial returns to the nation. However, under the Old Settler government the mineral deposits had been granted to Cherokee owners for their own profit. The most profitable saltworks was owned by John Rogers, the Old Settler chief. Rogers and the others who lost their saltworks by this act complained of the expropriation. According to the Cherokee constitution adopted in September 1839, all mineral deposits belonged to the nation and could not be developed by individuals except when rent was paid and a share of the profits went to the national treasury. The current Old Settler operators had no leases and paid nothing to the nation. Because the council failed to compensate the owners of these saltworks, they declared the action to be a prime example of the tyranny of the Ross government.[31] Whites considered the council's action a serious breach of contract, which further undermined support for Ross in the East.

In the spring of 1844, the council sent Ross and a new delegation to Washington. Ross was still trying to find some way to settle the financial problems the nation labored under because of its refusal to accept the validity of the Treaty of 1835. John Spencer had now been replaced as secretary of war by William Wilkins, who proved equally uncooperative. In fact, he held the Ross government chiefly to blame for the violence in the Cherokee Nation. He met not only with Ross but also with representatives from the Treaty party and the Old Settler party. Wilkins, concluding that there was no way to reconcile these three factions, returned to the solution that the Treaty party and Old Settlers had proposed three years earlier—a division of Cherokee territory into two separate nations.[32] When Ross protested, Wilkins said that the federal government could not assume that any one of the factions was truly representative but at least the Treaty party and Old Settlers seemed able to get along. Ross replied that as long as the federal government chose to ignore the duly elected government and treated groups of malcontented private citizens as though they were official representatives, these factions would be encouraged to promote further strife simply to justify their claims.[33] It was in the interest of these factions to destabilize the reunited Cherokee people.

However, Wilkins convinced President Tyler in the late summer of 1844 that it was necessary to send a special commission to the Cherokee Nation to undertake an official investigation of the charges of Ross's tyranny. Tyler appointed General Roger Jones, adjutant general of the U.S. Army; Colonel Robert B. Mason, commander of the dragoons at Fort Gibson; and federal agent Pierce M. Butler.[34] They were ordered to take public testimony from members of all the factions and report back on the stability and level of support for the Ross government. The violence of the terrorists and the alarmism among the politicians and journalists of Arkansas contributed to Tyler's decision.

Ross's position in Washington was not made any easier by a political decision of his second principal chief, George Lowrey, in September. When the Old Settler delegation returned from Washington in July 1844, its leaders decided to hold a convention in Tahlontuskey to prepare a memorial to the federal government listing all their grievances and asking for help. Lowrey believed this convention had been instigated by John Rogers and other Old Settlers living in Arkansas. He forbade the meeting on the ground that its only purpose was to promote more agitation within the already tense nation. Major William Armstrong, superintendent of Indian affairs for the western territory, acting on advice from federal agent Butler, persuaded the Old Settlers not to hold the meeting, fearing that it would lead to bloodshed.[35] This served the Rogers faction just as well, for it seemed to prove their point that there was no freedom for them to meet in their own country.

Ross remained in Washington until mid-October in order to marry Mary B. Stapler, the daughter of a wealthy Quaker merchant of Wilmington, Delaware. Ross had been a widower for five years, his first wife, Quatie, having died on the Trail of Tears.[36] Ross was now fifty-four; Mary Stapler was only eighteen. She had known Ross for three years. She was disowned by the

Society of Friends for marrying outside the faith (and probably also because she was marrying a slaveholder). They nevertheless had a long and successful marriage. Ross later entered into a partnership with her older brother, John, who opened a store in Tahlequah.[37]

The annual session of the Cherokee council began in September 1844, prior to Ross's return. Mounting violence from outlaw gangs led the council to strengthen its policing system. On October 18, 1844, it established eight police companies or light horse patrols, one for each of the eight electoral districts. Each patrol of twenty-five men elected its own captain.[38] Ross's opponents referred to these patrol companies as "vigilantes" who lacked discipline and sought essentially to arrest or shoot down Ross's opponents. While there were many occasions over the next few years when the light horse patrols and the outlaw gangs did shoot it out with each other, these patrols were not essentially political in nature. However, they were vindictive against those who shot law officers. Moreover, many of the outlaws (even those assumed by the Ross party to be politically motivated) engaged in robberies, horse stealing, slave stealing, and killings that had no political significance. The Cherokee Nation, like most frontier communities in the West in these years, was frequently the scene of gunfights and private vendettas; located on the open prairie, the nation needed a mounted patrol to deal with outlaw bands.

Tyler's three-man investigating committee began its work in the Cherokee Nation in November 1844. It held its first conference at Tahlontuskey, where it heard testimony from 546 members of the Old Settler party and 362 of the Treaty party. Most of the charges against Ross were made by 155 members of the latter party who were white men married to Cherokees. Some of the Ross party attended and cross-examined the complainants, but the Ross council complained that the commission should meet in Tahlequah in order to hear from those who supported the existing government. After taking testimony from General Arbuckle (now back as commandant at Fort Gibson) and Agent Butler, the commission did move to Tahlequah in December. It completed its work in mid-January 1845. To everyone's surprise (and the War Department's chagrin), its report to President Tyler constituted a strong endorsement of John Ross's position. The commissioners reported:

> The complainants in the Old Settler and Treaty Party [have] not shown in any case that life has been taken or endangered by the Cherokee authorities since the "act of union," except in the administration of wholesome laws. It cannot be denied that human life in the Cherokee country is in danger— great danger. But the danger lies in the frequent and stealthy incursions of a desperate gang of banditti—"half breeds" notorious in the nation as

wanton murderers, house burners and horse stealers, but whose fraternity is not of the dominant party. . . . The ample share in the offices of the nation by the Western Cherokees, especially in the judiciary (for the bench has been filled chiefly from among them) ought to lull suspicion of partial administration of the laws. . . . In view of all these ascertained facts, the allegation "that they cannot live in peace in the same community with their alleged oppressors" is of little weight and ought not, in the opinion of the commissioners, to be entertained. . . . The "old settler" and "treaty party" enjoy . . . liberty, property, and life in as much security as the rest of the Cherokees. . . . Nothing is more calculated to keep alive the flame of discord in the Cherokee nation than the belief that the restless or discontented, though comparatively few in numbers, will always find a ready audience in Washington.

The commissioners then recommended "that a new treaty be concluded on the just and liberal basis set forth and promised in the letter of his excellency, President Tyler, September 20, 1841." [39] John Ross could not have said it better himself. The commission also went on record in support of a resolution by the Ross council in October 1844 strongly opposing any division of the nation into two separate countries. [40]

While Ross later made good use of this report in his discussions with the secretary of war, President Tyler refused to accept its findings as definitive. The Cherokees remained adrift in debt, political confusion, and mounting turmoil for two more years. The failure of the light horse patrol to apprehend most of the outlaws, who continued to find a safe haven in western Arkansas and Missouri, led some of Ross's adherents to take retaliation into their own hands. In January 1845, a prominent Old Settler, Lewis Rogers (a member of John Rogers's family), was murdered in the nation. On February 22, John Fields, a leading figure in the Treaty party, was killed in the nation. No one was apprehended for either murder. The years 1845–46 were to be the bloodiest years of the factional dispute.

In the presidential election of November 1844, the Democrats, led by James K. Polk (a protégé of Andrew Jackson's), won the election. Tyler, the last Whig to serve as president, left office on March 4, 1845. Ross's delegation, with the same agenda it had been pushing since 1840, now met with Polk's secretary of war, William E. Marcy. Like Spencer and Wilkins before him, Marcy told Ross that he did not believe that the Ross party had any more legitimate claim to represent the Cherokees than the Old Settlers or the Treaty party. Also, like his predecessors, Marcy seemed to have less sympathy with Ross than with his opponents. He went so far as to tell the Ross delegation on

April 24 that, if violence continued in the Cherokee Nation, he would send the U.S. Army to maintain order. Ross later discovered that Marcy had written to John Rogers around this time, addressing him as "Principal Chief of the Western Cherokees."[41] The only concession Ross received from Marcy was the regularized payment of the annuities from the tribal trust fund—which, on its face, seemed a recognition of the legitimacy of Ross's council.[42]

Taking advantage of the awkward status of the Ross government, the outlaws in the Starr gang and other gangs, who considered it their function to keep the nation stirred up, launched a new series of murderous assaults in the fall of 1845, which led to some ardent reprisals by the Ross adherents. Between November 1845 and August 1846, there were thirty-three violent deaths in the nation. A letter from Jane Ross Meigs to John Ross, her uncle, on November 5, 1845, marks the beginning of this new reign of terror: "Excitement the most profound reigns around us. More deeds of horror have been committed. The torch and the deadly weapon have reeked the vengeance of the dark and hellish band of desperadoes who have so long infested the country."[43] The disorder brought itinerant missionary work to a standstill, made it dangerous to travel along the roads, and thoroughly disrupted normal trade. It successfully delivered the coup de grace to Ross's effort to reunite the nation on his own terms.

While the council was still in session on November 2, 1845, Tom Starr and his gang tortured and killed two full-blood Cherokees who had observed them spying on the home of Return J. Meigs, Jr., the husband of Jane Ross Meigs. Meigs, a white man, son of a former federal agent, was a very successful and wealthy trader in Tahlequah. He lived in a fine brick house at Park Hill, three miles from where the council was in session at the time. The Starrs planned to murder him in order to embarrass Ross in his own neighborhood. They also wanted to obtain Meigs's money and to demonstrate that not even in the heart of the nation, in the community where Ross and most of his most loyal supporters lived, was there safety from his enemies. Meigs managed to hold the robbers off long enough to escape through a rear window and hide in a copse behind his house. From his hiding place, he watched while the Starrs intimidated his slaves, then ransacked and burned his home. Meigs, unable to get immediate help, identified the marauders as Tom Starr, his brothers Washington and Ellis, Suel Rider, Samuel McDaniels, and Ellis West.[44]

Tom Starr was twenty-three years old in 1843. He was six feet, five inches tall, well-built, with a broad forehead, black hair, gray eyes ("generally with the lashes plucked out"), large feet, and great muscular strength, weighing 200 pounds. "He smiled a lot when he talked" and was a good horseman and a crack shot.[45] Tom Starr and his brothers shared a profound hatred of John

Ross and a deep conviction that there could be no reconciliation between the Treaty party and the Ross party. His motivation started as a political act, but his hatred quickly descended to personal vendettas and a desire for plunder. Tom Starr was said to have killed twenty men during the course of his career as an outlaw, fewer than half of whom could be connected in any way with the executions of 1839. Once the Cherokee light horse patrol began to arrest and punish the outlaws, they too were targets. Any police officer who shot a member of a gang became a candidate for execution by that gang.

A more political approach to vendettas was expressed by John Rollin Ridge, the son of the murdered John Ridge. He was only nineteen in 1846 and lived in Arkansas with his widowed mother and other relatives. He kept in close touch with his uncle, Stand Watie, and dreamed that someday he might waylay John Ross and stab him to death for the execution of his father. Early in 1846, after reading about various exploits of the Starr gang, Rollin wrote to his uncle Stand Watie, describing Tom Starr as a hero of romantic proportions to the younger members of the Treaty party: "I saw a man this morning from Boonsboro [in Arkansas] who had seen Tom Starr and Samuel McDaniels; they were in fine health and spirits. Those fellows, especially Tom Starr, are talked of frequently and with wonderment here. He is considered a second Rinaldo Rinaldina. Robberies, house-trimmings, and all sort of romantic deeds are attributed to this fellow, and the white people in town [Fayetteville, Arkansas,] and around say they had rather meet the devil himself than Tom Starr!"[46] A week after the Starr gang burned Meigs's house, a posse of 800 Ross supporters headed on horseback toward the Flint District of the nation on the Arkansas border, where James Starr lived. They surrounded his home, believing that the gang was inside. A gunfight ensued, during which the posse shot and killed James Starr and wounded two of his sons, William and Washington (aged fourteen), and Suel Rider, a member of the gang. However, Tom Starr and the rest of his brothers mounted their horses during the fray and escaped across the border into Arkansas. When the smoke cleared, there were eleven dead and eighteen wounded, most of them members of the posse. Believing that this would lead to all-out war against any Treaty party members still in the nation, hundreds of them fled to Arkansas too. Soon after this, the Ross council voted to strengthen the police force.[47] Ross was in Washington at the time.

General Arbuckle, now stationed at Fort Smith, Arkansas, sent an order to acting chief George Lowrey ordering him to disband his police companies on the ground that in hot pursuit they might cross the Arkansas boundary to capture the outlaws. He also ordered a company of U.S. dragoons to patrol the Flint District.[48] Lowrey refused to disband the police, claiming the sovereign right of the Cherokees to police themselves. Many of the Old Settlers who supported John Rogers joined the Treaty party extremists in flight to Arkansas and Missouri. Others, like Stand Watie, stood their ground. Watie gathered sixty men around him at old Fort Wayne (which was soon rechristened Fort Watie by his supporters). An abandoned army post, it was located on Honey Creek in Beattie's Prairie at the northeastern corner of the nation near the Arkansas border. Watie said he would defend himself against any police or posse sent to arrest him. He was not known to have engaged in any outlaw activity with the young hotheads, and no one sought his arrest. However, he had good reason to support the outlaws, for his brother, Thomas, was killed on November 14, 1845, by an unidentified man assumed to be of the Ross party.[49]

The murderous assaults on both sides mounted rapidly in the last months of 1845 and the early months of 1846. The light horse police in the Ross party were determined to rout out the bandits once and for all. The bandits, on the other hand, were determined to make as much trouble as they could. A sufficient number of deaths were connected to retaliations between Ross supporters and Treaty party members to give the appearance of a civil war. In January 1846, Granville Rogers, the son of John Rogers, was killed. That same month the Ross man who had shot Bean Starr was stabbed to death. In March, Stand Dougherty, who had been among the posse that killed James Starr, was killed by the Starr gang; a man implicated in Dougherty's murder, Wheeler Faught, was captured by the police, tried, and hung. The Starrs killed a Ross man named Cornsilk, and on March 29, a man named Turner of the Treaty party was killed in retaliation. That same month, Ellis, Dick, and Billy Starr were wounded in a gunfight with the police because they had killed a Ross man named Too-noo-wee; they managed to get across the border into Arkansas and took refuge with General Arbuckle at Fort Smith. The Cherokee council demanded their extradition, but Arbuckle said he would not deliver them until those in the Ross posse who killed James Starr were punished. In July 1846, Jim and Tom Starr killed two members of the Ross party named Baldrige and Sides; in retaliation the police killed Billy Rider of the Treaty party.[50]

By this time there were over 750 Treaty party and Old Settler refugees in Arkansas (150 families). Having fled with no provisions, they sought help from Arbuckle, and he provided them with army rations that he said the Cherokee Nation would have to pay for out of its annuities. The people of Arkansas once again demanded federal troops to protect their borders, but Arbuckle said there were sufficient troops at Fort Smith to protect the frontier. Nonetheless he issued guns and ammunition to the Arkansas militia in case there were incursions.[51] The *Cherokee Advocate*, which began publication in Tahlequah in 1844, was the official organ of the Ross council. Its editors explained the collusion between the citizens of Arkansas and the Starr gang in terms of the desire of the frontier whites to acquire the Cherokees' land: "Our comfortable cabins, productive farms, valuable mineral resources, clear streams, and beautiful prairies excite the cupidity and moisten the lips of those who have not failed to filch by fraud or rob by superior power of their native inheritance every Indian community with whom they have come in contact." The *Advocate* also noted that many citizens of Arkansas had loaned money or sold goods on credit to the so-called "refugees" of the Treaty party and Old Settlers, and "their only chance of getting a copper is to foment difficulties, creating dissentions to bedevil the Cherokees until, by a regular system of interference, slander, falsehood and misrepresentation, they can cajole the United States Government and create an apparent necessity for the adoption of some measure that will destroy our integrity and throw a few millions of dollars into the hands of those 'Chiefs' as indemnity for the supposed grievances they have sustained."[52] As General Taylor had said several years earlier, the western politicians and journalists purposely whipped up public fear while businesspeople in Arkansas expected to profit from any troops sent to the area.

However, some of the men elected to head the Cherokee light horse police were far from professional in their behavior. Knowing these gangs to be ruthless, they preferred to shoot first and ask questions later. The light horse police captains in the Saline and Delaware districts, Bug John Brown and John Potatoes, were particularly noted for their improper conduct.[53] Evidence that Ross party members were often ready to take justice into their own hands when robbed by one of the outlaw gangs was provided by Daniel Coodey, a nephew of John Ross, in a letter written in December 1844. Believing that the Starr gang had stolen several of his horses and others from his neighbors in Tahlequah, Coodey led a self-appointed posse in pursuit. The Starrs had fled to the Choctaw Nation, directly south of the Cherokees. The posse caught up with them there, wounding and capturing Bean Starr, who admitted that his brothers had stolen the horses. "We recovered ten horses and mules (including one that Bean Starr was riding when shot) which had been stolen from citizens of this country," Coodey wrote to his uncle. "Eight of the recovered horses and mules were taken there by the three Starrs" and their friends George Fields, Robin Vann, and Ta-ka ha-ka. "I was informed by William Harris, among other things, that the three Starrs came into the nation in the early part of the fall past for the purpose of house burning, robbing and killing the principal public men and those who were most active in attempts to arrest them shortly after their outrage upon Mr. [Benjamin] Vore and family," but "they had deferred the work of murder" because some of the gang refused to join them.[54]

When Coodey questioned Bean Starr, he revealed the mental outlook of the Starr family. Bean said that "but for his [Tom's] threats and the commands of his father, he would have some time since surrendered himself for trial. He further stated that it was their determination, in case either of them should ever be taken or killed, to rise and avenge him. He also declared that his father, James Starr and brother, Tom, were wholly to blame for his acts. . . . Much anxiety was manifested and expressed by him that we should not leave him because he said the other two would be certain to kill him since his Father had directed them to do so if he should ever leave them—a command which his brother Tom had at one time drawn a pistol to execute."[55]

Evidence of the lawless retaliations of the Ross party against the outlaws whom they considered to be tools of the Treaty party can be found in letters to Stand Watie. One of these, written in 1840, states that "not more than four days ago Jack Hawkins [a Treaty party member] came very near being killed by a member of the Ross party and when the party that came to kill him, found he had escaped [the Ross man] carried off a trunk containing nearly all that he [Hawkins] was worth."[56]

As the acknowledged leader of the Treaty party, Stand Watie was kept well informed of the killings and robbings that took place between 1840 and 1846. These letters indicate that the feuding included stealing slaves as well as horses and money: "Wheeler Faught was hung on the 23rd of last month for decoying Stand [Daugherty of the Ross party] out when he was killed. Two others were to be tried this week for the same offense. . . . Several persons have been killed since you left. . . . Old Corn Tassel who lived in Flint, he was killed at home and a negro boy was taken off. Some persons stole Two Negro boys from Wes. Creek and Two Mules, got away with them. M. Simon and others is charged with it. I heard today that five or six Negroes and several good Horses had been taken from Flint. Two Horses from Washington Adair."[57] Most of the persons reported as being robbed in this letter were members of the Treaty party. However, the outlawry was so indiscriminate that even Watie and his friends often did not know who had perpetrated the crimes and whether they were acting out of party motives or simply to enrich or avenge themselves. The same correspondent noted that the citizens of Arkansas were becoming worried over the number of thieves taking refuge in the border towns: "I think, from what I can gather, there is a company forming on both sides of the line to arrest these men that is killing and stealing negroes and horses."

By 1846, Ross had to face the fact that his enemies had succeeded in under-mining law and order and had seriously weakened his hand in negotiations with the government. Federal authorities were given regular evidence by the Treaty party and Old Settler delegations (as well as by the frontier press and the federal agents in the nation) of the breakdown of law and order. Even Ross's police force was out of control. Under orders from the men they elected as patrol captains in each district, the patrols now executed their own jus-tice—posse style—without waiting for warrants, courts, and trials. Stand Watie's wife, Sarah, who had taken refuge in Arkansas, wrote to her brother, James Bell, one of Watie's trusted allies, describing stories she had heard about the Cherokee police: "The police have taken David Knightkiller and run Eli Raper off and several others. I have not heard what they have done with David and them, but there is no doubt that they will either whip or hang him. Several have run over the line for refuge. Walter Ridge has just come in from Honey Creek [the Waties' home in the Cherokee Nation, now deserted]. He says John Watie has collected his men together again and is now building a fort at Hilierd Roger's [a relation of John Rogers] place. I wonder what they will do next. I expect they [will] all be scalped before long." [58] Another letter spoke of the ambushing of Treaty party followers: "An unprovoked murder was committed day before yesterday on Jack Elliot at his residence on Grant River. . . . [He was] fired on by some [persons] concealed in the bushes. . . . I have no doubt in my mind that his being with us and opposed to John Ross['s] measures was the cause of his death." [59]

Treaty party members held John Ross directly accountable for any and all harassment of their people. They believed he was determined to wipe out Watie and his friends or allow his supporters to do it. "The Ross party are out and doing," one Watie supporter reported. "They state that their inten-tions are to make a sacrifice of every respectable citizen belonging to the Old Settlers and Treaty Party they may fall in with and their Police Parties are all the time on the alert and doing mischief of considerable magnitude. . . . Dear Stand, you can form no idea of the situation of our distressed and unhappy people, we are, it is true, in the minority, and at this crisis can only act on the defensive. . . . Our mutual friend James Price has this moment informed me that the Ross police are seen every night recruiting [patrolling?] in the state of Missouri in search of those belonging to our party." [60] Much of what was reported were merely rumors, but the strong feeling of persecution on both sides was real enough.

By April 1846, the vindictiveness reached its highest pitch. John Candy, a relative and close ally of Watie's, sent him this report:

You will doubtless recollect that Stand, the murderer of James Starr, was killed and scalped and that Faught was caught for decoying him and has since been hung. Since that time old Cornsilk has been killed and robbed of a negro. Mrs. Pack has had some negro children kidnapped. Barrow Justin has been caught, tried and was hung yesterday. Ecoowee became State's witness against him. Bug John Brown and his [police] company caught a horse thief and they have killed him. It is now rumored that he and his company . . . have cut up another man in Flint in his own house. Bug seems to be the Constitution, law, Court and Executioner, yet our editor [of the *Cherokee Advocate*] can't see him in any light than a decent and clean man, all facts to the contrary notwithstanding. I forgot to mention that another man was killed at Ellis Hardin's. This man, it is said, was one of the company in Downing's gang in the mountains. He was scalped.

I think there is now to be no end to bloodshed, since the Starr boys and the Ridges have commenced revenging the death of their relatives. A dozen or so are implicated, and I am afraid that some of them will be more desperate than the first ones.

Murders in the country have been so frequent until the people care as little about hearing these things as they would [to] hear of the death of a common dog.[61]

Candy blamed Ross for the violence: "The question may be asked, 'Who first began the troubles in the Cherokee Nation?' The answer is obvious. We know it well." Candy referred to the murders of the Ridges and Boudinot as the origin of the civil war; he did not choose to see the betrayal of Cherokees by the Treaty party in 1835 as the cause of the trouble.

These actions did little to help John Ross's case among whites. They fit only too easily into the stereotypical picture of the supposed innate and ineradicable savagery and thievery of Indians. Similar bloodthirsty feuds among poor white southern mountaineers or bloody frontier town battles between white outlaws and sheriffs' posses fell into a different category in the minds of whites. In the 1850s, the murderous battles among white settlers for control of "Bleeding Kansas" were to demonstrate that frontier violence could be just as bloody and indiscriminate among whites as among Indians when it came to struggling for political dominance.

As usual, there were delegations from all three Cherokee factions in Washington in the spring of 1846. William Medill, who had replaced T. Hartley Crawford as commissioner of Indian affairs in October 1845, met with all three delegations and reported to President Polk that Ross's government was not protecting the lives and property of the Old Settlers or the Treaty party citizens. He rejected Ross's claim that the police and courts would soon have the situation under control. Believing that the civil strife was out of control, Medill recommended that there was no possible way to reconcile the three parties and that the only solution was to provide a territorial division of the country into two separate nations.[62] Cherokee sovereignty was to be divided.

Polk accepted this advice, and on April 13, 1846, he told Congress, "I am satisfied that there is no probability that the different bands or parties into which [the Cherokee Nation] is divided can ever again live together in peace and harmony and that the well-being of the whole requires that they should be separated and live under separate governments as distinct tribes."[63]

To counter this threat, the Ross delegation sent a long memorial to Congress blaming the bloodshed on the machinations of the two minority parties and various gangs of outlaws who had no party affiliation. Ross maintained that "the malcontents of the nation consist of idle, reckless and lawless men" and that "the number of these has been only increased by the mistaken policy of the government of the United States in encouraging" the unofficial delegations of "a few others, more intelligent and respectable, but whose purposes are wholly venal and selfish." The Ross memorial refuted the right of the federal government to interfere in the internal affairs of the Cherokee Nation or to divide the Cherokees' country without their consent. Ross cited the report of Tyler's commissioners (Jones, Mason, and Butler), who "attribute[d] all the dissensions and difficulties in the country to a portion of the western Cherokees, and the treaty party whom they properly designate as 'a desperate band of banditti.' "[64] The vast majority of the Cherokees, the memorial concluded, were peaceful, law-abiding citizens loyal to the prevailing government led by John Ross.

Nonetheless, the House Committee on Indian Affairs reported on June 2 that it supported the president's recommendation. A bill was introduced seeking legislation to divide the Cherokee Nation.[65] Ross faced a total loss of all he had worked for over the past seven years—that is, sustaining the unity and sovereignty of his people.

To avoid this catastrophe, he had no choice but to compromise. Most bitter of all, he had to accept the validity of the Treaty of New Echota. This probably was the goal of the federal government and of his enemies from the outset. Before Polk would agree to withdraw his plan for division of the nation from Congress, Ross had to agree to a number of other concessions, which he discussed with a commission that Polk appointed. The hard line taken by the United States at this time may have been instigated in part by the impending crisis with Mexico. Polk wanted no Indian dissension to the north of Texas while American troops were engaged in a war to the south.

Ross's delegates and Polk's commissioners met through the month of July to draw up a treaty that would resolve the internal difficulties that had so long plagued the nation. In effect, Polk's commission acted as a form of compulsory arbitration.[66] By the terms of this treaty, signed on August 6, 1846, Ross agreed to accept the Treaty of 1835 and work within its limits. This meant that he accepted the price of $5 million for the ancestral lands. He also agreed that the Old Settlers were part of the Cherokee Nation and therefore deserved a share of whatever per capita money was distributed as a result of that sale. He further agreed that the Cherokees who had escaped removal by hiding in the mountains and who now lived in North Carolina were entitled to a share of the per capita payments. Of course, the Treaty party would also receive such payments. This meant that there would be far less money available for Cherokee economic recovery and development in their new home. The thousands of dollars deducted from the original $5 million sale price to pay for spoliations and removal costs would result in a much smaller per capita payment for those in the Ross party who had borne the brunt of the removal process.[67]

However, Ross won some of his points. The Old Settlers finally gave up their claim to be the sole owners of the 7 million acres in the new homeland and thus yielded de jure control to the Ross party's government under the Act of Union and the new constitution. This was made palatable to the Old Settlers by Polk's agreement to ask Congress to provide additional funds to pay the Old Settlers a per capita rate equal to one-third of the total per capita payment under the Treaty of 1835. Ross succeeded in obtaining a patent in fee simple to the 7 million acres, as Jackson and Tyler had promised, but it was not worded in such sweeping terms as he wished. He agreed that the Treaty party should be allowed $100,000 (to be taken from the treaty money) to pay for validated claims of any losses they had suffered during the preceding five years when they were "forced" to abandon their homes and flee to Arkansas. In addition, $5,000 was to be paid as indemnity to each of the families of Major Ridge, John Ridge, and Elias Boudinot.

The Old Settlers and the Treaty party agreed to a general amnesty for all crimes committed by all parties over the preceding seven years. They also agreed that all "refugees" in Arkansas (including the Starr gang) would be encouraged to return under full protection of the law and with full rights as citizens of the nation. Furthermore, the light horse police companies appointed by the council were to be dissolved, and henceforth only civilian law officers were to maintain order.[68]

This treaty was ratified by the U.S. Senate on August 7, 1846. At its signing, Stand Watie and John Ross—whose enmity long preceded and long followed that date—shook hands and pledged to work together for peace, harmony, and the general welfare of the reunited Cherokee Nation. Presenting the treaty to the council for its approval on November 12, 1846, Ross said:

> It is the most favorable arrangement that could be made, and although not so liberal in some respects as was desired, yet it is a document of great importance to the Cherokees. Besides benefiting all parties more or less in a pecuniary point of view, it secures to us some of our most highly prized rights and privileges. . . . Among the advantages derived from it may be enumerated as of especial importance, the dissolution of former parties, the renewed recognition of our government, the possession in fee of our domain unimpaired, the restoration of peace.[69]

In short, the Cherokees, under Ross's leadership, were to be sovereign in their new land. However, he also noted that "it will be seen that no provision is made in the Treaty for private claims had by many [emigrant] citizens for losses they have sustained at the hands of the United States" between May 1838 and the time of arrival in the West. "The delegation labored to obtain a stipulation for this purpose, but were unsuccessful, and those claims consequently remain open for future adjustment upon principles of equity and justice."[70]

Two weeks later, after the council had ratified the treaty, Ross proclaimed a day of national thanksgiving "to the Author of all Good" for seeing the nation "through a long series of difficulties and dangers of the most perilous and alarming character." He asked the citizens to offer "the most humble and devout expression of our gratitude to Almighty God."[71] The Treaty of 1846 finally brought unity and order. It also brought the per capita payments so desperately needed for economic recovery. John Ross had kept the Cherokee Nation together once again. Now, seven years after removal, the Cherokee people looked forward to a quiet future with the funds and stability for revitalization. Only in 1846 did the removal crisis end.

3

Economics and
Traditionalism,
1846–1855

The common people are making slow but steady advances

in the science of agriculture; the more enlightened and intelligent

portion who have means, live much in the same style of the

southern gentlemen of easy circumstances.

—*Agent George M. Butler, 1853*

The Treaty of 1846 brought peace and political unity to the Cherokees after almost two decades of confusion and turmoil. Factionalism was not
dead, but it was temporarily subdued. Ross felt that he had given up much for
this; to accept the false Treaty of New Echota was a major pill to swallow.
He did so primarily for the sake of Cherokee unity and sovereignty. Sovereignty for Ross and most Cherokees meant the right to govern themselves in
their own way under their own leaders and to expect the federal government
to honor their treaties as it would honor treaty stipulations with any foreign
nation. Because the United States still dealt with Indian nations by treaty,
Ross maintained that the Cherokees were not subject to direct control from
Washington, D.C., in matters of taxation, criminal affairs, and citizenship.
The Cherokee constitution, though modeled on that of the United States, was
its own supreme law. Total sovereignty was limited only by treaty negotiations
mutually beneficial and voluntarily signed, and treaties were permanently
binding on both the Cherokees and the United States.

The first step in assuming control over their destiny as a nation was to establish economic stability. Ross was determined to squeeze every possible cent legitimately due to the nation from the federal government. These funds were to finance the rebuilding, the agricultural and mineral investments, the network of roads and ferries, and the government infrastructure that would enable the Cherokees to revive their economy.

The annual running expenses of the nation were met after 1846 essentially from the income of the trust fund of $500,800 that was established under the Treaty of 1835. Held in trust by the president of the United States and invested mostly in state bonds, it produced between $35,000 and $45,000 per year.[1] Ross knew that this "tribal annuity" would never be sufficient to meet the nation's annual expenses, nor would it do much to stimulate the nation's economic development. Out of this annuity, the Cherokees had to pay their governmental expenses (buildings, salaries, courts, police, tribal newspaper, delegations to Washington). It also had to support the nation's public school system, inaugurated by the council in 1841, and the national orphanage (to care for those children whose parents had died during and after removal). From 1839 to 1846, tribal expenses always exceeded this fixed income. The nation had been borrowing funds from private bankers against the next year's annuity without ever catching up. Efforts of the council to raise additional revenue from taxes met strong resistance. By 1850 the Cherokee Nation was in debt to private creditors for over $100,000, and this deficit continued to rise.

In 1846, having signed the Treaty of 1846 to pacify his opponents, Ross expected that he would soon be able to resolve the financial issues that were pending with the federal government. With part of the money due, he planned to establish a Cherokee National Bank that would make loans to enterprising Cherokees for business purposes and for developing the nation's resources. If he obtained all the money he believed rightfully due, he thought there would be sufficient funds remaining for a large per capita payment to help "the poorer class." The money due fell into four categories, each of which grew out of treaty stipulations. First, Ross felt the Cherokees who had resisted removal and refused to accept the validity of the Treaty of 1835 should now be fully remunerated for damages or loss of property during removal. Second, he believed that the government had not yet fully paid the nation back for some of the expenses in effecting removal and for the rations promised to them but never received during the year after removal.[2] Third, he claimed that the government had no right to deduct the removal costs from the $5 million it had agreed to pay for the Cherokee homeland. (The Treaty of 1835 seemed to imply that it could do so, but a later agreement with the War Department on June 12, 1838, said that the department would pay separately for the cost of removal.)[3] Because the per capita payment, which the Cherokees were counting on to relieve their private debts, would be drastically reduced if removal costs were deducted from the sale price, this was a critical matter for Ross. The fourth bone of contention involved Ross's conviction that the government ought, in equity, to pay the Cherokees 5 percent interest since 1838 on all of these unpaid sums due to the Cherokee Nation. Since the sums due constituted millions of dollars, this interest would add significantly to the total.

Needless to say the War Department vigorously resisted all of these demands, claiming that it had already paid in full everything it had promised except the per capita fund—the sum remaining after all costs of removal were deducted from the $5 million fund. Most of these deductions were charged not to the emigration costs per se but to remunerate the Cherokees for the improvements they had to leave behind (their homes, barns, stables, fences, cultivated lands, and other fixed assets, such as sawmills, gristmills, and ferries). The persistence with which Ross fought for these monies was central to his concept of the kind of sovereignty he considered due to all Indian nations. He was not asking for charitable support but for the payment of an international debt. To retain their independence, Ross and other tribal chiefs had to become masters of manipulating the minutest aspects of the contractual agreements inserted in treaties (with critical assistance from white lawyers specializing in "Indian affairs").

Ross's negotiations were complicated by competing claims from three other Cherokee groups—the Old Settlers, the Treaty party, and the Cherokees still living in North Carolina. Those Old Settlers who were formerly led by John Rogers (who had died in 1846) expected damages for the losses they sustained when they fled to Arkansas. Although the Old Settlers in general obtained a right to one-third of the per capita fund in the Treaty of 1846, nothing was said about where the remuneration to the so-called "Arkansas refugees" would come from. The Treaty of 1846 had granted $115,000 in damages to members of the Treaty party who had fled for safety to Arkansas during the tumultuous years from 1839 to 1846 (including $5,000 apiece for the families of the murdered Ridges and Boudinot). It was not clear whether this was to be deducted from the $5 million fund. The North Carolina Cherokees (who numbered close to 2,000 by 1846) demanded the right to share in the per capita payments, for it was also their homeland that had been sold and now they had no land to call their own.[4] Because all three factions agreed with Ross that their claims should not detract from the money available for the per capita fund, they seemed united. However, Ross fought all the factional demands on the ground that there was only one Cherokee Nation and the treaty recognized him as its chief. Moreover, he felt that those who had emigrated with him over the Trail of Tears (the "true" Cherokee patriots) were the most deserving. Each faction hired its own lawyers, as Ross did, and their handsome fees would ultimately detract from whatever payments were received.

It came as a great shock to all four Cherokee groups in 1848 when the federal accounting office tallied up what it believed remained from the $5 million to constitute the per capita payments. According to the accountants, after all sums were subtracted for remuneration of lost improvements, spoliations, and the costs of removal itself, all that remained was $627,603.95. This was less than one-fourth of the sum anticipated. The Treaty party had estimated in 1846 that there would be $2,475,734 left.[5]

Negotiations on these complicated items began in 1846 but were slowed down by the War Department's preoccupation with the Mexican War from 1846 to 1848. Indian affairs never had a high priority in Washington except when Indians were at war with the United States. Delays also resulted from the fact that the chief executive, the Treasury Department, and the Congress all had a hand in the matter. Congress would have to vote any appropriations needed to meet Cherokee demands not covered by the Treaty of 1835. Consequently, the negotiations dragged on year after year, and not until 1852 were all issues finally resolved. Ross's long and tedious efforts were successful on some counts but not on others. He could not persuade the government to pay for any spoliations or losses to his followers after May 1838. The Treaty of 1835 would have covered these only if Ross and his followers had accepted its legitimacy and met the deadlines set for claims. The government noted that the commissioners appointed to pay such indemnities had twice already considered extant claims and paid $1.5 million to those who had legitimate claims (mostly members of the Treaty party).[6] On a second important issue, Ross did succeed when the government accepted his argument that removal costs should not be deducted from the $5 million. Furthermore, he persuaded the government that nearly $1 million was still due to the Cherokees for removal expenses because the War Department had underestimated the cost of removal. He also won additional funds to cover extra costs paid for by bank loans to Cherokees when the federal contractors failed to provide sufficient rations during the year after they arrived in the West. Finally, he won his point that 5 percent interest should be added onto all of these sums when paid.[7]

Many years later, after Ross's death, Congress reconsidered the issues he had raised in these negotiations and concluded that another $961,368.66 was due to the Cherokees. That sum would have given Ross enough for a national bank had it been paid when needed most. Congress also voted in 1882 to give an additional $421,653.66 to the Old Settlers with 5 percent interest.[8] The Old

Settler faction won its request that $125,000 in damages was due to those families who had fled to Arkansas for their safety in the years 1839 to 1846. The North Carolina faction won the right to share in the per capita fund.

It was a measure of the loyalty of the great mass of Cherokees to Ross and of their confidence in his honesty in defending their rights that they continued to elect him chief during these difficult years. His success also speaks well for his careful record keeping, his skill with statistics, and his patience as a negotiator. Still, as during the removal crisis, many criticized him for causing hardship to his people by refusing for so long to compromise for smaller payments in federal negotiations.

The first breakthrough in negotiations occurred in December 1849, when a Senate committee voted to consider Ross's arguments that the costs of removal must be borne by the United States and not subtracted from the $5 million. After deliberating on his appeal, Congress then voted on September 1850 to add $189,422 to the money due for subsistence rations during the year from 1839 to 1840. Then in September 1851, Congress voted an additional $729,603.27 to cover the underestimate on the cost of removal itself.[9] The next victory came when Congress agreed in 1851 that 5 percent interest should be paid on all the funds now to be paid to the Cherokees. When this interest was added to the above sums, the total amount available for the per capita payments increased by almost $1 million, from $627,603.75 to $1,571,346.55. One-third of this sum was distributed per capita to the Old Settlers in September 1851. The North Carolina Cherokees received $197,534 for their per capita distribution. Not until April 1852, fourteen years after removal, was the remaining $1,032,182.33 distributed per capita to the members of the Ross party and the Treaty party. At this time there were 2,133 North Carolina Cherokees eligible for per capita payments, 2,495 Old Settlers, and 13,806 Cherokees of the Ross and Treaty parties combined.[10]

For the great bulk of the Cherokees, the per capita payment did little more than pay off the debts they had accumulated between 1838 and 1852. Each Cherokee received $92.79 or about $485 for an average family of five. Their creditors (mostly whites from Arkansas and a few Cherokee merchants) were on hand for the distribution process, collecting their debts from each Cherokee within minutes after the payment (in gold and silver) was handed over by the U.S. officials. The area surrounding the place of distribution was filled with white whiskey peddlers and faro gamblers who managed to take much of the money that was left in the hands of the poor.[11] So many Cherokees were taken advantage of by these whites that many observers deplored the per capita method of trying to help the poor. As one missionary in the Cherokee Nation reported to his board, "The recent payment of per capita monies has had a very injurious effect on the Nation, leading in very many instances to idleness, gambling and intemperance."[12] Another missionary wrote, "The intemperance and frequent murders" shortly after the distribution "are the evil results of the per capita payments."[13] However, missionaries were particularly prone to see most Indians as feckless and irresponsible. There were many Cherokees who used what little they received wisely, buying new tools or livestock for their farms.

The infusion of hundreds of thousands of dollars into the Cherokee economy after 1851 and the wiping out of years of private indebtedness helped considerably to restore national morale and to instill a new sense of hope for national revitalization. It provided the basis for new credit to the nation's treasury and to private citizens and brought renewed confidence in the Ross party's leaders. The smallness of the per capita fund and the demand that it be distributed among so many factions meant that Ross was unable to start a Cherokee bank or to reduce the necessity of annual borrowing to make up for deficits resulting from the small annuity that remained the only solid basis for national revenue. Soon after the distribution of the per capita payments, the national debt was estimated at $200,000.

Ross did his best to obtain other sources of income. Under the Treaty of 1835 the federal government had granted to the Cherokees 800,000 acres of national land in the southeast corner of what became, in 1854, the territory of Kansas. Known as "the Neutral Lands," this large tract was contiguous to the northern border of the nation, but it was not settled by any of the Cherokees. It was considered a national asset or investment to be sold whenever the nation needed money. Ross was convinced that the sale of the Neutral Lands was the best means to relieve the nation of its debt and at the same time provide a capital base for national development. He suggested to the council in 1846 that it authorize the annual delegation to enter into negotiations with the government for its sale.[14] The federal government had estimated its value at $500,000 in 1835. Ross presumed it would now be worth much more. However, selling tribal land was always a touchy matter, and the council rejected the proposal. Ross renewed his plea to the council in 1847. Still queasy about the matter, the council responded by calling a general council of all the citizens to meet at Tahlequah to see whether there was a national consensus for a sale. Ross appealed to the people for their approval, but his plea was rejected. Ross dropped the matter until 1851, when the long delays over payment of the per capita fund had left everyone frustrated. He himself called a general council of the people at Tahlequah to reconsider the sale. When the people assembled on November 17, he told them that the land was probably worth $1 million and that its sale would immediately relieve the nation of all its burdens. The

people finally acquiesced, and the council then authorized its annual delegation to Washington to approach the commissioner of Indian affairs and the
secretary of the interior early in 1852 to arrange to sell this tract back to the
government, thus making it available for white homesteaders. The delegation
offered to sell the 800,000 acres for $1.25 per acre. The federal government
showed no interest in buying it. In 1853, the Cherokees again proposed the
sale, but again the secretary of the interior turned it down.[15]

Despite the payment of the per capita money in 1852, the economy was slow
to revive and the national debt continued to increase. In addition, a terrible
drought in 1854 all but destroyed that year's crops, and it was clear, said Agent
George M. Butler, that famine conditions would prevail during the following
year.[16] Butler also told the commissioner, George W. Manypenny, that Ross
planned to use $200,000 of the sale money to pay off the nation's debts and
to invest the remainder in U.S. bonds to increase the size of the Cherokee annuity. The poorer members of the nation, however, wanted most of the money
to be distributed per capita so that they could have the cash to relieve their
personal debts and restock their supplies. As a result, the council voted on
October 11, 1854, that if the Neutral Lands were sold, no more than $30,000
could be invested after the debts were paid; the rest must be distributed per
capita.[17]

The negotiations with the federal government in 1855 were protracted.
Manypenny offered the delegation two choices: it could accept the sum of
$500,000 from the government in payment for the 800,000 acres, or it could
survey the land itself and accept the responsibility for selling it to white speculators or settlers.[18] The delegates protested that the land was worth at least
$1,250,000, based on their conviction that the government should pay inter-
est since 1835 on its original value. They were not interested in selling the land
themselves because they needed the money at once and could not afford the
time and expense of a survey and piecemeal sales. They then proposed that
the government pay interest on the land only since 1846 and lowered their
price to $700,000. When this offer was rejected, they lowered the price to
$625,000.[19] Although the land was clearly worth much more, the government
refused to go above $500,000.

The situation in the Neutral Lands was further complicated by the fact that
there were now thirty-three Cherokee families living on this land in Kansas,
cultivating a total of 922 acres. Some of these were Old Settlers, never reconciled to Ross's leadership; others were white men recently married to Cherokees and eager to obtain the best land in that area before it was sold in order
to obtain preemption rights.[20] Either these persons would have to be removed
or their land would have to be exempted from the sale price. Manypenny next

suggested that the Cherokees allow the U.S. Senate to set a fair price. This the Cherokees declined, fearing that the Senate would set the price at $500,000 and might require that this sum be shared with the Cherokees still living in North Carolina.

Despite the pressures brought by their creditors (U.S. banks) and the economic difficulties of the poor, the Cherokees refused to be forced into accepting a price they considered patently unfair. Fortunately, a good harvest in 1855 alleviated the famine. Creditors, still expecting that the Neutral Lands would be sold at any moment, continued to grant credit to the nation, and its debt continued to increase.

An earlier expedient utilized to help the nation's debtors was the passage of "stay laws." Starting in 1842 the council passed a law annually that prohibited a creditor from distraining and selling at a sheriff's sale any livestock, farm equipment, or other property of a debtor for failure to pay on time.[21] These laws were considered temporary in the expectation that negotiations with the federal government would soon bring about the per capita payments that would enable the poor farmers to pay their debts. However, as these negotiations continued year after year, the council renewed the stay laws year after year. While the advantages of these laws were obvious to the average farmer, they were often ruinous to creditors, both white and Cherokee. Many small creditors were forced into bankruptcy in the 1840s, which only made credit more difficult to obtain.

In the 1850s, the nation was forced to issue "scrip" to those creditors who had loaned money to the national treasury. The scrip was essentially an IOU redeemable from the Cherokee treasury by the holder at the time of the next annuity. As negotiable "certificates" backed by the nation, they served as a form of paper money—though at a discount. Unfortunately, the amount of the annuity was not fixed, and scrip had to be issued on the basis of what the revenue might be for the succeeding year. Ross tried to avoid the overissuance of scrip by requesting that the United States pay the annuity semiannually. The Treasury Department, however, refused. The value of scrip declined as more and more was issued and renewed rather than redeemed. By the end of the 1850s, the national debt had risen to $300,000.[22] The price of sovereignty was high even for a relatively acculturated and sophisticated tribe like the Cherokees. Conversely, the bonds of economic dependency were corrosive.

Nevertheless, the nation was now stable and rich in resources. More and more white entrepreneurs entered the nation after 1846, and several hundred Cherokee families became wealthy as merchants, tavern keepers, cattle ranchers, millers, and saltworks operators as well as from other occupations of manufacture and trade including trading in slaves. The nation had not only saltworks but also lead, coal, and considerable virgin timber. (No one had yet discovered marketable uses for crude oil and natural gas.) Wagon roads, bridges, and ferries were constantly improved, and a thriving riverboat traffic down the Arkansas River connected the nation with Mississippi River towns from Cairo to New Orleans and up the Ohio to Pittsburgh. (Railroads did not reach the area until the 1870s.) The Cherokee constitution required that the council must license and make a profit from the use of any timber or mineral resources on the communally owned land. However, the council preferred to lease these enterprises to Cherokees and therefore did not charge as much as it might have.

The overwhelming majority of the Cherokees were farmers, but only a few of them grew enough surplus to engage in profitable trade with the surrounding white communities or down the river. Corn, wheat, cotton, cattle, horses, and hogs were the chief surplus items. Wealthier farmers usually plowed the profits from these commodities back into their farms by purchasing fencing, cultivating more land, and buying more slaves. The council was unable to pass any system of taxation that was not strongly opposed by both poor and rich farmers. The nation made no money from selling public land or taxing it because tribal ownership of the land prevented speculation in this commodity among the Indian nations.

In many cases white traders and businesspeople were an asset to the nation since they provided capital, services, and jobs, but most of the whites who sought their fortunes in Indian nations were motivated by the thought that they would have easy pickings among people they considered ignorant. A common part-time occupation for white men in the nation was peddling whiskey—illegal both by Cherokee law and under the Trade and Intercourse Act of Congress. Many whites married Cherokees to obtain the right to use the common land (free of charge) for farming or ranching. Other whites made silent partners of Cherokees and took the profits for themselves while claiming to run a Cherokee business operation. The Cherokees by treaty had the right to expel "white intruders" who had no legitimate reason to be in the nation, but it was difficult, with an open border, to keep out intruders—some of them simply outlaws running from the law or debtors running from their creditors. The federal agent was supposed to expel such persons, but the nation was too large for one man to do this effectively. Many intruders simply went back and forth across the borders stealing Cherokee timber for their own farms or Cherokee salt and coal to sell in border towns. Some whites took up farming as squatters on Cherokee land, and where one started, many others followed.

In time whole communities of whites were living on what they considered "vacant" land. These intruders stubbornly refused to move until the agent called out federal troops to expel them.

Despite the intractable public debt, the erratic climate, and harvest-destroying pests, the Cherokee Nation gradually began to prosper in the 1850s. Not since the halcyon decade of 1817–27 had the nation been so well-off. The Old Settlers and the Treaty party kept their agreement to work within the structure of the constitution, and it was among them—or those of mixed ancestry among them—that the most prosperous elite developed. The nation's success stemmed from a number of circumstances. Their high percentage of English-speaking and intermarried white citizens knew how to make the most of business opportunities. The experience of their first era of revitalization from 1794 to 1830 had given them both knowledge and confidence in their ability to adapt to trade and agriculture in a market economy. Their successful evolution of a centralized government with an efficient political and legal system enabled them to sustain a participatory, if not consensual, form of decision making. Above all, they found dedicated and honest leaders committed more to the general welfare than to their own enrichment. Factionalism was common in all tribes, but seldom had the dominant faction produced leaders as dependable as John Ross and his party. The Cherokees continued to welcome missionaries, and, for many, the schools and churches they brought had provided a valuable alternative to the old religion. The Cherokees had more missionaries among them than most tribes and could choose among a greater variety of Protestant persuasions: Northern Baptist, Southern Methodist, Congregational-Presbyterian, Moravian, and, after 1856, Southern Baptist.

The most important lesson they had learned between 1794 and 1840 was that the original hope that they might be integrated as equals into the United States was impossible. Having accomplished so many of the improvements whites expected of them, they had assumed at first that despite differences in complexion they might find equality. After 1830 this hope was gone. The continuous efforts to remove them (in 1807, 1817, 1819, 1828, and finally 1838) had convinced them that they must rely on their own leaders and sustain their own autonomy. This had been a painful lesson, but it had been helped by the knowledge that they could now write their own language, manage their own economy, sustain their own political structure, and bargain effectively with the Bureau of Indian Affairs in the War Department (after 1849, in the Department of the Interior). As long as the United States lived up to its treaty obligations and guarantees (notably in regard to their self-government and self-determination), the Cherokees believed they could improve conditions for themselves and their children. John Ross had given them much of that confidence, but their own will was crucial. One of the most important lessons Ross himself had learned was that acculturation had to take place at different rates among different groups of his own people. He chose to let well enough alone when full-bloods ignored or rejected the white man's ways and sustained traditional practices. He was a patient leader, and he found more security in trusting the average Cherokee than in aligning himself with those who demanded rapid progress.

In the 1850s the large majority of Cherokees were poor subsistence farmers who built their own homes, cleared their own land, plowed it with a horse, a mule, or an ox, and harvested 8 to 10 acres of corn, wheat, and hay. Most parents had two or three children. They lived in double log cabins and owned some hogs and perhaps a cow or some beef cattle. The women had spinning wheels, perhaps a handmade loom, and a minimal amount of household furnishings. They cooked on an open hearth. The missionaries said that many Cherokees slept on the floor of their homes: "The little Indian girls," said a teacher at the Dwight Mission school, "sleep with no other accommodation than a blanket in which to wrap themselves, as they lie down upon the floor. This is their accustomed mode of sleeping at home and they prefer this way." [23] A farmer's wife kept a small vegetable garden where she grew potatoes, peas, pumpkins, and melons; some had peach or apple trees. Some grew cotton and flax or obtained wool to spin and weave the family clothes, but most bought manufactured cloth when they had the cash and sewed their own clothing. Women and children over ten were expected to help the men in the fields at planting and harvest. Cherokee farmers, in short, lived about the same way that the poorer frontier homesteaders did.

The one-horse plow cut a shallow furrow in the tough prairie soil, and small farmers planted only enough corn for their own use (including fodder and seed corn). Livestock generally ran loose most of the year, except the saddle horse and plow animals. Cattle and hogs were slaughtered in the winter, and the meat was salted or smoked. Wood for cooking and heating was gathered in the nearest woods by women and children. Few farmers had a wagon; they transported goods to and from markets on horses or mules.

In good years Cherokee farm families ate well; in bad years they did not. They liked to live near rivers or streams where the soil was richer and water easy to fetch, but spring floods made this hazardous. Two successive years of drought brought them to the brink of starvation and often caused them to move to a different location and start over. If they had been required to pay for their land and take out mortgages, these farmers would have soon been homeless paupers reduced to working as day laborers or sharecroppers. However, common ownership of the land enabled them to move about at will; it was an essential source of hope and perseverance. Even so, had it not been for extended family ties, clan loyalties, and the tradition of hospitality or sharing, the poverty would have been much more severe. Apart from droughts, the worst afflictions were diseases and maiming accidents. Though the nuclear family was the most common arrangement, aging parents, widowed aunts, crippled uncles, or husbandless daughters and their children also lived in many homes.

A sympathetic Baptist missionary, Evan Jones, whose mission board continually asked why his mission churches did not provide funds to help support their native pastors, explained the difficulties his full-blood members faced in the 1850s. There were "two distinct classes" of Cherokees, he wrote, "in very different circumstances with regard to property and the means of acquiring it." The first class were mixed-bloods; they constituted "the wealthy," English-speaking, more-educated class. "The other class, which constitutes the body of the Nation, and to which our labor have been chiefly devoted," were "the full Cherokees" who spoke nothing but Cherokee and had little schooling.

They are generally poor. They live by agriculture with the exception of a very few mechanics. Compared with their conditions 25 years ago, they have made great improvement, but on account of their deficiency in skill and industry, and general intelligence [knowledge], their progress is necessarily slow. And besides this, they have met with many reverses and disasters in their course toward civilization. . . . In 1845 in consequence of an unfavorable season, there was an almost total failure of crops and multitudes came near to starvation, although the Principal Chief procured many thousands of bushels of corn to be distributed among the destitute. Having somewhat recovered from this calamity, and in 1852 received from the United States government a small per capita, which has been due them since 1838, they were beginning to get into somewhat better circumstances, but in 1853 the crops were again cut off [by drought], and to a still great extent. The same calamity having visited the adjoining states, and the Arkansas River being so low that no supplies could be brought from a distance, provisions went up to enormous prices. So that those who had stock of any kind were compelled to sell it to procure food for themselves, their relatives and their neighbors. By this they were greatly impoverished and are not yet recovered from the effect of it.[24]

Jones also noted that it was more difficult for the poor to survive as self-sufficient farmers than it had been when the Cherokees lived in communal town settlements with common gardens, common granaries, and easy hunting and fishing. "The Full Cherokees are just now in a transition state. They have abandoned, to a great extent, their old mode of living and to a corresponding extent have adopted those of white people, which are much more expensive; while their proficiency as producers of the means of subsistence has hardly kept pace with their increased consumption" of manufactured goods for farming, clothing, and household items. Under such circumstances, "you will see how impracticable it would be to such a people to come forward with an offering of 300 to 400 dollars" to help the missionary cause by paying the salaries of their ministers. He pointed out, however, that they had built their own churches and supplied the food for their regular camp meetings. Also, their itinerant native ministers provided their own horses, and all missionaries relied on the food and lodging offered by their converts when they traveled about.

The lack of "proficiency" in husbandry among these full-blood farmers was explained by a knowledgeable federal agent, Justin Harlin, when he was asked to report on the agricultural progress of the Cherokees. "Nearly all the Cherokees, in a small way, cultivate their lands. Only a very small number cultivate largely." The large farms were cultivated chiefly by black slaves owned by the mixed-bloods. "Generally, with those who raise grain, a small field of corn[,] . . . a small field of wheat and a vegetable garden constitute their farm products. A few cultivate more largely, but too many, one-fourth perhaps, raise less than will make their bread. . . . The women are generally slow at their work but steady and industrious, and will do a considerable amount of labor. In too many cases the women have to do most of the work that is done." [25]

However, the major difficulty was their lack of experience and knowledge as farmers: "The cultivation by the best farmers among the Cherokees, I think, has always been defective, and with the poorer farmers, abominable. This country is subject to drought. Their lands are very rich. They plough for all crops too shallow; and corn, when grown, they cultivate too little. Their shallow ploughing on their rich land of a wet season produces a good crop. Of a dry season, their crops are poor. Their dry seasons are as common as their wet ones. If their grounds were broken deeply, and their corn kept clear of weeds, but few of their seasons are so dry as to prevent a large yield." As Harlin noted, to plow deeply required a much heavier plow and much stronger horses (usually two at a time) than most Cherokees could afford. The Cherokees as a whole had been horse-and-plow farmers for more than two generations by 1850, but they had only recently come to live in the more arid climate of the Southwest. Even white homesteaders descended from generations of farmers in the East (and before that in Europe) found it very difficult to cope with conditions west of Missouri and Arkansas on the edge of the Great Plains (then known as "the Great American Desert"). Harlin shared a common view that the "Indian men are generally indolent and careless" and "too frequently left cultivation to the women and children." He also noted that, by choice, they refused to adopt the hard-driving, competitive, materialistic values of frontier whites who came west "to strike it rich." Cherokee tradition operated under a different ethic. "Among the fullbloods, I think, most of them have discarded the notion that [farm] labor is disgraceful to a man, but I think few of them are covetous of any honors confirmed by industry." Self-sufficiency and not the amassing of wealth, land, and comforts remained the dominant outlook. They could adapt to the agricultural mode of life without abandoning their traditional value of living in harmony with nature and in equality with their neighbors.

Justin Harlin also noted that the full-bloods retained other traditional practices. Because "their law allows husband and wife to own separate property, it is not uncommon among full-bloods for the woman to own most of the [live]stock and generally as much as their husbands." Cherokee women guarded their independent right to own their own property after marriage as they did their right to a simple divorce and to control over their children. Cherokee law confirmed these rights. There were many aspects of white "civilization" the Cherokees found unattractive and unfair.

Cherokee farmers had long been accustomed to letting their livestock look after itself. "Horses, mules, cattle, sheep and hogs are reared with so little trouble and expense," said Harlin, that Cherokee farmers did not build barns or fenced pigpens. "They have not heretofore had to feed their stock of any kind [even] in winter, except a few for use [milk cows or saddle horses], but their herds of all kinds lived, and the grown ones, not too old, kept fat all winter." [26] In bad winters, however, they often lost many cattle and horses.

One New England missionary, Charles C. Torrey, noted another important reason why many Cherokee full-bloods were unwilling to drive themselves to build up large farms. "The people who had been greatly discouraged by their forced removal from the East" had become cynical about the possibility of obtaining permanent security in the face of the advancing white frontier. One man, when urged by Torrey to be more thrifty and industrious, replied, "I worked hard *once* and got a good farm [in the old homeland], and it was taken from me, and I am not going to try again." [27] This pessimism among the parents had its effect on the younger generation.

While parents wanted their children to go to school, they did not force them to attend and often called them home from school to help with planting or harvest or when there was sickness. Children often lacked shoes and could not walk long distances in winter.[28] However, the chief reason why full-blood school attendance was low was the frustration Cherokee-speaking children felt when the teachers taught and spoke only in English.[29] There was a certain pride in being able to write one's own language in Sequoyan that many full-bloods felt very strongly. Because the national Cherokee newspaper, the *Cherokee Advocate*, and the tribal laws were printed in both languages and because the missionaries translated the Bible and many other materials into Sequoyan, a Cherokee-speaking full-blood could participate in the life of the nation without knowing English. All speeches at the tribal council were translated from one language to the other. The virtue of learning English was only that it helped in coping with whites—as did arithmetic. Many preferred to avoid contact with whites and kept to themselves. Traditionalism in religious, medical, and social values, like speaking only Cherokee, was both a source of pride or strength and a sign of insecurity. It provided full-bloods with a sense of unity and a desire for isolation.

This same ambivalence was evident in the leisure activities and social life of the full-bloods. While English-speaking children were faithfully attending school, the full-blood children were often learning how to hunt bear and deer or practicing the skills of Cherokee ballplay, a traditional sport similar to lacrosse. Unlike the white-oriented mixed-bloods, the full-bloods enjoyed participation in traditional festivals and dances—the Green Corn (or harvest) Dance, the New Year's fire-lighting ritual, the purification ceremony (or "going to water"), and the all-night celebrations, during which the full-bloods danced around a fire singing ancient songs to the rhythm of rattles, gourds, and drums. Missionaries and white visitors to the nation often found this a sign of "backwardness" and "paganism," as deplorable as the barbarous behavior of frontier whites at horse races, drinking bouts, wrestling matches, and raucous shooting sprees. Female missionaries were particularly shocked at the lack of Victorian propriety among Cherokee men and women. Hannah Moore, a New England missionary teacher, was invited to visit the home of one of her pupils in 1844 during a vacation period.

They had a great corn dance while I was with them. Built a large fire and danced around it hold[ing] of hands, and roasted corn, baked their hough cake in the woods. But, Oh, their Ball plays and Saturday night dances are shocking to humanity. They play on a wager, staking their property for the success of an useless game at running. The night dances are frequently continued till the Sabbath sun dawns on them. Their passions become inflamed and they spend the day in a carousel wholly unbecoming its sanctity. . . . We had not proceeded far before a company of ballplayers over took us riding full speed, whisky bottles hanging at [their] sides. Though a great many females attend their play, my guides knew I did not relish for a moment to look on a scene so disgusting to refinement as Indians running in a state of nudity. When we came nearer the scene . . . I dare[d] not raise my eyes to look.[30]

Most Cherokee full-bloods also continued to make use of the services of medicine men or adonisgi. Whites called them "conjurors," and missionaries forbade converts to go to them for medical or other purposes (such as finding lost objects, love potions, detection of witchcraft, warding off evil spirits, or praying for rain). However, full-bloods found no contradiction in attending such ceremonies and also attending missionary services. Many full-bloods were attracted to revival meetings or camp meetings held in the open air by Methodists or Baptists and lasting for days at a time. The Cherokees were gregarious and enjoyed any opportunity to sing, relax, and meet with friends. Once missionaries began to license and ordain Cherokee-speaking preachers, the full-bloods found certain aspects of Christianity very appealing. The sharp dichotomy that whites perceived between Christians and "pagans" was lost on most full-bloods by 1850, and it is difficult to know how many Cherokees were so conservative that they held exclusively to their traditional practices. One missionary reported that he found most Cherokees "more than half hea-then."[31] He was a Congregationalist who had a mission station in a remote area called Lee's Creek where the people were chiefly full-bloods. "Many are pagans," he said, "and conjuring is universal."[32] He was convinced that if missionaries were to withdraw from the nation, "the people will revert to Barbarism" very quickly.[33] Elizur Butler, a medical missionary from New England, noted that in times of crisis the tendency to "return to heathenish practices" was particularly strong. "In the summer of 1845," he said, "there was a great drought . . . and the natives employed their conjurers to 'make rain.'"[34] During the epidemic of 1852, Agent Butler noted that "many of the fullblood Cherokees yet have a great aversion to the medicine of the regular [medically trained] faculty and prefer the roots and herbs of their own native doctors. The more enlightened portion are fast losing that prejudice and always call a physician when one can be had."[35] He found the full-bloods

very superstitious; they believe in demons, witches, ghosts, good and evil spirits. . . . They too frequently believe those [spirits], or some of them, to be the cause of their diseases, and doctor the patient more to appease the demon and drive him away, than otherwise to cure the disease. When medicine is left by a [white] physician, it is rarely taken as directed. Some old woman or old man . . . comes in and by charms and incantations drives off the physician, if not the demon and the disease. Intelligent Indians have discarded such a belief, but the unintelligent adhere to it; and this costs the nation many lives every year.[36]

Recent studies have shown, however, that at least one-third of the herbs and roots prescribed by Cherokee doctors were helpful, one-third were harmless, and only one-third may have been harmful. (Probably not too different from contemporary medicines, pills, drugs, and surgery.)

At a different level, traditionalism was delineated by one of the federal agents in terms of "the law of blood" or retaliation by clans (sometimes called "the law of familial revenge"). "Their quarrels are very bitter," he wrote, "their hatred and love of revenge are not momentary; they endure during the life of the parties. When an opportunity offers, the death of one or both parties alone settles the matter. Sometimes the quarrel is inherited by friends and relations, and many lives are lost every year from this cause." [37] Although "the law of blood" had been outlawed by the Cherokees since 1808, it never completely died. The matrilineal clans may have lost some of their power in this respect, but families sustained the practice even under a patrilineal structure, and it was just as strong among mixed-bloods as among full-bloods. The amount of violence (by guns and Bowie knives) remained high in the Indian nations, as it did on the white frontier, because of the high level of alcoholism and the low level of law enforcement. In the Cherokee Nation, as in most frontier areas, men normally went about armed. When they engaged in quarrels, they fought it out themselves. Often these quarrels were very personal and frequently between whites and Cherokees. Federal agent Pierce M. Butler wrote in 1842 that these fights "are eight out of ten provoked on the part of itinerant [white] citizens from all parts of the United States tempted or induced there [to the Cherokee Nation] by gain. It is too much the habit abroad to cry out 'Indian outrage' without a just knowledge of the facts." [38]

After the Treaty of 1846, tensions within the nation between the Ross party and the Old Settler and Treaty parties declined. However, a new kind of tension gradually developed between the mixed-bloods and full-bloods. While it reflected differences in wealth or social class, it was basically a cultural difference. The poorer Cherokees believed that the rich were abandoning sacred traditions and pushing the nation too rapidly toward the white man's ways and values. Missionaries, travelers, and federal agents frequently commented on this conflict. Sometimes they described it as the clash between "the progressive," "forward-looking," "more intelligent," or "better-informed" Cherokees and those who were "backward," "ignorant," and "uneducated." Sometimes they saw it in terms of mixed-bloods and full-bloods or Christians and "pagans." Often they talked of different "classes." Generally, whites held that the solution to the division, the equalizing force, was education. At first, the development of a large-scale system of free public education under the Ross council after 1841 seemed the best means to overcome this cleavage. Later, public schools may have accentuated the division. Some whites thought inter-marriage between whites and Cherokees would be the best way to "improve" the Indians, however, only when a white man married a Cherokee woman was intermarriage presumed to be effective, the man being the dominant figure in the Victorian perspective on marriage. Missionaries tended to place their faith in conversion to Christianity as the key to uplifting the masses, since they saw moral self-discipline as the key to a progressive social order.

Few mixed-bloods favored total assimilation or integration into white society, having encountered the racism of whites toward those of darker com-plexions. Conversely, many full-bloods were pious and dedicated Christians. Those of mixed ancestry often adopted the forms, but not the spirit, of the mission churches. The difference between the mixed-blood and the full-blood was best stated by the missionary who noted, "Those who have little Cherokee blood, in comparing themselves with white men, glory in being 'Cherokee,' yet look with contempt upon those who speak Cherokee only or chiefly as 'Indians.'"[39] The issue was not who was the better white person but who was the better "Cherokee." The basic problem of cultural division among the Cherokees after 1846 can be found in their effort to define whether the best Cherokee was the one who tried to adhere to traditional ideals or the one who proved he or she could do everything the white man or woman could. Hence the driving ambition of the English-speaking Cherokees was to demonstrate their talents as traders, planters, lawyers, businesspeople, housewives, and mothers. Because of their intense concern for the nation's economic progress and political self-sufficiency, they were as ardent in the defense of Cherokee rights as any traditionalist. They were determined to look after Cherokee interests in all relations with the federal government. In that sense, they were ardent "red nationalists." For them, national pride required both progress and sovereignty. The English-speaking believed they set the standards and deserved the leadership of the nation. However, they were also often patron-izing and paternalistic toward their non-English-speaking citizens. They did not forget their obligations to help their relatives, to practice hospitality, and to share food with the poor, but they were ambitious and eager for the praise of whites. They measured themselves by the standards of white Americans. As soon as they obtained enough money, they bought slaves, tore down their log cabins, erected clapboard, two-story frame houses, bought carriages and good rugs and furniture in the latest styles, and read the most recent maga-zines and books. The men wore frock coats and top hats on formal occasions;

the women wore calico, gingham, or muslin dresses. The women sewed or cro-
cheted but did not spin or weave. Girls were taught to play the pianoforte and
do fine needlework or watercoloring. Missionaries found mixed-blood children to be more highly motivated, better disciplined, and easier to teach. As
teachers in the public schools, mixed-bloods set the standards for the young.

By 1846 a group of about 300 mixed-blood families constituted a kind of
Cherokee upper class based on wealth, style, and influence.[40] Some of them
had plantations of 600 to 1,000 acres and cultivated wheat, cotton, corn,
hemp, and tobacco; most had large herds of cattle and horses. They owned
25 to 50 slaves; several owned over 100. In the 1850s some of these planters
were importing the latest reapers, mowers, and harvesters invented by Cyrus
McCormick. Their farms were "up-to-date." Some in this elite were merchants, traders, or businesspeople with important sources of credit. Several
owned steamboats that carried surplus cotton, corn, or tobacco to markets
in St. Louis or New Orleans and brought back manufactured goods—iron
cook stoves, farm machinery, dry goods, rugs—which they advertised for sale
in the *Cherokee Advocate*. Some became horse traders or supplied cattle for
eastern cities, and some were slave dealers.

The members of this elite liked blooded horses and drove in fine carriages.
When they entertained, they served wine, danced minuets or reels, and their
wives and daughters played and sang to the piano or the violin. They had
libraries in their homes, and on their living room tables were eastern newspapers and magazines. They understood the political issues before Congress
and in the neighboring states, and they were knowledgeable about the market
economy. They sent their daughters to mission schools and then to seminaries
or finishing schools in Arkansas and Missouri or farther east. John and Lewis
Ross sent their sons to Lawrenceville Academy, a private college preparatory
school, and then Princeton University.

Martha Tyner Swift, a member of the Sanders family and related to David
Carter, an important leader of the nation who was chief justice of its Supreme
Court, recalled some of the aspects of life among this elite. John Ross, she
said, "always drove a carriage with two horses. He had a driver and a little
black boy in uniform sat up on the back and Ross [in the carriage] between."
The Cherokee children used to watch him drive back and forth between his
large home on Park Hill (where he could entertain forty guests) and the council house in Tahlequah. John Carter "had many slaves. . . . He had large fields
where he raised wheat, oats, and corn, but he didn't make money out of his
crops as he raised it only for his own use. But Dave Carter had lots of money.
I remember he used to keep his money in big cotton sacks on the shelf of the
wardrobe," and, as children, "we used to get it down sometimes and play with

it"; it consisted of heaps of "gold and silver" coins. "He was more white than Cherokee" and attended the Southern Methodist church known as Riley's Chapel in Park Hill. "Dave Carter used to take a wagon and slave and go to Arkansas for his groceries and come back with the wagon heaping with sacks of sugar, green coffee, etc. He always used to drive horses, but most everyone used oxen for hauling."[41] Lewis Ross was one of the wealthiest men in the nation; he sent his sons to college. He was a merchant and owned a large plantation, and in the winters when his slaves could not work on the farm, he put them to work manufacturing salt in the saltworks he leased from the Cherokee government. He was said to own 300 slaves.[42]

Between this upper-class elite and the poor was a small group who could be said to constitute the economic middle class. Most of them were of mixed ancestry. They had farms of 100 acres, owned 3 to 9 slaves, and owned small herds of cattle and horses. Some were assistants or clerks to the larger traders; others were owners of sawmills, gristmills, cotton mills, taverns, tanneries, or saddleries or were lawyers. At the lower end of this class were the artisans—blacksmiths, wheelwrights, store clerks, and keepers of small shops. They lived lives of quiet respectability in double log houses with porches front and back, good barns and stables, and horses for their wagons. Many of these ran for office or held appointive office in the increasing bureaucracy of the Cherokee government—working as clerks to the council and courts, superintendents of the schools, or editors of the *Cherokee Advocate*. Even the artisan class did some farming to support their households.

At the bottom of the Cherokee social ladder—well below the average subsistence farmer—was a class of drifters, drunkards, day laborers, prostitutes, ne'er-do-well hangers-on, and outright criminals. Rootless and homeless, these Cherokees were supported at times by their families, but they provided little support for their wives and children. They were a constant source of irritation, but, except when they were participating in factional strife (as between 1839 and 1846), they did not seriously affect the nation as a whole. The sheriffs and courts managed to keep them under control. The most troublesome among them were the brawling drunkards (who frequently used guns and knives in their fights) and the gangs of horse thieves and robbers. Horse thieves established regular escape routes to the Creek Nation or to white accomplices in Arkansas and Missouri to market their stolen goods. Sometimes they sold horses stolen from the white frontier to people in the Cherokee Nation. Robbers occasionally invaded homes, but more often they waylaid travelers. By the Treaty of 1846, the Cherokees were forbidden to establish military companies, but they did utilize the light horse police to track down these gangs. The *Cherokee Advocate* contains many accounts of their trials.

Those convicted of murder were promptly hung; convicted thieves received 100 lashes. Crime in the Cherokee Nation, as in white society, had a class basis. Those at the bottom of society were much more often in conflict with the law than those at the top. As one missionary noted in 1849, anyone who tabulated the executions in the nation could see that it was the poorest full-bloods who were most often hung—and the majority of them were hung for killing other poor full-bloods. "It is a fact easily to be seen," the missionary wrote, "that the greater part of those who are murdered and those who are executed are full Cherokees."[43]

The Cherokee council did all it could to protect honest folk against criminals. The laws passed between 1838 and 1855 provide an overview of the kinds of problems the nation faced. The laws contained penalties not only for arson and horse stealing but also for burglary, larceny, treason, conspiracy, bribery, perjury, embezzlement, the burning of prairie or woodland, trespassing, and violating the Sabbath. There were laws regulating marriage and divorce, wills, the descent of property, the carrying of dangerous weapons in public, fencing land against stray cattle, and the branding of livestock. Other laws limited interest on notes, granted permits to hire whites for work, licensed traders, and protected the public domain (especially timber, grazing, and mineral deposits). Clearly these laws reflect the growth of the Cherokee economic system along the lines of a market economy as well as their acculturation to the white man's moral order. They resemble the laws of any western state or territory as it moved from a frontier society to a more settled community. Apart from protecting public property, however, there was little regulation of business and few taxes. Because land was free, Cherokees were expected to provide their own subsistence; there was no welfare legislation or protection for the poor, handicapped, or aged (except for the orphanage). The Cherokees helped each other.

Though missionary records make no mention of infanticide and rape, the Cherokee council passed laws against both in 1839. The latter was probably aimed not so much at Cherokees as at whites. This same council passed a law regulating intermarriage between Cherokees and whites to prevent white men from taking advantage of Cherokee women for the privilege of becoming citizens. The law required not only a marriage license (with a $5 fee) but also a certificate signed by seven persons testifying to the good character of the white man. It also protected the property and maternal rights of Cherokee women. In 1844 a special act was passed against horse thieves, reflecting not only the unrest due to party factions and bandits but also the increasing number of horses and the growth of their market value in the West. Stolen horses were difficult to track down, however, if they were sold outside the nation. A law of 1852 prescribed death to arsonists if anyone was killed as a result of their crime, arson being a common means of petty revenge in personal quarrels. That same year, laws were passed against gambling (probably a direct result of the influx of gamblers during the per capita distributions) and against carrying firearms (except for hunting). Some persons wanted to forbid the practice of whipping. In 1852 a decision was made to erect a jail at Tahlequah, but there were no funds to build and staff it until many years later.

Cherokee leaders accepted the view that poverty could be eliminated by promoting a market economy and developing the nation's resources. Chief Ross and the council tried many ways to raise additional revenue for the nation in order to pay off the national debt, encourage development, expand the school system, and raise official salaries. All of them failed. The effort to tax the per capita payments in 1847 was a total failure.[44] Two years later, Ross asked the council to place taxes on a number of sources: on income derived from grazing cattle or cutting timber on public land, on all merchants or traders doing business in the nation, and on mill owners and ferry keepers. He also proposed a small poll tax on all citizens.[45] The last was opposed by the poorer members of the tribe; the first three, by the more prosperous. The council consequently failed to enact any of these proposals. Ross tried to circumvent the elected council by calling for a general council of the people to assemble at Tahlequah to hear him explain the national benefits to be gained from such taxes. If this people's council endorsed the measures, the elected council would be obliged to accede to their will. However, the people's council also showed no interest in instituting the taxes.[46] The only part of his tax plan that Ross could get passed was the tax on ferry keepers and lawyers, which netted little for the treasury.[47] Much more popular was the law passed in 1850 to cut the salaries of all government officials by 50 percent.[48] A similar, but more hotly debated, measure cut the salaries of all public schoolteachers.[49]

Despite the mounting national debt, the standard of life slowly but steadily improved for the nation as a whole. There was a steady increase in the number of public primary schools, and two high schools (or seminaries) were built in the 1850s. The *Cherokee Advocate* began publication in 1844, and its pages gave citizens a full account of new laws, the negotiations in Washington, the messages of the chief, crimes and election campaigns in the United States and the Cherokee Nation, missionary activities, high school graduations, the temperance campaign, the building of new churches, the activities of the courts, social events, the state of the economy, and the activities of neighboring tribes and of various visitors who came in a steady stream from the East and abroad to see a model Indian state. The newspaper was subsidized by the nation, and the chief and council chose its editors. It appeared every two weeks and was bilingual, although it contained more in English than in the Sequoyan syllabary. Well-edited and well-written, it was the equal of any paper in the neighboring states. The advertisements of the local merchants in the paper indicate that there were people sufficiently well-off to purchase the latest fashions in clothing, books, household furnishing, and farm equipment from the East.

Statistical measurements of growth were not regularly tabulated by the nation, but the population steadily increased as did the number of black slaves and intermarried whites. The number of mills, bridges, and ferries increased, as did the size of farms, the number of acres under cultivation, and the size of livestock herds. A partial census taken in 1851 of those who had removed from the East between 1835 and 1838 reported that among "the emigrant Cherokees" there was now 65 blacksmith shops, 14 gristmills, 10 sawmills, 2 tanyards, and 5 saltworks, as well as 5,770 horses, 28,705 cattle, 35,832 hogs, and 233 mules. The nation had 27 schools (some of them mission schools but most publicly supported) and 38 Protestant churches or regular preaching stations. The combined population of Old Settlers and new emigrants was between 17,000 and 18,000 in 1851, and there were 1,844 black slaves and 64 free blacks. General Waddy Thompson, who had served as legal counsel to the nation in 1846, noted these figures in an article in the *Cherokee Advocate* after a visit to the nation in 1852. He added, "No general table can give an adequate idea of the general appearance of thrift and comfort of this . . . people. Their houses are generally built of hewed log, covered with shingles and with stone chimneys and neatly furnished. The farms all in good order and indicating industry and care. . . . I was three weeks in the nation and did not see anyone dressed in the Old Indian costume of leggings and hunting shirt out of more than 1,000 that I saw; what is more, I did not see a ragged, dirty or drunken Indian." [50] Like most visitors to the nation, Thompson spent the greater part of his time among Cherokees of mixed ancestry who lived in the Cherokee capital at Tahlequah or near the chief's residence at Park Hill.

One measure of the Cherokees' economic growth was the rise of three good-sized towns in the nation: at Tahlequah, Park Hill, and Fort Gibson. Tahlequah, located at the fork of the Illinois and Barren Fork rivers, was the largest. By 1850 it contained the legislative buildings, the Supreme Court building, the office of the *Cherokee Advocate*, a post office, eight stores, five hotels, three blacksmith shops, a tailor shop, a saddlery, a tannery, a shoemaker shop, a dentist, and several law offices, as well as residences of those who worked in the town. In 1849 a brick Masonic Temple had been built, and the leading members of the nation belonged to it. The town's population was about 1,600.[51]

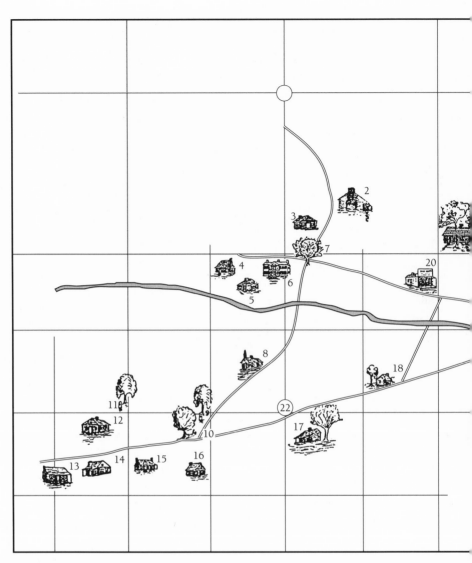

MAP 3. *Park Hill*

Source: Grant Foreman, *Advancing the Frontier, 1830–1863*
(Norman: University of Oklahoma Press, 1933).

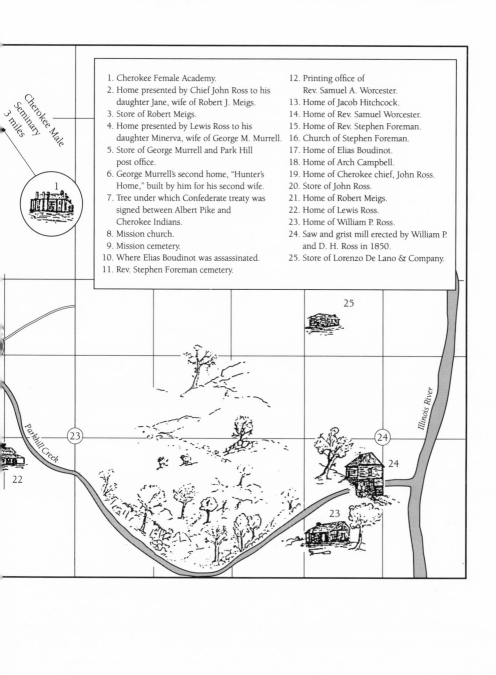

Cherokee Male Seminary 3 miles

1

1. Cherokee Female Academy.
2. Home presented by Chief John Ross to his daughter Jane, wife of Robert J. Meigs.
3. Store of Robert Meigs.
4. Home presented by Lewis Ross to his daughter Minerva, wife of George M. Murrell.
5. Store of George Murrell and Park Hill post office.
6. George Murrell's second home, "Hunter's Home," built by him for his second wife.
7. Tree under which Confederate treaty was signed between Albert Pike and Cherokee Indians.
8. Mission church.
9. Mission cemetery.
10. Where Elias Boudinot was assassinated.
11. Rev. Stephen Foreman cemetery.
12. Printing office of Rev. Samuel A. Worcester.
13. Home of Jacob Hitchcock.
14. Home of Rev. Samuel Worcester.
15. Home of Rev. Stephen Foreman.
16. Church of Stephen Foreman.
17. Home of Elias Boudinot.
18. Home of Arch Campbell.
19. Home of Cherokee chief, John Ross.
20. Store of John Ross.
21. Home of Robert Meigs.
22. Home of Lewis Ross.
23. Home of William P. Ross.
24. Saw and grist mill erected by William P. and D. H. Ross in 1850.
25. Store of Lorenzo De Lano & Company.

25

Illinois River

Parkhill Creek

23

22

24

24

23

Three and a half miles southeast of Tahlequah was the community of Park Hill. Here Chief Ross and many of the wealthy traders, planters, and political leaders lived. The town was also the center of the Methodist mission and the Congregational mission, which was led by the Reverend Samuel A. Worcester. On a printing press with fonts of Sequoyan type, Worcester and his assistants were publishing the various books of the Bible along with an annual almanac, pamphlets on temperance, and religious tracts. The Congregationalists also operated a mission school here. Park Hill was the social and intellectual center of the nation. The two large seminaries, the capstones of the public educational system, were in or near the town. These magnificently pillared structures were visible for miles around and were staffed at good salaries by young women from Mount Holyoke College and young men from Yale. The children of Park Hill families were sent to private academies in Arkansas or to college back east prior to the opening of the Cherokee seminaries. Park Hill was noted for its sophisticated social life, stately residences, well-stocked shops, ornamental shrubs, fine carriages, and well-kept farms and plantations. Every traveler to the nation paid a visit to this center of Cherokee society, and those who described the Cherokees as "progressive" and "well-informed" based such opinions on their observations during visits to this community. Far fewer visitors rode into the more distant parts of the nation where the poorer and more traditional Cherokees lived.[52]

Until 1857 the third largest village in the nation was at Fort Gibson in the southwest corner of the nation, located at the fork of the Arkansas, Grand (or Neosho), and Verdigris rivers, just across from the Creek Nation. The garrison's four square miles included the fort and homes of the armed units and their training grounds. The fort usually housed four to six companies of mounted soldiers or dragoons. Nearby were the stores and homes of those who served the garrison. The federal agent's office was also in this area. Because Fort Gibson was the last port for steamboats on the Arkansas River, it was the center of considerable activity in the receipt of visitors and goods from the East as well as in the export of cotton, corn, timber, and livestock. Because the troops received regular pay but had little work, the town attracted gamblers, prostitutes, and whiskey sellers. A racetrack added to the excitement, and when off the base the soldiers frequently became involved in fights with Cherokees who complained that the soldiers had a low opinion of them and commonly insulted them. Once its civil war ended in 1846, the nation was eager to get rid of the garrison. The Treaty of 1835, which established this post, stated that if the army ever abandoned it, the land would revert to the Cherokee Nation. Hoping to make a commercial river port at this spot and believing that the Cherokees' law enforcement officers were sufficient to keep the peace, Ross worked constantly in Washington to have the garrison withdrawn. He feared that it was too easy for the federal government to utilize the troops here for political purposes, as it had done in the days when Matthew Arbuckle was in charge.[53]

In the years 1846 to 1861, the Cherokee Nation was caught in a series of inauspicious contradictions. Its leaders wished to convince the white population that the Cherokees were capable of managing their own affairs in a stable, orderly, prosperous manner if only they were treated fairly and left to their own self-government. On the other hand, the very social and economic factors that enabled the Cherokee elite to make a good impression on visitors also marked the increasing division between the rich and the poor, the English-speaking and the Cherokee-speaking, and those ambitious for success according to the individualistic, self-reliant ethic of white America and those more interested in retaining as much as possible of their traditional culture and its values. As long as the great bulk of the full-bloods were left to themselves and able to support their families, they acquiesced in the able leadership provided by the mixed-blood elite. However, the two groups were working at cross-purposes that would eventually stir up a far-reaching and bitter confrontation over slavery and secession.

The conflict was masked during the decade from 1846 to 1856 by the Cherokees' search for political autonomy and economic prosperity. In addition, the mixed-blood elite were blinded to this schism by their profound belief (shared by white Americans in their search to maintain "a classless society" with advancement open to all) that free public education was the key to future harmony. By the late 1850s the public school system was a major factor in promoting class division. At that point, the nation was held together only by the need for a common front against white threats to its sovereignty.

4

Public Education and the Struggle for Independence, 1846–1860

Whereas the history of our race shows that whenever

the Indian and White man have been mingled together

promiscuously in the same community and under the same

government, the effect has ever been that the White man soon

owns everything and the Indian nothing . . . resolved, *that we do*

respectfully and earnestly protest against any change in our

present political relations to the United States.

—Cherokee and Creek resolution adopted at

North Fork, Creek Nation, December 7, 1854

The Cherokees undertook a major effort to restore national pride in 1840 when they decided to establish their own free public school system. Hitherto dependent on white missionaries for their schools, they now decided to accept responsibility for their own education. At the same time, they determined to throw off any dependence on the federal government to sustain law and order in their nation. If they were a sovereign people, they must take on the full measure of that status. Neither proved an easy task. The council, by establishing a nationwide school system, took on a heavy financial burden, especially after they added two public high schools in 1851. Furthermore, they required that the schools be taught in English, which placed a serious obstacle before the vast majority of children, who spoke only Cherokee. Ultimately, the children of mixed ancestry obtained the greatest benefit from the schools, and the more acculturated Cherokees began to wonder whether education for the poorer Cherokees should not be simply vocational in order to develop the skilled labor for a modern social order.

The effort to win greater freedom from federal supervision forced the nation into a long series of confrontations (some violent) involving the questions of who was entitled to trade in the nation, who was a legitimate citizen, who could license traders in the nation, and whether federal courts and the U.S. Army had any legitimate control over them. By the mid-1850s the Cherokees were fighting against the first demands of railroad companies that they be allowed to crisscross through the nation as well as against the efforts of western congressmen to transform the Indian Territory into a territory of the United States preparatory to statehood—a decision that could only lead to their detribalization.

One of the many great failings of Andrew Jackson's removal policy was that it did not place any geographical zone between the Indians and the white frontier. Texas, Arkansas, and Missouri were already well-populated states when the emigrant Cherokees, Creeks, Choctaws, Chickasaws, and Seminoles were resettled on their borders. From 1840 onward, the aggressive forces of white self-interest pushed into their new homeland as ruthlessly as they had into their old homeland. While bound by treaty to protect the transplanted Indian nations, the federal government served chiefly the voters of the advancing frontier, not the voteless Indians.

Totally committed to the goals of independence and prosperity for his people, John Ross believed that their security lay in their education. He asked no help from the United States or the missionaries. In his annual message to the Cherokee legislature in the fall of 1840, Ross recommended that it formulate a plan for a free public school system. As early as 1805 the Cherokees had made preparations for their own school system by including in a treaty a clause instructing the federal government to sell some of the nation's land and invest the proceeds in a Cherokee education fund. The government, however, failed to carry out this provision. Similar clauses were inserted in two later treaties, but still the government failed to act. Finally, in the Treaty of 1835, the government agreed that the Cherokee annuity would include the sum of $16,000 a year for public, Cherokee-controlled education. It was too small to finance all of Ross's plans for education, but the council at least had a starting point. There were between 3,000 and 4,000 children of school age dispersed over the nation's 7,800 square miles. Ross was well aware of the efforts of the eastern states at this time to inaugurate a free public school system. He wished to demonstrate that the Cherokee Nation could do the same for its people and meet the same standards.

The Old Settlers prior to 1839 had done little about education, relying chiefly on the missionaries. In 1832 their council had passed a law providing a public school in each of the four electoral districts. Sequoyah received $400 from the council to teach his syllabary in these schools at the same time that they were learning English.[1] However, these schools were not adequately funded or staffed. The plan adopted by the Ross council after 1840 was much more elaborate. Having expanded the electoral districts from four to eight, the council planned to start with one school in each district and, as funds became available, increase the number until every Cherokee child had a convenient local school. No charge was to be made to the parents of the children. The school law did not require attendance; it was voluntary. Each district provided what was called "a common school education" to all children between the ages of six and sixteen who wanted one, and most did. The teaching was to be in English, and the curriculum included reading, writing, and spelling in English as well as geography, arithmetic, and history. Teachers were encouraged to include religious and moral training of a nonsectarian kind but essentially Protestant. Eventually, more advanced schools were to be added in order to prepare the brightest youth for college or for positions as teachers in the common schools. The council set the salaries of common school teachers at $525, which was competitive with the salaries paid teachers in New England. At the outset, the Cherokees had to import white teachers. The school year was divided into two semesters of twenty weeks each from September 1 to July 30.

The Public Education Act of 1841 called for the appointment of a national superintendent of schools, to be paid from the national treasury, to supervise the system.[2] In each community where a school was located, the inhabitants were required to elect three local "school directors" whose duty it was to see that the community built and maintained a school building. The schools were built of logs by the inhabitants of the district. The superintendent, with the advice of these local directors, selected the teacher, who was paid out of the annuity fund. Schools were to have a minimum of twenty-five students who lived within walking distance; if the local directors could not maintain this number, the superintendent had the right to move the school to a more populous location in the district.

This plan proved very effective, and in 1843 the council increased the number of schools from eight to eighteen; in 1846 three more schools were added.[3] By 1860 there were thirty public schools in the nation. This was not sufficient to educate every child eligible, but the number of students in the schools rose steadily from 200 in 1842 to 1,500 in 1860. Financial difficulties forced the reduction of teachers' salaries from $525 to $333 in 1844. The school annuity was a fixed sum and, lacking other funds at first, the expansion of schools proceeded slowly. Once Cherokees were trained to be teachers, they were willing to work for lower salaries than the whites hired from the East.

Contrary to expectations, the schools quickly proved to have difficulty attracting the children of Cherokee-speaking parents, who were thought to be the children who would benefit most. Cherokee-speaking students found it difficult to learn from teachers who spoke no Cherokee. Frustrated and subject to ridicule by children of English-speaking, mixed-blood parents, most full-blood children dropped out of school. Gradually the student body came to consist predominantly of those of mixed ancestry, although two-thirds to three-quarters of the population were full Cherokees. The first school superintendent, the Reverend Stephen Foreman, was of mixed ancestry and had received ministerial training in Virginia at the expense of the American Board of Commissioners for Foreign Missions. Foreman himself was bilingual and such a skilled translator that Samuel Worcester employed him to assist in translating the Bible into Cherokee. However, Foreman found no bilingual teachers, and in order to recruit those capable of teaching the required courses in English, he had to ask the Protestant mission agencies to assist him. The necessity of cutting back teachers' salaries after 1844 seriously harmed this process. Moreover, some mission agencies expected that the teachers they recruited would be allowed to teach their denominational principles, and denominational rivalry became a problem. The Northern Baptists, based in Boston, sent a teacher for a school near their mission station and helped to support him; in the church's magazine it spoke of this Cherokee public school as "our school." A similar difficulty arose when a school was located in an area where many parents belonged to a particular denomination. The school directors they elected placed pressure on the superintendent to select a teacher for their community of the same denomination. There were reports from rival missionaries that Stephen Foreman was "too weak" to resist such pressure. Samuel Worcester, though a friend of Foreman's, reported that he had hired an inferior teacher simply because the man was a Methodist and the parents in that district had demanded a Methodist teacher.[4]

Other difficulties arose. In some school districts local parents failed to fulfill their commitment to maintain a good school building with adequate heat for the winter months. Charles Pulsifer, a Congregational minister, described this problem in 1844:

> In one of the districts, a school was opened about the first of the year in a very poor house. The people were very anxious for the school and promised to furnish a better house soon. But the business was neglected, nothing was done about a house, and Mr. Foreman told them he would continue the school until the cold weather and then, if no house was provided, he would discontinue it. Accordingly, later in the fall, he stopped the school. The people were offended and determined to have the school; they therefore employed another teacher and continued the school in the same house. After he had taught about one month, his employers petitioned the Council to grant him pay [and it did so].[5]

Pulsifer believed that both Foreman and the council had weakened their authority and lowered the standards of education by their failure to enforce the law. However, he also noted that teachers' salaries were lowered that year, which contributed to the problem: "The new law, enacted at the last council, provides for seven new schools (making the number of schools in all eighteen) and fixes the salary of the teachers at four hundred dollars. An effort was made to reduce it even to three hundred, and some even still lower—I believe to half that sum."

Pulsifer's observations were echoed by Thomas Frye and Willard Upham of the Baptist mission. Frye, a graduate of Waterville College, Maine, whom the Baptist mission board sent to teach at a public school in Going Snake District in 1843, had the same criticism of the willingness of the Cherokee council and school superintendent to yield to the people in the local district. He was promised a salary of $500 but received only $333. Then he discovered that the Methodists in the area were trying to have him removed and replaced by a Methodist teacher.[6]

Stephen Foreman resigned as superintendent in 1843, unable to cope with these problems, and was replaced by James M. Payne. Payne, in a letter to Ross on July 18, 1845, expressed several other criticisms of the system. Complaining that not enough money was available to provide adequate schoolbooks, especially for beginners, he said,

> I found many of the schools very much neglected by the Directors and teachers indolent even some who have a good knowledge of teaching, while some are totally ignorant and incompetent to teach. . . . It is difficult to get

a sufficient number of good, competent teachers to supply all the schools while the amount allowed for the salary of the teachers will hardly justify or induce men of competency and qualifications to come from the East. . . . It is to be regretted that without a change in the law and arrangement of our schools that the great and important design calculated to better the condition of our people will not be realized. . . . As the children advance more in the different branches, the more necessary it becomes to engage the services of good teachers, men of moral and religious endowments and competent qualifications. . . . I have found also that parents are much to blame and too indulgent in not sending their children to school regular[ly].[7]

Payne failed to note that one of the chief reasons for irregular attendance was that poor parents had to rely on their children to help on the farm. Cherokee girls were required to assist at home in cooking and caring for infants or the sick. In 1847 Payne reported that one of the chief reasons for the low attendance that year was extensive sickness, particularly from children's diseases such as mumps, whooping cough, and scarlet fever.[8] Payne's difficulty in obtaining competent Cherokee teachers was reflected in the large proportion of white teachers supplied by missionary agencies in the years prior to 1855. In 1847, out of a total of twenty-one teachers, Payne reported that five were Congregational missionaries, three were Baptists, and two were Methodists. Sixteen of the twenty-one were white, and nineteen were men. Because new schools were located where the population was densest, demography produced inequities among the eight districts. Three districts had four public schools each (Delaware, Going Snake, and Flint), four had two schools (Tahlequah, Illinois, Skin Bayou, and Saline), and the Canadian District had only one. The total amount spent on the schools in 1846–47 was $7,000, of which $200 went for books.[9]

The availability of free mission schools created complications in some districts. The school superintendents tried to locate public or "national" schools where there were no mission schools in order to avoid duplication of effort. The missionaries operated ten schools until 1852 and seven after that year. The Moravians conducted two schools throughout this period, one at Honey Creek and one at New Spring Place, and in 1852 they took over the Congregational school at Mount Zion, renaming it Canaan. Besides the school at Mount Zion, the Congregationalists managed four schools, at Dwight, Fairfield, Park Hill, and Lee's Creek. The Northern Baptists for a time had three schools in the Going Snake and Saline districts but closed them all by 1852 for lack of adequate funds. One of these, at Baptist Mission, became a Cherokee public school, although a Baptist missionary continued to teach there. The Southern Methodists and Southern Baptists took little interest in education and formed no permanent mission schools.

In order to train more Cherokee teachers, the council voted in 1847 to establish two seminaries or high schools, one at Park Hill for girls and one at Tahlequah for boys. The wealthier Cherokees supported this decision because tuition would be free, thus sparing them the expense of sending their children to academies in the states if they wanted them to have more education. The poorer Cherokees backed the seminaries because they wanted more Cherokee schoolteachers, preferably bilingual. Determined to prove their commitment to education, the Cherokees spared no expense. The extravagant sum of $70,000 was allocated to build the two seminaries, which ended up costing $80,000. A Cherokee committee studied the educational system of the New England schools and colleges to determine the appropriate curriculum and the equipment needed.[10] The Female Seminary was explicitly modeled on Mount Holyoke College in South Hadley, Massachusetts; the Male Seminary was modeled on classical high schools such as Boston Latin School and Lawrenceville Academy near Princeton. The Congregational missionaries were particularly helpful in this planning. A committee of three prominent Cherokees traveled to New England in 1851 and interviewed the graduating classes at Yale and Mount Holyoke to select the teachers and principals for the schools. Salaries were high enough to compete with those in the East, but an intense dedication was required to travel to the Cherokee Nation to teach Indians. The committee encountered difficulty recruiting a principal for the Male Seminary because religious New Englanders at this time were strongly opposed to slavery and it was known that the Cherokees owned slaves.[11] A young Baptist, Thomas Vann Horne, from Newton Theological School near Boston accepted the position.[12] After a brief lockout by the carpenters who built the seminaries because the funds ran out before they were paid, the schools opened in 1851.

The council appointed a committee of the new teachers, some missionaries and some educated Cherokees, to administer examinations to determine who would be admitted to the first class. One of the teachers, Oswald L. Woodford, of Connecticut, a Yale graduate, reported that he had to lower his standards somewhat in order to find a sufficient number of students.[13] Twenty-five were admitted and twenty-five more were to be enrolled in each of the next three years until the total at each seminary reached 100. Because the public primary schools accepted children up to age sixteen, many of the seminary students started at seventeen and graduated at twenty-one. All received free tuition, room, and board. As in the public schools, the various Protestant denominations in the nation vied to supply teachers. "A strong desire is manifest to bring the Seminaries under direct [Southern] Methodist influence," wrote Congregationalist Samuel Worcester. "The plan seems to be to let the funds run low, as they must unless new funds are provided by the sale of Kansas lands, and then urge that they do not need so large salaries, they can get good enough teachers at the South for much less, and avoid abolitionists [from New England] and (so say the Methodists), they can get Methodist teachers. And avarice may plead for a per capita distribution of the [Kansas] land money, and so avarice, proslavery, and Methodism may combine in the effort, and for ought I know, may succeed." [14]

As the slave-owning parents were chiefly English-speaking mixed-bloods, this problem revealed another difficulty at the seminaries. The small number of full-bloods who graduated from the public schools meant that few of them attended the seminaries, and many who did were not well prepared. Missionary Edwin Teele noted in 1853, after praising "the very commendable interest that is taken in the matter of the schools in the nation," that "the nation as a body [that is, the full-blood majority] do not care much for the schools. The mixed bloods are chiefly concerned in these movements. In the Seminaries there are not more than four or five pupils of fullblood. The majority have so much white blood in their veins that a stranger would pronounce them entirely of white parentage. The same is true to nearly an equal extent in all the public schools, so that the fullbloods are but little benefitted by these schools, and they compose about two-thirds of the whole nation." [15]

Elizur Butler, a Congregational missionary, wrote to the commissioner of Indian affairs in 1852 that many Cherokees were critical of the educational system, calling it "useless" and "expensive." [16] Missionary Asa Hitchcock, as early as 1845, commented that the public schools were "unpopular among the Cherokees." [17] Marcus Palmer of New England visited the nation in 1854 and criticized the small proportion of full-blood pupils in the public schools: "It does not satisfy their minds to be told that they may have the same privileges [of attending] in the public schools so long as they labor under the *great disadvantage* of not knowing the language in which learning is taught in the school. . . . In all the schools . . . there are probably 1,200 children, one-tenth of which, according to the estimate of the Superintendency, are full Cherokees. . . . The[se] children learn the English language . . . very slowly, become discouraged, and soon leave." [18] Samuel Worcester shared the view that the full-blood children often became "disheartened" by the difficulties they faced, and their frustration was increased because those children who had "little Cherokee blood" and came from English-speaking homes taunted them for their "stupidity"; "in some schools at least," the full-bloods "suffer reproach and contempt as 'Indians'"—a prejudice the mixed-blood children apparently learned from their parents. Worcester feared that "there is a danger that this growing contempt on one side and jealousy on the other, will provide a great obstacle to progress, if not the ruin of the people."[19] Worcester's insight proved to be correct. The full-bloods faced both external prejudice from whites and internal prejudice from mixed-bloods, and they resented the latter more than the former.

John Ross wanted to keep school standards high in order to win respect for the Cherokees. He had always favored rapid acculturation, though he had never tried to force it. Because the full-bloods generally wanted some education for their children, they resented the disadvantages they were under due to the absence of bilingual teachers. They concluded that the English-speaking Cherokees had no interest in training Cherokee-speaking teachers at the seminaries or in helping the full-bloods to learn English. The fact that the seminaries granted free tuition, room, and board to the wealthy (as well as to the poor) raised tribal expenses and provided a privilege for those who could have afforded to pay their children's way.

When the male and female seminaries were forced to close in 1856 for lack of funds, Chief Ross made strenuous efforts to revive them. He pushed even harder to sell the Neutral Lands but failed.[20] Even had he found the money, he might not have been able to persuade the full-bloods, who generally controlled the council, to vote to reopen the seminaries. Allocating what little money there was for education in 1858, the council voted "to add to the number of common schools rather than to revive the Female Seminary. Mr. Ross vetoed the bill and two-thirds of both houses passed it again."[21] The most successful aspect of the seminaries was that by 1858 they had trained sufficient Cherokees to provide teachers (but not bilingual teachers) for almost all the public schools; it was no longer necessary to hire white teachers. "The greater part of the [common] schools are now taught by seminary girls," wrote Samuel Worcester in 1858.[22] However, he feared this would not long continue. "As girls generally will get married, Mr. Ross thinks they will soon lack teachers unless they raise up more."

In its effort to cut costs and yet continue to enlarge the public school system, the Cherokee council tried to make missionary schools bear some of the burden. "I am told," Worcester wrote in 1858 of the public school taught by Willard Upham, a Northern Baptist minister, that the council "voted to remove Mr. Upham's school [to another location,] supposing that the Baptist Board would keep it up [at its present site] and so, by giving their [the council's] own support to another school, they should have two instead of one."[23] The Northern Baptists might have complied, for they were proud of their part in the school and Upham was also the pastor of the church nearby where most of his pupils attended, but in the end the council did not withdraw its payment of his salary.

Ross finally acknowledged the inability of the national treasury to pay for the seminaries, though he noted in 1857 that "they are . . . demonstrating beyond cavil the existence of mental powers in our midst which only require development to make us . . . independent."[24] For Ross the desire to be independent of any aid from whites in uplifting his people and developing their talents was his highest goal. He recognized that the full-bloods opposed the free tuition, room, and board at the seminaries for the wealthier parents' children, and he suggested that one way to reopen them would be to make those who could afford it pay part of the costs of room and board. However, the council declined this alternative.

Another side of public resentment against the seminaries may be seen in the report of the school superintendent, A. W. Duncan, in 1856. Duncan, representing a utilitarian or vocational position, maintained that the seminaries were not producing useful citizens but only aesthetes and intellectuals. The Female Seminary, he felt, was a ladies' finishing school for the rich to make their daughters eligible to become the wives of wealthy men. The Male Seminary graduates hoped to go on to colleges in the East or enter the learned professions: "All cannot live here without manual labor. Each cannot be a professor, lawyer, doctor, preacher, school-master. The means, opportunities and occasions are wanting" for so many to enter these prestigious, white-collar occupations. "All could not find such employment" in the nation, "and to seek it elsewhere would be to take one step towards the overthrow of the nation. For in that case it is clear that the ulterior result of our expenditures and labor would be to educate children for other countries." Duncan, fearing that the most talented youth would leave the nation for the kinds of work only a white community could afford, wanted the seminaries to train engineers, agricultural experts, and skilled artisans—people who would build bridges, roads, and mills and do the work the nation now had to pay whites to do. Publicly subsidized education should be for the nation's welfare, he believed, not for private advantage.[25]

In the long run, the Cherokee educational system, commendable as it was in principle, produced disunity; it increased rather than diminished class differences. Those of mixed ancestry were more interested in impressing whites with their own progress than in promoting the "Keetoowah" sense of harmony at the center of the traditional Cherokee ethic. This stress upon defining Cherokee progress in terms of white bourgeois standards of respectability was not unlike the use to which white Americans put their own public school system. It too was designed to make the poor (the peasant immigrant or "foreigner") conform to the ethnic model of the nativist bourgeoisie. The debate marked a new level in Cherokee acculturation as they tried to institutionalize the specialization of labor. However, it also created the more basic problem of preserving traditional identity while at the same time adopting an individualistic market economy.

A similar difference in values developed as the Cherokee Nation tried to free itself from the paternalism of the Bureau of Indian Affairs. Following removal, the United States had adopted an increasingly domineering outlook toward Indian affairs, insisting that it knew what was best for the Indians and constantly meddling in their affairs for the benefit of whites. The effort of the Cherokees to assert their political independence was not easy. The shifting of Indian affairs from the War Department to the Department of the Interior in 1849 had changed nothing. The Cherokees saw no reason why the federally appointed resident agent should grant licenses to white traders at his discretion. That should be done by the council. They saw no need for a military garrison of white soldiers occupying four square miles of their land at their best river port. They had long since given up warfare. They opposed the power claimed by the military commander and the federal agent to arrest Cherokee citizens at their discretion or on the order of the commissioner of Indian affairs. They could police themselves. They did not see any reason why the federal court in Arkansas should have the right to try Cherokee citizens involved in crimes between whites and Cherokees that occurred within the Cherokee Nation. They had their own judiciary. They also demanded the right to tax or exclude Texas cattle ranchers seeking to drive their herds through Cherokee lands and the right to prevent or limit the advance of railroads through their nation.

The most dangerous threat to Indian sovereignty arose from Congress's claim to have the right at any time to turn the Indian Territory into a territory of the United States. Such an act would open it to white settlement, destroy treaty boundaries, and ultimately denationalize the tribes. The essential feature in the various congressional territorial schemes—and the one that appealed to those who considered themselves reformers with the best interests of the Indians at heart—was the proposal for federal surveys of the Indians' lands, the abolition of communal landownership, and the allocation of tracts (usually 160 acres) to each Indian family as its own private property. The remainder of the land in the territory would then be designated "unused" and offered for sale to white homesteaders (who would soon outnumber the Indians in the territory, impose a white majority government, and seek statehood). Territorialization meant forced assimilation and the abolition of all tribal government, laws, and treaty rights. Only strict adherence to Indian sovereignty and treaty rights could prevent this ultimate catastrophe, for by treaties the federal government had pledged itself to protect the boundaries of each Indian nation, to expel white intruders, to allow each tribe to establish its own form of government, and to protect the system of communal ownership of all land within tribal borders. The Treaty of 1835 with the Cherokees explicitly stated that "the United States agree that the land herein guaranteed to the Cherokees shall never, without their consent, be included within the limits or jurisdiction of any State or Territory."

Opposing the five areas of federal interference in Cherokees' internal affairs—the licensing of traders, the military garrison, the use of federal courts to try Indian-white crimes, the question of white intruders and travelers through the nation, and territorialization—occupied much of the diplomatic efforts of the Cherokees after 1846. With great effort, the Cherokees succeeded in partially resolving two of these issues; on the other three, they met serious opposition and a penchant for postponing crucial decisions.

The Cherokees were able to make some headway in the matter of licensing white traders. Cherokee traders believed that licensing white traders created unfair competition and drained Cherokee money out of the nation. The federal government said white traders prevented monopoly practices. The practice of allowing the federal agent to license traders began in the 1790s to protect Indian tribes from unscrupulous traders. Now that the Cherokees felt able to manage their own affairs, such licensing seemed a serious infringement on their sovereignty.

When the eastern Cherokees arrived in the West, they found that Agent Montfort Stokes had granted trading licenses almost at will to any white who applied. A licensed trader was under the protection of the United States and was permitted to set up shop anywhere or to travel around the nation. Only the agent could expel a trader accused of corrupt practices. Many of those licensed by Stokes became engaged in the illegal sale of whiskey, cheated the Cherokees, or established silent partnerships with Cherokees to plunder the nation's timber and other resources. The Ross council repeatedly urged Stokes to expel some of the worst of these miscreants and to curtail the licensing of new traders. Stokes did little to curb the abuses and continued to issue licenses to dishonest traders.

When Pierce M. Butler replaced Stokes in 1841, he looked into the Cherokees' complaints and found them fully justified. He told the commissioner of Indian affairs that there were so many whites who claimed to have been licensed by Stokes, and Stokes's files were in such confusion, that there was no way to know which traders were operating legally and which were not.

The solution, Butler suggested, was to rescind all licenses and to require those who wished to continue to trade to obtain new ones. In that way, Butler could screen out the cheats and troublemakers based on the complaints of the Cherokees. He would then require every trader to post indemnity bonds. The War Department approved Butler's plan, and he put it into effect on February 1, 1842.[26]

The Cherokees welcomed this action but wished it to go further. They wanted the agent to exclude all white traders from the nation on the grounds that there were now a sufficient number of competent Cherokees to manage the necessary merchandising. Butler, however, continued to grant licenses to those whites he considered honest and efficient. Appeals to the commissioner of Indian affairs by the Cherokees led him to instruct Butler to suspend licensing from time to time when he thought there was a sufficient number of traders. The government was anxious to curtail surreptitious whiskey selling, and it seemed obvious that white traders found such sales too lucrative to stop. However, the Bureau of Indian Affairs had no intention of restricting white citizens from making money off of the Indians, and whites in Arkansas and Missouri chafed at any limitations on this form of enterprise.

In 1849, Butler's successor, William Butler, began issuing trading licenses more freely, and that year the council instructed its delegation to negotiate with the commissioner of Indian affairs for the total cessation of federal licensing of white traders.[27] In March and September of the next year, three leading Cherokee merchants (John Drew, David Vann, and William Potter Ross) signed protests to Secretary of the Interior A. H. Stuart, stating that white traders were so numerous that they drained away the funds circulating in the nation, which limited the self-improvement of the Cherokee people.[28] They asked Stuart to revoke all licenses to whites. W. G. Belknap, the acting agent after William Butler, wrote to the commissioner of Indian affairs in November 1850, stating his agreement with this position.[29] The acting southern superintendent of Indian affairs, A. S. Loughrey, instructed Belknap to suspend any further licensing for the time being.[30] While this did not invalidate licenses already issued, the decision seemed an important precedent for the Cherokees. However, it did not last long.

In March 1851, Loughrey was succeeded by Colonel John Drennen, who expressed strong opposition to Loughrey's suspension of licensing. "A very large majority of the [Cherokee] people are in favor of the admission of white men as traders," Drennen claimed. (He did not explain how he could know this, considering that he did not reside in the nation.) "The only persons opposed to the admission of white traders are white men intermingled with natives and natives who are themselves engaged in trade and who consequently desire to be freed from the competition."[31] Drennen ignored the fact that the Cherokee council, elected by all the Cherokee citizens, had long supported Loughrey's position. In most cases, poor Cherokees preferred to trade with Cherokee traders, who were more likely than whites to provide credit.

Cherokee traders disliked the competition of whites for another reason. White traders were able to obtain more and longer credit from wholesalers and manufacturers than Cherokee traders and therefore could undersell them. They also received preferential treatment in shipping goods and therefore could supply goods faster. The issue transcended private interests; the major demand for curtailing licensing of white traders came from the council as an issue of national sovereignty.

Nevertheless, the secretary of the interior supported Drennen's appeal, and the new Cherokee agent, George M. Butler, began to issue licenses again freely to whites after July 1851.[32] He required, however, that they post bonds for good behavior and that they give him an inventory of all the goods they planned to sell.[33] Butler licensed at least ten new white traders in the last six months of 1851. Not all of them established permanent shops; some were itinerant peddlers. Many of those licensed in 1851–52 were eager to take advantage of the per capita payments.[34]

In 1853 the Cherokee delegation to Washington, D.C., protested once again that the excessive licensing was an infringement of Cherokee control over its internal trade: "The exercise of this [licensing] power is clearly an incompatible power and its exercise is depriving the Cherokee Nation of a vital right and has become dangerous to its interests."[35] Economic independence was vital to a truly sovereign nation. Yet where treaties established contracts of economic assistance (or foreign aid), the Cherokees also wanted these honored. By its Treaty of 1833 with the western Cherokees, the U.S. government had agreed to provide the money to pay for public blacksmiths and wheelwrights. In 1850 the federal government tried unilaterally to curtail this subsidy. The Cherokees protested that these mechanics were essential for "the poorer class" of Cherokees.[36] Mechanics had previously been whites who came to live in the nation when hired; they provided services necessary for the poorest farmer as well as for the well-to-do. It is doubtful that many white artisans would have come to the Cherokee Nation to work if the federal government had not provided them with subsidized incomes. The council wanted these contracts to be given to Cherokee mechanics as well as to whites. Moreover, the council was entitled to specify where these mechanics should live, thereby making them available in more remote areas of the nation.

The federal government believed it knew what was best for Cherokee development. George Butler, replying to a complaint of the council regarding his continued licensing of white traders, told the commissioner of Indian affairs that in his opinion, the cessation of this practice "is calculated to retard the advancement of the Cherokee people" by making fewer goods available and probably increasing their price because Cherokee traders would gain "a monopoly."[37] (Why they would not compete with each other he did not say.) C. W. Dean, the southern superintendent of Indian affairs in 1856, supported Butler in a letter to George Manypenny, the secretary of the interior. Dean said that even if the government did agree not to license whites, whites could still trade in the nation by using the simple dodge of becoming "silent partners." By making Cherokee citizens their partners, white traders could continue to trade because any Cherokee could declare himself a merchant and trade without a license.[38] Manypenny accepted this argument, and licensing continued on the basis of the paternalistic rationale of protecting the Cherokees for their own good. The Cherokee council, in his opinion, would not be capable of finding a solution to the problem of "silent partners." In the end, the Cherokees were unable to persuade the federal government to acknowledge the nation's right to control the licensing of white traders.

However, the Cherokees did succeed in their long effort to remove the U.S. Army garrison from within the nation's boundaries. Fort Gibson had been founded in 1822 during the Osage Wars. Later the United States feared "domestic strife" among the Indians whom it had crowded into the area during the removal process.[39] Ross had opposed the right of the garrison commandant to interfere in Cherokee internal affairs as early as 1840, but General Matthew Arbuckle claimed the right to protect the Treaty party and the Old Settlers during the unrest ensuing from the execution of the Ridges and Boudinot.[40] Arbuckle had even gone so far as to assume the right to interfere for political purposes at that time. Many protests against the garrison's interference in the years 1839 to 1840 were filed by Ross and the council. When the Treaty of 1846 ended the "domestic strife," Ross tried again to have the garrison removed. The federal government argued that with the payment of the large sums due the nation as a result of the treaty, troops were needed to prevent disorders that might occur when the money was distributed.[41] For this reason Superintendent John Drennen had insisted that the per capita payments must take place at Fort Gibson. Ross and the council wanted the funds to be disbursed at the Cherokee Nation's capital, where Cherokee merchants and hotel keepers would have profited. Ross said, "I trust I may be pardoned for claiming for Cherokee citizens, farmers, hotel keepers and laborers, the pecuniary advantages which must accrue to any neighborhood in which so large a sum of money is disbursed" as opposed to granting such advantages to "others" who travel in and out of it (as white traders, whiskey dealers, and gamblers did at Fort Gibson).[42]

From the Cherokees' viewpoint, the military had always been a source of trouble besides its interference in tribal affairs. Off-duty soldiers were often drunk and disorderly, and if Cherokees became involved in disorders, they were subject to rough treatment when arrested. Soldiers sometimes married Cherokees, which led to family quarrels involving the wife's relatives. The racetrack at the fort provided other occasions for quarrels over betting.[43] Agent Pierce Butler reported in 1843 that the Cherokees considered the soldiers arrogant and racist.[44] He also noted the excessive drinking and brawling of the troops. When called on to arrest Cherokees, Butler said, the soldiers were often arbitrary and offensive.[45] In June 1847, recently discharged soldiers from the garrison entered into a plot to rob the federal agent's office at Fort Gibson, and they enticed some Cherokees and blacks to cooperate with them.[46] Quite apart from the issue of Cherokee sovereignty, the troops were clearly a disruptive element.

John Ross stressed also that the four square miles on which the fort was located constituted an important piece of Cherokee real estate that could and should be developed by the nation. He wrote in 1854, when the nation was struggling to relieve itself from debt, that the site was "the only eligible point for commercial advantages in this nation where a town of respectability might ere long grow up and flourish. It is therefore of utmost importance to the Cherokee nation that the Fort be abandoned."[47] However, none of these arguments had any impact on the government until 1857, when a serious depression in the United States made it essential that federal expenditures be retrenched. Moreover, the army's frontier had now expanded further west among the Plains Indians, and troops were clearly of little use in the Cherokee Nation.

Having decided to give up the post, the army tried, in June 1857, to auction off its military buildings to whites. The Cherokees protested that by treaty this land must now revert to the nation; the federal government had no right to sell Indian land for its own enrichment. Ross informed the secretary of the interior that "citizens of the United States cannot hold improvements in the Cherokee Nation."[48] On examining the treaty, the secretary discovered that Ross was right. He called off the sales, and all the land and buildings of Fort Gibson reverted to the Cherokees.[49]

Elated over this turn of events, the council immediately surveyed the four square miles into plots, christened the location "Keetoowah" after their ancient sacred town in the East, and offered the right to lease the plots to

Cherokee citizens. The auction netted $20,000 for the Cherokee treasury.[50] The council was so certain that Keetoowah would become the nation's most prosperous town that it voted to transfer the capital of the nation there from Tahlequah. John Ross vetoed the bill on the grounds that it was not as central a location for the nation. A commercial town did arise at the site of Fort Gibson, but it never fulfilled the Cherokees' hopes that it would become a thriving commercial center. Riverboats continued to bring merchandise to the town, but they also brought illegal whiskey. The location of the town just across the river from the Creek Nation attracted unsavory citizens of both nations. Criminals escaped arrest by fleeing across the river. The town continued to retain the unsavory reputation it had enjoyed when it was a garrison site.

Ironically, although the nation was happy to be rid of the fort, occasions arose when the Cherokees wished to have army troops come to their assistance. For example, when the Kansas Territory began to fill up with settlers, many of them intruded onto the Cherokee Neutral Lands.[51] When the council called upon the army to remove these intruders, troops had to be sent from Fort Smith, Arkansas.[52]

Having realized that Keetoowah would not be a thriving city or the nation's capital, the nation persuaded the federal government to transfer the headquarters of its resident agent from Fort Gibson to Tahlequah in 1858.[53] The agent had previously lived near the troops so that he could utilize them to exercise his authority; now he had no reason not to live in the nation's capital.

On the more crucial issue of the jurisdiction of the federal court in Arkansas over criminal cases involving whites and Cherokee citizens, the Ross government had no success at all, despite the obvious evidence that frontier racism seriously prevented justice from being administered to Indian plaintiffs or defendants. Under the Trade and Intercourse Act of 1834, the federal courts were assigned authority over all criminal cases in which both an Indian and a white citizen were involved within the Indian Territory, which, for judicial purposes, was annexed to Arkansas. Indian courts were not considered adequate to protect the rights of whites in criminal cases where jail, whipping, or capital punishment was involved. The fact that Indians were not treated fairly in white frontier courts was not considered. In the federal court in Arkansas, the sheriffs, marshals, deputies, clerks, judges, and juries were all white frontier citizens, and they shared the racial prejudices of their communities. Disdain for Indians and their rights was so ingrained in frontier society that even in a federal court Indians were regularly discriminated against and in many cases were subject to physical abuse, especially by the sheriffs and deputies who arrested and jailed them. Indians were arrested summarily in their own land and taken 50 to 100 miles away to jail in Arkansas. They were given no legal advice, they did not understand the white man's system, and most spoke little or no English. Even those who were simply witnesses to crimes were taken to Arkansas, where they were kept for weeks and even months in jail until the case was tried. Lawyers might be assigned to defend Indians, but their impartiality was negligible. No Indians sat on the juries. Their interpreters were whites. It was common knowledge that a white jury seldom if ever jailed, let alone hung, a white man who was convicted of assault upon or even the murder of an Indian.

Indians by reputation were considered treacherous, and their word was never accepted over that of whites. Moreover, it was common folklore that Indians were unable to hold their liquor and when drunk reverted to barbarous savagery and behaved like wild men. In "civilized" white communities, the Indian retained the image of a dangerous savage. This was difficult enough for full-bloods to bear, but it was particularly galling for those well-to-do Cherokees of mixed ancestry who spoke English, lived in good homes, and were respected citizens (judges, merchants, and civil officials) in their own nation. In Arkansas officials discovered that the wealthy, "uppity" Cherokees could be forced to pay high fees to cover costs even on trumped-up charges where no trial ever took place. No sheriff was ever tried for false arrest or other abuses of Indians' rights. The burden of proof always rested on Indians to prove that they were not savages. Officials in Washington, subject to the votes and political influence of white politicians in Arkansas, always assumed that justice was even-handed and fair in federal courts. Clear-cut evidence, supplied by whites, that trials were unfair was treated as exceptional. Cherokee claims that their citizens deserved the right to a trial in courts where witnesses and juries were their "peers" were dismissed as impossible.

One of the more thorny aspects of this problem was deciding who was a Cherokee citizen and who was a U.S. citizen. By Cherokee law, a white person married to a Cherokee was a Cherokee citizen and was both entitled to the rights of Cherokees and subject to the authority of Cherokee law. Many whites, however, believed that marriage to a Cherokee entitled them to the privileges of both societies. A white person married to a Cherokee who harmed an Indian or infringed on Indian law usually preferred to be tried in a white court before a white jury. Indians who harmed whites had no such option. It remained a moot point whether an intermarried white who preferred to be tried as an Indian in a Cherokee court could be denied that choice and forced to be tried in a white court. The problem of jurisdiction was compounded when the intermarried white had relatives in Arkansas (since most intermarriages were with border citizens) who had political influence or who might be officers of the federal court. Cases inevitably arose in which both the

Cherokee court and federal court claimed the right to try an accused criminal and fought over which had precedence. In some cases the accused might be subject to trial by both courts. The defendant's objection on the grounds of double jeopardy was denied if the first trial occurred in an Indian court; the decision of the Indian court was simply declared invalid. This created serious clashes between law enforcement agents in both jurisdictions, and when the Cherokees felt that the sovereignty of their nation was at stake, they sometimes engaged in shooting battles with the deputies of the federal court. To the Cherokees it was an inherent sovereign right that they, and they alone, could define who was or was not a Cherokee citizen.[54]

A concomitant problem involved the extradition of persons charged with criminal offenses. The officials of the federal court in Arkansas felt perfectly free to send marshals into the Cherokee Nation to arrest and bring back for trial Cherokees charged with crimes by whites. However, the Cherokee Nation was not free to take similar action when a Cherokee (married to a white or not) or a white (married to a Cherokee or not) charged with a crime in the nation fled across the border into Arkansas, Missouri, or Texas. These states acknowledged no right of the Cherokees to extradition of indicted criminals. Whites simply would not tolerate arrests made by "savages" in their sovereign states. Even when the Cherokee chief or council asked the federal agent to arrange for the return of criminals, this right was denied. White criminals therefore always found a safe and permanent haven across the border, whereas Cherokees were not safe in their own land from arbitrary arrest. No request was ever made by whites in Arkansas for permission to remove wanted criminals from Cherokee territory. The Cherokee Nation repeatedly requested that extradition agreements be established on both sides; at the very least, they wanted Cherokee police to make any arrests of Cherokees wanted in other states. Those Cherokees suspected of a crime, the council said, must be granted a formal hearing in a Cherokee court prior to extradition. The United States, however, never accepted the validity of these requests, and the western states loudly opposed them.

The Trade and Intercourse Act did not make clear precisely what kinds of criminal cases required trial in a federal court. Usually cases of murder, aggravated assault, or grand larceny were considered within the purview of the federal courts. However, in a wide range of criminal cases (including rape, petty theft, embezzling, importing and selling whiskey, and gambling), the decision whether to prosecute in a federal court was made in an arbitrary manner. The Cherokees tried in vain to have more specific definitions of criminal jurisdiction spelled out and uniformly applied. Cherokees might be arrested or tried on even the most petty of criminal charges by whites, but whites were seldom tried in Arkansas or Missouri on charges brought by Cherokees, even in major offenses. In the cases of white intruders who illegally entered the Cherokee Nation without licenses to trade or permission to settle, the authorities in white states took absolutely no notice. By treaty, the Cherokees were allowed to expel such persons, but they could do so only with the assistance of the federal agent. In most cases the agents needed federal troops for this purpose. Once an intruder was ejected—a task federal agents undertook reluctantly and rarely—there was nothing to prevent his or her return. No border patrols were ever established by the federal government to prevent such intrusions, even when hundreds of settlers invaded the Indian Territory, built log cabins, and began cultivating the land. Nor were those whites on the border who entered the nation to steal timber, salt, coal, or other minerals ever prosecuted. The Cherokee Nation struggled continually to obtain some effective means to prevent white intrusion and to prosecute intruders. A Cherokee proposal that intruders be prosecuted in Cherokee courts after arrests by Cherokee police and with Cherokee witnesses proved more than the federal government could tolerate, knowing full well the howl of protest this would arouse in states bordering the Cherokees.

The federal circuit court for western Arkansas was located in different places at different periods—at Van Buren, Little Rock, and Fort Smith. From 1836 to 1851 the court met at Little Rock. Congress passed a law in 1844 increasing the jurisdiction of this court over crimes involving whites and Indians in the Indian Territory. However, the 1844 enactment failed to clarify precisely what crimes were covered or how Indian citizenship was to be determined.[55] Some examples of the violence and injustice resulting from this overlapping authority, dual citizenship, and lack of formal extradition procedures indicate why this became so central and heated an issue for the Cherokees.

In 1842 a "native Cherokee" named David Downing killed a white man named Fred Fisher. Downing was arrested by Cherokee authorities, brought to trial, and acquitted on grounds of self-defense. Fisher was a white intruder; he had no right to be in the nation. Hence, the Cherokees believed jurisdiction in the case rested with their authorities. The federal agent, however, protested that, Fisher being white, Downing should have been tried in the Arkansas federal court. Downing was seized by marshals from Arkansas for a second trial in Little Rock. Agent Pierce Butler, realizing that Downing would claim double jeopardy, wrote to Chief Ross telling him to annul the verdict of the Cherokee court and officially turn Downing over to federal authorities for trial. Downing feared that he would stand little chance of acquittal in Arkansas. Ross was concerned chiefly with protecting Cherokee sovereignty. He refused to annul the decision on the grounds that under the separation of powers in the Cherokee constitution, neither the chief executive nor the council (the legislature) had the right to overrule a decision of the judiciary.[56]

At about this same time, two Cherokees who were intoxicated stole a horse from two white men, J. Hare and H. Jamison. The theft occurred in the Cherokee Nation, and Hare and Jamison had no license to be in the nation; they were intruders. Agent Butler believed that the case should be tried before the federal court. Ross disagreed: "The question of jurisdiction in this case, according to the long-established relations between the Cherokee Nation and the United States, cannot reconcile the Cherokees to surrender their citizens to the courts of the United States for the petty offenses alleged to be committed upon citizens of the States who, perchance, may have placed themselves out of the pale of protection of the laws of the United States by going into the Cherokee Country illegally."[57] Ross believed that too many whites claimed the right to enter and leave the nation at will, counting on the protection of their own courts while they were (illegally) in the Cherokee Nation. He held that treaty rights allowing the Cherokees to expel intruders clearly implied their right to try them for crimes committed in the nation.

The Cherokee delegation to Washington in 1842 protested to Secretary of War John Spencer concerning these matters: "It is not our wish that Marshalls of the adjoining States shall enter our Country (as they have heretofore) and arrest our citizens for any alleged offence and require their attendance at some distant Court under heavy penalties, or be put in prison until the meeting of the Court. We wish to know distinctly for what offences the Nation will be bound to deliver over its citizens for trial under the laws of the United States."[58] However, Spencer was unwilling to provide any clarification; that could only be done, he said, by an act of Congress amending the Trade and Intercourse Act. Ross and the Cherokees made the same complaint in 1846 to Secretary of War William Medill,[59] following the critical decision of the U.S. Supreme Court that year in *Rogers v. Cherokee Nation*—a decision that dealt a severe blow to the right of Indian nations to try intermarried whites for crimes and seriously undermined their claims to independence. William Rogers, a white man, had been arrested for killing Jacob Nicholson, also white, in the Cherokee Nation in 1843. Both were married to Cherokees but were tried at the federal court in Little Rock. Rogers demanded trial in the Cherokee Nation because he and Nicholson were considered Cherokee citizens because they were married to Cherokees.[60] Eventually the case made its way to the U.S. Supreme Court, presided over by Chief Justice Roger B. Taney, an appointee of Andrew Jackson. Indians, said Taney in the Court's majority decision, "have never been acknowledged or treated as independent nations by the European Courts nor regarded as the owners of the territories they respectively occupied." The Europeans who came to North America treated the continent "as vacant" and claimed it for themselves. "It is too firmly and clearly established to admit of dispute," Taney continued, "that the Indian tribes residing within the territorial limits of the United States are subject to their authority and when the country occupied by them is not within the limits of one of the states, Congress may, by law, punish any offence committed there, no matter whether the offender be a white man or an Indian." [61]

Interpreting Taney's decision in a letter to John Ross, Medill admitted that as "the red race" became "sufficiently advanced in intelligence" to adopt farming and regular government, the United States had "conceded to them the right to make and enforce laws" of their own. However, the United States had never "divested itself of the power to interfere when the laws of a tribe have been oppressive or unjust." As of 1846, "the original and unlimited sovereignty [of the United States] and right of control remains unimpaired." As "guardians" of the Indians, "the Government is called upon in the highest obligations of justice and humanity to interpose its sovereign and guardian powers" to maintain order. This would be true, Medill said, "even were it formally and specially stipulated in a treaty" that the Cherokees retained the right of self-government (as, indeed, it was stipulated in several treaties with the Cherokees). Such treaty clauses did not in any way limit Congress from asserting jurisdiction over crimes committed in the Indian nations, Medill told Ross.[62] "Unlimited sovereignty" meant just that. The Cherokees could hardly accept Taney's decision or Medill's interpretation of it without giving up all efforts to protect their treaty rights. Their status as a nation was being unilaterally altered from Washington. Taney had made a decision, but he offered no remedy to the anomalous situation. It was not to the advantage of the United States to work out a remedy.

In 1847 a significant concession was made to the Indian nations when the federal court in Arkansas at last permitted Indians to become witnesses in their own defense.[63] That same year, Ross again protested to the federal agent against U.S. marshals who entered the nation to serve court processes and subpoenas on Cherokees and on whites married to Cherokees to appear in the federal court in Arkansas. Ross said, "It is an unaccountable, illegal assumption of power, a direct usurpation, an imposition on the Cherokee people." He insisted that "it is the duty of the agent . . . when any property has been taken out of the Nation and found in the possession of the citizens of the States, say a Negro for instance" or a horse, "it is the duty of the Agent to have the Negro or Horse . . . taken by force and returned to the claimant in the nation." Agent James McKissick wrote to the commissioner of Indian affairs for advice, saying that he had so far declined to do as Ross demanded.[64]

The commissioner replied that it was within the legitimate power of U.S. marshals to arrest criminals in the Cherokee Nation, for if they did not have this power, the nation would become a haven of refugees from justice.[65] The response seemed to miss Ross's point. The sovereign power of the Cherokee Nation required a formal system of extradition and not simply an open field for unilateral action by authorities of the United States. Furthermore, if the United States had the right to apprehend refugees from justice in the Cherokee Nation, then the Cherokees had the right to expect the United States (through its agent) to apprehend refugees from Cherokee justice in adjoining states, lest these states become refuges for criminals.

A different but equally offensive process took place when the citizens of the United States made claims against unknown Cherokees for stealing horses or other property. The agent sent these claims to the War Department. If the War Department determined that a claim was valid, it deducted the sum claimed from the Cherokee annuity and sent that amount directly to the aggrieved white citizen. There was no formal process by which the Cherokee Nation could challenge the evaluations, and no attention was paid to the Cherokees' claim that the nation should not be held responsible for the crimes of its citizens. On the other hand, when the Cherokees made claims against white citizens for similar thefts or loss of property, there was no process by which they could bring action or be repaid except by private suits in state courts. Even when slaves or horses were stolen, as regularly occurred, no Cherokee court could try a white citizen. When Cherokees did bring suits in Arkansas, Missouri, or Texas, they received little attention.[66]

In 1853, the Cherokee delegation in Washington once again tried to obtain clarification concerning the jurisdiction of the U.S. courts. The delegation protested to the secretary of the interior that the federal district court in Arkansas "has proceeded to try and punish the citizens of the Cherokee Nation" for trading in liquor, which was a minor crime always punished in the past by the Cherokees against their own people or whites, who were usually unlicensed intruders or else they would have lost their bonds and licenses for selling liquor. The federal court was "also exercising a civil process of collecting fines" whereas the Trade and Intercourse Act gave federal courts jurisdiction only in criminal cases. The delegation also objected once more to the fact that the federal court continued to try intermarried whites who were citizens of the Cherokee Nation. "The exercise of this extraordinary jurisdiction is looked upon as subverting the regular progress of [our] laws," they asserted, and in the case of double jeopardy, this was "expressly prohibited by the Constitution of the United States."[67] The Interior Department replied that the resolution of these issues rested with Congress; it alone could clarify Indian rights.

By 1856 the situation had become so grossly unfair that both the federal agent, George Butler, and the southern superintendent of Indian affairs, C. W. Dean, joined the Cherokees in protesting against the actions of the federal court in Arkansas. Butler wrote to Dean on April 9, 1856, that although the Cherokee courts had a prior writ, a federal marshal had taken a Cherokee prisoner who was about to stand trial for horse stealing in the Cherokee Nation and carried him off to Arkansas for trial on another charge. The marshal wanted him to stand trial in Arkansas for stealing a mule from a white man and assumed that the right of the United States to try him preempted the right of the Cherokees. Butler wrote, "Instead of improving the Cherokees, as was the intention of the Intercourse Law, the course [being] pursued is calculated to embitter the good Cherokees against the United States, for if these people have no privileges as freemen and are to be treated as degraded Slaves, it is useless for Government officers to attempt to give them encouragement."[68] In short, Butler found his own position very awkward. He could not, as he felt it his duty, encourage responsible Cherokee self-government and at the same time allow the U.S. authorities in Arkansas to undermine it.

Superintendent Dean endorsed Butler's letter and sent one of his own to Washington. He could see no reason why "the Federal Court" should exercise such "interference . . . with the officials of the Cherokee tribunals." It was "an invasion of privileges and rights guaranteed by the United States" to the Cherokees in their treaties. "And it is among the very class, the more educated, refined and wealthy of the tribe, and whom it is most desirable to attach by sentiments of friendship and cordial goodwill to our Government and institutions, that the grievance is most deeply felt and the irritations the strongest."[69] Dean was concerned that the mixed-blood leaders, Cherokees of education and refinement dedicated to upholding law and order, would lose face. If the officials of the federal court showed no respect for these enlightened Indian leaders who were trying to uplift their nation, then the leaders would lose the respect of their people. Disrespect for Cherokee law by whites might, Dean said, lead the full-bloods to reject their enlightened leaders and conclude that the whole concept of acculturation was a worthless experiment. The United States, Dean argued, was driving the Cherokees back to barbarism by its failure to find a remedy for this conflict in legal jurisdiction.

Several months later, Chief Ross asked Agent Butler to request that the governor of Arkansas return to the Cherokee Nation four Cherokees (intermarried white men) wanted for murder who had fled to that state. Butler sent the request to C. W. Dean, who forwarded it to the U.S. district attorney in Little Rock, A. William Wilson. Ross maintained that return of Cherokee felons was guaranteed under article 2 of the Treaty of 1846: "All fugitives from justice . . . seeking refuge in the territory of the United States, shall be delivered up by the authorities of the United States to the Cherokee Nation for trial and punishment."[70] Wilson responded that he was reluctant to ask the governor of Arkansas to deliver these criminals. Dean told Ross that he could not enforce his request, and there the matter rested.[71] Wilson explained his refusal on the grounds that the treaty clause cited had "no practical operation or effect" without "an act of Congress specifying the manner" in which it was to be carried out.[72]

The Cherokees had reached such a state of frustration and anger by August 11, 1859, that Butler reported to A. B. Greenwood, commissioner of Indian affairs, that a group of "armed and painted Cherokees" had rescued Thomas Brewer, a Cherokee under arrest for killing a citizen of the United States, from the U.S. marshal who was taking him off to jail in Van Buren.[73] The persistence of an unjust system of law enforcement was leading to a breakdown of law.

In 1857, Elias Rector of Arkansas (who had formerly been a U.S. marshal there) replaced C. W. Dean as southern superintendent of Indian affairs and stated in his annual report that a drastic change in the federal relationship with the Indian Territory was needed. To overcome the objection of Indians that their people were carried miles away into Arkansas for trial, he proposed that federal courts be established among the Cherokees, Choctaws, and Creeks and that they be given very specific definitions of their jurisdiction.[74] This would not only clarify procedures but would mean that the juries would consist of Indians. Few whites on the frontier wanted to be tried before a jury of Indians, however. Rector also proposed that the federal agents have joint authority with the Indian legislatures in each tribe for the purpose of licensing white traders; that judicial power in minor cases be granted to the federal agents; and that the commissioner of Indian affairs be given the power to call upon military assistance in enforcing the laws governing Indians. Rector's proposals, however, were never implemented.[75]

As Morris Wardell, historian of Cherokee political development, wrote in his analysis of the arrogant behavior of the federal government toward the Cherokees, by 1859 "the imperialistic policy of the United States could not be stayed."[76] The forceful impingement of the dominant culture and power of the United States on the Cherokee Nation was demonstrated in several other crises in the 1850s. One of these concerned the increasing number of white intruders onto the Cherokee Neutral Lands in Kansas, especially following an act of the territorial legislature of Kansas to incorporate that land under its jurisdiction as counties. Another was evident in a statement by Robert J. Walker when he was inaugurated as governor of the Kansas Territory in 1857. Walker noted that white expansion into the territory (formerly reserved for Indians removed from the East) would soon be followed by expansion into the Indian Territory south of Kansas, an area frontier whites considered too rich in good land and resources to be left to Indians. "The Indian treaties will constitute no obstacle," Walker said, "any more than precisely similar treaties did in Kansas."[77] In 1859, Superintendent Elias Rector echoed Walker's statement when he said, "Necessity will soon compel the incorporation of [the Indians'] country into the Union, and before its [that is, necessity's] requisitions, every other consideration will give way, and even wrong find, as it ever does, in necessity, its apology."[78]

In effect, Walker and Rector articulated the prevailing feeling on the white frontier that all Indian land (whether protected by treaties or not) must soon be incorporated into the new states and territories as the white population moved steadily westward. The increasingly desperate effort of the Cherokees to sell the Neutral Lands in Kansas in the 1850s reflected their awareness that whites in Kansas could not long be restrained from settling on this tract and that the United States would not fulfill its treaty obligations to drive off these intruders. Next to their problems with the federal court, the Cherokees worried most about these intruders.

Ross had warned the Cherokee council on October 5, 1857, that the white people in the frontier were planning to expand onto their land in Kansas and perhaps even take away their control over the Indian Territory. He had quoted to the council the statements of Governor Robert Walker in Kansas "as evidence of the dangers with which we ourselves are threatened" and said that such a statement by a prominent western politician "encourages aggression upon our rights."[79]

Having failed to persuade the United States to buy their land in Kansas, the Cherokees demanded that the federal government remove all intruders on those lands. As early as August 1856, the Cherokees had asked Agent George Butler to do this, and Butler had requested that troops be assigned for the purpose.[80] Superintendent Dean, however, opposed the action in a letter dated January 17, 1857, stating that he did not believe in driving U.S. citizens out of their homes by means of the army.[81] In October 1857, Butler renewed his request for troops.[82] Superintendent Elias Rector, who had replaced Dean, also objected to forceful removal of U.S. citizens from the Neutral Lands, on the grounds that the Cherokees might soon sell the land.[83] In January 1858, Butler was still awaiting troops,[84] but not until May 1860 did the government finally authorize troops to take action. By that time the white intruders had concluded that the government would never act on its threat to remove them.[85] There were now 3,000 white squatters and 700 farms on the land. Federal agent Robert J. Cowart warned the squatters in 1860 that he would soon use the army to force them to leave, but he never carried out his threat.[86]

By 1860 the issue of squatters on the Neutral Lands was mixed with the slavery question. Southerners suspected that the white intruders on Cherokee land in the Kansas Territory were abolitionists who were aiding slaves to escape from the South on the underground railroad. Some Cherokee slaveholders had the same fears. Northerners, however, believed that these white intruders were proslavery people who wanted to make Kansas a slave state.

In addition to the problems raised by the refusal of the federal government to either buy the Neutral Lands or remove intruders from it, two other aspects of sovereignty caused the Cherokees considerable anxiety in the later 1850s. One was the increasing intrusion of white cattle herders on their land and the other the increasing pressure of railroad builders to obtain rights-of-way through Cherokee territory.

The establishment of the Indian Territory created a critical roadblock between beef producers in Texas and the nearest railroad terminals in Missouri where cattle were shipped to St. Louis and Chicago. The Cherokees and other tribes between Texas and Missouri were caught in a pincer movement as railroad builders aggressively sought rights-of-way southward through the Indian Territory to Texas, while cattle ranchers cavalierly moved their herds northward through the Indian Territory to the nearest railroad depot in St. Joseph, Missouri. Railroad builders also had a more distant goal than reaching Texas; they were eager to lay track (later the Southern Pacific Railroad) across the southern part of the country to California. The best southern route led directly through the Indian Territory. The Cherokee Nation in the northeastern Indian Territory would be the first link in that long chain.

As early as the 1840s Texas cowboys drove the first large herds of cattle north through the Cherokee Nation on their 800-mile trip to Missouri. The Texas herds started north in March each year, as soon as the grass turned green. The cattle moved slowly, grazing their way through the Choctaw and Cherokee nations under the watchful eyes of the cowhands. Six months later they reached their destinations, fat and sleek, ready for transport to St. Louis and beyond. Governor Robert Walker of Kansas said that the sale of Cherokee land to herders would make the Indians enormously rich, but from the Cherokee experience, such an enterprise was very destructive and not at all lucrative. Not only did the cattle eat the grass that might have fed Indian herds, but the cowboys often managed to pick up stray groups of Indian cattle as they traveled. In addition, ranchers did not believe that they should have to pay the Cherokees for the right to transport their herds to market. They considered the Indian lands to be "open prairie." Nor did cattle ranchers compensate the Indians when diseases from Texas longhorns infected and killed Indian cattle.

On October 23, 1853, the Cherokee council declared all stock grazing by whites on Cherokee land to be an illegal trespass. The law declared that those in charge of such herds were intruders who should be removed by the federal authorities responsible for maintaining Indian boundaries. The federal agent immediately sent a copy of the law to the commissioner of Indian affairs, George Manypenny, asking whether he should enforce it. Manypenny declared the law illegal and contrary to the Trade and Intercourse Act. Although the Trade and Intercourse Act forbade "malicious trespass" upon Indian land, it was never meant, Manypenny said, to prevent "travelers through their country."[87] Manypenny clearly did not choose to consider the "malicious" or injurious aspects of these cowherding "travelers," so the Cherokees attempted to explain the negative consequences of thousands of head of cattle on a leisurely six-month journey through the nation.

Thomas Drew, the superintendent for Indian affairs, told Manypenny in February 1854 that the cowhands or "stock drivers" commonly stole Cherokee cattle as they passed through the nation and that the diseases from their cattle (murrain and hoof-and-mouth disease) killed many of the Cherokees' cattle.[88] Manypenny was not concerned about these annoyances; they did not alter, he said, the principle of "freedom to travel." In early 1854 the Cherokees instructed Agent George Butler to order cattle herders off their land. Butler again wrote to Manypenny for instructions.[89] Manypenny again told him to do nothing. He went even further and instructed Superintendent Drew to issue passports to the cattle drovers, and twenty such passports were issued by February 16, 1855.[90] According to Drew, some of the large herds also went from east to west, from Arkansas through the Indian Territory, headed for California. Going through the Indian Territory saved 200 to 300 miles. Drew was well aware of Cherokee opposition to the cattle trade, but he followed Manypenny's principle: "The right of American citizens to pass through the Indian territory will be conceded by all, . . . and with them to take their stock or any other kind of property, and should the effect of the passage of large droves of cattle or horses prove injurious to the Indians by grazing along the line or by having disease among the cattle, it must be considered in the light of misfortune" for which no one is to blame. "The right of free passage . . . is a right too sacred to be called in question" by these Indians, and the U.S.

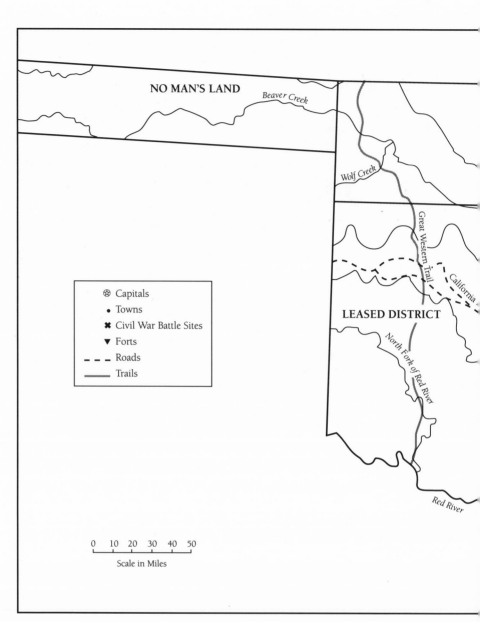

MAP 4. *Indian Territory*

Source: John W. Morris, Charles R. Goins, and Edwin C. McReynolds, *Historical Atlas of Oklahoma*, 3d ed. (Norman: University of Oklahoma Press, 1986).

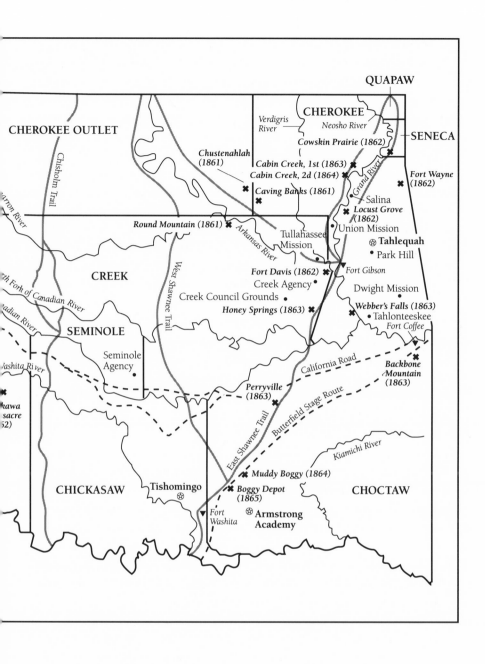

QUAPAW

CHEROKEE

CHEROKEE OUTLET

SENECA

Verdigris River

Neosho River

Chisholm Trail

Cowskin Prairie (1862)

Chustenahlah (1861) ✖

Cabin Creek, 1st (1863) ✖

Cabin Creek, 2d (1864) ✖

Fort Wayne (1862) ✖

Caving Banks (1861) ✖

Salina

Locust Grove (1862) ✖

Round Mountain (1861) ✖

Arkansas River

Union Mission

Tullahassee Mission

⊗ **Tahlequah**

• Park Hill

CREEK

Fort Davis (1862) ✖

Fort Gibson

West Shawnee Trail

Creek Agency

th Fork of Canadian River

Creek Council Grounds •

Honey Springs (1863) ✖

Dwight Mission •

Webber's Falls (1863) ✖

• Tahlonteeskee

adian River

SEMINOLE

Fort Coffee

Washita River

Seminole Agency •

California Road

Backbone Mountain (1863) ✖

✖

kawa sacre 52)

Perryville (1863) ✖

Butterfield Stage Route

Kiamichi River

East Shawnee Trail

CHICKASAW

Tishomingo ⊗

Muddy Boggy (1864) ✖

✖ *Boggy Depot (1865)*

CHOCTAW

▼ Fort Washita

⊗ **Armstrong Academy**

government would use its full authority to protect the right of free passage "from one ocean to the other."[91] White farmers or ranchers would never have tolerated the principle of free passage through their lands for a moment. However, white farmers held their land as private property; they believed the Indians had no private property and apparently little right to control their communally owned land.

In 1853, six months before the Cherokees passed their first law against white cattle grazing, the first overture from a railroad builder was made seeking land for a cattle depot in the Cherokee Nation. J. Sullivan Cowden of Ohio informed the War Department in 1853 that his company wished to obtain land and build a town called Ozark City in the northeastern corner of the Cherokee Nation. The land, he said, would be used as a railroad depot, and tracks would connect the stockyards in the Cherokee Nation with all the trunk lines heading north and east.[92] Cowden's offer was refused because the government could not sell the land without Cherokee permission and the Cherokees had no desire to sell land for railroad development. White business people never understood why the government could not serve their interests by taking land or rights-of-way from the Indians. Agent Butler in 1857 reported an offer by a railroad company to build a line from St. Louis through the Cherokee Nation, then southward to join the Southern Pacific Railroad in New Mexico. He supported the measure and thought the Cherokees could be persuaded to grant a right-of-way.[93]

In 1858, another railroad builder, J. B. Chapman, decided to deal directly with the Cherokees. He approached John Ross with a proposition to obtain a right-of-way for a railroad through the nation that would connect Fort Leavenworth, Kansas, with Fort Gibson in the Cherokee Nation. He may have hinted that Ross would personally benefit from such a grant. Ross simply referred Chapman to the Trade and Intercourse Act, which prohibited the nation from selling land to individuals; as a nation, the Cherokees granted land only through treaties with the United States. Ross then sent word to the federal agent that he had been privately approached by Chapman. The agent sent this information on to the commissioner of Indian affairs.[94]

When James Buchanan was inaugurated president of the United States in March 1857, he declared that the days of Indian recalcitrance against "progress" (meaning railroad building) and posturing about "Indian sovereignty" were numbered. Buchanan encouraged the pincer movement that would make the Indian Territory a corridor for commercial progress. "At no distant day," he said, to the delight of frontier speculators, the Indian Territory "will be incorporated into the Union."[95] Buchanan encouraged Congress to subvert Indian treaties and claims of sovereignty by passing a law that would transform the Indian Territory first into a territory of the United States and then into a state.

The effort to subvert Indian sovereignty through a territorial bill had begun in Congress a decade before Buchanan's inauguration. In 1848 Congressman Abraham R. McIlvaine of the Committee on Indian Affairs had introduced a bill to give the Indian Territory official status as a federal territory with its own territorial government merging all of the tribes into one and placing them under federally appointed officials. Ultimately Indians would be given citizenship, and whites would be allowed into the area to take land not in use by Indian families.[96] The *Cherokee Advocate* alerted the nation to the bill, and its editor voiced strong opposition. The bill was never acted upon, but thereafter the Cherokees kept a close eye on Congress for similar efforts. In his annual report in 1851, Agent George Butler expressed the view that the Cherokees would benefit greatly from citizenship under a federal territorial system.[97]

The territorial idea received its most serious consideration in Congress in 1854 when Senator Robert M. Johnson of Arkansas introduced the first carefully worked out bill to merge "the five civilized tribes" and other Indians within the boundaries of what is now Oklahoma into one territorial government.[98] The bill was closely coordinated with the effort to make the area then reserved for Indians to the north of the Cherokees into two new U.S. territories, Nebraska and Kansas. Under Johnson's plan all three territories would eventually become states, and all of the tribal structures within them would be abolished. In 1825 these three areas combined had been designated as a territory into which the eastern tribes should be removed and which would remain theirs "forever." However, the white frontier had quickly caught up with this region, and whites were eager to take the land once given to the Indians. The Cherokees had protested to Congress on November 29, 1851, against an earlier proposal to make Kansas a federal territory for fear that it would destroy the rights of Cherokees to the Neutral Lands as well as taking the land granted by treaties to other tribes in Kansas.[99] To make Kansas a federal territory, they believed, would set a precedent for opening their own territory to white settlement. Johnson made this fear a reality.

In order to temporarily preserve the separate identities of the major tribes, Senator Johnson's bill in 1854 called for the area that is now Oklahoma to be divided into three separate districts—one to be dominated by the Cherokees, one by the Choctaws, and one by the Creeks. After a brief time, however, these areas were to be merged into one single territory. Federal courts were to be established in the territory, with both criminal and civil jurisdiction over all activities. The Indians were to allow the federal government to survey their land and sell to whites any land plots not already settled by Indians. The Cherokee Outlet given by treaty to the Cherokees was to be immediately divided among whites since at that time no Indians were living there.[100]

None of the tribes in the Indian Territory was in favor of the Johnson bill. They all realized that detribalization not only meant loss of their own system of self-government but also placed them at the mercy of lawless or conniving whites who would try to settle on land along the railroad right-of-way. As usual, many officials and politicians convinced themselves that "the more intelligent and progressive" Indians favored the bill despite the fact that the Cherokees and Creeks were virtually unanimous in their opposition.[101] Agent George Butler, though he personally supported the Johnson bill, reported strong opposition among all classes of Cherokees.[102] John Ross had spoken out vigorously against any such measure in his annual message to the council in 1853 when the Kansas-Nebraska Bill was being pushed in Congress. In October 1854, he reiterated: "In my last annual message reference was made to the danger of encroachment being made upon our rights by the legislation of Congress on the subject of organizing the Territory of Nebraska." [103] The passage of the Kansas-Nebraska Act in 1854 seriously eroded the Cherokees' hold on the Neutral Lands in Kansas. Now, he said, referring to the Johnson bill, "There are . . . indications of further legislation to embrace the whole of our country and that of our neighbors . . . within organized territories of the United States on principles which must produce essential change in the relations of the several tribes." The Johnson bill, though not passed that year, indicated that Congress was preparing to abrogate the treaty system and conduct Indian affairs unilaterally through its own enactments. This change, Ross said, was "of such vast importance" as to demand "the utmost care and vigilance to guard our rights" to national independence under treaty guarantees.[104] Realizing the importance of uniting the various Indian nations against territorialization, Ross organized a meeting with the Creeks to obtain their support in opposition.

The council of Cherokees and Creeks met on December 7, 1854, at North Fork in the Creek Nation and concluded by endorsing Ross's position:

> Whereas the history of our race shows that whenever the Indian and White man have been mingled together promiscuously in the same community and under the same government, the effect has ever been that the White man soon owns everything and the Indian nothing, which has ever been followed by its natural results, the moral and social degradation and rapid extermination of the Indians . . . [and whereas] our respective nations . . . are rapidly changing from the character of a hunting to that of an agricul-

tural and commercial people, which change will fit them for living under the same government with the White man without ruinous results to either . . . *resolved*, that we do respectfully and earnestly protest against any change in our present political relations to the United States, as any propositions to that effect will at present only have a tendency to disturb the peace and quiet of our communities.

John Ross was requested by this joint council to present the memorial to the proper officers of Congress.[105]

The Johnson bill failed to pass at either of the next two sessions of Congress, despite strong support from the states bordering on the Indian Territory. This failure grew out of the difficulties in the Kansas Territory, which had provoked so much bloody strife and confusion over slavery that no one wanted another storm to the south of it. Northerners did not want another slave state created, as the Indian Territory was certain to be. Nevertheless, in 1857, Superintendent Elias Rector suggested that with some modifications, territorialization might win Indian support. His proposal included a clause making the private plots given to Indians (after the land was surveyed and allocated) "inalienable" for twenty or thirty years so that the Indian citizens would feel secure against white pressures (honest or fraudulent) to sell or lease it.[106] The prevailing western attitude toward creating a new territory or state of Oklahoma was expressed by Governor Walker of the Kansas Territory, who said in 1857, "It is essential to all the true interests, not only of Kansas, but of Louisiana, Texas, Arkansas, Iowa, and Missouri that this coterminous southwestern Indian territory should speedily become a State, not only to supply us with cotton and receive our products in return, but as occupying the area over which that portion of our railroads should run which connect us with New Orleans, Galveston, and by the southern route with the Pacific."[107] Territorial status would assure not only grazing rights to Texas cattle ranchers but also commercial advantages such as railroad rights-of-way throughout the Indian nations. John Ross told his people on October 5, 1857, "Years of trial and anxiety, danger and struggle have alone maintained the existence of the Cherokee people as a distinct community and such must continue to be the case if we would live as men."[108]

Failure of the Johnson bill led to efforts to detribalize the nation by other means. In 1859, A. B. Greenwood, the commissioner of Indian affairs, sent John Ross a proposal that the Cherokee Nation agree to have its land surveyed and divided in severalty, with a plot of 640 acres to be granted to each Cherokee head of family at the site of the family's present home or farm. Ross replied bluntly that the Cherokees were prosperous and happy as they now were and "will not voluntarily enter into any arrangement that may seem calculated to affect their Nationality." [109]

A year later, Ross, again seeking to sell the Neutral Lands before Kansans occupied it, reminded Greenwood that this land had "for so long a time been trespassed upon with impunity by white citizens of the United States against the repeated complaints and remonstrances of the Cherokee People" that if it was not sold soon, it would become useless to them. The Cherokees "are informed that the [white] intruders upon this tract of land since it has been included within the Territorial limits of Kansas . . . have greatly multiplied and are daily increasing—that there are now about 700 families upon it who have opened farms and are cultivating the soil." He reminded the commissioner that under the Treaty of 1835, the land in Kansas as well as the land on which the Cherokees were now settled had been guaranteed to them, the treaty stating that "in no future time, without their consent, [shall it] be included within the territorial limits or jurisdiction of any State or Territory." [110] However, the effort to convert the Indian Territory into a federal territory had only started.

Although the effort to develop a coherent system of public education had divided the Cherokee Nation during this period, the struggle to sustain and expand the nation's sovereignty against U.S. paternalism had united it. The forces working against Cherokee sovereignty, however, were growing stronger each year as the white frontier pressed harder and harder against the borders of the Indian Territory. During the 1850s tensions developed inside as well as outside the nation that were to force the worst of all possible situations upon the Cherokees—internal civil war. This catastrophe stemmed from frictions over the institution of black chattel slavery. Despite its efforts to maintain its distinction as a separate people and nation, the Cherokee Nation was too integrally linked to the political culture of white society to avoid entanglement in the sectional disputes that wracked the United States after 1850. Under the Democratic administrations of Pierce and Buchanan, however, the policies of the Bureau of Indian Affairs supported the slaveholders in the Cherokee Nation.

5

Cherokee Slaveholding and Missionary Antislavery Efforts, 1846–1855

The curse of slavery rests upon this nation.

—*The Reverend Edwin Teele, 1853*

The institution of black slavery among the Cherokees had a major impact on their economic growth after 1839 as well as on the emerging division between the full-bloods and the mixed-bloods. It also dealt a fatal blow to Cherokee sovereignty after 1861, forcing the nation to choose between siding with the Union or the Confederacy. However, the institution began so imperceptibly in the eighteenth century and grew with so little controversy among the Cherokees that its origins remain vague to this day.[1]

To the proslavery white citizens of the United States, and especially to those in the South, the adoption of the institution of black chattel slavery by the Cherokees and their Indian neighbors was a logical and inevitable step toward their social, economic, and political improvement. When Congress acquiesced in the policy of removing the southeastern tribes after 1830, it took care to relocate them below the Missouri Compromise line of 36°30' in the West as they had been in the East. To the Cherokees, slavery proved to be as thorny a problem as it was for white Americans. While Indian tradition had for centuries allowed a form of slavery for captured enemies, the southeastern Indians never had much economic use for Indian captives. Probably as many captives were adopted into the tribe of their captors as were enslaved, and more were simply killed in rituals of tribal vengeance. However, the kind of slavery that evolved into a fundamental feature of Cherokee society after 1794 was different. Not only did it involve racial distinctions not present in the slavery of Indian captives, but it became essential to the new economic structure. The antislavery crisis crept up on the Cherokees so slowly that it surprised them, as much as it did the whites of the United States, when it began to tear both nations apart after 1850.

Prior to 1794 the cheap labor of Africans had been of small use to a people whose chief income came from skill in hunting furs and hides and whose agricultural needs were easily provided by the communally cultivated farms tended by women, children, and old men. However, when horse-and-plow farming became the Cherokees' chief means of subsistence in the early nineteenth century and each family was responsible for raising its own food on its own isolated tract, the Cherokees faced serious difficulties. Frontier farming was hard for whites as well, but Cherokee difficulties were greater because they had no experience with this kind of agriculture nor with marketing a cash crop surplus to buy their manufactured necessities. From 1794 to 1822, the federal government gave the men plows, hoes, and seeds and hired artisans to teach Cherokee women to spin, weave, and sew, but only long years of trial and error could make Cherokee families self-sufficient by farming. Black slaves, who had grown up working on white farms, knew more about agriculture than most male Indians. The labor of clearing and fencing land, caring for livestock, building cabins, stables, springhouses, and smokehouses, and cultivating ten to twelve acres was difficult work for one man and his sons. It was a totally new and complex way of life for most Cherokees. Those who could afford it found that owning slaves provided many advantages, especially in a free-market, profit-oriented economy.

The intermarried whites who enjoyed living in Indian country where land was free and there were no taxes were the first to make regular use of black slaves in the nation. Many observers claimed that slavery began to play a significant role among the Cherokees after 1783 when the white Tories who took refuge with the southern Indian allies of George III stayed on with their slaves after the Revolution and institutionalized slavery. Resident federal agents and some missionaries encouraged the use of black slaves as well.[2] Cherokee women found that female slaves helped to decrease their labor as farmers' wives. Female slaves were often able to teach Cherokee women how to milk cows and make butter, cheese, candles, and soap as well as to spin, weave, and sew the family's clothing. They also performed the daily labor of drawing water, gathering wood, washing clothes, and cooking. Even the Cherokee diet changed with their new way of life.

Plowing behind a horse all day at first seemed degrading to Cherokee men.

By ancient tradition, men were hunters and warriors; women were the culti-
vators and food producers. The most sacred myth of the Cherokees explained
that this sexual division of labor started with the first man and first woman.[3]
However, a new creation myth developed among the southeastern Indians
after 1790 that explained that when the Great Spirit first created red, white,
and black people, he had given bows and arrows to the red man, paper and
pens to the white man, and hoes and axes to the black man.[4] This myth legiti-
mated the servant role for blacks in southern Indian culture; it smoothed the
transition for Indian males from warriors to slave masters. However, the in-
stitutionalization of chattel slavery was a long, uneven process, and buying
slaves required more money than most Cherokees ever had. At its peak in
1861, slave labor was utilized in less than one out of ten Cherokee families.

Poverty and a dislike for the white man's competitive system combined
to prevent most full-blood Cherokees from becoming slave owners. Frontier
cash crop farming fit neatly into the white man's concept of maximizing soil
production, but it ran counter to the Cherokees' social ethic. Accumulating
private property was not a value inculcated in most Cherokee homes, at least
among the full-blood majority, but acquiring both productive soil and black
slaves in the Cherokee Nation came naturally to intermarried whites and their
mixed-blood descendants.

Those Cherokees most admired by whites were from families with white
ancestry who raised their children to be like whites. The division that emerged
over time between slave owners and nonslaveholding farmers among the
Cherokees was not unlike that in white communities. The poor farmers ended
up with the worst land and seemed forever sunk in debt. However, poor, nonslaveholding whites in the southern United States identified with the values
of the planter class; they always hoped someday to own slaves and rise in
status. Nonslaveholding Cherokees, having a nonacquisitive tradition, did
not cherish this hope. Egalitarianism, sharing, and consensus government
played a greater role than material success in their culture. Hence the poor
nonslaveholders gradually moved from a neutral to a hostile attitude toward
the slave-owning elite who came to dominate the Cherokee political and economic system. The nonslaveholders came to regard the elite as no longer truly
Cherokee. The Civil War brought a social revolution against this slaveholding
elite in the Cherokee Nation instead of a desire to fight shoulder-to-shoulder
with them to preserve the institution of slavery, as in the South. This is not
to say that the nonslaveholding Cherokees felt much sympathy for African
Americans or wanted to free them. Being true to Cherokee ethnic values was
the paramount issue; they never viewed Africans as their brothers.

Contemporary evaluations of the benefits of slavery to the southeastern

Indians varied. White southern observers tended to agree with the suggestion of a federal agent to the Cherokees that the most effective way to civilize the Indians was to give each family a male and female slave.[5] However, northern white observers, especially after 1846, agreed with the missionary Edwin Teele, who said in 1853, "The curse of slavery rests upon this nation."[6] Northerners blamed slavery not only for the growing gap between the rich and the poor in the Cherokee Nation but also for what they perceived as the inveterate Cherokee aversion to hard labor. As the Reverend Charles Torrey wrote after living among the Cherokees from 1855 to 1860:

> The people were naturally indolent and despised labor, as is common in slave communities. A white man, a Methodist exhorter, found me at work in the field one day, and exclaimed, "What! Do you work?" "Of course I do, when I choose to," I replied. "Well," said he, "you have position, and it will do for you, but it would never do for me." This I found to be true in the case of a young Frenchman whom I hired to work for me. He was intelligent, had a good education, and was a very capable man who had been somehow stranded in that distant land. He worked for me very satisfactorily for several weeks and was paid good wages. But he gave it up because even the Negroes despised him for having to work.[7]

Hannah Moore, a New England schoolteacher among the Cherokees in the 1840s agreed with Torrey. Slavery, she said, led to ingrained laziness among the children of slaveholding families, killing any incentive to work. After one of her mixed-blood students invited her home during a school vacation, she wrote:

> I met a cordial reception and received all the attention and respect which seemed in their power to bestow. . . . Not withstanding all this, my heart was often pained at the supineness of parents and indolence of children. I regret to say almost all [family members] had slaves to perform all their laborious work while they, with folded hands, idly sat without any employment in their piazza, or open space through the midst of their house. The children, thus early accustomed to have a slave to fan them when they sleep and wait on and carry them when awake, early imbibe habits which need a large share of wisdom . . . to eradicate. This seems to me the great secret of the imbecility of their minds, why they do not expand faster. I feel confident [that] if slavery could be done away with, then they would make far greater progress in the arts and sciences.[8]

The division between those missionaries who felt slavery was a blessing to the Cherokees and those who felt it was a curse grew wider and sharper in the years 1846–60; the federal agents, all southerners, uniformly took the former view.

In 1809 there were 583 black slaves living among 12,395 Cherokees (2,400 families) in the nation. (Approximately 75 free blacks at that time made their living by mechanical skills or trading.) Slaves were unevenly distributed, with fewer than 125 families (or 5 percent) owning even one. By 1835 the number of slaves had grown to 1,592, living with about 300 families out of 3,300 families (or 16,395 Cherokees). About 8 percent now owned one or more slaves. The increase in the number of slaves resulted as much from their birthrate as from additional purchases.[9]

After removal to the West, Cherokees who owned slaves found it far easier to resettle than those who had no slaves. Slave labor built their new homes, cleared their land, fenced their gardens and pastures, cultivated their fields, planted and gathered their crops, and tended their herds of cattle, horses, and sheep. Slave owners made a quantum leap forward in wealth and influence in the years after 1839. Poor, full-blood, nonslave-owning families (most of them the last to arrive and choose land in the new country) fared badly after removal. By 1860 there were 3,500 to 4,000 slaves among 21,000 Cherokees; approximately 10 percent of the families (400 out of 4,200) owned one or more slaves.[10] All observers noted the close correlation between the highly acculturated, well-to-do, mixed-blood population and slave owning; conversely they noted the correlation between Cherokee-speaking, poor, conservative full-bloods and nonslaveholding. However, less than one-third of the mixed-bloods owned slaves. Assuming that the mixed-bloods constituted one-quarter of the population (by 1860 as high as one-third), only 400 out of 1,400 mixed-blood families owned one or more slaves. Some of these families had mixed ancestry extending back four or five generations; there was a decided tendency for mixed-bloods to marry mixed-bloods.

From 1846 to 1854 the nationalist policies of the Ross party appealed to the majority of the 4,000 voters, whether slaveholders or not, but after 1854, slavery (or "Southern Rights") became a very divisive issue.[11] As the Ross party leaders tried to take a moderate line on slavery and favored a neutralist approach to the growing cleavage between the whites of the North and South, they lost votes to an increasingly hard-line Southern Rights party that believed that alliance with white southerners in the defense of slavery was more profitable and wiser for the nation. In certain respects, the proslavery Southern Rights party in the Cherokee Nation tended to correlate with the old Ridge-Boudinot-Watie faction; to that extent the defense of slavery was a convenient way to undermine Ross's support among the elite. At the same time, however, it tended to strengthen Ross's support among the nonslaveholding full-bloods. The nation gradually divided along these new lines. Culturally, could a true Cherokee support slavery and material self-aggrandizement?

The Cherokee attitude toward the institution of slavery had shifted radically after 1839. Prior to that time, most Cherokees seem to have agreed with David Brown, a Christian convert and preacher who wrote in 1825 that blacks had no real place in the nation: "There are some African slaves among us. They have from time to time been brought in and sold by white men. They are, however, generally well-treated, and they much prefer living in an Indian nation to a residence in the United States. There is hardly any intermixture of Cherokee and African blood. The presumption is that the Cherokees will, at no distant day, cooperate with the humane efforts of those who are liberating and sending this prescribed race to the land of their fathers." [12] While Brown's statement clearly indicates race consciousness, it shows no sympathy for the institution. This changed rapidly in the West. Brown reflected the prevailing view of white Americans that slavery was "an unfortunate problem" that could be solved by the removal of the blacks to Africa. He supported the position of the American Colonization Society, which, in 1825, was the most popular of the antislavery societies in the United States. In 1830 more southern whites belonged to the society than northern whites. The Cherokee slaveholders had no objection to the organization of a Benevolent Aid Society among their slaves by northern missionaries in 1830, the object of which was to raise funds to emancipate slaves in the United States and send them to Liberia.[13] According to one well-informed missionary, "Before the Ridge Treaty [in 1835] there was an arrangement making by some of the most influential men in the nation to emancipate all the slaves among the Cherokees—receiving them as citizens and abolishing the system entirely. But, alas! that base instrument [that is, the treaty] prevented it." [14]

After 1831 the abolitionist movement, led by William Lloyd Garrison, began to change northern attitudes toward slavery. Few Cherokees and few missionaries among them adopted the abolitionist position, but for other reasons, the Cherokees' attitudes toward slavery began to harden after removal. Slavery had become highly profitable for those who owned five to ten slaves, and there was land in the nation where cotton could be cultivated. The number of slaves was growing so rapidly that it seemed essential to pass laws protecting the community from their misbehavior and disorder. The Cherokees were fully aware that the older view of the unity of the human race (upon which early federal Indian policy was based) could not withstand the growing prejudice among whites, which was rapidly winning support from leading scientists, against "people of color." All Indians knew that frontier whites had an inveterate prejudice against them, and, living in the South, the Cherokees also knew that whites treated blacks as basically inferior. Thomas Jefferson spoke for many Founding Fathers when he said that while the Indian was potentially the equal of the white, there were serious doubts as to whether this was true of Africans. It therefore behooved the "red" man to distance himself, and distinguish himself, from the "black" man if he wished to avoid being identified with him as a "colored" person, incapable of ever becoming the equal of the "white" man, no matter how civilized and Christianized he might be.

Consequently, many Cherokees accepted the necessity of the institution of slavery. Many also adopted the prejudices of whites against blacks. A series of laws passed between 1820 and 1827 by the Cherokee council stripped blacks (free or slave) of any opportunity to improve themselves or their position. Similar to the "slave codes" of the neighboring states adopted at this same time, the Cherokee black code reduced blacks to a permanently inferior caste. Even though they claimed that someday they hoped to be free of slavery, the Cherokees made it clear that as long as blacks remained among them, they would have to remain below them. The first Cherokee law in this code, passed in 1820, prohibited "any negro slave" from engaging in trade without the permission of his master and said that no slave may purchase "spiritous liquors and vend the same." This same act urged the Cherokees in every neighborhood "to organize a patrolling company" to keep an eye out for such offenses. The penalty for a slave who sold whiskey was to "receive 15 cobbs and paddles . . . from the hands of the patrollers of the . . . neighborhood." [15]

In 1824, a law forbade all "intermarriages between negro slaves and Indians or whites." [16] Another law that year made it illegal "for negro slaves to possess property in horses, cattle or hogs" and specified that slaves possessing such property had twelve months to dispose of it. [17] In November 1824, the first law regulating free blacks was passed: any "free negro" who entered the nation was henceforth to be treated as an "intruder" and "shall not be allowed to reside in the Cherokee nation without a permit" from the council. [18]

The revised Cherokee constitution, adopted after removal, retained the measures adopted in the Constitution of 1827 that denied political rights to blacks. Blacks (slave or free) could not vote or hold "any office of profit, honor, or trust under this Government." The same clause excluded all persons "of Negro or Mulatto parentage" from office. [19]

Long before 1839, the first Cherokees to go west took slaves with them, and these Old Settlers had instituted their own slave code. Between 1833 and 1835 the western Cherokee council voted that "no slave or slaves shall have the right to own any kind of property whatever"; all slaves were forbidden to gamble or drink spirits, the punishment for which was "25 lashes by the light-horse" patrol; and any slave who "shall abuse a free person" should receive sixty lashes.[20]

At the first session of the Ross council, after the Act of Union rejoined the easterners and westerners in September 1839, a law was passed "to prevent amalgamation with colored persons." By this law it was illegal for "intermarriage . . . between a free male or female citizen with any slave or person of color." It provided a penalty of 100 lashes for "any colored male" convicted under the act.[21] The following year a law was passed prohibiting any free black or mulatto from owning a farm or any other improvement in the nation.[22] In 1841 the council outlawed "the teaching of Negroes to read and write"[23] and permitted patrol companies to "take up and bring to punishment any negro or negroes that may be strolling about not on their owners' premises without a pass."[24] The patrols had power to mete out appropriate punishments without any judicial process. In 1843 a law expelled all "free negroes" from the nation "excepting such as have been freed by our citizens"[25] and required Cherokees who freed slaves either to have them leave the country or to post bonds for good conduct. That same year a law passed ordering 100 lashes for any slave or free black who counseled or helped a slave to run away.[26] In 1848 the law against teaching free blacks or slaves to read and write was amended to expel any person who broke this law (previously they had only been fined).[27] In 1850 a law prescribed death by hanging for any black convicted of raping a white or Cherokee woman.[28]

These laws were not peculiar to the Cherokee Nation. They were common in all southern states, and all of the southern Indian nations passed similar laws in these years. They constituted a significant aspect of acculturation, whereby the Cherokees assimilated the white man's racial prejudices (albeit for their own particular reasons) into their political and social structure.

Like whites who used the Bible to justify racist views (such as the curse on Ham), the Cherokees developed syncretic myths that asserted the superiority of the red man to the black man because of a divine curse upon blacks. The first missionaries among the western Cherokees in 1820 reported a prevalent version of this myth told by one of their oldest adonisgi, Ta-ke-e-tuh: "The first human pair were red, and the varieties of the color of the human race he accounted for by the influence of the climate, except in the case of blacks. Black was a stigma fixed upon a man for crime; and all his descendants ever since had been born black. Their [that is, the Cherokees'] old men, he said, were not agreed as to the crime thus marked by the signal of God's displeasures. Some said it was for murder, some cowardice, and some said it was lying."[29]

Ta-ke-e-tuh's version of creation had the virtue of maintaining the older view of the unity of man, racial differences being due to crime or environmental factors, while at the same time placing blacks in a special category. According to a Baptist missionary among the Shawnees (whose lands after removal were contiguous to the Cherokee Nation), they told a myth about how the Great Spirit had created an apple tree soon after creation and told the three human beings he had created not to eat any of the apples. One day he found some apples missing. " 'Did I not tell you,' " he asked, " 'not to eat of that fruit?' Whereupon, the one took his apple from his pocket [uneaten]. Unto him the Great Spirit said, 'I give you the bible and knowledge of letters to guide you in the troubles you will fall into.' Then the other took out his [apple] partly eaten. For his disobedience the great spirit changed the color of his skin [to red] and gave him his law in his heart only. The third, because of his having devoured the whole of his [apple], was blacked all over and left without moral obligation." [30] As white Americans tried to define more clearly "What is an American?," most of them concluded by 1830 that America was a "white man's country." The Indians thus had to ask "What is an Indian" and naturally upheld the view that America was, by the original design of the Creator, the red man's country.

As the Cherokees mastered their new environment in the West, some of them became prosperous and adopted a more advanced market economy. They learned many ways to exploit and profit from slavery. One of the easiest of these was to utilize slaves for herding cattle, horses, sheep, and hogs. The mild climate, open prairies, and woodland pastures made herding second only to farming—and far more profitable—as a source of Cherokee income. Blacks seemed to be particularly good herders or cowboys, just as they were good farmers. One missionary said that he would far rather have a black care for his farm and livestock than a Cherokee.[31]

Areas in the southern part of the new country, in the Arkansas River valley, were suitable for cotton growing, and several of the wealthier Cherokees obtained cotton gins to remove the cotton seeds, making this a profitable crop. Although small farmers could make a few dollars by growing small patches of cotton, they could not get rich from it. Most Cherokee farms were planted primarily in corn, oats, wheat, and barley. Large crops of corn were profitable only if the farmer owned a gristmill. Because unsettled land was free to any Cherokee, the more slaves a farmer owned, the more tribal land he engrossed—and usually it was the most fertile land.

Owning slaves was particularly profitable when the slaves were trained at some particular skill—as blacksmiths, carpenters, wheelwrights, or barrel makers. On a large plantation they saved the owner the cost of paying skilled mechanics to shoe horses, build barns, or repair wagons. When not working for their owners, slave "mechanics" could be hired out, their owners taking the pay for their labor. The federal agent discovered in the 1850s that slave owners were accustomed to bidding for the contracts for federally paid blacksmiths, gunsmiths, wheelwrights, and wagon makers (under the Treaty of 1833). "Public mechanics" were required to make, or repair cheaply, the tools the poor needed (spinning wheels, looms, horseshoes, plows, or hoes). However, when the agent found that the slave owners utilized skilled slaves to do the public work, he refused to allow the practice, arguing that the work should be given to Cherokee mechanics in order to train Cherokee apprentices and increase the number of skilled Cherokee workers.[32]

Slaves could also be trained to run a cotton gin, a gristmill, or a sawmill. They served as deckhands and engineers on the steamboats owned by wealthy Cherokee traders. They ran ferries and worked at hotels and taverns. Lewis Ross, who owned several hundred slaves, worked them on his large farm in the spring and summer, but once the harvest was in, he employed 150 of them to manufacture salt at the saltworks he rented from the nation.[33] Several slave owners (for example, John Ross and Avery Vann) owned kilns and employed their slaves in making bricks for buildings and chimneys, a business that became more profitable as prosperous Cherokees moved from log cabins into brick homes, as the nation constructed more public buildings (such as the brick seminaries), as merchants built stores in Tahlequah or Park Hill, and as missionaries constructed brick schools and churches. Joseph Lynch employed slaves to run his hide tannery.[34] Female slaves performed household chores— cooking, washing, woodcutting, sewing, and caring for children. Wives of wealthy Cherokees managed their plantation homes with the same skill as did southern white women. Slave labor helped them to dress fashionably, entertain lavishly, and find time to practice the art of fine needlework or piano playing.

Slaves were often used as collateral for loans, the debtor either giving a note to the creditor that entitled the creditor to own the slave if the debt was not paid or lending the slave to the creditor to work off the debt.[35] In a country where land was not privately owned and therefore not available as collateral, slaves were the most valuable private asset. In hard times slaves were mortgaged or sold to obtain necessary cash. Following any prolonged drought, the federal agent noted that there was always a great deal of slave selling by those whose harvests had failed.[36]

Some Cherokees made money as professional slave traders, among them John Drew, Andrew Nave, John Martin, and Lewis Ross. They often marketed (on consignment) for groups of Cherokee owners a hundred or more slaves at a time. In addition, they purchased slaves at slave markets in Little Rock, Van Buren, Memphis, and New Orleans. Tahlequah had a regular slave market, and slaves were frequently advertised for sale in the *Cherokee Advocate*. White slave dealers in Texas, Arkansas, and Missouri sometimes wrote to Cherokee dealers asking them to bring them slaves to sell.[37]

As slavery became more profitable ("prime hands" or mechanics sold for $800 to $1,500 in the 1850s), there was ample motivation for slave stealing, kidnapping slaves, and the illegal seizure of free blacks to be sold back into slavery. High profits produced daring thieves and presented a constant problem for Cherokee law enforcement. Gangs of "slave stealers" went from the Cherokee Nation into the Creek, Choctaw, Seminole, Chickasaw, and Osage nations to steal and kidnap, then hurried their booty across the border to sell them in Arkansas or Missouri. The traffic worked both ways, as gangs from other Indian nations raided the Cherokee plantations. Whites on the frontier also participated regularly in this lucrative traffic. Like horse stealing and the whiskey trade, it was almost impossible to stop. The records of the agent and the courts are filled with accounts of litigation and trials for these crimes.[38] On April 9, 1846, the *Cherokee Advocate* reported: "A whole family of negroes were stolen from Lydia Justice." Children were the easiest slaves to steal, for they could put up little resistance. In 1854 the Reverend Samuel Worcester sent a letter to Jefferson Davis, then secretary of war, about the kidnapping of the Beam family, who were freed slaves: "Five persons, including a little child, were recently offered for sale as slaves in Tahlequah in this nation who, a few days before, had been captured in the Creek Nation where they were living as free persons."[39] Worcester knew they were free because he had formerly hired one of them to work for him at the mission. Despite the combined efforts of the missionaries among the Creeks and Cherokees, the federal agent, the southern superintendent, and several lawyers hired by the government, it took three years to obtain a court decision freeing these kidnapped blacks; the lawyers' fees came to $3,723.24.[40]

Lawyers in the Cherokee Nation and in the neighboring states made money by collecting debts and settling the estates of slave owners, often utilizing slaves as the most tangible assets to pay creditors or satisfy heirs. Frequently slaves who thought they had been freed by their owners were told that their emancipation was invalid because their masters or mistresses owed debts that took precedence.[41] Few Cherokee slaves were emancipated by their owners until they became aged and unable to work; they were too valuable. One missionary claimed that superannuated slaves were sometimes given the choice of manumission or staying on to live in their slave cabins at the owner's expense.[42] Also, few owners freed slaves because Cherokee law required that persons who freed slaves must see that they left the nation or else put up bonds for their good behavior. From the reports available, there seem to have been very few free blacks in the nation in the early 1850s, but there were strong demands that the nation rid itself of these "potential troublemakers."[43]

Nearby slaveholding states feared that the Indian nations would become havens for runaway slaves because of their loose policing system, but there was little ground for their fears. The slaveholding Indian nations kept a close watch over their own slaves, and white owners of runaway slaves were given full cooperation when they came to search for runaways. Some questioned whether the Fugitive Slave Act of 1850 applied in the Indian Territory. John Ross may have considered enforcement of the act in the nation an infringement on Cherokee sovereignty, but he never made such a complaint. No Cherokee official ever prevented frontier whites from hunting down fugitive slaves, which would have turned whites even more strongly against them.

In a few cases, Cherokee masters agreed to allow slaves to purchase their own freedom by hiring themselves out as laborers. The slave retained part of the wages or gave them to the master as installments on the manumission price, and the master used part to support the slave and part as his profit until the bargain was completed. Such agreements were private, however, and not legally binding. If the master died before the slave completed the agreement, the heirs were not bound to honor it.[44]

One of the most effective ways for slaves to obtain freedom was to persuade their masters to arrange with missionaries to let them work out their value. Labor was scarce, and missionaries often hired slaves to assist at the mission farms or to help with the chores at the mission schools. Some missionaries from the North disliked this practice; others worried about how it looked to antislavery Christians on their mission boards. When Richard Taylor, the owner of many slaves, offered to loan a slave to work for nothing at a Congregational mission, the missionaries feared that "this seemed to partake too much of slavery" and preferred to pay the slave 50 cents a day. "We had rather labour the harder with our own hands than connive at the sin of slavery."[45] To avoid employing slaves, some mission stations used their funds or credit to purchase the freedom of a slave and then contracted with the slave to work off the purchase price at a fixed wage. Samuel Worcester wrote, "I would rather . . . purchase from [a slave's] master the deed of manumission, and if that were not possible, I would purchase him to hold no longer than as many minutes interchange of papers required, making him free the moment he is legally mine, and taking his note as that of a freedman for the sum his freedom had cost [the mission]. This I would consider an act of beneficence . . . though even that would excite the prejudices of the abolitionists."[46] This was a cumbersome process, however. Some manumitted slaves died before they had completed the contracts to repay the mission; some escaped. Samuel Worcester reported in 1842 that he lost $350 in such a case.[47] However, he rejoiced when a family of slaves whom he had redeemed from slavery by this process became devout Christians and decided to return to Africa as missionaries.[48] All of the mission stations, northern and southern, employed slaves during these years, claiming they simply could not get along without their labor. "Either stations must be abandoned or slaves must be hired,"[49] Worcester said.

Casual observers of slavery among the Cherokees seemed on the whole to believe that Cherokee masters treated their slaves well, worked them less severely than white slaveholders, and seldom punished them.[50] Most Christian slave owners allowed their slaves to attend church and Sabbath schools until the Cherokee council passed the law in 1841 prohibiting the teaching of slaves to read and write. As one northern missionary wrote, "The slaves have in general the same opportunity to receive religious instruction that the free members of the [Cherokee] family have. The slaveholding members of the church give their slaves the Sabbath [free] without exception. Indeed, this, and one week at Christmas is given to the blacks through the nation."[51] Another northern missionary said that "slaves among the Cherokees generally do not, I presume, perform half the labor that is required of hirelings at the North, and I am of the opinion that they are treated with much more attention than many, if not most, of the domestics in Northern cities."[52] Nevertheless, there are well-documented instances of cruelty toward slaves, the torture of slaves, and even the murder of slaves by Cherokee masters. James Vann once burned alive a slave whom he suspected of having robbed him,[53] and the Reverend Charles Torrey heard of a "cruel whipping" of a slave that he dared not publicly criticize.[54] A law passed in 1850 made the murder of a slave by a master or mistress punishable by death but not if the slave died while being given "justifiable correction." Some observers claimed that Cherokee masters tried not to separate slave parents from their children or husbands from their wives when they bought or sold slaves, but there is considerable evidence to contradict this.[55]

Off of the plantations, punishment of slaves was left to the neighborhood slave patrols and the Cherokee sheriffs. The *Cherokee Advocate*, edited by English-speaking, mixed-blood slaveholders of the Ross party, encouraged sheriffs and patrollers to be strict. An editorial on March 2, 1852, praised the sheriff of Tahlequah for his strictness: "Sheriff [Jesse] Wolf and posse caught a negro last Saturday night as his blackness emptied his jug and receipted him in full by a few stripes. Well done; go on. He that will wink at this traffic in whiskey by the negroes deserves the same punishment as the offender." [56] A year later, the editor urged more action:

We would take this time to say to all slaveholders in our country to draw the reins of government over the slaves with a steady and firm hand. The permitting of slaves at any and all times, without our consent, to run about over the country, generates a spirit of insubordination. They forget their stations and become impertinent and insulting. . . . They are permitted to meet and congregate in large crowds in various neighborhoods where drinking, gambling, and places of mischief are concocted and executed to their own detriment and the safety and good order of society. Patrol companies should be formed in each neighborhood as authorized by law to guard the interest and property of the country. The safety and good order will not only be guarded, but the companies would be a terror to "jug taverns." [57]

On the whole the Cherokee Nation was as efficient as the slaveholding states in keeping its slaves under control and "in their station." There is no record of any violent slave revolt in the Cherokee Nation, although there were occasions when a single slave killed his or her owner. Runaway slaves were sometimes so fearful of the punishment that awaited them when they returned that they fought back when about to be captured and lost their lives in the process.[58]

The number of runaway slaves was large among the Cherokees, but most were quickly caught and returned. The *Cherokee Advocate* regularly ran advertisements calling upon citizens to help locate runaways and offering rewards for their capture. The frequency of runaways may have been the result of either harsh masters or a certain looseness in the Cherokee system. Also, in a large, sparsely settled country, where plenty of horses were available, it was tempting for a slave to head off to freedom. Prior to 1848, most runaways headed for Texas or the Mexican border west of the Indian Territory; after 1854, they headed toward Kansas.

The most highly publicized "slave revolt" occurred in 1842 when the nation was suffering from the dissensions over the legitimacy of the Ross party government. The revolt was really a large-scale escape. Estimates of how many slaves were involved ranged from 21 to 200, but it was clearly well planned and well executed.[59] Although slaves from five or six adjoining plantations were involved, their escape was not detected until they were miles away, on horseback, armed, and heading for Mexico. They had gathered at four o'clock in the morning on November 14 at a prearranged spot near Webber's Falls on the Arkansas River. Their owners included Joseph Vann, James Mackey,

Joseph Talley, John Brown, and John Sheppard. Before leaving their plantations, these slaves had locked their overseers in their cabins, broken open the supply sheds, and stolen guns, ammunition, food, blankets, and horses for their long journey. Two days later, the Cherokee council voted to pay John Drew to outfit 100 men and go after them.[60] As the runaways were passing through the Creek Nation heading south, some Creeks tried to stop them, but the slaves fought them off. Later they met with two men who were returning a family of six runaway slaves named Hardy to their Creek master. The Cherokee slaves demanded their release, and when their captors (one a white man, one a Delaware) refused, they were shot. The Hardy family joined the Cherokee runaways, and they continued south. They were within seven miles of the Red River, 280 miles from the Cherokee Nation, when Drew's posse caught up with them. Outnumbered and outgunned, the slaves surrendered. Several apparently escaped at that time or on the return trip.[61] Three of the slaves, Moses, John, and Russell, were charged with the murders of the white man and the Delaware in the Creek Nation and sent to Fort Gibson. The rest were restored to their owners. The incident so frightened Cherokee slaveholders that the council passed a law severely punishing any slave found guilty of aiding or participating in a slave escape.[62]

In April 1846, Lewis Ross discovered that his slaves "had been collecting ammunition and guns," which they had hidden on his plantation. He "questioned" some slaves, but "he could not make them confess what they intended to do with these guns."[63] Four years later, a large group of Cherokee slaves, estimated at 130 to 150, ran away to the Seminole Nation to join Chief Wildcat, who was planning to start a community of Seminoles and blacks in Texas.[64] The slaves came from several different plantations. Their owners delegated three Cherokee slave owners, Martin Vann, William Drew, and Dick Drew, to recapture them. These Cherokee slave owners joined a group of Creek slave owners and some Seminoles in this effort in the summer of 1850. Late in July, William Drew told his brother John of their success: "We got eighty or ninety negroes. McIntosh and myself got 23 and brought home your black boy, Billy. I think we will get 25 or more in a short time. . . . The Negroes talked like fighting, but when we got there, we found no fight in them, the most of them ran off and put us to a great deal of trouble to gather them up. We collected 300. . . . There were a good many of these negroes that had been sold, or went off to the prairie with Wildcat. Among this number were Daniel Coodey's and yours."[65]

In 1847 some blacks (whether free or slave was not stated) were involved in an effort to steal several hundred thousand dollars in per capita money from the safe of the federal agent in Fort Gibson. The robbers included some soldiers (or former soldiers) at the post. They were foiled in the attempt by Agent R. C. S. Brown, and all went to jail.[66]

Much of the fear over slave revolts or slave escapes in these years was generated by increasing tension from the growing antislavery movement in the Northeast and by events in "bleeding Kansas" on the northern border of the Cherokee Nation. The rise of the Free-Soil party and later the Republican party added to the fear that slavery in the South might not be allowed to extend westward. Abolitionists, the radical fringe of the antislavery movement, also organized the underground railroad in these years and helped many slaves escape to Canada. Antislavery whites in the Kansas Territory were suspected of aiding Cherokees' runaway slaves. There is no evidence that any antislavery Cherokees participated in the underground railroad system to spirit slaves to Kansas.

Virtually all of the federal agents among the Cherokees (and other slaveholding nations), as well as most of the other appointees in the Bureau of Indian Affairs, were staunch proslavery advocates. It had become the custom of the executive branch to appoint as resident Indian agents persons who shared the views of the frontier whites living nearest to the Indians, hence southerners were assigned to southern Indians. Most of these agents brought their own slaves with them. As the political leaders of the South became more ardent in their support of slavery, federal officials from the South did their utmost to support the proslavery position of the southern Indians. Proslavery agents, finding John Ross and his party cautious and moderate in support of slavery, often allied with the ardent proslavery members of the Watie party. They also did all they could to hamper missionaries from the North, whom they suspected of being abolitionists, while favoring missionaries from the South, who preached that slavery for blacks was ordained by God.

Of the missionaries from the five denominational agencies at work in the Cherokee Nation between 1839 and 1860, those of the Congregational mission (or the American Board of Commissioners for Foreign Missions) were moderately and quietly antislavery, the Northern Baptists were actively antislavery, the Moravians (from North Carolina) tolerated slavery, and the Southern Methodists and Southern Baptists actively supported slavery. The proslavery Cherokees were convinced that there was little difference between being antislavery and being an abolitionist, yet both the Congregationalists and the Northern Baptists denied holding abolitionist views. Abolitionists were considered irresponsible fanatics, whereas northern missionaries considered themselves responsible reformers. This distinction became untenable in the Cherokee Nation after 1856.

Most of the slaveholding Cherokees, or would-be slaveholders, who were converts joined the Southern Methodists (the Southern Baptists did not send missionaries to the Cherokees until 1857). The majority of the church-going full-bloods were Northern Baptists. Each of these denominations had 1,000 to 1,200 members in the nation by the 1850s. John Ross had joined the Methodists as a probationary member, or "seeker," in 1829 before the sectional division of the denomination in 1845. Though he and his close relatives were slaveholders, their desire for tribal unity caused them to play down the slavery controversy; after all, their treaties were with the United States and not with any section of it.

From 1839 onward the Congregationalists and Northern Baptists had to walk a thin line between the proslavery Cherokees and the growing anti-slavery element among those churchgoers in the North who supported missions. In 1843 a group of abolitionist Baptists in the North formed the Free Mission Society to compete with the official Baptist Foreign Mission Board because the board was unwilling to urge its missionaries to oppose slavery. In 1846 the abolitionist Congregationalists and some northern Presbyterians formed the American Missionary Association as a rival to the American Board of Commissioners for Foreign Missions for the same reason.[67] These new abolitionist missionary associations raised money to hire their own missionaries and published periodicals accusing their official denominational mission boards of supporting slavery among the slaveholding Indians. Soon these new mission agencies were attracting sufficient support to jeopardize the work of the official boards. Consequently the official boards tried to persuade their missionaries in the field to dissociate themselves from any countenance of slavery.

The Congregational missionaries, almost all from New England, told their boards that while they personally abhorred the institution of slavery, it was not feasible for them to openly oppose it among the slaveholding tribes. Not only were missionaries supposed to avoid meddling in political affairs, but to do so would risk their being expelled. Moreover, due to the shortage of labor in Indian nations (since Indians did not like to work for missionaries), they often had to hire slaves to work for them.[68] (Missionaries from southern denominations actually bought slaves to work for them.)

In 1844 the Congregational board in Boston asked its missionaries to the southern tribes to expel from their churches any members who were slave owners and to admit no new members who owned slaves. Under Cherokee law, women could own their own property, so many women (married or single) were slave owners. This mandate raised a theological debate concerning the Christian requirements for church membership. Samuel Worcester among the Cherokee missionaries and most of the Congregational missionaries among the Creeks, Choctaws, and Chickasaws said they could find nothing in the Bible that made slave ownership a bar to church membership or Christian brotherhood. While they acknowledged that "the law of love" in the New Testament and the golden rule indicated that slavery was contrary to Christian ideals, nonetheless neither Jesus nor his apostles had barred slaveholders from membership; they treated slavery as a purely civil or political institution. Church membership depended solely on repentance and faith. Worcester's colleague, Daniel Butrick, told the board that ministers of God were not "authorized to wrest the sceptre from the hands of civil rulers."[69] The most they could do was to urge slaveholders in their churches to treat their slaves with kindness and love. (They also noted that they admitted slaves to church membership.)

Asked by the board whether they saw any possibility for the abolition of slavery among the Cherokees, some missionaries said they thought that most Cherokee Christians disliked the institution and wished to see it ended. David Vann, a Cherokee slaveholder but not a church member, told Elizur Butler in 1849, "Slavery is an evil which will, in fifty years, be gone from the nation."[70] Chief John Ross told Butler in 1852, "I wish there was not a black person in the Nation. I wish they were all in Africa where they belong."[71] Ross added, however, that he did not believe the institution would end among the Cherokees until it had ended among the whites of the United States. As Lewis Ross put it, "The Cherokees will undoubtedly give up slavery when the people of the United States do."[72] However, in answer to the board's question, Butler wrote, "I do not see any prospect of the abolition of slavery" by the Cherokee council; "little is seen or felt [among the Cherokees] with regard to the evil or injustices of it."[73] Butler seemed unaware of the growing antislavery views among the full-bloods.

When the board asked its missionaries whether they preached against the cruelties of slavery, they maintained that they knew of few instances of mistreatment of slaves by Cherokee owners. "Since I have been in the Nation," said Daniel Butrick, "I have had the privilege of baptizing fifteen slaveholders, including masters and mistresses," and he found them uniformly kind to their slaves.[74] They allowed slaves to attend church and Sabbath schools and provided them with clothing, food, and housing. Consequently no slave-owning church members among the Congregationalists had ever been disciplined for cruelty to his or her slaves. Samuel Worcester said he would resign his position before he would agree to exclude slaveholders from his mission church:[75] "Nor do I at present see how we can exclude them, or ever refuse to admit others, if they should give evidence of regeneration. . . . I regard it as certain that the apostles did receive slaveholders to their churches without requiring of them the emancipation of their slaves."[76] In 1848, 24 out of the 237 members of the Congregational mission churches among the Cherokees were slaveholders.[77]

Realizing that the Cherokees were aware of their personal distaste for slavery, the Congregational missionaries collectively signed and published a letter in the *Cherokee Advocate* on October 23, 1848, expressing their position on the whole issue: "We are aware that we stand between two fires; in danger of displeasing by what we may write, on the one hand, the people for whose good we labor, and on the other hand, the Christian community by whom we are sustained in our work." They admitted that they disliked slavery and that they would cease hiring slaves because it tended "to uphold and encourage slavery." However, they would also continue to admit slaveholders to their churches if they were truly moral and pious Christians. They might reject for membership a slave trader who acted with "manifest disregard to the welfare of the slave" (perhaps a reference to separating families for sale). Although they felt that slavery was "implicitly condemned by the general law of love" in the gospel, they expected this spiritual ideal to work its way gradually into the hearts of all Christians; it did not require political agitation. They promised never to preach from the pulpit against "what is generally regarded as simply a political institution," for churches should not meddle in politics.[78]

After printing this statement, the editor of the *Cherokee Advocate*, speaking for the Ross moderates, commented sententiously: "The position of the missionaries, as defined by themselves, is one that ought to satisfy people in the North, whose minds are not overcast by the darkness of slavery but beaming with the light of benevolence and the desire to do the greatest amount of good . . . without dragging religion into the mud and dirt of civil affairs and political dissensions and conflicts."[79]

The Northern Baptist missionaries received the same kind of prodding from their official board and at first reacted the same way. After the Baptist denomination split into a Northern antislavery denomination and a Southern proslavery denomination in 1845, the Baptist Foreign Mission Board in Boston changed its name to the American Baptist Mission Union. The Union wrote to Evan Jones, superintendent of its Cherokee mission in 1848, saying that it was pleased to learn from him that only 5 out of 1,100 Cherokee Baptists were slave owners (a fact, Jones noted, that was due to his working almost entirely among the full-bloods who were too poor to own slaves).[80] Jones wrote, as the Congregational missionaries had, that the Cherokees treated their slaves with kindness and were concerned for their conversion and moral improvement. Fifty members of the Baptist mission churches were slaves, though their masters were not. None of the Baptist missionaries owned slaves in the nation, Jones said, but they had all, at various times, hired slaves to work for them. Jones said this occurred "only in cases of absolute necessity in which other help could not be obtained."[81] Like the Congregationalists, Jones said that he and his colleagues never preached publicly against slavery: "No public instruction distinct from the ordinary Gospel precepts is given" with respect "to the righteousness or evil or sin of slavery." However, "in ordinary and private intercourse" with their members, the missionaries did say that "slavery is essentially evil in its nature." Jones believed that the Baptist missionaries' influence "has been in decided opposition to slavery and favorable to its extinction. We believe the hopes and anticipation of intelligent and pious Cherokees look forward to the extinction of slavery." However, with regard to excluding slaveholders from church membership, he agreed with the Congregationalists: "The march of public sentiment in the Cherokee Nation on the subject of slavery is not sufficiently advanced to justify the adoption of any measure on the subject in reference to church membership."[82] By 1850 there were 1,300 Baptist Cherokees in six mission churches and six native preachers. The native preachers, Jones added, "are decidedly and steadfastly opposed to slavery. . . . We have no apology to make for slavery nor a single argument to urge in its defence, and our sincere desire and earnest prayer is that it may be speedily brought to an end."[83]

However, the Union was not satisfied with this. It voted in May 1850 that it would exercise its right to deny financial aid to any mission churches "which persist in fellowshipping so great an evil as American Slavery."[84] This posed a dire threat to Baptist mission work, for none of its Cherokee churches was self-supporting; without financial aid they would collapse and their members scatter. Jones did not dare to ask the members of each church to vote on the issue of expelling slaveholders, although a majority in each might have voted to expel them. The resulting public excitement from such action might have lead to the expulsion of the Baptist missionaries. However, he did instruct the native ministers in the various churches to which the five Cherokee slaveholders belonged to issue them letters of dismission. Dismission was not excommunication, nor did it indicate any disciplinary action for sinful behavior. A letter of dismission stated that as a duly baptized Christian, the member was entitled to membership in another church; it simply assumed that the member was taking his or her membership to some other Baptist church. However, at this time there were no Southern Baptist churches in the nation; a letter of dismission left these slaveholding Baptist believers without a church.[85]

After these letters were issued, Jones wrote to the American Baptist Mission Union in March 1852 that "slaveholding has been separated from all our churches."[86] The Union expressed great satisfaction and immediately publicized the news far and wide. Jones's success led the Congregational board to ask its missionaries why they could not do the same. Worcester informed them that he considered Jones's action unscriptural and contrary to the Congregational principle of ecclesiastical government. He denounced Jones for acting like "a ruling bishop."[87]

The efforts of Worcester, Jones, and their northern colleagues to avoid controversy failed. In October 1853 federal agent George Butler wrote in his annual report to the commissioner of Indian affairs, George E. Manypenny, that certain missionaries in the Cherokee Nation were behaving "obnoxiously" concerning the slavery question. They were "fanatically pursuing a course which, if persisted in, must lead to mischievous and pernicious consequences."[88] Butler later wrote that slavery had been a positive asset to Cherokee progress, and he implied that by opposing it, these missionaries were a disruptive political force. He clearly had Worcester and Jones in mind, and he wanted Manypenny to give him the authority to expel them.[89]

A similar report from the federal agent to the Choctaws and Chickasaws, Douglas H. Cooper, predicted that if the northern missionaries in the Choctaw Nation continued "as they are now doing, in five years slavery will be abolished in the whole of" the southern Indian superintendency. "I am convinced that something must be done speedily to arrest the systematic efforts of the missionaries to abolitionize the Indian Country. . . . I see no way except secretly to induce the Choctaws, Cherokees and Creeks to allow [white] slaveholders to settle among their people and control the movement now going on to abolish slavery among them."[90] This seemed to indicate that, as agent, Cooper would encourage whites to enter the Indian nations and then become vigilantes to "control" abolitionists. Neither Cooper nor Butler trusted the Indian governments to manage their own problems with the issue of slavery, even though the chiefs and most of the leaders in all of the southern Indian nations were slaveholders.

These events, on top of the passage of the Kansas-Nebraska Act that year, made 1854 a critical turning point in Cherokee affairs. Worcester told his board in October that there was much "talk of having a law or resolution passed" in the council that fall "to have all abolitionists ejected from the nation. . . . They may possibly enact some sort of gag-law to which we cannot submit."[91] A bill of this sort was discussed, but no action was taken on it. The first serious action against northern missionaries took place the following year when the proslavery and antislavery Cherokees polarized into coherent political organizations.

After Manypenny received Agent Butler's charges against abolitionist missionaries, he asked for the names of the missionaries and for proof of the charges. Butler provided affidavits from slaveholders in June 1855 and specifically named Evan Jones and Samuel Worcester as the men he had in mind. The affidavits went back to events that took place in 1852. In Jones's case the affidavits came from four irate slaveholding Baptist converts: Mrs. Jesse Bushyhead, Mrs. William Musgrove, Tobacco Will, and Jack Foster, who, though formerly Jones's trusted assistant in translating the Bible, had joined the Southern Methodists after his dismission. Each of the complainants said that Jones had forced them out of their mission churches, denying them the right to worship Christ simply because they were slaveholders.[92] With regard to Worcester, Butler supplied an affidavit from Worcester's Cherokee translator, the Reverend Stephen Foreman. Foreman too felt that he had been unjustly driven from his mission post, but his case was more complicated, and he added other charges against Worcester.

Foreman was a highly influential mixed-blood slaveholder who had been appointed by the council as the first superintendent of the Cherokee public school system in 1841. He had been converted by the Congregationalists in the old nation in 1830, and they had helped to send him first to Union Theological Seminary in Richmond and then to Princeton Theological Seminary in New Jersey.[93] Ordained as a minister in 1833, he preached regularly in the nation. He became a key figure in translating the Bible into Cherokee for the American Board of Commissioners for Foreign Missions. In 1851, after Foreman purchased several slaves, Worcester asked him whether he intended to free them and let them work out their manumission expense under the usual contract labor plan followed by other missionaries of the board. Foreman said that he did not. When Worcester reported this, the board said it would no longer keep Foreman on its payroll unless he agreed to free his slaves, whereupon Foreman resigned before he could be fired. Worcester, desperate over losing his translator, managed to persuade the board to let him hire Foreman on an hourly basis, which would not require that he be listed on the official missionary payroll.[94] Worcester pointed out that "if he wants to, Foreman could do us much injury on the slavery question."[95]

Foreman felt very much abused and leveled four charges against Worcester. First, he complained of Worcester's criticism of Foreman for owning slaves. Second, "I was informed by the Honorable Lewis Ross that he had requested the Rev. S. A. Worcester to discontinue the visits to his negro house, which he had been in the habit of making, as it was injuring his negroes. I was further informed by the same Gentleman that the Rev. S. A. Worcester had been purchasing corn from a slave whereas it is contrary to the laws of the Cherokee Nation to trade with a slave without previous permission from the master."

Third, Foreman had heard "frequent remarks of citizens" of the nation describing Worcester as an abolitionist. "During the past year, Mr. Worcester preached several times in which the slavery question was made a prominent topic" (presumably a sermon on Hebrews 13:3 dealing with the treatment of captives and those held against their will). "There was considerable discussion upon the subject in the National Council at its last session [October 1854]." Foreman himself was convinced that "the [New England] missionaries . . . or their Board . . . were attempting to accomplish a political object under the garb of missionary labor," which "must have a baneful influence in this country." Fourth, Worcester's treatment of his slaves was "calculated to create dissatisfaction and insubordination in other negroes. . . . A slave cannot bear good treatment. . . . Mr. Worcester, for example, allows his servants to eat at the same table [with him], and not infrequently with the members of his own family. This they noise abroad in boasting manner, expatiating on this happy situation. As a natural consequence, the slave becomes dissatisfied with his situation and longs for a change, and hence he neglects his duty, becomes disobedient and hauty [sic], and hence, too, the reins are drawn tighter on him and the rod is more frequently applied." Trying to be fair-minded, Foreman said that though "all the missionaries of the board" were in his opinion "antislavery men," still, "none so far as I know are abolitionists." He concluded that "notwithstanding his ultra views on the subject of slavery," Worcester "has done much good for the whole Cherokee people."[96]

Butler, in his letter to Manypenny accompanying these affidavits, said, "I believe that the Rev. Jones of the Baptist Mission is an abolitionist and has been interfering with the Institution of Slavery in this Nation, first by refusing to admit slave owners as members of the church unless they would free their slaves and second removing slave owners from the church because they own slaves. . . . Mr. Jones," he added, "is only the instrument in the hands of the Baptist Board" in Boston. "If the course now pursued by that Board and its servants is persisted in, it must lead to mischievous consequences."[97] As for Worcester, Butler said, he "is also tinctured with Abolition sentiments." This was evident first "from the fact that he refuses to employ slave labor unless the slave shall receive wages, thus making a stab at the Institution of Slavery," second, from his practice of "admitting negroes into his family circle as companions, thus breaking down the distinction between owner and slave, which has a pernicious influence upon the slave portion of the community," and third, from his efforts at "inculcating anti-slavery sentiments from the pulpit."

For reasons not known, Manypenny did not respond to Butler's complaints. Nor did he write to the American Board of Commissioners for Foreign Missions and the American Baptist Mission Union, as Butler suggested, requesting them "to withdraw those instructions" regarding the exclusion of slaveholders from church membership. Probably Manypenny thought it inadvisable to arouse northerners by attacking missionaries.

By the summer of 1855 the slavery issue had become the central topic of political discussion in the Cherokee Nation. Kansas was in the throes of bloody battles between its proslavery and antislavery immigrants, who were to decide, by what Senator Stephen A. Douglas called "squatter sovereignty," whether the new territory should be admitted as a slave or free state. During the election campaign for new members of the Cherokee council in August 1855, Worcester wrote his board that some of the candidates "made the removal of abolitionist missionaries an electioneering hobby, and whether on account of that or in spite of that, were elected."[98] Worcester also reported that "a strong opposition was made in this district [that is, Tahlequah] to William P. Ross on account of his being favorable to missionaries," and he won only after John Ross stated publicly that the antislavery views of certain missionaries would have no effect on the nation's political interests.

In the same letter, Worcester informed his board sadly that Chief Ross had ceased attending the Congregational church at Park Hill that he had frequented for many years. He now attended the nearby Southern Methodist church, a political move calculated to dissociate himself from any tincture of abolitionism. Ross had always admired the New England missionaries and was good friends with Worcester; he would have joined Worcester's church, Worcester felt, "but for [his] apprehension of difficulty on the subject of slavery." Ross had recently told him, Worcester said, that "in some things in regard to the subject of slavery, I go too far." Ross also told him that he thought Evan Jones and the Northern Baptists went too far. By attending a mission church that was supportive of the institution of slavery, Chief Ross hoped to quiet the political controversy on this issue. Worcester added that although Ross owned many slaves, he "is very humane in his treatment of his slaves." Ross had commented to Worcester that he wished "there were no slaves" in America but that he thought "it would be ruinous both to them and the community to set them all free . . . and does not know *what* to do with them."

When the newly elected council met in October 1855, Worcester feared that "a strong majority in the National Committee [the upper house] will go for some strong legislation against abolitionist missionaries," as they had almost done a year ago. "But it must probably be defeated in the lower house or vetoed by the chief."[99] He was wrong in supposing that the lower house, though a majority of its members were full-bloods, would defeat the measure.

The bill that passed the legislature on October 24 began with a preamble asserting that the Cherokees had been and still were "a slaveholding people." It contained four parts designed to intimidate the missionaries. First, it called on the chief to write the boards of all mission agencies in the nation inquiring about "the institution of slavery as a church principle" and to report their answer to the next council. Second, it stated that it was "unlawful for any missionary to counsel or advise any slave in anyway whatever to the detriment of his owner"; solicitors of the nation were to report "missionaries so offending to the Agent, who is hereby requested to place them beyond the limits of our nation." Third, it stated that any Cherokee (for example, a native minister of one of the abolitionist mission boards) who "advised or counseled" any slave "to the prejudice of his owner" should be fined $25–$100 to be paid to the owner of the slave who had been counseled. Fourth, the superintendent of public schools was not "to employ or continue as teacher in any public school, . . . any person known to be an abolitionist or whose influence is opposed to the interest of slaveholders." (In several public schools whites supplied by mission boards were teachers.) [100]

The four most prominent leaders in the council at this time were W. P. Boudinot, Stand Watie, Alex Foreman, and Lewis Martin; all were slaveholders and at least two were of Watie's party (soon to be known as the Southern Rights party). The bill was vetoed by John Ross who did not want to arouse the northern mission boards by such action. The legislature tried to pass it over his veto but lacked the two-thirds necessary to do so. [101] Still the tension over slavery by no means abated, and the northern missionaries continued to be the chief scapegoats.

Antimissionary sentiment rose to new heights in June 1856 when the Reverend Charles C. Torrey of the Congregational mission at Fairfield was accused of abetting a slave to run away by giving him a pass and a horse. The slave, named Dave, was a member of the Fairfield mission church and a hired man at the mission. "He asked me," Torrey wrote later, "for my horse to go to Park Hill, and without any suspicion of his real purpose, I let him take the horse. He went to Park Hill, but instead of returning, struck out for Kansas." [102] Dave had run away because he heard "that he was to be taken from us and hired out at another place to which he dreaded to go." He was caught and returned to his master.

This incident aroused great excitement in the nation and great animosity toward Torrey and Worcester. Worcester was accused of helping Dave after he got to Park Hill. The council took up the matter of antislavery missionaries for the third time at its session of October 1856. Torrey, trying to head off a restrictive law, presented a long affidavit to the council declaring his innocence.

Nevertheless, the council passed a bill requiring all missionaries to appear be-fore the federal agent and explain to him their views on slavery; if he judged them to be opposed to the institution, he was given authority to expel them. Again John Ross vetoed the bill, and again it failed to pass over his veto. Torrey blamed the guerrilla war going on in Kansas for the overreaction of the Cherokees. "The Kansas excitement has rendered all northern men pecu-liarly obnoxious," he wrote to his board.[103] If that state were to become a free state, slaveholders in the Indian nations (and the neighboring southern states) expected a tremendous increase in runaways. Hence they desired to drive out or silence any person who might encourage such escapes.

Torrey's apprehensions about "the Kansas excitement" were paralleled by Agent George Butler's apprehensions about the growth of the Republican party. He wrote to Commissioner Manypenny in November 1856 that many of his personal friends had gone to live in Kansas (presumably to help pro-mote the proslavery sentiment there). Now they were being driven out by "bushwhackers" like James Lane (later territorial governor and U.S. senator for Kansas). "Until Lane and his Troops . . . commenced their depredations," these friends of Butler's had been peacefully farming in Kansas. "At the same time that these marauders were commencing their depredations in Kansas, the Emigrant Aid Societies were keeping up the Excitement in the states [of the Northeast] in order to elect Fremont and the Black Republicans, [and] were acting treasonally in the Congress and cooperating with abolition out-laws in Kansas." Butler wrote to Manypenny about this because he had been prepared to offer sanctuary in the Cherokee Nation to any proslavery farmers driven out of Kansas by the "bushwhackers." He said he was happy that troops of the U.S. Army were now being sent to Kansas to maintain order and that hopefully there would be no white refugees fleeing across the border into the Cherokee Nation.[104] Like his friend and fellow agent Douglas Cooper in the Choctaw Nation, Butler would have welcomed white proslavery settlers in the Indian Territory to help tighten control over abolitionist missionaries. Butler apparently had no intention of asking the council or chief to approve his sanctuary plan, believing that emergency aid to endangered citizens of the United States was sufficient ground for ignoring the sovereign rights of the Indians. Once they were in the nation, however, it would have been difficult to expel them.

The lull in fighting in Kansas in 1857 and the nationwide financial panic that plunged thousands of American enterprises into bankruptcy that year tempo-rarily distracted attention from the slavery issue. Torrey urged the American Board of Commissioners for Foreign Missions in July 1857 to stop agitating the slavery issue among the Cherokees. The "Southern unprincipled press," he said, distorted every word it heard from the North. Moreover, he optimistically declared that the financial panic that year had made slavery unprofitable among the Cherokees, and it might soon die out if left to itself. He believed the number of slaves was already on the decrease and that soon many slaves would flee to Kansas and further undermine the institution. The question could now be left to God to settle in his own good time.[105] Worcester offered similar suggestions. He thought that if the Indian Territory were made into a federal territory preparatory to statehood, as the Johnson bill proposed, it would result in ending slavery there (though he personally did not favor the bill). He urged the board to show more toleration for slaveholders under "the law of love" in the hope of soothing them.[106] Elizur Butler saw hope in the changing sentiment toward slavery among the full-bloods. Formerly he thought they were perfectly willing to tolerate the institution. Now, however, "there is, or could be awakening, more antislavery feeling [among them] than I had supposed." Butler believed this would be sufficient to block further antimissionary sentiment in the Cherokee legislature.[107] Evan Jones and his son John Buttrick Jones shared Butler's view, and they did their best to persuade the full-bloods to see that the ardent proslavery faction was not really acting in the best interests of the nation. The Joneses were actively engaged at this time in creating a secret political movement among the full-bloods to counter the proslavery faction.[108]

In the fall of 1857 the proslavery leaders in the Cherokee council tried once again to pass a law threatening missionaries with expulsion if they in any way opposed slavery. Charles Torrey, speaking for the missionaries of the American Board of Commissioners for Foreign Missions, appeared in person before the council to head off the law: "We disapprove of the system of slavery, but we came here not as abolitionists, not to make the blacks discontented or to stir up strife, but to preach the gospel of Christ and to educate your children." [109] Growing polarization within the council prevented any such bill from passing, but the matter did not die. As the full-bloods' resentment against the proslavery extremists grew, the nation once again was seriously divided.

Evan Jones and the Northern Baptists faced a new problem in 1857 when the Southern Baptists sent their first missionary among the Cherokees. In 1855 the Southern Baptist Convention voted to send proslavery missionaries to the Cherokees, Choctaws, and Creeks under the auspices of its Domestic and Indian Mission Board.[110] When John Buttrick Jones learned that he and his father would soon face proslavery missionary competitors from the Southern Baptists, he wrote to his board in Boston: "The Methodists en masse go for slavery. They admit slaveholders and make capital out of the fact that the Presbyterians [that is, the Congregationalists] speak against slavery and the

[Northern] Baptists have cut off all connection with it. . . . The Southern Baptist Board will soon send one Rev. Cobb . . . and 'free the Baptist Churches from the thraldom of abolitionism.' . . . We believe that is their intention."[111] This, he said, would add to the many "influences that are industriously used against us, growing principally out of our opposition on the slavery question."

However, Reverend Cobb never arrived. Instead, the Southern Baptists sent the Reverend James G. Slover, who reached Tahlequah in the spring of 1857 and at once began to undermine the position of the Northern Baptists. As he explained in a letter to the *Mississippi Baptist* magazine in 1857: "Since 1851 . . . a very large portion of this nation [that is, the slaveholders] have been deprived of the privileges in Baptist churches. An Act of the [Northern Baptist] Board . . . rendered it necessary for all slaveholding members to separate from the churches. . . . All persons in the nation holding slaves are barred from [Baptist] membership."[112] Slover's purpose was to provide Baptist churches for Cherokee slaveholders. He believed there were "many of this class" among the Cherokees—persons "who are Baptist in sentiment and will not be anything else." Exclusion from the Northern Baptist mission churches had driven some of these persons into the Southern Methodist churches, but the Methodists were scripturally unsound, according to Slover, because they practiced infant baptism by sprinkling and preached an Arminian rather than a Calvinist view of the gospel. He wished it known that he was in the nation to remedy this sorry state of affairs. However, he got off to a slow start in Tahlequah, making only two converts that year. He then moved into the area where the Northern Baptists were active, and by the end of 1858, he had gathered twenty-eight converts into two churches. Many others attended these services. Part of his success came from the large sums he offered to Cherokees to serve as interpreters and preachers.

For a Cherokee to be ordained as a Christian minister had become a source of considerable status and influence among many Cherokees by 1858. The Joneses had attributed their success largely to the work of their native preachers and ministers. However, the higher salaries offered by Slover now tempted some of their converts to switch to the Southern Baptists.[113] The Northern Baptist board, facing hard times during the financial crisis of 1857–58, had cut back on its mission funds. John Jones tried to persuade his board that this was a serious mistake. Slover, he wrote early in 1858:

has been laboring here for some time and is about to organize a pro-slavery Baptist church [near ours]. . . . Some who were formerly with us have joined his ranks. One man, by name of Young Duck who was a Deacon of the Pea Vine or Flint Church . . . has gone over to Mr. Slover. . . . I understand that Mr. Slover is offering salaries for more preachers. . . . He told me he had been trying to get Mr. [John] Foster. . . . He told me that he had told Mr. Foster to set his own price, and he should have it, if he would enter the services of the Southern Baptists. Mr. Foster is in the employ of the Methodist Episcopal Church South.[114]

Foster apparently did not accept Slover's offer, but other Cherokee Baptists did. Slover "takes great pains," Jones said, "to tell in certain places that he is not like the 'Jones' Baptists'; for circulating this information, of course, we are very grateful. He says he owns one 'nigger' and would own more if he were able." [115] When Slover succeeded in persuading a Northern Baptist Cherokee preacher named Thomas Wilkinson to become a minister for him, Wilkinson went to John Jones and asked for a dismission so that he could transfer his membership to the Southern Baptists. Since Wilkinson was a very active preacher whom Jones would be sorry to lose, he tried to convince him not to leave. Wilkinson first said he wished a dismission because he disagreed with the Northern Baptists' policy of refusing to baptize slaveholders; this, he said, was unscriptural. Next he claimed that "the Boston Board was doing everything it could" to subvert the Cherokee constitution, which upheld the institution of slavery. Then, after further questioning, he admitted that Slover was going to pay him $300 a year to become a preacher. Jones, believing that money was Wilkinson's main incentive, refused to give him an honorable dismission. Wilkinson wrote an angry letter to the *Western Recorder and Baptist Banner* in (Louisville, Kentucky), exposing what he considered the hypocrisy and lack of principle among the Northern Baptists. The editor of the newspaper expressed his support for Slover and Wilkinson, stating that he had traveled among the Cherokees and knew that "many of them were Southern in principle" and "baptist in sentiment." [116]

Although the Baptists in the United States had in the past prided themselves on their dedication to the separation of church and state, Southern Baptists by 1858 were frankly equating their principles with the political principles of their region and of the Democratic party. "Our politicians are every day becoming more religious and our religion more political," said the *Mississippi Baptist* in May 1858.[117] The editor wrote: "The Baptist church takes the lead in Scriptural soundness on the slavery question. . . . No man who admits slavery to be a moral evil is a fit man for the South. . . . We defend slavery because of our honest conviction that it is socially, politically, and morally right. This is the only true Southern platform and it is as Scriptural as Southern." [118]

Northern Baptists were becoming just as ardent in their belief that opposition to slavery was politically and spiritually correct. To them the Republican party deserved Baptist support. Christians found little place for the neutral ground between North and South that the Ross party leaders (who still considered themselves Whigs) believed to be the only hope for their future. Not only was the definition of "a good Cherokee" shifting, but the definition of Cherokee nationalism was also changing.

Evan Jones found himself involved in politics and secular affairs in 1858 when he tried to save a black woman from being taken back into slavery by William Penn Adair, a leader of the Watie party. This led Agent Butler to renew his effort to have Jones expelled. Butler had written to the new commissioner of Indian affairs, Charles E. Mix, on June 30, 1858, that the mission boards "at a distance [that is, in Boston] are governing the actions of, and acting in concert with, certain parties here whose sole object is the abolition of slavery in this nation. . . . The evils resulting from their course are already apparent, political strife and discord are showing themselves in every quarter of the nation." Butler was so alarmed that he asked to "confer with [Mix] in person" about the problem; "I respectfully suggest that I be ordered to your office [in Washington, D.C.,] without delay."[119] That same day, Butler wrote to Samuel Worcester, saying that he had been reported to be "an abolitionist, teaching and preaching in opposition to the institution of slavery in this nation."[120] Worcester wrote back on July 22 that he considered himself "not guilty" of the charge. In August 1858 Butler received concrete evidence from William Penn Adair of Evan Jones's meddling in slavery matters and took it with him on his trip to see Mix in Washington.[121] Adair told Butler that "Mr. E. Jones is interfering with the private property of Cherokee Citizens; that he is interfering with Slavery," and that "he is upholding abolition principles and doctrines." Jones, he said, "may 'gull' a few of the ignorant class" among the full-bloods by his religious pretensions, "but I think the more enlightened parties would rejoin [the church] at his removal."[122]

In Washington, Butler told Commissioner Mix in October 1858 that by requiring Jones to expel slaveholders from its Cherokee mission churches, the Northern Baptist board in Boston was "attempting to degrade slaveholders and place the institution of slavery upon the same level as murder, etc.," referring to other crimes deserving excommunication. He added that "Mr. Worcester and all of his denomination," though they had never expelled any slaveholders, "are believed to be Abolitionists." In his opinion, Mix must take "immediate action upon this subject" or the situation "must lead to bloodshed" (presumably mob action against the northern missionaries).[123]

Charles Torrey wrote to his board on October 11, 1858, that Butler was in Washington trying to obtain authorization from Mix to expel missionaries whom he considered abolitionist by his definition. It was important, Torrey told the board, not to push this issue any further. The missionaries must keep a low profile.[124]

Commissioner Mix, like his predecessor, declined to act on Butler's suggestions. Butler, however, maintained in his annual report that "there are Black Republicans who are particular fondlings of the abolition missionaries that have been, and still are, making themselves officious upon the subject of slavery" among the Cherokees. His report being a public document (unlike his correspondence with Adair and Mix), the newspapers in the states adjoining the Cherokees printed excerpts from the report in order to arouse public opposition to such missionaries. The *Fort Smith Times* in Van Buren, Arkansas, reported on February 3, 1859, that Evan Jones was "an abolitionist and a very dangerous man" who was "meddling with the affairs of the Cherokees and teaching them abolition principles." [125]

In the late fall of 1858, the American Board of Commissioners for Foreign Missions had requested the Cherokee council to permit them to bring a new missionary to replace the Reverend John Huss, a native minister in the pay of the board who had recently died. To their surprise, the council refused their request. Worcester told the board that this action was taken because to proslavery Cherokees, "we are abolitionists." He noted, however, that the lower house, in which the full-bloods were dominant, had favored their request.[126] During this same session of the Cherokee legislature, a petition was circulated in the vicinity of Tahlequah and Park Hill urging the commissioner of Indian affairs to expel Evan and John Jones for meddling in politics.[127] This petition was to be sent to Washington to bolster Butler's arguments and to persuade Commissioner Mix to act upon them.

The Cherokee people were by this time in almost precisely the same dilemma over slavery as were the citizens of the United States. There seemed no way to reconcile the proslavery and antislavery positions. A firmly entrenched and determined (though small) slaveholding class had achieved such power among the Cherokees that it assumed its interests and those of the nation must stand or fall together. This faction was perfectly willing to call in the power of the federal government to support its "peculiar institution," even if such an act weakened the case for Cherokee sovereignty. The nonslaveholding majority began to doubt the loyalty of this faction because it placed its special interest before that of national unity and independence. Slaveholders also threatened the religious freedom guaranteed in the Cherokee constitution by asking the federal government to expel ministers whom many admired. What ultimately would happen to those antislavery Cherokee ministers and laity in the Congregational and Northern Baptist denominations?

Slaveholding Cherokees had long since become convinced of black racial inferiority. Robert D. Ross, the son of Lewis Ross and a graduate of Princeton College, expressed this position bluntly in a letter to the *Southwest Independent* in Fayetteville, Arkansas, in 1854: "We will have ministers without abolitionism or no ministers at all. But good ones we can get to fill the place of these men who regard a negro above, or at least equal to, a Cherokee, for equal to *themselves* will Cherokee[s] regard [them] never!" [128] The federal agent to the Cherokees was convinced that the mixed-bloods who dominated the Cherokee legislature were the leaders of Cherokee progress and that their adoption of slavery had been the key to that progress. In his annual report to the commissioner of Indian affairs in 1859, George Butler wrote: "I am clearly of the opinion that the rapid advancement of the Cherokees is owing in part to the fact of their being slaveholders, which has operated as an incentive to all industrial pursuits, and I believe if every family of the wild, roving tribes were to own a negro man and woman who would teach them to cultivate the soil . . . it would tend more to civilize them than any other plan could." [129]

Unlike the nonslaveholders in the southern United States, the Cherokee full-bloods were not allied with the minority who owned slaves. The members of the Reverend Timothy Ranney's Congregational mission church at Lee's Creek petitioned the American Board of Commissioners for Foreign Missions on October 21, 1860, not to close its mission work among them. They wanted the Bible and other works translated into Cherokee because "about three-fourths [of the Cherokees] read only the Cherokee." They blamed the mixed-blood slaveholders for attacks on the northern missionaries: "We have among our people men half white who are very much opposed to missionaries, accusing them of being runners off of blacks." However, the full-bloods were gaining control in the Cherokee legislature, they said, and at the last council they had defeated "those [mixed-bloods] who wished to trample on the full Cherokees and on the poor." [130] New questions of Cherokee identity and tribal values began to enter into the opposition to the mixed-bloods. To some, a redefinition of Cherokee patriotism seemed to require both the end of slavery and the end of mixed-blood dominance. As surely as the disunited states of America, the Cherokee Nation was headed for a revolution in power.

6

The Start of the Keetoowah Revolt, 1858–1861

*The [Cherokee] Nation is fast tending towards a division
into two antagonistic parties—the mixed bloods and the full
Cherokees. The former constitute about one-third of the nation
and the latter about two-thirds. . . . Two classes are very
naturally collecting into distinct and separate settlements.*

—*The Reverend Marcus Palmer, 1854*

Despite a severe drought that ruined the corn crop in the summer of 1860, the Cherokees had never been so prosperous. In normal times prosperity was a strong force for national unity. However, in 1860 too many other forces were at work within the nation and outside of it to sustain a spirit of harmony. The people of the United States had reached an impasse in the struggle between the free-soil/free-labor views of the Republican party on one side and the "Southern Rights" demands of the proslavery Democrats on the other. Expansion of the white population westward required a decision as to whether the rapidly filling territories of the West were to be admitted as free or slave states—a decision neither Congress nor the president nor the Supreme Court seemed able to make. The policy of "squatter sovereignty" suggested by Senator Stephen A. Douglas had failed miserably in Kansas. The *Dred Scott* decision of 1857 only added to the confusion, and William

Lloyd Garrison's suggestion that the North should secede from the South exasperated common sense. Six years of guerrilla war in Kansas, the refusal of many northerners to uphold the Fugitive Slave Act, and John Brown's raid on Harpers Ferry in 1859 marked not only the failure of the Compromise of 1850 but also the fast rending of ties that bound the Union. As the southern states began to take secession seriously, the Indian nations pondered their own choices. Most of them hoped for neutrality in what they liked to think was a white man's controversy, but the tensions over slaveholding within "the five civilized tribes" undercut that evasion. Chief Ross of the Cherokees sounded the note of anxiety shared by the chiefs of all the slaveholding tribes in 1860 in saying, "Our only safety is in the Cherokee People being united." It proved a forlorn hope.

In May 1855, Ross had written a letter to his old and loyal friend, the Northern Baptist missionary Evan Jones, expressing his fear that a divisive spirit was at work among the Cherokees. He knew that Jones was committed to an antislavery position, but he also knew that Jones shared his view that national unity was the only way to sustain Cherokee independence against white expansion, imperialism, and aggression. "I have deemed it proper to send you the enclosed papers," Ross wrote, "from which you will see that the subjects on which they treat are well calculated, if agitated under the influence of political demagogues and through the prejudices of sectarianism on religious-doctrinal points, to create excitement and strife among the Cherokee people." Ross had discovered that "there has been a secret society organized in Delaware and Saline Districts" of the nation dedicated to the promotion of slavery and "auxiliary to a 'Mother Lodge' in some of the States or Territories of the United States." This effort of outsiders to interfere in the internal affairs of the nation posed grave problems. He enclosed a copy of "the oath said to be administered to the members of the Society." Ross said he did not believe the Cherokee people would be "duped" into abetting "this sinister plot." Nevertheless, he wanted Jones to be aware of it since several Northern Baptist mission churches were situated in the districts where the society already had a foothold. The fact that Jones's Baptist church members, all nonslaveholders and staunch supporters of Ross's nationalist party, were in the best position to observe and expose such an organization and to keep Ross informed of its actions possibly explains Ross's purpose in writing the letter, although he makes no specific request for help. The oath of allegiance to the secret society explained its objectives:

> You do solemnly swear that you will answer such questions as may be put to you? Are you in favor of supporting slavery in Kansas, in the Cherokee

Nation and in other countries? You do solemnly swear you will, for the support of Slavery, support any person that you may be instructed to by the Mother Lodge for any office in the Cherokee Nation or anywhere else, and to assist any member that may get into difficulty on account of being a Brother of the Secret Society and to keep secret the names of all the Brothers of the Society and other secrets of the Society?[1]

Ross did not say, and probably did not know, where the Mother Lodge was located, although it was most likely in Arkansas, where a number of such "Blue Lodges" had become active in the effort to promote the proslavery effort in Kansas. Ross also did not disclose how he obtained a copy of the oath. Evan Jones was convinced that concerted action was necessary to counter this effort to push the Cherokees into the ranks of southern proslavery politics. There were many among the Watie party in the nation who would support such an effort, and there were several well-connected members of the Watie party in Arkansas, such as E. Cornelius Boudinot, John Rollin Ridge, J. Woodward Washbourne, Elias Rector, and George W. Paschal, who might have aided the formation of these societies among the Cherokees.

Shortly after receiving this letter, Evan Jones and his son, John Buttrick Jones, conveyed its contents to the full-bloods in their churches. The Joneses hoped to unite the full-bloods into a well-informed, cohesive, and politically active force that could prevent the radical proslavery voters from controlling the electoral process and filling the Cherokee legislature with representatives committed to a proslavery, Southern Rights position. They probably started by talking about the problem to the native preachers of their mission, who met regularly with them for discussions about evangelistic activities. These leaders in turn expanded the discussions to concerned laypersons in the church. Eventually, the most politically inclined formed themselves into a group called the "Keetoowahs." The Keetoowah founders wanted to create a large secret society to counter the "Blue Lodges" or what later became known as the Knights of the Golden Circle.[2] The leading figures in the nascent Keetoowah organization were probably Budd Gritts, Lewis Downing, Smith Christie, Thomas Pegg, and James McDaniels, all leaders among the full-blood Northern Baptists.

The name Keetoowah had a double meaning for the Cherokees. It was the name of their ancient sacred town on the Little Tennessee River, said to be the first settlement of the Cherokee people after a long migration from the Iroquois country to the north. In ancient times the Cherokees spoke of themselves as "ani-Kituwah" or "Keetoowah people."[3] Long ago there had also been a Keetoowah Society composed of the most wise and experienced spiritual and political elders of the nation, who were charged with preserving the nation's sacred rituals and myths. Hence the name signified both the national roots of the people and their tribal values and ideals. To be loyal to "Keetoo-wah" meant to be loyal to the oldest and best parts of the Cherokee ethnic identity.[4]

However, the Keetoowah Society formed around 1855 was not strictly a traditionalist movement; most of its leaders were Christians. In spirit and structure, the Keetoowah Society was syncretic, seeking to combine both the traditions of the past and the virtues of the new religion. Its purpose was political, however, and the rituals and activities associated with its meetings were designed to unite the full-bloods for political action. Its primary goal, as Budd Gritts wrote in his early description of the founding of the society, was to create a nationalist organization that would assure full-blood dominance of the nation's council in order to preserve Cherokee sovereignty. Its negative goal was to prevent the mixed-bloods, in conjunction with intermarried whites, from directing the Cherokees' destiny as a people. Because the Blue Lodges and the Knights of the Golden Circle consisted predominantly of mixed-blood (and intermarried white) slaveholders, the Keetoowah Society was described by its enemies as an abolitionist society under radical northern missionary domination (that is, the Joneses). However, abolition was not the cause of its founding or its principal objective. The immediate purpose of the Keetoowah Society was to combat those mixed-bloods who wanted to link the Cherokees' destiny to that of the white southern nationalist movement in the United States. To that extent it opposed slavery, for if the Cherokee Nation could be separated from the peculiar (white man's) institution, it could better sustain its own identity and control its own future. However, the ultimate goal of the Keetoowah Society was to define a "true Cherokee patriot" as a full-blood, true to traditional values, national unity, and Cherokee self-determination through consensus. Its members treasured and sustained many of the ancient ceremonies, ideals, and spiritual aspects of their old religion. Quite apart from politics, this traditionalism was inherent in the full-blood life-style and therefore inherent in their loyalty to "the spirit of Keetoowah." The meetings of the Keetoowah Society included ceremonies and dances related to "the old ways" because these were the occasions on which the full-bloods came together. It was an all-male organization because its members pledged themselves to fight for its principles, either by voting or by participating in actual battles if necessary. Not all full-bloods became members of the Keetoowah Society just as not all slaveholders joined the Knights of the Golden Circle. However, these two organizations came to represent the polarization of the nation.[5]

For two or three years, those who called themselves Keetoowahs met without any formal organization simply to work out their views with respect to the issues facing their country. John Ross said in 1866 that the Keetoowah Society "had been thoroughly organized for two or three years" prior to 1861.[6] E. Cornelius Boudinot, the son of murdered Elias Boudinot and a leader of the Watie faction in the 1850s (when he edited a proslavery newspaper in Van Buren, Arkansas), said in 1866 that the Keetoowah Society "was organized five years before the war."[7] Budd Gritts, a major architect of the society, said that formal organization began in April 1858. By that time the Keetoowahs had already "discussed what the final result probably would be, caused by the existing state of affairs in the United States." They concluded that "the Cherokees were situated too far in the South, and the [leading] men were becoming reckless and seemed to be taking sides with the South." This was because "those who owned Negro slaves" wished "to preserve their property and the influence that went with it."[8] Gritts observed: "It was plain to be seen that the Cherokee people, without a full understanding, were taking sides with the South. It was plain that teachers from the North were objected to and were being forced out of the Cherokee Nation" by acts of the council, mobs, and efforts of the federal agents. The proslavery people, Gritts said, "believed if the missionaries were gone, all the Cherokee people would go to the side of the South."[9] "But they were mistaken," Gritts noted, for the majority of the Cherokees themselves were not slaveholders and did not want to be. By the spring of 1858, "These matters were already understood by the Keetoowahs," for they had met often to discuss them among themselves and with the Joneses. Also, the "Keetoowahs had already studied their means of defense" against the machinations of the slaveholders and their white allies in the nearby states. On April 15, 1858, "We decided best to affiliate with the North. I was then and there appointed to devise some plan that would be best for the Cherokee people and should place us [that is, the full-blood, nonslaveholding majority] in control of the Cherokee government." That was the goal of the organization—to seize the initiative from the slaveholders in setting Cherokee policies. They, as the majority, as the full-bloods, as those still true to the Keetoowah spirit of their ancestors, should and would direct the destiny of their people.

At their next meeting on April 20, 1858, the Keetoowah leaders read the constitution Gritts had drafted, approved it in principle, and began to gather in "confidential lodges" among the full-bloods "all over the Nation." After several of these lodges were formed, the leaders called "a general convention of the several districts" in September 1858 and presented the constitution of the society for formal ratification. This was to be a group organized from the bottom up, and the tradition of consensus decision making was to prevail in the Keetoowah Society.

The first paragraph of the constitution was a statement of tribal loyalty, self-determination, and self-government, reflecting "the long past history of our Keetoowah forefathers who loved and lived as free people and have never surrendered [their sovereignty] to anybody." Unity and harmony were the keys to this tradition: "They were just like one family. . . . They all came as a unit to their fire to smoke, to aid one another, and to protect their government." However, as of 1858, "we are separated into two parts and cannot agree," and the slaveholding Cherokees "have taken the lead of us." The source of this disunity, as Gritts and the Keetoowah members saw it, was the intervention of white people of the South, and all Cherokees should remember that these were "the people who took our lands away from us, which lands the Creator had given to us, where our forefathers were raised." Now, once again, "they have come in on us secretly, different organizations are with them and they have agreed to help one another in everything. They control our political offices because our masses of people are not organized."

The final paragraph of the original constitution stated that the Keetoowahs "bind ourselves together, the same as under oaths, to abide by our laws and assist one another" in order to regain control of the nation from the slaveholding minority and their interloping white allies. "Lodge captains" and national officers were prescribed, and secret membership lists were to be kept, like all their records, in the Sequoyan syllabary (unreadable to whites and most mixed-bloods). Membership was limited: "Only full blood, uneducated [that is, non-English-speaking] and no mixed blood friends shall be allowed to become a member."

In addition to recruiting candidates to run for national office, for whom they would all work and vote, the organization developed into a mutual assistance society—loaning money to needy members, assisting in burial rites, and looking after the sick. This fostered the Keetoowah spirit of unity and brotherhood. At some point prior to 1860, the members began to wear a special insignia on the lapels of their coats or hunting jackets consisting of two crossed pins.[10] E. Cornelius Boudinot claimed that the organization also had "its signs, grips and pass words." [11] Soon they were being called "Pin Indians" or "Pins." Estimates of the membership varied from 1,500 to 2,000 by 1861. As they grew in size and influence, their numbers proved more than a match for the Knights of the Golden Circle in votes; by 1861 both houses of the legislature were dominated by Pins.[12]

Much less is known about the proslavery, mixed-blood Blue Lodges and

Knights of the Golden Circle. Their memberships were so closely associated with the Watie party that they were known primarily by that name or as the Southern Rights party, although they were referred to jokingly by their enemies as "the Knaves of the Godless Communion."[13] Some believed Stand Watie was the leader of the Knights. According to the constitution and bylaws of the Knights, "No person shall be a member . . . who is not a proslavery man," and by oath they were required to protect their "country from the ravages of abolitionists or any other combination of persons wishing" to disrupt the nation.[14] They were organized into "encampments" or lodges and led by captains and lieutenants whose duty it was to call upon the members, whenever necessary, "to turn out and assist in capturing and punishing any and all abolitionists . . . who are interfering with slavery."[15] The Watie party had long been a close-knit group (many of them related by blood, clan, or marriage) that worked to elect their friends to office. As "ultraproslavery" advocates, the Knights had close ties with white extremists in the surrounding states and strong influence with the federal agents and officials of the Bureau of Indian Affairs. The major difference between the two secret organizations was that the proslavery activists, being almost entirely of mixed or white ancestry, did not bother to define themselves in ethnic or class terms; simply confining their membership to slaveholders was sufficient.

The full-bloods, who had never been politically organized (although most regularly voted for John Ross), added another dimension to their organization when they limited membership to those who spoke, wrote, and thought in Cherokee. Because slavery was the law of the land and assimilation was the goal of the Ross party, English being the official language of the nation, the Keetoowah Society was a subversive or radical organization striking against the established order and institutions. Secrecy was extremely important to its existence and success. However, because it was a grass-roots organization, representing the poor and the majority, it was also a populist movement. For all of its traditionalist aspects, as a political movement it represented a high level of acculturation for the full-bloods. The full-bloods had learned political organization from the congregational nature of evangelical churches; choosing their own leaders derived both from tradition and from the Baptist emphasis on developing a native ministry. For many Cherokees, Christianity (as understood and preached in their own idiom and subject to their own interpretation) had become a source of revitalization. The Joneses, by taking the lead in organizing the Keetoowah movement, unified Christians and non-Christians, galvanizing the majority to action for the self-preservation of the Cherokee people. This movement successfully integrated cultural identity, class identity, ethnic identity, and political idealism in a pietistic form of political action that closely resembled the Free-Soil and Liberty party movements in the northern states. In John Ross, they found their Abraham Lincoln.

John Ross, like Lincoln, preferred to avoid extremism. He always insisted that preservation of the Cherokee Nation, not the slavery issue, was the fundamental concern of his party. Although he had subtly led the Joneses to organize the Keetoowah Society to balance the proslavery party and the growing power of white extremists in the surrounding states, he never intended to split the nation by encouraging a populist revolt. Like Lincoln, however, he could not prevent the polarization of his nation; he called for union and got disunion. As one white observer wrote early in 1861, "The halfbreeds belong to the Knights of the Golden Circle, a society whose sole object is to increase and defend slavery, and the fullbloods have—not to be outdone—got up a secret organization called 'the Pins' which meets among the mountains, connecting business with Ball-playing, and this [group] is understood to be in favor of [the Lincoln] Government." [16]

The Knights of the Golden Circle and the Watie party were doing all they could to drive the northern missionaries out of the nation in the 1850s. With the assistance of proslavery federal officials, they succeeded. The Congregationalists withdrew from the nation in 1860. They had rallied behind Samuel Worcester's moderate antislavery position until he died in April 1859, but soon afterward they fell victim to the more heated struggle between their brethren in the Choctaw Nation and the American Board of Commissioners for Foreign Missions in Boston. The Congregationalists among the Choctaws, led by Cyrus Kingsbury, Cyrus Byington, and Ebenezer Hotchkins, stoutly rejected all efforts by their board to curtail their participation in slavery. In 1855 they had threatened to leave the Boston board and join the Old School Presbyterians, a proslavery group with headquarters in Philadelphia. In 1859 they were caught in an ugly scandal when one of their female church members among the Choctaws burned to death a female slave who was also a member of the same church (and the mother of eight).[17] Cyrus Kingsbury, pastor of the church, made no effort to discipline the Choctaw woman because, he said, she had acted out of irrational grief over the murder of her husband by a male slave who had later implicated the female slave in his act. That year the board voted to close its mission in the Choctaw Nation, and a year later, on September 18, 1860, it voted to close its mission in the Cherokee Nation. Abolitionists among the northern Congregationalists insisted that the board took these actions out of embarrassment for its long complicity with slavery. The board, however, insisted that it had acted because the Choctaws and Cherokees were, after fifty years of mission work, now "nominally Christian nations." [18]

The Boston board's decision to close its Cherokee mission, then consisting of four stations (at Park Hill, Fairfield, Lee's Creek, and Dwight), met the approval of Charles C. Torrey, the missionary who succeeded Worcester as mission superintendent. However, it angered two of the Congregational missionaries, Timothy Ranney and Worcester Willey. They told the board that Torrey had misrepresented the success of Christianity among the Cherokees and exaggerated the number of other missionaries and native preachers in the nation. They claimed that Torrey had also ignored the widespread paganism still remaining among the nation's full-bloods. Torrey had told the board that there were 60 licensed preachers, or 1 for every 450 persons in the nation, in the Baptist, Methodist, and Moravian missions (16 of them whites and the rest Cherokees). He had admitted that there were a few "pagans" but said most of these were inconsequential "conjurors and rainmakers" who had little influence.[19] Timothy Ranney, however, said that "many [Cherokees] are pagans and conjuring is universal."[20] His church members at Lee's Creek wrote to the board, pleading that it continue to support Ranney. "About ¾ read only Cherokee," they said, and they needed the missionaries to help them against "those who wished to trample [on] the full Cherokees and on the poor."[21] Ranney gave it as his view that "we are among a people more than half heathen." It was "a fiction," he said, to claim that the missionaries have "really christianized a pagan people. . . . If the Board should withhold their missionaries, there is no hope for them, but that the full Cherokees, constituting about ¾ of this nation, must return to their heathenish practices."[22] Worcester Willey concurred and wrote a blistering attack on the board, which appeared in the *Congregational Journal* on January 10, 1861. However, the board adhered to its policy and said it would cease all funding for its Cherokee missions by September 1861.

The proslavery Cherokees of the Watie party were delighted at the departure of the Congregationalists from the nation. They had been working for the northern missionaries' removal since 1854. In the final year of their mission, the Congregationalists continued to face hostility. Torrey wrote in October 1860 that the prejudice around Park Hill and Tahlequah against "Northern men" by "whites and halfbreeds" had become so great that "there is no point in my—or any American Board person—staying on here."[23] Torrey had been forbidden to preach in Tahlequah a few weeks before he wrote this. "A mob of disorderly men," he said, had surrounded his house and "demanded that I should come out to them." His wife, badly shaken, told the mob that her husband was not there. When he did return, he discovered that the reason for the mob was a rumor that he had criticized a Cherokee slave patrol for "cruelly whipping" two slaves they had caught in some misdeed.[24] Although he denied the charge, when he went to Tahlequah a few days later to hold his regular Thursday night service at the Masonic Temple, he was refused admission to the building. Torrey reported that the sheriff, Jesse Wolf, a Southern Methodist, had explained the reasons: "1st, that I had made invidious remarks as to the doings of a certain patrol company who had chastized two negroes at a house not far from our station; 2nd, I was in the habit of assembling negroes at my house on the sabbath for the purpose of teaching them to read and write; 3d, I was sustained by a Northern Board." Torrey denied the first two charges but admitted that privately he was "an anti-slavery man." He then met with the federal agent, Robert J. Cowart (from Georgia), who "proceeded to cathechize me" with respect to slavery. "He asked my opinion of the fugitive slave law and whether I considered myself bound to obey it." When Torrey declined to answer, the agent "threatened to remove me from the Nation." Torrey hoped that sooner or later he could persuade his congregation in Tahlequah to let him resume preaching, but he had no success. He and his family finally left the nation on February 9, 1861. Timothy Ranney left soon after, and Worcester Willey remained but not in the pay of the board.

The Northern Baptists felt the same mounting pressure in 1860. The Reverend Willard Upham, who had been a schoolteacher in one of the national public schools since 1847, reported to his board in February 1860: "We meet with intense hostility from those who fear our 'free soil influence.' Every effort is made to drive us from the country with threats of violence if we remained." [25] In the preceding year, John Buttrick Jones had told the board:

> On account of our position on the slavery question, we also have to contend with strong opposition from many of the politicians both in the Cherokee Nation and the State of Arkansas. The border papers vilify us and stigmatize us as abolitionists, and some of the slaveholders threaten us with the fist and the cowhide and expulsion from the Cherokee country. One man, who is now a member of the upper house of the National Council has said they would have us out of the Nation if they had to resort to a mob to accomplish their purpose. [26]

On April 21, 1860, Robert Cowart, who had succeeded George Butler as federal agent in March, received instructions from A. B. Greenwood, commissioner of Indian affairs (relayed through Elias B. Rector, superintendent of Indian affairs) to discover the identities of the white "counselors" of the secret "abolition" society in the Cherokee Nation and to expel them. He also ordered Cowart to investigate the Keetoowah Society and to "proceed at once to break it up." If it appeared that there might be resistance, Greenwood said the secretary of war had agreed to "place such force . . . as may be necessary at the disposal of the agent for this purpose."[27]

Cowart was successful in removing John Jones but not specifically for his part in the Keetoowah Society. Jones had unwisely given his board permission to publish in its missionary journal on May 1860 an account he had written of his persecution for promoting the cause of antislavery. After the account was reprinted in *The Arkansan* in July, a clipping was sent to Cowart along with a petition "from about five hundred of the citizens of the Cherokee Nation to remove" Jones. On September 7, Cowart sent Jones a letter giving him two weeks to leave the nation or else be forcibly seized by U.S. troops and expelled.[28] Cowart then informed Greenwood of the demand, adding, "There are a good many more that must be notified and put out before the Nation can have peace."[29]

John Jones could probably have obtained a petition signed by an even larger number of Keetoowahs opposing his removal, but he doubted that it would dissuade Cowart. He also feared that if troops were sent, there might be violence, and that if they did seize him, they would take him to the Arkansas border, where he probably would be met by a mob of whites who would treat him very roughly. He therefore took his family and, with an escort of full-bloods, made his way north to Missouri at night, ultimately finding a haven in Alton, Illinois.[30]

After his son was driven out of the Cherokee Nation by Cowart, the Reverend Evan Jones of the Northern Baptist mission expected his own expulsion. However, Cowart took no action against him, and he remained in the nation until June 1861. During the remainder of his stay, Jones reported that he had to curtail his circuit riding for fear that he would be subject to violence from the proslavery forces.[31]

In addition to driving out abolitionists, Cowart was under orders to expel from the Cherokee Neutral Lands in Kansas about 700 families of intruders who had illegally settled there. Butler had been repeatedly asked by the Cherokees to do this, beginning as early as 1857, but he had assumed that they were proslavery whites from the South, and for three years he had procrastinated. Greenwood and Rector seem to have concluded that the intruders were really free-soil or antislavery settlers from the North who were dangerous in part because of their participation in the underground railroad (to thwart the Fugitive Slave Act) and in part because they participated with James Lane, John Matthew, William Quantrill, and other border ruffians in "jayhawking" raids from Kansas into Missouri, Arkansas, and the Indian Territory. These raiders stole slaves, cattle, horses, and other items in the name of liberation or to frighten off equally rough "bushwhackers" from the slaveholding states who came to Kansas to harass free-soilers. Cowart obtained U.S. troops from Fort Smith, and in August 1860 he went to the Neutral Lands to expel these intruders.[32]

Despite his zeal to rid the Cherokee Nation of outside agitators with northern views, Cowart discovered that the task was far more difficult than he had imagined. In November 1860, he wrote to Greenwood: "I am peculiarly anxious to visit Washington. . . . The abolition party in and about the Nation are maturing their plans of operation in such a way that they cannot fail to give us troubles unless we prepare to mute them."[33] He was convinced that this would "require both the Interior and Military Departments of the Government" to act "before spring. It is the settled purpose of the antislavery part to abolitionize all this Indian Territory." When Greenwood failed to invite him to Washington, D.C., Cowart sent him a telegram in February 1861: "Want troops to protect Cherokees from threatened hostilities from above [that is, Kansas]."[34] With Lincoln's inauguration in March, Cowart left his post to return to assist his native Georgia in its rebellion. John Ross reported to federal authorities just prior to Cowart's departure that "Mr. R. J. Cowart is officiously advocating the secession policy of the Southern States and that he is endeavoring to influence the Cherokees to take sides and act in concert with the seceded states."[35]

Driving those northerners out of the nation who were identified as "abolitionists" was only one goal of the Southern Rights party. The other half of its program was to strengthen the proslavery minority by introducing more white slaveholders into the nation. In this, the Southern Rights party had the strong support of federal officials prior to Lincoln's inauguration. Many whites believed that the Indians were lacking in political skills, long-range foresight, and the kind of orderly discipline and planning needed to deal with complex problems. They were thought to be prone to ignore problems until they got out of hand. Hence, they maintained that the Cherokees needed the paternalistic guidance and direction of whites. Southern whites also doubted the leadership capabilities of the prosouthern mixed-bloods, although they were considered wiser than the full-bloods. As in the removal crisis, southern whites felt that the simple, "common" Indians were easily misled and that rich chiefs (like John Ross and his friends) duped the full-bloods in order to increase their own wealth and power.

This attitude had inspired George Butler's effort in 1856 to invite white proslavery farmers, then being harassed in Kansas, to seek refuge in the Cherokee Nation.[36] It led Commissioner A. B. Greenwood to suggest to John Ross in December 1860 that the Cherokees should let the government survey their land, divide it into small tracts, give each Cherokee family its own home-stead, and open the remainder to white settlement (since, being a slaveholding nation, it would naturally attract slaveholders).[37] It led George Butler, Robert Cowart, and Elias Rector to inform their superiors regularly from 1856 to 1861 that more military troops were needed in the Cherokee Nation.[38] The most explicit statement of whites' belief that Indians could not manage their own affairs without white help came from Douglas H. Cooper of Missis-sippi in February 1861. Cooper was the federal agent to the Choctaws and Chickasaws and an ardent proslavery secessionist who later became a Con-federate colonel heading Indian regiments. He had expressed admiration for those Congregational missionaries among the Choctaws who had opposed their board's efforts to force them (against their consciences, he believed) to take a public stand against slavery.[39] Such missionaries he considered to be a stabilizing influence on the Choctaws. Cooper wrote to the superintendent of Indian affairs, Charles W. Dean, in 1854, when the Congregational missionar-ies were under pressure from their board to adopt an aggressive stand against slavery: "If things go on as they are now doing, in five years slavery will be abolished in the whole of your superintendence." He then added a note that he marked "*Private*":

> I am convinced that something must be done speedily to arrest the sys-tematic efforts of the [northern] missionaries to abolitionize the Indian Country. Otherwise we shall have a great [slave] run-away harbor, a sort of Canada—with "underground rail-roads" leading to and through it—adjoining Arkansas and Texas. It is of no use to look to the General Gov-ernment—its arm is paralyzed by the abolition strength of the North. I see no way except secretly to induce the Choctaws and Cherokees and Creeks to allow [white] slaveholders to settle among their people and control the movement now going on to abolish slavery among them.[40]

Exactly how these slaveholding whites would "control" the abolitionists, Cooper did not say, but presumably he believed they would cooperate with the proslavery agents, send petitions to the Cherokee legislature and to Wash-ington, and, if necessary, take vigilante action.

These ideas received constant reinforcement from white politicians (as well as from newspaper editors and land, cattle, and railroad speculators) in the states surrounding the Indian Territory. It was not surprising that Blue Lodges and Knights of the Golden Circle began to filter into the Cherokee Nation after 1854. "Abolitionism," as defined by the people of Arkansas and Texas, in-cluded far more than dislike for William Lloyd Garrison's approach to eman-cipating the slaves. It was considered an alien, un-Christian, and un-American ideology opposing the southern white man's view of the good society. Indian nations had to accept this ideology and unite with the South or face a white southern invasion.

A series of letters in the *Arkansas Gazette*, published in Little Rock, entitled "Cherokee Abolitionism" began to appear in June 1860. The tone of the letters indicated that the whites on the Cherokees' eastern border were not prepared to tolerate any deviance among the Cherokees from the South's proslavery position. It also indicated the prevalent frontier expectation that whites would soon be allowed to occupy all of the Indian Territory. The danger of abolitionism, wrote the author (who signed himself "Q" and lived in Fayetteville, near the Cherokee border), "can be met and crushed out with proper effort . . . on the part of the South. . . . A few years ago Mr. Johnson introduced a bill in the U.S. Senate for the formation of new territories of the Nation's west. . . . The full-bloods . . . manifested the greatest opposition" to the bill and were also cool toward slavery. "The Southern people, including the pro-slavery portion of the Cherokees, can hardly tolerate the large convenient outlet now in process of opening for the escape of slaves. . . . The present state of affairs in the country requires the interposition of the South" in Indian affairs. "There is nothing necessary but a readiness for occupancy and immediate settlement . . . of the [Indian] country. Necessity awards that country to our people."[41] The author went on to say that "a Southern organization is needed . . . to counteract the designs of the abolitionists and give abiding security to all identified with the Peculiar Institution."[42] The object of this organization "should be to counteract any decline in Southern feeling" among the Cherokees and other tribes.[43]

The election of Abraham Lincoln in November 1860 on a platform of containing slavery within its present boundaries (with the implicit hope that this would soon stifle and extinguish it) convinced the majority of white southerners that separate nationhood was the only way to sustain their way of life and the ideology they had constructed to sanctify it. As a southern Whig, John Ross had probably hoped for the election of John Bell on the Union party ticket, but he must have known that this was unlikely. The people of the United States, he had said in May 1860, "should choose some great and good conservative Patriotic Man . . . under the banner of the Union and the Constitution."[44] After the election, he expressed no opinion that has survived, yet concerning a choice between North and South, those who knew him best were convinced that he would choose the North. The South, a section tied to the Democratic party (the party of Andrew Jackson and Indian removal), continued to represent to him the spirit of majority tyranny and anti-Indian prejudice. On the other hand, William Seward, when campaigning for Lincoln in the fall of 1860, said in a widely quoted speech in Chicago: "The Indian territory, also, south of Kansas, must be vacated by the Indians."[45] Ross could hardly embrace a party with such views.

Arkansas, the most immediate neighbor of the Cherokees, had voted for the Breckenridge wing of the Democratic party, and its governor, Henry M. Rector (brother of Elias Rector), was ardent in the proslavery cause. The state rejected secession in December but then accepted it on May 6, 1861. Typical of the more ardent proslavery whites in Arkansas who worked closely with Stand Watie's party was J. Woodward Washbourne, the wayward son of a Congregational missionary. He kept Watie informed of political affairs in Arkansas and wrote to him in May that Lincoln, according to rumor, had appointed "Jim Lane, the notorious Abolitionist, robber, murderer and rascal," as commissioner of Indian affairs to replace A. B. Greenwood.[46] This appointment, he said, "portends" the "subjugation of the Cherokee to the rule of Abolition . . . to enslave the Cherokees." Later, when Washbourne discovered that William G. Coffin had been appointed, not Lane, he denounced him too as "a Black Republican" who would be just as bad.[47]

The people of Arkansas felt particularly threatened. They believed that the Indians to their west could mount at least 25,000 "warriors" if they banded together. Some Arkansans had declined to support secession until they were sure which side the Indians, particularly the Cherokees on their immediate border, would choose. During the early months of 1861, John Ross was besieged with inquiries about the political stance of the Cherokees from officials in Arkansas, Texas, and the Confederate government. He tried desperately to steer a course that irritated neither the North nor the South.

Ross had spent many months in Washington with a Cherokee delegation during the spring and summer of 1860. He had endeavored to clarify the legal jurisdiction of the federal court in Arkansas, to assert the right of the Cherokees to tax white traders, to force more prompt payment of Cherokee annuities, and to sell the Neutral Lands—all issues that had been debated for years.[48] When he addressed the National Council in October 4, 1860, he had to admit failure on all of these matters; the United States was too preoccupied with the sectional division over slavery to consider the Cherokees' problems. Ross addressed the slavery question in this message, but he handled it gingerly. "It is a cause of deep regret that the subject of slavery has become paramount to all other considerations in the opposite sections of the United States. . . . Slavery has existed among the Cherokees for many years, is recognized by them as legal, and they have no wish or purpose to disturb it. . . . Agitation in regard to it of any kind can be productive of good to no one. We should discountenance everything of the sort."[49] In order to reassure the frontier whites, he stated: "Our locality and institutions ally us to the South." To balance this, he added: "To the North we are indebted for a defence of our rights in the past and that enlarged benevolence to which we owe chiefly our progress in civilization. Our political relations are with the Government of the United States," because of their treaties. "Our duty is to stand by our right, allow no interference in our internal affairs from any source, comply with all our engagements, and rely upon Union for justice and protection." By "Union" he may have meant both the unity of the United States and the unity of the Cherokee Nation.

Commissioner A. B. Greenwood, in his annual report on Indian affairs to President James Buchanan on November 30, 1860, had stressed the acute divisions among the Cherokees. "Much excitement is reported to exist among the Cherokees and during the past year many murders and other crimes and outrages have been perpetrated. A secret organization has been formed by the full-blood members of the Tribe and the cause of the present existing difficulties is attributable, it is alleged, to the missionaries among them who are charged with interfering with the institution of slavery among the Cherokee Nation." Greenwood went on to suggest "the importance of establishing a military post within the near limits of Cherokee Country [for] . . . the enforcement of law and order in the limits of that country." Because Cherokee law recognized slavery, law enforcement meant the suppression of antislavery agitation.[50]

Ross's position in the months between Lincoln's election in November and his inauguration in March 1861 seems to have been to adhere to his nation's treaty obligations and to hope that the Cherokees would be left to pursue their own internal affairs without being drawn into the conflict. The income of the nation was, after all, provided from trust funds administered by the federal government, and that government was committed to protecting the Cherokees from outside intervention as long as they fulfilled their treaty obligations. Presumably he expected that Lincoln would not interfere with slavery within the Indian Territory, hence the Indian nations should be allowed to remain in peace as long as they took no part in any political intrigue or military action on either side of the sectional division. His major concern was to assure his white neighbors in the proslavery states that the Cherokees would never act against their interests. He leaned over backward, therefore, to display friendship for the South while refusing to break his nation's ties with the federal government. Like most white Americans, he had no expectation of a long and bloody civil war.

On January 25, 1861, J. S. Dunham, editor of the *Arkansas Gazette*, wrote an editorial asking rhetorically where the Cherokees stood on the question of secession. "In the event that Arkansas secedes from the Union, a war on her Western frontier is inevitable. That Abolition enemies of the South will hiss the Indians upon her . . . for the indulgence of their hellish passions" seemed obvious. The people of Arkansas "must look to Tennessee, Kentucky and Missouri" for protection from "devastation by savages" and their northern allies. Recent border raids from Kansas upon Missouri and Arkansas had put the state on edge, although no Indians were involved in the raids.

John Ross felt obliged to take issue with Dunham's stereotype of the Indian lest the editorial be a precursor to white invasion in the name of self-defense: "However savage and uncivilized they may be in the opinion of gentlemen of the press abroad, the fact cannot be denied that they have important interests at stake in the issue of the present crisis. . . . Their first wish is for peace and protection by the General Government. . . . But if ambition, passion, and prejudice blindly and wickedly destroy it—with a fair guarantee of their rights, they will go where their institutions and the geographical position place them,—with Arkansas and Missouri." [51] As for being like dogs who reacted to whistles and hisses, Ross said angrily, "We are not dogs to be hissed on by abolitionists." [52] Ross had hoped that the other Indian nations would adopt a similar position of neutrality and remain calm. They should be friendly to both North and South while honoring treaty obligations to the government of the United States. He was disturbed when he learned that the Chickasaws, Choctaws, and Creeks decided on January 5 to call a convention in the Creek Nation and invited him to attend. These three nations were dominated by their mixed-blood, proslavery leaders, and Ross suspected that they would assume a prosouthern position. He agreed to send a delegation headed by his nephew, W. P. Ross, but he instructed them to oppose making any commitment to either side. [53] "Guard against any premature movement on our part," he said; "should any action of the Council be thought desirable, a resolution might be adopted to the effect that we will in all contingencies rest our interest on the pledged faith of the United States."

On January 29, two weeks before this Indian convention, Ross received a letter from Governor Rector of Arkansas, delivered to him at Park Hill by Lieutenant Colonel J. J. Gaines, Rector's aide-de-camp. Rector wished to know where the Cherokees stood. "Your people, in their institutions, productions and natural sympathies are allied to the common brotherhood of the slaveholding states. Our people and yours are natural allies in war." He reminded Ross that "the incoming administration of Mr. Lincoln" was looking at the Indian Territory "as fruitful fields, ripe for the harvest of abolitionism, freesoilers, and Northern mountebanks." He therefore hoped that the Cherokees were "willing to cooperate with the South in defense of her institutions" and asked Ross to confer "confidentially upon these subjects" with Gaines.[54]

Ross had no intention of entering into secret negotiations leading to a national alliance with the South. "The Cherokees," he said, "cannot but feel with deep regret and solicitude for the unhappy differences which at present disturbs [sic] the peace and quietude of the several States," but they "have placed themselves under the protection of the United States and of no other Sovereign whatever." Therefore they could enter into no alliance with any "foreign power or with any individual States." They were "inviolably allied with their white Brethren of the United States." However, he assured the governor that he was correct in one important respect about the Cherokees: "Their institutions, locality and natural sympathies are unequivocally with the slave holding States."[55]

The nine states of the Deep South that seceded from the Union met in Montgomery, Alabama, on February 8, 1861, and declared themselves united into a new nation, the Confederate States of America. A week later, John B. Ogden, commissioner of the federal circuit court in Van Buren, who still felt bound to the federal government by reason of his position, wrote to Ross saying that he had heard that "commissioners are now visiting the Indian nation on our frontier—preparatory to forming an alliance to furnish them with arms and munitions of war." Therefore, "in discharge of my duty," he inquired whether any such actions were being undertaken, reminding Ross that they would be "in violation of subsisting treaties and the laws of the United States." Ogden had evidently learned of the efforts of J. J. Gaines to enter into "confidential talks" with the Indian nations.[56] He described Gaines as "the late editor of a secession sheet in Little Rock." After leaving the Cherokee Nation, Gaines had gone to visit the other Indian nations in the territory and then attended the general Indian council in the Creek Nation on February 17, to which Ross had sent delegates. While there, Gaines "announced to the Council his mission to be that of a Commissioner from Arkansas accredited by the Governor to consult with them in relation to cooperation with the seceding States," even though Arkansas itself had not yet seceded.[57] In his reply to Ogden, Ross did not mention Gaines, but he did tell Ogden that he thought federal agent Robert J. Cowart had been trying to stir up trouble in the Cherokee Nation and should be removed.[58] After receiving Ross's reply, Ogden wrote to Jacob Thompson, the secretary of the interior, confirming Ross's view that Cowart was an agent of "disunion" in Arkansas as well as among the Cherokees. Ogden may not then have realized that Thompson was himself prosouthern and ready to support secession; Thompson was well aware of Cowart's proslavery activities.[59]

The state of Texas joined the Confederacy on February 1, and on February 27, it commissioned three men, led by James J. Harrison, to visit the Indian nations to persuade them to do the same. These commissioners appeared at a council of the Choctaws and Chickasaws and, after discussion, said they found these tribes to be "entirely Southern" in their views and willing to provide troops for the South.[60] They visited the Cherokees in March, and, according to their report, they "were received with courtesy but not with cordiality." They had a long conference with Ross but "without, we fear, any good result. He was very diplomatic and cautious. His position is the same as that held by Mr. Lincoln in his inaugural; declares the Union not dissolved; ignores the Southern Government." Sizing up public opinion among the Cherokees generally, the Texans concluded: "The intelligence of the nation is not with him," meaning the educated, English-speaking slaveholders. They noted in Ross's favor, however, that "he frequently avowed his sympathy for the South" and said that "if Virginia and the other Border States seceded . . . his people would declare for the Southern Government." They recognized Ross's difficulty: "The fact is . . . that among the common Indians of the Cherokees there exists a considerable abolition influence created and sustained by one Jones, a Northern missionary of education and ability, who has been among them for many years and who is said to exert no small influence with John Ross himself."[61] After seeing Ross, the Texans went on to visit the Creeks, whom they found "Southern and sound to a man," a gross misestimate as it turned out.[62]

When Arkansas voted for secession and union with the Confederacy on May 8, 1861, the secretary of their convention was Elias Cornelius Boudinot. The son of the Treaty party leader murdered in 1839, Boudinot had lived in Arkansas ever since. His selection for the post was obviously a bid by the Arkansans for Cherokee support, but his appeal only extended to the Watie faction. The vast majority of Cherokees had always considered him a traitor like his father. He in turn nursed such bitter hatred toward the Ross party that he devoted his life to destroying the Cherokee Nation.

The day after the vote, a group of citizens of the frontier community of Boonesborough, Arkansas, led by Mark Bean, addressed a letter to Ross stating that they had "a right to know what position will be taken" by the Cherokees—"whether you will cooperate with the Northern or Southern section. . . . We prefer an open enemy to a doubtful friend."[63] Ross gave Bean the same equivocal answer he had given to Governor Rector and the Texans: "The Cherokees are your friends and the friends of your people, but we do not wish to be brought into the feuds between yourselves and your Northern Brethren. Our wish is for peace." As yet, the United States had not declared war, nor had the Confederate States. "Your difficulties may be ended soon by compromise or peaceful separation." The best answer Ross could give was that "the Cherokee Nation will not interfere with your rights nor invade your soil," and he hoped the same would be true of the people of Arkansas.[64]

Such equivocal answers were not acceptable, and on May 15, Ross received a letter from Captain J. P. Kanady at Fort Smith, Arkansas, formerly a federal garrison but now in the possession of the Confederacy. Kanady informed him that Senator James H. Lane of Kansas was preparing to raise troops to enter the states of Missouri and Arkansas on behalf of the United States. He demanded to know whether the Cherokees "mean to support the government of the Southern confederacy" in resisting such an invasion.[65] Responding on May 17, Ross reiterated his continued obligation to obey treaties with the United States but said the Cherokees wished to "take no part in the present deplorable state of affairs." He hoped "they should not be called upon to participate in the threatened fratricidal war. . . . We do not wish our soil to become the battle ground between the states."

On the same day he wrote this letter, Ross issued a formal declaration of Cherokee neutrality. In it, he urged his people to continue "in their ordinary vocations" and to abstain "from partisan demonstrations" on either side. They must "cultivate harmony among themselves and observe, in good faith, strict neutrality." [66] In some respects, Ross's declaration of neutrality appeared to be a shift in his position, for clearly he had never cut his ties with the North. However, to him, the measure was a tactical emphasis on his commitment not to take part in any hostile actions against the South. He was also serving notice to the Southern Rights party, led by Watie and his friends, that he would not tolerate their making any secret agreements with the South.

Two days before this, on May 15, 1861, the Confederate Congress in secret session had passed an act establishing its authority over the Indian Territory, obligating itself to pay all annuities and other claims due the Indian tribes within it, and establishing a commissioner to travel among the Indians to raise troops for the Confederacy.[67] A few days later, Albert Pike, an attorney (and Mexican War veteran) from Van Buren, Arkansas, who was well acquainted with the Indians, was appointed special commissioner for the Confederacy to negotiate treaties with all the western tribes. David Hubbard was appointed superintendent of Indian affairs for the Confederacy, and General Ben McCulloch was given command of the Indian Territory west of Arkansas, with headquarters at Fort Smith. He was instructed to raise two regiments of Indian troops and three regiments of white troops as soon as possible to protect Missouri, Arkansas, and the Indian Territory.

Pike and McCulloch traveled to Fort Smith, and just prior to their departure for the Cherokee Nation on May 23, they were approached by "some five or six Cherokees . . . representing those of the Cherokees who sympathized with the South." These "Southern Cherokees," as they preferred thereafter to be called, probably included E. Cornelius Boudinot, Stand Watie, John Bell, and William Penn Adair. Since they were members of a nation whose declared policy was neutrality, their visit to Pike and McCulloch was clearly leaning toward treason. They came to Pike and McCulloch "in order to ascertain whether the Confederate States would protect them against Mr. Ross and the Pin Indians if they should organize and take up arms for the South." [68] Pike and McCulloch assured them that "they should be protected." At Pike and McCulloch's suggestion, they sent letters to five or six prominent members of the Southern Rights party to bring them into the conspiracy. They were invited to meet Pike at the Creek agency two days after the meeting scheduled with John Ross on June 5. If Ross refused to treat with the commissioners of the Confederacy, then, Pike wrote, "my intention was to treat with the heads of the Southern party, Stand Watie and others." He intended to ask them to break the policy of neutrality and raise troops to fight for the Confederacy. The Southern Rights party never had any intention of being neutral in the controversy. They had no respect for the authority of John Ross, and they were determined to use the war and their alliance with the Confederacy as a means to unseat him.

Pike and McCulloch's meeting with Ross proved unsuccessful, even though Pike offered to make a very generous treaty and even to buy from the nation the Neutral Lands that Ross had been trying to sell for so many years and to which the South would probably never have a claim. Pike reported that Ross "refused to enter into any arrangement with the Confederacy." Like the Texans before him, Pike discovered that the full-bloods were strongly behind Ross's policy of neutrality and that the Joneses had organized them into a secret society to combat the proslavery faction. Pike reported that after he left the Cherokee Nation, "We learned that some attempts to raise a Secession flag in the Cherokee Country on the Arkansas border had been frustrated by the menace of violence" from the Pins. The Southern Rights party had told Pike that the Pins were "a Secret Society, established by Evan Jones, a Missionary at the service of Mr. John Ross, for the purpose of abolitionizing the Cherokees and putting out of the way all who sympathized with the Southern States." However, when Pike checked into this, he learned "with certainty, [that] the Secret Organization . . . was established for the purpose of depriving the half-breeds of all political power . . . and it was organized and in *full* operation long before Secession was thought of"; it was not a movement organized to promote abolition and oppose those favoring the Confederacy.[69]

In order to avoid appearing hostile to the Confederacy, Ross told Pike and

McCulloch (or so they reported) that "all his interests and all his feelings were with us and he knew that his people must share the fate and fortunes of Arkansas." Pike and McCulloch told Ross frankly that "the Cherokees could not be neutral"; it was too late for that. McCulloch did promise to respect Cherokee neutrality to the extent that he would not invade the nation with the troops he was raising unless "it should become necessary . . . to expel a Federal force or to protect the Southern Cherokees." There was, however, little respect for neutrality in these statements. The commissioners in effect had destroyed Ross's neutrality by secretly agreeing to defend his opponents against him. Ross must have realized that negotiations to arm the Southern Rights party were about to take place. His efforts to adhere to his treaty obligations with the United States were being undermined by the Watie party's determination to make its own bargain with the Confederacy. When Pike left Ross on June 6, 1861, he told him that by his refusal to abandon neutrality, he had lost his chance for a treaty with the Confederacy and that the offer he had made to purchase the Neutral Lands was withdrawn. Ross's only power now lay with the Pins. The Southern Rights party did not show up at the meeting they had plotted with Pike, later explaining that they did not come because they feared for their lives if the Pins discovered the treasonous actions they were plotting.

David Hubbard as Confederate superintendent of Indian affairs sent Ross a letter on June 12 stating his confidence in a southern victory and noting what Ross had to lose if the South did not win. "First, your slaves they will take from you," then they would "settle their squatters" or free-soil homesteaders in the nation; they would allocate small plots to Indian families but "totally destroy the power of your chiefs and your nationality." Ross had only to look at the miserable confusion of the northern tribes to see what lay in store. Hubbard reminded Ross that virtually all of the trust funds upon which the Cherokee annuities rested were invested in the bonds of the southern states, and they would be worthless if the North won.[70]

Ross responded several days later, saying that he had no "cause to make war against the United States or to believe that our Treaties will not be fulfilled and respected." As for the way the North had treated Indians, Ross reminded Hubbard that it had been the southern states that had unilaterally dispossessed them in the 1830s and driven them from their land. "Few Indians now press their feet upon the banks of either the Ohio or the Tennessee."[71] He claimed that there was still hope for some compromise and reconciliation between North and South. "If you remain as one Government our relations will continue unchanged. If you separate into two Governments upon the sectional line, we will be connected with you," he wrote, apparently meaning that if Lincoln allowed a peaceful separation, the Cherokees might work out some realignment.

McCulloch wrote to Ross shortly after their talk on June 5, requesting that Watie and those Cherokees who wished to serve as volunteers in the Confederate army should be permitted to do so. Ross replied firmly on June 17 that such a course was improper and dangerous. "Your demand that those people of the nation who are in favor of joining the Confederacy be allowed to organize into military companies as home guards for the purpose of defending themselves in case of invasion from the North is most respectfully declined. I cannot give my consent to any such organization. . . . It would be a palpable violation of my position as a neutral" and "it will place in our midst organized companies not authorized by our laws who would soon become efficient instruments in stirring up domestic strife and creating internal difficulties among the Cherokee people."[72] He clearly foresaw clashes between such companies and the Pins, which would enable the Watie faction to call upon the promised protection of the Confederacy. That would bring white armies into the nation, and Ross would be a captive in his own country.

When General McCulloch ignored this protest and commissioned Stand Watie as a colonel in the army of the Confederacy in July 1861, then issued arms to over 300 Cherokees who enlisted with Watie, Ross realized that he had all but lost control of the situation. With Watie's supporters not only armed but under the protection of the Confederate troops at Fort Smith, the possibility of a coup d'état, which would displace him from power, became very real. Only the Pins stood between him and deposition. If President Lincoln did not send help soon, Ross knew he would have to rethink his whole strategy. National unity was now perilously fragile.

7

The Cherokees Abandon Neutrality for Unity, 1861

The permanent disruption of the United States into two governments is now probable.

—*Chief John Ross, 1861*

The narrow edge of neutrality along which Ross walked for seven months in 1861 became even sharper when all of the other major Indian nations in the Indian Territory signed treaties of alliance with the Confederacy. The Creeks signed such a treaty on July 10, the Choctaws and Chickasaws on July 12, and the Seminoles on August 1.[1] Only the Cherokees of all the major tribes now remained on the fence. The other four nations had been strongly prosouthern from the outset of the crisis. All were governed by mixed-blood slaveholders and had strong majorities in favor of repudiating their treaties with the United States. Nonetheless, there were strong full-blood factions within them—especially among the Creeks and Seminoles—who regretted this realignment and continued to support either neutrality or loyalty to the United States. Only among the Cherokees were the opponents of an alliance with the Confederacy in a large majority and also in control of the council, but their position was now tenuous.

The efforts of the Watie faction to obtain an alliance with the Confederacy had been obvious from the beginning, and the Confederate government was eager to reciprocate. As early as May 13, 1861, Leroy P. Walker, secretary of war for the Confederacy, had written to Douglas Cooper (by then a major in the Confederate army), authorizing him to raise regiments among the Choctaws and Chickasaws and stating confidentially that "it is designed also to raise two other similar Regiments among the Creeks, Cherokees and Seminoles, and other friendly tribes for the same purposes."[2] On May 18, a group of secessionist citizens in Fayetteville, Arkansas, led by J. W. Washbourne, wrote to Stand Watie: "We are happy to inform you in accordance with our promise of said letter [from Walker], that we would afford you all the aid we could, that a certain number of guns, good guns, have been granted to the State of Arkansas [by the Confederacy] for the use of the Cherokees in the defense of their and our frontier. So push on the good work and train your men and apply for these guns."[3] Washbourne also reported that Jefferson Davis, president of the Confederacy, "is determined to arm the Cherokees, Creeks and Choctaws." However, he urged that "the [Southern] Cherokees ought to be silent in their preparations" so that they could "ambush" any troops from Kansas that thought they could march unimpeded into the Cherokee Nation. It is not clear exactly when Watie did obtain guns, but Evan Jones reported that Watie had 300 armed men under his command in the late spring of 1861. Watie was commissioned a colonel by the Confederacy on July 12, 1861. Soon after, his regiment was actively engaged in border raids into Kansas from the Cherokee Nation.[4]

While the southern pressure upon Ross to abandon neutrality mounted, he received no official support from Washington, D.C. Realizing that time was running out, he finally sent his trusted old friend, the Reverend Evan Jones, to Kansas in June 1861 to try to find out when Lincoln was planning to come to his assistance.[5] Although Ross well knew that under President Buchanan the secretary of the interior and the entire personnel of the Bureau of Indian Affairs were proslavery and prosouthern, he was appalled that the agent whom Lincoln chose to replace Cowart, a man named John Crawford, was also an ardent secessionist. Crawford arrived on April 21. He did nothing to assist Ross, but he did all he could to aid the Watie party. Although he officially resigned on June 15, Crawford remained in the nation for another two months, consorting with the Watie faction and the Arkansas secessionists.[6] In his letter of resignation to Lincoln's commissioner of Indian affairs, William P. Dole, Crawford said that he had accepted the post only because he thought "the Cherokee Indians was Southern in their feelings and did not wish a Northern man sent among them" but that after two months, he found he could not continue to act "under the administration of A. Lincoln."[7]

During the period from January to April, every federal military garrison in the Indian Territory was withdrawn, leaving no source of federal authority to fulfill the treaty obligation of the United States to protect the Cherokees from foreign intervention.[8] Lincoln and his cabinet were too busy dealing with the secession crisis after March to take much interest in the Indians. Lincoln appointed William P. Dole to replace Greenwood as commissioner in April and William G. Coffin to replace Elias Rector as superintendent. Although both were eager to keep the Indians in the Union, they had to wait until May 15 to obtain a proclamation from Lincoln that the federal government intended to honor all its treaty obligations and to do all it could to protect the Indians against Confederate aggression.[9] Coffin planned to take this to the chiefs himself, but due to illness, he did not reach Kansas until the end of June. He then started to the Cherokee Nation but became fearful for his safety (probably because of Watie's border raids). When his illness recurred, he stopped at Blue Eye Shotoes in the Neutral Lands and sent Ross a letter on June 22, which did not reach him until July 27. Meanwhile, Evan Jones, who had moved to Lawrence, Kansas, met with Dole and Coffin on Ross's behalf, but he too was unable to get messages through to Park Hill.

Coffin's letter, as paraphrased by Ross, said "that he intended coming down to this place but learning it would not be altogether safe for him and that it might be embarrassing in the present unfortunate difficulties of the Country— and he being 'really too unwell to travel,' " he had determined to return northward. He "would be gratified if I could go up there to see him with Mr. John Crawford, the Agent, to confer with him as to the money due the Cherokees and other matters—that he had all along intended to stop at this place" and would do so "as soon as it can be done safely." [10] This statement could only have confirmed Ross's worst fears since Coffin did not even realize that Agent Crawford was an ardent secessionist. Coffin thought that it might be embarrassing to Ross to receive Lincoln's new superintendent, but he did not appear to consider how embarrassing it would have been for Ross to leave his nation and travel to Kansas for a meeting. Coffin said he had "other matters" to discuss with Ross, which most likely involved the Cherokees' commitments to the Union. However, there was no evidence that the federal government had sufficient troops to assist the Indians. If it had, why would Coffin have feared to enter the Cherokee Nation? Coffin's fears were obvious signs of federal weakness, and the worst news of all was that Coffin would not be delivering the Cherokee annuity for 1861 that the deeply indebted Cherokees needed in order to manage their affairs. If Ross had gone to Kansas to meet with Coffin, then Watie and the Southern Rights party would certainly have seized the opportunity to take control of the nation. There was nothing to stop Watie and his Confederate soldiers from taking control of the nation, unless the Pins or the members of the Keetoowah Society took arms against him and started a war of Cherokee against Cherokee.

Ross's situation was so weak, so exposed, and so tenuous that he decided not to visit Coffin. Instead, he called an emergency meeting of his Executive Committee for July 31. "The object of the meeting," he told Joseph Vann, the second principal chief, "was to take into consideration the request of numerous citizens that a general meeting of the Cherokee people should be held for the purpose of harmonizing their views in support of the common good." This probably indicated that the Pin leaders on the one hand and the Ross moderates on the other were worried over the growing strength of the Watie party and Ross's inability to maintain control. Ross gave as a second reason for calling the meeting his desire "to remove false allegations as to the opinions of the 'full blood' Cherokees on the subject of slavery and of their sentiments towards white and 'half breed' citizens." [11]

The Southern Rights party was not the only group stirring up trouble in the nation at this time. As the Cherokees drifted toward war, the Pins were willing to use threats to try to intimidate those who sympathized with the Watie party. James G. Slover, a Southern Baptist missionary who worked among both the Cherokees and the Creeks, wrote from Tahlequah on June 26, 1861:

I think [Evan] Jones and party have learned that it would be dear blood for them to shed mine. My brother, help me praise God for the preservation of my life. . . . The Native minister, an inoffensive and pious man was murdered—called out of his own house at night and shot; he ran—they followed and cut his throat. The cause is hard to ascertain. Three rumors here. 1st, Because he would not leave the Southern Baptist Church and go back to the Northern, of which he once was a member. 2nd, Because he had withdrawn from a secret organization known here by the term "Pins," he refusing to unite again; 3rd, Because of his money of which everybody that knew him knew that he did not have a *red* cent. The first seems to be the most plausable [*sic*], for another Cherokee minister similarly situated (except he is not a Pin) has been waylayed but escaped, others have been threatened that if they preached in certain quarters that they would be killed, this is the game they (Jones party) have been playing for the last three years. If we are not mistaken, every man in Jones churches is more or less tinctured with abolition sentiments, and some of them, yea a large majority, are *deep* black in the warp and *sable* African in the filling, for I heard one of his preachers say "if Abraham David and all the ancient worthies of the O. T. being slave holders were here on earth, he could not fellowship them[.]" Now would you not think such a man as this was an abolitionist of the deepest die? The strong hold of these is in the Southern part of the Nation, some squads on Lee's Creek, and in Flint District south of the latter place.

In writing this letter to his colleague, the Reverend E. L. Compere, who was worried about entering the Cherokee Nation because he feared the Pins, Slover advised:

On the South of Arkansas River, they are all right side up and out for the South, you need not fear any danger from Fort Smith up the River to Webber's Falls and South to Canadian River. At some points you could preach without an interpreter, others it would be better to have one, in fact out from the river toward the Canadian they are all full bloods. . . . Our interest is quite weak, however at Webber's Falls there are a few Baptists mostly colored. Brother Vore is a noted and worthy Brother. . . . P.S. If you say anything about the contents of this letter, keep my name secret." [12]

The danger of violence between the Ross party and the Watie party was hardly new, but it gained importance after an incident at Webber's Falls in June 1861. Although knowledge of the event was widespread, the details are unclear. A group of Southern Rights activists decided to raise a Confederate flag in the small village of Webber's Falls, formerly a center of the Old Settlers, now a center of proslavery sentiment and the Watie party. Word of the plan got out, and the Pins decided to prevent the raising of the flag. They were officially defending the nation's policy of neutrality and expressing their support for Ross, but at the same time they probably wanted to demonstrate to the mixed-bloods that they would not tolerate any effort to push the nation into an alliance with southern whites. Each side, tense over their constant maneuvering, seemed ready to test its relative strength. Fortunately the potential for violence was defused, and the two groups dispersed without any result except that the Confederate flag was not raised. John Drew, a mixed-blood slaveholder who was at this time loyal to Ross and the moderate position of neutrality, wrote to Ross and Joseph Vann about the incident, urging that something must be done to prevent such flare-ups from dividing the nation into hostile camps. They wrote back on July 2: "We regret very much indeed to hear that difficulties of a serious character exist in your neighborhood between some of the half and fullblood Cherokees . . . particularly so at the present time when surrounded by the Commotions that exist among the People of the States. . . . There is no reason why we should split up and become involved in internal strife and violence on account of the political condition of the States. We should really have nothing to do with them." [13] They asked Drew to "impress upon your neighbors the importance of harmony and good feeling." Drew formed a local committee to discuss the subject, and several weeks later they came to Tahlequah to talk with Ross. On July 28, Ross wrote Vann: "They reported that the misunderstandings among some of the citizens in the vicinity of Webbers Falls have been peaceably and satisfactorily adjusted." [14] However, they must also have informed Ross that the situation was still volatile.

Ross also informed Vann of the contents of the letter he had just received from Coffin. He then said he felt it important to call a meeting of the Executive Committee, which consisted of Ross, Joseph Vann, James Brown, John Drew, and W. P. Ross. They discussed the division within the nation over the policy of neutrality. Unable to resolve the issues among themselves, the Executive Committee agreed to call a general council, to which all members of the nation were invited. The ostensible purpose of this council was to resolve the tense situation between "the 'full blood' Cherokees" and "the White and 'half breed' citizens" over "the subject of slavery" and to seek "the common good." [15] The committee said that the council was being convened at "the request of numerous citizens." Presumably it was hoped that some consensus might emerge. No more detailed agenda was provided, but when the people gathered for the council on August 20, they heard an address from Ross that seemed to indicate a sharp reversal of national policy.

Apparently, at some time between July 31 and August 20, Ross and his Executive Committee had decided to abandon the policy of neutrality. Because no explicit reason was ever given for this shift (other than "the common good"), the answer has to be found in the various events of that period. The incident at Webber's Falls, the growth of Watie's regiment, the absence of support from Washington, the disappointing letter from Coffin, and the apparent military weakness of the Union all contributed to push the nation toward an alliance with the Confederacy. The battle of Bull Run in Virginia on July 10 demonstrated how woefully unprepared the federal army was for war. Then on August 10, 1861, the first effort of the federal forces in Kansas to invade Missouri and Arkansas (offering support to loyal Indians in the territory) failed miserably. General John C. Frémont and General Franz Sigel conducted the expedition, but it met sharp defeat at the hands of General Ben McCulloch and General Sterling Price at the battle of Wilson's Creek (also called Oak Hills or Oak Ridge) in southwestern Missouri. The federal army withdrew, and there was no indication when it might return. [16]

To make matters more difficult for Ross, Stand Watie's Cherokee soldiers participated very effectively in the Missouri engagement and received high praise from the Arkansas newspapers. Though Watie himself was not present, he and his men became heroes to those Cherokees who admired a courageous warrior.[17] As Watie's star rose, Ross's waned. The influence of the old chief was being eroded by events over which he had no control. Soon it would become known that no annuities would be received that year from the federal government. Hitherto Ross and his closest advisers seem to have thought the war would be of short duration; now it looked as though it would either lead to a quick Confederate victory or a very prolonged struggle.

Accounts of the general council held at Tahlequah on August 20–21 differ markedly. Ross's account states that 4,000 male citizens attended, but W. S. Robertson, a Presbyterian missionary from the Creek Nation who happened to be present, said there were only 1,800 present.[18] Evan Jones reported that some of Watie's officers attended, bringing with them 70 to 80 of their soldiers "with the intention to break up the meeting."[19] Ross reported that the meeting was characterized by "good order and propriety . . . and of marked unanimity." Most accounts held that this unanimity sanctioned a critical change of policy from one of neutrality to one of support for the Confederacy, but W. S. Robertson said that the vast majority of those present left under the assumption that they had voted to sustain the policy of neutrality.[20] Some accounts also assert that the meeting was a victory for the Southern Rights party. Yet the statements by leading members of that party indicate that they considered it a terrible defeat, for it left Ross, not Watie, in charge of national affairs. Watie himself was not present at the council.[21] Ross shrewdly saw the council as a means to thwart Watie and promote national unity.

Ross opened the second day of the council on August 21 with an address noting the increasing fierceness of the war between the states and the "peculiar" position of the Cherokees who wished to be friendly with both sides. He said that although the nation had agreed on a policy of neutrality, "alarming reports" had been circulating at home and abroad that the nation was deeply divided. "The object" of these reports "seems to be to create strife and conflict instead of harmony and good will" among the Cherokees and "to engender prejudice and distrust" among "the Officers and citizens of the Confederate States." The purpose of this council, he continued, was to quiet these reports and demonstrate "the harmony of the People." This council must disprove the rumor that "the people . . . are arrayed in classes one against the other— the full-blood against the white and mixed blood citizens." They must speak with one voice as to "whether you abide by all the rights" guaranteed in the laws and constitution, "particularly including that of slavery and whether you have any wish to abolish or interfere with it in the Cherokee Nation?"[22] Ross was not asking for a referendum on slavery but on loyalty to the nation's laws and constitution. "The great object with me has been to have the Cherokee People harmonious and united in the full and free exercise and enjoyment of all their rights of person and property. Union is strength; dissension is weakness, misery, ruin. In time of peace, together! In time of war, if war comes, fight together. As Brothers live; as Brothers die!" Ross believed that his stance was consistent. The important thing was unity: Cherokees must not fight Cherokees; Indians must not fight Indians. Continued national independence (whether under the United States or under the Confederacy) required the submerging of class, ethnic, and social differences and the burying of the slavery issue. The preservation of Cherokee sovereignty required this. "When your nationality ceases here, it will live nowhere else. When these homes are lost, you will find no others like them." It was necessary to be "prudent," not excitable. "The preservation of our rights and our existence are above every other consideration."

Ross then pointed out that the situation around the nation had changed greatly since he had first argued for neutrality. "The permanent disruption of the United States into two governments is now probable. The State on our border [that is, Arkansas] and the Indian Nations about us have severed their connection from the United States. Our general interest is inseparable from theirs, and it is not desirable we should stand alone." In short, Ross said, to survive as a people, the Cherokees must side with their neighbors and not wait any longer for distant and perhaps futile help. "I say to you frankly, that in my opinion, the time has now arrived when you should signify your consent for the authorization of the Nation to adopt preliminary steps for an alliance with the Confederate States upon terms honorable and advantageous to the Cherokee Nation."

To the Pins and other Ross supporters who heard this message, it conveyed three major points. First, it expressed loyalty to the Keetoowah spirit of national preservation, which required unity of the nation regardless of which side had to be taken in the white man's war. Second, the question of slavery must be secondary; if John Ross believed they had more to gain by uniting with their southern neighbors, loyalty to the chief required loyalty to his advice. Third, loyalty to Ross would reaffirm their opposition to the Watie faction and strengthen Ross against it. Because Ross carefully noted that they would be approving only "preliminary steps" for a treaty, they knew that eventually any formal alliance would have to come before their council for final ratification. Abolishing slavery had always been a means, not an end, for the Keetoowahs. Their aim was to gain control of the nation from the mixed-bloods. To throw their weight behind Ross at this point assured this.

This decision at Tahlequah was a tactic in the more important struggle over who would control the destiny of the nation.

After Ross spoke, former agent John Crawford, now a colonel in the Confederate army, was allowed to make some remarks to the assembly. He stressed the importance of the slavery issue and its connection with southern rights and Cherokee rights. However, Crawford was not highly respected among the Cherokees, even by the Watie faction, and his remarks carried little weight.[23]

The end result of the meeting was the adoption of eight resolutions by acclamation, drafted by a staunch Ross supporter, Pickens M. Benge, probably with the assistance of Ross and the Executive Committee.[24] The resolutions were ambiguous and seemed to contradict each other, which explains why W. S. Robertson thought the voters were confused. The first resolution stated, "We fully approve the neutrality recommended by the principal chief in the war pending between the United States and the Confederate states."[25] The last resolution stated that "reposing full confidence in the authorities of the Cherokee Nation, we submit to their wisdom the management of all questions which affect our interests growing out of the exigencies of the relation between the United and Confederate States of America and which may render an alliance on our part with the latter States expedient and desirable." The six other resolutions did little more than assert the nation's desire to be all things to all people. By voting to accept these resolutions, the council renewed the friendship toward the people "of all the States, and particularly those on our immediate border"; professed "brotherly feeling" toward the neighboring Indian nations; disavowed any wish to perpetuate distinctions between full-bloods and mixed-bloods; proclaimed "unwavering attachment to the constitution and laws"; declared that "property in negro slaves" was protected in the constitution and swore that they were not "abolitionists" (a designation few anywhere in the United States then espoused); and asserted that their greatest concern was for unity and harmony among the Cherokee people.

Ross took this vote as permission to arrange a treaty with the Confederacy, if he thought best, and once the scales tipped in that direction, they were not easily tipped back. W. S. Robertson's eyewitness account of this council, written by a man basically supportive of Ross, deserves attention because it offers a very different interpretation of the event from that commonly accepted:

Of the 1800 persons present at the "Mass Meeting," not one in ten understood the purport of their Chief's speech or of the resolutions passed, and the great majority of the people went home supposing that "The Cherokees with marked unanimity had declared their adherence" not to the "Confederate States" but to the past neutral policy of their Executive. No Rebel flag was displayed until the next day, after the greater part of the people had dispersed. When I left, Agent [Crawford], Merchants, teachers and even [southern] missionaries were using great efforts to prejudice the people against the U.S. government, assuring them that they were to be robbed of their country, stock, crops, in a word of everything. If the Commissioner's [that is, Dole's] advice to march a force against the Southwest Indians is carried out without their being assured of the friendly feeling of the people of the U.S., of being protected in their rights, it will tend, in my opinion, to unite all parties as one man against those . . . invading [Union] armies.[26]

Robertson closed by suggesting that President Lincoln send a friendly, supportive letter to the Cherokees immediately and that John B. Jones translate it into Cherokee so that all could read it.

The Southern Rights party was exasperated by the result of the council. Watie and his colleagues considered it a tremendous victory for Ross and the Pins, even though it threw the nation on the side of the Confederacy, since it kept Ross in power. Backed by the support of the Pins, as well as by the votes of his close supporters among the mixed-bloods, Ross was not beholden at all to the Southern Rights party. A week after the council, Watie's two closest advisers, William P. Adair and James M. Bell, wrote to Watie about it and gave them their pessimistic assessment:

You have doubtless heard all about Ross's Convention which in reality tied up our hands and shut our mouths and put the destiny and everything connected with the Nation and our lives, etc. in the hands of the Executive. . . . Pike is disposed to favor us. . . . The Pins already have more power in their hands than we can bear, and if in addition to this, they acquire more power by being the Treaty making power, you know our destiny will be inalterably sealed. It seems we should guard against this. Now is the time for us to strike, or we will be completely frustrated. Ross's Resolution adopted at the Convention endorses 1st his Neutral policy, 2nd his correspondence with Gen. McCulloch . . . and . . . they give the Executive the sole right in his wisdom to transact all matters of interest. . . . They don't say a word about [the terms of] a Treaty with the Southern Confederacy, which is the most essential thing. Everything is yet left open.[27]

Watie and his friends felt shut out by Albert Pike's negotiations and they were right. Pike had accepted Ross's right to dictate the terms of an agreement with the Confederacy. Watie's friends were correct in their belief that this meant new power for the Keetoowahs. Adair and Bell told Watie in this letter that it was essential, somehow, to "have this pin party broken up." It was equally essential to have "at least" some "equity with this old Dominant party that has for years had its foot upon our necks."

By agreeing to make an alliance with the Confederacy, Ross not only achieved political dominance over the Southern Rights faction but also soon obtained military dominance over, or at least parity with, Watie at Confederate expense. As soon as he received the mandate of this council, Ross wrote to General McCulloch at Fort Smith on August 24, 1861, enclosing the council's resolutions and stating, "We are authorized to form an alliance with the Confederate States." He warned that northern troops might invade the Cherokee Nation as soon as the alliance became known. Consequently, "we have deemed it prudent to proceed to organize a regiment of mounted men and tender them for service. They will be raised forthwith by Col. John Drew." [28] Drew was married to Ross's niece. Although sympathetic to the Confederacy because he was himself a slaveholder, Drew's familial loyalty to Ross was equally strong. The Watie faction could see in this action that Ross was creating a counterforce to Watie's regiment and that McCulloch would commission and arm it.

On the same day that he wrote to McCulloch, Ross also wrote to the editor of the *Fort Smith Times and Herald* to inform the people of Arkansas that the Cherokees, having "declared their allegiance to the Confederate States," were now their allies. He informed the Arkansans that "a regiment of mounted men will be immediately raised and placed under the command of Colonel John Drew," but that this force would be utilized only "for service on our northern border," where an attack from Kansas might be imminent once news of the Cherokees' shift from neutrality to a southern alliance was known. [29]

Ross next made arrangements for Albert Pike to come to Tahlequah early in October to negotiate the details of a treaty of alliance. Pike suggested that Ross invite delegates from the Osage, Shawnee, Quapaw, and Seneca nations to attend at Tahlequah to draw up their own treaties of alliance with the Confederacy. [30] Ross agreed. Meanwhile, Ross continued to enlist men in Drew's regiment, even though McCulloch had replied that he could not officially commission such a unit until the treaty was signed. Nonetheless, by the time all the parties assembled at Tahlequah on October 2, Drew's regiment already had over 900 men enlisted. Ross had acted swiftly because he feared that Watie might yet try to disrupt this course of events as he saw his favored position with the Confederacy slipping away. To ensure that Drew's regiment would be loyal to him, Ross appointed as officers men who were either directly related to his family or otherwise known supporters. Most of the officers were English-speaking mixed-bloods, but almost all of the enlisted men were full-bloods, and the overwhelming majority of these were members of the Keetoowah Society. The chaplain of the regiment was to be Lewis Downing—an ordained Northern Baptist minister, a leader of the Keetoo-wahs, and a Cherokee-speaking protégé of Evan Jones. General McCulloch perhaps was not aware that the new regiment would be dominated by Pins, but he did know that Ross was assembling a full-blood unit to counter Watie's predominantly mixed-blood unit: "Colonel Drew's Regiment," McCulloch wrote, "will be mostly composed of full-bloods, whilst those of Col. Stand Watie will be half-breeds, who are educated men and good soldiers."[31]

After the Osages, Shawnees, Quapaws, and Senecas worked out their treaties with Pike on October 2–4, Ross and his Executive Committee worked out the Cherokee treaty. This treaty, which had yet to be ratified by the Cherokee council to become effective, included many of the arrangements for Cherokee sovereignty that Ross had tried and failed to obtain from the United States over the previous fifteen years. He called it the most favorable treaty the Cherokees had ever made. One of the key provisions protecting sovereignty was the agreement that the Cherokees would have the right to obtain extradition from the surrounding states of any person who fled the nation after committing a crime in the Cherokee Nation.[32] It agreed to the important principles that the Cherokee people had the right to decide who was or was not a citizen and the right to try all civil and criminal cases in their own courts. It granted the nation the right to have a delegate in the Confederate Congress and limited the right of Indian agents to license white traders. The Confederacy agreed to purchase the Neutral Lands (though for only $500,000), and it guaranteed the payment of all Cherokee annuities. The Confederacy even agreed to pay all unsettled claims by the Cherokees for losses sustained during the removal crisis in 1839. Furthermore, this treaty contained no clause like the provision in the Treaty of 1835 that permitted the white man's government to intervene in Cherokee affairs in order to prevent "domestic strife."[33] Ross was in a good bargaining position with Pike at this time, for consolidation of the Indian Territory in Confederate hands required the cooperation of the Cherokees.

From Ross's immediate point of view, the key phrase in the treaty asserted that no Cherokee troops raised for the Confederacy would be asked to serve outside the Cherokee Nation. Drew's regiment and Watie's regiment were to be strictly home guards defending their land from northern invasion and thereby protecting the western flank of the Confederacy. They were not to fight in the white man's battle over southern independence.[34] However, like the southern states that had seceded from the Union, the Cherokee Nation also issued an official "Declaration of Independence," stating its reasons for breaking its treaties with the United States. This document did not claim that the North had failed to protect the Cherokees from invasion and thus had itself broken its treaties with the Cherokee Nation. Rather it said that "the war now waging is a war of Northern cupidity and fanaticism against the institution of African servitude" and that Cherokee institutions "are similar to those in the Southern States and their interests identical with theirs." However, it also noted their fear that the United States would make the Indian Territory into "what they term free territory and after a time a free state, and they have been also warned by the fate which has befallen those of their race in Kansas, Nebraska and Oregon, that at no distant day they too would be compelled to surrender their country at the demand of Northern rapacity and be content with an extinct nationality." Although Pike claimed to have written the declaration, it was an assertion of Cherokee national sovereignty. It asserted the Cherokees' inalienable right to break off from a power that threatened their freedom, "the security of their rights and liberties," and by allying with others to "declare themselves a free people, independent of the Northern States of America." On the other hand, they admitted that they were too weak to defend themselves and needed the protection of a more powerful ally.[35]

When the Cherokee council met to consider the treaty on October 9, both houses were controlled by the full-bloods (and consequently by the Keetoowahs). Once again, the tension was increased by the presence of 80 to 90 of Watie's soldiers and a much larger number of armed Keetoowahs in Tahlequah. John W. Stapler, Ross's brother-in-law, reported to Ross from Tahlequah just prior to this council that Watie and his friends had come to make trouble.

> Our Town is filling up with Strangers. [James M.] Bells Company [of soldiers] arrived here late last night, quartered at Wilson's Store and John Freemans. [E.] C. Boudinot with them, and Stan[d] Watie with his Companies expected tonight. The issuing of the inflammatory sheet denying unity of feeling; copies of Carruths letter to you—(an unheard of breach of trust) . . . endangering a bloody Civil Conflict. . . . Anderson Downing was killed late last night. . . . I furnish these items to give you an index to the current work here. *Please destroy this.*[36]

The "inflammatory" broadside was designed to prove to Pike that there was no real unity in the nation and that the full-bloods were still basically pro-Union. What was in the private letter of Edwin H. Carruth (a Union supporter at work in Kansas) to Ross is not known, but the correspondence indicated that Ross was in touch with Union officials. Also, evidently someone Ross trusted had given copies of Carruth's letter to Watie. Anderson Downing was related to Lewis Downing and Huckleberry Downing and, like them, was probably a member of the Pins. His murder demonstrated that the unanimity of the general council in August was extremely fragile. Perhaps Watie hoped to stir up a confrontation. In any case, Stapler was warning Ross that the Watie party was doing all it could to prevent the treaty from being negotiated by Ross.

After the treaty was signed, Albert Pike met with Watie and his friends to try to placate them. Pike had previously led them to believe that he favored their party and was prepared to work with it as the official liaison with the Confederate States. Now he had reversed his position and Ross was the official with whom the Confederate States would deal directly. "They censured me," Pike said, "for treating with Mr. Ross and were in an ill humor, saying that the regiment [of John Drew] was raised in order to be used to oppress them."[37]

Ross had bested the Watie party for the moment, but the cost of making the treaty with the Confederacy proved, in the long run, to be a heavy one for the Cherokee Nation. Ross presented the treaty for ratification at a regular meeting of the National Council on October 9, 1861, two days after the treaty was signed. If the full-bloods, who controlled the council at that time, were surprised to find that this treaty was the outcome of the ambiguous resolutions they had adopted on August 21, there is no record of it.[38] The treaty was ratified without dissent. Some were led to believe by later events that Ross had made the treaty only to thwart Watie and the Confederacy until such time as the federal government was able to send troops to rescue him from his dilemma. Some claimed that the full-bloods, through the Keetoowah Society, were aware of this plan and hence went along with it. However, the evidence is purely circumstantial, and Albert Pike insisted later that "I no more doubted then that Mr. Ross' whole heart was with the South than mine was. . . . I believed Mr. John Ross at this time and for long after to be as sincerely devoted to the Confederacy as I myself was. He was cheerful, earnest and evidently believed that the independence of the Confederate States was an accomplished fact."[39] He added, however, that "Colonel Drew's Regiment of Cherokees" in 1861 consisted of "chiefly fullbloods and Pins." Within a year, Ross was to swear that he had always supported the Union and had agreed to a treaty only as a dire necessity and under overwhelming pressure from the surrounding power of the Confederacy. That he had little choice at the time between signing the treaty and facing an effort by Stand Watie to replace him as head of the nation seems certain. That he did not at the time think that the treaty was a good one or that the Confederacy would win the day is not so easy to prove. Ross's sympathies may have been with the North, but his chief concern was the welfare and security of his own nation.

Ross's message to the Cherokee council on October 9, 1861, was grandiloquent. "Since the last meeting of the National Council [in October 1860] events have occurred that will occupy a prominent place in the history of the world." The formation of the Confederacy and its war for independence "has been attended with success almost uninterrupted on their side and marked by brilliant victories. Of its final result there seems to be no ground for reasonable doubt."[40] He seemed convinced that the Cherokees had chosen the correct side. "When there was no longer any reason to believe that the Union would be continued, there was no cause to hesitate. . . . Our geographical position and domestic institutions allied us to the South," and local developments "clearly pointed out the path of interest." He claimed that the Cherokee people themselves had seen this, and they, not he, had made the decision on August 21. While Colonel Drew's regiment would now "tender its services to General McCulloch," he told the council, it was raised "for the purpose of aiding in defending their homes and . . . the Indian nations about us." It would not fight in the white man's country. The whole treaty was designed for "self preservation." "The Cherokee Nation may be called upon to furnish troops for the defense of the Indian Country but is never to be taxed for the support of any war in which the States may be engaged."[41]

Ross then explained to the council the many benefits of the generous treaty arrangements—including true control of its own affairs, just compensation for claims, and adequate financial support—that had "long been withheld from the Nation" by the United States. In recommending ratification, he said: "The Cherokee People stand upon new ground" of security, prosperity, and national destiny.

Following ratification, the council took up the problem of the nation's debts and the financial crisis resulting from the failure to receive their annuity that year from the United States. Now that the northern missionaries had gone and their houses, schools, churches, and farms were vacant, the council voted on November 6 to confiscate them and put them up for sale to "the highest bidder for the benefit of the Cherokee Nation." The proceeds were to be applied to redeem "national tickets and warrants."[42] However, the bill seemed to reflect resentment over the divisive aspects of the various missionary positions on slavery. Before passage, a clause was exscinded that required those who purchased the missions to permit Evan Jones's family and Worcester Willey "to reside on said stations for the term of one year from the passage of this act." Another clause stated that "the Printing Press and building at the Baptist Mission does not belong to the Mission Board" but to the nation. Ross vetoed the bill because he felt it unjust to remove "the missionary families out of possession as intruders" and because "this bill would be viewed as an act of ingratitude toward those who had toiled and labored in the years past for the moral and religious improvement of the Cherokee people." He may have feared that confiscation of northern mission improvements without compensation, while leaving the missions of the Southern Baptists and Methodists untouched, would look unjust. He said there were "many other whites in the Nation without authority" who "are to be dealt with as Intruders as soon as our treaty can be executed in conjunction with an agent of the Confederate States." A general bill ridding the nation of intruders was preferable to one that singled out northern missionaries.[43] The bill was not passed over his veto. Ross expected the Confederacy to help them out of their financial straits by sending them the money for their annuity and a down payment on the sum promised for the Neutral Lands. Although he ultimately discovered that there was a considerable gap between Pike's promises and the Confederacy's ability to deliver on them, during the first months after the alliance, Ross seems to have done all he could to support the treaty.

A series of unexpected shocks slowly undermined the euphoria Ross felt in October 1861. First he discovered that he was not able to prevent Cherokees from fighting other Indians or even other Cherokees. The divisive animosity between the Pins and the Watie party could not be resolved, even for the sake of self-preservation. In addition, the first "brilliant victories" of the Confederacy did not, as he expected, presage a quick end to its war with the United States. In fact, the Confederacy began to suffer serious military reverses in the West. Finally, as he might have guessed, whites in the South were no more concerned, in the long run, with preserving the "nationality" of the Indians than were whites in the North. Pike himself was sincere about this, but when he pressed his superiors for more help for their Indian allies, he soon fell out of favor. The worst blow of all to Ross was the realization that having turned over control of the military defense of the nation to the commanders of the Confederate forces, he had himself lost control of the nation's destiny. The critical decisions concerning the nation's fate were now in Confederate hands. By July 1862, he was facing an even more excruciating dilemma than he had faced in July 1861. Though far from the eye of the military storm, the Cherokees suffered increasing losses from its backwash.

Within weeks after signing the treaty, Ross received his first shock, which involved his relations with the Creek Nation to the west of the Cherokees. The two nations had been closely associated for centuries. During the American Revolution, they had fought together for the British. They had shared a friendly border in the East as they now did in the West. Like the Cherokees, the Creeks were deeply split between their mixed-blood elite and their full-blood conservatives, who also were nonslaveholding and favored a policy of neutrality. However, the antisouthern party was not a majority. The leader of the Creek full-bloods was Opothleyoholo, now an old man but long an opponent of the assimilationists and the Southern Rights party, led by Motey Kennard, Daniel N. McIntosh, Rolly McIntosh, and Echo Harjo. However, unlike the Cherokees, the full-bloods had not been as open to missionary evangelism from the North. Opothleyoholo, however, had stood with Ross in the early months of 1861 in support of Indian neutrality, and he had established ties with some of the leaders of the Keetoowah Society who shared his dislike of "ultraproslavery" and well-to-do mixed-bloods. Opothleyoholo was shocked and angry when he learned that Ross had decided to ally the Cherokees with the Confederacy. He declined Ross's overtures to put unity first among the Indians.[44]

Rather than allow his followers to be conscripted into the Confederate army to serve under mixed-blood officers in the white man's war, Opothleyoholo made plans in September 1861 to gather together all who shared his Union views and move to Kansas. The Creek leaders became alarmed, especially when many of their slaves ran off and joined Opothleyoholo. They requested the assistance of Colonel Douglas H. Cooper, who commanded the Choctaws, and Colonel Daniel N. McIntosh, who commanded the Creek regiment raised for the Confederacy to put down Opothleyoholo's "insurrection." David McIntosh, another Creek leader, wrote to Colonel John Drew on September 11, 1861, giving him "reports from Hopoithyala [Opothleyoholo] of an alarming character. . . . It is now *certain* that he has combined with his party all the surrounding wild tribes and has openly declared himself the enemy of all the South. Negroes are fleeing to him from all quarters—not less than 150 have left within the last three days." Such a rebellion "should be put down immediately. . . . I hope you will come over in haste and join us in an undertaking for the interest of all." McIntosh pointed out that "this state of things cannot long exist here without seriously effecting your country"—a hint that the Cherokee full-bloods might undertake similar action or try to join Opothleyoholo.[45] On October 1, John Ross received a letter from Motey Kennard, the principal chief of the Creeks, explaining these activities by "the dissatisfied party." Kennard said that he had visited Opothleyoholo and that Opothleyoholo was convinced that "a large majority of your people is against you and with him" in opposing any alliance with the South.[46] This "has greatly encouraged them. If some timely remedy is not used for its arrest, it will and must end in civil war" among the Creeks, and the Cherokees might be dragged into it.

Alarmed, Ross sent a delegation, led by Joseph Vann, to meet with Opothleyoholo on October 8 and tell him that Ross's advice "to all the red Brethren was to be united and friendly among themselves."[47] At about the same time, Colonel Douglas Cooper heard that Opothleyoholo was about to attack Kennard's forces and ordered several regiments of Texans who were on their way to join the Confederate garrison at Fort Smith to the Creek Nation to assist him. Opothleyoholo took this as the start of offensive action and hastened his plans to depart.[48] He also sent messengers to Union officials in Kansas asking for protection.[49] Kennard wrote Ross on October 18: "If they get aid from the North, which they are making every effort to do, they will be our most formidable enemy." Moreover, "they are causing our negroes to run to them daily to the injury of many of our best citizens." Consequently, the Creek council had decided that it was "necessary for them to be put down at any cost." As soon as they were reinforced by enough Texas troops, Kennard said, they planned to attack Opothleyoholo's camp.[50]

Ross was horrified. Not only would Indians soon be fighting Indians, but both sides would be calling upon whites to assist them. "We are shocked with amazement," he wrote to Kennard on October 20, "at the fearful import of your words." He begged him to hold off and argued that the Cherokees might yet bring about reconciliation before blood was shed.[51] However, it was too late. At the news of the Creek council's preparation for war, hundreds of other Creeks left their homes and flocked to Opothleyoholo's camp. Perhaps 6,000 of the 12,000 people in the nation were behind him; his fighting force included 1,200 to 1,500 Creeks and 700 armed blacks. The task of getting this large body, including women, children, and the elderly, 200 miles to safety in Kansas was formidable. He decided as a first step to move them into the Cherokee Nation, where he expected assistance from "the dissatisfied" Union sympathizers among Ross's full-bloods.[52]

Acting on Confederate orders, Colonel Drew, with 480 Cherokees, left Fort Gibson on November 14 to join Douglas Cooper, Motey Kennard's soldiers, and the Texas troops. Meanwhile, Cooper's forces marched to Opothleyoholo's camp on November 15, but he had already left. Cooper's force of about 1,350 pursued them and caught them in Creek territory on November 18. Motey Kennard and Echo Harjo talked to Opothleyoholo under a flag of truce, but he refused to yield. Kennard told Ross that Opothleyoholo "affirmed that they were looking for Cherokees to aid them, that they [that is, pro-Union Cherokees] had promised to come to their assistance." The next day the first Indian battle of the war took place at Round Mountain; it lasted six hours. Four Texans and two Creeks were killed on the Confederate side, and a larger, but unknown, number on Opothleyoholo's side. (Colonel Drew's contingent had not yet joined Cooper.)[53] The battle was inconclusive. At the end of the day, Opothleyoholo moved his contingent northeastward toward the Cherokee Nation. Kennard asked Ross to "stop them" before they got to Kansas; "they have a quantity of our [slave] property which they are taking Northward."[54]

Cooper caught up with Opothleyoholo again on December 8. They were now within the Cherokee Nation at a place called Bird Creek. By this time the Cherokee regiment under Drew had been incorporated into Cooper's forces. To the dismay of Cooper and the chagrin of Drew, on the night before the battle, about 420 of the 480 Cherokees under Drew's command deserted and joined Opothleyoholo. The next day they fought side by side with Opothleyoholo against Cooper, the Creeks, the Texans, and the remnants of Drew's regiment.[55] Called the battle of Bird Creek (or Caving Banks), this was the first time that Cherokees had fought against Cherokees in the war. Again Opothleyoholo held off the attackers long enough for his people to load their wagons and supplies and move north, but Cooper claimed the victory. Drew returned to Fort Gibson with the few Cherokees still loyal to him. Around 150 of the deserters stayed with Opothleyoholo; the others drifted back to their homes in the Cherokee Nation, no doubt hoping that Ross would protect them from court-martial.

Cooper's forces continued their pursuit of Opothleyoholo, and on December 22 they were joined by a Confederate regiment from Van Buren, Arkansas, led by Colonel James M. McIntosh of Arkansas.[56] At this time Colonel Stand Watie's regiment replaced Drew's. Of the various contingents, James McIntosh's regiment was the first to catch up with Opothleyoholo on December 26. A third battle took place at Shoal Creek or Chustenalah (sometimes called Patriot Hill) about twenty miles south of Kansas. Watie's troops, hastening to join McIntosh, arrived too late.[57] Opothleyoholo fought at this time with only 500 or 600 soldiers, who quickly ran out of ammunition. He was badly defeated, and his people now fled in total disarray to the north, abandoning their wagons and supplies. McIntosh's and Watie's forces pursued them through heavy snowstorms, finally catching them again seven miles from Kansas. Another fight took place, but again Opothleyoholo broke off and retreated.[58] His party was pursued no further but reached Kansas only after suffering terrible hardships in the bitter cold. They were among the first "Loyal Indian refugees" to reach that state but not the last. Neither state nor federal officials in Kansas had sufficient supplies, blankets, tents, or food to give them, and many Creeks died of sickness and exposure during the winter. Some of the Cherokees who had deserted from Drew's regiment suffered and died with them. Later, hundreds of these Indian refugees enlisted in the Union army.

Ross could hardly believe the disaster that had occurred. Frightened and disgruntled Cherokees began to leave their homes and move to Kansas. The Watie faction was furious at the bad name the deserters gave the Cherokees, and Drew was highly embarrassed. Ross did not know what to do about the deserters who had returned to the nation. Finally he decided that they had been confused because of his own efforts to seek reconciliation with Opothleyoholo and by the treaty that promised they would fight only to defend their nation. Ross's enemies said he hid some of the deserters in his home.[59] Douglas Cooper wanted to court-martial the deserters. Ross said he persuaded Cooper to let him handle the matter. On December 19 Ross reconstituted Drew's regiment (including many of the deserters) and addressed the men. He criticized the deserters but pardoned those who agreed to rejoin the regiment.[60] Without Drew's regiment, he would have been powerless against Stand Watie.

Watie's supporters believed that those Cherokees who fought with Opothleyoholo deserved death, and bitter feelings developed between them and Drew's men. Late in December 1861, the rising tension between Watie's party and Ross's supporters resulted in the murder and scalping at Tahlequah of a well-known Pin leader named Chunestotie. Chunestotie had deserted from Drew's regiment and fought with Opothleyoholo, but he later rejoined the regiment. He had also played a prominent part in preventing the raising of a Confederate flag in Tahlequah previous to the signing of the treaty—an incident similar to the one that had occurred a month earlier at Webber's Falls—and was assumed to be a member of the Keetoowah Society. The murder was therefore said to be political in nature. Watie's nephew, Charles Webber, was accused of killing him. Drew called it a "barbarous crime" and demanded the arrest and trial of Webber. Stand Watie opposed Webber's arrest.[61] Ross supporters, by identifying the murderer as "Watie's nephew," sought to hold Watie's party responsible. Webber never stood trial, and the murder marked the beginning of an increasingly bloody feud between the Pins and Watie's soldiers that lasted throughout the war.

When confronted with the murder, Watie said he regretted it but saw no great significance in it. He claimed his nephew was "besides himself with liquor" at the time. Watie insisted that the Ross party was simply trying to tarnish his reputation and cover up the treachery of Drew's men. Ross asked Colonel Cooper to investigate "certain complaints against the reckless proceedings of Colonel Watie and some of his men towards Cherokee citizens."

In February 1862, Watie replied to a letter from Cooper that he was "well aware that the personal relations of myself with the unfortunate faction is seized upon with avidity by those whose only ambition seem to be to misrepresent and injure me."[62] He added, "Chunestotie has been for years past hostile to the southern people and their institutions; he was active last summer in repressing southern movements with a strong hand, with advice and assistance, as I am assured, of Captain John Ross[, Jr.] . . . He went at the head of many others of like opinions in Tahlequah last summer, for the avowed purpose of butchering any and all who should attempt to raise a southern flag—the flag was not raised as you perhaps remember." Watie advised that no action be taken against Webber for the time being because it would only stir up further trouble. He also referred to the recent murder of Arch Snail, one of the deserters from Drew's regiment, who was shot with his own pistol by some of Watie's men who accused him of trying to ambush them.[63] To Watie, this murder was justified even if the murder by his nephew was not. Watie's own dislike of Ross, as well as Drew, whom he considered a tool of Ross, revived his own long-standing grievance against Ross for the murder of his brother, cousin, and uncle in 1839. Webber's act, Watie said sarcastically, "is called a barbarous crime and shocks the sensitive nerves of Colonel Drew, Mr. Ross, and others, who of course never participated in the shedding of innocent blood."

The animosity between Ross and Watie supporters in January 1862 was also reflected in the comments of the Reverend Stephen Foreman. Foreman, an ardent "Watie man," an ordained Congregational minister, and a mixed-blood slaveholder, recorded in his diary that on January 11, "Col. Drew's Regiment left Gibson today to go to Park Hill . . . to winter." One of the soldiers told Foreman that they were relocating "to protect Chief Ross, that it was thought he was not safe." Foreman suspected that Ross was frightened in his home "because a drunk boy goes there, calls him a Pin and an abolitionist." This "boy" was Return Foreman, Foreman's nephew. Foreman was convinced that Ross had never been truly committed to the southern cause and was suffering from "a guilty conscience." Ross had referred privately to Drew's regiment as "my regiment," and Foreman wrote sarcastically: "His regiment showed their hand and his hand too at the Bird Creek fight when they fought against our men. Mr. Ross showed his hand also in pardoning all those men without even a trial. Mr. Ross also showed his hand harboring the leaders of those traitors of their country. It is said that two or three of those traitors were in his house."[64] Foreman lived in Park Hill, only a quarter of a mile from Ross, and kept a close eye on his activities.

Ross obtained no satisfaction for Chunestotie's murder from Douglas

Cooper's investigation, and Watie supporters continued to provoke incidents involving Pins and others suspected of being antisouthern. On February 25, 1862, Ross complained to Albert Pike, Cooper's superior, about "the unwarrantable conduct on the part of many base, reckless and unprincipled persons belonging to Watie's Regiment" who were causing divisions in the nation. Watie's men, he said, were "under no restraint of their leaders in domineering upon the rights of peaceable and unoffending citizens,"[65] but he did not specify what these actions were. Watie's task at this time was to patrol the northern border of the nation, scouting for any northern troops or jayhawkers. Probably his troops had harassed Cherokees they suspected of sympathizing with the Union or Cherokees caught trying to flee to Kansas.

Ross received a further blow in March 1862, when a significant battle took place between Confederate and Union troops at Pea Ridge (or Elkhorn Tavern) in the northwestern corner of Arkansas near the Missouri border. Although, under the treaty agreement with Pike, no Cherokee soldiers were to be used outside the Cherokee Nation without the consent of the council, Drew's replenished regiment and Watie's regiment were both ordered, late in February, to join General Earl Van Dorn in Arkansas to repulse the invasion of a strong federal force. Choctaw and Chickasaw troops also joined the Confederate force. Three days of fighting took place on March 6–8, and the battle resulted in a serious defeat for the Confederates. Watie's regiment retreated to the Cowskin Prairie in the Cherokee Nation, Drew's regiment fell back to Webber's Falls on the Arkansas River, and Pike withdrew the main body of Confederate soldiers into Choctaw country at Boggy Depot.[66] This left the Cherokee Nation open to the Union forces. Fortunately for the Confederates, the Union troops did not follow up their advantage, but Ross was astonished at how drastically the military situation had altered in six months. "There is no force to withstand the invasion of the Federal Army," he wrote to Pike from Park Hill on March 22. "This state of affairs naturally begets apprehension and anxiety."[67] He requested that "Drew's regiment or a portion of it, be stationed in this immediate vicinity" to afford some protection, especially for "the funds of the Nation and all its public records." Pike agreed to send part of Drew's regiment to Tahlequah. He had deposited $70,000 in gold and $150,000 in Confederate bills with the Cherokee treasury on March 1 as a first payment on the Neutral Lands.[68] Ross used the money to pay off national debts and redeem scrip.

In April, Ross complained to Pike that "the impoverished condition of the Country," resulting from last year's drought, a lack of national revenue, and various levies to support troops, caused mounting concern.[69] Pike, however, was unable to obtain further funds, either for Cherokee annuities or for the payment of Cherokee soldiers. Ross therefore called a special session of the legislature to gain its permission to use some of the funds received for the Neutral Lands to pay the salaries of the troops guarding Tahlequah.[70] The council also passed a law urging more volunteers to join the Cherokee regiments and requesting President Jefferson Davis of the Confederacy to take some action for the release of Cherokee prisoners of war in Kansas.[71] In conveying this resolution to Davis, Ross took the liberty to note that guarantees made to the Cherokees in the treaty of October 7 were not being complied with—notably financial support and military protection. "A very large proportion of their [that is, the Cherokees'] effective men are now in the service, but their efficiency is much impaired by the want of suitable arms, which have not been furnished according to treaty. The unprotected state of the country makes this circumstance the cause of more regret and solicitude." The white regiments were all at Pike's headquarters, "more than two hundred miles south of the northern border of the Cherokee Nation." Ross hoped that "we may be supplied, if possible, with means to defend ourselves." Albert Pike later admitted these deficiencies. "After the actions at Pea Ridge," he said he had paid the Cherokee soldiers "$25 cash" each in Confederate money for their first six months of service. "Nothing more, owing to the wretched management of the Confederate government, was ever paid them," Pike said.[72]

When the situation did not improve over the next two months, Ross wrote a much stronger letter on June 25 to General Thomas Hindman, commander of the Confederate troops in Arkansas. He reminded Hindman that Drew's regiment "were to be armed by the Confederate States and placed upon the same footing with other troops" but that "no arms have been furnished and nothing paid them except a very scant allowance of clothing and recently the bounty . . . for the first six months of service." General Pike's force was still "more than 200 miles" from the Kansas border, where they had been since March, "which was virtual abandonment of this nation." Ross reported that Union troops had recently made a foray into the nation, attacked Watie's men, "dispersed them, captured a large number of horses and cattle, took some prisoners, and returned" to Missouri.[73] He asked that some attention be given "to the destitute condition of the Cherokee troops and of their families" and to the "protection promised the nation." On the day Ross sent this letter, the nation was invaded by a major expeditionary force from Kansas that reached Park Hill on July 8.

Ross's confusion was reflected in his growing fear that he might be attacked and assassinated by Watie's supporters. "One of the soldiers told me yesterday," said Stephen Foreman on January 11, 1862, "that they were all going to Park Hill to protect Chief Ross. . . . It is a guilty conscience; he is afraid his duplicity is becoming apparent."[74] Foreman had always been suspicious of Ross's loyalty to the Confederacy. However, there were many reasons for Ross to be discouraged in the early months of 1862. Despite his best efforts, after the treaty with the Confederacy, Ross rapidly lost control of his country.

The disastrous battle of Bull Run in July 1861 had thrown the federal government into a frenzy, and for a year Lincoln gave little thought to the western frontier, despite the constant pleas of Kansans worried about possible Indian attacks, especially from the Cherokees on their immediate borders. Persons well acquainted with the Cherokees assured the Kansans that this was very unlikely. Evan Jones had assured them in June 1861 that the Cherokees were loyal to the Union. Edwin H. Carruth, who had lived for twelve years among the Cherokees, Choctaws, and Seminoles, said in July 1861 that all the full-bloods were "loyal to the Government" and that "no one is a firmer friend of the Union than John Ross."[75] Lincoln's effort, through Superintendent William G. Coffin, to reassure the Indians that the government had not forgotten them had failed; without a strong Union force, federal officials dared not enter the Indian Territory. Still, Evan Jones found it incredible when told that Ross had signed a treaty with the Confederacy. In a letter to Commissioner William P. Dole on January 21, 1862, he said,

I was unwilling to accept a report which implied anything dishonorable or even unstable in John Ross because I was so well acquainted with his long settled principles and policy. . . . Since I have had free conversation with the Cherokee messengers for Opothleyoholo's camp, . . . I am satisfied that I was not mistaken. . . . Whatever unfavorable shade may rest on his movements is the result of causes beyond his control. . . . The perpetrators of that enormous crime against their people—the treaty of 1835—and their successors, are the chief actors in the present rebel movement. . . . Since the secession question has been agitated, it has broken out with renewed virulence. Though it [that is, secession sentiment] would not have proceeded to overt acts but for the incitement of emissaries of rebellion from Arkansas, Texas and finally from the so called Confederate States . . . under the secession stimulus this inimical party, last spring, raised a military force of five or six hundred in the interest of and for the service of the Confederate States in defiance of the laws of the Nation. . . . In addition . . . there was the defection in the same interest . . . of portions of each of the neighboring tribes, the pressure of the Commissioners and other emissaries of the Confederate States, the presence of their army, the declaration of McCulloch that unless the Cherokees would join the Confederates he would march his troops into the territory whenever he might deem it proper . . . (and the urgent petitions to the Principal Chief of certain citizens of the nation). In view of all [of] which the best friends of the Union and of the nation were brought to their wits end and . . . to avert the over-running of the country by the Secession troops, and having no military force of their own, nor any other means of defense, the only choice seemed to be to accept the best conditions they could obtain. . . . [Drew's regiment] was raised for home protection . . . the great majority of the officers and men in this case being decidedly loyal Union men.[76]

The efforts of Jones, Carruth, and others to defend the Cherokees met considerable skepticism once Ross became allied with the Confederacy. Nonetheless, the federal government felt obliged to drive the Confederate troops from the Indian Territory in order to protect the western states. The people of Kansas were particularly anxious to have a Union force enter the Cherokee Nation. However, this expedition proved difficult to organize given the desperate military situation in the eastern part of the United States and the conflicting factions in Kansas seeking political advantage from it. Meanwhile, Ross's problems mounted daily in the summer of 1862 as the Watie faction, the Confederate commanders, and the citizens of Arkansas began to doubt his loyalty to the southern cause. By July 1862, he was caught in an unwinnable position. The future of the nation was in serious doubt.

8

The Civil War in the Cherokee Nation, 1862–1865

This war has been disastrous in its effect on the welfare

of our people. The operations of our government have been

paralized by the incursions of an overwhelming force. . . . Our

legitimate protection, the government of the United States, was

far away and every channel of communication cut off, every

military post in our vicinity abandoned. . . . Our wisest men

knew not what to do.

—Thomas Pegg, a Cherokee leader, 1863

When John Ross signed the treaty with the Confederacy in October 1861, it sent tremors through the state of Kansas. Now the whole Indian Territory was united against them. There was no telling when hordes of savages, led by white Confederate commanders, might sweep across their borders to attack the weakest frontier settlements. Fearful Kansans sent urgent demands to Abraham Lincoln and Congress to turn their attention to this menace on the Union's western flank. Meanwhile "jayhawking" raiders from Kansas entered the Cherokee Nation to "liberate slaves," steal cattle, and capture "rebel" Cherokees.[1]

Fears of "savage" invaders were matched with a sense of new opportunities. Political leaders of Kansas vied for the honor of a high command among the Kansas regiments to invade the Indian Territory in order to reap military honor as protectors of the frontier. Land speculators, railroad promoters, and ordinary homesteaders, never doubting the ultimate victory of the Union, looked forward to the day when the Indian Territory would be opened for white settlement and development. Once again the "treachery" of the Indians, their breaking of treaties with the United States, made it clear that they could never be civilized and their land should be forfeited.

Controversy broke out over how to react to the threat. Officials of the Bureau of Indian Affairs, like Commissioner William P. Dole and Superintendent William G. Coffin, took the ground that there were "Loyal" Indians, like Opothleyoholo among the Creeks and Billy Bowlegs among the Seminoles, who, with their followers, were seeking refuge in Kansas but would be willing to return and fight their disloyal countrymen. Dole and Coffin tentatively accepted the view of the Reverend Evan Jones that Chief John Ross was fundamentally loyal and only needed an opportunity to bring his nation, the largest and most advanced of the southern tribes (and the closest to Kansas), into support of the Union. Also, they had to acknowledge the truth of the argument made by Jones and the Cherokee, Creek, and Seminole refugees that the United States had not honored its treaty pledges to protect the Indians against foreign enemies.

For all of these reasons, concern over "the Indian menace" united the disparate political elements in Kansas and in the federal government behind an "Indian expeditionary force" to drive "the rebels" from the Indian Territory and to rescue those Indians who remained loyal to the Union. The primary argument was protection of the white frontier. A secondary reason was to end the steady flow of Indian refugees into Kansas. They placed a heavy burden for their support on the government and aroused anxiety among Kansans that these thousands of Indians might settle among them for the duration of the war. Honor and policy, duty and expediency, obligations and cupidity, combined in 1862 in the effort to save John Ross and the Cherokees. Ultimately, after the Cherokee Nation was liberated and its warriors joined the Union forces, the army commanders expected that the federal expeditionary force would cross the Arkansas River and drive the rebels from the Creek, Chickasaw, Seminole, and Choctaw nations further south and west—a plan that never came to fruition.

Some controversy arose over whether the Indian refugees should be allowed to enlist in Indian regiments. Kansans like Senator James Lane favored this, but Edwin Stanton, Lincoln's secretary of war, opposed it.[2] The War Department held that Indians were too undisciplined to be reliable soldiers and that in the heat of battle they would resort to their "savage" practice of scalping and otherwise mutilating the dead and dying.[3] Reports had circulated that Creek and Cherokee Indians at the battle of Pea Ridge (some of them under Watie and Drew) had done this.[4] However, on March 19, 1862, the War Department relented and allowed Indian refugees to enlist. However, General Henry Halleck issued a caveat: "These Indians can be used only against Indians or in defense of their own territory and homes."[5]

By late spring of 1862, there were 8,000 to 10,000 Indian refugees in Kansas from many different tribes. Perhaps one-fifth of them were able-bodied men eager to enlist, the majority of whom were Cherokees, Creeks, and Seminoles. The U.S. Army proposed to raise two Indian regiments from among these refugees, but it provided little in the way of uniforms or supplies. They were enlisted officially as infantry, but most of them, preferring to fight on horseback, provided their own horses.[6] Creeks and Seminoles predominated in the first Indian regiment; Cherokees, Osages, Delawares, Quapaws, and Shawnees made up the second.[7] The main body of the 10,000-man expedition consisted of white regiments from Wisconsin, Ohio, Indiana, and Kansas. Because the force was so small, the leading generals and politicians (like David Hunter and James Lane) lost interest in commanding it. Colonel William Weer (also spelled Weir), a lawyer, was put in charge. The force organized at a camp near Baxter Springs in southeastern Kansas and embarked on its mission on June 28, 1862, entering the Cherokee Nation near Cowskin Prairie from Missouri.[8] The Indian expedition was of minor importance in the war as a whole, but it was of the utmost consequence to the Cherokees.

Accompanying the troops were a number of civilians with special missions from Dole and the Bureau of Indian Affairs. Evan and John B. Jones went along as close friends and advisers of Ross. Edwin H. Carruth and H. W. Martin from the bureau had official messages for Ross from Dole and Coffin.[9] Colonel Weer was confident that Ross would welcome his arrival: "John Ross is undoubtedly with us and will come out openly when we reach there," he wrote just prior to departing.[10]

The Confederate States of America had taken as little care to help the Indians after they were allied with them as the Union had.[11] General Albert Pike had been succeeded in authority by Major General Thomas Hindman. Hindman placed Douglas Cooper in charge of all the Indian forces and Colonel James Clarkson in charge of the Confederate forces in the Cherokee Nation. Watie, lacking sufficient guns and ammunition, had not been able to continue patrolling the Neutral Lands in Kansas and had established his headquarters at Spavinaw Creek, not far from where Weer entered the nation. When news of the invasion reached the Confederates, Clarkson was ordered to unite the forces of Watie and Drew with a contingent of Confederate regulars to stop Weer. Watie left his Spavinaw camp to meet Clarkson at Locust Grove, forty miles to the southwest. Shortly after he left, on July 3 Weer's troops entered the camp, overran the small guard Watie had left there, and seized most of his ammunition and supplies.[12] Later that day, a sharp engagement took place at Locust Grove. Weer's forces, ably assisted by the two Indian regiments, captured Clarkson and many of his Missouri volunteers. In this engagement, Drew's Cherokee regiment faced the Union Cherokees, and many of them deserted to Weer.[13] Watie's men fled to the south across the Arkansas River to Fort Davis, opposite Fort Gibson in the Creek Nation, leaving the way clear to Tahlequah and Fort Gibson. The desertion of Drew's men and their enlistment a week later as a third Indian regiment in the Union army confirmed the view that Ross was indeed loyal. As Lieutenant Colonel David E. Corwin, commander of the Second Indian Regiment, later wrote: "We were in constant communication with the loyal portion of the Cherokees" prior to leaving Kansas, "and it was then perfectly understood between us, before Colonel Weer's expedition had been finally decided upon, that as soon as the United States troops advanced into the Nation, the loyal Indians, including Colonel Drew's regiment, would join us. They said at that time, and I believe with entire truth, that Colonel Drew's regiment had been raised [by Ross] in order to protect the loyal portion of the Cherokees from the outrages of Stand Watie's rebel band."[14]

Weer's force moved southward from Locust Grove toward Fort Gibson and camped at Wolf Creek, twelve miles from John Ross's home at Park Hill. While some of the troops moved on to chase the last Confederate forces from Fort Gibson, Weer sent a small body of troops under Captain Harris S. Greeno to John Ross's home on July 7. Greeno carried a flag of truce and was accompanied by fifty Union Cherokees and one company of white soldiers. When they arrived, they found Ross's home surrounded by several hundred men from Drew's regiment, who were guarding Ross as much from Watie's men as from Weer's. The Union army surgeon, Rufus Gillpatrick, presented Ross with a letter from Weer inviting him to Wolf Creek for negotiations. Greeno learned that just prior to his arrival, Ross has received orders from General Cooper to draft every Cherokee from age eighteen to thirty-five and have them report to Fort Davis to fight the invasion. Ross declined to execute this order, but he also declined to go with Greeno. In his response to Weer, written on July 8, Ross explained that in allying with the Confederacy he had acted under "the authority of the whole Cherokee people" and that he would faithfully observe his "treaty obligations." "I cannot, under the existing circumstances, entertain the proposition for an official interview between us at your camp." After Greeno brought Ross's reply to Weer, he returned to Park Hill on July 15 and, acting on Weer's orders, placed Ross, his brother Lewis, and his nephew William under arrest in their homes.[15] None of Drew's soldiers offered any opposition (Drew himself was at Fort Davis). Evan and John B. Jones were also present during these discussions with Ross, who apparently was trying to protect his political position in case the Confederate army returned and drove off the expeditionary force. To be arrested by a superior force was not the same as embracing them.

Weer's forces cleared Fort Gibson of Confederate troops. However, most of them simply went across the Neosho River to Fort Davis, where the main body of Cooper's Confederate force was gathering. Uncertain what to do next, Weer waited for a long-overdue supply train to reach him from Kansas. Temporarily he had freed the Cherokee Nation of Confederate forces, but no one knew when they might return. Some of Weer's officers feared they might circle behind them and cut off the supply train. The summer was extremely hot, and water was scarce, as well as forage for the horses. Many soldiers became ill, and as supplies dwindled, Weer's officers urged him to return to the north to see what had happened to the supply train. Weer ignored their advice and began drinking heavily. Finally, on July 18, Weer's second in command, Colonel Frederick Salomon of the Wisconsin regiment, with the full support of the other officers, placed Weer under arrest for "incompetence" and took command of the expedition. The next day, Salomon ordered the force to regroup and move back to Kansas.[16]

This retreat was catastrophic for the Cherokees, and it left John Ross in an awkward position. Once the expedition retreated, the Confederate forces would obviously reenter the nation and take revenge upon all who had shown friendliness toward the Union (including the families of the Keetoowahs who had deserted Drew's regiment). Salomon ordered the Cherokee regiments under Colonel William A. Phillips and Colonel Robert W. Furnas to remain in the area. At this point they became known as the First and Second Cherokee Home Guard regiments. Ross and his entourage remained at Park Hill under guard. On July 27, some of Watie's men returned to the Cherokee Nation and were engaged by Phillips's Cherokee regiment at Bayou Menard. Though Watie's troops were beaten back, both Phillips and Furnas feared their position was untenable.[17]

When General James G. Blunt, the commandant of the Union forces in the Southwest, heard of Salomon's retreat, he was irate. He accepted the necessity of the mutiny, but nothing was ever done to discipline Weer. Blunt was particularly annoyed that John Ross had not been brought out of the nation. On July 26, he ordered Lieutenant William F. Cloud to take a force of 1,500 men back to Park Hill to seize Ross and his entourage and conduct them to Fort Leavenworth, Kansas. Blunt was convinced that Ross had always been loyal and that he would sign a treaty that would in effect transform the Cherokee Nation into an ally. This, presumably, would assure Kansans that their border would be safe.[18]

With Cloud went Evan and John Jones and Rufus Gillpatrick to convince Ross that his surrender was necessary and that his country would be protected from Confederate reprisals. Although Ross could have used the interval to contact Cooper or Hindman, he did not. When Cloud arrived, Ross readily agreed to leave with him, taking several days to pack his official records, the Cherokee treasury, and the household goods of some forty members of his family and friends. They left Park Hill on August 3. Also returning with Cloud and Ross were the two Cherokee home guard regiments, who set up camp in Kansas near the Cherokee border at Camp Corwin. They lacked sufficient men and supplies to defend the Cherokee Nation. However, Blunt had promised them that a new expedition would take place that fall or the following spring. Meanwhile, thousands of Cherokee refugees fled to Kansas with the home guard, fearing Confederate reprisals in the defenseless nation.

After Ross talked to Blunt on his arrival at Fort Leavenworth on August 12, Blunt told Ross that he must talk to President Lincoln and offered to give Ross an honorable parole for that purpose. Ross agreed, and he left Kansas with his family on August 13 for Washington, D.C., ostensibly to arrange a treaty of alliance with the United States. However, that task did not prove so easy. He obtained a meeting with Lincoln on September 12 and convinced him of his loyalty. Lincoln asked him to put his case in writing, and Ross wrote on September 16:

> In consequence of the want of protection [from the United States] . . . and of the overwhelming pressure brought to bear upon them, the Cherokees were forced, for the preservation of their Country and their existence, to negotiate a treaty with the "Confederate States." . . . No other alternative was left them, surrounded by the power and influences that they were [faced with]. . . . As soon as the Indian Expedition marched into the Country, the great mass of the Cherokee people rallied spontaneously around the authorities of the United States.[19]

In this letter, Ross urged Lincoln to send Union troops immediately to reside in the Cherokee Nation to protect his people from their former allies: "The withdrawal of that Expedition and the reabandonment of that people and the country to the forces of the Confederate States, leave them in a position fraught with distress, danger, and ruin. What the Cherokee people now desire is ample military protection." He also said that the Cherokees would welcome a proclamation from Lincoln stating his friendly intentions toward them. This Lincoln declined to provide, but he did write to Colonel Samuel Curtis at Fort Scott, Kansas, asking whether it would be possible for him to send troops to protect the Cherokees.[20] Curtis replied that he hoped soon to have troops in the Indian Territory, but he made no promises. Ross stayed in Washington, hoping to work out a treaty with Lincoln, but he was not able to do so.

The departure of John Ross from the Cherokee Nation looked very different to Stand Watie and those who remained loyal to the Confederacy than it did to Union supporters. They considered Ross a traitor and suspected that he had plotted the entire scenario from the beginning. Watie now assumed the role of principal chief. On August 21, 1862, Stand Watie and his soldiers, who now numbered around 700, entered Tahlequah and held a self-constituted National Council.[21] Hannah Hicks, the daughter of the Reverend Samuel A. Worcester, who, now widowed, continued to live in Tahlequah, wrote in her diary on August 24: "Stand Watie has been elected Chief; Sam Taylor, second Chief; S[tephen] Foreman, Treasurer, and [they] are now making new laws." [22] The new council voted to affirm the Constitution of 1839 and the laws made since that time. They reaffirmed their treaty with the Confederacy and declared all who had deserted Drew's regiment to be outlaws. On September 3, General Hindman instructed Watie to treat all deserters, and any who tried to flee to Kansas, as "disloyal" enemies of the Confederacy.[23] Hannah Hicks heard on August 31 that the Watie council had passed "a conscript law compelling boys and men from 16 to 35 into the Army." [24] Anyone who did not obey this law identified himself as disloyal to the nation, and in the months ahead, many Cherokees were killed on such suspicion.

Watie served both as civilian chief of the nation and as the commander in chief of its armed forces (under the Confederate commandant). He proved to be a very capable leader despite the fact that the Confederacy seldom kept his men well supplied with ammunition, guns, horses, uniforms, or food; he and his men learned to live off the country. John Drew, despite Foreman's suspicions, remained loyal to the Confederate cause but was not given troops to command. Joseph Vann, who had served as second principal chief with Ross until July 1862, also served in Watie's force. At various times over the next three years, Watie's soldiers met as the nation's council, chose national officials, and passed laws. These councils also passed many resolutions addressed to the secretary of war of the Confederacy, asking for supplies for their families and ammunition and back pay for themselves.

Blunt was unable to launch a major Indian expedition into the Cherokee

Nation in the fall of 1862; he first had to defeat the Confederate troops in Arkansas and Missouri. He did send a small force into the nation on October 22 that defeated General Cooper at old Fort Wayne in the northeastern corner. Also, on December 27, Colonel William Phillips and the Indian regiments crossed through the Cherokee Nation and drove the Confederates from Fort Davis. However, the major battles in the area were fought by Blunt in Missouri at Cane Hill on November 28 and at Prairie Grove on December 7. Both were Union victories, but the Cherokee Nation itself remained without any Union garrison during the winter of 1862–63.[25]

The two Cherokee regiments spent the winter at Cowskin Prairie on the Cherokee-Missouri border. On February 17, 1863, they crossed into the nation to hold a council on their own soil in order to affirm that they, and not Watie's council, were the true government. The actions of this "Loyal" council (consisting chiefly of the members of the two regiments) greatly encouraged John Ross in Washington as he struggled to assert his right to speak for the Cherokee people. The council reelected Ross as its chief and Major Thomas Pegg as acting principal chief. Lieutenant Colonel Lewis Downing was chosen president pro-tem of the upper house, and Spring Frog (Toostoo), Speaker of the lower house. John B. Jones, now serving as chaplain of the Second Cherokee Home Guard Regiment, was chosen clerk of the Senate.[26] The council voted to depose from national office all persons still allied with the Confederacy, thereby nominally unseating Watie and his council. Next, it abrogated the treaty with the Confederate States and asserted its continuing loyalty to the United States and to the treaties made with it.

On February 20, the Loyal council passed an act emancipating all slaves in the Cherokee Nation as of June 25, 1863. This emancipation act freed few slaves, however, for most of them were owned by those Cherokee mixed-bloods allied with the Confederacy. This council would also vote at a later session on November 14, 1863, "that liberated slaves not having rights and privileges as the Citizens of the Cherokee Nation, shall be viewed and treated as other persons, members of other Nations or communities, possessing no right to citizenship." That is, they were to be expelled as "intruders." "But if such persons desire to become laborers within the Cherokee Nation, they shall be admitted upon the same terms as others who are not citizens. But the person so employing said liberated persons shall first obtain a permit for that purpose." In short, former slaves could work as contract labor for Cherokees. "Be it further enacted that all acts prohibiting to teach Negroes to read and write or to trade with them, making it unlawful for them to own and use fire arms, or other acts which may oppress any Negro, . . . [are] hereby repealed, except so much as forbids amalgamation with Negroes or Coloured persons."[27] The Loyal Cherokees shared the views of most northern whites at the time. They were willing to end the institution of slavery but unwilling to allow civil or social equality to former slaves, and they were not eager to have them living in their vicinity. They were, however, willing to exploit the former slaves as cheap labor. If the Keetoowahs or Pins were "abolitionists," as has been claimed, they were not of the radical Garrisonian variety.[28]

Also on February 20, the council chose four delegates to proceed to Washington to join Chief Ross: Lewis Downing, James McDaniels, and Evan Jones, who had been serving temporarily as a chaplain of the First Indian Home Guard Regiment. This delegation was instructed by the Loyal council to make a treaty with the United States, to obtain the nation's unpaid annuities and due compensation for losses suffered from Confederate depredations, to urge the government to send food and clothing immediately to Cherokee refugees in Kansas, and to demand that a military expedition free their nation from "the rebels" so that the Cherokees could return to their homes and live in safety.[29]

The people of Kansas were finding the thousands of Indian refugees among them a great burden, and his superiors told General Blunt to find some way to get them out of the state. Blunt commanded Colonel Phillips to return in force to the Cherokee Nation in April 1863 and to order the Cherokee refugees to return with him. Phillips and his command met little opposition as it marched southwest across the nation to Fort Gibson with the refugees in wagons and on foot trailing along after him. The Confederate forces, unable to hold the fort, retreated to the southwest across the Arkansas River. They made several forays back into the nation but were defeated in small battles on April 25 and May 20.[30] It appeared to General Blunt that the Union forces would now be able to hold the Cherokee Nation, so all the Cherokee refugees who had left Kansas with Phillips were ordered to return to their homes and begin to plant crops. As Justin Harlin, the newly appointed federal agent to the Cherokees who had accompanied Phillips, wrote to William Coffin later,

The military authorities, no doubt, believed, and assured me and the Indians, that with the force they had they would be fully able to hold that post and protect the Indians in their homes. Under this fair assurance I procured a supply of garden seeds, potatoes, and some farming implements and caused them to be distributed as equally as possible. . . . The able bodied men of the Cherokees were nearly all in the army. The labor of planting and cultivating devolved almost entirely on the women and children. Most of the families with commendable industry, planted their gardens and fields, and the prospect was fair for good crops.[31]

However, Phillips did not reckon on the daring and mobility of Watie's men, who, knowing that Phillips was dependent on supply trains from Kansas, were able to circle around Fort Gibson, sneak into the nation, and wait to ambush the trains. While waiting, they lived off the country and mercilessly raided and pillaged the homes of the returned refugees. Harlin reported:

About the 21st of May, the rebel Indians under the command of Stand Watie, entered the Territory and robbed the women and children of everything they could find, and took off horses, cattle, wagons, farming utensils, and drove off the inhabitants and laid open their farms to be entered and eaten up by stock. Crops were not sufficiently forward to mature without further cultivation, and were consequently mostly lost. Robbing, sometimes murdering and burning, continued until about the fourth day of July without abatement.... The military authorities were, or seemed to be unable... to afford protection to the nation at their homes. They were compelled to leave their crops and homes and seek protection at Fort Gibson.

Meanwhile, the Confederate forces under General Cooper were building up their supplies at Honey Springs, fifteen miles southwest of Fort Gibson across the Arkansas River. General Blunt decided to proceed with reinforcements to Fort Gibson and from there to engage Cooper in an effort to prevent his reentering the nation. He arrived at Fort Gibson on July 13 and, after building barges, crossed the Arkansas River with his troops and supplies and marched directly to Honey Springs. Although Cooper had 6,000 men and Blunt only 3,000, Cooper's troops were poorly armed and Blunt had more artillery. The two forces met in battle on July 17. The Cherokee regiments fought well, and the battle was a complete defeat for Cooper, who lost almost all of his supplies. The Confederate forces retreated to the Red River on the Texas border. Afterward, some of the Confederate Cherokee families moved into Texas with their slaves for the duration of the war, including Stand Watie's wife and children. In August, Blunt fought successfully against another Confederate force under General Frederick Steele at Perryville, Arkansas, and on September 1, the Union forces captured Fort Smith in southwestern Arkansas.[32] It seemed at last that the Cherokee Nation was safe. The refugee families at Fort Gibson returned to their homes and started to rebuild, plant, and cultivate.

In May 1863, prior to Blunt's arrival, the Loyal council had held a second meeting and passed one of the most controversial acts of the war, authorizing the confiscation and sale of all personal property and improvements owned (and now declared "abandoned") by "disloyal" (that is, Confederate) Chero-kees. In part this act was designed to compensate those whose property had been stolen or destroyed by Confederate soldiers, and in part it was designed to raise funds to provide food and equipment for the refugees. However, its deeper purpose was to inform the wealthy, mixed-blood Confederate sup-porters that when they returned after the war, they would no longer enjoy the large homes and plantations they had possessed before. In a sense, it was an effort to redistribute the wealth by the Keetoowahs who dominated the Indian home guard regiments and who were determined to carry out their plan for full-blood control of the nation.[33]

However, the war was far from over. The Cherokees had yet to face the worst of it. General Blunt withdrew his troops from the nation in August 1863, and while Colonel Phillips and the home guard troops remained at Fort Gibson with some Creek, Seminole, and Kansas troops, a part of Phillips's command was withdrawn for action in Missouri. Although the Confederate army under General Cooper was too ill-equipped and demoralized to under-take a major effort to reconquer the Cherokee territory, the 700 soldiers under General Watie never ceased their guerrilla warfare. As soon as Blunt left the nation, Watie returned, once again stealing and burning the property of the hapless Cherokee loyalists and driving them from their homes and back to Fort Gibson for protection. Agent Harlin wrote,

> In the rebel Indian raids, everything which could be found, and which could be eaten by an Indian—every article of clothing that could be worn by men, women and children, and every article of bedding and blankets—was eagerly seized upon and carried away by them. . . . School-houses are fast suffering a general wreck, like[wise] all kinds of buildings, fences, etc. in the nation, and there is not enough farming done this year to show what kind of farmers they are. . . . Their houses, barns, fences and orchards, after two years of partial or total abandonment, look as hopeless as can be conceived. From being the once proud, intelligent, and wealthy tribe of Indians, the Cherokees are now stripped of nearly all. . . . This is a sad picture, not overdrawn, and which no good man can see and not feel real sorry for their condition.[34]

Colonel William P. Ross, who was with the Indian home guard troops at Fort Gibson, wrote to his son in December 1864: "Everything has been much changed by the destroying hand of War. . . . But few men remain at their homes. . . . Nearly all the farms are growing up in bushes and briars, houses abandoned or burnt . . . [giving] some idea of the great and melancholy change which has come over our once prosperous and beautiful country. . . . Livestock of all kinds has become very scarce. . . . We have not a horse, cow or hog left that I know of. . . . [There is a] great increase in the number of wild animals. The wolves howl dismally over the land, and the panther's scream is often heard."[35]

From 1863 to 1865, when the Cherokee countryside was deserted, the Watie forces were not the only ones who pillaged and robbed. White citizens from Arkansas crossed the border to steal from abandoned homes and to round up all the horses, cattle, mules, and hogs they could find to sell to the U.S. Army. According to Agent Harlin: "What proportion of [Cherokee] property has been stolen by white men professing to be loyal to the United States, and what portion by the rebel Indians, I have no means of knowing. . . . Large herds of cattle were raised. . . . Probably a majority of the Cherokee cattle south and all north of Grand River are gone, and from the best information, entirely reliable, I can get, I think it is safe to say that more than four-fifths have been taken by white men." He added, "Many of their horses have been worn out in the service of the United States; many have died, and still a larger number have been stolen and taken out of the Territory."[36]

Watie's men justified the destruction of their country not only as part of the war effort—to scorch the land—but also out of their own necessity to feed and clothe themselves and their families. They also did so out of revenge, for in 1862, when the home guard regiments were left behind after Weer's expedition retreated, they took their own toll on the homes of rebels and Confederate sympathizers. Stephen Foreman reported in July 1862: "The Pins are robbing the people of their negroes, houses, guns, etc. . . . Major Murrell, it was said, lost seven blacks and a number of horses and mules." Foreman himself was robbed by the Pins: "They first took from before my eyes, my two black men, Joe and Charles, and one horse and a mule. Afterwards they took five head of horses and two saddles and bridles. But that did not satisfy them. They came and helped themselves to my oats . . . and they are now at work on my apple orchard. . . . I am expecting them every day to begin on my wheat and standing corn."[37] In September 1862, Hannah Hicks, though a Union sympathizer, wrote in her diary: "We hear today that the Pins are committing outrages on Hungry Mountain and in Flint, robbing, destroying property and killing. It is so dreadful. . . . Last week some of Watie's men went and robbed Ross's place up at the mill; completely ruined them. Alas, alas, for this miserable people, destroying each other as fast as they can."[38]

The worst conditions resulted from the overcrowding in and around Fort Gibson. Harlin reported that by the end of 1863 there were 3,000 soldiers and over 6,000 refugees crowded within a mile and a half of the fort, the only place they felt safe. They lived in tents or crudely constructed hovels without any sanitary provisions. The elderly and children suffered from dehydration, dysentery, and malnutrition; ultimately smallpox and malaria epidemics broke out. During the winters, pneumonia took many more lives.[39] Harlin and Phillips did all they could to provide supplies and medical care to the refugees, but there was never enough. Those who did not flee to Fort Gibson went back to Kansas, where they suffered almost as badly. In September 1863, Harlin urged that Congress be told of "the necessity of an appropriation . . . immediately for their winter clothing and subsistence of not less than two hundred thousand dollars. . . . They have no clothing or blankets for winter, and not subsistence for more than sixty days."[40] On top of this, a general demoralization among the soldiers at Fort Gibson led to a high rate of drunken disorder, brawling, and minor crimes. Gambling and prostitution flourished around the camp. One problem played upon another.

Matters were not much better for the Confederate Cherokees. The booty from guerrilla raids hardly made up for their lack of food and clothing. The Confederate Cherokee families in the Choctaw Nation and in northern Texas lived separated from their men and with virtually no money, for the Confederate army seldom paid its Cherokee soldiers. Watie's council met from time to time and sent requests to the Confederate Congress to send them money, supplies, clothing, guns, and ammunition but to little avail. The council chose E. C. Boudinot to represent the Cherokee interests as a delegate to the Confederate Congress. Although he sometimes succeeded in having annuities or supplies sent, the funds that were sent were in depreciated Confederate currency.[41] Eventually, the dispirited Watie council lost confidence in Boudinot and in the Confederate Congress and its army. Watie's brother-in-law, Lieutenant Colonel James M. Bell, threatened to resign his commission, but Watie persuaded him to remain in the army. Bell wrote his wife on September 2, 1863: "There is so much expected of us. People in Texas think we have an army standing in line well equipped for fighting [but] . . . one thousand are without arms and many have no clothing to change [to], without shoes, and what anyone in their right senses would say was in a deplorable condition, looking more like *Siberian exiles* than Soldiers."[42] Later that month, Bell told Watie: "Circumstances preclude the idea of me reporting myself for duty to this Brigade any longer. . . . I am not inclined to be an idle observer of the wrongs of my people any longer. . . . What have they ever received but slights and neglect. . . . Will you command us to bear it longer; if so, you are knowing to the wrong . . . and we must regard you in the light of an Enemy."[43]

Through losses in battle and from sickness, Watie's regiment fell farther and farther below its regular strength, and his council sought desperately for some way to obtain replacements from white volunteers in the South. In 1863

E. C. Boudinot, with the support of the Confederate Congress, suggested that the best way to obtain white volunteers was to offer them a land bounty in the Indian Territory after the war. Boudinot had no interest in preserving the Cherokee Nation; he wanted it divided in severalty and opened to white settlers, and he considered military bounties a step in that direction. Proposing this measure to the Watie council at Prairie Spring in May 1863, Boudinot met with strong resistance.[44] James Bell described the meeting to his wife: "Our convention has been in session for several days," and one proposal "to offer inducements [to white enlisters] of 160 acres of land is meeting with considerable opposition." With these land grants would go official citizenship in the Cherokee Nation. Bell had been appointed to a committee to consider and report on Boudinot's proposal. The committee debated for five days and could reach no resolution. Few wanted whites living in the nation as equal citizens after the war.[45] In their own way, the Watie Cherokees were also committed to the nation's independence. Finally, three of the leading members of the Watie council—Samuel M. Taylor, the second principal chief, John Spears of the Executive Council, and Alexander Foreman, president of the convention— sent a letter to President Jefferson Davis:

> We are informed . . . that you think it best for us to give part of our lands to our white friends. . . . That to defend our country and keep troops for our protection, we must raise and enlist them . . . and that it is actually necessary that they are citizens of our country. . . . To do this would be the end of our national existence and the ruin of our people. Two things above all others we hold most dear, our nationality and the welfare of our people. Had the war been our own, there would have been justice in the proposition, but it is that of another nation. We are allies, assisting in the rights and independence of another nation. We . . . cannot agree to give part of our domain as an inducement to citizens of another Government to fight their own battles. . . . It would open a door to admit as citizens of our Nation, the worst class of citizens of the Confederate States. Against such a scheme we respectfully, earnestly, and solemnly protest, and in doing so we express the sentiments of two thirds of our people.[46]

The Watie party was beginning to understand that the whites of the South were as eager to detribalize them and take their lands as the whites of the North. Though Watie continued to support his nephew, Boudinot, the three protesters against this scheme went on to inform President Davis: "We have no longer any confidence in our delegate, [E. C. Boudinot] and take this means of expressing to you our disapprobation of his course" in persuading the Confederate Congress to adopt such a measure. The one-third of the council who favored the plan probably consisted of white men married to Cherokees.

Watie was not a politician, nor was he ambitious for personal power or fame. Had Ross's friends not murdered his brother and two nephews, he might have led the full-bloods in opposition to Ross rather than siding with the mixed-bloods, who seemed to have little attachment to the common people. Watie's strength as a leader stemmed from his steadfast devotion to his friends, his relatives, and his country's welfare as he understood it. His correspondence with his wife reveals these loyalties. Watie had gone to mission schools and, though not pious, was a believer in the Christian idea of God. His wife, Sarah Bell, the sister of James Bell, was more deeply religious. She worried when her fifteen-year-old son, Saladin, joined Watie's regiment and seemed to enjoy the fighting and killing of war: "I am afraid that Saladin never will value human life as he ought." [47] She wrote to her husband, "Tell my boys always to show mercy as they expect to find God merciful to them." She asked Watie: "If you should ever catch William Ross, don't have him killed; I know how bad his mother would feel, but keep him till the war is over. I know they all deserve death, but I feel for his old mother, and then I want them to know that you do not want to kill them just to get them out of our way. . . . Always do as near right as you can." [48] A few months later, Watie made a raid on Park Hill, burned down John Ross's mansion, and captured several members of the Ross family. He wrote to Sarah: "Took Dannie Hicks and John Ross[, Jr.] Would not allow them killed because you said William Ross must not be killed on old Mrs. Jack Ross's account. . . . Poor Andy Nave was killed. He refused to surrender. . . . I felt sorry, as he used to be quite friendly towards me before the war, but it could not be helped. I would a great deal rather have taken him prisoner." [49] Yet in the same letter he said, "Killed a few Pins in Tahlequah. . . . I had the old council house set on fire and burnt down, also John Ross's house. They found some negro soldiers at Park Hill; killed two and two white men." Watie's mercy was contingent on private loyalties.

Toward the end of the war, Watie's wife expressed the deep despair and depression of the Confederate families living in Texas: "I hope the war will close soon, and we will get time to sit down in peace. . . . This war—it will ruin a great many good people. They will not only lose all their property but a great many will lose their character, which is [of] more value than all their property. . . . I am almost ashamed of my tribe. . . . I want to see the end of this war and then I will be willing to give up the ghost." [50] Watie too became discouraged, but he did what loyalty and duty required. Only occasionally did he stop to reflect on what the war was doing to his friends and his nation.

Once, when falsely accused of killing a member of his own regiment in a fight, he wrote to Sarah:

> I am sorry that I should be charged in public of an act of that kind, but it seems that is my doom; let me act as I will, my conduct is always considered wrong. No charity was ever shown me, yet I have lived through it, and I trust and hope that justice and right will be meted out to me some day. Although these things have been heaped upon me, and [it] would be supposed that I became hardened . . . it still hurts my feelings. I am not a murderer. Sometimes I examine myself thoroughly and I will always come to the conclusion that I am not such a bad man at last as I am looked upon. God will give me justice if I am to be punished for the opinions of other people. If I commit an error, I do it without a bad intention. . . . I call upon my God to judge me; he knows that I love my friends and above all others, my wife and children.[51]

It was one of the ironies of Cherokee history that Ross, and not Watie, was the leader of the full-bloods. Watie had the sturdy temperament of a full-blood; Ross was a well-meaning bureaucrat. Watie stated his views in a simple, straightforward style; though Ross had strong feelings, he always expressed them in a formal, self-conscious way. Writing to his daughter on September 18, 1865, when he had returned to the nation to see the remains of his home that Watie had burned, Ross commented: "I then hastened to our once lovely home and witnessed the ruins and desolation of the premises— the only buildings standing was Johnny's chicken house, the carriage house, and Peggy's cabin. We found the old dun mare and the broken leg horse in the garden, and riding through the orchard, found a few peaches, other fruits being all gone—I cannot express the sadness of my feelings in rambling over the place."[52]

From 1862 to 1865, John Ross worked in Washington with his delegation to obtain military protection for the nation and food and clothing for the refugees in Kansas and those stranded at Fort Gibson. His immediate family and several of his house slaves lived in the homes inherited by his second wife from the Stapler family, one in Philadelphia and one in Wilmington, Delaware. The Rosses were supported by funds provided by the commissioner of Indian affairs out of the tribal trust. His enemies said that he lived in luxury while his people starved during these years, but he asserted quite correctly that his work in Washington was essential to their survival. He was able to obtain more for his people from the Lincoln government than Watie obtained from that of Jefferson Davis, though it was not much. Ross's primary function was to provide accurate, up-to-date information on Cherokee affairs to the government and to the eastern public; he informed the former through memorials and the latter through letters to the press. Ross saw to it that the Cherokees were not forgotten by a Congress that would have preferred to forget them. In general, his efforts were supported by William P. Dole and, to a lesser degree, by William G. Coffin. Dole, however, came to resent Ross's constant requests for money to support his family. Coffin believed that Ross had deserted his people (and ultimately came to doubt that Ross had really been forced into a treaty with the Confederacy). Still, both men did all they could to provide supplies to Cherokee refugees and military support to reclaim and protect their country.

Ross's efforts were hampered by several measures that Congress took against all the Indian nations that allied with the Confederacy. In July 1862, Congress voted to suspend all treaties with any Indian nations that allied themselves with the Confederate States. At the same time it placed the annuities due to the five major tribes in a common fund that was thereafter drawn upon for relief to loyal Indian refugees (including, after 1862, the Cherokees).[53] This act was strengthened by the Indian Confiscation Act of March 1863, under which the secretary of the interior was to make treaties with those Indian nations which, prior to 1861, lived on reservations in Kansas for their removal to the Indian Territory (although none of these tribes was disloyal).[54] In 1864, General John Pope proposed that Congress stop making treaties with Indian tribes and simply legislate at its own discretion all Indian affairs. Congress postponed its decision on the proposal.[55]

Throughout the last years of the war, determined efforts were made by Senators James Lane and James Harlan of Kansas to obtain passage of a bill that would convert the Indian Territory into a federal territory under government supervision, open it to homesteaders, railroads, and cattle grazing, and lead to the denationalization of all the tribes there.[56] All of the things that in 1861 David Hubbard of the Confederacy had warned Ross the northerners would do seemed to be coming true. Ross was especially concerned over the fact that 98 percent of the Cherokee trust funds in the prewar years had been invested by the government in the bonds of those states that joined the Confederacy, and he feared they would become worthless. Somehow the federal government had to be required, as trustees for the Cherokee annuities, to make good on these bad investments.

During the summer of 1864, Ross and the other Cherokee delegates worked out what they thought would be a useful treaty to bring at least temporary financial support to the nation. It included the resumption of annuity payments, the sale of the Neutral Lands (for $500,000 plus interest since 1835), agreement to permit the Delawares from Kansas to live in the Cherokee

Nation, the privilege of joint U.S.-Cherokee consultation in choosing Indian agents, the payment by the United States for all losses and injuries suffered by Cherokees "since the commencement of the present rebellion," and, most important, recognition of Cherokee sovereignty.[57] The commissioner of Indian affairs reviewed the proposal but declined to enter into any negotiations while the war was in progress.

Consequently, Ross had to rely on piecemeal efforts to obtain relief for his people. He succeeded in obtaining some money through the pool of tribal annuity funds. After discovering, through Dole, that over $130,000 had accrued to the nation from the sale of twelve square miles of Cherokee land in Alabama designated in the Treaty of 1819 for a school fund, Ross tried, unsuccessfully, to have the sum granted to the nation. He attempted several times to negotiate the sale of the Neutral Lands,[58] but by now too many other interests were connected with this tract and the government preferred to deal with the issue later. During the winter of 1863–64, Ross and Evan Jones finally turned to the philanthropic public and churchgoers for help for their starving and homeless people. Letters to the press and to church leaders brought in gifts of clothing and blankets, which Dole agreed to have transported to the nation free of charge.[59]

One of the more difficult problems for Ross to solve resulted from an order issued by General Blunt on April 16, 1864, that permitted army quartermasters and contractors to force Cherokees who owned livestock to consign it to them for any use.[60] Not only legitimate army officers but a host of whites posing as quartermasters or army contractors entered the nation and virtually stole every cow, horse, mule, and hog they could find. Vast herds were taken to Kansas, Missouri, and Arkansas by bogus contractors and sold to the army. Ross received many complaints from the Loyal Cherokees about this, one of which came in the name of the Keetoowah Society on July 7, 1864:

> By request of Captain Smith Christie, Acting Chief, I desire to address you on behalf of the Keetoowah Society, that large and loyal class of Cherokee citizens who, in point of fact, constitute 7/10ths of the male population. . . . We complain that while our men are bravely battling for the Union cause, United States citizens and soldiers are stripping our country of the last vestige of cattle and horses. . . . This is done by contractors and officers of the United States army [and] . . . the great motive power that they secured [with] the issue of General Blunt's Order No. 7. . . . These parties are literally robbing the government and our nation.[61]

Despite concrete evidence of the misuse of this order, Ross was unable to have it rescinded or its abuses investigated.

Ross's most successful effort for his people occurred only days before the war ended, when Secretary of the Interior John Usher provided $50,000 from tribal funds for Cherokee relief.[62] It was not enough to do much for the devastated nation; reconstruction would take hundreds of thousands of dollars and many years of hard work. Peace came on April 9, 1865, although Stand Watie did not surrender until June 25, the last Confederate general to do so.[63] When the war ended, most of the Southern Cherokees and their families were fearful of returning to the nation. Their homes had been confiscated, and private, if not public, retaliations seemed likely for their actions during the war. Many of their leaders were convinced that, as in 1839–46, their only safety lay in a division of the homeland into two separate Cherokee nations.

The Loyal council met in Tahlequah on July 13, 1865. With Ross still in Washington, Lewis Downing served as acting principal chief. The council voted an act of amnesty and pardon to all who had fought with the Confederacy. The rebels would be readmitted to full citizenship upon taking an oath to support the constitution and laws of the nation. Downing urged reconciliation, but because the council refused to rescind the act confiscating rebel homes and farms, his attempt to arrange a preliminary reunion with a delegation from the Watie party failed.[64]

After Lincoln's death, President Andrew Johnson appointed Senator James Harlan of Kansas secretary of the interior. In September 1865, Harlan appointed six commissioners to go to Fort Smith to sign articles of peace with the five major tribes. Three of the commissioners were from the Department of the Interior (Dennis N. Cooley, commissioner of Indian affairs; Elijah Sells, southern superintendent of Indian affairs; and Thomas Wistar, a Quaker philanthropist); two were from the War Department (General W. S. Harney and Colonel Ely S. Parker, a Seneca Indian and aide-de-camp to General Ulysses Grant). The sixth appointee did not attend. The commissioners were instructed that the treaties must be signed by both loyal and rebel factions in tribes that were divided (the Cherokees, Creeks, and Seminoles), that all of the tribes must agree to abolish slavery, that they must admit their former slaves to full citizenship, that provision should be made for land to be used by the tribes being moved from Kansas, that they must agree to grant rights-of-way (including large land grants) to railroad companies, and that they must agree in principle to the merging of all tribes into one government with quasi-territorial status under federal supervision.[65]

When the Cherokee delegates from the Ross and Watie factions appeared before the commissioners at Fort Smith on September 8, 1865, they discovered that the major question facing them was whether the commissioners would recognize John Ross as the legitimate chief of the Loyal Cherokees. Ross had just returned to the nation, but he did not immediately appear at Fort Smith for this meeting. The commissioners had been reading for the first time some of the captured Confederate correspondence between Ross and various Confederate officials during the period the Cherokees were allied with the Confederacy. They were shocked at what now appeared to be Ross's ardent espousal of the southern cause.

The second pressing question was whether the commissioners would accept the demand of the Watie delegates that any peace treaty must include the division of the Cherokees into two separate countries. To the surprise of the Loyal delegates, the treaty commissioners not only seemed inclined to support this proposal but also acted far more cordially toward the Southern delegates than toward those representing Ross. Underlying these two problems was the personal antagonism of Dennis Cooley toward Ross. Cooley realized that Ross was not inclined to accept most of the conditions set down for the treaty. He was also well aware that Ross, considering his people to have been loyal to the Union cause throughout the war, expected to be treated differently from the other tribal leaders and wanted the United States to make full compensation for the losses the Cherokees had suffered from the failure of the United States to protect them from the Confederate forces that had "overwhelmed" them.

Ross was now seventy-five years old. His country lay in ruins. He had three sons and three grandsons who had served in the Union army, and many close members of his family had died in the war. One of his sons and a nephew had been killed in the war. His plantation was in weeds, his home burned, and his slaves (fifty to one hundred) freed. His people were demoralized and poverty-stricken. All the prosperity of the year 1861 had disappeared; the Cherokees were back virtually where they had been in 1839 when they were dispossessed, divided, and driven from their ancient homeland. Counting the losses from battle, guerrilla action, disease, and related causes, the Cherokee Nation had lost over 4,000 persons in the war years and found itself with 1,200 orphans and many maimed veterans. Ross firmly believed that three years of loyal service to the Union by the overwhelming majority of the Cherokee males in the Indian regiments deserved a reward and not a punishment from the federal government.

The negotiations went badly. The Loyal Cherokees negotiated first, from September 8 to 15. Lewis Downing, Smith Christie, and H. D. Reese led the delegation. They protested that they were being treated as though they had been rebels throughout the whole war, as were the Choctaws and Chickasaws. When Ross finally appeared at the negotiations on September 14, he was told by the commissioners that they did not recognize him as chief of the

Cherokees. Ross protested angrily and gave them an account of the sacrifices he had made for the Union.[66]

In the end, the commissioners found they could not negotiate official treaties with any of the tribes because the tribal delegates said they had not been given the power to sign a treaty. Instead, Cooley had to settle for articles of peace that mentioned the various stipulations he wanted in only the most general terms but left all of the details to be worked out in subsequent negotiations to take place in Washington. Ross's nephew, William P. Ross, presented a protest for the Cherokee Nation against the unwarranted "deposing" of his uncle.[67]

Before adjourning, the commissioners met with the delegates of the Southern Cherokees—E. C. Boudinot, Stand Watie, William Penn Adair, and James M. Bell. These Cherokees said they would gladly agree to all of Cooley's stipulations except two: they did not want the former slaves to be incorporated into the nation as citizens, nor did they favor any form of detribalization and territorial status under federal supervision. However, they made a strong argument for the necessity of a division of the nation. Cooley tried to persuade the Loyal and Southern delegations to reach agreement on a reunion, but he failed. The Southerners argued that by the confiscation of their homes, they had become a dispossessed and homeless people, and their lives would be in danger if they set foot again in the old nation.[68]

The peace talks had brought no peace to the Cherokees. Their factional rivalry remained as strong as ever. Their nation was as riven as the two sections of the United States. Sovereignty, unity, and harmony never seemed more unattainable.

9

Reconstruction and National Revitalization, 1866–1870

Bad as is the condition of all these southern Indians,

that of the Cherokees is much worse than the remainder of

the tribes. They have a domestic feud of long standing which

prevents them from coming together for mutual aid and support.

—Commissioner William P. Dole, in Annual Report of the

Commissioner of Indian Affairs *(1865)*

The Loyal Cherokees, having reaffirmed John Ross as their chief in October 1865, and insisting on their loyalty and sacrifice for the Union cause, appointed a delegation to go to Washington, D.C., in January 1866 to work out a treaty that would clarify their status and provide the income the nation needed to reconstruct itself. Led by John Ross and including Smith Christie, White Catcher, Sam Houston Benge, D. H. Ross, and John B. Jones, the delegation was instructed to obtain a just settlement of Cherokees' claims against the government for its failure to protect them from the Confederate invasion, to obtain all monies due from their trust funds (frozen during the war), to secure pensions and bounties for veterans and their widows and children, to repulse the Indian bureau's drive for a territorial government, and to thwart the Southern Rights party's plan for two distinct Cherokee nations. The council also authorized the sale of the 800,000 acres in the Neutral Lands in southeastern Kansas.[1] However, the underlying goals, as always, were Cherokee unity and sovereignty, both of which would have seemed beyond hope to anyone but John Ross.

The Confederate Cherokees (now known as the Southern party or Southern Cherokees) appointed their own set of delegates as though they were the legitimate authority of the nation, Commissioner Dennis N. Cooley and the other envoys having rejected Ross's claim to represent his people at the September 1865 meeting at Fort Smith. In addition to working for a division of the nation and a proportional share of all tribal funds on hand or to be obtained from land sales, the Southern delegates, headed by Stand Watie and including E. C. Boudinot, John Rollin Ridge, Saladin Watie, James M. Bell, J. A. Scales, and William Penn Adair, were instructed to make whatever concessions Cooley demanded in order to establish their legitimacy. In effect, they hoped to persuade Cooley to make two separate peace treaties, one with them (forever separating them from the Loyal Cherokees) and one with the Loyal Cherokees, conceding their right to a share of tribal land and funds. They knew that this would weaken Ross's position and enable Cooley to play each side off against the other in order to obtain his stipulations, but their bitterness was so great that they had no qualms about proceeding with their plan.

The reasons for division of the nation went beyond the enmity between the two sides during the war, according to the Southern delegates: "The 'Pin Society' [or the Keetoowahs] was organized five years before the war" and "the purpose of this secret society was to secure and perpetuate the power of Mr. Ross and his friends by arraying the great mass of fullbloods against the halfbloods and white men of the Nation; to inflame and excite the innate prejudices of caste among the Indians and thus enable demagogues, peculators of public funds, and murderers to enjoy in security their ill-gotten gains." This feud between the Pin Society and the Watie party, the Southern delegates continued, sprang from the earlier division between the proremoval and antiremoval parties in the 1830s and 1840s. "We acknowledge that the great injustice and wrong we have endured at the hands of this pretended loyal party have utterly destroyed all sentiments of brotherhood between us. For thirty years we have had neither a community of interests, tastes, or aspirations. We are two different peoples, to all intents and purposes."[2] This argument, while it served the purpose of the Ridge-Boudinot-Bell families who dominated the delegation, was not true for most of their followers, as subsequent events demonstrated.

No two estimates of the sizes of the Southern and Loyal parties were the same. The Southern delegates at one time claimed to represent "at least 8,000" Cherokees as opposed to 10,000 Loyalists. The Loyal Keetoowahs claimed to represent seven-tenths of the male population. More realistic estimates placed the upper limit of the Southern party at 6,500 and the Loyalists at 9,000–10,000. The confusion arose because no one knew exactly how many Cherokees there were in 1865. In 1860 the population (including slaves and intermarried whites) had totaled 21,000 to 22,000, but estimates in 1865 ranged from 14,000 to 17,000.[3]

John Ross and his delegates did their best to "wave the bloody shirt" and described the Southern party as "a few factious men who were among the instigators of the rebellion." "It is not peace, security and fraternity these lately disloyal leaders want, it is political power." Ross himself claimed to speak for 11,000 out of 17,000 Cherokees.[4] However, the negotiating strength lay with Cooley, who managed to play the parties off against each other until he had squeezed out of them as many concessions as he could.

Dennis Cooley, Elijah Sells, and Ely Parker, whom President Andrew Johnson commissioned to treat with all the western tribes in Washington, managed to work out treaties with the Creeks, Choctaws, Chickasaws, and Seminoles by June 1866. They persuaded them to make large land cessions, grant extensive railroad rights, and agree to take steps leading toward a territorial government. However, the two Cherokee parties remained so far apart that there seemed no way to write a treaty that both would sign. Finally, the commissioners decided to make separate treaties with each faction. It was to the government's advantage to treat first with the Southern party. Ross and his delegates had become so annoyed with Cooley by May that they appealed over his head to the president and Congress.[5] This delighted the Southern delegates. J. Woodward Washbourne, the secretary of the Southern delegation, wrote to a friend in Arkansas on June 1: "The Ross delegation has been dismissed by the Commissioner because they would not agree to a division" of the nation. The Southern delegates "are all in high spirits. The President has ordered that a treaty be made with us for our own prorata share of the Nation. . . . Ross is going to try to beat us in the Senate. He is trying to make public sentiment through the *New York Tribune*. Rollin [Ridge] has answered it in a scorching reply and went himself to see Greeley of the *Tribune*. . . . Ross will be beaten there. His day is done. Ours is fast rising and bright. We will get what we asked for."[6]

The treaty that Cooley concluded with the Southern party on June 13, 1866, included all of Cooley's stipulations, although there was some dissension among the delegates about accepting former slaves as citizens and about agreeing to work toward a federally managed territorial government. The Watie delegates agreed to give the railroad corporations all the rights-of-way they wanted and to grant them alternative sections of land (amounting to millions of acres) along their tracks through the Cherokee Nation. They agreed to sell a strip of land between Kansas and the Cherokee Nation known as the Cherokee Strip, the Cherokee Neutral Lands for $500,000 (without interest), and the Cherokee Outlet to the government. They also agreed to give their former slaves civil and political rights, although they expected that ultimately blacks would be removed from the nation and given a separate tract of land to themselves on the Outlet. They agreed to a territorial government based on a confederation of all the tribes and supervised by white officials appointed by the secretary of the interior.

In exchange for these concessions, Cooley agreed to their demand for an autonomous country with a separate government under their own elected officials to be supported by their proportionate share of all tribal funds. Cooley expected, however, that the two separate nations would be considered as one in any diplomatic negotiations with the United States and would send only one delegation to Washington, with a proportionate share of members from each division. The area of the Cherokee Nation given to the Southern Cherokees in this treaty was southwest of the Arkansas River (the Canadian District of the prewar nation), and it was to extend northward along the Creek border far enough to provide 160 acres for every man, woman, and child in the Southern party, a determination that would require a census after the Southern Cherokees returned from their wartime homes in Texas and the Choctaw Nation. All Cherokees in the Ross or Loyal party would be required to emigrate out of this area, which was designated for the Southern party's "sole use and occupancy." [7]

This treaty so exhilarated the Southern delegates that they instructed Stand Watie, who had already returned to the West and would obviously be elected the chief of this new nation, to begin organizing the Southern residents of the Canadian District area into a political unit. He and J. A. Scales (who had served as a major in Watie's regiment) were to start moving as many Southern families as they could into the area and were to issue a proclamation announcing the inauguration of the new Southern Cherokee Nation. "In God's name be swift about it," J. W. Washbourne wrote to Scales: "Let General Watie issue his Proclamation in the Canadian District declaring the existence of the Southern Cherokee Nation. . . . Organize the Government as soon as it can be done. You will be protected against any interference" from the Pins.[8] "Even should General Watie's Proclamation not be able in time to collect a thousand voters," he should proceed to organize the region "with a few hundred votes. . . . We have won the day. . . . Ross is appealing to the sympathies of the [Republican] Radicals" in Congress, but, Washbourne said, he was too late.

Cooley transmitted this treaty to President Johnson, who was to send it to the Senate for ratification. However, whether the whole procedure was simply a gambit to force the Loyal party to negotiate on Cooley's terms or whether Johnson did not want to risk a fight over it in the Senate, he never transmitted it. The possibility that he would transmit it was sufficient to insure that the treaty with the Loyal faction would be favorable to the U.S. government. Ross and his delegates met with Cooley and agreed to yield to some of his stipulations. Cooley knew that Ross would do anything to prevent a division of the Cherokee Nation. A divided nation would too easily be manipulated by the federal government, as demonstrated in the past by the way the eastern and western Cherokees were played against each other from 1819 to 1835. Moreover, Ross, now seventy-six years old, had suffered a severe illness in April that confined him to his hotel bed. Though still mentally alert and able to understand completely all that his colleagues were doing, he lacked the strength to attend long, argumentative meetings. The delegates kept him fully informed, and he personally approved every clause of the treaty.

The Southern delegates were distraught when they learned of this new turn of events. "I wrote to you some time ago," E. C. Boudinot wrote to his brother, William P. Boudinot, on July 2, 1866, "that we had signed a satisfactory treaty. Since then things have taken a change under a mistaken apprehension that a compromise can be made. The President directs that another treaty shall be made" with the Ross party.[9]

This second treaty was signed by the commissioners and Loyal delegates on July 19, 1866 (including a shaky signature obtained from Ross in his hotel room). It contained thirty-one separate and complex articles. The most important article from Ross's point of view was Cooley's agreement not to divide the nation. Instead, the Southern Cherokees received only semiautonomous control of the Canadian District within the nation (electing their own council representatives and local sheriffs, judges, and court officers) and were required, just as any other district, to obey the laws passed by the majority of the council. They also lost control over any part of the nation's land or funds. All Cherokee funds remained in the hands of the national treasury and its Loyal majority in the council. In return for this, Ross had to agree, against his private objections, to give citizenship to former Cherokee slaves, to repeal the act confiscating rebel improvements (providing compensation to those who had bought them and might be reluctant to return them to rebel owners), to sell the Cherokee Strip, to allow other tribes to be settled on Cherokee land (for a fair price to be paid by such tribes into the Cherokee treasury), and to allow two railroad rights-of-way—one north to south and one east to west—through the nation. Ross succeeded in limiting railroad rights-of-way to 100 feet on each side of the track. He argued that "if we were to make the grants of alternate sections for five miles on each side of each road, with a compensatory grant to supply deficiencies reaching for ten miles on each side," as the railroads requested, the nation would have to give up "more than a million acres of our land to private companies"; as they sold these sections, "a tide of white population would set in upon us which would begin by settlements[,] . . . be followed by disturbances with our people, and probably end by forcing us from our country . . . guaranteed to us as a permanent refuge." [10] Ross agreed to sell the Neutral Lands for $500,000 plus interest but refused to sell the Cherokee Outlet. He obtained the right to all the annuities of the national trust funds frozen by the government during the war and an immediate payment of $150,000 in back annuities to pay the nation's debts. Furthermore, the government agreed to pay all bounties, pensions, and pay arrearages due to the Loyal soldiers of the Cherokee home guard regiments or their widows.

Other clauses in the treaty gave the Cherokees alone the right to grant or withhold licenses to white traders and stated that the federal government would establish a district court within the Cherokee Nation (and therefore draw upon Cherokee juries) to replace the U.S. District Court for the Western District of Arkansas, where white juries tried all cases involving crimes between whites and Cherokees. The only serious problem for Ross was the concession he had to make to Cooley's prime concern, that is, to allow some steps to be taken toward establishing a territorial government. However, Ross saw to it that this clause was carefully drawn so that an agreement among all the Indian tribes in the territory was necessary before any white-supervised, federally appointed territorial structure could be established. He was prepared to allow a confederation of Indian tribes to act in concert on certain intertribal issues but insisted on the right of each tribe to continue its own government. [11] To quiet the fears of the Southern party, complete amnesty was granted to all Cherokees on both sides for crimes committed during the war. [12]

This complex and sometimes ambiguous treaty was sent to President Johnson, who transmitted it to the Senate, ignoring the treaty that had been worked out with the Southern party. The Senate ratified it on July 27, 1866. [13] John Ross died four days later. He had been principal chief of the Cherokees for forty years and a major leader for ten years before assuming that post. While at times devious and artful, he was never dishonest, either with the Cherokees or with the government (with the possible exception of the Confederate treaty). [14] He had once been very wealthy, but he died in debt. The secret of his success lay in his ability to sustain the loyalty of the full-blood majority while at the same time encouraging the mixed-bloods and intermarried whites to develop the nation's resources to the fullest extent. On controversial issues, he had always called the whole nation together to make decisions, thereby honoring the ancient ideal of harmony and government by consensus. He never chided the full-bloods, who adhered to their old values and religion, though he was always cordial to missionaries and insisted that the nation's public schools be taught in English. Ross was a strange blend of paternalist and democrat, whose political sympathies, for obvious reasons, lay with the old Whig and the new Republican parties of the United States. He served his people well, and the full-bloods were always loyal to him. None of the chiefs who succeeded him proved capable of maintaining his strong and sustained leadership in the difficult years ahead.

The second principal chief at this time was Lewis Downing, who spoke no English and hence was considered a full-blood, though he was of mixed ancestry. He was a devout Baptist preacher, a founder of the Keetoowah Society, and a veteran of the Cherokee home guard and had always been an ardent supporter of John Ross. The question of whether the National Council, which under the constitution had to choose a replacement for Ross at its next meeting in October 1866, would endorse Downing to complete Ross's term (which ran until 1867) or whether it would select Ross's nephew, William Potter Ross, a well-educated, mixed-blood lawyer and merchant, cast uncertainty over the immediate future.

The Southern party added to this uncertainty by its resentment of John Ross's victory over its delegates in Washington. Despite the pledge of amnesty, most Southern Cherokees remained fearful about returning to the nation. Watie and most of his followers believed that many Cherokees, particularly among the Pins, would take vengeance upon them for their ruthless guerrilla tactics. They also felt certain the majority would deny them any role in political affairs, and they knew that whoever became chief would follow the policies of John Ross. Downing had once said that he would never consent to the repeal of the confiscation act, but that was before Ross had signed the treaty including such a stipulation. Downing had participated in most of the worst fighting during the war, and the Southern party had good reason to be wary of him. They had equal reason to be wary of William P. Ross, whose bitterness toward the Southern party had been increased by its efforts to divide the nation. He also lacked the spirit of harmony and charity that tended to soften Downing's anger toward the Watie faction.

The signing of the treaty with John Ross had been a startling reversal of fortune for the Southern party. Victory was snatched from its hands at the last moment. William Penn Adair, one of the Southern delegates, called the treaty "the worst ever entered into with the Government." He argued that it "is not binding upon the Southern Cherokees, as we refused to sign it, and fought to the last and [are] still fighting it," and that the "Ross delegation were bribed to make this Treaty."[15] James Bell said, "We refused to accede to the Ross Treaty and fought it from H—l to breakfast. . . . Tell our friends not to despair. The President is [still] on our side, but wants some further excuse, and he has left the way open" for the treaty's revision by stating that he would bring the treaty up for reconsideration in the next Congress.[16] E. C. Boudinot thought it best to acquiesce in the treaty for the time being. He expected that many Cherokees would resent the concessions the Loyal delegation had been forced to make, and, in the end, there might be a total rejection of it and those who made it: "They shoulder all the responsibility of the negro matter," he wrote, and he was certain that most Cherokees (full-bloods as well as mixed-bloods) were not ready to accept former slaves as "black Cherokees."[17]

Both delegations returned home in August 1866 and waited for the council to meet. After choosing a new chief, the council would have to amend the Cherokee constitution and make some new laws in order to enact the articles of the new treaty. The former Cherokee slaves were particularly anxious to see what their new status would be and how much freedom and equality they would obtain as citizens of the Cherokee Nation.

On October 19, to the great surprise of many Keetoowahs, the council passed over Lewis Downing and chose William P. ("Will") Ross to complete his uncle's term. While the choice of worthy nephews to succeed uncles had ancient precedent in Cherokee politics, it seemed a betrayal of the Keetoowah movement. Just when the full-bloods seemed to have national power within their grasp (the original purpose for which they had been organizing), they had to accept as chief one of the most haughty, elitist, and acculturated of the mixed-bloods.

Will Ross was the son of John Golden Ross, a Scotchman. His mother was John Ross's sister, and his wife was the daughter of Lewis Ross, John Ross's brother and right-hand man as treasurer of the nation for many years. John Ross had taken this nephew under his wing at an early age, sent him to Princeton College, and then helped him acquire many important offices in order to gain experience in leadership. Will Ross had edited the *Cherokee Advocate*, served as director of the Cherokee seminaries, been a member of the Cherokee council, served as a frequent delegate to Washington, and fought through the war as a colonel in the home guard. In addition, he was a lawyer, trader, saw-mill owner, scientific farmer, and businessman. He had little in common with the full-bloods except his loyalty to his uncle and his policies. The Southern Cherokees were equally unhappy at the council's choice because they knew how bitter and unrelenting Will Ross was toward them. While some of the

Southern families moved quietly back into the Canadian District that fall, the majority, including Stand Watie, remained in the Choctaw Nation or Texas until they could determine how the new chief would act.

The council had chosen Will Ross because it felt that the nation needed an experienced leader during this period of reconstruction and doubted that Downing had the requisite experience. Much had yet to be negotiated with the federal government, and some worried that an uneducated chief who could not speak or read English would be at a disadvantage.

Once Will Ross was installed as chief in October 1866, he proceeded to implement the treaty by amending the constitution and laws of the nation. Reconstruction in the Cherokee Nation was similar to that in the slaveholding and secessionist states between 1865 and 1875 as they struggled to reenter the Union. However, the Cherokees had no carpetbaggers among them and fewer committed to the "Lost Cause." The first amendment that the council passed struck out all references in the old constitution to the institution of slavery. The second granted citizenship, voting rights, and the right to hold office to all former Cherokee slaves who returned to the nation by January 17, 1867. Many former slaves were living in Kansas, some on the Neutral Lands where they had started farms (technically the Neutral Lands were no longer part of the Cherokee Nation but were held by the United States in trust until they would be sold). Many more former slaves were still working for their Southern Cherokee owners in Texas or the Choctaw Nation. Some had been captured or sold to slave dealers during the war and carried off and sold in other states. It was not going to be easy for all of these former slaves to gain their rights as citizens of the Cherokee Nation; most Cherokees hoped that few would return in time to claim their new status.[18] Another constitutional amendment acknowledged the semiautonomous status of the Canadian District, where the Southern Cherokees were expected to settle. The amendment granted them the right to choose local judges and sheriffs as well as representatives to the National Council, as the treaty required.[19]

Several minor amendments unrelated to the treaty or the war were adopted to improve the efficiency of the nation, including new methods for selecting national judges and changes in the terms of office for certain positions. A census was to be taken every ten years to assure representation in proportion to the population of each of the nine electoral districts (though no district was to have less than two members in the lower house and two in the upper). The upper house was to be called the Senate instead of the National Committee; the principal chief and the second principal chief were to be called simply the chief and the vice chief.[20]

When a committee of the council had drafted these amendments, Chief Ross called a general council or convention of all the Cherokee people at Tahlequah to meet on November 26. The people's ratifying convention voted to accept all of the constitutional amendments for the reconstituted and reunified Cherokee Nation.

Although a few of the Southern Cherokees attended the ratifying convention, and several had been elected to offices in the Canadian District and other parts of the nation, most remained wary. Stand Watie, J. A. Scales, W. P. Adair, William P. Boudinot, and other Southern leaders called a convention of their party in the Canadian District on December 31, 1866. At this convention, the Watie faction voted to send its own delegation to Washington in January since Ross had no intention of appointing any of its members to represent the nation in its efforts to make further settlements with the United States. Southern delegates Adair, Scales, and Richard Fields arrived in Washington at about the same time as the Ross delegation. To the consternation of the latter, the new secretary of the interior, Orville H. Browning, accepted the Southern delegates as legitimate representatives of their party and proceeded to hold official meetings with them. Nothing in the treaty justified this; the nation was presumed to be reunited and therefore could have only one official delegation representing its interests. However, President Johnson still had a concern for the rights and well-being of the Southerners.

Nonetheless, a steady return of Watie party refugees from Texas, the Choctaw Nation, and the Creek Nation took place after January 1, and by no means all of them settled in the Canadian District. Many preferred to return to their old homes (or what was left of them) and to expel those who had purchased them under the now-repealed confiscation act of May 1863. The new federal agent, John P. Humphreys, wrote optimistically at the end of 1866 that both factions of the Cherokees had "a disposition to forget the past and unite as one people."[21] Probably this view did prevail among the rank and file, but the Watie-Ridge-Boudinot-Bell families were determined never to forgive or forget.

The many problems the Cherokees still had to settle in Washington in January 1867 included the sale of the Neutral Lands and the Cherokee Strip and the questions relating to railroad rights-of-way through the nation. Any railroad entering the nation from the north would have to cross through the Neutral Lands or the Cherokee Strip. Many white squatters and some Cherokees and former slaves were already farming there. Arrangements had to be made to remove these illegal squatters and settle their claims before the land could be sold. The Cherokees desperately needed the income from the sales to rebuild their nation.

Furthermore, the Cherokees, led by the adroit and businesslike Will Ross, had some hopes of gaining an interest in these railroads. The railroad company most likely to enter the nation from the north was the southern branch of the Union Pacific, led by President N. S. Goss and Secretary P. B. Maxon. On October 26 the Cherokee council passed an act appointing Ross, Lewis Downing, S. H. Benge, Daniel H. Ross, and Redbird Six Killer as a committee to meet with Goss and Maxon to negotiate a means by which the Cherokees could become shareholders in the southern branch and obtain membership on its board of directors.[22] Goss and Maxon came to Tahlequah on October 31 and agreed to build a railroad from Kansas to Fort Gibson and from there across the Arkansas River toward Texas or perhaps eastward to Fort Smith, Arkansas, within one year. The agreement also stated that "the Cherokee Nation, by its said Commissioners, agrees to take stock in said Railway Company to the extent of 500,000 dollars to be raised from the proceeds of the sale of lands belonging to the Cherokee Nation laying west of the 96 degree of west longitude [that is, the Cherokee Outlet]. . . . The Cherokee Nation may at any time within three years take a further amount of stock . . . [and] shall be entitled to two Directors in said Railway Company."[23] A 100-foot right-of-way was provided to the Union Pacific but did not include any sections of land along its track. If the railroad failed to build within one year, the contract was void, and the nation would be free to make another contract with any other railroad.

When the terms of this contract became known, the Southern Cherokees claimed that it was a corrupt bargain to line the pockets of Ross and his friends. Adair said in February 1867 that the Southern delegates would demand a thorough investigation of the whole matter by the secretary of the interior and would "try to knock it into a cocked hat if we find fraud in it."[24] The majority of Cherokees were also unhappy about the arrangement because they were vehemently opposed to selling any of the nation's land.

The plan fell through for other reasons. The Osage Nation had once owned a large tract of land stretching across the length of southern Kansas, from the Neutral Lands to the western border of the state. In the general effort of the government to move all Indians out of Kansas, the Osages had been forced to sell this tract and in exchange were promised the right to settle on land directly to the south of it on the Cherokee Outlet (for which they would have to pay the Cherokee Nation). The government expected to settle other "wild tribes" upon the Outlet, and the Treaty of 1866 had given them the right to do this as long as the Cherokee Nation agreed in each case to a suitable sale price. Consequently, the Bureau of Indian Affairs was unwilling to sanction the agreement to sell any part of the Outlet so that the Cherokees could raise $500,000 to buy shares in the southern branch of the Union Pacific and obtain two seats on the board of directors. The precise right-of-way for the railway was further held up by the complications over selling and surveying the Osage tract and the Cherokee Strip. A year went by with no start for the railway, and the contract was declared void by the council in December 1867.[25] Nevertheless, the episode demonstrated an imaginative entrepreneurial effort by the Cherokee Nation to participate in a major aspect of American postwar economic growth.

Meanwhile, another railway company, the Atlantic and Pacific, had already begun negotiations with the federal government for the purchase of the Neutral Lands, through which it planned to extend its line into the Cherokee Nation from the north. By treaty, only one railroad was to be allowed to pass through the Cherokee Nation from north to south. The federal government had ruled that the first railroad company whose tracks reached the border of the Cherokee Nation would obtain that right. The Union Pacific (later the Missouri, Kansas, and Texas Railroad) was consequently in sharp competition with the Atlantic and Pacific to be the first to reach the Cherokee border.

In making their plans to cross through the Indian Territory, capitalize on the increasing cattle trade from Texas, and push on to the Mexican Gulf to the south and to the Pacific Ocean to the west, the railroads wished to assure themselves that they would be subsidized by enormous grants of land from the public domain, which they expected to sell to white homesteaders to recoup their investment. In 1862 Congress had passed an act granting alternate sections of land along the tracks to major western railroad lines, but there was some doubt whether this act applied to land through the Indian Territory. Consequently, shortly after treaties were signed with the five major tribes in the Indian Territory granting rights-of-way (and in some treaties, alternate sections of land), Congress passed acts (on July 25, 26, and 27, 1866) promising that land grants would be given to railroads through the Indian Territory "as soon as the Indian titles are extinguished." [26] The railroads assumed, as did many in the Bureau of Indian Affairs, that Congress would very soon pass a bill making the Indian Territory into a federal territory and that under the terms of that bill, the Indian nations would be denationalized, their lands allotted in severalty, and the remaining area opened to white homesteaders. Railway companies consequently sold stock on the basis of the land they expected to acquire once a territorial bill was passed. Inevitably the railroad lobbyists in Washington became the most powerful group seeking federal ownership of the Indian Territory. The economic expansion of the United States was now clearly on a collision course with the sovereignty of all Indian nations in the West, whatever their treaty guarantees of perpetual ownership of their lands.

Within a month after the Cherokee Treaty of 1866 was ratified, Secretary of the Interior James Harlan made a contract with the American Emigrant Company to sell the Neutral Lands for $800,000 to, James F. Joy, an agent for the Atlantic and Pacific Railroad.[27] According to the Cherokee treaty, however, this land could be sold only for cash, which Joy did not have. After Harlan's resignation in December 1866, his successor, Orville H. Browning, invalidated the contract. Early in 1867, John F. Tremont, president of the Atlantic and Pacific, said he would pay $1 million for the Neutral Lands, and despite a protest by the Southern Cherokee delegation in March 1867, Browning agreed. The U.S. Senate rejected the contract because it made no provisions to deal with the thousands of squatters (red, white, and black) who were already on the land. Finally, in 1868, an agreement was reached whereby the original title (granted to the American Emigrant Company) was transferred to James F. Joy, as agent for the railroad, who would then buy the Neutral Lands on an installment plan.[28] Joy made an immediate down payment of $75,000, but it was four years before the land was surveyed, the squatters were satisfied, and the income from the sale began to come regularly into the Cherokee treasury. Cherokee recovery from the devastation of war was not, as John Ross had hoped, financed by the sale of land but, as in 1839, by the hard labor and mutual aid of the Cherokee people themselves. Meanwhile the Cherokee treasury sustained a steadily mounting national debt. The Atlantic and Pacific got its right-of-way through the Neutral Lands, but it was not the first to reach the Cherokee border.

While these complex negotiations were going on in Washington, and while the Southern Cherokees continued to agitate for money and power, the vast majority of Cherokees were trying to rebuild their homes, fence their overgrown pastures, plant crops on their weed-covered land, and acquire the implements and livestock necessary for small, self-sufficient farms. The winter of 1865–66 was unusually severe, and seeds for planting were used to feed livestock. Consequently, the harvest was lean in the fall of 1866. Horses, cows, mules, hogs, and plows were expensive. Clothing and blankets were scarce, and few had spinning wheels and looms. Some Cherokees reverted to deerskin clothes and clay pottery as they had after the Trail of Tears.

The Bureau of Indian Affairs, convinced that the western Indians were rapidly dying out and eager to crowd as many as possible into small areas in order to open up land to white settlement, persuaded Congress to establish a commission to investigate the status of the Indians. The Doolittle Commission sent long questionnaires to federal agents, army officers, and others believed to have firsthand information on the condition of the various tribes. The questions indicated that the committee expected confirmation of a series of self-serving assumptions, namely that the population of all tribes was rapidly declining; that the Indians were incompetent to manage their own affairs; that the Indians would be better off living under close white supervision under a federally managed territorial government; and that the best incentive for the Indians' improvement would be to allocate their land in severalty. The replies to these questions by Agent Justin Harlin described the status of the Cherokees at the end of the war as well as revealing the customary bias of even well-disposed whites, who saw all Indians as exhibiting bad habits, a weak character, primitive ways, and ineradicable indolence and superstitions. Harlin gave credit to the "natural sagacity" of the Cherokees but had little hope for their recovery from the devastation of war. He had worked among other tribes before becoming agent to the Cherokees in 1863. Having spent two years at Fort Gibson during the war, he was highly critical of the white military officers who failed to provide good leadership to the Indian regiments and did little to improve their morale. His detailed eyewitness report is the best available account of the economic, social, and cultural condition of the Cherokees at the end of the war, especially of the full-blood majority.

Harlin estimated that in 1861 there had been 22,000 Cherokees and "of these 8,500 joined the rebellion and about 13,500 remained in the nation" after the rebels were driven south in 1863.[29] He concluded that from disease, exposure, and warfare, the population had decreased by at least 2,500 (he referred only to the Loyal Cherokees, however, having no information on the Southern refugees who fled the nation after 1862). "I think the Cherokees, like all other tribes of Indians will decrease . . . by all the causes which have decreased other tribes." The most common illnesses were "bilious fever and fever-and-ague . . . and some inflammatory disease." In addition, "intoxication generally prevails." He observed that "some Indians are wholly temperate; some take a dram and no more, and are never drunk; some get drunk occasionally, and some get drunk at all times when they can get it." Speaking of his experience at Fort Gibson during the war, he noted that "prostitution, to a lamentable extent, does prevail and the diseases consequent upon it. . . . Their laws on the subject of marriage and marital rights are most crude. . . . They have what is called 'blanket marriages.' . . . A man may at any time after his marriage abandon his wife and children. They are frequently left very poor, to be raised by the mother." He did not mention that wives were equally free to leave their husbands.

The chief cause of the population decline, apart from wartime conditions, was, in Harlin's view, the old system of clan revenge, now distorted into factional, familial, or personal vendettas. "Their quarrels are very bitter; their hatred and love of revenge are not momentary; they endure during the life of the parties. When an opportunity offers, the death of one or both parties alone settles the matter. Sometimes the quarrel is inherited by friends and relations, and many lives are lost every year from this cause." The second leading cause of population decline stemmed from their aversion to modern medicine:

> They are very superstitious; they believe in demons, witches, ghosts, good and evil spirits, and many other kindred beliefs. They too frequently believe those, or some of them, to be the cause of their diseases, and doctor the patient more to appease the demon and drive him away, than otherwise to cure the disease. When medicine is left by a physician, it is rarely taken as directed. Some old woman or old man, the uglier, more deformed, and more ignorant, the better, comes in and by charms and incantations drives off the physician, if not the demon and the disease. Intelligent Indians have discarded such a belief, but the unintelligent adhere to it, and this costs the nation many lives every year.

Harlin's reports reveal that he was an honest and sympathetic social observer but that he shared many of the prejudices of whites. Although a strong advocate of acculturation, he opposed removing the Cherokees, or any other tribes, further west to make room for the advancing white frontier. He felt it was the duty of the government "to educate, civilize, and Christianize the Indians" and then "to admit them as citizens of the United States." He thought that "a great evil befell the Cherokee Nation when Sequoyah invented the Cherokee alphabet," and "the sooner the Cherokee alphabet and Cherokee language cease to be used, the better." Speaking and writing Cherokee promoted cultural nationalism and obstructed their assimilation.

Harlin stressed that the Cherokees were capable of self-improvement. Before the war they had built "saltworks, mills, farms, houses—many fine ones" and could build them again. "Their country is a fine country for stock, and they had vast herds," which could be restored. He firmly opposed their denationalization. "To deprive them of their country and all these improvements . . . would be national folly, sin, and everlasting disgrace. . . . The whole Indian country is one of the finest on this continent. For that reason the white man wants to get it. . . . Just what excuse we can have or feign [to take it] I cannot at present see." As for forcing the Cherokees to abandon communal ownership of their land and dividing it up, giving each a small tract of privately owned land, Harlin considered this a recipe for social disaster: "As it now is, and ought to continue, if an Indian gets tired of the place where he lives, he can sell [the improvements] and go on to any other common land . . . and call it home . . . but if they had to buy [land], they would soon have nothing to buy with. . . . A vast number of Indians who are comparatively poor and indolent" would suffer. Harlin estimated that it would take another twenty-five years to educate the full-blood Cherokees to be able to manage land as private property. Even then, he thought they should be allowed to sell their land only to other Cherokees, never to whites. Whites interspersed among the Indians would despoil and defraud them.

Describing the Cherokees' use of their lands, Harlin wrote:

Nearly all the Cherokees, in a small way, cultivate their lands. Only a very small number cultivate largely. Generally, with those who raise grain, a small field of corn[,] . . . a small field of wheat, and a vegetable garden constitute their farm products. . . . One-fourth perhaps raise less than will make their bread. The Indian men are generally indolent and careless. The women are generally slow at their work, but steady and industrious and will do a considerable amount of labor. In too many cases, the women have to do most of the work that is done.

He considered the Cherokees on the whole to be bad farmers:

The cultivation by the best farmers among the Cherokees, I think, has always been defective, and with the poorer farmers, abominable. This country is subject to drought. Their lands are very rich. They plough for all crops too shallow; and corn, when grown, they cultivate too little. Their shallow ploughing on their rich land of a wet season produces a good crop. Of a dry season, their crops are poor. Their dry seasons are as common as their wet ones. If their grounds were broken deeply, and their corn kept clear of weeds, but few of their seasons are so dry as to prevent a large yield. Their grounds, properly cultivated of a wet season, produce as fine crops of grain as I ever saw.

The greatest asset of the nation, Harlin believed, was its suitability for livestock:

Horses, mules, cattle, sheep, and hogs are reared with so little trouble and expense that at the beginning of the late rebellion almost all Cherokees had some stock. Many had large stocks and [a] few had them of their own raising by thousands. They have not heretofore had to feed their stock of any kind [even] in winter except a few for use; but their herds of all kinds lived, and the grown ones, not too old, kept fat all winter. . . . In a country where all stock winters itself, natural increase even from a small beginning soon swells into vast herds. The half-breeds generally attend to their farms and stock and many grew wealthy. The fullbloods generally did not so well, it seems, attend to their stock, and too frequently left cultivation to the women and children who could only raise a scant subsistence and but few grew wealthy. Among the fullbloods, I think, most of them have discarded the notion that labor is disgraceful to a man. . . . It is not uncommon among fullbloods for the women to own most of the stock, and generally as much as their husbands. Among half-breeds, the women generally own separate property but not to so great an extent.

Harlin especially praised the Cherokees' dedication to their public school system, which he felt indicated that "the Cherokees, as a people, do not lack capacity. Their indolence is their drawback." However, "English schools only should be supported. Schools to teach the Cherokee language should receive no encouragement whatever." For the time being, the best teachers were those "who speak both languages. . . . This is a great advantage in teaching the children who speak the English language imperfectly. Manual labor schools, I am satisfied, would do a vast amount of good." The Cherokees needed training in "patient industry and perseverance." He believed that the 1,200 orphans resulting from the war should be placed in such vocational schools.

Harlin did not tell the Doolittle Commission what it wanted to hear about territorialization. He favored honoring treaty rights and cooperating with elected Indian leaders, not unilateral federal paternalism. The government had granted the Cherokees a patent to their land, he noted, and by treaty they were entitled to keep it to themselves as long as they chose. "We have but to comply with our treaty stipulations. Protect them on their present reservations, as we are bound by treaty" to do. "It is not an open question what we think would be the best for us or for them, but what we *and* they think and what they will agree shall be done. We have so long and so often recognized in them a sort of sovereignty, the treaty-making power, and the obligatory force of these treaties on us, that it would be unjust in us, and unjust to them, now to deny them any of the rights heretofore conceded or implied." It would be best of all "for the present, and for a long time to come, to leave them just as they are." He observed: "There is no want of the keenest sagacity among the Indian tribes and among the Cherokees," and they could take care of themselves if not hindered or harassed.[30] However, Harlin spoke for allowing Indians a diminishing voice in their own affairs. Even avowed friends of the Indians had begun to advocate denationalization.

In the end, the Doolittle Commission made no recommendation either for territorial status or for allocation in severalty. Its only recommendation was for the creation of regional boards of inspection to supervise government agencies and white contractors. The commission was convinced that whites in the West were corrupt and dishonest in their relations with the Indians.

Congress, finding no help from this report and lacking any consensus in public opinion on "the Indian question," simply pressed on with the process of making treaties to place Indians on smaller and smaller reservations, trying to consolidate them all in the Indian Territory. For the next fifteen years, the pressure constantly mounted among white homesteaders, railroad promoters, land speculators, and entrepreneurs to open up all Indian land to white development on the familiar claim that Indians were a roadblock to progress.

Meanwhile, the Cherokees did their best to cope with their problems on their own. Their population did not decline; it increased steadily through the rest of the century, as did their prosperity. As they rebuilt their farms, their production of corn, wheat, and cotton rose and their livestock herds thrived. Slowly they rebuilt their bridges, gristmills, sawmills, blacksmith shops, wagon shops, and cotton gins. Experience improved their skills. The more prosperous Cherokees purchased new farm machinery and planted orchards. The public school system revived. A jail was built, which resulted in ending the practice of whipping. The *Cherokee Advocate* resumed publication. The missionaries returned and built new churches.

Gradually, as income began to come in from soldiers' back pay and pensions, various land sales, and the payments by various tribes who were settled on Cherokee land (Delawares, Shawnees, and Osages), the national income grew and the interest on it grew as well. Nevertheless, the average subsistence farmer seldom made ends meet, and the nation's income remained below its expenses from 1865 to 1885. The national debt remained at $175,000– $200,000 throughout this period. When harvests were good, people managed, but when harvests were bad (as in the early 1870s), they suffered. The Cherokee government borrowed in bad years to distribute "bread money" (corn, flour, and seed) to help the small farmers survive. At such times, the indebted farmers clamored for "per capita" payments from whatever income the nation was receiving; cash in their hands was what they needed most. However, the wealthier Cherokees constantly opposed this, urging instead that all major income from land sales and war reparations be deposited in the national trust funds so that the nation's interest or annuities would increase and enable it to meet the expenses for administration, law enforcement, schools, and care of the orphans and poor without resorting to taxation. Cherokee politics in the postwar years focused on quarrels over the disposal of funds, the reduction of individual and national indebtedness, and the increasing tensions between the poor and the rich, which, to put it another way, involved traditional communal values versus the advantages of development through free enterprise.

Nevertheless, there were sufficient areas of agreement or compromise to permit the National Council to function effectively and to satisfy most of the demands upon the annuity. The annuity, based on the interest from the national funds held in trust by the United States, mounted from $35,000 a year to $130,000 a year over the next decade as a result of new income from the sale of the Neutral Lands, the Cherokee Strip, and land sold to the other tribes that the government moved onto Cherokee land. By treaty, 35 percent of the trust fund annuity was to be devoted to public schools, 15 percent to the care of orphans, and 50 percent to running the national government (for example, salaries for officials, court costs, sheriffs' pay, and maintenance of government buildings). Virtually all Cherokees agreed on the importance of public education for their children, and one of the first tasks of reconstruction was to rebuild the school system.

In 1866 the 35 percent of the annuity available for schools came to less than $10,000, but the nation was prepared to go into debt to rebuild its public school system. The council voted that year to establish and equip thirty-two schools and to provide them with teachers. The schools were scattered throughout the nation wherever population density was sufficient to guarantee an average attendance of twenty-five or more students. The population was shifting a great deal in these years, so the school locations constantly changed. By 1870 the nation had increased the number of schools from 32 to 54, including two segregated schools for the children of former slaves. By 1875 there were 65 public schools, 7 of which were for blacks, and by 1885 the nation had 100 schools, 14 of which were for blacks (a number considered proportionate to their number). However, the number of students in school did not grow by the same ratio. In 1871 regular school attendance averaged 1,948 (out of 2,153 enrolled), and in 1881, 1,883 (out of 2,300 enrolled). This was attributed by many mixed-bloods to the failure of full-blood parents to compel their children to attend, allegedly because they held education of little value and believed the ability to read and write in the Cherokee syllabary was sufficient. More sympathetic observers attributed the low percentage of full-blood students in part to the fact that they were needed to work at home and in part to their frustration at trying to learn in a school system where all the teaching was done in English and hardly any of the teachers were bilingual. For a time after 1865, the schools experimented with bilingual education, but it proved very expensive to provide bilingual textbooks, and few teachers could be found capable of teaching in both languages.[31] Also, primarily because of the increase of whites in the nation, more and more full-bloods learned enough "pidgin" English to be described as "English-speaking," but there was no doubt that the language problem exacerbated conflicts between the rich and the poor, between the large-scale rancher, cash crop farmer, or businessperson and the poor subsistence farmer with one horse and a plow.

Lack of funds also made it difficult to care for the 1,200 war orphans. Fifteen percent of the annuity in 1866 was such a small sum that it allowed only a few dollars to support each orphan. There was no money to build an orphanage. Again the nation accepted its responsibility and went into debt to provide money to pay volunteer families a per diem fee to care for the children. To assure that they attended school and did not simply become cheap labor, the orphan fund was administered by the school districts; five orphans were allotted under the budget for each school district. The pay to foster parents was distributed by the local school committee. Smaller children were housed at first at the Female Seminary, which had closed in 1856; the building had served as a hospital during the war and was badly run down. At this "manual labor school," these orphans received practical training designed to make the boys self-sufficient farmers or mechanics at eighteen and the girls capable housewives.[32]

Ultimately, as the orphan fund increased and the seminaries were refurbished and reopened in the 1870s to train secondary school pupils who would become the nation's teachers, money was available to rent and then to build or buy a large orphan asylum. Again, however, controversy surrounded the decision to expend such a large sum on a state institution. Claims were made that certain national leaders were making money out of the orphan fund. Blacks also complained that their orphans were not admitted to the orphanage and, rather than suffer discrimination at an integrated establishment, asked that the orphan fund be divided and a separate orphanage under black supervision be established for black children.[33] Over time, the number of orphans decreased, and the expenses did not exceed the amount allotted within the annual budget. However, in the first fifteen years after the war, the number of Cherokee orphans far exceeded the funds available, and Cherokee families (probably related in some way) took them in for little or nothing, virtually adopting them.

Another continuing problem was the shortage of labor following the abolition of slavery. Those former slaves admitted to Cherokee citizenship (as well as those who were not) chose to stake out their own farms on the tribal land and to become self-employed. The Cherokees who had been nonslaveholders were generally too poor to hire extra labor. To solve the labor problem, the wealthier Cherokees embarked on the risky policy of admitting whites by the hundreds into the nation on white labor permits. Under the laws passed for this purpose, hiring permits were issued to those Cherokees who agreed to employ whites. The employers were required to pay a small fee (usually on a monthly basis) for each employee; they were also held responsible for the behavior of the whites they hired either as farmhands or mechanics, store clerks or millhands. Some of these workers were given wages out of the profits their employers made from their labor, but most became tenant farmers or sharecroppers for their employers. The permit system was subject to abuse and corruption, which ultimately led to a major confrontation between the full-bloods and mixed-bloods.

Under the communal system of landowning, any Cherokee was permitted to stake out a piece of farmland or pasture anywhere in the nation and place a hired hand, tenant farmer, or sharecropper on it. Thus those who could pay for permits became absentee landowners—some on a grand scale. Many sharecroppers brought their families with them; some married Cherokees and became adopted citizens. Not all of them paid their employers the rent due or the employers' share of the crops they grew. Many white mechanics and store clerks stayed on after their permits expired and entered into silent partnerships with Cherokees in order to run their own businesses. Whites from Kansas, Arkansas, and Texas were willing to become permit labor because they expected that Congress would soon transform the Indian country into a federal territory, after which they would be able to purchase the farm on which they had been working as sharecroppers or other tracts they wanted. Meanwhile, they paid no taxes and could profit from growing cotton, raising livestock, or making crafts.[34]

While white laborers proved helpful in alleviating the labor shortage, they posed serious difficulties for the nation when they refused to leave after their permits expired. Technically they then became illegal intruders, but it proved difficult to expel them, and their numbers increased rapidly from year to year. Many of them were unsavory characters in the first place—renegades who dared not return to their places of origin because of warrants for their arrest, lawsuits, angry wives, or unpaid debts. In the Cherokee Nation, some of these whites drifted into criminal behavior, becoming cattle thieves, whiskey peddlers, timber thieves, or robbers. A more complex aspect of the white labor permit problem arose when poor Cherokee farmers came to believe that wealthy farmers were using white labor to enhance their own landholdings, thereby engrossing more and more of the good land, pasture, and timber. Thus the rich were getting richer and the poor poorer under this system.

The Keetoowah Society and the Christian mission churches both played important roles in sustaining morale during Reconstruction. Missionaries returned to the nation as soon as the war ended, among them the Moravians, the Northern Baptists, the Southern Presbyterians, and the Southern Methodists. However, they were no longer sent by foreign mission societies that brought the gospel to the "heathen," since the Cherokees were now considered a Christianized nation. The missionaries returned under the auspices of home mission societies devoted to assisting Christian Cherokees to form congregations for worship, hire pastors, and build churches out of their own free-will offerings rather than depending on funds donated by white mission agencies. Recognizing that at the moment most Cherokees were too poor to support regular pastors, the home mission societies sent ministers to act temporarily as preachers until the congregations were able to hire pastors. As before the war, the Christian Cherokees worked cooperatively to fell and haul trees and erect their own hewn-log meetinghouses. Camp meetings remained popular, and the Baptists and Methodists in particular utilized them to recruit new members and reactivate old ones. Christianity provided a sense of community and spiritual hope—especially for the poorest.

The churches grew slowly, however, and thrived best in areas like Fort Gibson, Park Hill, and Tahlequah, where the population was most dense. The Northern Baptists remained the most numerous. According to William B. Davis, the federal agent in 1868, one-fourth of the nation's population before the war had been Baptists. Evan and John B. Jones, who had helped to found the Keetoowah Society and who had both served as regimental chaplains in the Indian home guard regiments, returned to the nation in 1866 to play influential roles as agents of the Northern Baptists. Southern Baptist missionary J. S. Murrow had served as a chaplain in Watie's regiment, but his denomination was not active in the nation during the immediate postwar years. The Northern Baptists remained popular among the Pin Indians; the Southern Methodists, among the Southern party. Southern Methodists quickly reestablished their itinerant preachers and circuits. Like the Baptists, they trained native preachers and ordained native pastors. Southern Methodist missionary John Harrell, who had served as a chaplain in Watie's regiment, returned in 1866 as superintendent of missions for his denomination. The Congregationalists from New England, who had played so large a part in the prewar years through the American Board of Commissioners for Foreign Missions, did not return after the war, but the Reverend Stephen Foreman, who had been ordained by the board, transferred to the Southern Presbyterian denomination and opened a church in Park Hill after the war. The Reverend E. J. Mack of the Moravian denomination returned to the nation in 1866, but the old mission station at New Springplace was too run down to reopen, so the Moravians preached at Tahlequah and Park Hill.

The Keetoowah Society, having achieved political dominance during the war and one of its leaders, Lewis Downing, having served as acting chief in

1866, no longer needed to maintain its policy of secrecy. Its members met openly at annual conventions, which, while they were still active in politics, they viewed as essentially social and cultural activities. Family members attended, and dancing, ballplays, and festivities predominated. In many respects, the Keetoowah Society rivaled the churches as a unifying force and an organization for mutual assistance, and many Cherokees held membership in both institutions.

Other organizations arose for social and educational purposes. By 1870 there were farmers' clubs that began to hold annual fairs to show off prize produce and livestock and share information about the newest kinds of hybrid seeds, fertilizers, varieties of hogs and cattle, and planting, mowing, and harvesting machinery. The Cherokee Agricultural Fair took place in Tahlequah in 1870 and became an annual event thereafter. Later it became the International Indian Fair, meeting annually in different Indian nations and providing intertribal social exchange and agricultural information. By 1872 there were several lodges of the Patrons of Husbandry in the nation, part of the Granger movement then spreading among white farmers throughout the United States. On the whole, the more well-to-do mixed-bloods were the most interested in scientific farming and breeding to improve their farm yields. The poorer farmers lacked the money to invest in fertilizers and complex new machinery or to pay for special breeds of cattle and hogs. However, many of them did take up fruit cultivation and began to plant apple and peach orchards.

Cherokee war veterans, though not formally organized into the Union veterans' organization, the Grand Army of the Republic, shared a common interest in obtaining back pay, pensions, and bounties. Over 3,000 Cherokee males were veterans out of a total adult male population in 1866 of 4,300. Veterans' benefits, usually in cash or bounties saleable for cash, were a major asset for the average Cherokee. The Treaty of 1866 called for full payment of all monies due to Cherokee veterans, but often administrative procedures were slow, complex, and confusing. A whole class of lawyers arose specializing in obtaining veterans' claims (for a portion of the funds retrieved). Some lawyers obtained rights of attorney from scores of veterans, and a few of them swindled both the veterans and the federal government. So many technicalities arose in proving claims that many veterans were still suing for their pensions, pay, and bounties well into the 1870s, though the great bulk of them were paid off within a few years after the war.

The Cherokee Nation, through its annual delegations to Washington, proved resourceful in obtaining monies due. The federal government was often slow in remitting funds from the sale of Cherokee land, but the delegations were very persistent. Because Cherokee voters kept a watchful eye on all relations with Washington, especially on the delegations sent to negotiate with the Bureau of Indian Affairs, there was far less corruption and scandal among the Cherokees over financial matters than in most Indian nations in these years.

The Cherokee Nation also proved rich in natural resources and in people with the business skills and resourcefulness to exploit them. Waterpower was effectively harnessed for sawmills and gristmills. Timber, salt, coal, copper, and zinc were exploited. Although their full value was not yet recognized, the dirty "oil springs" that welled up here and there were seen as having commercial prospects since it was thought that drinking oily water had medicinal value. No one had yet been able to utilize the natural gas that abounded. There was much enterprise in trade and merchandising. Tahlequah became a thriving mercantile center with stores, hotels, tanneries, livery stables, and blacksmith and wheelwright shops. By the end of the 1860s, Cherokees were once again growing large amounts of cotton, ginning it, baling it, and shipping it down the Arkansas River to New Orleans. Tobacco became a popular product, and in 1868 the first Cherokee tobacco manufacturing company began. It was followed by several others, until controversy arose over whether or not payment of the federal excise tax was required. Some Cherokees invested in steamboats and entered the shipping business. However, the most successful and profitable business, and one in which many Cherokees engaged, was cattle and horse raising on the nation's rich pasturelands.

Overcoming the bitter internal animosities growing out of the Cherokees' civil war proved, in the end, less troublesome than many had expected. Once again the Cherokees recognized that survival required unity, and, for the national good, factionalism gave way to the need for unity. In October 1868, Agent William Davis wrote in his annual report: "The unhappy differences existing between them at the close of the rebellion was [sic] in a great measure settled by the provisions of the treaty of 1866, and the so-called southern Cherokees availed themselves of the opportunity of making their friendship and alliance complete by uniting with a portion of the so-called loyal Cherokees in their national election of 1867 so that at present, the Cherokees may be regarded as one people, all working harmoniously for the advancement and prosperity of their tribe." [35]

Davis referred here to the creation of the Downing party in 1867 and its successful effort to replace Chief William P. Ross with Lewis Downing through an adroit alliance with Watie's Southern party. Agent John P. Humphreys, Davis's predecessor, had reported in January 1867 that the Cherokees were making gradual progress toward recovery and displaying "a disposition to forget the past and unite as one people," [36] but as long as the Southern party remained afraid to return to the country and continued to send its own delegation to Washington to compete with that of the Ross or National party, unity was impossible. However experienced and dedicated Will Ross was as a chief, his hatred for the members of the Watie faction and their intense dislike for him prevented any cooperation. Stand Watie himself was still living with his family in the Choctaw Nation, farming on the Red River, in the summer of 1867. Seeing no future for himself in his country, he volunteered his services to the War Department to raise a regiment of Cherokee war veterans (from his old regiment) to go West to fight the Cheyennes, Sioux, and Arapahoes.[37] His request was not granted.

Northern Baptist missionaries Evan and John B. Jones are generally given credit for devising the political strategy in 1867 that overcame the continued division of the nation. As old friends of John Ross and leaders of the Keetoowahs, they remained in the thick of political affairs after the war ended. It troubled them that Will Ross lacked his uncle's skill at relating to the common people and that he stubbornly insisted on excluding the Southern Cherokees from any political influence. He lacked the spirit of the traditional harmony ethic. Working through their Northern Baptist friends among the Keetoowahs, the Joneses suggested that a compromise candidate should run against Ross in the election in August 1867 and that he make overtures to the Southern party leaders in order to gain their support. For many in the Southern party, defeating Ross was their highest priority, but they did not trust the Pin Indians.

Lewis Downing seemed the most suitable compromise candidate, and he apparently made the first overtures to the Southern party. There is little record of Downing's negotiations with the Southern party, but he was a member of the Ross council's delegation in the spring of 1867 to Washington, where he had ample opportunity to meet with the delegates of the Southern party, who still insisted on negotiating separately with the government. From what transpired later, it appears that he made several promises in return for their support: if elected, he would appoint Southern Cherokees to important positions in the nation, and he would see that they became members of the official council delegation. Southern delegate E. C. Boudinot was not interested in an alliance, but some in the Southern party who were not particularly fond of Boudinot and who did not, as he, favor territorialization of Indian country agreed to use their influence for Downing's election. In April 1867, William P. Boudinot, Watie's nephew (and brother of E. C. Boudinot), wrote to Stand Watie in the Choctaw Nation about the coming election: "The Pin ticket for Chiefs next election is Bill Ross and Jim Beam (Csomanatah) on one side, Louis Downing and Crab Grass [Joseph Vann] on the other. The offices are worth a little now and with [John B.] Jones and Ross in the foreground to intrigue, backbite, and blarny, the race is expected with some interest by the Southern lookers-on." [38]

In June, William Penn Adair, one of the Southern delegates, wrote to Watie with a different perspective: "At this time I think our prospects in Washington are much better than they have been, provided we can beat Bill Ross for Chief, which I feel assured can be done with proper management. I will go today and see [John Porum Davis, another influential Watie supporter] and others and consult [with] them as to the course we shall pursue. . . . Should the opposition to Ross act in concert to defeat him, I feel confident of our success in closing the Cherokee business in Washington." [39] Because Adair later became a leading figure in the Downing party and was, after the election, appointed by Downing to the nation's official delegation, it seems likely that he was one of those approached in Washington by Downing. William Boudinot evidently had heard from his brother, E. C. Boudinot, of negotiations between Adair and Downing, since he wrote Watie on April 11, 1867: "If you proceed [to Washington] give my respects to Cornelious [E. C. Boudinot], Adair and [J. A.] Scales. It is reported that the latter [two] are likely to be bought off and that they will be paid a handsome sum by way of 'compromise' with the other Delegation so that the latter may swindle without further opposition." [40] Adair preferred Cherokee unity in dealing with the federal government and strongly opposed the territorial bills in Congress that E. C. Boudinot was backing. After Downing's election, Scales too was appointed to the official Cherokee delegation by Downing. Boudinot's information was apparently correct that Scales and Adair acted in collusion with Downing.

W. P. Boudinot also told Watie that the division between the Ross and Downing factions was in part over whether to grant "head rights" (that is, full Cherokee citizenship) to the various Indian tribes in Kansas (as well as to the eastern Cherokees in North Carolina) whom the Bureau of Indian Affairs wished to move into the Cherokee Nation. "The Pins, I heard, are going it pretty lively on the Head right question, pro and con. Downing [is] expected to win next August on that hobby in a canter over Ross. . . . The Pins are generally friendly [toward us] but are organized in each District with a fair supply of arms, ammunition and speeches." [41] The Pins who were friendly were undoubtedly those who supported Downing against Ross and wanted the Southerners to return and add their weight to the effort to place the full-bloods back in control.

Whether the Southerners remained observers or whether they made a bargain with Downing, most of them who voted apparently cast their votes against Will Ross. Downing was elected in August 1867 by a narrow margin, but he would not take office until the council met in November and ratified the election tabulation. During the interim, a Ghost Dance movement took place among the full-bloods that reflected the anxieties felt by many over the nation's future. It was not easy for some of them to reject their old chief's nephew or share power with the Southern party. There is no evidence that Watie or his friends made any public statement about where they stood, but for a time, Downing's decision to run against Ross created considerable tension.[42]

After his installation as chief, Lewis Downing appointed W. L. Gordon Miller as his executive secretary, a post that did not exist in the constitutional structure but that Downing had created because, unable to either read or write English, he needed a bilingual assistant. Born in Scotland, Miller had come to Montreal in 1832 and moved a few years later to North Carolina and the Cherokee Nation, where he married a Cherokee woman, automatically making him a Cherokee citizen. He was outraged by the removal process and went west with the Ross party in 1839. Thereafter, he lived in Tahlequah, working as a merchant and a lawyer until the Civil War. Indefatigable in defense of Cherokee rights and an admirer of the full-bloods, Miller was able to read and write Cherokee fluently and served the Downing party faithfully in the years ahead.[43]

After the election in 1867, Will Ross retired temporarily to private life as a merchant and a lawyer in Fort Gibson. The remaining Southern Cherokee refugees—perhaps 2,000–2,500—finally returned to live in the nation. The Downing party provided an important impetus toward national reconciliation, which supplied an additional source of talent and enterprise for the nation's economic revitalization. Stand Watie himself returned from the Red River in November 1867 and was soon rebuilding his farm at Breebs Town on the Canadian River.[44]

At the end of his first session as chief of the Cherokee council, late in November 1867, Downing appointed the members of the annual delegation to go to Washington to resolve the nation's perennial problems. Evidently true to his promises, he chose an equal number of leaders of both parties. Besides himself, the three from his own party were H. D. Reese, Archibald Scraper, and Samuel Smith; the four from the Southern party were E. C. Boudinot, W. P. Adair, J. A. Scales, and John Porum Davis. In January 1868, after reaching Washington, Adair wrote to Stand Watie's son Saladin: "It may be some news to you to know that Boudinot, Judge [Richard] Fields and Scales and myself have all made friends again."[45]

The best measure of Downing's success as chief of the reunited nation can be seen in the new treaty that this delegation worked out in Washington in the spring of 1868 with Nathaniel G. Taylor, the new commissioner of Indian affairs. Taylor proved to be one of the most congenial commissioners the Cherokees had ever faced, and he had a genuine respect for the members of the delegation. "As a body," Taylor said, "the men representing all these tribes in Washington will compare favorably with any like number of representative men in our State legislatures and in our national Congress as respects breadth and vigor of native intellect, thoroughness of cultivation and propriety and refinement of manners." He went on to note that the troubles of the Indians were caused chiefly by the unscrupulous whites on the frontier, who intruded upon and harassed them: "Beyond the tide of emigration and hanging like the froth of the billows upon its very edge is generally a host of law-defying white men, who introduce among the Indians every form of demoralization and disease with which depraved humanity and in its most degrading forms is ever afflicted." [46]

The treaty that the delegation of 1868 worked out with Commissioner Taylor was signed by Secretary of the Interior Orville H. Browning on July 9, 1868, approved by President Johnson, and presented to the Senate for ratification. It was a landmark in Cherokee affairs, resolving most of the major difficulties still pending between the Cherokee Nation and the government. The preamble indicated that its purpose was to cement the reconciliation between the Loyal and Southern wings of the nation:

> Whereas the feuds and dissensions which for many years divided the Cherokees and retarded their progress and civilization have ceased to exist and there remains no longer any cause for maintaining the political divisions and distinctions contemplated by the treaty of 19th July, 1866; and whereas the whole Cherokee people are now united in peace and friendship and are earnestly desirous of preserving and perpetuating the harmony and unity prevailing among them; and whereas many of the provisions of said treaty of July 19, 1866, are so obscure and ambiguous as to render their true intent and meaning . . . difficult to define and impossible to execute and may become a fruitful source of conflict. . . . therefore, with a view to the preservation of that harmony which now so happily subsists among the Cherokees, and to the adjustment of all unsettled business . . . between the Cherokee Nation and to the Government of the United States . . . [47]

The treaty went on in twenty-one clauses to settle the obscurities and ambiguities of the Treaty of 1866. The first three clauses declared the "abolition" of all party distinctions in the nation in order to prevent any further efforts of factions (like the Southern party) to deal with the U.S. government through their own delegations, defined the nation's boundaries precisely, and asserted the responsibility of the United States to carry out all of its obligations arising from the treaty rights of the Cherokees (such as expelling intruders from Cherokee land). The treaty also committed the United States to pay the Cherokees $3,500,000 for the Cherokee Strip, an area of 13,768,000 acres to be sold to homesteaders as part of the state of Kansas. Another clause asserted the obligation of the United States to pay 5 percent interest on the $500,000 owed the Cherokees for the Neutral Lands. The United States also agreed to pay all arrears owed to the nation for annuities withheld during the war. Perhaps most important of all, this treaty conceded that crimes involving intermarried white Cherokee citizens and Cherokees would no longer have to be tried in the federal court in Arkansas but should be tried only before the courts of the Cherokee Nation, in effect permitting the Cherokees to define who were its citizens. A minor but significant concession required the United States to reimburse those Cherokees who had been dispossessed when during the war the United States reoccupied Fort Gibson, where a garrison continued to be maintained. A commission was to be appointed to review all claims by the nation and its citizens for losses sustained during the war due either to Confederate or to Union depredations (on the grounds that the United States was, by treaty, obliged to protect the Cherokees against all such invasions and loss). The United States was also to see that all back pay and bounties still due Cherokee Union soldiers were paid.[48]

Agent William Davis commented at the time this treaty was being discussed by the U.S. Senate: "If the pending treaty is ratified, the financial pressure [on the Cherokee Nation], which is at present experienced, will be relieved at once." As he saw it, "The financial affairs of the nation are of the greatest importance. . . . The success of the merchant, mechanic, professional man and farmer all depends upon the promptness with which the national obligations are met." By expediting the sales of Cherokee land at a fair price, the treaty would redeem the nation's credit and "liquidate all their outstanding liabilities and leave a surplus in the treasury. . . . The warrants [that is, scrip] on the treasury would be at par; industry and enterprise properly rewarded, and life and energy diffused throughout every department of business. . . . The past season has been one of unusual good health. . . . The blessings of peace have rested upon us and genuine friendship and kindness have been manifested by all parties."[49]

However, the U.S. Senate was not pleased with the treaty. According to its opponents, it did little to help the railroads, made no advance toward territorial status, gave the Cherokees too much money for its land sales, and diminished the ability of the U.S. district court to protect white citizens of the United States who lived in the Cherokee Nation. In other words, the elected representatives of the white citizens of the United States believed that this treaty came too close to asserting Cherokee sovereignty. The failure of the Senate to ratify this treaty did not rest with the Downing party or the Southern party but was the result of a major shift in the official attitude of Congress toward "the Indian question." The United States was no longer willing to settle disagreements with Indians in terms of binding contracts embedded in treaties that then became "the supreme law of the land." It would be much easier for the United States to procrastinate, quibble, and make ad hoc bureaucratic decisions through the Bureau of Indian Affairs until such time as Congress decided to pass a statute that settled Indian controversies in terms satisfactory to white interests. To put it in the government's terms, the United States would henceforth decide what was in the best interests of the Indians without asking their advice or consent. This shift took disastrous form in 1871 when Congress voted to abandon the practice of dealing with Indians by treaties. With one stroke, the question of sovereignty was settled unilaterally. Whether this decision was constitutional remained debatable.

Despite the Senate's refusal to ratify the 1868 Cherokee treaty, harmony continued to prevail between the Southern party and the Downing party, and certain aspects of the failed treaty were accomplished through ad hoc agreements with the Bureau of Indian Affairs. In August 1868, federal officials agreed to appraise all of the improvements that were destroyed either by the Union army, by the Confederate forces, or by expropriation for use in the Union army (the latter being mostly cattle, horses, or wagons confiscated for army use). The payment of these claims went far to soothe the Southern party and to help the Loyal Cherokees who were trying to pay off their debts. Good harvests in the years 1868–72 and the absence of epidemics or pestilence further contributed to the recovery. Although the Cherokee Nation had suffered greater losses proportionately in lives and property than the most war-torn border state in the Union, its road to reunion was surprisingly rapid.

One of the thorniest problems remaining, and one that the Downing administration proved unable to resolve despite its best efforts, concerned the status of former Cherokee slaves—namely, how many were eligible to become citizens and how they were to be treated once they became citizens. Once again Cherokee nationalism required a clear definition of who was, or could become, "a true Cherokee."

In 1865 Congress had sent General John B. Sanborn to the Indian Territory to report on the status of former Indian slaves. He reported early in 1866 that while most of the former slaves were industrious and wanted to take responsibility for the care of their families, they were not willing to settle down on farms because they expected—and wanted—to be given a separate, segregated tract in the Indian Territory, on which the former slaves of all the five southern tribes would be allowed to settle and run their own community. Sanborn had talked to Downing (who was at that time acting chief) and reported that Downing was willing to give former Cherokee slaves a separate tract on Cherokee land. The former slaves, Sanborn said, "all desire to remain in that territory upon lands set apart for their own exclusive use." He favored this plan and believed that the former slaves should be given homesteads, owned in fee simple, as well as citizenship in the United States so that they could protect their property.[50] Nothing ever came of the plan, however, because Congress did not want the former slaves to live in a separate community and many Cherokees did not feel that they had enough good farming land to spare for 8,000 to 10,000 former slaves. Integration of the former slaves of each tribe as citizens of that tribe with full tribal rights and the responsibility for caring for themselves was the preferred solution. That was the treaty agreement, and the Cherokees were prepared to honor it. However, they hoped to keep the number of former slaves admitted as citizens to the barest minimum.[51]

One of the first acts of the Downing party in November 1867 had been to introduce a bill that would grant citizenship to those former slaves who had not been able to return to the nation by January 27, 1867, the date that the Treaty of 1866 had set for admission to citizenship. The bill had not passed because of strong opposition both in the Downing party and in the Southern party. While racial prejudice against blacks played some part in the bill's defeat (as seen in the emancipation act of 1863 that continued the prohibition against intermarriage between blacks and Cherokees or whites), the major objection involved the fact that Cherokee citizens were equally entitled to utilize the common land of the nation and to share in per capita payments from any sales of tribal land. Thus the more former slaves admitted to citizenship, the more rapidly good land would be taken up by their claims (leaving less for future generations of Cherokees) and the smaller the per capita payments to each Indian. This problem was also complicated because many former slaves from the southern states moved westward into the Indian Territory and made false claims to being former Cherokee slaves or their relatives; some intermarried with Cherokees. Antagonism against former slaves was intensified when it became clear that most of them favored territorialization and denationalization of the Cherokee Nation since they would then each obtain a 640-acre homestead in fee simple. By holding strictly to the date of January 17, 1867, the Cherokee council created great hardship for those former slaves who, for reasons beyond their control, were not able to meet that deadline. By refusing to extend the deadline as Downing recommended, the council in effect proclaimed all latecomers (known as "too-late Negroes") to be aliens or intruders and demanded that the federal government remove them from the nation since, by treaty, it was required to remove all intruders.

In 1867 there were 2,000 to 2,500 blacks living within the Cherokee Nation, less than half of them admitted to Cherokee citizenship.[52] The number grew annually because of the return of more latecomers, the influx of former slaves from the southern states, and natural increase. According to a census taken in 1868, the Cherokees had admitted 1,576 former slaves to citizenship out of an estimated 4,000 who were Cherokee slaves in 1861, but there were many disputed cases. In December 1869, the council voted that these disputed cases should be settled by the Cherokee Supreme Court and ordered all former slaves who claimed citizenship to bring their claims before the court for final adjudication. The court heard 177 applicants (representing wives and children who brought the total number of people involved to five times that figure). It rejected 130 families and admitted 47. Downing requested the council to show leniency toward the "hardship cases" and to pass a law admitting them to citizenship, but the council refused.[53] Once the Supreme Court had made its rulings, the council ordered the chief to present a list of former slaves living in the nation who had not been accepted as citizens to the federal agent with orders to have them removed. However, the federal agents and the Bureau of Indian Affairs were reluctant to take such action during the era of Radical Reconstruction, hence the problem remained unresolved during Downing's administration.[54]

Those former slaves who were accepted as citizens found that they did not obtain full equality with Cherokee citizens. There was no overt violence, no Cherokee Ku Klux Klan, and no lynchings, and blacks not only voted but also eventually elected a black council member in 1875. They were allowed to take up unclaimed land in the nation, build homes, and start farms without molestation. Many blacks with mechanical skills found work as blacksmiths, wheelwrights, mill workers, and farm laborers. However, their children were not provided with adequate schooling, and black children were not admitted to the orphan asylum. When black schools were created, they were built only in areas where the density of black population provided an average of twenty-five children in daily attendance. In less populated areas of the nation, blacks were not admitted to Cherokee public schools. Black schools, as in the South, were more poorly equipped and less well taught than Cherokee schools.[55]

Downing and some of the leading full-bloods in his administration tried repeatedly to solve the problems concerning the former slaves. Six Killer and Oochalata (Charles Thompson), two of the most distinguished full-blood members of the Cherokee Senate, introduced bills year after year to extend citizenship to the latecomers, but they were never passed.[56] The former slaves organized associations to defend their rights and sent petitions to the federal agent, the Bureau of Indian Affairs, and even to President Ulysses Grant. One petition, written by Louis Rough to Grant during the last year of Downing's administration, forcefully expresses their feelings about racial discrimination:

Mr. Grant. . . . most of the Cherykees is down on the darkys. The Cherykees says they aint in favour of the black man havin any claim, that they had rather any body else have a rite than us poor blacks. . . . [Lewis] downing is for us, Chelater [Oochalata], and mr. Six killer, them tree [*sic*] is in our favour, and what can they doo with so many [on the other side]? . . . [We] all dont think it rite to[o], after we have made them rich and built their land, doo you[?] . . . Now mister grante, i want a mesig from [you] rite away. . . . Please give me a litle infermation what the dark population is too doo about theys school funds to have our Children educated[?] Are we to rais them up like hethens[?] [57]

The election of Lewis Downing in 1867 and his subsequent reelection in 1871 were major steps on the Cherokees' road to reunion and revitalization in the postwar years, but Downing could not solve all of the nation's problems. In particular, he could not persuade the United States to help solve the problem of white intruders, railroad trespasses, and territorial efforts to undermine Cherokee sovereignty.

10

Free Enterprise and "the Indian Question," 1867–1872

As exaggerated reports of the excellence of the [Cherokee]
country go out, and the people of the States become more eager
and clamourous for its possession in consequence of these
railroads passing through it, this feeling of displeasure is still
more intensified in the minds of the masses of the Cherokee
people. This state of things, together with the fact that at each
session of Congress bills are introduced and pressed for the
establishment of a territorial government over the Indians and
looking to the opening of this country to settlement by whites,
causes among the Cherokees a deep feeling of insecurity.

—*Agent John B. Jones, 1871*

With considerable political skill and magnanimity, the Cherokee
people had, by 1870, overcome the bitter internal factionalism that had divided them for so long. John Ross's proficiency at the negotiation of the peace
in 1866 and Lewis Downing's statesmanlike overture to the Southern party in
1867 laid the basis for successful Cherokee reconstruction. But the external
forces now playing upon the nation were stronger than they had been since

1830. The eagerness of homesteaders and cattle ranchers to possess their land, the insistence of the railroad companies on obtaining large tracts to subsidize construction, and the prevailing belief of white Americans that Indians were now only a pesky nuisance in the way of national expansion produced a major shift in Indian policy in the 1870s. Denationalization of the tribes and the allocation of their land in severalty was advocated by paternalistic reformers as well as those who had little regard for Indians. The first step toward the final resolution of "the Indian question" was generally considered to pass a law to replace tribal self-government with federal administration of the Indian Territory.

Cherokee recovery from the war was hampered in the years 1866–70 by the rapid turnover among federal agents and acting agents. During these five years, the nation had five different agents and two acting agents, none of whom stayed long enough to acquaint themselves with the nation's problems or culture.[1] Not until President Ulysses Grant inaugurated his "Indian Peace Policy" and appointed John B. Jones as agent in December 1870 did the Cherokees acquire a man fully capable of understanding and sympathizing with their goal of sovereignty. Even Jones, however, could do little to forestall the pressures that concerned the Cherokees. Jones was an ardent supporter of the Downingites and had little use for either William P. Ross or the Watie-Boudinot-Bell faction. No Downingite was more strongly committed to sustaining the Cherokees than Jones; none more opposed to territorialization, white intruders, or railroad machinations. However, the more he was trusted by the Cherokees, the less he was trusted by frontier politicians and Washington railroad lobbyists. Jones was a helpful ally, but the battle for national survival had to be borne by the Cherokees themselves.

Jones endeavored to impress the Bureau of Indian Affairs by describing the enormous progress the Cherokees had made since the war in his various annual reports. He stressed their interest in scientific agriculture, their schools, their good relations with their neighbors, and the skill with which they were coping with the difficult task of incorporating other tribes who were relocated onto Cherokee land. Jones persuaded the bureau to transfer the agency headquarters from Fort Gibson, where it had been located during the Civil War, to the nation's capital at Tahlequah and encouraged the Cherokees to grant a tract of 1,280 acres on the northern edge of the town for the agency. He devoted a large section of this land to an experimental farm where he planted new varieties of grain and fruit trees. The seeds and saplings that he grew, he gave to Cherokee farmers in order to help them increase their yield. In 1871 he reported to the commissioner of Indian affairs: "In most branches of agriculture, the people are making very commendable progress. . . . The large stockraisers, who number their cattle by the thousands . . . are again slowly coming into existence here. . . . In fruit culture the Cherokees are perhaps more backward than in any other branch of agriculture. . . . By this effort, I hope it will be rendered easy for every family in the nation to have an orchard and fruit garden."[2] Jones had undertaken a careful study of the soil and rainfall and found that certain kinds of apple trees grew especially well in Cherokee country. He encouraged the formation of the Cherokee Farmers' Club in 1870, which sponsored the nation's first Cherokee Agricultural Fair at Tahlequah that year. He was also enthusiastic about the International Indian fairs that began meeting annually in different Indian nations after 1872 and were mutually supported by funds from the Cherokees, Choctaws, Chickasaws, Creeks, and Seminoles. In addition to competitions among farmers for prizes in livestock breeding and farm products, farmers' wives competed in displays of their spinning, weaving, sewing, and needlework as well as exhibiting their skills at making jellies, preserves, cheeses, and baked goods.

Jones provided valuable statistics in his annual report in 1871 on the rebuilding of farms and estimated that the population of the nation had reached 16,500 after its low point of 14,500 in 1865. He reported that the nation contained 3,792 log houses, estimating one per family: "More than a thousand of them are good, comfortable residences built of hewn timbers with stone or brick chimneys. They are equal to the best hewn-log houses in the Southwestern states. Many of them are weather-boarded so as to present the appearance of frame buildings. . . . Many families have large double-houses, a storey and a half high, with hall between, and all necessary outbuildings." As for the 5 million acres of land in the nation (excluding the Cherokee Outlet, which had another 7 million), he tried to cool the ardor of white frontier people and land speculators to acquire it by explaining that much of it was low-grade soil. "At least two-thirds are entirely unfit for agriculture," he wrote (knowing that his report would be published by the Bureau of Indian Affairs and avidly read in the surrounding states), and "a large share of the tillable land is of inferior quality."[3] If the Cherokee farmers were making a living on it, it was due to their hard work and their effort to improve produce and livestock with new hybrids and not because they were situated in a land rich in soil, rain, and timber, as the frontier whites tended to believe.

Jones maintained that if the government was serious about helping the Indians to advance in "civilization," it should provide some assistance to them and not expect them to lift themselves by their own bootstraps. "Cannot an agricultural school be established[?] . . . Can there not be an experimental fair and garden stocked, furnished and conducted in such a way as may be required? . . . I recommend that the Government aid the Cherokees in establishing and operating such school, farm and garden." He also recommended that "the Government come to the aid of the Cherokees in their noble efforts to educate their children" and "grant to the Cherokees the means necessary to carry on two high schools" to train schoolteachers, the prewar seminaries at Park Hill and Tahlequah requiring more money to repair and staff than the current state of Cherokee indebtedness would permit them to spend.

While stressing the Cherokees' herculean efforts to rebuild their nation and educate their children, Jones also noted that they operated under continual fear that their country might soon be taken from them, which was psychologically debilitating:

> They have so often been told by the newspapers and windy orators, both white and Indian, that the United States will take their country and open it for settlements, treaty or no treaty, whether they are willing or not, and that the railroads will hasten on this inevitable event, that these feelings of insecurity and dissatisfaction have become very general and intense. . . . A feeling akin to that of despair is generally prevalent among the common people, for they know that they (the common people) will be the victims in case these evil prognostications are realized.[4]

Jones summed up his own concept of proper Indian relations in 1871: "If the Government would give them assurance that white settlers will not be permitted to force themselves into their country—that the treaty guarantees will be maintained—a vastly better feeling would prevail; a more cheerful effort would be made for improvement. The Cherokees would then hail the railroads as helps and blessings" instead of a curse.[5] Jones's program for positive government assistance to the Indians ran directly counter to the prevailing ethos of self-help and survival of the fittest in the Gilded Age.

Federal Indian policy at this time concentrated on "consolidating" the western tribes onto smaller and smaller "reservations" in the eastern half of the Indian Territory. The Osages were moved from southern Kansas to settle on the Cherokee Outlet in 1870; the Delawares were resettled within the Cherokee Nation in 1867–68; and the Shawnees became part of the nation in 1870. Each of these tribes received payment from the government when it sold its older lands and with that money paid the Cherokee Nation for the right to settle on its land, paying the amount that the federal government assessed per acre for the land on which they were to settle. The Treaty of 1866 allowed the Cherokees to negotiate individually with the tribes seeking admission to their country (several negotiated but never came) and to require a contract for their admission sufficient to pay not only for the land but for the costs

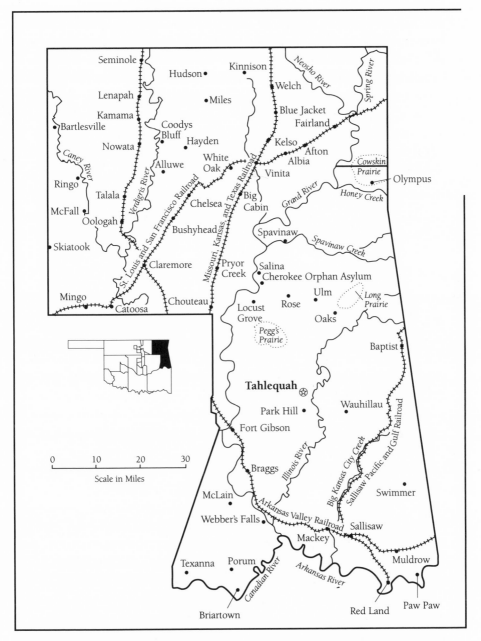

MAP 5. *Cherokee Nation, 1889*

Source: John W. Morris, Charles R. Goins, and Edwin C. McReynolds, *Historical Atlas of Oklahoma*, 3d ed. (Norman: University of Oklahoma Press, 1986).

of Cherokee administration, schools, and orphanages, which they gained the right to use. According to article 15: "The United States may settle any civilized Indians . . . within Cherokee country" provided they paid the sums required by the Cherokees, and according to article 16, any uncivilized or "wild" Indians could only be settled west of 96° on the Cherokee Outlet. The "wild tribes" were to be autonomous and paid only for the land. The "civilized tribes" received citizenship and paid amounts proportionate to their numbers for participation in Cherokee institutions.

The Delawares who had lived in Kansas were the first nation to work out an agreement for Cherokee citizenship. They purchased at $1 per acre 160 acres for each of their 985 members at a total of $157,600 and then paid an additional $121,843 into the Cherokee national trust fund to cover their share of school, orphanage, and administrative costs.[6] The Shawnees paid $50,000 for their allotted space and an annual fee of $5,000 for institutional fees so that 770 of their people could settle in the nation and become citizens.[7] Among the other tribes that settled on Cherokee land in these years were the Kaws, the Munsees, and the Chippewas. The Canasauga tribe of Mohawks negotiated but never came to settle.[8] For a time, in 1868, the Navajos talked about moving into the Cherokee Nation provided they could live east of 96°, but they wanted 900,000 acres, and the Cherokees refused to sell that much land unless it was west of 96°, the area of the Outlet.[9]

These new citizens kept to themselves and settled in the less populated Cooweescoowee District along the Verdigris and Caney rivers. They had their own local schools and sent representatives to the Cherokee council. Some of the Delawares were not happy with their land, however, and 200 of them moved out to try to find better land in the Cherokee Outlet. Chief Downing persuaded them to reconsider and later they moved back.

The settlement of the Delawares was marred at first by the efforts of some unscrupulous Cherokees to take advantage of them. Because the new tribes were not permitted to remove any Cherokee who had already settled in the area assigned to them, schemers moved into the area just prior to the Delawares' arrival, laid down four logs for a presumed house location, and then set up stakes for the perimeters of a claim. The Delawares were then fleeced to buy out each of these specious claims for several hundred dollars apiece. Agent Jones complained about these fraudulent impositions, but there was little he could do about it.[10]

The first of the "wild tribes" to move onto the Outlet were the Great and Little Osages. They left Kansas for a tract of 640,000 acres just west of 96° along the upper Arkansas River. They quarreled for years over how much this land was worth before agreeing to pay 70 cents an acre.[11]

Jones also complained that when the federal government assessed the land on the Outlet where the Osages were to settle, it did so at less than 50 percent of its real value "because it was for Indians." The land was worth $1 an acre, but the government valued it at 47 cents an acre. The Cherokees protested, and Jones supported them: "The Cherokees feel that they have been wronged by the valuation of that portion of their land lately assigned to the Osages," he wrote. The land was worth "a much higher price." Ultimately, the government agreed to raise the price to 90 cents an acre.[12]

All of these sums of money provided useful income for the indebted Cherokee Nation. However, the new citizens produced an additional burden on the nation's expenses. They also utilized large areas of Cherokee land, thus curtailing the mobility of the Cherokees within the nation. For those tribes who settled on the Cherokee Outlet, there were few problems other than the usual white encroachments on their land. However, those who settled within the nation proper and became citizens raised other issues. One of these concerned linguistic problems in the schools and in the council. More serious was the weakening of Cherokee national identity as a people. In addition, the Cherokees had qualms about sharing with these citizens the per capita income from the sale of Cherokee lands. They believed, for example, that the Neutral Lands belonged only to the Cherokee people and saw no reason to share the sale price with newcomers who were not Cherokees. The new multiracial, polyglot makeup of the Cherokee Nation by 1873 was summed up by Agent Jones:

> The Cherokee Nation consists of a heterogeneous population, differing from each other in language, race, and degree of advancement in civilization. For this reason they require a great variety of appliances to secure their further progress in all that pertains to civilization and religion. The various classes may be thus enumerated:
> 1st. The fullblood Cherokees.
> 2d. The half-breed Cherokees.
> 3d. The Delawares, both fullblood and half-breed.
> 4th. The Shawnees, both fullblood and half-breed.
> 5th. The white men and women who have intermarried with these.
> 6th. A few Creeks who broke away from their own tribes and have been citizens of the Cherokee Nation for many years.
> 7th. A few Creeks who are not citizens but live here without any right.
> 8th. A few Natchez Indians who are citizens.
> 9th. The freedmen adopted under the treaty of 1866.
> 10th. Freedmen not adopted but not removed as intruders.[13]

Of these groups, Jones said, "the fullblood Cherokees form the most numerous class, outnumbering all other classes combined." The question was, what constituted "a true Cherokee" in the nation?

Jones failed to list another group of Cherokees who spoke the same language and had the same customs but whom the western Cherokees did not acknowledge, considering them citizens of the United States. These were the Cherokees who still lived in the East, most of them in western North Carolina. In 1871 there were over 2,300 eastern Cherokees, almost all Cherokee-speaking full-bloods. During the Civil War they had, with a few exceptions, sided with the Confederacy.[14] They were so destitute in 1866 that most of them would gladly have moved to join their brethren in the West had the federal government agreed to pay for their transportation. Will Ross and Lewis Downing both said the nation would be happy to welcome them. However, the refusal of the federal government to provide money for their transportation and their internal political quarrels among rival chiefs (each of whom claimed to speak for the entire "Eastern Band") prevented any concerted action. Between 1866 and 1876 about 300 North Carolina Cherokees did make their way to the West and became Cherokee citizens, but the majority never moved. The council required those who emigrated to the West to apply for citizenship before they were allowed to enter the nation because, it said, they were U.S. citizens and the council dared not grant them the right to settle and participate as Cherokees without first applying for citizenship for fear that white citizens would somehow claim the same right.[15]

The eastern Cherokees who remained in North Carolina, nonetheless, claimed to be an integral part of the Cherokee Nation and insisted that any funds deposited into the national treasury in the Indian Territory (from land sales, war reparations, or payments by other tribes settled among them) must be prorated so as to give the Eastern Band its due share. The easterners also claimed the right to share in any per capita payments made to the nation in the West. Neither the federal government nor the western Cherokees ever accepted these claims, but considerable time and expense went toward paying lawyers' fees and the efforts of council delegations in Washington, D.C., to fight off these eastern Cherokee claims. Many in Congress and the Bureau of Indian Affairs considered it strange that blacks, Delawares, and Shawnees could become Cherokee citizens, but members of the Eastern Band had to seek individual admission in person to the nation in the West.

While the Cherokee national treasury gained almost a million dollars from the admission of other tribes to their land, the nation still could not balance its annual budget or clear its debt. Although the interest from the nation's trust funds increased year by year, the nation's expenses increased even more. For

example, administrative and school costs far outstripped the annuity allotment for them. One of the most expensive items in the nation's administrative
costs were the annual delegations to Washington. Usually four to six persons
were sent to lobby and negotiate on behalf of the nation's interests. They arrived in January and received a per diem rate of $8 to $10 per person for
the duration of each congressional session, which often lasted until July or
August. By the 1870s, the cost of the delegation sometimes reached $30,000
a year. It was difficult for the average Cherokee to understand how this enormous sum benefited the nation, especially since most of the delegations' work
went toward preventing the passage of harmful legislation (such as territorial and allotment bills) and not toward positive measures that brought in
new income. Many Cherokees came to believe that the money was used for a
luxurious binge by the delegates at the nation's expense. Because most of the
delegates were English-speaking mixed-bloods, the full-bloods came to resent
the delegation process. The delegates, of course, reported their activities each
year to the council and argued that without their efforts the nation would soon
be destroyed. Among friends, they also hinted that their most effective work
was done by bribing congressmen to vote against bills that were harmful to
the nation's interests.[16]

Added to the high cost of lobbying was the money spent to pay lawyers'
fees. Indian law became an important specialty in Washington in these years,
and lawyers who were experts in Indian affairs not only profited from adjudicating Indian claims for pensions and reparations but acted as lobbyists
and influence peddlers, many of them having been officers of high rank in the
Union army. The Cherokee delegations hired the best lawyers money could
buy and learned to know which ones they could trust and which ones they
could not. However, the fees were high either way. According to one account,
the delegations spent $64,171 for lawyers' fees in the years 1870–78.[17]

Delegations also had high costs each year for printing memorials and reports that were distributed to congressmen and to the newspapers to plead
their case on each issue. They may also have had to pay to influence certain
journalists for favorable reporting on their issues. While the full-bloods resented these expenditures, most knowledgeable Cherokees agreed that lobbying was an unfortunate prerequisite for national survival.

Another major expense not covered by the annuities was aid to needy
farmers and their families during times of drought, floods, or pestilence. Serious droughts occurred in 1866, 1873, and 1874. A prolonged drought not only
meant a small harvest but the loss of livestock. Meager harvests were con-
sumed by the end of winter, leaving no seed to plant in the spring and no food
to live on until the next harvest. For a time a farmer might survive by eating

his livestock, but ultimately horses, cows, and pigs had to be bought to replace them. Meanwhile there was no cash income for necessities like clothing and blankets, new harnesses or tools, repairs to wagons and plows, or horseshoes for the farm horses. The Cherokee hospitality ethic remained strong, and those who had food shared it with those who did not. Hard times thus affected the wealthy as well as the poor, the big farmer as well as the subsistence farmer. In earlier times, each Cherokee town had kept a communal warehouse or granary to store food for hard times. Now the burden fell on the generosity of the well-to-do and the Cherokee treasury.

Although the federal government had paid $150,000 in frozen wartime annuities to the Cherokees in 1866 to help pay off the nation's debt, it was not enough. During the next decade, the debt amounted to about $150,000 annually, and by 1878 it was up to $197,611.20. The same situation had prevailed in the prewar years, but then the nation had smaller public expenses and its delegations were much less costly. In the immediate postwar years, every family went into debt, and those who invested in the complicated new farm machinery (which promised higher yields), who tried to utilize fertilizers, who purchased better breeds of livestock, or who planted large orchards relied on credit with their local merchants. Those with big farms and herds paid off their debts, but usually they poured their profits back into expanding their farms and herds. Average Cherokee farmers seldom managed to break even, and often their debts mounted year after year. Apart from cattle and horses, cotton was the only major cash crop, and not many grew it in large quantities.

Basically the economic difficulties of the Cherokee Nation resulted from its inability to attract outside capital. There were timber and mineral deposits that could have been exploited, but the Cherokees lacked the money to invest in the manpower and equipment needed. Whites in the neighboring states expected that sooner or later the Cherokee land would fall into their hands, and they would not invest to enrich the Cherokees and keep them independent.

Cherokees did enter into small-scale enterprises, often with white partners. Gristmills and sawmills were profitable, but, run chiefly on waterpower, they often suffered damage from floods or declining use during droughts. Merchandising was done mostly on credit. Whiskey peddling was profitable but illegal. Shipping, for those who could afford to buy and maintain steamboats, was highly competitive, and accidents were common. The Arkansas River, the only major waterway through the nation, was too shallow even for Mississippi steamboats during most of the summer and fall. The only industry that seemed to offer a chance for good profits was tobacco manufacturing. It required some investment in machinery and buildings, but the fact that no excise tax would be required from Indian manufacturers would enable the sale of tobacco at competitive prices in the neighboring states.

E. C. Boudinot was one of the first to seize upon this possibility, which derived from a clause in the Treaty of 1866 that stated: "Every Cherokee and freed person resident in the Cherokee Nation shall have the right to sell any products of his farm . . . or any merchandize or manufactured products . . . without restraint, paying any tax thereon, which is now or may be levied by the United States on the quantity sold outside of the Indian Territory." [18] The tobacco grown in the Cherokee Nation and surrounding states was not of high quality, but it was suitable for "cut plug" chewing tobacco, which was very popular in the south and west. In 1868 Boudinot persuaded his uncle, Stand Watie, to lend him some money and his good name and enter into a partnership as the Watie and Boudinot Tobacco Company. Watie cared little for business but was willing to act as a silent partner; apparently he and Boudinot each put up $2,500.[19] Boudinot obtained the machinery to cut, pack, and package tobacco from a company in Hannibal, Missouri, and erected factory buildings a few feet inside the Cherokee Nation boundary at Wet Prairie, not far from Maysville, Arkansas. He was to pay for the machinery out of the profits. Boudinot found that it cost about 43 cents per pound to manufacture chewing tobacco but that the federal excise tax raised the price to 75 cents a pound. Taking advantage of the tax break for Cherokees, he could undersell his competitors by up to 32 cents a pound.

The plant began large-scale production in January 1870 and soon was turning over a very good profit. Watie needed money to rebuild his farm at Honey Creek, so Boudinot offered to buy him out. However, he kept Watie's name because it helped to sell the product. Boudinot worked also as a lobbyist for the railroads and as clerk for the congressional committee on land claims and railroads, so he had inside information on their business plans. Based on this information, he used his profits to speculate in land, particularly for hiring white permit labor to maintain claims he staked out along the right-of-way near the town of Vinita in the Cherokee Nation where the Missouri, Kansas, and Texas Railroad (MKT) was expected to intersect with the St. Louis and San Francisco Railroad (going east and west) within a year or two. Among other things, he planned to build a hotel there.

However, after several other entrepreneurs also built companies inside the Cherokee Nation, the Watie and Boudinot Tobacco Company ran into a snag when competing tobacco companies in the neighboring states began to feel the competition. The tobacco manufacturers in Missouri and Arkansas complained to their congressmen, and it was discovered that in July 1868 Congress had passed a revenue bill that imposed a tax on liquor, tobacco, snuff, and cigars manufactured "within exterior borders of the United States whether the same shall be within a collection district or not."[20] Somehow the Cherokee delegation had not been aware of this legislation Although the law was designed to curtail foreign competition, the commissioner of internal revenue was persuaded that it applied also to businesses within Indian nations. Boudinot had been aware of the law but had been told by this commissioner in October 1869 that it did not apply to his company. However, the pressure from his competitors on the government became too strong, and the commissioner changed his ruling for political reasons. The whites had votes; the Indians did not. On December 20, 1869, the U.S. marshal for the Western District of Arkansas seized the Watie and Boudinot Tobacco Company for unpaid tobacco taxes. The marshal confiscated its hydraulic press, pumps, scales, molds, and 4,500 pounds of tobacco, sugar, licorice, and grape juice. Warrants also led to the confiscation of the contents of four other tobacco companies in the nation. Boudinot found himself facing serious criminal as well as civil charges.

Boudinot's experience demonstrated that white businesspeople in the United States were not prepared to accept competition from Indians. When Indians demonstrated the ability to make money in a competitive business, they were not praised for learning the rules of capitalist enterprise and exhibiting business acumen. If an Indian nation's ambiguous status gave it any competitive edge, the advantage was promptly taken away by unilateral action; tariffs against foreign competition served the same end for overseas competitors. American free enterprise was quick to define "unfair competition" by others.

The Boudinot case raised two legal and constitutional issues: first, whether acts of Congress could supersede treaty guarantees, and second, whether Boudinot was subject to criminal charges. Boudinot managed to get his criminal case postponed until the U.S. Supreme Court could rule on the treaty power question. Meanwhile, he appealed to Chief Downing and the Cherokee council. The Downing party had no particular liking for Boudinot, but it recognized the importance of this issue for the economic future of the nation. The council voted in December 1869 to spend $1,500 to hire lawyers to argue on behalf of the nation's sovereign rights before the Supreme Court.[21] It declined to vote money to help Boudinot pay his own legal fees.

In their plea before the Court in 1870, Albert Pike and Robert W. Johnson, lawyers for the Cherokee Nation, stated that the Treaty of 1866 clearly exempted Cherokees from excise taxes, that treaties under the U.S. Constitution were the supreme law of the land, and that consequently the revenue act of 1868 could not be used to prosecute Boudinot or undermine the nation's rights. The Court, however, was not interested in protecting treaty rights. Even before the Court gave its decision, Congress had voted in January 1871: "Hereafter no Indian nation or tribe within the Territory of the United States shall be acknowledged or recognized as an independent nation, tribe or power with whom the United States may contract by treaty."[22] The days of treaty making were over, although the law did not invalidate extant treaties. On May 1, 1871, the Court handed down its decision. The majority of the Court said that there was ample precedent for the fact that "an act of Congress may supersede a prior treaty. And that the consequences in all such cases give rise to questions beyond the sphere of judicial cognizance. In the case under consideration, the act of Congress must prevail as if the Treaty were not an element to be considered."[23]

Boudinot correctly called the decision "the Death Knell of the [Indian] nations." He now faced criminal charges for breaking the law.[24] The Cherokee Tobacco Case was a major blow to the Cherokees (and all other Indian nations). With it they also lost one of the few economic advantages they had to improve their economic conditions through business enterprise. Coming on top of Congress's decision to forego treaties and to legislate whatever Congress thought best for its "wards," the Court's ruling dealt a severe blow to Indian efforts toward self-help. The Cherokee council sent a memorial to Congress in 1871 stating that these actions made them "justly solicitous as to the security and stability of their rights." They found the claim that acts of Congress could supersede treaties to be a great "departure from" their "conceptions of justice and supremacy of treaties" as stated in the U.S. Constitution. "It imperils, we fear, all our rights. It commits us wholly to the 'political department of the government.' " Treaties were contracts that "could be abrogated only by mutual consent," but by this decision, "our treaties are now dependent wholly upon the forebearance of the political department of Government."[25]

William P. Boudinot, brother of E. C. Boudinot and now editor of the *Cherokee Advocate*, wrote an editorial in which he concluded, "The decision is monstrously wrong, we think . . . and it means that Congress can take away our lands, while we hold them in common, and give them to others. The only way to save the country now is to cover it with individual titles, which Congress can't touch and the Courts can and will protect."[26] This, of course, would entail not only private ownership of land (which both the Boudinot brothers had long advocated) but an end to the tribal government, for it would require that Cherokee citizens become U.S. citizens in order to protect their title to property in U.S. courts.

A secondary but equally disturbing result of the Cherokee Tobacco Case was its effect on frontier whites. A politician in Kansas named Laughlin was reported to have given a speech telling his fellow citizens "that all Indian lands are the property of the United States and subject to the disposition of Congress." Some whites began to argue that the decision "authorizes squatters to settle on vacant Indian lands."[27] E. C. Boudinot, speaking as a business entrepreneur, thought the worst consequence of the decision was that it discouraged Indians from entering manufacturing for sale outside the nation and thus takes "from them every inducement to manufacture for themselves."[28] It also deprived them of a future source of internal taxes.

Comparatively few individuals were personally affected by the tobacco case, but all the Cherokees faced the problem of paying the national debt. Some Cherokees urged greater economy in the government, while others wanted more pressure placed on the federal government to complete the land sales entrusted to it under the Treaty of 1866. John Ross had recognized that only by selling some of its unused land and investing the proceeds could the nation hope to find the capital to secure economic self-sufficiency. Hence he had agreed to sell the 800,000-acre Neutral Lands in Kansas and the Cherokee Strip, a 435,000-acre tract 2.5 miles wide and 276 miles long stretching across the northern border of the nation from the Neutral Lands to the western border of Kansas. The Treaty of 1866 had ceded both these areas to the United States with the understanding that as soon as possible, the government would survey and sell them, turning the sale money over to the Cherokees. The treaty also said that these lands were not to be sold for less than $1 an acre; they would therefore net the nation $1,235,000, which it badly needed. Lewis Downing and his delegations worked hard from 1867 to 1872 to press the government to carry out these sales expeditiously, but it proved to be a very complicated process in which the railroad companies became deeply involved.

The Cherokee Outlet, as Will Ross had discovered in 1866 when he tried to persuade the Cherokees to invest in the Union Pacific Railroad, could not be sold because the government wanted to hold that land for relocated Indian tribes. The Neutral Lands were tied up in the efforts of James F. Joy and the southern branch of the Atlantic and Pacific Railroad to settle the claims of 20,000 squatters. The Cherokee Strip produced income only as it was purchased tract by tract by white homesteaders. The wording of the Treaty of 1866 with regard to the Cherokee Strip was so vague that the secretary of the interior did nothing to carry out his trust until May 1872, when Congress made its own provisions for the survey, appraisal, and sales.[29] Congress said the land on the Strip should not be appraised at less than $2 per acre if it was east of the Arkansas River and not less than $1.50 west of it. To avoid its being sold to land speculators, Congress required that the first sales should go to persons who occupied the land. The day that sales were to begin, thousands of homesteaders lined up on the edge of the Strip in Kansas and at the appointed moment rode their horses and wagons at breakneck speed to plots that they had previously determined to buy. However, the appraisal prices proved too high for many of them, and Congress had to pass an act giving them an extension of their payments until January 1875. Two years later, Congress voted to sell all the remaining land on the Strip for $1.25 an acre for one year and then lower the price to $1 an acre. Desperate for cash, the Cherokees agreed to all of these measures, but they did not receive the final payment until late in the century.[30]

Long before this, the Cherokees had decided to make one more effort to go into the railroad business for themselves. While the southern branch of the Union Pacific was still raising funds from eastern and foreign investors in 1867, and there was still no railway within sixty miles of Cherokee territory, E. C. Boudinot concocted a scheme. "I have drawn up and had introduced [in Congress] an important railroad bill," he wrote to Stand Watie from Washington in January 1868. "It is my own invention and I am entitled to a patent right therefore. The bill incorporates the Central Indian R.R. Co., the first directors to be apportioned to the several nations [in the Indian Territory] according to population, and the subsequent directors to represent the several nations in proportion to the stock subscribed. My plan is to allow the Indians to build their own road and own it. They have got the land and money to do it, and it will be their own fault if they don't. The bill takes well and is already printed."[31] Boudinot was at this time one of the national delegates appointed by Chief Lewis Downing to lobby for the nation. His comment that "the bill takes well" meant that Downing and the other delegates supported his plan. The bill required congressional approval because it was a joint venture of the five major southern tribes in the Indian Territory. The railroad was to be financed with monies from the respective trust funds that the federal government held for the nations. "The Secretary of Interior," the bill read, "for and in behalf of said nations, is hereby authorized to subscribe to the stock of said road after said nations shall signify, through acts of their several national councils or legislatures, their assent and desire for the same, so much as the said nations respectively may deem proper of the funds so held . . . by the government."[32] The secretary was to pay the funds "to the officer of said railroad company authorized to receive the same."

A combination of fear of white railroad corporations and trust in Downing's leadership led the full-bloods to go along with the plan. Though often charged with being traditionalists, backward, and ignorant, the full-bloods were never opposed to competing with whites in "civilized" activities as long as they trusted their leaders and felt that control remained in their own hands—and provided the plan worked on behalf of the general welfare of the nation.

Boudinot's bill named the first board of directors from each of the five major tribes. The combined trust funds of the five tribes who were to finance the railroad totaled over $10 million. Boudinot thought the board of directors would also be able to attract outside capital. Many railroad companies had been started with fewer assets, and at the very least, the existence of this company might force some other company to buy them out in order to avoid competition.

That the Cherokees took this plan seriously, at least for their own national purposes, is indicated by their continued efforts over the next three years to persuade Congress to enact Boudinot's bill. In 1869 the delegates of the Downing party presented a petition to Congress on this subject:

We know that all the varied forms of territorial government are but an initiatory step to crowding white settlers among our people. We are told that it would make no difference how we are secured and protected so it is effective, and that it would be done as effectually by legislation as by treaty; but to us it appears that when once cut loose from our treaty moorings, we will roll and tumble upon the tempestuous ocean of American politics and congressional legislation and shipwreck by our inevitable destination. . . . The Cherokees wish to build and own, by such company of Cherokee citizens as shall be organized under the authority of the Cherokee National Council, the railroads crossing their own lands. . . . They wish to do this for reasons above and of pecuniary considerations. They know that to have the roads contemplated through their country owned by the capitalists who are strangers to them, who will only look upon their nationality as in incumbrance and perhaps their presence in any form as a nuisance, would result in the loss of their lands and destruction of their people. They have the means to build their [rail]roads. . . . By allowing them to do so, a nation will perhaps be saved. By refusing . . . the last eager hope of a race [will be] extinguished.[33]

This petition was signed by Lewis Downing, W. P. Adair, Arch Scraper, James Vann, and Spencer S. Smith (Boudinot was not a delegate in 1869). Subsequent appeals were made in 1870,[34] but Congress never considered the bill. To have done so would have aroused too much opposition both from the railroad companies and from the paternalistic Indian reformers in the East who feared that venal chiefs might fritter away tribal funds to enrich themselves. In hindsight, it would have been a poor investment.

From 1868 onward, the federal agents among the Cherokees reported the increasing anxiety over the coming of the railroads. Agent John Craig said in his report in 1870, "The Cherokees have for many years past been uneasy about the security of their possession of the lands they occupy," and the railroads "excited great uneasiness" because Congress had already promised them huge land grants in Indian country. Craig did not think that freight in cattle would be sufficiently profitable to support a railroad: "No company would select a route through [the Indian Territory] . . . unless with the prospect of securing grants of land to pay expenses of construction and yield a profit" since "from Kansas to Texas . . . there will be no resources for the support of a railroad among a people entirely agricultural, excepting a limited business in transporting cattle."[35] Why, he asked, should the government violate "every principle of right" with respect to Indian treaties and take away Indian lands "to enrich railroad corporations" when everyone knew of "the unscrupulous capacity of these corporations"? Agent John B. Jones reported the following year that whites had tried to convince the Cherokees that railroads were the harbingers of prosperity, but "desirous as they are of maintaining their nationality and of holding their lands, the great majority of the people regard these roads as the introducers of calamities rather than of blessings."[36] They would even forego prosperity to avoid them.

A friend wrote to Stand Watie's wife in 1872 expressing the same foreboding: "It strikes me that Rail Road Combination[s] and their accomplishments threatened to overwhelm your Nationality."[37] Few expected that Congress could long withstand the pressure from the railroads to pass a territorial bill that would extinguish Indian title and give the railroads their millions of acres of promised land.

The MKT, successor to the southern branch of the Union Pacific, was the first road to complete a track to the border of the Cherokee Nation. In June 1870, it won from President Grant the north-south right-of-way granted in the Treaty of 1866.[38] The directors of the railroad fully expected to obtain very soon the land grants in the Cherokee Nation promised by Congress in 1866 once Indian title was extinguished by means of a territorial bill. Meanwhile they anticipated making good profits from the transporting of cattle and produce from the Southwest to the cities of the North and East. Ever since the conclusion of the Civil War, Texas cattle ranchers had been driving enormous herds of cattle through the Indian nations each year to railroad terminals on the Union Pacific—first at Kansas City and later at Dodge City and Abilene. The MKT had planned to build its line southward through the Cherokee Nation along the old Texas cattle trail and to establish big stock-loading corrals at various points along its route to obtain the freight charges that would result from their rapid means of transport to the North. The Cherokees had just started to tax these herds, but as the railroad moved southward, out of their nation, that income would disappear.[39]

The MKT was in stiff competition with the Missouri, Fort Scott, and Gulf Railroad to be the first to reach the border of the Cherokee Nation, for with only one right-of-way, there would be only one set of land grants available. There is strong evidence that in winning the race, the MKT engaged in considerable dishonesty and fraud.[40] After crossing the border just south of Chetopa, Kansas, the MKT continued its tracks southward to what became the town of Vinita (or Downingville, as the Cherokees called it in 1872) and then into the Creek Nation to Muskogee, which it reached in 1874.[41]

The second railroad to enter the Cherokee Nation, which claimed the single east-west right-of-way, was the Atlantic and Pacific Railroad (later the St. Louis and San Francisco Railroad). It entered from Missouri through the old Shawnee Reservation in 1871 and was certified for the east-west monopoly. After intersecting with the MKT at Vinita in 1872, it built no more track until the 1880s when it turned southwest to Claremore and then entered the Creek Nation at Tulsa.[42] Neither of these railroads made large profits, but they were self-sufficient. Together they combined to make a forceful lobby to persuade Congress to denationalize all of the tribes in the Indian Territory.

In 1872 the House Committee on Territories held a hearing on one of the many bills to create "the Territory of Oklahoma."[43] The committee's majority sent the bill on to Congress with its approval, but the minority report, written by Congressman H. E. McKee, so clearly expressed the views of the Cherokees that they had it reprinted and distributed for many years thereafter whenever a territorial bill came up: "The real root of this movement [for territorial bills] springs from the fact that Congress, in an unwise moment [in 1866], granted millions of acres belonging to the Indians to railroad corporations contingent upon the extinction of Indian title. And now these soulless corporations hover, like greedy cormorants over this Territory and incite Congress to remove all restraints and allow them to sweep down and swallow over 23 million acres of the land. . . . And why must we do this? In order that corporations may be enriched and railroad stocks advanced on Wall Street."[44] McKee spoke with the rhetoric of the Grangers and Greenbackers of the South and West, but he spoke for the full-blood Cherokee farmers as well.

As soon as the two authorized railroads entered the Cherokee Nation, their presidents wrote immediately to the Cherokee council, asking it to grant them alternate sections of one square mile of land on each side of their tracks. The council bluntly turned them down, but how long could they hold out against Congress?[45]

The Cherokees never found the railroads of much help to their economy. The first impact of the railroad invasion was the great number of white intruders who came into the nation with the railroads or following after them. The second was the havoc the building of the railroads wrought as tracks were laid across Cherokee farms and pastures. Agent John Jones reported that white intruders from Kansas settled all along the railroad line of the MKT as it moved into the Indian Territory because they expected that land to be particularly valuable as soon as Congress established a territorial government. Other intruders came as railroad employees—surveyors, engineers, and work crews—or as "camp followers," such as prostitutes, gamblers, and whiskey peddlers, who preyed upon the workers on paydays in the tent cities that sprang up along the newly laid tracks. These people were not particularly cordial toward Indians, and fighting frequently broke out. As the tracks were laid, severe damage was wreaked upon Cherokee timber, public and private; railroad crews cut trees indiscriminately for railroad ties, embankments, and bridges. The railroad agents were supposed to pay for all timber used, but even when they did, they paid far less than its full worth. Large numbers of Cherokee livestock were killed, sometimes shot for food by work crews, but many of them killed when engines plowed through herds grazing along the tracks.

Lewis Downing and the council frequently complained to the agent about the excessive cutting of Cherokee timber. Agent Jones wrote to the commissioner of Indian affairs that "the first effect of building these roads was to despoil the country, along their respective lines, of timber, which was already scarce."[46] The council knew that some Cherokees were in the business of supplying the railroads with ties and passed laws regulating this business and setting the price to be paid per tie, but it was difficult to monitor the process along hundreds of miles of tracks.

In December 1871, a group of Cherokee farmers applied to Jones for help in pressing claims against the MKT for damages to their livestock. Jones sent their complaints to the Bureau of Indian Affairs and substantiated the fact that the railroads had "killed and maimed" hundreds of horses, cows, and hogs. When he tried to bring these claims to the attention of the railroad managers for compensation, he was told: "The agents of the road have orders not to pay for livestock destroyed in the Indian Territory."[47] The company claimed that the owners were to blame for not fencing in their stock. In the end, Jones and the Cherokees had to gather evidence and affidavits and press their individual claims in federal courts before the railroads would even consider them. Even then, the railroads appealed many claims to the Bureau of Indian Affairs, which tended to take the companies' side or else to lower the amount awarded to the Cherokees for their claims.

Other claims were brought by Cherokee farmers who said that the railroad agents had expropriated valuable parts of their land for the right-of-way and had not paid them what the land was worth. Among the most persistent of these claimants were James P. Audrain, James Fields, and Whiteday. Audrain asked Jones to evaluate the land that the MKT took from his farm, and Jones put the value at $1,270. The railroad claimed that it was worth only $70 and refused to pay any more. The case came before the secretary of the interior who appointed a committee to examine it. After the committee approved the sum set by the agent, the railroad appealed to the secretary of the interior. The secretary overruled his own committee, and Audrain was paid only $70. The process of pursuing this claim took over two years and considerable time, effort, and money, but power, not justice, called the tune.[48]

One of the most effective means the five large southern tribes found to wage their struggle against the railroads was through their annual international councils. Some of the tribes had agreed in 1866 to work in principle toward an acceptable type of territorial structure for the Indian Territory. In order to promote this effort, the federal government agreed in 1870 to spend $10,000 a year to pay the expenses for an intertribal gathering. The international councils included representatives from over thirty tribes located in the Indian Territory, but the five large southern tribes dominated the proceedings. The Bureau of Indian Affairs delegated Enoch Hoag, head of the central and southern superintendency, to implement and supervise these international councils.

The first one was held in Ocmulgee in the Creek Nation in the autumn of 1870. The Cherokees sent Stand Watie and thirteen other delegates led by Will Ross. After long discussions of their common problems—particularly the railroad land grant laws, the Cherokee Tobacco Case, and the decision pending in Congress to end the treaty-making process—the council adopted resolutions deploring all of these conflicts. It then appointed a committee to draw up a constitution for an Indian confederacy. One of the promises the government had made to encourage the Indians to participate in forming a territorial government was that it would allow such a government to send a delegate of its own choice to Congress who would be able to speak for the Indians (although not to vote). E. C. Boudinot thought he should be that agent and hoped to use the position to advance the schemes of his railroad clients and his own plans for territorial government and allotment of the land in severalty. It was he who had persuaded the aged Stand Watie, who generally stayed out of politics, to accept the position as a delegate to the international council in 1870: "With the help of Mr. Geo. Reynolds and friends of ours among the Creeks and Seminoles, I think I could get a majority of their votes if you could be in your seat at the time of Election. . . . Let us be stripped for the fight, for now is the time when our family, so long under the ban, may assert its just position of honor among our people."[49] Boudinot always had a skewed view of what would bring honor to his family and the Cherokee people.

Will Ross was chair of the committee that drew up the Ocmulgee constitution. The document allowed every tribe to retain its sovereignty but called for each to send annual delegates, according to its population, to a confederated congress where matters of common interest could be decided. The intertribal congress was to have no power to enact laws governing all the tribes unless each member nation, through its council, voted to do so. The convention approved the constitution. Enoch Hoag, however, was not pleased with it, his aim being to break down tribal sovereignty, but he approved it as a small step in the right direction. Unfortunately none of the tribal councils ever ratified this constitution. They feared that if they ratified it and sent it to Congress, Congress would assume the power to modify it toward its own goals into a document supporting a centralized, white-supervised territorial system preparatory to statehood and detribalization. It would be easier to avoid territorialization if the nations did not give any indication that they favored territorial government in any form. Still, the international council did serve a useful function, and Agent Jones wrote the commissioner of Indian affairs in 1871: "In regard to the Ocmulgee constitution, I need make only one remark. If it should receive the sanction of the Government as it passed the [international] council, or without any radical changes, I have no doubt it would be adopted by the Cherokees. They are, however, utterly opposed to any alterations that will weaken the treaty obligations of the United States. They cling to their treaties as the sheet-anchor of their rights and immunities."[50]

Enoch Hoag continued to convene the international councils for five years and Congress voted the funds to finance them, but he could make no further headway toward his goal. In fact, the council came to see itself as a powerful tool for consolidating Indian resistance to government infringement of treaty rights. Year after year it passed strong resolutions deploring all efforts by Congress to transform the area into a federal territory. Congress finally ceased to appropriate any more funds for the gatherings in 1875. However, the tribes continued to call regular meetings at their own expense for some years after-

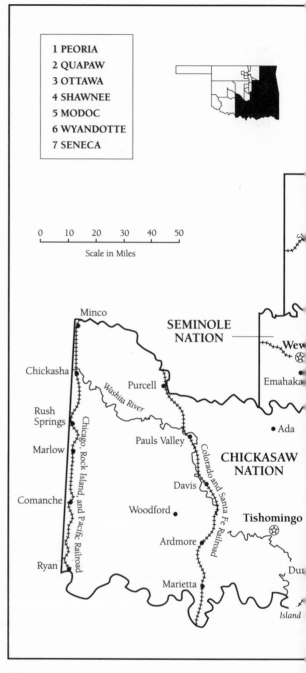

MAP 6. *Indian Territory, 1889*

Source: John W. Morris, Charles R. Goins, and Edwin C. McReynolds, *Historical Atlas of Oklahoma*, 3d ed. (Norman: University of Oklahoma Press, 1986).

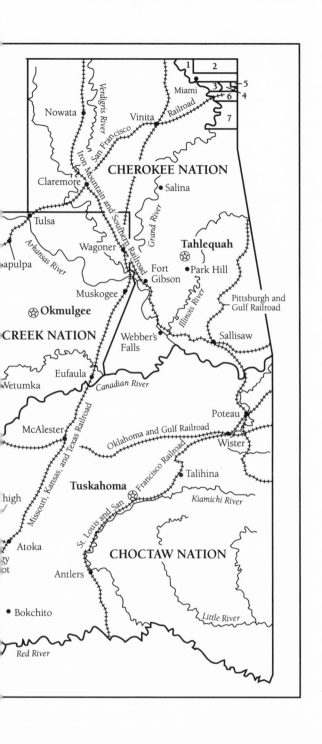

1
2
3
5
4
6
7

Miami

Nowata

Vinita

Verdigris River

Iron Mountain and Southern Railroad

San Francisco Railroad

CHEROKEE NATION

Claremore

Salina

Grand River

Tulsa

Tahlequah ⊛

Wagoner

Fort
Gibson

Park Hill

Arkansas River

apulpa

Muskogee

⊛ **Okmulgee**

Illinois River

Pittsburgh and
Gulf Railroad

CREEK NATION

Webber's
Falls

Sallisaw

Eufaula

Canadian River

Wetumka

Poteau

McAlester

Oklahoma and Gulf Railroad

Wister

Missouri, Kansas, and Texas Railroad

Talihina

Tuskahoma ⊛

Kiamichi River

St. Louis and San Francisco Railroad

high

Atoka

gy
ot

CHOCTAW NATION

Antlers

Bokchito

Little River

Red River

ward and often called international councils at times of special crisis affecting them all.

The full-bloods expressed no opposition to this effort to confederate the Indian nations. In fact, many of them agreed with Downing that it had a very useful purpose in strengthening national sovereignty and consolidating Indian unity. In most tribes the full-bloods remained the majority, and they found common ground in opposing those of mixed ancestry who claimed to see benefits in territorial status or allotment of land in severalty and clamored for protection of their private property through U.S. citizenship. The issue of tribal sovereignty was firmly allied to the issue of holding tribal lands in common. Ironically, the movement toward Pan-Indian confederation, which had started as a "progressive" effort from the federal government's position, ended as a conservative one from the Indian tribes' viewpoint. There is no doubt that the uniform and repeated opposition of all the tribes to territorialization was a major factor in defeating territorial bills in Congress in the 1870s.

On August 31, 1872, the editor of the *Cherokee Advocate* spoke with exasperation of "these everlasting territorial bills" that the nation had to combat every year at such expense. Every year after 1866 there were from four to eight different territorial bills introduced in Congress, usually by senators or congressmen from frontier states clandestinely backed by railroad promoters, land speculators, and entrepreneurs. (The only group that did not favor them were the cattle ranchers, who had worked out leasing arrangements for their herds in the Indian Territory and who knew that territorialization would introduce homesteaders who would fence off the grazing lands.) No sooner was one major territorial bill defeated than another was introduced. On December 9, 1871, the *Cherokee Advocate* reported that there would be thirty territorial bills of various kinds before the next session of Congress.

The full-bloods continued to complain about the expense involved in sending delegations to fight the bills, but there seemed no option. Downing assured them that delegations were a vital expense and that without them the nation would be destroyed.[51] To emphasize the growing frustration that he and the entire nation felt, Downing (a Baptist preacher) called a national fast day in October 1870 because it seemed that only God or the Great Spirit could relieve them of this emotional drain on their energy. In an address to the Cherokee people, Downing stressed the feeling of despair that gripped the Cherokees: "Today the Cherokees, and the whole Indian race, are in distress and danger. Powerless we lie in the hands of the government and people of the United States as did the Jews in the hands of Ahasueris and the Persians. . . . All this prosperity under God and his gospel we owe to our separate national existence and the protection and security afforded by our treaties," but now "rapacious land grabbers," "the tide of [white] immigration," and the lawlessness of "the liquor dealers" and various white outlaws within the nation were combining to overwhelm the Cherokee Nation.[52]

The following spring, Downing and the Cherokee delegation went to Washington to remonstrate against the bill that would end the practice of treaty making and to oppose the newest wave of territorial bills. The Cherokee protest against the territorial bills stated that through such schemes "the rights of [Indian] self-government are invaded and the attempt is made to render them subject to the political and municipal jurisdiction of the United States Government at Washington and the local control of white men at home." Although the delegation conceded that the Cherokees were, as John Marshall had said, "a semi-dependent nation," it insisted that they were still a nation and that "dependence does not destroy sovereignty." "We wish this fact to be kept constantly in view, that we have the inherent and inalienable right of self-government, recognized and guaranteed by treaty." The delegation declared that "every attempt to territorialize us is an attempt to break down the treaty barriers which keep the speculators and railroad land-grabbers off our possessions" and that "there are several hungry railroad corporations awaiting the extinguishment of 'the Indian title' to our lands in order that they may appropriate them to their own uses."[53]

In 1870 William P. Adair, a perennial delegate of the nation because he had become an expert on the territorial question, wrote to his cousin, James M. Bell, in April: "Thus far we have strangled four territorial bills. . . . Keep our people firmly united against this measure."[54] Then he added a significant statement that marked the growing division of opinion within the nation over whether territorialization could be held off much longer and what strategy was best to cope with that possibility. If territorialization could be held off for the time being, he suggested to Bell, "we may hope for success until our lands shall have been divided among ourselves, and then we need not fear anything from railroad or land pirates since we will have no lands for which they may maneuver." Adair was referring to a strategy increasingly popular among the wealthier mixed-bloods and the intermarried whites. Men like Bell, Adair, E. C. Boudinot, William P. Boudinot, Sut Beck, and Richard Fields had concluded that the only hope for saving the country (or "the red race") lay in abandoning communal ownership of land and dividing the whole of the nation up so as to give each family its own portion of the total. Once there was no "public land" in the nation, or no land not owned by some individual Cherokee, then there would be nothing for the railroads or white homesteaders to appropriate if a territorial bill were passed. This division would not be an equal division, of course; the richer Cherokees would obtain large tracts of land because they already had large farms. The nation had never limited the amount of land a citizen could occupy.

Virtually all territorial bills were based on the assumption that the Indians of each nation had far more land than they could ever use. The bills therefore supported the idea of allotting to each Indian family a plot of 160 acres and then throwing all the rest open to white homesteaders, railroads, or other entrepreneurial interests. By this system, approximately two-thirds of the land in the Indian Territory would be available to whites, and under a territorial (or eventually a state) government, the white inhabitants rapidly would come to dominate the legislature. The mixed-bloods like Adair, Bell, and Boudinot found this 160-acre allocation plan simply another form of communism based on the white assumption that all Indians were equally poor and deserved an equal (and small) amount of land. The mixed-bloods had worked hard to improve and enlarge their farms and pastures. They managed many different tracts, on which they raised herds of cattle, grew corn or cotton, ran sawmills or gristmills, and exploited valuable mineral resources. Any system of equal distribution would be an enormous setback to them as the most enterprising and forward-looking Indian citizens. However, if the National Council could be made to see the futility of fighting off territorial bills and steal a march on their enemies by themselves voting to divide up all their land, granting to its present occupants what they now used and then dividing the rest pro rata among the Cherokees, white land-grabbers and railroad promoters would be thwarted, for the government would not dare to take from individual property owners the land that these outsiders wanted. However, the mixed-bloods' effort to protect their personal holdings did not square with the full-bloods' economic needs and their traditional adherence to communal ownership.

Embedded in the mixed-bloods' strategy were three other implicit, seldom articulated ideas. First, the strategy was based on a conviction that the full-bloods were a backward element who never would, and never wanted to, become responsible, industrious, hardworking cash crop farmers or business-people. Mixed-bloods would find it intolerable to live under the domination of full-bloods, whose policies were based on a nativistic adherence to cultural norms repugnant to people of more "progressive" ideas. Second, the rich mixed-bloods were not unwilling to take the step from owning private property to accepting citizenship in the United States. Ultimately, only under white American law could the courts be forced to protect Indians against whites. A third unspoken assumption in the scheme of intratribal allotment in severalty was that private property would be alienable—it could be bought and sold by anyone. While this was frightening to the non-English-speaking full-bloods, who feared they would be cheated or harassed out of land allotments by whites, it was welcomed by some of the more acculturated mixed-bloods, who fully expected to be able to cope with whites and who might themselves buy out poor neighbors whose land they wanted. The Bells, Adairs, and Boudinots did not often assert these views outside of their private correspondence, but most full-bloods were aware of them.[55]

Downing's first four-year term ended in 1871, and he stood for reelection. He had lost some ground because of his generosity toward the Southern party and his willingness to give its members high positions in the nation. His desertion of the Ross or National party had alienated others, though he had certainly not denied appointments to Ross men. In addition, his lenient attitude toward the "too-late Negroes" bothered some voters who accused him of simply seeking the votes of former slaves who were now citizens.[56] Nonetheless, Downing again defeated Will Ross in the election of August 1871, and he persisted in his efforts to solve the dilemma over the former slaves, which was becoming one of the most aggravating internal problems next to that of white intruders and white labor permits.

Cherokees who opposed admitting more former slaves to citizenship felt perfectly satisfied by 1871 that they had done all that was required for them (and far more than they had anticipated in the emancipation act of 1863).[57] However, the Radical Republicans in Congress were convinced that they had not done enough. As the former slaves returned to the nation and discovered that the federal government stood behind their obtaining full citizenship, they scattered throughout the countryside, laid claim to land for farms, and struggled like most of their Cherokee neighbors to become self-sufficient. Those unable to reunite with their families found new wives or husbands and started new families. Most agents considered the former slaves to be more capable farmers than the full-blood Cherokees and reported that their farms were more prosperous and that they were more industrious. Agent William B. Davis said in 1868 that in some cases former slaves returned within the deadline "while their children, who were not large enough to travel alone, and who had been sold and separated from their parents, did not get back within the time provided. . . . In some cases such children were, under the provision of the statutes of the State where they were living at the close of the war, bound out until they should arrive at maturity, and were not allowed to return"; others had not learned of the deadline until it was long passed.[58] Davis requested that he not be forced to remove all the latecomers as intruders, for "in discharging my duty I would have to separate husband and wife, parents and children." The Bureau of Indian Affairs procrastinated.

Matters came to a head when preparations were being made for the decennial census that was to be taken in 1870. The council voted to give the census takers the right to determine who was a citizen and who was an intruder. Any former slave who disagreed with their decision was instructed to appeal to the Cherokee Supreme Court in December 1870. The court in effect was to become for this purpose a commission on citizenship status.[59] In September 1870 Agent Craig reported that only 1,545 former Cherokee slaves had been recognized as citizens and that 700 were classified as intruders.[60] "The colored people who are Cherokee citizens seem to be in some degree dissatisfied with their condition" and the "leading men among them . . . have applied to me on the part of all saying they wish to have a part of the country to themselves to own their lands individually." He said he thought the Cherokees "will accede to a proposal for setting aside a portion of the country sufficient to give each head of family 160 acres, and with this the colored people will be fully satisfied."[61] However, he was wrong.

In November 1870, Downing, noting the reluctance of the federal government to remove the latecomers and rightfully fearing the anger of Congress, urged the council once again to consider a bill to admit them to citizenship, but the bill was defeated. Meanwhile the Cherokee Supreme Court began hearing claims for blacks and whites who believed they had been unfairly declared intruders by the census takers. The court rejected all but those blacks who claimed citizenship by virtue of marriage to a Cherokee. As required by the council, Downing then presented the names of those rejected to the agent and demanded their removal from the nation as intruders. Agent John Jones was as reluctant as Agents Davis and Craig had been to carry out this order. He told the commissioner of Indian affairs that most of those rejected were latecomers who missed the deadline through no fault of their own. They had now been back in the nation for three or four years and had "opened farms and built houses." He asked, "I respectfully recommend that some step be speedily taken to ameliorate the condition of these unfortunate freedmen."[62] Again the Bureau of Indian Affairs procrastinated.

When Downing began his second term in November 1871, he once again introduced a bill to admit latecomers, and once again it failed. William P. Boudinot wrote of the defeat of the bill in the *Cherokee Advocate* on December 9, 1871:

> The bill to admit the Blacks, formerly slaves of Cherokees who failed to return to the Nation in the time required by the treaty, was lost this week in the Senate. We admire the generous feelings which must have actuated the Principal Chief in recommending such a measure. . . . We share [his] sympathy with the unfortunate colored persons whom accident or inability

prevented from realizing the greatest boon ever given to any of the Race. But there is one consolation for us. It is the reflection that what land these persons missed accepting still belongs to those who owned it before, and that their shares, already too small, are not any further reduced.

"As much as we feel for the former slaves of Cherokee masters, we confess to feeling more for those Cherokees who did not own any slaves at all," he wrote, for they would be forced to give up much of the common land to former slaves when they had never had any part in the institution of slavery. Holding onto their land was the major reason given by the Cherokees for taking a hard line against admitting the latecomers. Boudinot agreed, pointing out that for every black admitted as a Cherokee, the nation must "consent to give away a part of each share" of land properly owned by all Cherokees. "The fact is, the share of each individual Cherokee is small enough now, and there are settled causes actively operating to lessen it without seeking new ones,"[63] wrote Boudinot, meaning the railroad land grants and territorial bills. As a leader of the group of mixed-bloods who favored the division of all the land in the nation among the Cherokees prior to any territorial bill, Boudinot also stressed that former slaveholders like himself and his family would lose their "fair share" as much as any nonslaveholding full-blood if a congressional allocation took place.

Agent Jones, having heard nothing from the Bureau of Indian Affairs by February 1872, posted notices and an advertisement in the *Cherokee Advocate* announcing that all persons designated as intruders by the council must leave the nation within thirty days or he would obtain government troops to expel them.[64] Two weeks later, he wrote to the commissioner requesting advice and instructions. He could not go on ignoring the council's orders. It was unfair, he wrote, that these former slaves "must be driven out, leaving their native land, houses, farms, friends and kindred—leaving the labor of years and having blasted their fondly cherished hopes" of becoming good Cherokee citizens. "Many have been dragged South by their [Cherokee] masters or had fled North to escape, and either did not hear [of the time limit for returning] . . . or were unable to reach the nation" before it expired. The Cherokee Senate, by rejecting Downing's bill, "did not take into account the fact that these colored people and their ancestors have labored for Cherokees unpaid for many years, and that the fruits of such unpaid toil have afforded the means of defraying the expenses of educating many of the most highly cultivated Cherokees. As far as I am concerned, the class thus educated are the loudest and most influential in opposing the adoption as citizens of their former slaves." He also admitted that "many of the fullbloods share their sentiments."[65]

Jones did not at this time suggest that the latecomers be allowed to remain until the Cherokees admitted them as citizens; he saw no hope of that. He said the best solution would be for the federal government to purchase from the Cherokees a tract of land on the Cherokee Outlet where they, like the Osages, could manage their own affairs: "Perhaps some arrangement may be made by which a tract of [Cherokee] country may be set apart to them west of 96° meridian and by which they may be paid for their improvements on which they now live," so that they would not be left paupers as well as landless. If the government could provide reserves for hundreds of "wild Indians," it surely could find land for a few hundred civilized and Christian black farmers.

The Bureau of Indian Affairs instructed him not to remove the former slaves designated as intruders.[66] Although the decision was made on humanitarian grounds and was meant only to persuade the Cherokees to reconsider their vote against admitting the latecomers, it was considered by the Cherokees as a very serious abridgment of their sovereignty. Once again they were denied the right to define who was a Cherokee. It was also an infringement of treaty rights and of the Trade and Intercourse Act, which required the government to expel intruders at the request of the Cherokee council. If the Cherokees could not decide who were and were not Cherokee citizens, who should be expelled as intruders and who could live in their country, then the whole basis of their sovereignty was undermined. Even more worrisome than the refusal to remove the former slaves was the implication that the government could refuse to remove white intruders, who were much more numerous and more dangerous.

Jones, however, made it clear that the two cases were totally different. There were no humanitarian grounds at issue in removing white intruders. As a friend of the Cherokees and a Cherokee citizen by adoption, Jones was more than anxious to expel the whites whom the council had designated as intruders. White intruders took many forms. The most serious and numerous were squatters and timber thieves from Kansas who had moved across the southern border of that state into some of the most valuable tracts in the nation. Here they cut trees, built cabins, fenced in land, grew crops, herded cattle, and simply waited for the railroad companies or their agents to persuade Congress to pass a territorial bill that would give them preemption rights to purchase the land they had settled on. Many of these lived on the Cherokee Strip or the Cherokee Outlet, expecting these lands to be the first put up for sale, but many hundreds also moved into the Cherokee Nation proper, east of 96°. They knew very well that they were breaking the law; the Cherokee authorities told them so, but they paid no heed to Cherokee authority. Some of them settled on land already claimed by Cherokees, and when the Cherokees protested, the intruders simply drove them off by force. "These intruders," Jones reported to the Bureau of Indian Affairs in September 1871, "are quite defiant and cannot be removed without military force."[67] Complaints by previous agents seeking military assistance had been ignored both by military officials and by the bureau, which always disliked the expense and political agitation when whites were removed from Indian land. Frontier whites generally regarded Indian land that was unsettled as open to their settlement. Jones asked for military assistance but found it hard to obtain. At times it seemed that intruders were tolerated by the bureau as a means of destabilizing the Cherokee Nation and thus justifying detribalization.

In 1871 the army commandant for the southwestern region had sent orders to reduce the garrison at Fort Gibson to a dozen men; the rest were sent off to fight the Plains Indians.[68] When Jones wrote to Fort Gibson for assistance in removing the squatters, the commandant said he could not spare any of his men for this long and tedious duty. Jones then wrote to the commissioner of Indian affairs, stressing the possibility of violent confrontations on the border of Kansas if the squatters were not checked. "On this frontier line [south of Kansas] and along this railroad [that is, the MKT] intruders are [apt] at any moment to come into the Cherokee country and depredations are liable to be committed by whites upon Indians and vice versa. Complaints have already been made of [white] depredations" by some of the Cherokees in that vicinity. White squatters had stolen livestock and abused Cherokees who protested.[69] The army was of no assistance to him, he reported, because the commandant of the Department of Missouri, General John Pope, had prohibited "any soldiers or officers of the army from lifting a hand unless I am present to give the order in person." Jones did not see why he had to be present every time an intruder whom he had identified in writing had to be expelled. However, General Pope feared that some squatters might fire on soldiers, claiming to be protecting home and family. Pope wanted the Interior Department to bear any burden of responsibility if any soldiers or settlers were shot.[70] "No agent was ever required" before to be present when intruders were removed, Jones complained. "I wish to have this order [of General Pope] revoked as soon as possible."[71]

Rather than wait for the order to be revoked, he was prepared to accompany a body of troops to the Kansas border to remove the hundreds of squatters there. "I wish to have a company of cavalry stationed at Fort Gibson for the service which this state of things renders necessary," he told Commissioner Ely Parker. "This is a matter of great importance—the peace of the country, the protection of the people, cannot be secured unless the Agent can enforce his orders" against intruders.[72] Written orders to army officers by previous agents had simply been ignored, and the squatters, after living several years in their cabins, were convinced that the government would never remove them. Jones visited the area in 1871 and reported the serious inroads they had made into the Cherokees' limited stands of timber. "The timber in the Cherokee Nation adjoining the town of Parker[, Kansas,] and extending south on both sides of the Verdigris River for many miles, is said to have been excessively fine. . . . Its value was greatly enhanced by the scarcity of timber in that vicinity, for that whole country . . . consists of prairie." However, since the coming of the squatters and transient white timber cutters who carried the logs back to Kansas for sale, the timber "has been cut off to a great extent for some miles inside the Cherokee country and has been taken into Kansas; much of it sawed into lumber, but more of it used as rails for fencing." Three Cherokees had complained to him that good woodlands in this area "have been stripped of timber" by white intruders. Jones noted that legally the Cherokees "can claim indemnity under the intercourse laws" for the government's failure to protect their property. If an Indian war did not break out, a legal battle would. He said that he would testify on behalf of the Indians, and the federal government might have to foot the bill for these losses.

When he received no troops from Fort Gibson to help him, Jones said, "I have determined to send a United States marshal to that part of the Nation and have him arrest the offenders and bring them before the United States District Court for the Western District of Arkansas for trial to prevent further depredations." However, he doubted whether the marshal could do it alone. "I would advise [that] an officer with twenty or thirty men (cavalry) be stationed near Parker," and that they be given instructions to prevent any more intrusions from Kansas. Commissioner Parker did not reply to these requests because at this time he was at odds with President Grant over the undermining of his authority by the civilian Board of Indian Commissioners, whom Grant had appointed to reform the bureau. Parker tendered his resignation in November 1871, in the middle of this correspondence from Jones. No new commissioner was appointed until March 1872. Jones wrote in February 1872 that there were now 1,005 white squatters south of the Kansas line. "The settlers are sanguine of holding their claims and say that if they are not molested till the first of March, their number will be so great that [the] government will not dare to attempt their removal."[73] "Shall I proceed with the troops?" he asked. "Shall we arrest them?" Of course, he added, "their removal will be of little use unless measures are taken to prevent their return," hence the need for stationing troops on the border.

Ely Parker's successor, Francis Walker, reviewed the situation that Parker had let drift and concluded that Jones was right. Not removing the intruders now might cause much more trouble in the long run. He therefore authorized the use of the cavalry needed to assist Jones. Accompanied by these troops under Major J. J. Upham, Jones arrived among the squatters in April 1872. Although he had informed them in advance that he was coming, the intruders did not "start until they see the troops. . . . They believe, or pretend to believe, that the Indians have no right which the white man is bound to respect." It is "another article of their faith . . . that all unoccupied land belonging to the Indians is, or should be, free booty. The hundreds of farms or small fields and cabins built by the intruders will constitute an additional temptation to these or other intruders to come and settle on the lands" as soon as the cavalry had departed. Furthermore, "I am of opinion that efforts will be made by these bands of men [to] get up an Indian war on the border during this season."[74] Even rumors of Indian fighting would bring immediate sympathy for the squatters, and hundreds of other whites armed with guns would pour across the border to help them. If the Cherokees fought back, that would be the end of the Cherokee Nation. The governors of the adjoining states would consider this the final excuse needed for denationalizing all the tribes and turning their land over to whites.

Between May and July 1872, Jones and the cavalry succeeded in removing 1,500 intruders from this area of the nation. This was a unique achievement. No other major effort was authorized during Jones's tenure or those of his successors. Within six years, white intruders had returned to the same area in equal numbers.

Against most other white intruders, Jones was compelled to take action one at a time, for they were scattered throughout the nation. Many were whites who traded in whiskey or itinerant peddlers who came into the nation with a wagonload of goods and left after they had sold them. Others obtained licenses to trade or took on silent Cherokee partners and went into business claiming to be Cherokee enterprises. Those white businesspeople who were honest and respectable were probably an asset to the nation. They gave bonds for their good behavior, and their names were on record in the agent's office. However, many who were unwilling to give bonds or too unsavory to obtain licenses nevertheless managed to find ways to do business. One white man, S. H. Day, said he and a Cherokee partner were in the business of selling firewood to the army at Fort Gibson. However, their business consisted simply of cutting down trees in the public domain and selling the logs to the army, thus profiting from timber they did not own.[75]

A white lawyer named J. W. Wright, who had been a judge, set up a law office to handle Indian veterans' claims against the government. Wright found it easy to persuade Cherokees to grant him power of attorney; for many other claimants, he apparently forged powers of attorney. Then he pocketed the payments without informing his real or alleged clients. Wright's son, J. B. Wright, married a Cherokee and thereby became a Cherokee citizen. He accepted a position as a silent partner in a firm with two unscrupulous white traders. J. B. Wright, the agent said, "seems to be an irreclaimable drunkard and entirely unfit for business of any kind." Nonetheless, Jones reported, his two white partners, Cuthbertson and Clapperton, claimed that they were doing business for or with Wright in their store at Salt Springs in the nation. They charged high prices, cheated customers, and took all of the profits for themselves.[76] When Cuthbertson was threatened with expulsion, he was heard to say "that he can successfully override the United States Intercourse laws and set at defiance the agent" of the Bureau of Indian Affairs.[77]

The federal agent was often frustrated in his efforts to remove or prosecute such knaves when the commandant at Fort Gibson refused to provide him assistance and the U.S. district attorney in Arkansas would not prosecute. Lewis Downing protested to the commissioner of Indian affairs when the troops at Fort Gibson were removed. Considering the scope of the intruder problem, withdrawal of these troops was, Downing said, "an abandonment of the Cherokee Nation to the harpies that, in violation of United States laws and treaty stipulations, have settled within our limits and who now throng our borders waiting for such a manifestation or other weakness on the part of our government . . . and they will seize upon it as an authorized encouragement to seize upon our land with greater boldness than ever." [78] However, the troops were not returned to Fort Gibson, and future agents in need of troops had great difficulty convincing the commissioner of Indian affairs to make arrangements to have them assigned on temporary duty from some distant post.

Cherokee affairs stood in a delicate balance in the fall of 1872. Congress was whittling away at the nation's rights and leaning toward those who favored denationalization. Lewis Downing still had the confidence of the people, but in November 1872, after a two-week bout of pneumonia, he died. He was one year into his second term, and under the constitution, the council was required to choose someone to complete the last three years of his term. For reasons that are difficult to conceive, the council chose his archenemy, Will Ross, and the nation entered upon one of the stormiest periods in its peacetime history.

11

The Loss of Social Coherence, 1872–1875

It has been repeatedly charged that crime has greatly increased in the Cherokee Nation. . . . This charge, I am compelled to admit, is true. It is also true that the representations of this increase of crime have been exaggerated and distorted.

—Agent John B. Jones, 1873

The second term of William P. Ross was fraught with controversy. Few of the Watie-Boudinot-Bell faction supported him, and many of the full-bloods in the Downing party were fearful that his election would undermine their hard-won dominance and swing the nation back into the hands of its English-speaking, mixed-blood, wealthy class. Nonetheless, he was an experienced diplomat and as committed as his uncle John had been to sustaining Cherokee sovereignty.

Ross was not entirely to blame for the loss of unity that had grown under Lewis Downing from 1867 to 1872. Even a more charismatic chief would have had trouble. The Watie-Boudinot-Bell faction was determined to pursue its own agenda, and a constant stream of pressures bore down upon the nation from outside. So many lawless whites intruded onto Cherokee land that public order was bound to suffer. The problems over the two railroads, newly completed in 1872, were compounded by problems with the continuing cattle drives through the nation each year. The Radical Republicans in the U.S. Congress insisted on interfering on behalf of the latecomer former slaves and tried to dictate who was a Cherokee citizen. White homesteaders and western politicians continued to push for territorial bills that would open the Indian Territory to development. A nationwide panic and depression in the United States after 1873, coupled with a severe western drought that year, created tremendous economic strains on all farmers in the West (Indian, white, and black). Although frontier whites saw the increasing factionalism, crime, and violence among the Cherokees as further evidence of the inability of "savages" to sustain a civilized social order, the entire West was increasingly wracked by violence and political divisions in these years. The populist movement among white farmers sprang from the same dissatisfaction with the major political parties and the economic system that prevailed among the Cherokees. The Cherokee budget remained unbalanced. The federal government continued to be tardy with its payments from the sale of the Cherokee Strip and the Neutral Lands. Conflicts of jurisdiction with the U.S. District Court for the Western District of Arkansas reached new levels of hostility; several of these jurisdictional controversies reached the point of pitched gunfights. Ross struggled with all of these and failed.

In February 1874 Ross presented to Congress a thoughtful and provocative memorial against some of the perennial territorial bills before Congress, prefacing his argument by noting that violence was not peculiar to his or other Indian nations but was endemic throughout the United States. He told the House Committee on Territories that he was well aware of the many newspaper reports headlining the fact that "there are murders and outrages" committed in the Cherokee Nation: "Alas, there are. . . . And yet those who most loudly wail over such things in the Indian Country are most familiar with them at home [that is, in the border states]. Kansas, on our borders, had its Benders [an outlaw gang], its mob at Lacygne, and its shootings along the line of its railroads and border towns; Arkansas offers rewards [for wanted men], it is stated in the issue of a single paper, for fourteen murders, to say nothing of the proceedings of mobs, white and colored, and individual acts of violence which occur in the swamps and mountains" of that state. "In Missouri, the Knights of the Hood, in broad daylight, cause the gate keepers of city fairs to stand and deliver; mobs stop railway trains, plunder or murder their passengers, shoot down the officers of the law in order to hang men who have been consigned to imprisonment." Even in Washington, D.C., "murders [are] frequently committed" as well as in Virginia. Within the Cherokee Nation, "in view of the surroundings" and despite "the agitations allowed to be kept up here by unauthorized persons . . . fomenting mischief in their midst, there is no undue proportion of unpunished crime. . . . Life and property are as secure as anywhere else in the surrounding states." In fact, Ross claimed, "I appeal to experience to show that the charges of lawlessness are exaggerated." In the Cherokee Nation, there were no travelers molested, no railroad trains stopped and robbed, no telegraph poles chopped down or wires cut. All of the outcries about violence were simply "a new chord to the Territorial Harp of a thousand strings," repeating the old anthem that Indian "country stands in the way of progress and is the abode and harbor of crime."[1] Yet crime did increase in the Cherokee Nation after 1872, and before Ross's administration ended, many Cherokees held him personally to blame for tolerating criminal gangs, which they said he utilized for his own ends.

Few of the violent episodes in these years involved former slaves. Whatever prejudices the Cherokees had against blacks, they did not take them out in violence or harassment. Social segregation was practiced but often as the preference of the former slaves. Ross, like Downing and two of the leading full-bloods in the council (Six Killer and Oochalata), believed that all the latecomers should be admitted as citizens. Although, if enacted, such a measure would mean a slight loss of common land, some diminution of per capita payments, and an increase in school and orphanage expenses, it would rob the Radical Republicans in Congress of one of their most persuasive reasons for interfering with Cherokee sovereignty. However, the Southern party and most full-bloods remained opposed to admitting the latecomers. Ross introduced a bill to grant citizenship to them in November 1873, but the council once again defeated it. Ross tried to explain his position when he spoke before the House Committee on Territories in Washington in February 1874. "You are told that the freedmen . . . are in a most deplorable state, houseless, homeless, friendless, despised and neglected." He noted that by the Treaty of 1866 the former slaves were given "all the rights and privileges of native citizens." The Cherokees "have been munificent towards them, placing them upon an equal footing with native citizens, and this signified equal rights under their laws in political franchises, in lands, and moneys." The fact that several hundred "colored people" were "there by sufferance and enjoy no rights of citizens" was the result of the wording of the treaty to which the United States was itself a party. By the terms of the treaty, these former slaves "have no legal claim to be admitted. . . . The treaties make them intruders. . . . Whatever may be our sympathies, and I have shown mine[,] . . . they have no legal rights there, and the government cannot more fairly force their admission to a participation in the property of the people of that country than in that of the people of Missouri or New York."[2] For Ross and the Cherokees, the issue was national sovereignty, not racial prejudice.

The committee made no official answer to Ross's memorial, but when George W. Ingalls, successor as agent to Jones, posted a notice in November 1874 that black intruders must leave the nation within thirty days, a number of these latecomers at once sent a petition to the commissioner of Indian affairs.[3] Ingalls added a personal note to their petition requesting that he not be required to enforce their expulsion. Commissioner E. P. Smith had finally made official on May 17, 1874, what had hitherto been muted: he asserted the power of the federal government to determine Cherokee citizenship. He ordered Ingalls to keep three separate lists of noncitizens of the nation: one list of those whom he was convinced were truly intruders (such as white squatters or former slaves from the southern states); one list of North Carolina Cherokees in the nation who had not yet applied for citizenship because they believed they already were citizens; and, most important, one list of those blacks or whites who, in Ingalls's opinion, had some legitimate claim to remain in the nation, either because they were married to Cherokee citizens, they were whites with labor permits, or they were former slaves who had missed the deadline. Ingalls was instructed not to expel as intruders any persons on the second and third lists but to forward the lists, along with all evidence and affidavits, to the commissioner's office.[4] Actions of the Cherokee council and courts to determine citizenship were now subject to review and approval by the commissioner of Indian affairs.

The Cherokees were shocked by Commissioner Smith's action and protested vigorously against it. However, Smith had already made his views on Indian sovereignty very clear in his annual report to Secretary of the Interior Columbus Delano in 1873:

> We have in theory over sixty-five independent nations within our borders with whom we have entered into treaty relations as being sovereign peoples, and at the same time the white agent is sent to control and supervise these foreign powers and care for them as wards of the Government. This double condition of sovereignty and wardship involves increasing difficulties and absurdities. . . . So far, and as rapidly as possible, all recognition of Indians in any other relationship than strictly as subjects of the Government, should cease. To provide for this, radical legislation will be required.

Pending the enactment of a territorial law giving the secretary of the interior the right to govern the Indian Territory as a federal territory, Smith clearly intended to act (in concert with the secretary of the interior) to treat the Cherokees as wards of the government and make his office responsible for control over them through the federal agent.

The Cherokee National Council proceeded to make matters worse by ruling that a per capita distribution of "bread money" to be made in July 1875 to help those Cherokees facing starvation because of the severe drought in 1873–74 would be given only to Cherokees identified "by blood."[5] In effect, the council created two types of citizens: those who were Cherokees by biological inheritance and those who had been adopted into the tribe (including whites, Delawares, Shawnees, Creeks, and former slaves). Four hundred black citizens, whose families were suffering as much from the drought as any of the Cherokees "by blood," protested that the council's racial limits on the per capita payments were an infringement on their rights as citizens guaranteed under the Treaty of 1866. The Delawares, Shawnees, and Creeks adopted into the Cherokee Nation were equally angry.[6] Agent Ingalls tried unsuccessfully to delay distribution of the per capita payments until the former slaves' rights to it were adjudicated. Commissioner Smith told him that the immediate need among the Cherokees was too great, but he was perplexed about how to proceed. He told Ingalls to warn the Cherokees that no citizens should be denied their rights to obtain this or any other per capita payment. However, the money was distributed "by blood" only.

Ingalls carried out the instructions from Smith to make lists of persons he thought may be entitled to citizenship. Moreover, he offered to help former slaves against whom the Cherokee Supreme Court had ruled to get on his list of potential citizens by collecting evidence and signing affidavits for them. Chief Ross protested in June 1875 that the Bureau of Indian Affairs had no right to tell its agent to substitute his judgment about citizenship decisions for that of the duly constituted authorities of the nation. Nor, said Ross, did the commissioner or the secretary of the interior have this power. As a sovereign nation, and under its treaty right to expel intruders, the Cherokees had the power to define their own terms for tribal membership.[7]

The Cherokees were particularly upset because Ingalls had listed many white intruders as possibly having legitimate claims to reside in the nation. A. J. Watts was a case in point. Watts and members of his family (eventually joined by other squatters) came into the nation from Arkansas in 1871, and by 1875 they had farms and pastures for their cattle along the Arkansas River covering thousands of acres. Watts claimed to have some Cherokee ancestry, but the Cherokee Supreme Court had denied his claim. Despite this, Ingalls had included Watts on his list of possible citizens.

Agent Ingalls further angered the Cherokees by providing "certificates" for those on his potential-citizens lists stating that they were not to be removed by Cherokee sheriffs or other officials.[8] Such certificates became highly desirable items for blacks and whites whom the Cherokees considered intruders. It also left such persons in political and legal limbo since it was not clear whether sheriffs or courts had jurisdiction over them for misbehavior. When the Cherokee delegation to Washington in 1875 insisted on the nation's "unequivocal right" to decide who were and were not its own citizens, the acting secretary of the interior, Columbus Delano, simply ordered his own investigation of the status of the former slaves on Ingalls's list.[9]

Ross was unable to resolve this vital question of citizenship during his administration, nor could he resolve the equally complex white labor permit system that had evolved after the war. The practice of employing whites (permits were not granted to hire blacks from outside the nation) to cultivate farms as sharecroppers or tenant farmers or to take care of large herds of cattle on pastureland was subject to growing abuse. Wealthy Cherokee farmers were employing whites in order to engross larger and larger tracts of land. Claiming to be "progressive" and "enterprising" agriculturists who used new scientific methods and machinery, these Cherokees generally profited handsomely from the permit law. The law was difficult to police. When permits expired, the white sharecroppers often remained in the nation although by law they were required to leave. Resentment was strong among the full-bloods against this system; their farms were small and they had no money for extra labor. To them the rich were perverting the ancient communal system. A growing class consciousness developed among small and large farmers that reanimated the prewar bitterness between slaveholders and nonslaveholders.

An egregious example of corruption in the white labor permit system developed in the arrangement between E. C. Boudinot and A. C. Larkin. Boudinot had borrowed money from Larkin, a citizen of Arkansas, in 1870 and as a result of the Cherokee Tobacco Case was unable to pay him back. He worked out a scheme with Larkin to obtain a permit for him to settle on some of the best land in the Cherokee Nation (on the Kansas border), where he would ostensibly work as a farmer and cattle herder for Boudinot. However, after several years, Boudinot ceased to renew the permit. Larkin was then cited by the sheriff as an intruder, but he refused to leave and sought help from the federal agent. The nation also claimed that Larkin owed the treasury $500 in back taxes for grazing his cattle on Cherokee land during the years after his permit lapsed. Larkin refused to pay, and the sheriff seized some of his cattle and sold them to pay the taxes. Larkin then became involved in a lawsuit with the nation that went on for many years. However, the U.S. district attorney in

Arkansas, William H. Clayton, had no doubt that Larkin was guilty and that Boudinot had assisted him.

> I remember very distinctly the evidence of Mr. August C. Larkin. . . . He stated that at that time [1871] there was a bill known as the Parker Bill, pending in Congress which had for its object the opening to white persons of the Indian Country. It was thought this would become a law. Upon the strength of this, he entered into a contract with Colonel E. C. Boudinot by which they were to secure for themselves a large tract of valuable land. This contract was to the effect that Colonel Boudinot was to procure for Larkin a permit from the Indian authorities Authorizing him to live in this country, and Larkin was to move on[to] this land and hold it until the Parker bill should become law. Then they were to divide the land between them. Pursuant to this contract, Boudinot obtained the permit and Larkin moved on[to] the land . . . [but] the Parker bill did not pass. This permit was renewed at the end of the first year. . . . He lived there about five years altogether, the last three years without any authority whatever. . . . At the time his property was taken . . . he was an intruder. . . . His avowed purpose in moving into your country was to possess himself of a large and valuable tract of your land without consideration. He had lived and pastured large herds of cattle on your lands for five years without charge and in fraud of your rights.[10]

Federal agents had little control over the permit system because they were expected to grant a permit to anyone who could pay the fee, usually $3 per year or 25 cents per month. Most of the agents in the postwar years agreed that white permit labor meant greater economic productivity and increased the nation's prosperity. John B. Jones said in 1872: "Individual Cherokees are constantly applying for permits to hire white men as laborers, mechanics, clerks, etc. Such applications are multiplying."[11] However, he worried that such jobs did not attract very respectable whites because frontier people did not think whites should work for Indians. "Men leave the states to escape paying taxes, and they take up their residence in the Indian country" on these permits. "They are instigated to hire [out] to Cherokees more particularly by the hope of the Indian country being soon opened for white settlement. Many such laborers finally become intruders when their permits expire." Jones said he found it difficult to catch up with and expel these men or to persuade the U.S. district attorney in Arkansas to prosecute those who became swindlers of the Cherokees. He suggested to Chief Ross that some way be found to tighten up the permit law.

Ross brought a new permit bill, with higher costs and stricter terms, before the council in November 1872, which ultimately produced serious conflict. According to the account of J. R. Trott, a member of the Southern party, although Ross was not eager to raise the price of permits much higher, after he discovered that the Downing party members of the council were determined to make the cost of white labor prohibitive, he supported a high charge for permits in order to put the Downingites in an embarrassing position. However, they passed it. As a result, Trott said, "this permit bill is a fatal stroke at all the vitality that was left in the country." He told James M. Bell: "John Landrum tells me that this bill was passed for spite. That the Ross Party got it up, thinking the Downing Party would defeat it, thereby making [political] capital for Ross, and in order to evade it, they voted for it." [12] The new law aroused a storm of protest from those with a large investment in permit labor. The well-to-do who utilized the labor considered it malicious class legislation. The law took the granting of permits out of the hands of the federal agent and placed it in the hands of the Cherokee treasurer. It declared all current permits invalid, raised the fee to $2 per month, and limited the duration of new permits to one year (though they were to be renewable). Cherokees who broke any of these provisions were liable to fines of $500 to $1,000, thus holding the employers responsible if white laborers stayed on beyond their permits' duration. The law also enjoined the federal agent to strictly attend to expelling any whites whose permits had expired.

Agent Jones and the commissioner of Indian affairs received a flood of letters and petitions objecting to the law, some urging that he refuse to enforce it. One such letter from E. C. Boudinot, James M. Bell, and Sut Beck demanded that the commissioner of Indian affairs order Jones to ignore the law and continue to sign permits on request as he had done under the old law. This law, said the petitioners, "requests the U.S. Agent to have removed all white men now employed as laborers from the Nation as intruders. . . . Our large farms cannot be carried on without employment of labor obtained from the States. . . . We submit that the agent is not bound to comply with the infamous law . . . and thus to aid to destroy the industry and enterprise of our people. . . . If a poor widow, who is dependent upon the products of her farm for the support of herself and her little ones (and there are hundreds of such in our Nation), should dare to employ a white man to plough her land, she is liable to a fine of $1,000." [13] The fact that these well-to-do farmers refused to appeal to the council to revise the bill and instead sought direct intervention of the Bureau of Indian Affairs typified the contempt many mixed-bloods had for the full-bloods who dominated the council. It also indicated their willingness to put their private well-being ahead of the majority. If they could not control the council, the mixed-bloods were prepared to subvert its authority.

However, the mixed-bloods failed to consider the fact that if the commissioner could instruct the agent to ignore this law, as they demanded, he could also ignore other laws.

Always concerned about the "enterprising" members of "the Indian race," the commissioner of Indian affairs wrote to Agent Jones for his views on this issue. Jones responded that he could not agree with the large landholders that he should flout the laws of the nation but that perhaps the new bill was "too sweeping." He said he would suggest to the next council that it modify the law. He added, however, that some revision of the older permit law was essential, for the system was getting out of hand: "The present system was being greatly abused by many citizens of this Nation who made it the pretext for bringing into the community many white families. With these I have had much trouble, as difficulties have arisen between them and their employers and other Cherokee citizens. Intruders were also multiplied thereby."[14] The more disreputable white laborers often got drunk, caused fights, and frequently cheated unwary Cherokees.

Jones pointed out that the "general outcry against" the new permit law was made by the wealthier farmers and herders. "They complain . . . that the[ir] cotton farms in the Arkansas [River valley] and other farms in all parts of the Nation must to a great extent go uncultivated" without some form of cheap labor. He agreed with them that "many widow women have entered the bitterest complaints."[15] The commissioner decided to take Jones's advice and leave the matter to the council. Chief Ross, however, had so angered the Downing party by his effort to embarrass them that they refused to revise the law.

Adding to the confusion over the white labor permit law, a new kind of intrusion grew to major proportions in these years. The growth of the cattle business in Texas and nearby states had stimulated railroad growth throughout the Indian Territory, but the railroads were not yet capable of absorbing all the livestock traffic and many cattle ranchers still preferred to move their herds slowly through the good grazing land in the Indian Territory, fattening them up as they went northward into Kansas. These cattle drives lasted for months and caused constant trouble every year. More than once, quarreling and shooting resulted between Cherokees and cowboys. Having been forbidden by the United States to prevent the cattle traffic moving across their land, the Indian nations thought at least they ought to be able to collect some revenue from it. Most of the nations, including the Cherokees, passed laws in the 1870s taxing every head of foreign cattle grazing on their land. The Cherokees required a tax of 10 cents per head of beef; with foreign herds of 8,000 to 10,000, this seemed a good way to improve the nation's income. However, few cattle herders paid the tax. "Intrusions this year have taken a new form," Agent Jones reported from the Cherokee Nation in 1873. "This spring, men with droves of cattle have come down from Kansas and up from Texas and are herding on Cherokee lands. The Cherokees have a heavy tax imposed by law on such herders, but they refuse to pay such tax and the officers [of the nation] have not the power to collect it, so that a large portion of their country is overrun with men and cattle." [16]

In order to be fair to the cattle ranchers, the commissioner of Indian affairs sought advice from the U.S. attorney general as to whether the Indians had the right to tax the use of "open range" within their boundaries. The attorney general ruled that the Indians did have the right to collect the tax, but his opinion helped little. The cattle ranchers still refused to pay it. Jones reported that a man named William Brown had refused to pay the tax levied on the 10,000 cattle he grazed for six months each year on Cherokee land. Brown, Jones reported, was "an overbearing, law-defying speculator on a large scale." He had started grazing his cattle on Cherokee land in 1868, and in 1873 he had still not paid a cent. Brown's excuse was that he was an adopted member of the Osage Nation and thus did not have to pay. However, the Osages denied that he was a citizen of their nation.[17] Neither Jones nor the Cherokees found a way, during Ross's administration, to enforce the taxes on Brown and other lawless ranchers, further undermining the nation's status.

The general farm depression in the 1870s also added to the influx of whites into the nation. Jones reported gangs of armed white outlaws who camped in different parts of the nation; they engaged in stealing horses or cattle and robbing traveling peddlers or Cherokee citizens. Because many Cherokee citizens carried guns, they fought back when attacked, and a mounting toll of lives caused apprehension. The Cherokees had no mounted police, and the local sheriffs were left to maintain order through posses. In some cases the locally elected sheriffs found it more profitable either to ignore the outlaws or to collaborate with them. In theory the Cherokees and the agent could call on the U.S. marshal and district attorney of the U.S. District Court for the Western District of Arkansas to prosecute whites who committed crimes against Indians. The court and its marshal, however, proved totally unreliable. White law enforcers were usually anti-Indian, like most whites on the frontier. They claimed that the Cherokees were "wild savages," treacherous, and bloodthirsty. Some of the court's officers were former Confederate veterans who disliked the Cherokees for having sided with the Union. Several marshals in Arkansas were said to be former members of William Quantrill's infamous Confederate raiders, a group so bloodthirsty that the Confederate army eventually disowned them.[18]

Agent Jones informed the commissioner of Indian affairs in 1872: "From what I can learn [of] the whole United States Court [at Fort Smith] they are all, from the Judge and District Attorney down to their Deputy Marshalls, in the habit of trumping up charges for the sake of fees and extorting money from the accused [Indians]. Many cases of the most distressing character occur" involving the Cherokees they arrest. "An innocent [Cherokee] man is accused, thrown into jail, is compelled to fee lawyers, to deplete his means of living for his family, and pay out. This has been repeated many times, and, as I believe, maliciously." [19] At one time during his first term in office, Chief Ross was arrested and taken to Arkansas by these marshals for allegedly refusing to let them arrest a man who Ross claimed was a Cherokee citizen and subject to Cherokee law.

In the Treaty of 1866, the United States had pledged that "the United States Court" in Arkansas was to be replaced by one "to be created in Indian Territory," but no action had been taken on this. Consequently, the problem regarding who was a Cherokee citizen and who was not in cases involving crimes between whites and Indians became a major issue as more and more whites intruded into the nation. After 1872, some of these jurisdictional disputes erupted into such bloody gun battles between Cherokee sheriffs and U.S. marshals as to cause white concern far beyond Arkansas.

The two most notorious gun battles were known locally as the Going Snake Tragedy in 1872 and the Tahlequah Riot in 1874. The first took place at the Going Snake District Courthouse on April 25, where a Cherokee named Ezekiel Proctor was being tried for the murder of Polly Chesterton. Since Polly and Proctor were citizens of the nation, the Cherokees brought Proctor to trial in their courts. Polly was married to a white man, William Chesterton. She had been killed when she stepped in between Proctor and her husband as they were quarreling with drawn guns. Proctor admitted firing the shot that killed her, but his Cherokee attorney was planning to argue that her death was an unpreventable accident. Because there were no degrees of manslaughter in Cherokee law, Proctor would either be hung for murder or set free. The relatives of Polly Chesterton feared he would go free and felt this would be a miscarriage of justice. William Chesterton, acting as a citizen of the United States (although by Cherokee law he was not), swore out a warrant in the Arkansas federal court for Proctor's arrest on the charge of attempted murder, and the court sent a U.S. marshal to apprehend him. The marshal, realizing that he would probably face opposition, swore in over fifteen deputies to assist him. Some were William Chesterton's relatives, including Sut Beck, also a white man married to a Cherokee; some were renegade Cherokees related to Polly. This group of armed men rode up to the courthouse as the trial was in progress. The Cherokees had been warned of their coming and had their own armed deputies waiting. Beck stood in the doorway of the courthouse while the marshal from Arkansas presented his warrant for Proctor's arrest. When it became clear that the Cherokee judge would not honor the warrant, Beck pulled his revolver and shot at Proctor, wounding him. The Cherokee sheriff and others in the courtroom returned the fire while the marshal's deputies fired back. During the ensuing gun battle, the Arkansas forces killed Proctor's attorney and wounded six other Cherokees, including the judge. The Cherokees killed eight of the Arkansas deputies and wounded three. The marshal and his deputies then beat a retreat.[20]

When the marshal got back to Fort Smith, he and his deputies swore out warrants for the arrest of the wounded judge and many of those who had fired at them. The Cherokee judge and six Cherokee citizens were arrested and taken to jail at Fort Smith. Agent Jones, who had been away removing white intruders at the Kansas border at the time of the "tragedy," conducted a thorough investigation and wrote a long report to the commissioner of Indian affairs. He said the Arkansans had fired first and the Cherokees were simply defending themselves. He also stated that the case was rightly under Cherokee jurisdiction and that the U.S. court had no right to issue a warrant for Proctor. The affair produced headlines all over the United States, and a loud cry went up in Arkansas for the hanging of those Cherokees who had dared to fire on and kill white deputies of the U.S. marshal who were only doing their duty. The commissioner, not content with Jones's report exonerating the Cherokees, ordered Enoch Hoag, the superintendent of Indian affairs, to make another investigation. Hoag's report substantiated that of Jones: "Have visited Tahlequah," Hoag telegraphed. "All is quiet; the tragedy originated from impudent interference by Federal authority with Cherokee laws while being duly executed."[21]

The U.S. Congress was not satisfied and conducted its own inquiry. Meanwhile the seven accused Cherokees languished in jail at Fort Smith. Eventually the congressional investigation agreed that the blame rested with the federal marshals. Meanwhile, the Cherokees had demanded that the marshal and his deputies be placed on trial. Not until May 1873 was Jones able to work out a deal with the secretary of the interior in private negotiations. It called for the Cherokee prisoners to be released (much against the wishes of Arkansans) and for the Cherokees to press no charges against the marshal and his deputies.[22] Enoch Hoag saw only the tip of the iceberg when he said, "There appears to be an unfortunate conflict of jurisdiction by the United States's claiming continuance of jurisdiction over United States citizens who have become Cherokee adopted citizens in certain cases."[23]

The jurisdictional dispute was never satisfactorily settled and continued to wreak havoc on the Cherokee judicial system and Cherokee national pride for years to come. The investigations into the kinds of officers employed by the Arkansas district court were so damaging that a year later, after the Going Snake Tragedy, charges of corruption and bribery were added to those alleging the mishandling of this case, and the federal judge, the district attorney, and the chief marshal were forced to resign.[24] Year after year, Cherokee delegations claiming that a Cherokee citizen was entitled to a trial before a Cherokee jury pressed for the implementation of the article in the Treaty of 1866 specifying that a district court should be established in the Cherokee Nation. However, the federal government never enacted the clause. Instead, Congress constantly threatened to pass a law instituting a federal court in the Indian Territory that would supersede the judicial systems of all Indian nations in all criminal and civil cases. Though some mixed-blood and intermarried whites favored this because they believed it would provide greater protection to private property, the Cherokee majority consistently opposed it as another outrageous effort to undermine the sovereignty of Indian nations.[25]

The Tahlequah Riot in 1874 only indirectly involved the U.S. district court, but it did point up the appalling decline in Cherokee law enforcement. The fact that it happened in broad daylight in the nation's capital emphasized the general breakdown of law and order during Ross's administration. The "riot" was perpetrated by the murderous behavior of two drunken Cherokee citizens, John Proctor and John Ice, which the local sheriff and his deputies did nothing to stop. In fact, it appeared that the sheriff's deputies participated in the riot. On the morning of November 24, Proctor and Ice got into a quarrel with a Cherokee from North Carolina named James Murphy and killed him in broad daylight on the main street of town. They then proceeded down the street to McDaniel's Liberty Stable, where they tried to kill Thomas Hatcheets and several others who had been indirectly involved in the quarrel. The sheriff, Eli Spears, stood by through all of the fighting, along with his deputy, Henry Barnes, and other law enforcement officers. According to eyewitnesses, "They did not take any measures to quiet the riot . . . or to arrest any of the parties engaged . . . save two members of their own guard . . . after those two persons had emptied their revolvers or pistols, and not until after the riot or disturbance was over."[26]

In the view of Agent George W. Ingalls, whom Chief Ross requested to investigate the riot, "the said Spears possessed neither fitness nor other qualifications necessary for the position" he occupied, and his appointment as sheriff "has served to create a feeling of uneasiness and apprehension of danger in the minds of the people instead of a feeling of security." Spears, it seems, was closely associated with various members of a gang of local outlaws who had somehow engineered his election and then arranged to have themselves, though "men of bad repute," placed on the police force as Spears's deputies.[27]

Ross immediately removed Spears from his position, but many thought Ross had previously approved his election. Ingalls therefore added a note to his report saying, "It is proper and just for me to state that there is nothing in this testimony to show that the Chief or his other officers have in any way been responsible for this riot." The mere fact that Ingalls felt it necessary to say this indicates that many suspected some collusion between Ross and the criminals who terrorized the area around Tahlequah.

Two years before this riot, John B. Jones had written to the commissioner of Indian affairs: "There existed, and still exists, evidence that a strong combination of bad men [live] here [in Tahlequah]. That they introduce liquor and sell it; that they steal horses and other things, and that a party of them have murdered Teigle and Phipps," two Germans traveling through the nation who were shot and robbed. Jones added, "The Sheriff of this district is the intimate friend of those constituting this combination; that men of this character . . . have at various times of late been summoned by the said Sheriff as guards and posse. That while on guard, they have committed wanton deeds of violence."[28]

In the aftermath of the riot, John Proctor was put on trial for the murder of James Murphy, and the Cherokee Nation agreed to pay the attorney's fees. The trial of Proctor took place in the Arkansas district court because James Murphy had not yet applied for Cherokee citizenship; consequently, the U.S. court claimed jurisdiction because, as the Cherokees themselves maintained, the North Carolina Cherokees were citizens of the United States.[29]

Another major anomaly in the Cherokee legal system that caused considerable difficulty and debate concerned the absence of any legal process by which a civil suit involving a Cherokee and a citizen of the United States could be adjudicated. Parties with claims involving contractual problems, unpaid debts, or fraud generally came to the federal agent for assistance. Agent Jones complained about this in 1873: "There is no tribunal where civil suits can be tried between citizens of the United States and Indians or even where citizens of the United States are the only parties, if the cause of action arises in Indian Territory."[30] He and other agents did their best to arbitrate such cases, but they had no power to enforce any decision. Some irate creditors who were U.S. citizens demanded that the commissioner of Indian affairs deduct the sums due from the Cherokee annuity and pay them directly to the creditors. Jones saw no merit in this arbitrary and unilateral proposal. "The object of these claimants is to present the[ir] claims before the Government and get the amount of this claim out of the Cherokee Nation. This seems to me a very unjust proceeding as the Nation has no means of giving redress. I do not think that the Cherokee Nation should be held responsible for the acts of individuals."[31]

No action was taken on the problem. In 1880 another agent noted, "The duties of the agent . . . are of a judicial character. There is no court with jurisdiction to try cases when an Indian is one party and a citizen of the United States or corporation is the other, so the agent is compelled to act as arbitrator. . . . By this arrangement several hundred cases have been tried as the time of the agent permits."[32]

The only serious effort at legal reform came from the Cherokees themselves. The council decided in 1873 to strengthen its own system of law enforcement. Crime in the Cherokee Nation, wrote Agent Jones in 1873, "results largely from the existence of organized cliques and parties, said to be pledged to defend each member when arraigned for the violation of law."[33] Four years before Jones wrote this, agent John Craig had said the same: "The [Cherokee] villages and trading stations, especially Fort Gibson, are constantly made scenes of lawless affrays by desperate characters, generally half-breeds, whom the Cherokee courts will not convict or sentence for fear of consequences to their members at the hands of the criminal and his associates."[34] Emboldened by weaknesses in the Cherokee judicial system, the corruption of the district court in Arkansas, and the inability of the federal agents to muster troops to assist them, these organized gangs intimidated sheriffs, judges, juries, and witnesses.[35] As Jones put it,

Instances have occurred where the basest of crimes have gone unpunished, apparently owing to the operations of such parties. Witnesses have been intimidated, others have been run off, so that their testimony could not be obtained. Truth has been suppressed on the witness stand. Particular friends of the criminals have been placed on the juries to try them. Cases have occurred where men have been afraid to testify against, or even to charge, crime on those who are most clearly guilty. This has occurred in the midst of a people of widespread intelligence, where the great mass of the people read and write either English or Cherokee, where schools fill the land and large and active churches exist. How to remedy this state of affairs, I can hardly say.[36]

Jones's point was that crime in the Cherokee Nation could not be explained away simply with the stereotypical image of Indians as "backward" or "ignorant savages" existing in a wild state of nature. The same situation existed in many towns in the frontier states where outlaws such as Jesse James, Billy the Kid, and the Dalton gang were active.

An examination of the records of the district and circuit court cases in these years indicates that 85 percent of the cases involved assault with guns and knives occasioned by quarrels when one or both parties were under the influence of alcohol.[37] Attempts to curtail the liquor traffic, however, were futile. Furthermore, many Cherokees resented the fact that they were presumed to be so irresponsible and lacking in self-control that the federal government prohibited liquor sales in the nation.

The problems in the Cherokee legal system arose from the fact that it had been devised for an earlier, simpler era, when the nation was more homogeneous, more distant from external influences, and more loyal to its original code of honesty and respect for others. By 1870 the nation was far more diverse in its makeup and more individualistic in its behavior. Life was much more complex, and there were many new causes of frustration, anger, and violence. One glaring problem involved intermarriages, as new tribes, former slaves, and black and white intruders used this old method of admission to tribal membership to obtain the rights and privileges of Cherokee citizenship. The council had withdrawn validation of certain cases of citizenship by marriage and limited the privileges conveyed by intermarriage. Valiant efforts were made to sustain the rights that Cherokee women had always enjoyed over their own property and their children as well as their rights to divorce and remarriage. Cherokee law specified that a white man lost his citizenship after his Cherokee wife divorced him or died and he then remarried a white woman, but when did this loss of citizenship go into effect? Did it subject the white man to immediate expulsion? Did it affect his property rights? Such cases became almost impossible to adjudicate. Situations changed faster than new laws could keep up with them.

"The Cherokee law is very slender in its provision, and its punishments do not properly meet any case but those of treason, murder and arson," said Agent Craig in 1869.[38] Too much leeway was left to the judge or jury in some cases, and in others, as in regard to various degrees of manslaughter, there was too little leeway. Until the Cherokees erected a jail in 1875, the only punishments were whipping and death. Few judges kept written records of their reasons for making decisions, so there was no way in which precedents could be established or cited. Virtually every case became a case of equity, the jury and judge making decisions based on their own principles of common sense. However, what was common sense in simpler times was not so clear in 1870, and the common man's idea of justice was insufficient in most civil suits.

An editorial in the *Cherokee Advocate* on October 21, 1871, touched on some of the procedural problems: "There are no forms of pleading fixed by statute. . . . The issue taken therefore is always general and an appeal of the whole case is taken to the Supreme Court when appealed at all." The editor noted that the Supreme Court then relied only on the written report of the lower court in making its judgment; instead, he asserted that the court should see and hear the witnesses in order to judge the character and veracity of their testimony.

Cherokee tradition often entered into jury decisions. For example, an honest man of good reputation, claiming self-defense, was almost always acquitted if he shot or killed a man in a brawl who was known to be of bad character or reputation. Being drunk was considered a legitimate excuse for violence in many cases, especially if both parties were wounded or injured. The ancient custom of clan revenge (now often transformed into revenge through a patrilineal rather than matrilineal system) influenced some jurors toward leniency. Acculturation created the need for a more complex legal system, but the effort to integrate traditional Cherokee values and usages into a free-market economy dominated by Anglo-Saxon concepts of due process and fair trials would have taken more time than the Cherokees had.

In 1873 the *Cherokee Advocate* began to print letters from people who wanted a major overhaul of the Cherokee legal code and a better definition of the qualifications for lawyers and judicial positions. Commenting on one letter (signed "J. S.") the editor said, "J. S. sees a necessity for amending our criminal law. Other intelligent citizens see the need as well. . . . The glaring defect of some part of our Judicial system is constantly made apparent to the commonest apprehension." Laws were not carefully drawn and did not cover all cases; the wording of many laws was unclear; and there was no definition of certain crimes. "We heartily agree with J. S. in his desire to see our criminal law amended. . . . The more faithfully [the current laws] are enforced, the more glaring will the errors" be revealed. "For instance, our system authorizes anyone to make a criminal charge against anyone else, founded upon sworn belief of guilt." There was no grand jury system requiring at least prima facie evidence of a crime and substantial factual proof. "What is the result? It is an unquestioned fact that real criminals have been prematurely charged and tried before the evidence of the crimes had time to develop. In such cases Justice has been scandalized and cheated of its dues." A man whom later evidence demonstrated to have been guilty could thus be tried and declared innocent for lack of that evidence when he was tried. "A mere Judge cannot help this. It is his duty to try a charge once fairly before him. Again, and worse still, an innocent man may be convicted by false charges being made against his witness or witnesses, their testimony thereby being barred." With his best witnesses disqualified, such a defendant faced the lies of the accusers, which might convict him; mere circumstantial evidence or bad reputation might do the same. "We have a law against perjury which, like most of our criminal law, is a mere outline, which the Courts are left to fill out at their discretion." The court often had to deal with people who spoke little or no English and who used words or understood terms differently from the lawyers, judge, or jury. Delawares, Shawnees, Osages, and former slaves with little education and different cultures could seem to be lying simply because they understood terms differently or misunderstood a question. "The vagueness of our statutes leads often to ridiculous mistakes, and outraged decent citizens."[39]

The editor of the *Cherokee Advocate* praised Chief Ross, who, recognizing the need for legal reform, "has advised the Council of its importance" and urged them to undertake a total revision of the legal code. The editor also suggested that this revision include higher qualifications for circuit judges than for district judges, for under the constitution no qualification beyond a minimum age was required for either.[40] Full-bloods, however, were uneasy about the adoption of the complex structure of Anglo-Saxon law.

Finally, in 1873, the council appointed a commission to draft a new legal code and to make any other revisions needed in the legal structure. The commission presented its revision to the next council in November 1874. That council adopted the new code, ordered it printed in English and Cherokee, and ruled that it would go into effect on November 1, 1875. Most agreed that the new code would be a major improvement, but it ran into technical difficulties before it could get started. The law required that it be printed in Cherokee and distributed six weeks prior to the date that the new code was to go into effect so that those who read and spoke only Cherokee could become familiar with it. A fire in the Boston printing establishment that was responsible for the Cherokee language edition prevented its being ready six weeks before November 1, 1875. The council and the judiciary then wrangled over whether it could be put into effect on that date or whether parts of it must be suspended (particularly the criminal section) and cases tried under the old code until the Cherokee edition was in distribution for six weeks.

These tensions continued to mount from year to year, and Ross handled them poorly. Negative publicity about Cherokee law and order was fomented by nearby state newspapers and relayed to the East by the Associated Press. The reports tried to show that the situation was the result of political factionalism; they ignored the indecisions and contradictions in federal Indian policy and administration. The Cherokees, who had long had a reputation as a very orderly, civilized, law-abiding people, were now equated with the "unruly" and "undisciplined" Indians of the Plains. Agent Jones, who saw the situation from inside the nation, did what he could as agent from 1870 to 1874 to counter the newspapers' charges that a "crime wave" was sweeping through the nation. However, he had to admit that the number of unresolved murders perpetrated by lawless individuals was increasing every year; by 1875 it had reached two or three per month. "It has been repeatedly charged," he told the commissioner of Indian affairs in 1873, "that crime has greatly increased in the Cherokee country within the past few years. This charge, I am compelled to admit, is true."[41] However, he thought it unfair to call the whole nation "lawless" just because a few outlaw gangs behaved violently. He claimed that sensational frontier newspaper reports "have been greatly exaggerated by those who want to emphasize the failure of Cherokee civilization." For example, he said the recent "disturbance at Coody's Bluff" was not a result of factional rivalry at the polls as the press portrayed it. The fight had indeed taken place at a polling booth during an election, but it was simply happenstance that a drunken brawl outside the polling booth ended when one of the parties tried to escape from the other by running through the polling place. There was not any "greater insecurity of life and property" in the Cherokee Nation, Jones claimed, than in any other frontier community.

However, some vital elements of social coherence had broken down in the nation. A pervasive unease and distrust suffused the body politic. It extended to distrust of the chief himself, who was rumored to protect some of his nephews who were involved in lawless "cliques." Faced with such a volatile situation, the Cherokees' national newspaper was as vehement as any in deploring the breakdown of law and order.

Another major source of social confusion arose from the actions of those who clustered around the remnants of the old Watie-Boudinot faction. After Stand Watie's death in 1871, James M. Bell became the patriarch of this group. Closely associated with him were E. C. Boudinot, Sut Beck, William West, John Porum Davis, James Taylor, William P. Boudinot, S. S. Stephens, John Landrum, John Candy, J. J. Trott, Richard Fields, J. A. Scales, and James Barker. These persons, closely related by family ties, Civil War comradeship, or business relationships, had no use for either Ross and his party or for the Downing party. Active in politics, law, and business affairs, they had their hands in everything but political control over nothing. Generally well-off (though some tied to them by familial or business relations were ne'er-do-wells), they chafed under the inadequacies of the legal system to protect their property, the disorder from the outlaws, and the political machinations in the council that led to such results as the white labor permit law of November 1872. For them, the ancient tradition of communal landownership was fundamentally contrary to the nation's adoption of a system of private enterprise. Their general alienation manifested itself in their willingness to connive secretly with E. C. Boudinot's efforts in Washington to obtain passage of a territorial and allotment bill that they believed would guarantee law and order and the protection of their property interests. Some of them hoped first to persuade the council to divide up the nation's land, as W. P. Adair had suggested, so that when a territorial bill was passed, most of the good Cherokee land would be the private property of the well-to-do. Some of them supported Senator James Harlan's bill before Congress in 1873 that called for the establishment of a territorial government under confederated Indian control. They had little sympathy for efforts to preserve tribal sovereignty and communal landownership.

James Bell was the son of John A. Bell, a signer of the Treaty of New Echota, and the younger brother of Sarah Bell Watie, Stand Watie's widow and after 1871 the matriarch of the family clan. Born in 1826, he was an active lawyer, large-scale farmer, and aggressive entrepreneur. He was elected to the Cherokee Senate for one term from the Canadian District in 1869. His correspondence reveals his effort to direct his faction and combine its energies for twenty years after the war. He was E. C. Boudinot's partner in many political and business activities, cooperating with Boudinot in his efforts to acquire most of the land around the railroad junction in Vinita. He was also Sut Beck's defense attorney after the Going Snake Tragedy. His attitudes were well known, though many of his political activities were secret, and he was generally persona non grata with the Ross party and the Downing party. Twice in his career he was placed under arrest for treason, and once the Keetoowahs warned him to leave the nation for treasonous behavior.[42]

Typical of the actions that led the Cherokees to distrust the Bell-Boudinot group was their effort to persuade the secretary of the interior to instruct Agent Jones not to enforce the white labor permit law in 1873. William N. West of the Saline District expressed the faction's general contempt for the full-bloods in a letter to Bell in March 1873: "The delegation [in Washington] is destroying the [Cherokee] Government by degrees, and the Kee-too-wahs, which is the great majority, is supporting them. I am, and a great many others are, in favor of a change of government." West felt that he represented "the enterprising class, not the Hog and Hominy class that care for nothing further" than bare subsistence on their ill-kempt farms.[43] West congratulated Bell for writing the protest to the secretary of the interior against the new white labor permit law. Another letter of the same temper was sent by Bell's friend, William Stephens, to President Ulysses S. Grant on March 23, 1873:

Dear President Grant,

Being a citizen of the Cherokee Nation by birth [I write to oppose the recent law] refusing to grant permits to us to employ proper help to enable us to carry on our legitimate business, which is that of farming. [This law] ought to be abolished [for] said law is oppressive and detrimental [to the nation. If carried out,] we are no better than slaves, for it deprives us of our only means of support and confines us to the whims of a class of people who have always been, and still are, opposed to improvements of any kind. I mean the fullbloods.[44]

Stephens went on to say that he had read the Cherokee treaties and believed the president had the power "to suspend or abolish" any Cherokee law that "is found to be oppressive to us." In his opinion, the white labor permit law was "both unjust and oppressive and tends to degrade instead of enlighten the inhabitants of the Nation." He then went on to suggest the need for forcing the nation to adopt a policy of private ownership of the land:

If the land in the Nation were allotted to us equally, according to families, and we were all allowed to open our farms to be cultivated by whites, it would be much better, for each family would own enough land to start a small neighborhood and establish schools and our children would grow up and be educated together, and in time to come the [Indian] race would be extinct or, if you thought better, to give each citizen his own part or portion of land to keep or sell as he pleased, it would be only fair and just, for why not let the red man have the same right to sell his land for $1.25 per acre or retain it, as best suits himself.

He concluded by expressing his disgust with the annual Cherokee delegations sent to Washington because of their misguided efforts to preserve the communal system of landholding.

On March 8, 1873, E. C. Boudinot wrote to Bell from Washington that he was appalled that Ross had ordered Bell's arrest "for treason."[45] Ross considered appeals by private citizens to federal authorities for intervention as efforts to abridge the Cherokee constitution and attacks on the nation's sovereignty. However, he did not pursue the case, and Bell was released. Bell's interest in abridging the white labor permit law sprang from the fact that, like many other large-scale farmers, he had utilized it to engross more land for himself. Bell had hired a white man named Dodson to be his tenant farmer on some valuable land in the Cooweescoowee District, but there was some confusion over his permit and Dodson was told to leave by the federal agent.

A friend told Bell that Agent Jones was about to expel Dodson for lack of a permit and that "Dodson told some one that you promised him that you would give him half of the place or half the value of it when the Nation was sectionized, if he would hold it [for you]."[46] Bell had paid for the permit, however, and Dodson was allowed to stay.

In June 1873, Samuel H. Payne wrote to Bell saying that it was time to start "a reform party" in the nation to challenge Ross and the full-bloods. He thanked Bell for sending him copies of a printed circular explaining a petition that Bell and Sut Beck were taking to Washington, urging Congress to pass a bill dividing the nation's land up among its own people.[47] When George Harkins, a prominent mixed-blood leader of the Choctaw Nation, heard of Bell's plan for Cherokee land allotment, he wrote to say that many Choctaws of mixed ancestry favored the same plan and sent him a copy of the Choctaw proposal.[48]

Bell and Beck went to Washington in January 1873 to present a memorial with "several hundred" signatures to Secretary of the Interior Columbus Delano. The petition protested against the white labor permit law and supported a bill requiring the nation to divide its land in severalty and to divide all tribal funds into equal shares for each family. In their "Address to the Citizens of the Cherokee Nation" explaining their reasons for this action, they said frankly that they had no confidence in the council:

> Some who favor allotment say that the petitions should be made to our National Council. We do not think so. A council so utterly oblivious to the interests of the enterprising, industrious classes of our people, and so cruelly indifferent to the welfare of the hundreds of widows and orphans amongst us, as to pass a law which practically prohibits them from employing labor to work their farms, is not a body before which we care to present any petition. The Government of the United States has the power to survey our lands and have them allotted to us in severalty.[49]

They also reminded the Cherokees that the government had already surveyed the land of the Chickasaws, Creeks, and Seminoles. Bell and Beck said they were confident that in any fair referendum on the question "a majority of the [Cherokee] people would be found in favor of allotting the lands." The reason they had not obtained more than a few hundred signatures for their petition to Congress was that, because of the utter breakdown of law and order in the nation, many refused to sign "for fear of being assassinated by those who are opposed to allotment." In an oblique reference to the Keetoowahs, they stated: "How shameful that there should be found among the Cherokees a set of men so ignorant and malicious as to threaten the lives of those who petition for what the treaty guarantees and what a large majority of our best citizens [think] is our *only salvation*."

Bell and Beck went on to say that while "we have not agreed with Colonel Boudinot in his territorial schemes," they considered him very farsighted in realizing that sooner or later Congress would pass some territorial bill. If left to Congress, such a bill would grant only a small proportion of the present Cherokee land to the Cherokees; most of it would be given to white homesteaders. Meanwhile, the misguided National Council failed to see the handwriting on the wall. "Not less than $150,000 [of tribal funds] have been expended" to fight both allotment and territorial bills and to cling blindly to the ancient system of communal ownership of the land. Although it was true that Boudinot had not been able to get Harlan's territorial bill passed so far, he had already drawn up a revised version of it that would be reconsidered by Congress. Bell and Boudinot complained that their homeland was already shrinking rapidly—thousands of acres had been sold to the Osages, Delawares, and Shawnees, and who knew how many other tribes would soon be given more of it. Since the war, the nation had been reduced from 7 million acres "to our present reservation of about 3,600,000 acres." They defended their petition to the Congress to abrogate the white labor permit law because "this odious permit law will do more to hasten a territorial government than anything else" and denounced the law as "a stupid and malicious attempt to ruin the best class of our citizens." They claimed, "How much better it would be for every man to own his own land in severalty and cultivate it as he sees fit, employing such labor as is necessary to produce the crops for the support of his family. The only objection we have heard to this policy of dividing the lands is that of one of the Delegates here who says it would prove disastrous to the blanket Indians." Bell and Beck noted that the "several hundred" signers of the petition to Secretary Delano had evidently agreed with them:

> Our affairs are in a very precarious condition. . . . It is notorious and a lamentable fact, that there is no security for life or property in the Cherokee Nation. . . . Our laws are trampled upon. The honest and quiet citizens are at the mercy of desperadoes and outlaws. The officials of the Nation protect criminals and assassinations because they can control, in a great measure through their baneful influence and lawless intimidation, the popular elections.

They asked, "Is this carnival of crime and blood to continue" just because the delegations to Washington insist that "all is peace and quiet among us?" These truths could not be hidden and Congress must act. Meanwhile, "We shall also continue to urge the division of our lands and money before any more is squandered and given away." They asserted, "We have no doubt of ultimate success."

Neither Delano nor Congress took action on this petition, but in subsequent sessions over the next decade, many bills for "survey and allotment" of Indian lands were introduced. Ultimately, under the Dawes Severalty Act of 1887, this policy was enacted for all but "the five civilized tribes" (though not in the manner Bell and Beck suggested). Despite the claims of Bell and Beck, no other civilized tribe had a majority in favor of allotment any more than did the Cherokees.

After Bell returned home from Washington in 1873, he stood for election to the Cherokee Senate and lost. He ran for office several other times in the years ahead, but despite his claim that a majority agreed with his policy, he was never elected. The protests of this alienated group continued throughout Ross's administration, and in 1874 one of their number suggested that the only answer to the "reign of terror" in the nation was "a citizens' army." [50] As "enlightened" men of standing, they disputed the claim of some that the full-bloods or the Keetoowahs deserved to be called "conservatives." Traditionalism was not conservatism. So far as Bell was concerned, the full-bloods were "radicals" of the sort who led the reign of terror in the French Revolution—fanatical peasants or anarchists in favor of "no government." [51] True conservatism favored industrious people of property and enterprise.

The policies and actions of the Bell-Boudinot faction did not lead to a reform party or a citizens' army, but in the summer of 1874, a new party did emerge, the National Independent party, led by Dennis W. Bushyhead and Rabbit Bunch, to challenge both Ross and the old Downing party full-bloods. The Downing party held a convention in Tahlequah in August 1874 and issued a platform appealing to those who opposed Ross. The Bell-Boudinot group were not prominent in either of these parties. People like Bell, Payne, and Stephens had now been alienated from Cherokee culture for many years, and whatever participation they had in tribal affairs was chiefly to advance their own private or familial interests. Nonetheless, they were very intelligent, highly acculturated, knowledgeable Cherokees. Their decision to advocate division of tribal land in severalty indicated a growing sense that the nation was facing impossible choices—that their chances of salvaging their wealth out of the nation's confusion were diminishing year by year. They believed it impossible to persuade the majority of Cherokees to support land allotment and unrealistic to think that Congress would pass an allotment bill that would give Indian land to Indians only and not to white homesteaders. These disaffected Cherokees whom Bell led, assisted by intermarried whites, felt frustrated by the limits that ancient tribal customs and the Keetoowah Society's traditionalism placed on their efforts to be "progressive." They believed that, as enlightened Cherokees, they had the right to develop the nation's resources, not the whites on their borders. They had become a small bourgeoisie without power.

William P. Ross, though himself a very enterprising and highly acculturated Cherokee, had little in common with this group and devoted himself ardently to sustaining the sovereignty of the Cherokee Nation. For this he needed the votes of the full-bloods. He made good use of the monies the nation received from its land cessions to strengthen the institutional structure of the nation. He appointed strong delegations to work with him in Washington to oppose territorial bills, and he made excellent use of the international councils to create a Pan-Indian consensus against any inroads on the sovereignty and self-government of each tribe. During his tenure, he successfully improved and extended the public school system, promoted agricultural fairs to improve Cherokee farm production, and did his best to solve the citizenship problems. Through his efforts, the council voted to erect an imposing brick capital building in Tahlequah in 1875, constructed a jail in 1875, and built a new orphan asylum in 1873 and a home for the indigent, deaf, dumb, and blind in 1874. He also took steps to reopen the two seminaries in order to train teachers for the public schools (which increased to sixty-seven during his administration, including seven for black children). The Cherokee population, despite the famine in 1873–74 (for which he obtained "bread money"), had grown steadily to 19,000 by 1875.

However, Ross's decision to limit per capita payments to only Cherokees "by blood" added greatly to the general unrest. He was also unable to eliminate the national debt or to curtail the expenses that produced it. In fact, the high cost of delegations to Washington became a major campaign issue in 1875. Ross's major difficulty was his conviction that he was the best and wisest man to run the nation, and he was determined that in 1875 he would win election at last by the popular vote of the people. He seemed blind to the mounting resentment he inspired. He did not share "the blanket Indians'" allegiance to older, traditional beliefs and values; he was equally appalled by the Bell-Boudinot efforts for allotment. While there was a large group of Cherokees who admired his ability to fight for treaty rights and his efforts to promote productivity and institutional development, he lacked the personality needed to pull the nation together.

One outcome of the dislike of Ross was a growing populist movement among the poorer farmers. It is not surprising that the first Grange was formed in the nation in 1870 and others were added in the next few years. A second result, visible in Dennis Bushyhead's new National Independent party, was a greater public emphasis on fiscal responsibility, and a third was an ardent desire for law and order. Ross's determination to hold onto power led some of his minions to believe that intimidation of his opponents was permissible. This aspect of the political struggle resulted in a serious gun battle on Christmas Day, 1874, which inaugurated seven months of armed tension prior to the election. The federal agent, George W. Ingalls, began to wonder as the election of 1875 approached whether open civil war could be avoided.

12

The Full-Blood
Rebellion of 1875

I find as the time for general election for officers of the

Nation draws near, the number of local disturbances, quarrels,

fights and murders rapidly increasing. One of the Cherokee

citizens informed me yesterday [that] the whole country is much

like a volcano on the eve of an eruption.

—*Agent George W. Ingalls, 1875*

The alienation of the Bell-Boudinot faction at the top of the social hierarchy in the Cherokee Nation was matched by a growing dissatisfaction at the bottom, which can be defined as a form of populism. Cherokee populism became an organized social and political movement in 1874, although it began before that time. It was both a cultural and a class movement, pitting the full-bloods against the mixed-bloods, the poor majority against the rich minority. Oochalata (Charles Thompson), who ran against William P. Ross in 1875, was not a compromise candidate to divide the mixed-blood vote as Lewis Downing had been in 1867. He was the candidate of the poor subsistence farmers against the rich commercial farmers and businesspeople.

This dramatic shift in Cherokee politics marked a turning point in Cherokee history. Previously, dedication to national survival had surmounted internal divisions. Only White Path's Rebellion in 1824–27 came close to social rebellion by the full-bloods, and it too ended in a compromise for national survival that sustained mixed-blood leadership. The division during the Civil War was not based on class (despite the importance of the Keetoowah movement). Many slaveholders and mixed-bloods were members of the Ross party in 1861, and the full-bloods in general remained loyal to that party under both the treaty with the Confederacy and in service to the Union. The partisanship of 1839–46 and 1865–67 was political, not economic, and the minority were the rebels in both instances. Downing's victory in 1867 came the closest to representing a class movement, yet its whole purpose was to heal the divisions between Loyal and Southern factions for the good of the nation. It grew out of the full-bloods' continued willingness (for the sake of national unity) to share power with the mixed-bloods (although a full-blood chief was to keep the minority in check).

The election campaign of 1874–75 broke with a long tradition of national unity. The party led by the Cherokee-speaking Oochalata called for full-blood domination of the nation in the interest of the full-blood majority. Mixed-bloods might join them, but only if they accepted the full-blood agenda. No promises were made either to the Ross party, to those mixed-bloods tired of the Ross party, or to the remnants of the old Southern party. The attempt of Dennis Wolf Bushyhead and Rabbit Bunch to launch an National Independent party (independent of Ross on one side and the Bell-Boudinot faction on the other) was buried in the tense struggle between Ross and Oochalata.

The year 1874 began with the usual delegation to Washington, D.C., appointed by Ross and ratified by the council. It had the perennial agenda—to oppose territorial bills, to negotiate for completion of the sale of the Cherokee Strip, to obtain back pensions due to Cherokee veterans, to persuade Congress to create a U.S. district court in the Cherokee Nation without disturbing Cherokee courts, and to persuade the secretary of the interior to get army help to remove over 1,000 intruders. The only new item was an effort to obtain congressional approval to convert some of the national income (from land sales) to a per capita payment to assist those suffering from the long drought of 1873–74. Ross had persuaded John B. Jones to take a leave of absence from his job as federal agent in order to serve (in his capacity as an adopted Cherokee citizen) on this delegation along with Ross, W. P. Adair, Rufus O. Ross, and Dennis Bushyhead.

Ross had not been particularly friendly toward Jones ever since Jones helped to organize the Downing party against him in 1867, but they shared a deep interest in preserving and protecting the rights of the nation as well as in advancing its political unity and its economic prosperity. Most Cherokees agreed that the nation was fortunate to have such an effective, dedicated, and helpful agent. His annual reports were models of what a federal agent's report should be—defining the difficulties in the way of Cherokee progress and offering specific means by which the government could assist them. On certain issues he differed with the majority of Cherokees, most notably in his defense of the "too-late" former slaves (some of whom he, like George W. Ingalls, assisted in obtaining evidence of their right to citizenship).[1] Two other matters of interest to Jones bothered some Cherokees: his strong stand in favor of bilingual education in the public schools and his objections to what he considered the mismanagement of the Cherokee orphan asylum.

Jones's support for bilingual education developed out of his many years of experience as a missionary among the full-bloods. All Protestant mission schools had been taught in English, but Jones and his father, two of the few missionaries to learn to speak and read Cherokee, noticed that children from Cherokee-speaking families soon dropped out of school under that system, while children from English-speaking families stayed on. When the Cherokee public school system was instituted in 1841, the council had retained the requirement that all teaching must be in English. Consequently the Cherokee seminaries did not train teachers to read or write Cherokee, and most seminary pupils were from English-speaking families. Jones found that full-blood children continued to do poorly in school and usually dropped out without having acquired much formal education. While a student at Madison University in Hamilton, New York, in the 1850s, Jones had discovered that a German linguist, Heinrich G. Ollendorf, had developed an original and highly successful method of teaching foreign languages by asking students to answer questions about everyday life (an early version of the Berlitz method). After the Civil War, Jones persuaded the council to provide funds so that he could publish bilingual textbooks for the Cherokee public schools utilizing the Ollendorf method. He had produced at least one of these, an arithmetic book, by 1870. After a brief trial period, however, the Cherokee council abandoned this experiment because it was too expensive. As a federal agent, Jones continued to advocate and work for bilingual education, at least in schools where the full-bloods predominated. In his annual report in 1872, he wrote:

The schools attended by the half-breeds, speaking English, are going well and are of great benefit to the children. But those attended by fullbloods, speaking only the Cherokee language, are accomplishing little good. The children learn to read, spell and write the English language, but do not understand the meaning of words. They are engaged in the slavish labor of learning the forms and sounds of letters, syllables, words, without connecting with them any ideas whatever. The great desideratum for this class of children is a system of education which shall take their own language and also make it a medium of conveying to them the rudiments of common education. Then, by the time they would have learned the English language so as to use it with facility, they would have acquired a considerable knowledge of arithmetic, geography, and history and the structure of both languages. . . . Instead of being a hindrance, [the Cherokee language] could be made the means and medium of more extensive and accurate knowledge of the sciences, of both languages, and of more varied culture of the intellect.[2]

In short, he wanted the Cherokees to be able to speak, read, and write both English and Cherokee—to be truly bilingual. Jones realized that this would require training bilingual teachers and providing bilingual textbooks, but he hoped that the federal government would provide the necessary funds.

Having revived the issue, Jones found himself in the midst of a major controversy. An editorial in the *Cherokee Advocate* by John L. Adair on March 7, 1874, summed up the issue: "We now have 67 common schools at an average expense of $400" each and with a total school population of 1,800 (out of perhaps 3,600 school-age children). "The average is not more than fifteen" pupils in attendance at each school, "and if facts were known, it is very probable that it is much less. There are at least 20 schools [in the full-blood areas] . . . which will not average over five students. . . . Some of them will even go below that number." The editor believed that, in view of the nation's increasing indebtedness and the inefficiency of the expanding school system, the cost-benefit balance needed to be reassessed. "Eight or ten thousand dollars go annually to teachers who have no interest at all in their schools further than their salaries are concerned, and half the [school-age] children in our country are not benefitted" because they do not attend. Everyone knew that it was the full-bloods who did not attend. Some thought this was because full-bloods preferred to keep their old language and were not interested in acculturation. However, Adair took Jones's view that the difficulty lay in the full-bloods' "not being able to understand that language in which . . . instruction is given." He wrote, "To this is mainly due the want of attention to education among the full Cherokees, and they, constituting the majority of our population, the cause of the low average of [attendance in] our schools is easily understood." Adair, noting all the experiments the nation had tried to solve this problem, took a pessimistic view: "The Cause of education among the full Cherokees is dead, without the hope of resurrection under the present system." He laid out the options: "The full Cherokee children must have a knowledge of the English language," therefore either "books in the English language with definitions in the Cherokee must be had," or "they must be placed in continual intercourse with those who speak the language and be educated at the same time" (that is, by working together at manual or farm labor with English-speaking children from an early age), or "teach them in their own language and give them all possible intelligence" via schools taught in Cherokee only. Adair's phrase, "all possible," indicated the common mixed-blood view that the Cherokee language was incapable of conveying the most advanced scientific knowledge.

Ross favored a combination of the first two alternatives. For those from English-speaking families, public schools would be taught in English; for those from Cherokee-speaking families and the poorer mixed-blood families, there should be manual labor schools in which the emphasis would be on learning a trade or learning to farm and not on book learning. In such schools, the teachers would speak and teach in English, but the full-blood children would keep their own language by working, learning, and playing with children who spoke Cherokee. Ross had inaugurated such a plan at the Cherokee orphan homes, and most Cherokees considered it very successful.

Ross's views were reflected in an anonymous article signed "Native" that appeared in the *Cherokee Advocate* shortly after Adair's editorial: "The Ollendorf or other like system of educating full-blooded Indians might prove highly satisfactory to Congress and its chief agent [John B. Jones]. It would no doubt prove lucrative to those who had the making of the books, maps, etc., and yet it might, and we believe it would, be a complete failure when compared with the plan of the Principal Chief of this Nation, that is the family or boarding industrial school plan."[3] As boarding schools, the industrial schools would of course take the children away from their parents. This constituted a regression to the old Protestant mission schools, which had been based on the missionaries' belief that acculturation required separation of the child from the home environment. Many mission schools were part of a "model farm" on which the pupils worked for part of each day. "Native" made no bones about the fact that the industrial school plan was favored by the educated to help the poor. "This is the plan that our leading men favor for our full-blooded children. Cheap, comfortable buildings on the plan of the old Dwight Mission, with a good farm, is what we deem necessary. We believe this to be the true plan, the most practicable, quickest and quite as cheap as any other."

Because most of the full-bloods seemed unconcerned about formal education, believing that if their children could read and write Cherokee they were sufficiently educated to manage their lives, Jones feared that the mixed-bloods would institute the industrial education plan and ultimately reduce the full-bloods to an underclass, unable to develop to their fullest potential. At a time when everyone was worried about the nation's debt and the depreciation of Cherokee scrip, the high cost of bilingual education was worrisome. Jones made the mistake of suggesting that perhaps the Bureau of Indian Affairs and the commissioner of education ought to take charge of Indian education. He did this in his annual report for 1873, which did not appear in print until 1874. He wrote:

> I recommend that the educational interest of the Indians be placed under the supervision of the Commissioner of Education; that provisions be made by Congress for the appointment of such subordinates as may be necessary to inaugurate and carry into effect efficient measures to promote the work of education among the Indians. . . . A well-devised scheme for the cooperation of the Bureau of Education with the local managers of the work in the several tribes of nations, would result in giving far greater efficiency than has hitherto been attained in the educational institutions among these tribes.[4]

It was some time before the Cherokees discovered Jones's proposal, but when they did, they united in opposing it, and he found himself in serious difficulty.

Jones's second quarrel with Ross, over the orphan asylum, arose from complaints brought to him that the orphanage was not providing care for all those entitled to it and that black orphans were not being admitted at all. After the war the Cherokees had been too poor to build an orphanage. The money allotted for the care of 1,200 orphans was too small to do more than pay a small sum to foster parents to take these children into their homes and see that they attended the nearest school. Most of the orphans were Cherokee-speaking; many who took charge of them were English-speaking. Living with adults who spoke English (although they spoke Cherokee with each other), the younger orphans picked up English without much difficulty. As more funds became available, the council acquired buildings that were transformed into orphanages staffed by English-speaking teachers and families. The children were given manual training in household and farm duties at the orphanage.

Jones first became involved in the affairs of the orphan asylum in 1873 when some former slaves sent him a letter stating that no black orphans had been admitted. Jones passed the letter on to the commissioner of Indian affairs, stating that blacks' "orphan children are cut off from participation in the Cherokee Orphan Fund." The blacks who complained were former Cherokee slaves who were now citizens of the nation, therefore they had a right to share in the fund. They told Jones that they had petitioned the council about this but had received no satisfaction. "They further state," Jones reported, "that owing to the prejudice existing in the minds of many Cherokees against associating with the people of African blood, they urge, or even request, that their orphans not be taken into Cherokee Asylum, for they do not wish to obtrude any portion of their people on those who dislike to associate with them. But they ask that their proportionate share . . . of this asylum fund be set aside for the benefit of the colored orphans of this Nation."[5]

The commissioner sent the petition and Jones's letter to Chief Ross. Ross was irate at the charge that any racial prejudice existed in the nation or in the orphan asylum. He replied that if, at that moment, there were no black children in the orphanage, this was simply because there was a shortage of space and funds.[6] He admitted that "only a limited number" of orphans could be accommodated in the orphanage but insisted that priority was given based on need, not race or color. He noted that many Cherokee orphans were also not getting the care they needed and were in foster homes. He pointed out that, as chief, he had always tried to help the former slaves and was well known to have advocated admitting to citizenship those former slaves who had returned too late to meet the six-month deadline. Ross firmly opposed any effort to divide the orphan fund because if blacks demanded a share, perhaps the Delawares and Shawnees would do the same, and then the sum would be too small to have a competent orphanage for any of them.

Over the years, the annuity for the orphans had steadily increased, and plans were maturing in 1873 to buy or build a large enough building to house all the orphans under one roof. In 1872 the council had authorized the board of trustees for the orphanage to purchase a suitable house or, if none was available, to erect a new building. The trustees consulted an architect who told them it would cost $42,000 to build a home for 150 orphans, so they decided it would be cheaper to buy one. The home they chose was the former home and farm of the recently deceased Lewis Ross and the adjoining home and farm of his son, Robert Ross, also recently deceased. The former would be used for white orphans, the latter for black orphans. The price being asked for both properties, plus the cost of some necessary renovations, would come to $28,000, a considerable savings over building a new home. However, everyone knew that Lewis Ross was the uncle of Chief William P. Ross and Robert Ross was his cousin. At their deaths, he became the executor of the two estates, and consequently he stood to profit handsomely from this arrangement. Furthermore, since he had appointed the trustees, some suspected that there was collusion in the choice.

Some of Jones's Cherokee friends, with his support, protested the plan, and at the next council meeting, the trustees were asked to reconsider their decision. After agreeing to reconsider, they confirmed their original plan. One of the protesters, Sam Houston Downing (a close friend of Jones), took the case to court, suing the trustees for malfeasance. The judge, Riley Keys, was a close friend and ardent supporter of Chief Ross. He ruled, on a technicality, that the suit was improper. Again collusion was suspected.[7] Jones believed that even if there was no collusion, the price Ross was asking for the two houses was far too high and that he was swindling the nation to line his own pockets. Jones planned to use his influence with the commissioner of Indian affairs to propose that the funds for the orphan annuity not be released until Ross had been called to answer for this. Consequently, when Jones was asked to join the Cherokee delegation in January 1874, he accepted, knowing that he had some items on his agenda that were not on the agenda of the other delegates.

From January to March, Jones worked hard and effectively with the delegation to address its major concerns. He helped to lobby against, and defeat, four new territorial bills; he tried to obtain an advance payment against the sale of land on the Cherokee Strip in order to relieve those suffering from the drought; he worked for stricter controls over the cattle grazers who passed through the nation; he argued for back pay for veterans' pensions and the payment of indemnities for Confederate damages during the war; he drafted a memorial opposing the claim of the North Carolina Cherokees for a share of the annuities and of the income from the sale of Cherokee lands in the West; he supported the delegation's effort to obtain the transference of the U.S. district court from Arkansas to the Cherokee Nation; and he argued against two bills calling for the sectionalizing (via survey and allotment in severalty) of Indian lands.[8]

After this, he then made his case to the commissioner that the payment of the education and orphan funds in the annuity be withheld by the Bureau of Indian Affairs until the Cherokees agreed to build a new orphan asylum and until Congress considered a bill implementing his plan that Indian education be managed henceforth by the commissioner of education and the bureau. When the other delegates learned of his actions, they were so angry that they expelled Jones from the delegation and wrote back to the nation about his perfidy. Letters and editorials began to appear in the *Cherokee Advocate* denouncing his efforts to undermine Cherokee sovereignty and self-government. "Our affairs in Washington," said the paper's editor, "had become fearfully complicated, leading to the rupture of the delegation, a suspension of payment of all Cherokee moneys, a move to wrest the cause of education from the control of our National Council, and it is believed that moves [are] in Congress for a partition of lands and moneys in favor of those citizens of our Nation who might wish to withdraw their interest in our common heritage."[9]

Jones also received a letter from his wife stating that a leading supporter of Chief Ross was "trying to get the Colored people to sign a petition to have you removed from the nation."[10] This petition accused Jones of meddling in the internal affairs of the nation. Later he received information in another letter concerning a possible plot to assassinate him when he returned. Rumors had circulated that his "object was to put down the Rosses—to have a Territorial Government, divide up the lands [in severalty], draw all the money and distribute it per capita." Rumors also circulated that he and the leaders of the Downing party "had a plot to kill W. P. Ross, [Vice Chief] James Vann, and others." On receiving this information, Jones wrote to his wife: "It is Bill Ross's vengeance for the Orphan Asylum business. It means to arouse wrath against me, if possible to procure my assassination." He held James Vann responsible for the rumors. That Jones truly feared for his life indicates how serious the breakdown of law and order had become in the nation. Before he left Washington, he evidently relented in his effort to hold up the tribal annuity, for the commissioner released the funds and the storm died down.

When Jones returned to the nation in July 1874, he probably played a part (along with his full-blood friends Sam Downing, Smith Christie, and Spring Frog [Toostoo]) in organizing the political convention of the Downing party in Tahlequah in August. This convention drafted and published a platform containing sixteen articles as the basis for the election campaign in 1875. The populist aspects of this campaign went back long before Jones's quarrels in the spring of 1874 with the Ross delegation. He had been working since 1870 to improve the lot of the Cherokee farmers with his support of a botanical nursery at the agency and his encouragement of farmers' clubs and agricultural fairs. "The great majority of them use the most primitive kinds of [farm] implements," he wrote in one of his reports, "and confine themselves to raising corn and a very small number of vegetables. Their hogs are of a very inferior kind" with little meat or fat.[11] He had encouraged them to plant cotton because it was the one crop that had a steady cash market. He had sympathized with farmers about the misuses of the white labor permit law. However, what brought the populist movement to its peak in 1874 was two years of prolonged drought and the worst grasshopper plague in many years.

The Downing party held its convention during the first week in August and on August 11 adopted a manifesto and platform, which it published as a broadside, "To the Cherokee People." It called for "the speedy payment of a per capita to the Cherokee people" to help them cope with severe problems caused by the drought and grasshopper plague. It demanded "an equitable and judicious application of the School and Orphan funds so as to bring the advantages of education within the reach of all classes." It assailed the breakdown of law and order and urged "a just and rigid administration of the laws of our country without regard to person or party or previous condition," meaning blacks. With regard to the national debt, the platform supported "opposition to any useless or extravagant expenditure of the public funds for the benefit of a few individuals and to the detriment of the interests of the masses of the people." The white labor permit system was not mentioned because the strong law against it still remained on the books. The final plank asserted: "We are utterly opposed to the establishment of a territorial government of the United States over the Indian Country"—a stance with which all but the Bell-Boudinot faction concurred. Other planks called for recognition of the "paramount authority" of treaty stipulations over congressional statutes (a reference to the Cherokee Tobacco Case); unity with other Indian nations against "unjust aggressions upon their rights"; "speedy removal" of the North Carolina Cherokees "to this Nation" at federal expense, since the more Indians were in the nation, the less land whites with labor permits could get; and opposition "to any monopoly of the public domain for speculative purposes." This last item was a direct attack on those wealthy mixed-blood farmers and herders who were engrossing more and more of the best public land for their own families (sometimes establishing fraudulent "sleeper claims" in the names of their children) or by means of the white labor permit system.[12]

The platform omitted some planks that might have been expected in a populist campaign. For example, there were no attacks on railroads and their efforts to obtain land grants along their rights-of-way (although the *Cherokee Advocate* in one recent issue was horrified at the extortionate prices charged after a new rise in passenger rates).[13] There were no attacks on Wall Street bankers or the grain futures market in Chicago, for Cherokee farmers had no dealings with these. The platform did not mention the familiar populist concerns over greenbacks or cheap money but instead included a plank calling for a balanced budget and the abolition of the national debt since the chief currency among the Cherokees was paper scrip and warrants, which were already depreciated by 40 to 60 percent. It would be easier for farmers to obtain credit from merchants once the debt was paid and the scrip returned to par value.

The essential message of the Downing party's platform was that "the masses" were angry that a privileged few, special interests within the nation, were manipulating the system to their advantage, while the party in power was abetting them by an unfair administration of the laws. To help the masses, the government's first duty was to provide cash to the needy through a per capita payment. National income distributed directly to the people reached the hands of those who needed it most, while the practice preferred by the well-to-do was to deposit all income in the nation's trust fund and then, through the actions of the council, spend it on expensive delegations or public buildings.

This convention did not present a slate of candidates or choose a party spokesperson, but the most distinguished full-blood in politics at this time was Oochalata, and many expected him to be their candidate for chief. Oochalata was probably born in North Carolina in about 1821. His father was a full-blood; his mother a white woman. Both of them spoke only Cherokee, and both became devout attendants at a Northern Baptist mission church led by Evan Jones. After removal, they lived near Spavinaw Creek in the Delaware District and probably attended the Baptist church at Taquohee. Prior to 1874, Oochalata was converted, baptized by immersion, admitted into the Baptist church, and ordained as a deacon. A dedicated Christian, he felt called to be a preacher. His church had licensed him to preach, though it had not yet ordained him. He made his living primarily as a storekeeper. A member of the Keetoowah Society, he had fought in the Indian home guard regiments during the war, though he was never called by his military rank, indicating that he was not a commissioned officer. After the war, he took up law. It was said that his church hesitated to ordain him because the legal profession was considered an improper career for a preacher.[14]

In 1867 Oochalata had supported the Downing party and was elected to the upper house of the National Council from the Delaware District. He was reelected in the next three elections and acquired a reputation as a forceful speaker and a conscientious politician. As a protégé of the Joneses, he was sympathetic to the admission of the latecomer former slaves as citizens and supported the Downing and Ross bills proposing that they be granted citizenship. He also worked hard to win passage of a bill that outlawed carrying guns, except when hunting, traveling, or in performance of police or military duty. He firmly opposed the white labor permit laws, which he thought were being abused by the wealthy farmers, and he defended Cherokee interests against the railroads. Though elected president of the upper house, Oochalata was never chosen as a delegate to Washington, perhaps because he could neither read nor write English. Not until early in the summer of 1875 did the party ask him to run for the position of chief.

During the summer of 1874, John B. Jones regained the goodwill of his friends in the Downing party. He worked hard obtaining long-overdue pensions, bounties, and back pay for Cherokee veterans, and he presented complaints of railroad depredations to the Bureau of Indian Affairs. In September he wrote a long letter to the commissioner of Indian affairs noting that "the number of intruders is perhaps greater now than at any previous time." As in the past, most of them had come down from Kansas and settled by the hundreds in the very areas from which he and Major J. J. Upham had driven them two years before. However, now there were "a large number of intruders in all the Districts of the Cherokee Nation. Some of these I find to be the same as those reported previously and notified to leave." [15] He had recently asked the commandant at Fort Gibson to furnish troops to assist him in removing these intruders. The commandant told him he "could not furnish him any troops on account of there being only a small guard on duty at the post." Jones asked the commissioner for troops to be sent from Fort Smith: "The Indians are in great danger of having their country more and more overrun by white intruders." [16]

Jones became ill at the end of the summer of 1874 with the recurrence of a tubercular complaint that eventually took his life in 1876. He sent in his resignation and asked that a replacement be sent. In his last official report, written in September 1874, he said, "The contentions between the Downing and Ross factions are often bitter and sometimes bloody." [17] In November, Jones turned over his post to George W. Ingalls and warned him to pursue the problem of intruders and to be wary of the increasing violence in the nation. However, as agent for "the five civilized tribes," Ingalls maintained his office in the Creek Nation and at first seemed out of touch with the mounting political struggle in the Cherokee Nation.

When the council met in November, it faced the problem of implementing the new legal code. It voted to suspend implementation, but Judge Abraham Woodall of the Canadian District Court said that this did not apply to the semiautonomous district where he presided. Chief Ross promptly suspended him. A letter from Calvin J. Hanks of the Canadian District in October 1874 to John L. McCorkle, a friend who, like him, was deeply involved in Cherokee politics, reveals the complicated situation at this time:

There is no general news of importance except that I hear the Ross Party is losing ground in all parts of the Nation. Starvation is threatening one half of the people through the entire Nation; it is the general belief that the Council will have to feed them at the Nation's expense or a great many will surely starve. Ross would not act on the petition to Reinstate Judge Woodall, although it was signed by at least half of the people of the District, but the Council will certainly reinstate Woodall. . . . [J. A.] Scales and Co. are trying to work up a case against Poram [John Porum Davis] and [Richard] Fields—charge them with Bribery in the passage of the Markham claim.[18] Have no doubt but the charges are true, but think there is too many fingers in the pie to cause them any trouble. Huston Benge has got afraid of his own party and moved into Town. He lost some horses; took up two men, hung and whipped them to make them talk on some others and has got scared at his trick; [he] did not attend the Ill[inois] Court [though he] had several important cases; he was afraid he would be killed. . . . The permit law has been tried in nearly all the districts without success, but the different judges have all shirked it without deciding on the Constitutionality of the act, and there has been no appeal to the Supreme Court. . . . Scales himself told Lipe a few days ago that they had given up the contest and the show was slim for any of them at the next election.[19] It is believed by knowing ones, that Ross will lose Illinois District in the next election as the negroes will not support the party. The Nomination of Chief has been talked of, but neither Party has settled on anyone as yet. Dennis Bushyhead seems to be the foremost Ross Man, while Judge [David Rowe] is favorably spoken of by the Downing Party.[20]

The council tried to amend the white labor permit law in November. The first attempt to pass a more lenient bill succeeded in the Senate but failed in the lower house, where the full-bloods were dominant. A somewhat stricter bill, but more moderate than that of 1872, passed on a second attempt. This bill allowed a Cherokee to employ no more than one white person per year and required the employer to post a bond of $250 for the good behavior of the employee. A fee of 50 cents per month was also to be paid to the national treasurer. Laborers who failed to pay the fee were to be fined and imprisoned for thirty days.[21] The well-to-do farmers and businesspeople were not much happier with this law than the old one. Ross undermined the law somewhat when he permitted the federal agent instead of the national treasurer to issue labor permits at will, a decision that greatly angered the small subsistence farmers.[22]

Late in November the National party held its convention in Tahlequah. It is not clear whether Ross or Bushyhead was behind this, for the convention did not nominate a candidate for chief or vice chief. There were many in the Ross party who felt that Bushyhead, who had been a very competent treasurer of the nation, would make a better candidate than Ross. In the slate of candidates for the council, Ross was not listed, though Bushyhead appeared as a candidate for the council from the Illinois District. The ticket and platform attempted to appeal to as wide a group of voters as possible, but it had no real populist emphasis. Its platform called for maintaining "the existing form of government" (that is, Cherokee sovereignty as opposed to any territorial system). It advocated retention of "the national domain, entire"—a rejection of the idea of allotment in severalty. Like the Downing party platform, it advocated "impartial administration of laws" and called for "an economical administration" and rapid payment of the national debt. To save money, the party called for an end to "the employment of needless delegates or attorneys in transacting the public business elsewhere." It also followed the Downing platform in supporting reunion with the eastern Cherokees and a per capita payment, although it hedged on the latter by suggesting that some of the income from land sales should be placed in "the nation's trust fund." To attract the "enterprising" and "progressive" voter, the party committed itself to support "industry and the encouragement of enterprise and the development of the resources of the Nation." It parted company with the Downing party in demanding "a liberal policy toward labor" (that is, a liberalized white labor permit law) and in promising "to develop especially the agricultural and mechanical fairs," which would improve farm production.[23]

Its slate of candidates for the council included members of the Ross party (S. H. Benge, Bushyhead, J. A. Scales, and Daniel H. Ross), but it also included full-bloods like Rabbit Bunch, Naked Head, Tahanesee, and John Tulsie. For some reason it saw fit to nominate Eli Spears as one of the representatives from Tahlequah, the sheriff Ross had removed after the Tahlequah Riot. That this was a middle-of-the-road party was evident in its failure to mention the rights of the poor farmers or the dangers of giving too many benefits to the few. The National party, whether it was for Ross or Bushyhead, was trying to maintain a moderate position against the more populistic Downing party.

Agent Ingalls said that his major problem in the Cherokee Nation in 1874 was trying to cope with "the immense illegal whiskey transactions" in the area that bordered on Arkansas, Missouri, and Kansas. "I have been led to investigate some recent disturbance and murders at Tahlequah," he wrote in December, after the Tahlequah Riot; "while there were causes which led to serious and bad feelings between the two political parties in the Cherokee Country, whiskey was the immediate provoking cause" for the murders.[24]

The failure of the fall harvest led to petitions for aid from the poorer farmers as they faced the winter with no resources. One petition, signed by 154 persons, asked Chief Ross "for immediate relief as we have fail[ed] with our crops and have no means of purchasing food" for the winter.[25] However, there was no money in the treasury to provide relief. The winter proved one of the harshest in a decade, and great suffering prevailed by February. "It makes my heart ache to hear the pitiful stories of our full blood Cherokees, many of whom are now sick and dying," wrote W. P. Adair to Agent Ingalls. "It is no fault of theirs that they are destitute. They all put in their crops and worked them, but the drought and grass hoppers ruined them. For God's sake do all you can for our people as soon as possible."[26] By April 1875, Ingalls's assistant, Major E. R. Roberts, wrote, "The industrious are really suffering as well as the idle and shiftless. . . . I am credibly informed [some] are boiling and eating bark from some kind of trees. There is no chance to overstate the want and suffering."[27] The council had instructed its delegates in Washington that winter to make their prime goal the attainment of $500,000 for "bread money" to be distributed per capita to feed the people as quickly as possible.

Just as the delegates left for Washington late in December, a shocking gun battle took place near the town of Choteau in the district of Cooweescoowee. Whiskey was later given as the cause, but it was politically motivated and it had far-reaching results. Ingalls learned of it from J. M. Bryan, a Cherokee who had lived in that part of the nation since the 1830s. Bryan wrote him on January 1, 1875, about "the trouble that now surrounds this Neighborhood" along the railroad tracks near Vinita. "On Christmas day a party was given in Saline District near the line of Coowayskooway District about 9 o'clock P.M. The Deputy Sheriff of Saline District, with three others, visited the place as they said 'to waste whiskey,'" meaning to find and destroy illegally imported whiskey. Bryan believed they used that as an excuse to break up and intimidate a meeting of the Downing party leaders in Cooweescoowee District. "The posse came to the home of John Lewis [a Downing party leader] and found a respectable group of Cherokees there." As Lewis and his men were standing "outside the yard fence, the sheriff met three or four men and disarmed them of their Pistols, but no whiskey was found" anywhere on the premises. Then "three others rode up who proved to be Tom Cox, J. T. Beamer [Doubletooth], and Nawly [Noel] Mayes. . . . Suddenly . . . firing commenced." In the fray, "the Deputy Sheriff was wounded in the shoulder, one of his party, named Alex Colston, killed; J. T. Beamer shot through and Tom Cox killed." Bryan reported also that Beamer was "one of the Executive Councillors" of the nation, a person high in the Ross party and a nephew of Chief Ross. Alex Colston, on the other hand, was "a desperate man," formerly "accused of killing Turu Foreman" at the "last council" in Tahlequah. Cox was described by Bryan as a simple "vapid fellow," and Mayes as "quite a young man" but related to Judge Joel Mayes who had recently broken with Ross and was being wooed by the Downingites. "While I am now writing," Bryan concluded, "130 men from Saline District, armed . . . [are here] searching for men accused of resisting the Deputy Sheriff and some arrests have already been made."[28]

Bryan did not give Agent Ingalls any explanation for the shooting or say who had fired the first shot, but he clearly implied that it would have political ramifications. The shoot-out had occurred not far from the new railroad line of the Missouri, Kansas, and Texas Railroad. Passengers traveling between Choteau and Chetopa heard of the event and began to spread rumors of a major crisis in Cherokee affairs. The local stringer for the Associated Press heard the rumors in Kansas and began filing stories of a new "reign of terror" among the Cherokees. His dispatches were picked up by the border papers and reached the eastern press by telegraph the next day. Ingalls had recently gone to Washington to clear up his accounts at his previous post in Indiana and received news of "the Christmas shoot-out" from newspaper stories before he got Bryan's letter. He wired Roberts, his assistant, in Muskogee, asking him to investigate. Ingalls then received telegrams from Chief Ross and from R. S. Stevens, manager of the Missouri, Kansas, and Texas Railroad. Ross asked that an investigation of the trouble be undertaken but tried to play down its importance. Stevens said he feared there would be interference with the railroad and wanted federal troops to protect passengers and the U.S. mail. Ross told Ingalls that he had ordered the arrests of those involved, but when his agents arrived on January 1, those for whom warrants had been issued fled to the town of Vinita, thirty miles north of Choteau, where they had been joined by "friends" who were prepared to help them fight against arrest.

Ingalls also read letters received by the Cherokee delegates in Washington describing the affair. He summarized all the information he had gathered on the incident in a report to E. P. Smith, the commissioner of Indian affairs. His report indicated that this was a politically motivated incident. "The present troubles," he said, "commenced at the residence of Mr. Lewis, who is a son-in-law of Colonel W. P. Adair." Since Downing's death, many considered Adair the titular head of the Downing party, and after 1872 it was sometimes referred to as "the Adair party." At Lewis's home, only a short distance from the railroad line, "a select party of friends of the family were assembled on Christmas. This party was made up of what is known as . . . the 'Downing' also called the 'Adair' party." The deputy sheriff had appeared at the door with his men, "as they stated, for the purpose of seizing whisky and firearms." He "proceeded to disarm the party," and "some sharp words passed." Ingalls reported that one of the deputy sheriff's party shot one of the Downing party, "which was followed by a general shooting on the part of both parties, resulting in two or three men being killed and some wounded. The sheriff's party, I have been informed . . . are members of the Ross Party," and while they may have been authorized to search for whiskey and firearms at this party, "such are the intense feelings existing between these two political parties, as plainly shown to me in the late Riot at Tahlequah, which I investigated, that I think the least imprudence in the discharge of official duties by the Ross Party would be likely to provoke a fight." [29] Ingalls assured Commissioner Smith that Stevens was unduly worried about the railroad passengers and the U.S. mail: "I am fully convinced there is no immediate necessity for the employment of government troops to protect the railroad"; this was simply another effort of the railroad promoters to persuade the government that only a territorial government could preserve order in the nation. Ingalls was more fearful that some of the white intruders in that region whom he had recently instructed to leave the nation would try to take advantage of the confusion, involve themselves on the grounds of self-defense, and provide a pretext for white vigilantes to enter the nation from Kansas. What had started as a political quarrel might become a major crisis on the frontier.

Meanwhile, Roberts took the train from Muskogee to Vinita to begin his investigation. He wired Ingalls on January 7 that he would send a full report soon but that he thought he had managed to defuse the controversy by persuading "Chief Ross to quash indictments against Judge Mayes and party at Vinita" for gathering armed guards around Mayes and his friends. Ross had assured both sides full "protection" against any further violence.[30] When Roberts's full report reached Ingalls, it contained new and confusing facts. According to him, the incident occurred "on the night of Tuesday, December 29," not on Christmas Day, and illegal whiskey traffic definitely had been involved. "Two men, Jack Doubletooth, alias J. T. Beamer, a fullblood Cherokee, and Thomas Cox, supposed to be a halfbreed Cherokee, had brought a load of whiskey from Kansas and had made their way down as far as Pryor's Creek, some 35 miles south of Vinita and 15 or 20 miles east of the railroad, where they were discovered by a Cherokee deputy sheriff named Frank Kousine . . . with his posse. . . . A fight occurred during which Cox was killed. . . . The whiskey was finally spilled, and the sheriff's party withdrew." Alex Colston had only been wounded in the fray, Roberts reported, but was later shot by "Wash" Mayes who had "a grudge against him." Those involved in the attack on the posse "declared they would not be taken" and fled to the Choteau railroad station. Later the sheriff "gathered a large party" and went after them with warrants from Ross. Rumors flew "that a large force were marching to Vinita, causing temporary alarm among the inhabitants," who feared they would be caught in the cross fire between the posse and the defenders of the murderers. Roberts said that the posse "was composed mainly of bad characters" and that Beamer and his friends "were desperadoes" and "were inflamed by old grudges assisted by whiskey. . . . The vicinity of Pryor's Creek . . . is a notorious rendezvous for desperadoes, whiskey smugglers, and counterfeiters." Only rough characters would dare to volunteer for a posse sent to that area.[31]

In summing up, Roberts contradicted the political explanation of the incident offered by Ingalls. "My opinion is that the affray had no political significance whatever, neither the Ross or Downing party being cognizant to . . . the affair." Roberts believed, or had been led to believe by his informants, that it was all an "attempt of certain parties in Kansas in making [it appear] a party [that is, factional] affair, and keeping up the excitement is for purposes of their own." E. C. Boudinot, who was in Washington and privy to most of this information, wrote to James M. Bell on January 6, expressing total disbelief in Roberts's version: "That fellow Roberts, clerk of Agent Ingalls, who is in the interest of Ross, has telegraphed here that the fuss at Choteau all grew out of whiskey, that a couple of Downing men were introducing whiskey and the Ross Sheriff and posse were trying to stop it according to law. . . . Get a statement from Judge Joel Mayes and the best men you know of who know all about it, get them to swear to it and send [it] to me. I will spoil Ross's little game. Don't fail to act quick; there isn't an hour to lose."[32] Though no friend of the Downing party, Boudinot would do anything to embarrass Ross.

Roberts may well have been given a cover-up story by persons in both parties in order to avoid any federal intervention or railroad machinations. It was in the best interests of the nation to keep internal factional quarrels among themselves. In order to display his own impartiality, Ross agreed to withdraw some of the warrants he had issued, particularly against the distinguished Judge Mayes, even though Mayes had assembled fifty to sixty of his friends at Vinita (they claimed for self-protection) when the local sheriff, with 300–400 men, started out for the town to arrest Mayes and fifteen others.[33] Ross did, however, sustain his warrants against the minor participants.[34]

Roberts's report left Ingalls rather confused, but he persisted in his conviction that the incident had major political implications and that troops might be needed to maintain order between the white intruders and the Cherokees. He wrote to the commissioner of Indian affairs on January 8 that from his "previous knowledge and experience with the two political parties . . . I feel it my duty to recommend securing at once an increased number of troops at Fort Gibson, there being at present but ten or twelve soldiers at the post." He thought "at least one company of Cavalry" would be needed to prevent the "large class of unprincipled white men who take refuge in the territory," escaping from penalties for crimes committed in adjoining states, from "fomenting troubles among the Indians."[35] Ingalls said he had consulted Senator John Ingalls of Kansas, William P. Ross, Colonel W. A. Phillips in Kansas, and the commanders at Fort Gibson, "all of whom agree with me as to the necessity of troops."

Meanwhile Ross had sent Dennis Bushyhead to the scene on January 5 to investigate "the difficulties at the house of Mr. Lewis, Christmas night, in which Thomas Cox and Alex Colston were killed and Sheriff Conseur and John T. Beamer wounded." Bushyhead reported that the incident was "greatly exaggerated by fabrications and misrepresentations through the telegraph and otherwise" by persons anxious "to disseminate" bad reports about the Cherokees. He felt certain that "the affair at the house of Mr. Lewis was regarded simply as a drunken row" by those who knew the facts. In order to dissipate animosities, Ross had agreed to withdraw all arrest warrants "except those for Nolly Mayes, John T. Beamer and John Hatchet."[36] Bushyhead seems to have ignored the incident at Pryor's Creek that Roberts had made the center of his report.

Ross revealed his desire that the affair be forgotten in a letter to Agent Ingalls on January 13 stating that the incident was inconsequential compared to the more serious problems facing the nation. One of these was the "considerable suffering among many of our people in consequence of the failure of their crops." Another was "the recommendations of the Board of U.S. Commissioners who visited Muskogee the 11th and 12th of December" and "contrary to the wishes of the Indians" had "created a feeling of disappointment and apprehension" with regard to the probable passage of a territorial bill before Congress. He was now happy to report, he said, that "no territorial bill would pass this Congress," a fact that had "restored confidence" somewhat.[37]

However, the affair was not so easily glossed over. The *Cherokee Advocate* finally printed its version of it on January 16:

Chief Ross, according to one report, has two nephews and sundry friends whose conduct is disgraceful to him. If he cannot prevent such outrages by persons closely connected with himself, he ought at least to be swift and sure in punishing them, but the report asserts that no effort has been made to arrest the offenders, that a general reign of terror exists, and that many persons think that he winks at this lawlessness in order to prevent any action favoring a Territorial government. . . . The [Cherokee] Territory is held by bitterly hostile factions and besieged by railway operators and land speculators and it is utterly impossible to determine how much truth there is in the statements telegraphed or written. . . . But it is very clear that no such state of things as is described in the telegram from Chetopa can exist without grave responsibility on the part of the chief. A correspondent whose letter we publish today gives the other side of the story. He sets forth that the attacking party was a Sheriff's posse, searching for whisky illegally brought into the Territory and was led by a Deputy Sheriff who was shot. He says that the leader of the Downing party was a notoriously bad character who had been a typesetter and translator in the office of *The Cherokee Advocate* but had been discharged for drunkenness.[38]

The typesetter referred to was "a member of the Chief's Executive Council, appointed by the National Council, but Chief Ross had refused to have him in council of late on account of his bad habits," a description that would identify him to most Cherokees as John T. Beamer, or Doubletooth, though the paper did not mention his name. The day after this criticism of Ross appeared, the office of the *Cherokee Advocate* burned to the ground and publication was not resumed until March 1876.

Secretary of the Interior Columbus Delano took Ingalls's recommendations seriously and wrote to the War Department, asking it to consider sending troops to Fort Gibson. When the War Department wrote to Major General John Pope at Fort Leavenworth, Kansas, he replied, "I would not send troops to meddle with these affairs. There is no war and no likelihood of war." The army, he said, should reserve its fighting for handling open hostilities between Indians and whites and not inject itself into the internal politics of the five civilized tribes. However, Pope dispatched Colonel R. C. Drum to the Cherokee Nation to make his own investigation.[39] Drum did little more than speak to Ross, who confirmed Pope's opinion.

Subsequent events proved Ingalls closer to the mark. "On my return to the territory" in mid-April, he wrote, "I found political matters so exciting, very frequent murders being committed on that account, and thinking that if I recommended a thorough examination of the different claims present, most of the cases being persons belonging to the Downing Party, the opposition party represented by Chief W. P. Ross, not knowing my instructions, might construe my acts as an interference with Cherokee matters for political purposes," he decided for the time being to drop all plans for further investigations.[40] By mid-July Ingalls became worried that the situation was so volatile that the two parties might become engaged in open warfare. "I find, as the time for general election for officers of the Nation draws near, the number of local disturbances, quarrels, fights, and murders rapidly increasing." While whiskey often instigated these acts, Ingalls said, it was not the root cause. "One of the Cherokee citizens informed me yesterday [that] the whole country is much like a volcano on the eve of an eruption. The excitement among the leading men of both parties is constantly increasing and so intense is the feeling of hatred" that murders were becoming a common occurrence; there had been "at least ten within a few weeks." "It will require but little cause to throw the entire nation into a scene of bloodshed never before known here." This would mean the end of the Cherokee Nation, for it would "result speedily in the establishment of a government, for them by the United States," and "while the result may be desired by the government, the cost and manner of bringing it about is sad to think of." He therefore counseled "the leaders of both parties to do all they can to control the bad blood" between their followers.[41] By this time a troop of cavalry had been sent on temporary duty to Fort Gibson.[42]

Ross and the Cherokee delegation had been hard at work in Washington since early January and found the news from home very disturbing. Daniel H. Ross, one of the delegates, wrote to Bushyhead in July, explaining their efforts with regard to "the sale of the Strip lands, the question of jurisdiction raised by the Wright case, the removal of intruders involving our right to determine who are entitled to citizenship, the 'Old Settler' back claims." Their most signal success had been the release of $500,000 of funds from Cherokee Strip sales for use as "bread money," which was distributed in the midst of the turmoil over politics. However, the fact that Will Ross insisted that it be distributed only to Cherokees "by blood" added to the tension, though Ross undoubtedly thought it both necessary and good for his campaign. Daniel Ross ended his letter to Bushyhead by saying, "I am pained to hear of more killing. It is fearful to contemplate. St. Louis accounts say that Big Jo Coody and two others (Downing men) were killed. Please let me know at once who was killed, by whom killed, and to what political party they belonged. State cause of difficulty. We must have the facts in order to refute the hundreds of lies in circulation" in Washington.[43]

Ingalls did not provide in his reports any details of the political issues that produced the bitter quarreling. He did note in July 1875 that Ross was now the avowed candidate of the National party (not Bushyhead) and that both sides were scrambling hard to get votes for their respective leaders. Oochalata had beaten out David Rowe as leader of the Downing party and was its candidate for chief. Rowe ran as candidate for vice chief. Ingalls accused the Ross party of manipulating the election in a letter to the commissioner of Indian affairs on July 22: "The whole Judicial System of [the] Cherokees today presents a laughable farce, and serves more as a shield for rogues than a safeguard against them, and is but a political machine for [the] purpose of serving the interests of the present administration." By accusing the judicial system of being "a shield for rogues," Ingalls meant that when gangs of white and Indian outlaws were accused of killing Downing party members for political reasons, the Ross party did not bring them to trial. By calling the Ross party's judicial appointees "a political machine," he referred to a report that "one or two Judicial District Judges (Downing men) . . . were recently removed to give place to Ross men, though charged by the Chief of some irregularity in office" in order to cover the political motivation for removal. "These Judges appoint Election judges, and it is apparent to [the] Downing Party [that] the object is for election purposes, the general election for Chief coming off next month."[44] Ingalls later asked the commissioner of Indian affairs to withdraw this statement "concerning the Judicial system" because, though it was "I believe, correct, it may not be good taste to so express it."[45]

Despite Ross's continual claim that all was tranquil in the nation, this was not the case. Sarah Watie, Stand Watie's widow, in a letter to her nephew, James Bell, a month before the election said she had learned that "there was forty men armed themselves and went to Ross and told him that if there was one other man killed that was of the Downing Party, that he would be held responsible for it." [46]

Ingalls claimed that the Ross party was using renegade gangs to intimidate and even murder Downing party members in a letter to the commissioner on July 30, three days before the election. He identified several areas of the nation that were headquarters for "the most desperate set of desperadoes that ever went unhung," including Coody's Bluff, Pryor's Creek, Choteau, Vinita, Fourteen Mile Creek, Going Snake, and Tahlequah. Many of them were whites from Texas. Their identities and hangouts were well known, Ingalls said, but "there has been no successful effort of the Cherokee authorities to arrest them, although for the past nine months they have, with others of their gang, undoubtedly been interest[ed] in or assistant in the murder of probably 41 persons within nine months and 17 of these within 60 days." He mentioned a Cherokee he knew whose home was in Tahlequah who, with "several other Citizens (Downing men) have been compelled to flee their homes because of [the] bitter feeling of some of the Ross party and the 14 Mile Creek 'outfit' who support the Ross party at present and for the past year." Only recently one of this gang had entered a Baptist meeting and shot Richard Fields through the head. Fields, Ingalls said, was "a worthy Cherokee Citizen . . . an Auditor of the Cherokee Nation, but a Downing Man." [47] The criminal was never apprehended. "I trust the Department will secure the early reinforcement of Fort Gibson with cavalry," he wrote. "There is great probability of serious fighting this fall among the Cherokees if the Downing Men do not succeed in carrying the Election." Ingalls had heard that "the Downing party claim a majority of 600, and the Ross leaders say they will carry their ticket by 600 majority." [48]

Ingalls annoyed Ross by his constant insistence that troops were, or might be, needed to maintain order. Ingalls reported that he had "visited Chief Ross at Fort Gibson when the excitement was so intense because of the murders which were being committed and offered my services in calling the leaders of both parties together in convention to discuss mutual plans to secure" order and "to stop the frequently occurring murders in the country." However, "my services were declined with the statement by Mr. Ross that he was not aware of any trouble" and that the murders "were a few old personal feuds but none of a political character, etc." [49] After the election, Ross complained to the Bureau of Indian Affairs that Ingalls had been guilty of meddling in Cherokee politics.

The secretary of the interior did not order the cavalry back to patrol the nation during the election on August 3–4. Little violence occurred, although there was confusion and evident fraud in some of the polling areas. As soon as the election was over, Ross claimed he had won, while the leaders of the Downing party claimed they had won. However, the leaders of the Downing party presented Ingalls with a petition "signed by Charles Thompson [Oochalata]" and others stating "that it is feared that upon the assembling of the Cherokee Council on the first Monday in November, when the election returns will be canvassed and the result declared, there will be disorders and bloodshed" and an attempt by the Ross party to invalidate sufficient votes to give its candidates the majority.[50] Again Ingalls requested military assistance. The acting secretary of the interior, B. R. Cowen, presented the matter to the secretary of war. Chief Ross again protested against any "military interference" in the internal affairs of the nation.[51] In a telegram to the secretary of the interior on October 19, Ross wrote, "Application through the agent for troops at Cherokee Council should not be granted. Country thoroughly quiet. No trouble anticipated."[52] Ingalls insisted that the petition from Oochalata "is . . . evidence that danger was apprehended by intelligent, prominent Cherokees, at the Council." However, no troops were sent. To avoid charges of meddling, Ingalls wrote to Oochalata "and urged him to withdraw the petition for troops as I was afraid if troops were ordered to the Council at his request, the fact might be used by his opponents and embarrass him."[53] Ingalls decided not to attend the council himself.

That the Downing party's fears of trouble were correct was evidenced by the fact that "there were several hundred Ross men assembled, well armed, during the Council and the contest for its control." The Downing party also gathered 500 people at Tahlequah, "fully armed to maintain their rights and secure the fruits of the election."[54] Perhaps because of the fears expressed and the awareness by the Bureau of Indian Affairs of the tensions within the nation, both sides decided to avoid a confrontation. During the first weeks in November, the council examined the votes reported from each district, ordered investigations of areas where voting results were challenged, and, after considerable wrangling, declared on November 27 that Oochalata and Rowe were elected.[55] The full-bloods took control of the management of the nation, but they had only a slim majority in the council.

Ross, bitter over his loss of the election, complained to the commissioner of Indian affairs about Ingalls's "unprofessional" conduct. The secretary of the interior ordered General G. P. C. Shanks to act as special commissioner to investigate the charges. Shanks reported that Ingalls had been guilty of certain improprieties and questioned his competence. Ingalls was asked to come to Washington to explain his actions. His defense was so effective that he threw doubt on the veracity of Shanks. The Bureau of Indian Affairs then sent Colonel E. C. Watkins to investigate the general nature of law and order in the Cherokee Nation.[56] In the end, Ingalls was cleared of all charges and reinstated as federal agent for the five civilized tribes. He continued to work hard to remove intruders, "to stop the traffic in intoxicating liquors," and to make the judicial system more efficient and fair in the U.S. district court in Arkansas. However, he never again took such a close interest in Cherokee politics. Besides, Oochalata proved to be a very competent and effective chief, although his narrow margin of victory (by only eleven votes) in a hotly contested election made it difficult for him to fulfill all of his campaign promises. The Cherokee Nation was faced with too many problems beyond its control.

13

The Twilight of
Cherokee Sovereignty,
1875–1879

*I have received a communication from the Superintendent of
Indian affairs which staggered my belief. . . . His department . . .
suspended the law of the United States and the operation of
Treaties in relation to intruders. . . . We are then berated as unfit
for self-government . . . and more peremptorily required to
abandon our right to self-government guaranteed to us by treaty
and ours by nature.*

—Chief Oochalata, 1877

Oochalata tried, after his election, to speak for all of the Cherokee people, not just for the full-blood subsistence farmers. He appointed
William P. Ross to the delegation that went to Washington, D.C., in January
1876. However, he stressed, far more than his predecessors had, the social
and economic inequities that had produced the populist movement leading
to his election. His populism, however, was redolent with traditional Cherokee ideals and values concerning social harmony, sharing, and cooperation,
or what the Bell-Boudinot faction called primitive "communism." In his first
annual message to the council in November 1876, he said, "I see in various
portions of our country that there is greed and avariciousness manifested by

some of our citizens to hold whole sections [that is, one square mile] of land to the exclusion of other citizens, which I deem contrary to the constitution and should not be permitted."[1] Actually there was nothing in the Cherokee constitution that limited the amount of land a Cherokee could occupy, for in 1839 no one suspected that Cherokee farms would ever become so large. What Oochalata meant was that the engrossment of thousands of acres of nationally owned land for private profit was contrary to the ancient Keetoowah spirit. As the population expanded, the diminishing quantity of arable land since 1865 had created a problem for the poor. Hence, Oochalata continued, "I am satisfied that further legislation is necessary to fully protect the public domains and to prevent the attempt [of the rich] to monopolize the same for Speculative purposes. . . . The effort of some of our citizens to get possession of large tracts of land and timber and to hold an unlimited number of claims should be stringently prohibited." Small farmers throughout the United States were facing this same crisis in these years; like the Cherokees, white populists attacked speculative greed and monopoly as the heart of the problem. Cherokee populists were no more popular in the industrial United States than white populists. Both were considered too backward-looking and unprogressive in a rapidly industrializing, urban society where the new ideology spoke of "survival of the fittest," and "bigness" was touted as "efficiency."

Like the white populists or Grangers, the Cherokees saw the railroads as a major threat, but for different reasons. In his annual message, Oochalata stressed his opposition to "the heavy siege that these Railroad adventurers are prosecuting against our Country." Their goal was to seize millions of acres of Cherokee land promised to them by Congress: "These cunning adventurers, in 1866, while the attention of the Congress . . . was absorbed in healing up the wounds of war . . . slipped through Congress three Rail Road Bills, the benefit of which are now claimed by the Rail Road Corporations known as the Missouri, Kansas and Texas and [the] Atlantic and Pacific companies." The railroad companies had now sold stocks and bonds to speculators in the United States and abroad on the basis of the wealth they expected to reap, not only from their freight traffic but also from the sale of these gifts of public land. They "have mortgaged entire lines (real and prospective) of their roads and have . . . already issued and sold, chiefly to foreigners and New Yorkers, about $16,300,000 in Bonds on these mortgages or on the lands belonging to our People. . . . In other words, these Railroad companies have sold the finest portion of our country and are endeavoring to make these sales valid by throwing our lands into a territory of the United States and robbing us."[2] Populists Henry George and Tom Watson could not have said it any better.

Behind the railroads, Oochalata saw the bankers and financial interests who held the stocks and bonds that controlled them. "There is a class of the people in the United States, embracing a powerful minority, chiefly speculators, that have but little, if any, respect for our national or individual rights, who lust for our lands. I have no doubt this last-named class is led not only by wealthy men, but also by men of very strong ability who, by their shrewdness, have managed to occupy generally the chief seats of financial and political power in the United States and have, through Congressional legislation and otherwise, preyed upon the people." The chief was trying to give his people a lesson in American political economy, and like most populists, he portrayed the issues in simple, moral terms, denouncing the oppression of the honest, hardworking masses by the cunning few in high financial and political places. Oochalata was not only a Cherokee populist but also an evangelical Baptist preacher. He may well have belonged to one of the Grange lodges in the nation. He did not suggest any alliance with white Grangers, but he believed they were engaged in the same battle to save their way of life. Big business interests "have, through Congressional legislation, and otherwise, preyed upon the people of the United States as long as they will submit and have now turned their eyes upon the beautiful lands of the Indian nations." [3]

His reason for not suggesting an alliance with white populists was the same as his reason for opposing the opening of the Indian Territory to poor white homesteaders. "All experience has proven that Indians (the weaker party) perish when commingled indiscriminately with the whites under the same local government of the white race." [4] Cherokee populism was profoundly nationalistic and ethnic, despite its awareness of class issues. Cherokees and other tribes began in these years to speak of "the red race." While acknowledging the tremendous power that bankers, railroad magnates, and land speculators had over the destiny of the Cherokees, Oochalata asserted that the Cherokees could look after themselves if whites would simply leave them alone. His rhetoric was neither consistent nor logical, but it was emotionally satisfying. "The matter of intrusion in our country has necessarily grown to be a subject of considerable annoyance to our Nation. There are now thousands of intruders (citizens of the United States) squatted upon our lands. . . . The majority, at least, of them appear to have fled from the states to avoid taxation and to acquire, by 'sharp practices,' an interest in our lands and funds." The poor outcasts from white society, corrupted by their own economic system, now preyed upon their weaker Indian neighbors and tried to corrupt them. Separatism—Cherokee sovereignty—was the only answer. [5]

In this populist version of Cherokee nationalism, the Cherokees were still one people. The mixed-blood land monopolizers and land allotment advocates in the nation were simply being misled by the corrupt white intruders and their alien values. They could be reclaimed and the nation reunited if the Cherokees returned to their ancient values. Oochalata considered himself an enlightened leader, dedicated to traditional national ideals, and not, as Bell and Boudinot portrayed him, a radical, revolutionary fanatic. Congressional bills that undermined treaty rights and land aggrandizement that betrayed Cherokee communalism were the truly radical proposals for change.

It is not clear how many full-blood dirt farmers accepted Oochalata's populist ideology, since those who spoke and wrote only Cherokee left few written records. However, their support of Oochalata speaks for them. A letter by a farmer written in poor English that appeared in the *Cherokee Advocate* in 1878 may express some of the reasons for his victory. "The theory of white people laboring for Indians" under the white labor permit system was "bad," the writer said, and the efforts of the mixed-bloods to liberalize the permit law was a mistake. "They would flood our country with a white population as great or greater than our own; I am of opinion from our past experiences that the presence of such a population would be serious to us as nation. The law relative to employing citizens of the U.S. should be rigidly enforced and not repealed by our next council. Our people should learn to work their own farms." The use of white permit labor was the way of the speculator and the idle rich as opposed to hardworking citizens.[6] In other words, better to be poor and independent than rich and corrupt.

Other evidence that Cherokee populism had a broad base was the reorganization of the Keetoowah Society a few months after Oochalata's election. Frustrated by the inability of the council to move swiftly and decisively to help the poor over the past three years, the full-bloods decided to make the Keetoowah Society once again a source of political power vis-à-vis the English-speaking minority. The society met on February 15, 1876, and voted to "reorganize" and "to discuss what we Keetoowahs were leading to. We have been united together for many, many years," but since Lewis Downing's election in 1867, they had ceased to concern themselves with politics as a group. Most of their meetings had been given over to social activities. Now, in 1876, it seemed necessary to return to older principles. "At this time it might seem that our society was scattered on account of other different lodges, societies, and companies being organized amongst our people." These smaller divisions— the Masons, the Granges, and political parties—were undermining the spirit of national harmony that should transcend local organizations and factions. The nation had lost its Keetoowah spirit. "The purpose of some [of these new societies] is greed, some to oppress your own fellow man . . . some to swindle, some to assist railroad companies, some to deprive each individual of his property, some to destroy the Cherokee National government" by working for territorial status. To counter this disintegrating, contentious, and "un-Cherokee" spirit, the Keetoowahs decided to reinvigorate a national patriotic party. The convention voted to renew its dedication to Keetoowah ideals and said that henceforth "all laws of Keetoowah accumulated shall be sacred and recognized; we therefore go back to the act of April 29, 1859, wherein it provides it shall be a secret society; we reiterate and reinforce this law."[7]

Once the Keetoowahs became a secret society again, their activities cannot be traced, but they clearly had three basic goals: to unite all full-bloods behind a defense of the nation's sovereignty; to oppose the greed and self-interest of the English-speaking elite; and to support the Downing or Oochalata party. Oochalata's victory had not yet enabled the majority to gain a firm grasp on the government. His opponents remained strongly entrenched in the upper house of the council and would try to thwart his program. The situation seemed as desperate as in the pre–Civil War years when the Southern Rights party, the Knights of the Golden Circle, and the Blue Lodges were ready to divide the nation in order to defend the institution of slavery. The rich plantation owners and big ranchers had ignored the interests of the nonslaveholders on their small farms and were willing to abandon their treaty pledges to the United States. Now, once again, many of the English-speaking Cherokees were opposed to the best interests of the poor and of the nation. Violence and fraud had been used to try to thwart Oochalata's election and the will of the majority; the old Ross party had become as corrupt as the Southern party in defense of its prerogatives.

In the years ahead, the Keetoowah Society provided steady political support for Downing party candidates, but there is evidence that it did more than that. In the heated election of 1875, the Keetoowahs had provided vigilante groups to protect their candidates from the assassins whom they believed to be tools of the Ross party; their own armed men had served notice on Ross to stop the killings. Having succeeded in electing Oochalata, they had no intention of allowing his opponents to intimidate his supporters in the council. They rallied when a movement was made in 1877 to impeach Oochalata. Though Oochalata was undoubtedly a member of the Keetoowah Society, he never appealed openly to it for support, but it provided a focal center for those who put traditional values first, defining Cherokee patriotism in ethnic or cultural terms rather than economic and political terms.

One of Oochalata's first acts as chief was to try to end the senseless feuds and murders that had caused such havoc and confusion since 1872. He began by advocating a general amnesty bill for all crimes committed prior to August 1, 1876. When the council passed this bill in November 1876, the law-and-order advocates, like James M. Bell and Spencer S. Stephens, were certain it was a mistake. They wanted the culprits punished. A friend writing to Bell about the bill said, "This wholesale refusal to keep order in the country will hardly be [allowed] by the United States. This is the d—dest council for thirty years. They are going backward at a big rate."[8]

The Cherokees also came together over a bruising blow to the national and ethnic self-esteem from President Ulysses Grant. In February 1876, Grant had nominated William P. Ross as federal agent to "the five civilized tribes" to replace George W. Ingalls. The *Cherokee Advocate* was elated at "the choice of an Indian by the President. . . . It should be considered a recognition of Indian merit, creditable to the Indian name, and in the honor of which all parties . . . may share alike."[9] However, for reasons Grant never made clear, he withdrew Ross's name from consideration a few weeks later. The *Advocate* expressed the general shock: "The question of Colonel Ross' capacity and personal fitness for the office was not, we believe a disputed one." There were some who said the president was told that an Indian was not eligible for such an office—though Grant himself had appointed Ely Parker, a Seneca of mixed ancestry, as commissioner of Indian affairs several years earlier. To deny Ross the position because of "his Race," said the *Advocate*, was to "strike at the privileges of all Indians. . . . He is a Red Man." It would "humiliate all red men" to say that race was the reason Grant withdrew his name. For whites to question "Indian eligibility to hold the Office of Indian Agent" was "a public degradation" of all Indians. If a man like Ross, a graduate of Princeton University, was considered incapable of fulfilling that job, it indicated that the Indian "will be consigned permanently to a state of inferiority" from which nothing "will ever elevate him."[10] The Cherokees preferred to believe, with some reason, that Ross was denied the position because of his well-known opposition to the railroads and territorial bills. Still, the rejection was difficult to take.

When the council met in November 1875, Oochalata summarized the major problems facing the nation: as usual there were territorial bills to be fought off; the invasion of a third railroad, not authorized under the Treaty of 1866, to be halted; white intruders to be expelled; the national debt to be reduced; and the monopolizing of land to be outlawed. Also, the problem of the "too-late" former slaves and their status remained unsettled. On this issue Oochalata urged once again that the easiest and best solution was to pass a law admitting them all to citizenship, for it had become clear that the government was determined not to remove them from the nation.

To fight off the latest territorial bills, Oochalata suggested sending a small delegation to Washington. To prevent the invasion of a third railroad, he wrote a protest to the federal government insisting on the treaty limitation to two railroads. However, the other three issues were more complicated. The white intruder problem had become mixed up in the view of the Bureau of Indian Affairs with the latecomer former slaves; both were technically intruders, but the government failed to see the difference between former Cherokee slaves who had missed a deadline in claiming citizenship and white renegades who deceitfully claimed citizenship by false marriages or unproven assertions of Cherokee ancestry. Former slaves constituted a small and finite number; the stream of invading white "con men" was endless.

The reduction of the national debt was a promise of the Downing party platform, but the problems of how to cut the budget and how to increase the national income were not easily solved. As for monopolization of the nation's best land by the more well-to-do farmers, the tight white labor permit law was some help, but a new law to register and keep a check on all land claims in the nation would require an expensive survey and a large bureaucratic system. Populist idealism was difficult to put into daily practice, and class conflict was a threat to national unity. Moreover, Oochalata's majority in the council was slim. In power, the idealist had to be a pragmatist.

The council of 1875 passed no innovative legislation to cope with any of these problems. The first act of the new populist legislature was to suspend until August 1, 1876, the institution of the new legal code that was supposed to go into operation on November 1, 1875, but had been held up by the failure to have it printed in Cherokee and circulated prior to that date. However, the reason for this suspension was a strong belief on the part of many full-bloods that the penalties for criminal actions under the new code were too severe. Before this section of the code went into effect, the populists wanted to amend the criminal part of the code by reducing the mandatory sentences and the requirement of heavy bonds for bail. Such burdens would fall heaviest on poor offenders. However, Oochalata had campaigned on a platform plank that called for an end to the lawlessness that prevailed under Ross, and he supported heavy penalties for vicious criminals (as did the middle-class mixed-bloods). As a Baptist minister, Oochalata may have believed that swift and condign retribution was essential to good order and a deterrent to crime. In any case he vetoed the bill suspending the new criminal code, arguing that it was not too severe considering some of the crimes being committed. The populists nevertheless passed the bill over his veto and then proceeded to pass another bill revising the code by reducing the mandatory ten-year sentences to five years and the five-year sentences to two years.[11] Jail sentences replaced whipping after the national jail was built in 1875, but many Cherokee traditionalists disliked incarceration, and some may have preferred quick corporal punishment.

The suspension of the legal code caused a confrontation not only between Oochalata and his constituents but also between him and the Cherokee Supreme Court. While Oochalata favored law and order, he found himself at odds with the Supreme Court over exactly which parts of the new code had been suspended by the council. As the *Cherokee Advocate* described it, "A conflict of opinion between the Supreme Court and the Executive Department in regard to the extent which the New Code was suspended" caused the court to suspend "not only the penal part of the Code but all that portion in reference to the trial as well as to the punishment of criminal offenses." In this situation, the Supreme Court "decided to exercise jurisdiction under the authority conferred by the [new] Code and to enforce its provisions in criminal trials so far as they were not restrained by their construction of the act of suspension."[12] The editor questioned the propriety of this course, as did Oochalata. The chief determined that it was not appropriate for the court to take such a loose construction of the suspension act, and he consequently suspended the judges. More than that, he recommended their impeachment for manifestly defying the will of the council. This, in turn, led Oochalata's political opponents in the council to threaten to impeach him.[13]

The controversy, which dragged on through the next two years, marked the slim margin of Oochalata's victory and the sharp tensions within the nation. It was not resolved until late in the council session of 1877, when a compromise permitted Oochalata to withdraw his suspension of the Supreme Court judges, and, in return, his opponents dropped their effort to impeach him.[14] In this same session, the populists inserted into the new code a "section . . . imposing a tax of $500 on any white man who should marry a Cherokee and desired to become a 'full citizen.'" However, this aroused such a storm of protest from whites in the nation that it was quickly repealed.[15]

Oochalata learned in June 1876 that the new commissioner of Indian affairs, J. Q. Smith, had reported that the full-bloods in the Cherokee Nation and the other civilized tribes were in favor of territorial government and that the will of this majority was being thwarted by the mixed-blood minority. This was Andrew Jackson's old argument for Indian removal updated. As Smith put it,

> In the so-called [civilized] "nations" are a number of educated, intelligent, ambitious men who, under the present system, are leaders of their people, controlling their affairs and the expenditure of their revenue. They very naturally deprecate any change which will endanger their power. They argue with great earnestness that the adoption of a territorial form of government would be followed by an influx of white men into the Territory, and

that the ultimate result to the Indians would be dispossession of homes and pauperism.[16]

Because the sentiments were exactly the opposite in all of the major Indian nations, Oochalata was astonished that Smith could be so ill-informed. He called a special meeting of his Executive Committee to seek their advice on how best to handle this situation. He had recently received a letter from Ward Coachman, principal chief of the Creek Nation, suggesting that a convention of the five civilized tribes should meet at Eufaula to discuss this matter. Chief Coleman Cole of the Choctaw Nation had sent him a similar message. When Oochalata discovered that the federal government would no longer pay for the expenses of the international councils that had met annually from 1870 to 1875, he said, "It means that we shall be left to fight . . . a Territorial Government . . . with the loss of the most efficient weapon we have heretofore had."[17] He proposed to his Executive Committee that the various tribes revive this Pan-Indian effort and pay for it out of tribal funds.

In July 1877 Oochalata informed the Executive Committee that a "false report raised by our enemies" was circulating in Washington to the effect "that the fullblood Indian of the Territory is in favor of the Territorial scheme called 'the Oklahoma bills' and that the agitations kept up against them are formulated and kept up by those of the half blood and white, seeming to forget that our Councils are largely made up of full bloods who faithfully represent the views of their class," which were then carried to Washington by the delegations they instructed. "Love of race and country" animated his delegates, he said, even though they were English-speaking and of mixed ancestry. Some congressmen were now arguing that silence from the full-bloods indicated their "tacit consent" to territorial bills. Oochalata suggested that perhaps a mass meeting or people's council of all Cherokee citizens should be called to allow the full-blood majority to make a public statement in support of its delegates.[18]

The Executive Committee agreed with Oochalata that he should meet with the principal chiefs of the other civilized tribes, but it had misgivings about a mass meeting of the Cherokee people. Such a meeting might give "the imputation that our protest is the work of a packed convention." Commissioner Smith and the congressmen in favor of territorial bills might dismiss such a protest as having been manipulated by the mixed-blood leaders. If "the people's views" could "come direct from themselves" through a grassroots petition movement, that would have far more authenticity, the council believed.[19]

The highwater mark of the populist effort to prevent "monopolizing of the public domain" during Oochalata's administration was a new white labor permit law. It was passed as part of "An Act for the Protection of the Public Domain" in November 1878. The white labor permit law of 1872 that had caused so many protests and petitions had been slightly modified by Ross in 1874, but his lowering of the permit cost from $2 per month to 50 cents per month (payable in cash or national certificates) had been offset by limiting permits to two per employer and requiring a $250 bond for the good behavior of such employees.[20] The well-to-do Cherokee farmers were far from satisfied with this, and they had hoped that if Ross were reelected they could modify it. Biding their time under Oochalata, they somehow managed to push through a modification in November 1877. However, Oochalata vetoed it, and the populist members of the council, bitterly resenting their effort, then passed the strictest white labor permit law ever enacted and Oochalata signed it. Its purpose was clearly to put an end, once and for all, to the practice of hiring whites to work in the Cherokee Nation.[21]

Oochalata had vetoed the first version of the bill because, he said, "I am convinced the first section of the bill will dismiss every employee in the nation except mechanics, . . . and that if the bill became a law, its effect will be to dismiss our school teachers and perhaps ministers of the Gospel as well as other employees not excepted as mechanics." However, "with these objections obviated, I would sign the bill."[22] The council corrected these defects and, over strong objections from members of the Ross party, sent it back to the chief for his signature. The bill had three sections. The first ordered the chief to have all sheriffs in each district arrest all trespassers upon the public domain and to "deliver to the authorities of the United States . . . all persons found trespassing . . . whether the same be in removing timber, salt, coal, wood, lumber or minerals of any kind." Any Cherokees involved in such trespasses "shall be held for trial" in the Cherokee courts. The second section required the chief "to report all intruders . . . to the Commissioner of Indian Affairs and ask for the removal of such intruders"; if he did nothing by August 1, 1879, then "it is hereby the duty of the Principal Chief to remove" them, for which purpose he was authorized "to call upon the sheriffs of the several districts." The third section stated that "it shall not be lawful for any citizens of the Cherokee Nation to employ any citizens of the United States" with the exception of "school teachers, ministers of the Gospel, and missionaries following their profession." It also excepted "mechanics working as such" in mills or cotton gins but stated that "such [Cherokee] citizens desiring to employ a citizen of the United States . . . shall pay to the clerk of the district in which such citizens may live, twenty-five dollars per month in advance for every citizen" of the

United States so hired. Failure to pay this sum would result in heavy fines or imprisonment.[23]

"The twenty-five-dollar permit law" constituted a major victory for the Downing party and the populist movement. Its clear intent was to wipe out the efforts by wealthy Cherokees to lay claim to large tracts of valuable land and mineral resources in the public domain by employing white citizens as sharecroppers, tenant farmers, or caretakers or by promising to divide that land with them once the Indian country became a territory of the United States. The law was an effort to return the nation to an egalitarian society of small farmers. The full-bloods hoped with this law to redistribute the wealth or at least to make what was left of the nation's best land available to the poor. Its passage caused an uproar among the mixed-blood elite. Many doubted that the nation would ever be able to remove all of the white intruders who were benefiting from the permit system. The sheriffs alone could not have done it, and any attempt by large posses to drive whites out of the nation would have resulted in violence. Nor did it seem likely that the United States would provide the agent with the soldiers necessary to enforce the law. Some of the district solicitors evidently brought suits against the more egregious violators of the act (Cherokee employers who held many rich claims), but according to reports, "No jury could be found that would convict the violators and the law was repealed soon after its passage."[24]

Recognizing that the law was too stringent, Oochalata recommended its repeal. The populists reluctantly acquiesced. The new law in 1878 returned to the terms of the law of 1874 except that those requesting permits had to obtain testimonials of the white employee's good character and the permit had to be signed by the commissioner of Indian affairs.[25] It was not going to be easy— if possible at all—at that late date to release the national economy from the meshes of the white labor permit system. The Cherokees did not train their own young people to become mechanics or artisans, and the public treasury lacked the funds to develop the nation's timber and mineral resources as publicly owned businesses. To the white public, the twenty-five-dollar permit law seemed to substantiate the claim of the mixed-blood elite that the full-bloods stood for regressive traditionalism.

Another effective but temporary populist effort of Oochalata's administration was his halting of the third railroad company to enter the Cherokee Nation. The Little Rock, Fort Smith Railroad (later the Kansas and Arkansas Valley Railroad), without bothering to ask permission either of the Cherokee Nation or of the secretary of the interior, ran its railroad line into the southeastern corner of the nation just west of Fort Smith in the summer of 1876.

It had advanced fifteen miles into the nation and established its first station before Oochalata was able to persuade the secretary of the interior to halt its work. As Oochalata told the council in November, by the Treaty of 1866 "no other [rail]road has any legal right to be operated or built on our land without our consent. . . . It was on these grounds that as soon as I received information last May that the Little Rock, Fort Smith Railroad had entered our border, I promptly protested to the proper authorities against such illegal action. . . . But from some cause or other . . . the action of the Interior Department was so delayed that the Company had time to complete their Road and make their [first] terminus some distance within our limit" before it was ordered to desist.[26] Resistance to this new railroad continued for another decade, but the company did not remove its tracks; it simply bided its time.

The one populist platform plank that received total support from the opposition party was the demand for parsimony in national expenses and payment of the national debt. "I am sorry to say," Oochalata told the council in 1876, "that our nation is still largely in debt, but I must say I do not blame any person or party. . . . The circumstances transpiring under which that indebtedness was incurred were beyond our control. Consequently, as we value the good name and credit of our nation, I would advise that you so legislate as to relieve our Government of the pecuniary embarrassment and to so curtail our national expenses as to bring them within our income."[27] Other than recommending sending smaller delegations to Washington, he offered no advice as to how to control expenses until 1877. That year the national debt reached $189,316.63 and there was only $560.66 in the treasury as of September 30. "The principal part of the debt," Oochalata said, "has been caused by the issue of certificates [that is, scrip] in criminal trials for the board and pay of guards and the board of prisoners, thus virtually placing our financial affairs at the mercy of the lawless, and to the too easy acquiescence of officials in allowing unlimited continuances [of trials], often on the most trifling pretenses." The real culprits were the sheriffs and their deputies who had been enriching themselves by inflating the prices they set for the care of prisoners, but judges and lawyers had been guilty of such practices as well. Oochalata recommended that "a stringent law . . . to limit continuances of criminal cases and . . . a stricter rule to prevent the employ of guards or posses to search for ardent spirits, etc., etc.," would help curtail national expenses. He was happy to announce, however, that after some delays, the national prison would go into operation in 1877, and this would provide a much less expensive system of retaining prisoners.

In addition, he recommended that delegates to Washington be required to provide a more stringent accounting of their expenses. Henceforth, they would have to provide receipts and explanations for every cent they spent, and the national treasurer would have to certify the validity of each item. However, the most effective way to end the debt and restore the nation's credit was to apply some of the money that was due to the nation from the sale of the Cherokee Strip and from renting land on the Outlet (to "wild" tribes) to wiping out the debt. This would require approval from Congress or the secretary of the interior, for by treaty all such income was to be deposited directly into the national trust funds. The council therefore requested its delegation to seek such permission and to assure Congress that thereafter the nation would have a more sound economy because its credit would be restored and its scrip would circulate at closer to par value. It would also free the nation from paying heavy interest on its debts.

Oochalata was seriously concerned about the depreciation of the national scrip (also called certificates, warrants, or tickets) because government employees were paid in this paper money. Deflation of scrip meant lower salaries for these employees. Because the scrip was not immediately redeemable for gold or silver when the treasury was empty (as it was most of the time), the scrip itself was used for money when Cherokees bought merchandise and purchased cattle, horses, or farm equipment. In 1877 Oochalata told the National Council: "The great depreciation of all kinds of our national scrip, warrants and certificates proves a serious loss to our people, who are in general the owners of the scrip, but who, from necessity, are compelled to part with it at the fancy price [that is, the discount or markdown] put on it by the traders or speculators varying from twenty cents on the dollar up to forty cents." Thus the wages of public officials, which "are none too large" anyway, "are in many instances" reduced by 20 to 40 percent. "It is truly a hardship for them to lose two-thirds of their salaries[,] . . . the burden of the debt [thereby] falling on the most needy or our people, and really in violation of contract [with them]. Something should be done to . . . give early relief."[28] The low salaries also meant that government work was not attracting the best people.

One of the anomalies of the Cherokee populist movement of the 1870s was that it favored hard money rather than soft money. Having no taxes, liens, or mortgages to pay, the Cherokees were mostly in debt as a nation, not as individuals. They wanted hard money to pay off their debts that had accumulated through the use of depreciated paper scrip. This was not new. The nation had been perennially in debt since 1839 to the sum of $150,000 to $200,000. The national annuity came into the treasury only twice a year, so most expenses had to be met by warrants or scrip, and, since the annuity and costs varied from year to year, the budgets often exceeded the income. The problem was exacerbated not simply by the "fancy" discounts charged by merchants but also by the fact that if hard cash was needed, the paper money was redeemable from moneylenders at a heavy discount. Some well-to-do Cherokees made a practice of "buying up" warrants and scrip at discounts and then redeeming them at par whenever the treasury had cash on hand.

Oochalata tried his best to curtail expenses and to obtain funds to pay off the debt, but he never succeeded. The main reason for this failure was the inability of the federal government to sell off the Cherokee Strip to white farmers or parts of the Outlet to "wild tribes" in an orderly or consistent fashion. The best land on the Strip went quickly, but the less desirable land, at a fixed price, went slowly; only when Congress lowered the price did sales increase for a time. As for the Plains Indians, they did not wish to be cramped into small reservations and to become farmers or cattle herders in the Indian Territory. The effort to force them to move to the Outlet became so costly that Congress eventually gave them reservations farther west.

Moreover, Oochalata was caught in the conflict between the debt reduction plank of his party and the per capita payment plank. Had money from the federal government become available to the nation in large amounts during his administration, he might have applied some of it to the national debt, but it usually came in small amounts that the council felt obliged to pay to its citizens in cash to relieve their private debts.

Oochalata had been elected in part to reduce the costly practice of sending four to six delegates to Washington each year. Although he did keep the number of delegates small in 1876 and 1877, he was forced to expand the number after learning that many in Washington believed that the mixed-blood delegates being sent did not represent the views of the full-blood majority, who, they claimed, supported territorialization. This problem was impressed upon him in November 1878 when Congress sent a committee of senators to the Indian Territory to look into the matter. Senator Lafayette Grover of Oregon came to the Cherokee Nation, and on hearing the senator express the view that full-bloods supported territorialization, Oochalata called for a mass meeting of the Cherokees to disabuse him of this notion. Within two days, 2,500 persons arrived in Tahlequah to meet the senator. Determined to dramatize the Cherokee position on this question, Oochalata brought Grover before the assembled throng in the public square. He told all those present who favored the establishment of a federal territory to move to the east side of the speaker's stand. No one moved. He then asked all those who opposed territorialization to move to the west side, and the throng moved en masse.[29] Oochalata then circulated a petition among the crowd opposing territorialization and obtained 1,470 signatures. When the council made its usual recommendation that two delegates be sent that year, Oochalata recommended "adding two more delegates [both full-bloods] . . . and that the appropriation be increased" to include them and also that money be paid "to employ attorneys to assist them." He justified this expense by pointing out that "our Nation and people are in great danger of extermination by the passage of a territorial bill" and "our delegation at this time should have a fullblood element in it to show Congress that our fullbloods, as well as halfbreeds, are opposed to these territorial schemes." He also added that the agenda of matters to be addressed was so large that two delegates could not manage it all. He provided a list of twelve items that he would instruct the delegation to pursue:[30]

—"unsettled business" about the Outlet land
—"the citizenship question"
—"the intrusion question"
—"depredations upon our public domain"
—"bounties and pensions due to our people" from the war
—"the collection of back annuities misapplied during the war"
—"claims . . . for property furnished the U.S. Army during the war"
—"payment of our national debt" by authorizing advance payments from land sales
—"the North Carolina Cherokee question"
—opposition to efforts for "the Transfer of the Indian Office to the War Department"
—"repeal of the grants of lands claimed by the Railroad companies for our lands"
—"annulment of the $16,000,000 of railroad bonds issued on our lands" in 1866

The delegation that addressed these problems in Washington was enlarged by the addition of more full-bloods than usual, but it made no headway with the Bureau of Indian Affairs. The following year, 1879, Oochalata stood for reelection. His opponent, Dennis W. Bushyhead, published a statement saying that Oochalata had broken his election promise to reduce the debt and compared his record on the expense of delegations to that of Ross. During the three years under Ross, from 1872 to 1875, the nation had spent $100,298 on its delegations; during the three years under Oochalata, the nation had spent $54,494. It was an improvement, of course, but still far from the kind of reduction the people had been led to expect.[31]

Oochalata claimed that the new legal system and the various compromises he had worked out on other issues during his first two years in office had restored peace, harmony, and civil order to the nation. "The Cherokees are more friendly and peaceable than at any former period within my memory," he said in November 1878. "The laws are well executed and for the first year I have had no occasion for the suspension of any officer for neglect or refusal of duty; crime has been less frequent," and there had not been "more than one case of murder . . . within the past year." Good harvests and the absence of pestilence had led to some financial recovery. "Our people have materially increased very much in the resources of personal wealth." He still hoped that the federal government would provide funds "out of the proceeds of the un-sold balance of our lands in Kansas known as the Cherokee Strip" to pay off the national debt. The sum of $270,000 was due on the Strip lands, and the council had agreed to apply it to the debt. If the money was not available, he hoped the government would give them an advance on it. He suggested that some money might be saved by having smaller juries and by speeding up trials so as to shorten the time witnesses had to be provided with room and board. He was even prepared to endorse the start of a library for the two seminaries, an expense that he had opposed in 1877. The only serious internal problems in the past year had been some cases of yellow fever and the continued stealing of coal, timber, slate, and other resources by white intruders. It was one of the most optimistic messages of the whole decade.[32]

Still, the nation remained very uneasy about the fundamental question of its right to define who were its own citizens and its right to expect the United States to remove those who the nation judged were not. Ever since 1872 fed-eral agents had refused to expel from the nation those former slaves whom the nation considered "aliens," and since 1874 federal agents had been under instructions from the Bureau of Indian Affairs to compile their own lists of black or white persons who, in their opinion, had some claim to citizenship despite previous rulings of the Cherokee courts on their claims. Oochalata recognized that no other issue was more pressing. If the bureau refused to re-move blacks designated as intruders and extended the same leniency to whites who claimed to be unfairly treated (not to mention those North Carolina Cherokees who came west but refused to apply for citizenship), the nation would soon find itself in a precarious position. Many other undesirable aliens with no real claim to citizenship would take advantage of this situation to press fraudulent claims, and a growing number of persons with an ambiguous status would settle on Cherokee land, engage in business, or simply pursue criminal activities in the nation while the Cherokees and the government haggled over how to deal with them. Under the Trade and Intercourse Act and under treaty stipulations, the government was obligated to protect the nation from intrusion. If that obligation was not honored, the security of the entire nation was jeopardized. The long debate over the status a few hundred former slaves had somehow escalated to involve the status of thousands of whites in the Cherokee Nation. Virtually all Cherokees were united in seeing this as a deliberate effort to undermine Cherokee sovereignty and flood the nation with whites. If granted Cherokee citizenship, they would press for territorialization; if not, they would cause trouble and provide Congress with an excuse for detribalization.

Oochalata had worked hard for a resolution of this thorny problem since his election in 1875. In so doing, he entered into a tug-of-war with the government that ended in one of the most disastrous rulings ever rendered by the U.S. attorney general against the Indian nations. The confrontations began over the continued meddling in the citizenship question by the federal agent, George W. Ingalls, who was steadily adding to his list of persons he considered to have been unfairly excluded from Cherokee citizenship. In 1875 Ingalls went so far as to advertise in the *Cherokee Advocate*, soliciting affidavits and other information from those who claimed citizenship.[33] When a person submitted what to him seemed convincing evidence, Ingalls issued a signed certificate to the individual, tantamount to a visa, forbidding the Cherokee council or its law officers from expelling that person. Those with certificates were left free to do as they wished in the nation, although they had no legal standing and were thus subject neither to Cherokee nor to U.S. law in the territory.

On the basis of the affidavits and reports submitted, the secretary of the interior, Zachariah Chandler, sent E. C. Watkins to the nation in 1875 to investigate the citizenship problem and gather information that Chandler could use to ask Congress to take action on behalf of these "men without a country."[34] Watkins reported in February 1876 that many of those on Ingalls's list were "clearly entitled" to Cherokee citizenship.[35] Oochalata denied it. He countercharged that Ingalls was meddling in Cherokee affairs and wrote to the Bureau of Indian Affairs to complain. Receiving no satisfactory response, he wrote directly to President Grant on November 13, 1876, enclosing a petition from the Cherokees in Cooweescoowee District, complaining that the agent had not removed thousands of intruders in their area though ordered to do so by the council. Some of these intruders were former slaves from the Deep South, but most were white U.S. citizens from Kansas, Missouri, and Arkansas.[36]

Grant referred this letter to Commissioner J. Q. Smith. Annoyed that Oochalata had gone over the head of the Interior Department to the president, on December 8 Smith wrote Oochalata a long, assertive, and highly provocative letter outlining for the first time the department's position on this question. Smith said that from the evidence he had received, both from various federal agents and from the investigations of E. C. Watkins, the Cherokee

Nation had failed to deal consistently and impartially with the problems of former slaves and others who claimed Cherokee citizenship. Therefore the Bureau of Indian Affairs would continue to compile its own list of those who had "prima facie" evidence for citizenship (whether the Cherokee courts had acted negatively on their claims or not), and it would take no action to remove them until the Cherokees carried out four stipulations to resolve the issue. First, the council must establish a clear, legal procedure providing due process for adjudicating all prima facie claims. Second, the rules by which such cases were decided must be approved by the secretary of the interior to insure their impartiality. Third, he suggested that the Cherokee circuit courts be designated as the appropriate bodies for such hearings. Finally, claimants' appeals of the decisions of the Cherokee circuit courts must be forwarded to the secretary of the interior, and no claimant for citizenship should be removed from the nation until the secretary had made his own ruling. In effect, Smith asserted the right of the Bureau of Indian Affairs to decide who was and was not a Cherokee citizen.[37] A crucial decision concerning the issue of the sovereignty of Indian nations was about to be reached.

Oochalata was stunned and wrote a 139-page letter to Smith explaining why this procedure was totally unacceptable and contrary to law, treaties, precedent, and the U.S. Constitution. Although Oochalata, like Downing and Ross before him, sympathized personally with the latecomer former slaves and regretted the intransigence of the council with respect to them, he could not allow the Bureau of Indian Affairs to threaten the nation's sovereignty by this new and arbitrary policy.[38] Either the Cherokee Nation could define its own identity, or it would cease to be able to determine its own destiny.

That the Cherokees had been inconsistent in some of their decisions regarding the former slaves was true. For example, blacks who had settled on the Neutral Lands in Kansas during the war, thinking they were on Cherokee soil, had not returned to the nation proper prior to January 27, 1867, and were therefore denied citizenship. In another embarrassing case, several of the slaves of Chief John Ross, who had accompanied him to Washington and served the Ross family there from 1862 to 1866, had been unable to get back to the nation before the deadline and were denied citizenship. Such examples seemed inconsistent with others, such as a case involving a former Cherokee slave in North Carolina who came west after the war, married a Cherokee, and was allowed to become a citizen and the case of a former slave from a southern state who came to the nation, married a former Cherokee slave who had acquired citizenship, and was then allowed to become a citizen. The principle of citizenship through marriage to a Cherokee was honored for blacks, but failure to meet a formal deadline set in the Treaty of 1866 was sufficient to deny citizenship.

One of the more ambiguous problems involving white intruders concerned nineteen white women who married Cherokee citizens. Cherokee law said that a white man who married a Cherokee woman was automatically adopted into the nation, but it did not mention white women who married Cherokee men. In the past the Cherokee courts had permitted white women to gain citizenship by marriage because there were so few of them, but now that the question of intermarriage involved scores of former slaves and whites seeking some claim to citizenship, the Cherokee courts became much more strict. In 1871 the Cherokee Supreme Court ruled for the first time that marriage of a former slave to a Cherokee woman did not convey citizenship; this was the first time any ruling had been made on such cases.[39] This reversed a policy that had allowed such claims from 1867 to 1871.

Acting on instructions from Oochalata, the Cherokee delegation sent another letter to President Grant on January 9, 1877, insisting that treaty rights, the Trade and Intercourse Act, and precedent gave the nation the right "to determine the question as to who are and who are not intruders."[40] The president referred their letter to Secretary of the Interior Carl Schurz, who, on April 21, 1877, told the delegation that he supported Smith's four stipulations for settling the matter.[41] Oochalata ignored this response and in August 1877 sent to the new commissioner of Indian affairs, Ezra A. Hayt, a list of all the intruders whom the Cherokees wished to be immediately removed. On November 7, Hayt replied flatly that the Bureau of Indian Affairs would not do so: "While the department reserves to itself the right to finally determine who are and are not intruders under the law, it expects the Cherokee National Council to enact some general and uniform law by which the Cherokee courts shall hear and determine the rights of claimants to citizenship, subject only to the review of the Secretary of Interior after a final adjudication has been reached."[42]

The controversy was deadlocked. In his annual message to the council on November 13, 1877, Oochalata expressed his exasperation. In answer to all his petitions and "reasonable requests," he said,

I have received a communication from the Superintendent of Indian affairs which . . . staggered my belief as to its being genuine, as it is in many respects so unstatesmanlike and [so] much different from any communication ever received. . . . The Honorable Commissioner starts out by voluntarily informing us that since the 26th of September, 1874 . . . his department had, without the authority of United States law, suspended the law of the United States [that is, the Trade and Intercourse Act] and the operation of Treaties in relation to intruders . . . on the ex parte say-so of parties [that is, the intruders] whose very acts proved them to be inimical to the Cherokee Nation. . . . We are also told that this is done on the report of Inspector Watkins, who is converted into a common detective . . . to find fault with the Cherokee authorities surreptitiously . . . [and] that he went through the nation without either notifying or consulting the authorities. . . . We are then informed that there are certain persons, that are classed [as intruders], who have rights that we ignore. . . . We are then berated as unfit for self-government . . . and more peremptorily required to abandon our right of self-government, guaranteed to us by treaty and ours by nature. . . . In short, the letter is an open avowal of the determination of the Department to coerce us . . . under the threat that unless we submit—that intruders shall not be removed from our soil.

Furthermore, Oochalata continued, he had received an arrogant letter from Agent G. W. Marston, stating that "he had been officially informed that these two last documents [from Smith and Schurz] . . . contained the view of the United States government," and would uphold them. "From which," Oochalata said, "we are to infer that the Government of the United States have adopted the rule to not observe any Treaty that clashed with the individual opinion of the Secretary of Interior or his subordinate, the Commissioner." The department's claim that it had the right to judge intruders was, in Oochalata's opinion, "a new doctrine for construing treaty or contracts in writing, to add to it verbally, a new clause, after the expiration of 92 years from date of that compact or treaty and without the consent of [one] party. . . . It is a dangerous doctrine to which I can never agree." [43]

While he urged the council to send a protest through its delegation, Oochalata also asked it to enact a law that would establish a court to decide citizenship claims in a legal and uniform manner. The council complied on December 5, 1877, but the compromise was fatally weakened by the council's failure to address two aspects of the law governing the citizenship court's actions. First, the law provided no guidelines for deciding cases that would meet the demands of the Bureau of Indian Affairs, and consequently, in cases involving former slaves, the citizenship court relied, as the Cherokee Supreme Court had in 1870–71, simply on the wording in the Treaty of 1866. Second, the council explicitly refused to allow the right of the secretary of the interior to review the decisions of the court, stating that the Cherokee citizenship court was "a tribunal of last resort." [44] The three persons appointed to the court were John Chambers, O. P. Brewer, and George Downing. Also referred to as the Chambers Commission, the court began to hold hearings early in 1878. All persons claiming to have grounds for citizenship were required to present them or to be declared intruders.

The Bureau of Indian Affairs refused to consider this court a legitimate response to its demands and continued to refuse to remove any intruders. When the Cherokee delegation presented its demand for the removal of 2,500 intruders on February 18, 1878, they were told they were to blame for the problem: "You are shutting the door and rendering it impossible to expel these men because you are not willing to make a law that will be considered fair among men."[45] The citizenship court nonetheless continued to hold hearings and make decisions. Many former slaves were loath to appear before it; if rejected for citizenship, they were declared intruders, and the sheriffs were instructed to seize their farms, sell their improvements at auction, and remove them. The former slaves appealed to the commissioner of Indian affairs for help. Acting Commissioner W. M. Leeds told them in July 1878 that they need not bother to appear before the Cherokee court because the Bureau of Indian Affairs did not recognize the authority of the court to make final decisions.[46] While Leeds instructed the agent not to expel any of those judged to be intruders by the court, he did nothing to prevent the Cherokee authorities from ejecting them from their homes and selling their improvements. The former slaves had become pawns in a much bigger game.

By the end of 1878 Oochalata was struggling to find some new approach to the problem. On December 3, he went over the head of the Bureau of Indian Affairs again and wrote to President Rutherford B. Hayes, forwarding a complete account of all the cases adjudicated by the citizenship court and asking him to order the expulsion of those rejected and all other intruders. He told Hayes that the Cherokee Nation had an "inherent national right" to define its own citizens, while the United States had a well-established obligation to expel noncitizens.[47] Suspecting that Hayes would reject this request, Oochalata approached Commissioner Ezra A. Hayt and tried to work out a compromise. He said that the Cherokees would stop confiscating the property of those former slaves judged to be intruders pending the appointment of a joint commission of Cherokees and members of the bureau to review the rejected claims. Hayt agreed only on the condition that decisions of this commission must be unanimous or the bureau would retain the right to make its own decision in each case. Oochalata and the delegation could not accept such a condition, and the negotiations broke down.[48]

Finally, as a last resort, the council decided to submit a series of questions to Secretary of the Interior Carl Schurz about their right to determine citizenship and the obligation of the United States to accept their determinations. They asked Schurz to present these questions to Attorney General Charles Devens for his opinion. They sent the letter on March 3, 1879, and after Hayt informed Devens of his views on the matter, Devens held hearings at which both sides presented their views.[49] Realizing the importance of the decision, the Cherokees spent the money necessary to hire the best lawyers they could find to assist them. Hayt said that the status of at least 1,000 persons was at issue;[50] the council argued that there were over twice that many intruders whom the department was refusing to remove. Throughout the dispute, the Bureau of Indian Affairs declined to act against intruding squatters from Kansas who made no pretense to citizenship.

The three questions that the council asked Devens to answer were: Did the Cherokee Nation have the right to determine its own citizenship? Did the former slaves who were citizens have any claim to share in the use of Cherokee land or in the money derived from the sale of Cherokee land? Was it, or was it not, the duty of the federal government to remove intruders under treaty stipulations and the Trade and Intercourse Act?[51] By the time Devens sent his reply to Schurz in December 1879, the citizenship court had heard 416 claims for citizenship and rejected 338.[52]

Devens's opinion was a shattering blow to the concept of Cherokee sovereignty: "It is quite plain," he said, "that in exercising such treaties, the United States are not bound to regard simply the Cherokee law and its construction by the council of the Nation, but that any Department [of government] required to remove alleged intruders, must determine for itself, under the general law of the land [that is, U.S. law] the existence and extent of the exigency upon which such requisition is founded."[53] This decision, along with the Cherokee Tobacco Case of 1870 and the law ending treaty making in 1871, served as a coffin nail in the concept of Cherokee sovereignty and self-determination.

One other action taken in 1879 marked the setting of the sun on independent tribal government for all the nations in the Indian Territory. In the various treaties made with the five civilized tribes in 1866, they had all been obliged to give up control over their lands in the western part of the Indian Territory and to withdraw toward the east in order to make room for those tribes in Kansas, Nebraska, and elsewhere who were being removed to the western part of the territory. Although numerous tribes had been settled on the land ceded in 1866, there remained in 1879 some 2 million acres in the central part of the territory that were still vacant or "unassigned." In addition, the western part of the Cherokee Outlet, though still nominally belonging to the Cherokees until it was sold to make way for other tribes, was also called "unassigned." Frontier homesteaders and land speculators, convinced that any land not actually settled by Indians should be open to whites, persisted in arguing that these unassigned lands should fall within the stipulations of the Homestead Act of 1861. Consequently, when an article appeared in the *Chicago Times* in the spring of 1879 declaring that the unassigned lands in the Outlet and in the central part of the Indian Territory were in fact "public land" and open to settlement, there was a tremendous surge of squatters into these areas and a strong demand on Congress to declare officially that these areas were open to settlement.

The article in the *Chicago Times* was written by E. C. Boudinot, who was well known to be an authority on territorialism and, as a clerk of the Senate Committee on Land Claims, was thought to have inside and quasi-official knowledge of such matters. Boudinot, as usual, was lobbying for passage of several territorial bills and speaking widely around the country to promote support for them. Boudinot wrote to James M. Bell on February 3, 1879, that "I am in for establishing a colony west of 98 [on the Outlet]. We can do this *without* authority of the U.S. or anybody else." [54] His unauthorized article declaring the unassigned lands open was the first step in this private plot. The tense situation that developed from Boudinot's machinations demonstrated the mounting pressure toward territorial legislation in this decade that eventuated (a decade later) in the act of Congress officially declaring the unassigned lands open to white settlement.

Throughout Oochalata's administration, the Cherokee delegations had successfully defeated territorial bills at the rate of two to five each year. "Territorial bills," said the *Cherokee Advocate* in March 1876, "are launcht at our heads like so many blows of a hammer . . . without ceasing. These blows must be warded off if we would not be struck down as a Nation never again to rise." [55] The Voorhees and Franklin territorial bills of 1878–79 were designed specifically by Boudinot, who knew that a general public dislike in the nation for the railroads made it difficult to counter the claim that all territorial bills were special interest legislation to obtain land grants for them. The Voorhees and Franklin bills specifically called for rescinding the laws of 1866 that had granted Indian land to railroads once Indian title was extinguished. This, of course, turned the railroad lobbyists against the bills, and the public witnessed the odd spectacle of Cherokee delegates and railroad lobbyists working together to defeat the same legislation.

The Voorhees and Franklin bills had other features that attracted support from some Indians. They mandated only minimal supervision of a consolidated Indian legislature for the territory (similar to the terms of the Ocmulgee constitution of 1870). The Franklin bill specifically prohibited the entry of whites into the territory without special permission from the Indian tribes. It tried to address the overlapping jurisdiction of Cherokee law and that of the U.S. District Court for the Western District of Arkansas by calling for a U.S. district court within the territory. It also included the privilege of a delegate to Congress to be chosen by the Indian legislature. The delegate would be given a seat (but not a vote) in Congress and would present the Indian viewpoint on all issues. (Boudinot hoped this position would go to him.) However, the key feature of both the Voorhees and Franklin bills provided for a survey of all Indian land in the territory and its allotment in severalty to Indian families— the policy that many mixed-bloods in the five major tribes favored.[56]

When the *Baltimore Gazette* published a long editorial denouncing the Franklin bill, Boudinot wrote a strong response. He said he was doing all he could to find some consensus between the growing movement among Indian reformers to grant land in severalty to the Indians and the view of Indians like the Bell-Boudinot faction in the Cherokee Nation, who also favored division of the land in severalty but under tribal self-government. Boudinot's letter was reprinted in the *Cherokee Advocate* in April 1877. The Baltimore newspaper had denounced the bill as an abrogation of treaties and said that 80,000 Indians now lived in the Indian Territory in a civilized way of life that should not be disturbed. Boudinot, in his response, pointed out that the Choctaws and Chickasaws had agreed to territorial status in their treaties of 1866, that the Ocmulgee constitution of 1870 had supported territorial status, and that there were now 20,000 white citizens of the United States in the Indian Territory who needed the protection of U.S. courts. He claimed that there were only 25,000 full-bloods in the territory while there were 16,000 whites and 6,000 blacks who favored territorial status as well as 3,000 intermarried whites. He also called attention to the thirty trials for murder in the Indian Territory since the previous May that were pending in the U.S. district court and added there were 100 warrants for murderers now in the hands of the U.S. marshals, which indicated that the Indian Territory was hardly safe or civilized. He asserted, "The Territory is the refuge for the worst characters from the contiguous states and will in the very nature of things remain so until there is established a general government over the Territory" because these criminals knew there was no effective way "to crush out the desperadoes and villains who now seek an asylum where there is no local authority which can arrest or punish them." He also noted that "the United States has extended its internal revenue laws over the Indians" in the Cherokee Tobacco Case and so Indian businesspeople were being taxed without representation. Boudinot pointed out that the Cherokee delegation was at that moment "fighting hand in glove and side by side with the railroad bondholders" against this bill at a cost of $20,000 a year to the poor full-bloods. "In short, Sir, is the civilized

Indian to remain in perpetual pupilage? Is he never to become a citizen of your government which taxes him for its support and drags him out of his country to be tried by aliens and strangers" in Arkansas?[57] Boudinot had caught the tone of eastern Indian reformers perfectly: save the Indians from their own inept governments, allot them tribal land in severalty, and lead them by paternalistic steps toward U.S. citizenship.

This was the essence of the speeches Boudinot gave throughout the United States in these years. He seldom noted that all territorial bills called for the denationalization of the Indian tribes, thereby ending treaty obligations and leaving Congress free to legislate any regulations it wished for the territory. Though the Voorhees and Franklin bills would inaugurate a federal territory run by Indians, that structure would quickly disappear under Boudinot's plan. A good example of what white speculators and business interests expected would emerge out of any territorial system can be seen in the letter written by Kansas entrepreneur Jeff Hibbetts to James M. Bell in 1874. Hibbetts had formed a mining company and wished to give shares to Cherokees who would assist him in seizing control of all the mineral resources in the nation once it became a territory. "I am about completing the organization of my 'Oklahoma Milling and Manufacturing Co.,'" he wrote to Bell from Chetopa, Kansas. Hibbetts said he had told

> my friends, who are to furnish the money, that no shares shall be placed except for money or in consideration for important discoveries and information valuable to the company. Colonel [E. C.] Boudinot is to be a shareholder for his having disclosed to me the location of the Zinc mine [in the Cherokee Nation] which I believe to be very valuable. . . . If you are willing to show me the copper mine . . . , it will establish your right to be a shareholder. . . . The object of the company is to obtain control—as soon as it can legally be done—of the best mineral claims in the Territory. . . . The share [you will get] can be made very valuable when the country is opened for settlement. I think I need hardly tell you that the whole affair is to be worked very quietly and that whatever arrangements we enter into will be strictly confidential.[58]

For Boudinot, passage of a paternalistic territorial bill, cooperation with enterprising businesspeople like Hibbetts, the use of the white labor permit law to settle his contract with A. C. Larkin, and white settlement on the unassigned lands were all part of the same general effort by other enterprising Indians to line their pockets. Hence, he had no qualms about asking James Bell, Spencer S. Stephens, James Barker, and other friends to join him and entrepreneurs like Hibbetts or the owners of the railroads in support of these schemes. The impasse that had developed between Oochalata and the Bureau of Indian Affairs over the removal of intruders between 1875 and 1879 played directly into Boudinot's hands. Boudinot wished to test the right of whites to settle on any land not occupied by Indians. In 1877, Samuel H. Payne of Arkansas led a group of whites to settle on land in the Cherokee Outlet. Oochalata wrote to W. M. Leeds in the bureau that the council had passed a law on December 9, 1877, "declaring Dr. S. H. Payne and others, intruders upon the public domain of the Cherokee Nation." Leeds, without bothering to investigate, replied in March that by action of the department, no one would be removed until the problem regarding all those who had "a color of right" to be in the nation was settled.[59] Clearly, as since the days of Andrew Jackson, federal refusal to honor the requirement of removing intruders was to be the means of forcing the Indian nations to do what they did not want to do.

Aware of this new policy, Boudinot urged James Bell to gather persons for a similar colony who would settle upon the unassigned land in the Cherokee Outlet. "Get up your colony," he urged Bell in June 1879, even "if not more than 20 or 30."[60] Bell had no qualms about this plan, even though he knew that the area west of 96° not sold to other tribes had been leased by the Cherokee Nation to cattle ranchers for grazing and that the nation depended on this income to help pay off its debt. Bell's colonists settled at a spot named Chilocco late in 1879 and began to build cabins. Payne and Bell were the first "Boomers."

Fortunately the appeal of the Cherokee delegates to President Hayes earlier in 1879 had convinced Hayes that there might be a difference between the latecomer former slaves or others with "a color of right" and the colonizing groups led by Payne and Bell who had no right whatsoever. Troops were therefore sent to remove both colonies. Payne was tried and fined in the U.S. district court in Arkansas, but he never paid the fine, and during the 1880s he continued, as did David H. Payne of Kansas (no relation), to organize additional white colonies on Cherokee land. Being a Cherokee citizen, Bell was indicted for treason in the Cherokee courts, but the case was not pressed. Oochalata left office before the trial was scheduled. When it became clear that his successor, Dennis W. Bushyhead, would not push the case against Bell, the reorganized Keetoowahs determined to take action themselves. On September 12, 1881, they wrote letters to Bell and to Boudinot threatening them with execution. To Bell, they wrote,

We, the undersigned Committee of Safety, have organized for the purpose of driving you from our midst; traitors and all persons that are laboring to bring the allotment and sectionalization of our country[. We] do hereby order you and your family from our midst. . . . In all secret and underhanded ways you are laboring against our Government, our people, and our interest, and in favor of railroad corporations, land grabbers, and such arch traitors as Cornelius Boudinot. . . . You are ordered to leave this country within 60 days . . . as you have forfeited all right to a common property, a common government, and a common protection. . . . Remember the fate of the Ridge family.[61]

The tradition of execution of traitors seemed about to be revived against the Bell family. However, Bell was neither expelled nor assassinated, probably because wiser Keetoowah leaders felt that it would only play into the hands of Boudinot and his friends. The federal government managed to hold the line against these well-organized and persistent white squatters on unassigned Indian lands until 1889, but it clearly lacked the will to make its position convincing.

As the Cherokee election of August 1879 neared, it was apparent that Oochalata would not run again. He was not in good health and was slowly going blind. His efforts to sustain tribal unity were not successful, nor had he reduced the national debt. The populist movement had faded away with the return of good harvests, and the full-bloods were upset at his inability to resolve the problem of the former slaves or to persuade the federal government to remove the thousands of intruders crowding in upon them.

William P. Ross hoped to be chosen to run on the National party ticket in 1879, but Dennis Bushyhead finally engineered the break with Ross that he had been considering since 1875. By calling their party the National Independent party, Bushyhead and his friend Rabbit Bunch emphasized their distinction from the old Ross or National party. The National Independent party sought to attract disaffected members of the Downing-Oochalata party. Another political coalition movement was under way. No platforms were published during this campaign, and there was no violence by either party. When Oochalata withdrew from politics, David Rowe ran on the Downing-Oochalata party ticket to succeed him.

Bushyhead won handily over Rowe in August 1879 and served two four-year terms. However, in the end, it did not matter any more who was chief; the handwriting was on the wall. The fight to sustain Cherokee sovereignty and self-government was all but over by 1880. The best Bushyhead could hope for was to postpone the inevitable for awhile. The turning point was reached in 1887 when Congress passed the Dawes Severalty Act.[62] The act expressed what was now the national consensus among white voters (including Indian reformers, railroad magnates, and entrepreneurs)—that the solution to "the Indian question" was to denationalize the tribes in the Indian Territory, survey and allot their land in severalty, and establish a white-dominated territorial government over "Oklahoma," the Choctaw word for "red man."

Oochalata was the second and last full-blood chief elected after 1827. His administration had, for a time, restored the full-bloods to power as in the days of Lewis Downing. The Keetoowah Society had done its best to lend weight to his program to help the small farmers against the businesspeople and big farmers. However, too many outside forces impinged upon the nation and too few alleged reformers (or "friends of the Indians") in the East understood the Cherokees' desire for tribal sovereignty. With the last of the Plains Indians (under Geronimo) defeated in 1886, the white citizens of the United States could now claim that the territory of the United States from coast to coast belonged to them to do with as they pleased. According to the prevailing ideology of the era, the United States was to be based on individual self-reliance and survival of the fittest races in the name of progress. No one expected the Indians to succeed in that contest, but, allegedly, equal opportunity would be theirs once they abandoned their primitive nationalism and became citizens of the United States.

Epilogue:
The End of Sovereignty, 1880–1907

[The Dawes Severalty Act] is only one step in the systematic attempt on the part of those who covet the lands of the Indians to dishonor the obligations of Indian Treaties. . . . It sweeps away, at a stroke of the pen, treaty guarantees of tribal ownership of lands [and] . . . must necessarily result in the acquisition of the great body of lands by a few strong and unscrupulous hands, with poverty and misery for the masses of the [Indian] people.

—Appeal of the Delegates of the Chickasaw, Creek and

Cherokee Nations to the President of the United States *[1887]*

After 1880, the Cherokees' stubborn fight against territorial bills gave way to a much more difficult struggle against division of their land in severalty. While political factions within the Cherokee Nation continued to contest elections for another twenty years, all tribal attention focused on the allotment issue. The story of this struggle, involving all of the Indian nations, is too complex to do more than summarize here.

Although Oochalata was the last of the full-blood chiefs of the Cherokees, he was not the last to struggle to sustain sovereignty. Other chiefs continued that fight until 1898 and thereafter the Keetoowahs fought on alone. In 1887, eight years after Oochalata left office, the United States drastically altered its Indian policy with the passage of the Dawes Severalty Act. By that act, the denationalization of all the tribes within the Indian Territory became the answer to "the Indian question." To soften opposition to the policy, "the five civilized tribes" were at first exempted from its terms. The last years of Cherokee national existence from 1880 to 1898 were essentially a history of futility. Oochalata was probably the last chief to believe that the Cherokees' sovereignty could be preserved. Dennis W. Bushyhead, who succeeded Oochalata, said in 1889, "The more intelligent of the Cherokees realize that the present order of things cannot long exist."[1] A year later, Congress established the Oklahoma Territory in what had been called the "unassigned lands" in the center of the Indian Territory. In 1893 the Dawes Commission was authorized by Congress to negotiate with the five civilized tribes for allotment of their land in severalty. In 1896 this commission was authorized to take a census of all the members of these tribes to determine who among them was eligible to receive the allotments. Two years later the Curtis Act effectively put an end to tribal governments in the Indian Territory. The state of Oklahoma, as it now stands, came into being in 1907. Thereafter the Cherokees (like all the other tribes crowded into the Indian Territory) were a people without a country.

As Oochalata and his successors realized, the federal government (after 1865) followed the same policy of attrition that Andrew Jackson adopted in 1830. It subverted the effective government of the Indian nations by refusing to carry out its obligation to remove white intruders until their numbers became so great and their behavior so uncontrollable that they undermined all efforts to maintain order. The government did this by denying the right of Indian nations to define who were their own citizens and by refusing to expel (as the law required) those who were not. The Cherokees compared themselves to the Trojans: "It was the contents of the wooden horse emptied inside the walls of Troy that enabled the Greeks to take that ancient city."[2] By encouraging and protecting white intruders, federal officials were responding to the incessant demands of the frontier citizens and business interests who coveted the Indians's land and resources. Having destabilized their countries, Congress declared the Indians incapable of self-government. The myths of white supremacy and manifest destiny created the aura of "inevitability" to cover this naked imperialism and paternalistic ethnocentrism.[3] In 1884 a historian of the Cherokees, Charles Royce, wrote, "They felt that they were, as a nation, being slowly but surely compressed within the constricting coils of the giant anaconda of civilization; yet they held to the vain hope that a spirit of justice and mercy would be born of their helpless condition."[4]

The resistance of the five civilized tribes to the severalty policy caused the U.S. Senate to send an investigating committee to the Indian Territory. It reported in 1894 that these five tribes were "non-American" because they held their lands in common.[5] This conclusion echoed the views of countless well-meaning but ill-informed Indian reformers in the East who had been telling government officials since 1880 that, for the Indians' own good, Congress must end their ancient practice of owning land in common. Only by owning their land as private individuals would the Indians ever develop the initiative, self-discipline, and desire for improvement essential to their survival. A committee of reformers, led by Albert Smiley, a Quaker philanthropist, informed the secretary of the interior in 1880 that "the greatest good for the Indian" would be "the speedy enactment of the pending bills in Congress providing for lands in severalty . . . and ultimate citizenship. This much-needed Congressional action secured, the problem of Indian destiny would be of easy solution. The policy of seclusion would soon give way to that of absorption; industrial pursuits [would] take the place of idleness and the chase."[6] Another Quaker philanthropist, Philip Garret, wrote in 1886, "Let [the Indian] lay aside his picturesque blankets and moccasins, and clad in the panoply of American citizenship, seek his chances of fortune or loss in the stern battle of life with the Aryan races."[7]

The clash of cultures that led to the denationalization of the five civilized tribes, a title they had earned by 1825, had its ideological roots in the expansionist nationalism of white Americans, their religious sense of chosenness, and their capitalist ideology. The sacred essence of private property and the free market economy were first explained to generations of Americans by the Reverend Francis Wayland, the devout president of Brown University, in his popular college textbook, *The Elements of Political Economy*, first published in 1834 and still widely read in the 1880s. Wayland had much to say about Indians. To him the Indian was an anachronism. In explaining "progress," Wayland used "Indian" as a metaphor for humanity in its primitive or savage stage of development. The concept of political economy that Wayland's book taught to young Americans was based on the natural laws of the Creator. Wayland incorporated within "God's laws" "manifest destiny," republican political science, and the economic theory of Adam Smith. "Without a knowledge of the laws of nature, we should all be savages," Wayland wrote. "That nation which is most assiduously cherishing the means for availing itself of the benefit of the laws of the Creator will most rapidly provide itself with the comforts and conveniences and luxuries of life."[8] Two of the most basic laws of creation were that every man must "be allowed to gain all that he can," and that "having gained all that he can, he be allowed to use it as well." To Wayland, the fundamental failing of the "savage" was the folly of holding land in common. The root of human progress was "that property be divided. When property is held in common, every individual . . . has an equal but undivided and undetermined right to his portion of the revenue. . . . There is, therefore . . . no connection between labor and the rewards of labor. There is rather a premium for indolence. . . . The forest of an Indian tribe is held in common and a few hundred families barely subsist upon a territory which, were it divided and tilled, would support a million civilized men." Progress included a steady increase in human population through the development of land and resources. To accomplish this, God instilled in each man a desire to increase his own wealth. Progress derived from enlightened self-interest. All nineteenth-century college presidents (most of them ordained evangelical Protestants) were fond of reminding their students that the laws of political economy (which the classical economists "discovered") were really God's laws. This was explicit in Genesis, where God commanded all creatures to "be fruitful and multiply" and told man "to have dominion over the earth and all that is in it" and "to live by the sweat of his brow." "You see a man diligent in business," said the biblical proverb, "shall stand before kings."

The American rationale for destroying the Indians' sovereignty, religion, ethnicity, culture, customs, treaty guarantees, and self-government was that only this would (or might) save them from extinction. After 1870, with the new Social Darwinism, Wayland's Creator was said to have imposed on human history an ethic of survival of the fittest, and the fittest were those who followed God's natural laws of progress. It applied to races or nations as well as to individuals. This deeply ingrained ideology numbed the sensibilities of even the most dedicated Indian reformers and blinded white voters to the cruelties of their new Indian policy. Denationalization caused much greater hardship for the poorer Indians and the traditionalists. However, "tough love" required that Indians face up to their savage ignorance and relegate their heritage to the scrap heap of history.

In a memorial presented to Congress against the Dawes Severalty Act in 1887, the Cherokees, Creeks, and Chickasaws stated that the act unilaterally abrogated the treaties made with the tribes. It also went on to explain the religious significance of communal landowning. "Ownership of lands in common . . . is with them a religion as well as a law of property. It is based upon peculiarities and necessities of the race."[9] Whites responded that this only proved how erroneous their religion was. It was not only "non-American" but, as Wayland said, contrary to God's natural laws.

After 1889, the Keetoowah Society was restructured. It concentrated its attention on the politics of preventing denationalization.[10] The Keetoowahs took a nonviolent stand, but this proved no more effective than the armed resistance of the Apaches or the Ghost Dance movement of the Sioux. When John B. Jones was the federal agent of the Cherokees in 1872, he tried to point out to his superiors in Washington, D.C., that part of the reason the Plains Indians were fighting so desperately to save their homeland was their perception of the way in which the federal government treated the tribes it had defeated. "One of the strongest motives which can be brought to bear on the wild Indians to induce them to adopt a civilized life," Jones wrote, "would be for the civilized Indians to point to their own condition of elevation and comfort and to testify to the wild Indians that the Government and people of the United States fulfill all obligations to the civilized tribes and secure them in the enjoyment of all their rights and immunities. This testimony they cannot render while they stand in constant dread of being crushed by a territorial government." [11] The passive resistance of the Keetoowahs did little more than reveal the iron fist within the velvet glove of the civilizers. Hundreds of them were sent to jail after 1898 for refusing to enroll for their allotted tracts of land, which would then make them citizens of the United States.

A map of the Indian Territory at the time Oochalata left office in 1879 reveals the crazy-quilt pattern of forced Indian resettlement that constituted official Indian policy since 1866. Over thirty different Indian nations, ranging in size from several hundred to 25,000 persons, were placed on different patches of land in what is now Oklahoma. Some tribes were resettled on the Cherokee Outlet; some were settled within the Cherokee Nation itself; some were located in the "unassigned lands" ceded by the Chickasaws, Creeks, and Seminoles after 1866 in the central part of the Indian Territory. Originally the goal of the Bureau of Indian Affairs was to fill up the Indian Territory with the remnants of the Plains Indians as they were conquered. However, whether this haphazard policy would lead to a federal territory of confederated tribes, a territory with a single Indian legislature under the secretary of the interior, or statehood was never agreed upon. Every new territorial bill from 1866 to 1880 offered a different solution.

As of 1880 two large areas of the Indian Territory—the Oklahoma panhandle in the northwest and Greer County in the southwest corner—were still claimed by Texas. Toward the end of Oochalata's administration in 1879, the frontier whites in Kansas decided to force the government to adopt a new

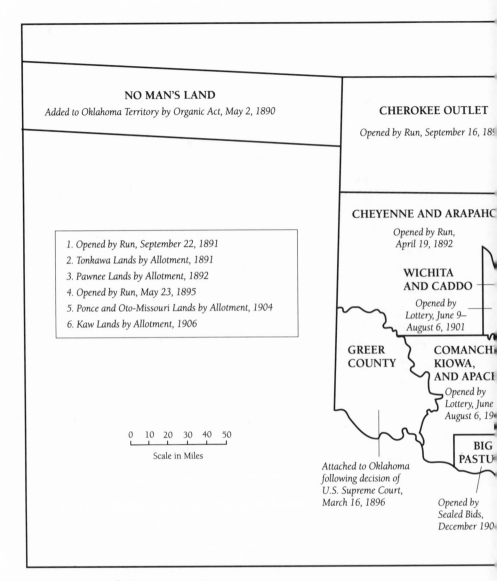

NO MAN'S LAND

Added to Oklahoma Territory by Organic Act, May 2, 1890

CHEROKEE OUTLET

Opened by Run, September 16, 189

CHEYENNE AND ARAPAHO

Opened by Run,
April 19, 1892

WICHITA
AND CADDO

Opened by
Lottery, June 9–
August 6, 1901

1. *Opened by Run, September 22, 1891*
2. *Tonkawa Lands by Allotment, 1891*
3. *Pawnee Lands by Allotment, 1892*
4. *Opened by Run, May 23, 1895*
5. *Ponce and Oto-Missouri Lands by Allotment, 1904*
6. *Kaw Lands by Allotment, 1906*

GREER
COUNTY

COMANCHE
KIOWA,
AND APACHE

Opened by
Lottery, June
August 6, 19

0 10 20 30 40 50

Scale in Miles

Attached to Oklahoma
following decision of
U.S. Supreme Court,
March 16, 1896

BIG
PASTU

Opened by
Sealed Bids,
December 190

M A P 7 . *Land Openings, 1889–1906*

Source: John W. Morris, Charles R. Goins, and Edwin C. McReynolds, *Historical Atlas of Oklahoma*, 3d ed. (Norman: University of Oklahoma Press, 1986).

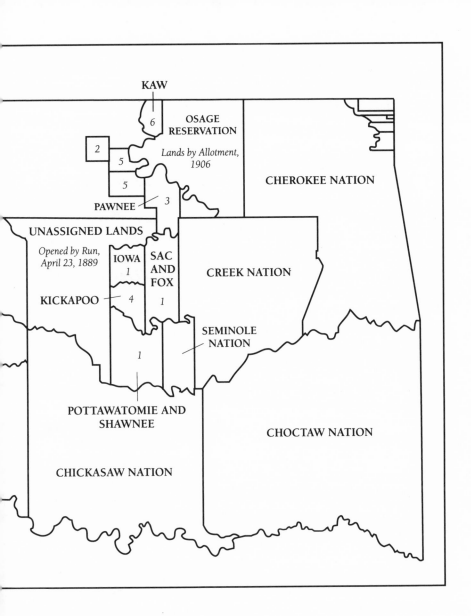

KAW

OSAGE
RESERVATION

Lands by Allotment,
1906

6

2

5

5

PAWNEE — 3

CHEROKEE NATION

UNASSIGNED LANDS

Opened by Run,
April 23, 1889

IOWA
1

SAC
AND
FOX

CREEK NATION

KICKAPOO — 4

1

SEMINOLE
NATION

1

POTTAWATOMIE AND
SHAWNEE

CHICKASAW NATION

CHOCTAW NATION

policy by arousing national support for opening all unsettled or "unassigned" parts of the Indian Territory to white homesteaders. The "colonization" efforts of Samuel H. Payne, David H. Payne, James M. Bell, and other lawless entrepreneurs from 1879 to 1885 brought thousands of whites into the Cherokee Outlet and the unassigned lands that were awaiting the resettlement of conquered Plains Indians. These squatters were called "Boomers" because they were beating the drum for a white invasion of "vacant" land. They were also called "Sooners" because they entered the territory sooner than the government allowed settlement there. The Cherokee Outlet was directly across the border from Kansas; intruders had been settling there more or less quietly for decades. However, the Boomers' colonization schemes were, by design, the opposite of surreptitious. Illegal colonizing was undertaken amid the most blatant forms of high-flown publicity. They wanted to galvanize public opinion against the fact that the government was resisting development of vacant land by solid citizens and reserving it for primitive savages. The Outlet, however, was used at this time by cattle grazers from the various border states who leased it from the Cherokees. The combined interests of the cattle grazers and the Cherokees helped at first to persuade the government to resist colonization in the Outlet. However, the unassigned lands to the south of the Outlet (utilized as part of the Chisholm Trail by cattle drovers) were still under federal control. The Boomers contended that there was no reason why that land still unoccupied by Indians should not be opened to white homesteaders.

Public opinion persuaded Congress to support this claim, although the first illegal colonizers were removed in 1885. However, they were removed only so that Congress could develop a more orderly structure for opening up the lands to white settlement. In 1889 the unassigned lands were surveyed and renamed Oklahoma and declared open to white settlers; they were allowed to settle wherever they chose. Within months, there were 60,000 whites in the heart of the Indian Territory, directly between the five civilized tribes to the east and a dozen resettled Plains tribes to the west. As these unruly settlers required law and order, the movement grew in Congress to declare this a federal territory. In 1890, Congress reconstituted the area as the Oklahoma Territory.

This was considered too small an area to justify statehood. Since the Dawes Severalty Act had already put the seal of approval on the plan to free the whole of the Indian Territory from Indian control, the process of taking over more Indian lands continued. After 1887 negotiations had begun with the tribes adjacent to the unassigned lands, and they were persuaded to sell their tribal lands to the federal government. Each tribe was promised that its land would be surveyed and that every Indian would be given a tract (roughly 160 acres) on which to sustain his or her own homestead. Once this was accomplished, the land not selected for Indian homesteads was declared "surplus." In 1891 the tribal lands owned by the Iowas, Sacs, Foxes, Pottawatomis, and Shawnees were allotted and the surplus thrown open to white homesteaders. Later that year the surplus lands of the Tankawas, Wichitas, Caddos, Comanches, Kiowas, and Apaches, which were much larger in extent, were opened to whites by lottery.[12] However, this still did not expand the Oklahoma Territory enough to warrant statehood.

The Cherokee Outlet north of the Oklahoma Territory separated it from Kansas, and white homesteaders in the territory pressed the government to buy it. However, the Cherokee Nation refused to sell. Ever since 1883, the Cherokees had maintained profitable leasing arrangements with the Cherokee Strip Livestock Association (a conglomerate of cattle ranchers) to graze their herds on a part of the Outlet where no tribes had been resettled. This lease brought $150,000 annually to the Cherokee treasury. To obviate this profitable incentive, the Dawes Commission obtained a ruling from the U.S. attorney general in 1892 that it was illegal for the Cherokees to lease land on the Outlet because it was in effect under federal control as a potential area for Indian resettlement.[13] Seeing the handwriting on the wall, the Cherokees struck a hard bargain and sold the Outlet for $8,595,736.12 in 1892.[14] The next year the area was opened to homesteaders in the most famous of all the homesteader land rushes (or "runs") for good tracts; 50,000 to 100,000 whites in wagons, on horseback, or on foot took part.

Three years earlier the Oklahoma panhandle area (hitherto a no-man's-land) had been added to the Oklahoma Territory by Congress, and in 1896 the U.S. Supreme Court ruled that Greer County belonged to the Indian Territory, not Texas. These two areas were then opened to whites. By 1896 the now-enlarged Oklahoma Territory was greater in size than the land still held by the five civilized tribes in the eastern area of what was left of the Indian Territory. Meanwhile, the Oklahoma Territory had filled up with 350,000 whites who clamored for statehood. The Dawes Commission sought more power to overcome the resistance of the five civilized tribes to accept allotment and become part of a new state. It recommended that Congress simply nullify the self-government of these tribes and declare their lands open to survey and allotment whether they agreed to negotiate or not. Congress was reluctant to do this, but in 1896 it did give the commission the right to draw up a census identifying the true members of each of the five tribes. Between 1895 and 1898, the commission finally persuaded the Choctaws (1897), Chickasaws (1897), and Seminoles (1898) to agree to allotment, but it made no headway with the Creeks and Cherokees.[15]

By 1898 Congress was ready to compel the Cherokees and Creeks to agree to allotment. It passed the Curtis Act, drawn up by Senator Charles Curtis of Kansas. Entitled "An Act for the Protection of the People of Indian Territory and for Other Purposes," this law abolished all tribal law and tribal courts as of July 1, 1898. It also prohibited tribal councils from instituting any new laws without the express approval of the president of the United States. The Dawes Commission was then able to obtain agreements granting each Creek citizen 160 acres (1901) and each Cherokee, 110 acres (1902). Once these citizens accepted their tracts, the remainder was thrown open to white homesteaders. There were so many claimants for Cherokee citizenship by that time that there was no surplus land in that nation.[16]

An effort by the five civilized tribes to create a separate Indian state (to be called Sequoyah) out of the eastern third of the Indian Territory failed in 1905. Congress did not want to create an Indian state. In part because of the Keetoowahs' refusal to accept their allotments, Oklahoma did not become a state until 1907. It immediately fell under the control of the white homesteaders who outnumbered the Indians seven to one. Within twenty years, two-thirds of the Indians had lost the small allotments given to them—partly through their inability to pay their taxes, partly through agreeing to sell it to whites, and partly through outright fraud (especially when Indian farms happened to have coal, oil, gas, or other valuable mineral deposits). The Keetoowahs, some of whom went to jail after 1900 rather than enroll for their tracts, finally capitulated in 1910—the last resisters in the lost cause of Cherokee sovereignty.[17]

It has been argued by both Indian and white historians that racism had much to do with the destruction of Indian sovereignty. There is no doubt that it did. Whether racism was implicit in "God's natural laws" (interpreted as "survival of the fittest race" in the name of progress), it was nonetheless clear to the scientists of the day that "objective" empirical evidence demonstrated the superiority of the white (Caucasian or Aryan) race over all of the "colored" races. So widely accepted was this "evidence" that even the Indians began to argue that their right to separate nationhood and sovereignty should rest upon their special and peculiar characteristics as "the red race." Racism was of course inherent also in Francis Wayland's concept that "savage" people were backward people. Their refusal to give up their savage culture despite so many years of white "tutelage" confirmed whites' belief in their biological and mental inferiority.

Commissioner of Indian Affairs E. P. Smith expressed in 1873 a different justification for the abolition of Indian tribal government and land bases. The difficulty lay in the problem of dual sovereignty. The Indian tribes claimed to be independent nations, Smith said, when they were in fact merely "wards" of whites: "A radical hindrance [to Indian progress] is in the anomalous relation of many of the Indian tribes to the Government which requires them to be treated as sovereign powers and wards at one and the same time. The comparative weakness of the whites made it expedient in our early history to deal with the Indian tribes as with powers capable of self-protection and fulfilling treaty obligations, and so a kind of fiction and absurdity has come into all our Indian relations."[18] Might made right in the long run. Denationalization, allotment, and citizenship did away with the early fictional absurdity. Wards, after all, are considered people lacking in the ability to care for themselves, so inherent in Smith's argument was the implication of a kind of racial inferiority that had often been subsumed in the sentimental claim that Indians were "the children of the forest." This same line of reasoning also led after 1898 to American imperialism in the Philippines, where the United States joined other "Teutonic" nations in carrying "the white man's burden."

The reaction of the Cherokees to their ultimate defeat is not easy to describe in their own words. Clearly the more acculturated mixed-bloods like James M. Bell, Spencer S. Stephens, and E. C. Boudinot had decided long before 1887 that they could live without their old tribal system. Stephens, who had been superintendent of the Cherokee public school system, made this clear as early as 1882 in his pamphlet *The Indian Question Discussed*: "It is necessary for the better condition of the Indian to set aside as soon as possible the ineradicable spirit of communism which is part and parcel of their tribal life, habits, faith and traditions. Among the Cherokees, it is only individuality that provokes ambition. We have no landed security [under communal ownership] consequently we cannot accumulate. . . . The whole country must be open to the progress of commerce."[19]

The situation was somewhat different for the full-bloods. Because they spoke and wrote only in Cherokee and little has survived of their writing in this period, it is difficult to find expressions of their feelings other than in the actions of the Keetoowahs. One letter by a full-blood, written to Oochalata in 1877, provides some insight into their despair. It was written by Ganenulisgi. He had been elected solicitor of the district of Going Snake and had for several years tried to carry out his duties as faithfully as he could. His job included, among other things, warning white intruders out of the district and informing the federal agent to expel them when they did not heed his warning. Oochalata had recommended to the council that it raise the pay of solicitors, for it was difficult and dangerous work. They served as prosecuting attorneys in the district courts and were important in the nation's law enforcement. To be elected, they had to have the respect of their neighbors and to know the people well enough to distinguish between perennial and temporary troublemakers.

However, few of them had any legal training, and most of them, little education, and under the new legal code of 1875, law enforcement had become very complex.

Ganenulisgi did his best to carry out his duties, but after several years he felt that he was doing little to improve the life of his community. Going Snake District bordered on Arkansas and contained many whites who illegally entered the nation to sell whiskey, work as sharecroppers or tenant farmers, or squat on land and farm it in the expectation that it would soon be open to white settlement. These intruders were truculent and well armed and paid little attention to Ganenulisgi's efforts to warn them off the land. Every year he made a list of the intruders who failed to heed his warnings and sent it to the federal agent (in Muskogee in the Creek Nation), who was responsible for removing all intruders from all five of the civilized tribes. The agent never once responded.

Finally, in March 1877 Ganenulisgi wrote in Cherokee to his chief, "Friend Oochalata," that he was going to resign. He had done his best, but his efforts were futile. "I have just relinquished the District Solicitorship," he said. "My head is simply too small for official work and the new law is very difficult to interpret rightly. That is the reason why I have decided that it would be good to get a replacement. Personally, I do not desire to keep the job just because of the salary. I know my capabilities [and limitations in] enforcing the law. It has become desirable to do the right thing and to ask someone [else] to finish out my unfinished year." In the course of the letter, he referred to Oochalata with the traditional address, "Beloved Principal Chief," indicating his respect for the office. "All of this has become very difficult," for the district was large and "visiting the homes of white intruders" was a nerve-racking business; they could be violent men. Because the federal agent paid no attention to the lists he had so carefully made of offenders, the intruders paid no attention to his orders. "We do not know [here] the reason why it has become this way. For I do not have the authority to remove them firmly in my hand, and I cannot continue to do the work of two persons," that is, prosecuting Cherokee criminals and expelling white intruders. "Since it has become [so] difficult, I have just decided that those who live here in the District should think that I have done right. . . . I now relinquish the commission that you bestowed upon me."[20]

The great mass of Cherokees were neither as ready for denationalization as those like Bell and Stephens nor as desperate to hang onto their old ways as the Keetoowahs. Some insight into the feelings of the ordinary Cherokees can be found in the letters of Ann Bell Shelton, a niece of Sarah Watie (Stand Watie's widow). Shelton was a Christian and a member of the mixed-blood

Bell family. Her husband had died and left her with four children and no means of support. She moved to Roxton, Texas, in order to find work as a schoolteacher among whites, but she kept informed about Indian affairs and wrote regularly to her "Aunt Sallie" (Watie) and "Uncle Jim" (Bell) to express her views on "the future of the Cherokees." "What do you think will be done to the Nation?" she asked her uncle in October 1873. How could the Cherokees sustain their independence and dignity? "What sort of people will we be? We are already regarded as inferior. Let us do nothing to bring ourselves any lower in the estimation of the world. . . . I never see anything in the papers about Indians but something that is low and mean, and I have almost concluded that there is no good in us, and all I wish is to get some obscure place and be poor and beggarly all to myself."[21] Shelton, though a mixed-blood with respectable family connections and some education, felt demeaned both by her own treatment by whites and by the federal government's treatment of Indians in general.

Recognizing the fragility of the Cherokee reputation for "civilization," Shelton feared its further degradation by association with "wild" Plains Indians. Four years later, after the Custer affair in 1876 and the effort to move some of the defeated Sioux to the Indian Territory, Shelton wrote to her aunt: "It was a great source of satisfaction to me to see that Col. [E. C.] Boudinot protested against all that wild, savage element coming into the—your—territory. Not that I have not great sympathy for them. I have. But charity begins at home, and plenty want to send them there to produce confusion so [as] to have an excuse for extermination."[22] Her cynicism had reached the point where she suspected the federal government of putting wild tribes into close contact with civilized Cherokees in order to provoke hostilities that would justify sending in troops to exterminate both. Yet she could not dissociate herself from the plight of the Plains Indians. During the uprising of Sitting Bull, which was fearfully portrayed by the frontier press, Shelton wrote,

I must leave some room to ask you, how do you feel on the indian question? My soul sickens at the very mention of it. The talk of extermination—just the same as if it were rats they were talking of. For my part, I don't see what else they can do, I mean the Sioux, but fight when the last reserve has been taken from them. I wish sometimes the whole of us, from the pure Indians to the last one with the millionth part of a drop of blood, could be cut off in a moment and the vexed question stopped forever. But then again, God knows best. I can't see through these things. But I admire Sitting B[ull] amazingly and I don't want blood shed on either side. But I don't want him to come to any harm. Poor Indians, what do you suppose they were created for? I tell you, Aunt Sallie, all my life I have tried to live so that the [Cherokee] Nation would never suffer in reputation by the least act of mine.[23]

Where could a Cherokee turn for help and respect? For Ann Shelton, "the Indian question" stemmed from white racism, not "primitive communism," dual sovereignty, or "expedient" treaty rights.

The social and psychological dilemma of the Cherokees lay in the inability of white Americans to accept the fact that the United States was, had always been, and would always be a multiracial and multicultural nation. The Enlightenment outlook of the Founding Fathers had said that all human beings were created biologically equal; the Christian missionaries said that "God hath made of one blood all nations." However, most nineteenth-century U.S. citizens assumed, without question, that this was "a white man's country." Social Darwinism reinforced this myth. It enabled whites to relegate blacks to segregation by law after freeing them from slavery at such heavy cost. It excluded Chinese immigration in 1882. It justified the reduction of Indians to second-class citizenship under the mask of bettering their condition.

Some Indian nations have vanished, but most endured. Today there are over 232,000 Americans who identify themselves in the census as Cherokees.[24] Contemporary efforts among many Native American peoples to assert tribal sovereignty continue, sometimes with considerable violence. The struggle is not likely to disappear, and in the process factionalism continues to wrack the tribes. The Cherokees have no land base today for the 150,000 members on their tribal roll. Though they have legal recognition as a tribe and elect their own chief, they lack sovereignty. They have left a remarkable record of their struggle against overwhelming odds to remain a sovereign people.

Notes

INTRODUCTION

1. George Fredrickson, *The Black Image in the White Mind* (New York: Harper and Row, 1971), p. 42.

2. Andrew Jackson, Message to Congress, December 3, 1833, *House Executive Documents*, 23d Cong., 1st sess. (Washington, D.C.: Gales and Seaton, 1833), 254:14.

3. Chief Lewis Downing, quoted in *Cherokee Advocate*, January 30, 1871.

4. Gail H. Landsman, *Sovereignty and Symbol* (Albuquerque: University of New Mexico Press, 1988), p. 61.

5. Ibid.

CHAPTER ONE

1. For the Cherokee struggle over removal in the years 1828–38, see Thurman Wilkins, *Cherokee Tragedy*, 2d ed. (Norman: University of Oklahoma Press, 1986). For the federal removal policy, see Ronald N. Satz, *American Indian Policy in the Jacksonian Era* (Lincoln: University of Nebraska, 1975), and Dale Van Every, *Disinherited* (New York: William Morrow, 1966). For the Trail of Tears, see Grant Foreman, *Indian Removal* (Norman: Oklahoma University Press, 1932).

2. Van Every, *Disinherited*, pp. 236–37.

3. Andrew Jackson, Message to Congress, December 3, 1833, *House Executive Documents*, 23d Cong., 1st sess. (Washington, D.C.: Gales and Seaton, 1833), 254:14.

4. Gary E. Moulton, *John Ross: Cherokee Chief* (Athens: University of Georgia Press, 1978), p. 6.

5. The Camp Aquohee resolves are quoted in Emmet Starr, *History of the Cherokee Indians* (New York: Kraus Reprint, 1969), pp. 104–5. Between 600 and 800 Cherokees escaped the military dragnet in 1838 and joined another 800 Cherokees living in North Carolina to form the Eastern Band of Cherokees, which remains there to this day. See John R. Finger, *The Eastern Band of Cherokees, 1819–1900* (Knoxville: University of Tennessee Press, 1984).

6. See Moulton, *John Ross*, p. 232, n. 40.

7. For the conflict between full-bloods and mixed-bloods over acculturation in the years 1794–1830, see William G. McLoughlin, *Cherokee Renascence* (Princeton: Princeton University Press, 1986). President Jackson told John Ross in the spring of 1836 that he refused to recognize any self-governing body over the eastern Cherokees. Charles G. Royce, *The Cherokee Nation of Indians* (Chicago: Aldine, 1975), p. 161.

8. See Richard Peters, *The Case of the Cherokee Nation against the State of Georgia* (Philadelphia, 1831), pp. 281–82.

9. The precise count of those who died is debatable. See Russell Thornton, "The

Demography of the Trail of Tears Period: A New Estimate of Cherokee Population Losses," in William L. Anderson, ed., *Cherokee Removal, Before and After* (Athens: University of Georgia Press, 1991).

10. For statements regarding the poor quality of food provided by the firm of Glasgow and Harrison in the six months after the emigrants arrived, see Government Microfilm Series, Bureau of Indian Affairs, Record Group 75, M-234, Letters Received by the Office of Indian Affairs, 1824–1881, reel 83, 0016 (April 19, 1839), 0023 (April 19, 1839), and 0026 (April 23, 1839). See also Foreman, *Indian Removal*, pp. 310–12; Grant Foreman, *The Five Civilized Tribes* (Norman: University of Oklahoma Press, 1934), pp. 286–87; John Ross, *The Papers of Chief John Ross*, introduction by Gary E. Moulton, 2 vols. (Norman: University of Oklahoma Press, 1984), 2:8; Moulton, *John Ross*, p. 108; and Ethan Allen Hitchcock, *A Traveler in Indian Territory*, ed. Grant Foreman (Cedar Rapids, 1930), pp. 41, 69, 71, 81–82.

11. Starr, *History*, p. 106. Starr provides most of the documents on this council.

12. Cephas Washburn to David Greene, August 12, 1839, in Papers of the American Board of Commissioners for Foreign Missions, Houghton Library, Harvard University, Cambridge (hereafter cited as ABCFM), quoted in Wilkins, *Cherokee Tragedy*, p. 332.

13. Ross, *Papers of Chief John Ross*, 1:712–13.

14. Wilkins, *Cherokee Tragedy*, p. 333.

15. Ross, *Papers of Chief John Ross*, 2:9, 35. Ross consistently argued that cupidity, "secretly grasping at the common purse," a desire to share in the money from the removal, lay behind the opposition of the Old Settlers and the Treaty party to his leadership of the majority. From his point of view, the Treaty party members deserved nothing because they had betrayed their country. The Old Settlers deserved nothing because they had emigrated voluntarily (and in many cases at federal expense); they were expatriates who had given up any share in the mother country.

16. Starr, *History*, p. 106.

17. Ibid., p. 109.

18. Ibid., p. 110.

19. Wilkins, *Cherokee Tragedy*, p. 333; Foreman, *Five Civilized Tribes*, p. 292; Morris Wardell, *A Political History of the Cherokee Nation, 1838–1907* (Norman: University of Oklahoma Press, 1938), p. 15.

20. Wardell, *Political History*, p. 15.

21. Ross, *Papers of Chief John Ross*, 2:715. Ross wrote to Montfort Stokes on June 21 that the difficulty with the Old Settler chiefs arose because "they require the unconditional submission of the whole body of the people who have lately arrived, to laws and regulations in the making of which they have had no voice. The attempt of a small minority to enforce their will over a great majority, contrary to their wishes, appears to us . . . repugnant to reason." Ibid., 2:716. He wrote again to Stokes and General Matthew Arbuckle on June 30: "Two [Cherokee] Governments cannot and ought not to exist in the Cherokee Nation any longer than arrangements can be made of uniting the two communities. . . . We have used our best endeavors to bring about this desirable event. . . . We have claimed no jurisdiction over our Western brethren, nor can we . . . consistently with the responsibilities with which our constituents have invested us, recognize their jurisdiction over us. We claim to stand on equal

ground." Ibid., 2:522. In other words, he claimed that two equally sovereign Cherokee governments existed, but "the nation" could only survive by merging them into one.

22. Starr, *History*, pp. 110–11.

23. For example, prior to major structural reforms in the Cherokee system of government in the years 1817–20, all treaty negotiations took place before a council of the whole people. See Rennard Strickland, *Fire and the Spirits: Cherokee Law from Clan to Court* (Norman: University of Oklahoma Press, 1975), and McLoughlin, *Cherokee Renascence*. Ross explained this to William Armstrong, the western superintendent of Indian affairs, on June 30, 1839: "At a later general council held at Takattokah by the joint appointment of the chiefs of the Eastern and Western Cherokee for the purpose of forming a reunion of the people and taking preliminary measures for remodelling their governments and laws . . . the representatives of the people having failed to effect the desired object, the people, therefore took the matter into their own hands and appointed a National Convention." Ross, *Papers of Chief John Ross*, 1:725. When Armstrong later told Ross to revoke this council, Ross responded, "I cannot adjourn them inasmuch as the meeting was called by the people." Ibid., 1:728.

24. Starr, *History*, p. 111. Summarizing this impasse at a later date, Ross maintained that the Old Settlers had taken the perverse view that "the emigrants [the Ross party] . . . have no right . . . either to soil, jurisdiction or government in the country only by coming under the government and laws of the Old Settlers" because the Old Settlers had been given that land in the treaties of 1817 and 1828. The Old Settlers also seemed to argue that "the Emigrants have no rights in the country and are intruders," and if the government of the United States had granted such a right to the eastern Cherokees in the Treaty of 1835, it had unjustly taken the western Cherokees' land from them. Ross, *Papers of Chief John Ross*, 2:19. This was, in fact, the key to the problem, for the Treaty of 1835 failed to consider the question of political reunion of the two governments—a blindness due in part to the stereotypical view that "Indian tribes" were too rude and uncivilized to have any serious political structure and in part to the government's inconsistent behavior toward what it often called the "Eastern Nation" and the "Western Nation." Four years later, on February 18, 1843, T. Hartley Crawford, the commissioner of Indian affairs, stated emphatically that the Old Settlers had no claim to being a separate nation and were always part of the Eastern Cherokee Nation because the Western Cherokee Nation consisted of nothing but a continuous stream of easterners who moved west from 1794 onward. Far from establishing the westerners as an independent nation, the Treaty of 1828 had specifically noted that the 7 million acres given to them was for the express purpose of allowing their brethren to unite with them there. "The Western Cherokees were only contingently a separate community" and were "subject to increase by the emigration." "They were not consequently a separate, independent community nor have they any ownership of the land except that which belongs to them in common with the whole Cherokee people." M-234, reel 87, 0934. Had the government made this explicit in 1839, the Old Settler question would have been much more easily settled. Instead, the government, and especially Crawford, encouraged the obstructionism of the Old Settlers out of dislike for John Ross and the difficulties he caused. As Crawford finally said flatly in 1843, "All the annuity and vested funds under the treaty of 1835 are common and belong to the tribe or *nation* which . . . embraces all Cherokees" (italics added). Had this been

clearly said in 1839, the long and bitter struggle among the different parties to split up the annuities and vested funds among themselves might have been avoided. However, many government officials in the years 1839–42 insisted that the Old Settlers or Western Cherokee Nation was the only true government over all the Cherokees now living in that country. See, for example, General Matthew Arbuckle, November 10, 1839, M-234, reel 84, 0111, and statement by the western chiefs, December 27, 1839, M-234, reel 84, 0076.

25. Although no copy of this statement by Sequoyah and Bushyhead or any indication of how many of the Cherokees assented to it has been located, there is no reason to doubt Ross's claim that this occurred. See Ross, *Papers of Chief John Ross*, 2:10; Wardell, *Political History*, p. 16; Starr, *History*, pp. 111–12. The wording probably closely resembled the statement made by George Lowrey quoted above.

26. Ross, *Papers of Chief John Ross*, 1:716–17; John Ross and Richard Taylor to Montfort Stokes, June 21, 1838, M-234, reel 83, 0267.

27. Montfort Stokes to Joel Poinsett, M-234, reel 83, 0275.

28. For clan obligations in questions of "blood revenge," see John P. Reid, *The Law of Blood* (New York: New York University Press, 1975). For Allen Ross's firsthand account of this secret meeting, see John Howard Payne Papers, Newberry Library, Chicago, and *Chronicles of Oklahoma* 12 (March 1934): 23. The list of those to be executed has not survived.

29. Wilkins, *Cherokee Tragedy*, p. 289.

30. Wardell, *Political History*, p. 18.

31. Foreman, *Five Civilized Tribes*, p. 296.

32. For a similar execution of a Cherokee chief named Doublehead as punishment for selling tribal land, performed by Major Ridge in 1807, see McLoughlin, *Cherokee Renascence*, pp. 120–21.

33. John Howard Payne Papers, Newberry Library, Chicago; *Chronicles of Oklahoma* 12 (March 1934): 23.

34. Wilkins, *Cherokee Tragedy*, pp. 334–39.

35. Starr, *History*, pp. 114–15; Wardell, *Political History*, p. 21.

36. Starr, *History*, p. 116.

37. Ross, *Papers of Chief John Ross*, 1:732, 735.

38. Foreman, *Five Civilized Tribes*, p. 299.

39. Wardell, *Political History*, pp. 25–26; Moulton, *John Ross*, p. 116.

40. Starr, *History*, p. 119.

41. Ibid., p. 121; Foreman, *Five Civilized Tribes*, p. 300.

42. Wardell, *Political History*, p. 28; Starr, *History*, 121.

43. Ross, *Papers of Chief John Ross*, 1:738.

44. Ibid., 1:745; Wardell, *Political History*, p. 23; Wilkins, *Cherokee Tragedy*, p. 342; Foreman, *Five Civilized Tribes*, pp. 299–300.

45. Kenny A. Franks, *Stand Watie* (Memphis: Memphis State University Press, 1979), pp. 63–64, 67.

46. Official correspondence regarding the Old Settler position at this time is contained in M-234, reel 83, 0278–94. See also Foreman, *Five Civilized Tribes*, p. 305, and Moulton, *John Ross*, p. 116.

47. See Elizur Butler to David Green, October 14, 1839, in ABCFM.

48. Starr, *History*, p. 122.

49. Foreman, *Five Civilized Tribes*, p. 307.

50. Ross, *Papers of Chief John Ross*, 2:24.

51. Foreman, *Five Civilized Tribes*, p. 307.

52. Wardell, *Political History*, p. 35.

53. Moulton, *John Ross*, p. 133.

54. For Ross's Cherokee National Bank proposal, which he placed formally before the Cherokee council on October 23, 1841, see M-234, reel 85, 0143. The best discussions of the per capita payment and its relation to other financial aspects of the removal process can be found in Moulton, *John Ross*, pp. 101–6, 127–30, 153–54; Foreman, *Five Civilized Tribes*, pp. 170–84; and Royce, *Cherokee Nation*, pp. 183–91.

55. Wardell, *Political History*, p. 34.

56. Ibid., p. 35.

57. Ibid. Arbuckle wrote to Poinsett shortly after receiving the letter that instructed him to force Ross to produce the Ridge-Boudinot murderers: "If he had not been prepared to start for Washington on business . . . I would have caused him to be arrested and placed in confinement until the pleasure of the government was known." Foreman, *Five Civilized Tribes*, p. 306; Matthew Arbuckle to Joel Poinsett, April 13, 1840, M-234, reel 84, 0161.

58. Ross, *Papers of Chief John Ross*, 2:33; Foreman, *Five Civilized Tribes*, p. 306.

59. Moulton, *John Ross*, pp. 119–20. Other members of the Old Settler and Treaty parties later joined Brown there.

60. For a discussion of the Treaty of 1828, see Royce, *Cherokee Nation*, pp. 101–9. For Rogers, see Ross, *Papers of Chief John Ross*, 2:731–32.

61. See the report of T. Hartley Crawford to Joel Poinsett, November 25, 1839, in *Annual Report of the Commissioner of Indian Affairs* (Washington, D.C., 1840).

62. Crawford also implied that Ross might be trying to foment an Indian uprising because he had "sent beads and tobacco and friendly talks to the chiefs of the Creeks" and transmitted his view to "a Choctaw chief" as well as to "a Seminole chief of note." Ibid.

63. Quoted in Ross, *Papers of Chief John Ross*, 2:12. Ross here used the quotation to his advantage. See also William Armstrong to Joel Poinsett, January 29, 1840, M-234, reel 84, 0095.

64. Wardell, *Political History*, p. 35; M-234, reel 84, 0066; Ross, *Papers of Chief John Ross*, 1:773. Rogers was reluctant, however, and said the Old Settlers would never give up their sovereignty to majority tyranny. John Rogers to Joel Poinsett, December 27, 1839, M-234, reel 84, 0076.

65. Wardell, *Political History*, p. 36; M-234, reel 84, 0102, 0106, 0121, 0126–31. Most of the Cherokee documents and official correspondence with the commissioner of Indian affairs and the secretary of war for the years 1839–41 are contained in "John Bell's Suppressed Report," in *House Executive Documents*, 29th Cong., 1st sess. (Washington, D.C., 1839), n. 185 (hereafter cited as Bell's Report).

66. Montfort Stokes to Joel Poinsett, January 28, 1840, M-234, reel 84, 0588; Matthew Arbuckle to Joel Poinsett, January 29, 1840, M-234, reel 84, 0098.

67. Arbuckle wrote to Poinsett on January 29, 1840, a week after the council called by Stokes: "I do not believe that the vote in favor of the new Government of the

Cherokee Nation at the late assemblage is a majority of the voters of that Nation. Yet I have no doubt that a decided majority of the Cherokee people are in favor of that Government [the new Ross government]. . . . I now regard it my duty . . . to notify the Old Settlers that their Government has ceased." M-234, reel 84, 0098.

68. Moulton, *John Ross*, pp. 121–22; Wardell, *Political History*, pp. 36–43; Franks, *Watie*, p. 69.

69. Matthew Arbuckle to Joel Poinsett, February 10, 1840, M-234, reel 84, 0133. See also Arbuckle's letters of January 28, 1840, M-234, reel 84, 0121, and April 13, 1840, M-234, reel 84, 0161. On March 6, 1840, Poinsett suspended Stokes for being partial toward the Ross faction and turned over solely to Arbuckle the power to end "the tyrannical and oppressive conduct of the emigrating party toward the old settlers." See Poinsett to Arbuckle, March 6, 1840, M-234, reel 84, 638. It should be noted that throughout this controversy the Old Settlers, though fully supported by Poinsett, made the same claims for "sovereignty" as those of the Ross party. As the Old Settlers under John Rogers wrote on February 7, 1840, their sovereignty rested on the treaties of 1817, 1819, and 1828, "which plainly demonstrate that we were considered as a separate community." In 1828 they had agreed to give eastern emigrants "a free participation in our own sovereign rights. But never have we yielded any of our rights as a sovereign and independent nation." Reply of the Old Settlers, February 7, 1840, M-234, reel 84, 0126–31. The several uses of the term "sovereign" by the federal government, the Old Settlers, and the Ross party in this long dispute constitute the crux of the ambiguity in Indian diplomacy in the pre–Civil War years.

70. Matthew Arbuckle to Joel Poinsett, January 28, 1840, M-234, reel 84, 0121, and December 26, 1839, M-234, reel 84, 0061; Wardell, *Political History*, p. 36; Moulton, *John Ross*, p. 121.

71. Franks, *Watie*, pp. 69–70; Wardell, *Political History*, pp. 36–37. See also Bell's Report.

72. Franks, *Watie*, p. 69; Moulton, *John Ross*, p. 123.

73. Joel Poinsett to Matthew Arbuckle, March 7, 1840, M-234, reel 85, 0434–37; Wardell, *Political History*, pp. 37–38.

74. Wardell, *Political History*, p. 36; Foreman, *Five Civilized Tribes*, pp. 307–8; M-234, reel 84, 0126.

75. Ross, *Papers of Chief John Ross*, 2:6–17; Foreman, *Five Civilized Tribes*, pp. 308–9.

76. Ross, *Papers of Chief John Ross*, 2:23–39.

77. Bell's Report; Moulton, *John Ross*, p. 123; Foreman, *Five Civilized Tribes*, pp. 311–12.

78. Joel Poinsett to Montfort Stokes, March 6, 1840, M-234, reel 84, 0638. For Stokes's querulous response, see September 22, 1840, M-234, reel 84, 0617. Moulton, *John Ross*, p. 121; Wardell, *Political History*, pp. 37–38.

79. Joel Poinsett to Matthew Arbuckle, March 7, 1840, M-234, reel 85, 0434–37.

80. Matthew Arbuckle to Joseph Vann, April 21, 1840, M-234, reel 84, 0167; Joseph Vann to Matthew Arbuckle, April 22, 1840, M-234, reel 84, 0179–82.

81. Matthew Arbuckle to Joseph Vann, May 27, 1840, M-234, reel 84, 0200. As Arbuckle put it, if Vann did not send official delegates, he would call "together the Representatives of all that are willing to establish a Government for the Cherokee

Nation." See also M-234, reel 84, 0212, 0215, 0221, and 0232, for documents concerning this council. See also Moulton, *John Ross*, pp. 121–22, and Wardell, *Political History*, pp. 39–40.

82. Joseph Vann to Matthew Arbuckle, June 23, 1840, M-234, reel 84, 0215.

83. Matthew Arbuckle to Joel Poinsett, June 28, 1840, M-234, reel 84, 0215.

84. Wardell, *Political History*, pp. 39–40.

85. Matthew Arbuckle to Joel Poinsett, June 28, 1840, M-234, reel 84, 0221–35. No record exists of any resignations or elections by the Old Settlers to replace them. On January 17, 1840, W. S. Coodey had told Arbuckle that nearly half of the officers of the government were already Old Settlers. M-234, reel 84, 0110.

86. Wardell, *Political History*, pp. 41–42; Moulton, *John Ross*, pp. 121–22; Bell's Report.

87. Foreman, *Five Civilized Tribes*, p. 309; Bell's Report.

88. Moulton, *John Ross*, p. 12.

89. See T. Hartley Crawford to Joel Poinsett, August 22, 1840, and Poinsett's response, November 30, 1840, M-234, reel 84, 0661; *Annual Report of the Commissioner of Indian Affairs* (Washington, D.C., 1840); and Wardell, *Political History*, p. 42.

90. Moulton, *John Ross*, p. 128.

91. During his travels in the nation in 1841, Colonel E. A. Hitchcock heard much about the hotly contested election, the rumors that Ross had embezzled national funds, and the debate over per capita payments. See Grant Foreman, ed., *A Traveler in Indian Territory: The Journal of Ethan Allen Hitchcock* (Cedar Rapids, Iowa: Torch Press, 1930), pp. 40, 52, 58, 83–84, 238. Hitchcock concluded, however, that Ross was fundamentally honest and concerned only for the good of his people. Ibid., p. 234.

92. For Cherokee food shortages in 1840–41, see M-234, reel 84, 0136 (February 11, 1840), and reel 85, 0056 (August 13, 1841).

93. Ross, *Papers of Chief John Ross*, 2:93; Moulton, *John Ross*, p. 132; M-234, reel 85, 0143. For Ross's response, see M-234, reel 85, 0143 (October 23, 1841). The council members expected at this time a per capita payment of $150 per person from an anticipated $2 million remaining in the $5 million settlement for the homeland.

94. Moulton, *John Ross*, pp. 129–30.

95. Ross, *Papers of Chief John Ross*, 2:104–5. Ross reported to the council in November 1841 that Tyler's administration was very favorably disposed to the Cherokee government as now constituted. Address of John Ross, November 29, 1841, M-234, reel 86, 0143.

96. Moulton, *John Ross*, pp. 132–33.

97. For Ross's view of his opponents in 1841, see Ross, *Papers of Chief John Ross*, 2:25–35.

98. Moulton, *John Ross*, p. 131.

99. Ibid., p. 132.

CHAPTER TWO

1. Quoted in Grant Foreman, *The Five Civilized Tribes* (Norman: University of Oklahoma Press, 1934), p. 283.

2. Grant Foreman, ed., *A Traveler in Indian Territory: The Journal of Ethan Allen Hitchcock* (Cedar Rapids, Iowa: Torch Press, 1930), pp. 54, 87, 89, 240. Hitchcock noted that the English-speaking, more well-to-do Cherokees referred to the full-bloods as "the poor," "the common people," or "the ignorant people." "The more wealthy," he said, lived in comfortable, well-furnished houses and had "horses, cattle, hogs, sheep and poultry and cultivate extensive fields of corn with pumpkins, etc." He added, however, that a sense of charity and sharing (the old hospitality ethic) prevailed. The harvests of the well-to-do "are shared among the poor with kindliness and liberality that have not been learned from the whites. . . . I heard of grain having been purposely left in the field for gleaners." Ibid., p. 240. Hitchcock did not note that black slaves provided most of the field labor among the wealthier Cherokees.

3. John B. Jones, federal agent to the Cherokees, report to the commissioner of Indian affairs, September 1871, in *Annual Report of the Commissioner of Indian Affairs* (Washington, D.C., 1872), p. 364. Jones had lived in the Cherokee Nation since 1841. The Cherokee's new land in the West was divided into three distinct areas: the Neutral Lands in Kansas, consisting of 800,000 acres; the Cherokee Outlet west of 96°, consisting of about 7 million acres (mostly grazing land); and the area in the northeastern corner of present-day Oklahoma, the new nation proper, consisting of about 5 million acres. The total of 12,800,000 acres was roughly 10,000 square miles, but the Cherokees were allowed to settle only on the area in the northeast, which constituted roughly 4,000 square miles.

4. It was against federal law for whites to sell alcohol to the Indians, but there was no way to enforce this regulation without a much larger army garrison in the Cherokee Nation to patrol the borders of Arkansas and Missouri. Cherokees themselves helped to break the law, believing they had as much right as whites to drink whiskey. Many whites set up "grog shops," "doggeries," or "groceries" at the edge of Indian lands to make it easy for them to obtain liquor. (No scientific studies have ever proved that Native Americans are more prone genetically to alcoholism than any other ethnic groups, despite the stereotype of the "drunken Indian.") Some Cherokee women also turned to prostitution, especially near the U.S. Army camp at Fort Gibson. See Grant Foreman, *The Advancing Frontier* (Norman: University of Oklahoma Press, 1933), pp. 25–34, 66, 72–73; Pierce Butler to T. H. Crawford, May 17, 1842, Government Microfilm Series, Bureau of Indian Affairs, Record Group 75, M-234, Letters Received by the Office of Indian Affairs, 1824–1881, reel 86, 0110; and John Ross, *The Papers of Chief John Ross*, introduction by Gary E. Moulton, 2 vols. (Norman: University of Oklahoma Press, 1985), 2:143.

5. While Colonel E. A. Hitchcock did not distinguish between the houses of Treaty party members, the Old Settlers, and the wealthier members of the Ross party in his 1841 account, he does provide a good description of the life-style of the wealthier Cherokees: "There are many houses, though of logs, that are perfectly comfortable; double [houses] with a covered passage between them and a porch, front and rear; embracing a second story with floors planed . . . with good doors with iron hinges and locks, glass windows with moveable sashes, the interior of the house neatly white-washed and suitably supplied with needful furniture; good bed-steads with beds, chairs, tables and bureaus, with clocks with brass movement. . . . The dress and general deportment of the prosperous correspond very nearly to those of a white population.

Shoes are almost universally in use; cloth coats and pantaloons are extensively worn, and hats are common, though many prefer a shawl turban. . . . The common people wear leggings of dressed deer skin and sometimes coats of the same material. . . . The women nearly all dress comfortably well and many would not be singled out in our cities." Foreman, *Traveler in Indian Territory*, p. 240.

6. See M-234, reel 84, 0136 (February 11, 1840), on starvation.

7. See the report of the Cherokee federal agent, Pierce M. Butler, March 4, 1842, in *Annual Report* (1842). Butler estimated the number of Cherokees to be 18,000 at this time. Ibid., p. 453, and in M-234, reel 86, 0030. Butler to T. H. Crawford, March 1843, M-234, reel 87, 0049.

8. P. M. Butler to T. H. Crawford, March 4, 1842, M-234, reel 86, 0030, and in *Annual Report* (1842), p. 454.

9. M-234, reel 87, 0035 (1843), reel 88, 0015, 0018 (1844); Butler's report, March 4, 1842, in *Annual Report* (1842), p. 455.

10. The lawyer for the Ross party was General Waddy Thompson, the lawyers for the Old Settlers were Samuel E. Stambaugh and Amos Kendall, and the lawyer for the Treaty party was George W. Paschal at this time. Morris Wardell, *A Political History of the Cherokee Nation, 1838–1907* (Norman: University of Oklahoma Press, 1938), pp. 72, 98; Gary E. Moulton, *John Ross: Cherokee Chief* (Athens: University of Georgia Press, 1978), p. 150. For the connection between Paschal and John Rogers, see Ross, *Papers of Chief John Ross*, 2:187–88.

11. P. M. Butler to T. H. Crawford, December 20, 1841, M-234, reel 86, 0126. See also M-234, reel 86, 0149 and 0159.

12. Ross, *Papers of Chief John Ross*, 2:145.

13. Ibid.; Moulton, *John Ross*, pp. 133–34; Charles G. Royce, *The Cherokee Nation of Indians* (Chicago: Aldine, 1975), p. 174.

14. Royce, *Cherokee Nation*, p. 176.

15. M-234, reel 88, 0689 (July 2, 1844), 0704 (August 19, 1844). By this time, the original appointees, John H. Eaton and Edward Hubley, had been replaced by George C. Washington and John T. Mason as the claims commissioners.

16. M-234, reel 89, 0589 (May 27, 1845). George C. Washington and John T. Mason note that the Cherokees had presented them with 4,075 claims. That these claims totaled $4 million was stated by Edward Harden, February 17, 1847, M-234, reel 91, 0445.

17. The work of this commission was extensive. Important aspects of its reports are found in M-234, reel 89, 0399–0452 (February–May 1845); Moulton, *John Ross*, p. 133; M-234, reel 89, 0651, reel 95, 0445, reel 96, 0353, and reel 86, 0354. This commission also adjudicated outstanding claims made by the Treaty party and the Old Settlers and by the Cherokees still in North Carolina. M-234, reel 88, 0443, 0689, 0704.

18. Pierce Butler to T. H. Crawford, April 25, 1842, M-234, reel 86, 0100; Ross, *Papers of Chief John Ross*, 2:124, 126, 139, 143; Foreman, *Five Civilized Tribes*, p. 324.

19. Stand Watie was much admired by many whites in Arkansas, and it seemed important to them to clear his name. M-234, reel 86, 0107 (May 24, 1842). He was defended by a white lawyer in Arkansas, George W. Paschal, who had married Major Ridge's daughter and was thus related to Stand Watie. Pierce Butler to T. H. Crawford, May 17, 1842, M-234, reel 86, 0110; Kenny A. Franks, *Stand Watie* (Memphis: Mem-

phis State University Press, 1979), pp. 64, 80–83, 85–87; George W. Paschal, "The Trial of Stand Watie," ed. Grant Foreman, *Chronicles of Oklahoma* 12 (September 1934), pp. 305–39.

20. Foreman, *Five Civilized Tribes*, pp. 325, 328–29. For additional examples of the efforts by Governor Yell and other Arkansans to promote the fear of a Cherokee uprising, see M-234, reel 87, 0252, 0259, 0357, 0393, 0423, and reel 88, 0326, 0603.

21. Ross, *Papers of Chief John Ross*, 2:158–59.

22. Ibid., 2:179; Moulton, *John Ross*, pp. 134–35.

23. Moulton, *John Ross*, p. 135.

24. Petition of certain citizens of Arkansas, July 3, 1843, M-234, reel 87, 0393. The Arkansans constantly played up any sign of tribal collaboration or tribal disorder on their borders, calling for more soldiers and federal support to protect them. See n. 20 above.

25. Ross, *Papers of Chief John Ross*, 2:166–67, 172; P. M. Butler to T. H. Crawford, November 12, 1843, M-234, reel 87, 0361, 0423, 0440; Moulton, *John Ross*, p. 136; Foreman, *Five Civilized Tribes*, p. 327.

26. See P. M. Butler to T. H. Crawford, M-234, reel 87, 0443, 0447, 0472; Foreman, *Five Civilized Tribes*, p. 327; and Ross, *Papers of Chief John Ross*, 2:169, 170–71, 175, 177, 185.

27. Quoted in Foreman, *Five Civilized Tribes*, pp. 328–29. For efforts by Arkansas newspapers and politicians to incite a constant popular fear of the Cherokees, see M-234, reel 86, 0326, reel 87, 0252 (May 21, 1843), 0393 (July 3, 1843), 0412, 0443–90, 0505–14, and reel 88, 0603 (July 16, 1844).

28. Foreman, *Five Civilized Tribes*, p. 328.

29. Moulton, *John Ross*, p. 137.

30. Foreman, *Five Civilized Tribes*, pp. 331–32. See also Ross, *Papers of Chief John Ross*, 2:188. There were four major saltworks in the nation and six to eight smaller ones. The council exempted from this law the saltworks that had been given to Sequoyah by the Old Settler government many years earlier. See T. L. Rogers letter, M-234, reel 88, 0074.

31. Foreman, *Five Civilized Tribes*, pp. 331–32; Royce, *Cherokee Nation*, pp. 178–79.

32. M-234, reel 88, 0488–0521, 0526, 0543, 0549–69, 0575; Ross, *Papers of Chief John Ross*, 2:200–202; Moulton, *John Ross*, pp. 137–38; Franks, *Watie*, pp. 91–93.

33. For the discussions between Secretary of War Wilkins and the Ross delegation over these issues in 1844, see Ross, *Papers of Chief John Ross*, 2:216–27, and Moulton, *John Ross*, pp. 137–39.

34. Moulton, *John Ross*, pp. 145–47.

35. Wardell, *Political History*, p. 57.

36. Moulton, *John Ross*, pp. 139–45. His marriage to Mary Stapler was Ross's second marriage. Missionaries reported that in the early 1840s Ross had taken a Cherokee woman into his home as a "concubine." See Samuel A. Worcester to David Green, November 24, 1843, in Papers of the American Board of Commissioners for Foreign Missions, Houghton Library, Harvard University, Cambridge (hereafter cited as ABCFM).

37. Moulton, *John Ross*, p. 155.

38. Wardell, *Political History*, p. 83; Moulton, *John Ross*, pp. 149–50.

39. For this report, see M-234, 89, 0399–415. See also Ross, *Papers of Chief John Ross*, 2:217, 222, and Foreman, *Five Civilized Tribes*, pp. 332–35.

40. Moulton, *John Ross*, pp. 145–46. For Ross's utilization of this report to attack the terrorist efforts of the Old Settlers and the Treaty party, see Ross, *Papers of Chief John Ross*, 2:249.

41. Foreman, *Five Civilized Tribes*, p. 336; Wardell, *Political History*, p. 67; Moulton, *John Ross*, pp. 151–52; Ross, *Papers of Chief John Ross*, 2:269–71.

42. Moulton, *John Ross*, p. 147. For Ross's dealings with Marcy, see Ross, *Papers of Chief John Ross*, 2:268–71, 274–79.

43. Ross, *Papers of Chief John Ross*, 2:271–72; Foreman, *Five Civilized Tribes*, p. 347. For examples of the serious impact of this violence on the missionaries, see William G. McLoughlin, *Champions of the Cherokees: Evan and John B. Jones* (Princeton: Princeton University Press, 1990), pp. 237–39.

44. Ross, *Papers of Chief John Ross*, 2:272–74, 279–80.

45. Foreman, *Five Civilized Tribes*, pp. 338–39; Moulton, *John Ross*, p. 148; Wardell, *Political History*, p. 54.

46. Edward E. Dale and Gaston Litton, *Cherokee Cavaliers* (Norman: University of Oklahoma Press, 1939), pp. 38–39. Rollin Ridge never joined any of the outlaw gangs, but he did kill a man in a quarrel in Arkansas and had to flee to Missouri to escape trial. See ibid., p. 63, n. 18. Later he became a journalist and poet in California.

47. George Starr and Joseph Starr to Commissioner of Indian Affairs, November 11, 1845, M-234, reel 89, 0499; Foreman, *Five Civilized Tribes*, pp. 338–40; Wardell, *Political History*, p. 63.

48. Foreman, *Five Civilized Tribes*, p. 341.

49. Wardell, *Political History*, p. 53; Franks, *Watie*, p. 96. Many of those who joined "Watie's army" at Fort Wayne were involved in numerous murders and thefts.

50. Moulton, *John Ross*, pp. 149–50. Moulton says that "the Cherokee agent reported in one ten-month period in 1845–1846 a total of thirty-four killings, mainly of a political nature. Certainly the situation was near anarchy." James McKissick to W. Medill, August 28, 1846, M-234, reel 90, 0579. See Royce, *Cherokee Nation*, pp. 181–82, and Foreman, *Five Civilized Tribes*, pp. 338–48, for accounts of the various murders in this period. See also M-234, reel 90, 0505–79.

51. Foreman, *Five Civilized Tribes*, pp. 338–39, 344, 346. Eventually, the outlaws who sought refuge in Arkansas caused so much trouble in the border towns that the local citizens petitioned to have them removed. Foreman, *Five Civilized Tribes*, p. 345. The deaths (by natural causes) of two important leaders of the Old Settlers (John Looney and John Rogers) in the spring of 1846 helped to bring sufficient quiet to the country to permit the negotiations for peace. Both men died in Washington, while pressing for various claims of the Old Settler party. Ibid., p. 342.

52. *Cherokee Advocate*, November 27, 1845.

53. See, for example, the complaint against John Potatoes in the affair that led to the death of James Starr, November 11, 1845, M-234, reel 89, 0499.

54. Ross, *Papers of Chief John Ross*, 2:255.

55. Ibid. For other references to the activities of the Starr gang, see Dale and Litton, *Cherokee Cavaliers*, pp. 29–30, 32–33, 37, 39, 41.

56. Dale and Litton, *Cherokee Cavaliers*, p. 18.

57. Ibid., pp. 29–30.

58. Ibid., p. 37.

59. Ibid., p. 41.

60. Ibid., pp. 43–44.

61. Ibid., pp. 32–33.

62. Foreman, *Five Civilized Tribes*, pp. 347–48.

63. Wardell, *Political History*, p. 69.

64. See Ross, *Papers of Chief John Ross*, 2:285–97, for the statement of the Ross delegation on April 30, 1846, in opposition to Polk's proposal. The delegation had told Polk on April 11 that the best way to end the terrorism in the Cherokee Nation was for him to order General Arbuckle to cease protecting Stand Watie and his "lawless band of armed men at Old Fort Wayne. . . . To put an end to these disturbances, we respectfully request that orders be given to disburse the armed band . . . to discontinue the issue of rations to them and the so called 'refugees' in the State of Arkansas and that they be advised to return in peace into their own country." Ibid., 2:283–85.

65. Moulton, *John Ross*, p. 152; Foreman, *Five Civilized Tribes*, p. 349.

66. The terms of this treaty are described in Royce, *Cherokee Nation*, pp. 182–86, and in Moulton, *John Ross*, p. 152.

67. For the documents of the treaty negotiations, see M-234, reel 90, 0081–1240 (June–July 1846), and 0303 (July 21, 1846); Ross, *Papers of Chief John Ross*, 2:309–14; Royce, *Cherokee Nation*, pp. 176–82; Wardell, *Political History*, pp. 73–74; and Moulton, *John Ross*, pp. 153–54.

68. Royce, *Cherokee Nation*, p. 177; Moulton, *John Ross*, pp. 152–53; Foreman, *Five Civilized Tribes*, pp. 349–50.

69. Ross, *Papers of Chief John Ross*, 2:317.

70. Ibid.

71. Ibid., 2:320.

CHAPTER THREE

1. Annuity payments can be found in the *Annual Report of the Commissioner of Indian Affairs* (Washington, D.C., 1846).

2. The chief discrepancy between what the government had advanced for removal and what Ross claimed was due stemmed from the different estimates of the actual cost per person for the march over the Trail of Tears. The government at first estimated $20 per person or 16 cents per day for two months. When the War Department turned over the management of removal to the Cherokees themselves in June 1838, John Ross and his brother Lewis recalculated the expense at $65.68 per person. After the arrival of all the emigrants to their new home, the Rosses found that the actual expense came to $103.25 per person, a sum the War Department found outrageously high and for which it declined to reimburse the Cherokee Nation, which had borrowed money to pay the extra costs. The War Department accused John and Lewis Ross of inflating the cost to enrich themselves. For these estimates and other financial details of the negotiations, see Gary E. Moulton, *John Ross: Cherokee Chief* (Athens: University

of Georgia Press, 1978), pp. 85–86, 101–5, 151–54; Charles G. Royce, *The Cherokee Nation of Indians* (Chicago: Aldine, 1975), pp. 182–91; Morris Wardell, *A Political History of the Cherokee Nation, 1838–1907* (Norman: University of Oklahoma Press, 1938), pp. 77–84; John Ross, *The Papers of Chief John Ross*, introduction by Gary E. Moulton, 2 vols. (Norman: University of Oklahoma Press, 1985), 2:323–29, 341–42, 362–68; and Government Microfilm Series, Bureau of Indian Affairs, Record Group 75, M-234, Letters Received by the Office of Indian Affairs, 1824–1881, reels 83–96.

3. Royce notes that as of June 1838, the secretary of war made "a new contract with the Ross party, outside the treaty [of 1835] . . . by which the Secretary of War agreed that the expenses of removal and subsistence . . . should be borne by the United States" and should not be covered by the $5 million the Cherokees were to receive for their homeland. *Cherokee Nation*, p. 189.

4. Ibid., pp. 191–95. Ross had no objection to the North Carolina Cherokees' receiving their share of the per capita fund, but only if they came west and rejoined the nation. He could foresee endless complications if a second Cherokee group continued to exist in the East demanding a continual share of tribal funds. Many of the North Carolina Cherokees might have gone west if the government had agreed to pay for their transportation.

5. Ibid., p. 184; Moulton, *John Ross*, pp. 151, 153.

6. Royce, *Cherokee Nation*, p. 184. In 1840 Ross received $23,323.18 for his loss of improvements on his farm in the East. Moulton, *John Ross*, p. 124. Royce provides the following summary by the accounting office of the government's tabulations for the removal costs under the Treaty of 1835:

For improvements	$1,540,572.27
For ferries	159,572.12
For spoliations	264,894.09
For removal and subsistence	2,952,196.06
For debts and claims upon the Cherokees	101,348.31

7. For a detailed explanation, see Royce, *Cherokee Nation*, pp. 125–90.

8. Moulton, *John Ross*, p. 154.

9. Royce, *Cherokee Nation*, pp. 184–90.

10. Ibid., p. 187. The total in each category included only persons living in 1852 who were Cherokee citizens in 1835. It is significant that Ross had to ask a council of the people in November 1851 for permission to deduct 5 percent from the total of the per capita money in order to pay the nation's lawyers. Moulton, *John Ross*, p. 156.

11. Moulton, *John Ross*, p. 154; Wardell, *Political History*, p. 83; Royce, *Cherokee Nation*, p. 190. A census taken in 1850 placed the total Cherokee population at 16,593 (not including over 2,000 in North Carolina). In addition, there were about 2,500 black slaves and several hundred intermarried whites in the nation. Wardell, *Political History*, p. 84.

12. Samuel A. Worcester to S. B. Treat, June 23, 1852, in Papers of the American Board of Commissioners for Foreign Missions, Houghton Library, Harvard University, Cambridge (hereafter cited as ABCFM).

13. Marcus Palmer's report, April 19, 1854, in ABCFM.

14. For a discussion of the sale of the Neutral Lands, see Wardell, *Political History*,

pp. 89–91; Moulton, *John Ross*, pp. 157–58; Royce, *Cherokee Nation*, pp. 197–99, 226; and *Cherokee Advocate*, January 6, 1846.

15. Documents to and from the commissioner of Indian affairs relating to these proposals may be found in M-234, reel 95, 1394 (November 29, 1851), 1187 (July 16, 1852), and reel 96, 0278 (February 17, 1853), 0107 (March 2, 1853).

16. George Butler to George Manypenny, M-234, reel 96, 0486; letter of David Harden, September 16, 1854, M-234, reel 96, 0478.

17. George Butler to George Manypenny, October 11, 1854, M-234, reel 96, 0486.

18. These negotiations are described in M-234, reel 97, 0271–83, 0297–0305, 0313, 0316, and 0517ff. (1855).

19. Cherokee delegation of George Manypenny, M-234, reel 97, 0272–83.

20. George Butler to George Manypenny, December 2, 1854, M-234, reel 97, 0046.

21. Wardell, *Political History*, p. 85.

22. See Moulton, *John Ross*, p. 157; Wardell, *Political History*, pp. 86–87. The "scrip" was also known as "warrants" or "tickets."

23. Cassandra Lockwood to S. B. Treat from Dwight Mission, in ABCFM. This composite portrait of the average Cherokee is taken from a variety of sources including missionary letters, reports of federal agents, and various visitors.

24. Evan Jones to Solomon Peck, January 22, 1857, in American Baptist Mission Union Papers, American Baptist Historical Society, Rochester, New York.

25. Harlin's report is in *Condition of the Indian Tribes: Report of the Special Joint Committee* (Washington, D.C.: Government Printing Office, 1867), p. 444.

26. Ibid.

27. Charles Torrey, "Notes of a Missionary among the Cherokees," ed. Grant Foreman, *Chronicles of Oklahoma* 16 (June 1938): 171–89.

28. See letters of Mary Denny and Elizabeth Hancock to S. B. Treat, April 19, 1854, and December 12 and 14, 1858, vol. 12, letters 15–25, in ABCFM.

29. See William G. McLoughlin, *Champions of the Cherokees: Evan and John B. Jones* (Princeton: Princeton University Press, 1990), pp. 34–38.

30. Hannah Moore to S. B. Treat, September 10, 1844, in ABCFM.

31. Timothy Ranney to S. B. Treat, April 23, 1861, in ABCFM.

32. Timothy Ranney to S. B. Treat, June 16, 1860, in ABCFM.

33. Ibid.

34. Elizur Butler to David Greene, April 26, 1845, in ABCFM.

35. George Butler's report, in *Annual Report* (1853).

36. Ibid.

37. Harlin's report, in *Condition of the Indian Tribes*, p. 443.

38. P. M. Butler's report, in *Annual Report* (1842).

39. S. A. Worcester to S. B. Treat, June 5, 1851, in ABCFM. Typical of this attitude was the effort of the more acculturated Cherokees to impress upon white visitors that the old traditions had all but disappeared in the nation. As early as 1841, Colonel E. A. Hitchcock was told that "the ancient customs of the nation are all gone" and "savage customs and manners have disappeared." The old clans and exogamous marriage had "grown into disuse. . . . The 'physic dance' . . . [and] the greencorn dance . . . are no longer known . . . and the race of Conjurors has disappeared almost as completely as the race of witches from Salem." Grant Foreman, ed., *A Traveler in Indian Territory:*

The Journal of Ethan Allen Hitchcock (Cedar Rapids, Iowa: Torch Press, 1930), pp. 35, 48, 241. Reports from the missionaries among the full-bloods indicate that this was far from true.

40. Statement of Martha Tyner Swift, in Foreman Papers, Gilcrease Institute, Tulsa, Oklahoma.

41. Ibid. See William G. McLoughlin and Walter Conser, "Cherokees in Transition," *Journal of American History* 64, no. 3 (1977): 678–703.

42. Theda Perdue, *Slavery and the Evolution of Cherokee Society, 1540–1866* (Knoxville: University of Tennessee Press, 1979), pp. 96–97, 102, 105. Perdue gives good descriptions of the other members of the slaveholding class in this volume.

43. Elizur Butler to S. B. Treat, January 25, 1949, in ABCFM.

44. Wardell, *Political History*, p. 87.

45. Ibid.; Moulton, *John Ross*, pp. 156–57.

46. Wardell, *Political History*, pp. 87–90.

47. Moulton, *John Ross*, p. 156.

48. Wardell, *Political History*, p. 88.

49. McLoughlin, *Evan and John B. Jones*, p. 241.

50. *Cherokee Advocate*, March 9, 1852.

51. Carolyn Foreman, "History of Tahlequah," typescript, in Foreman Papers, Gilcrease Institute, Tulsa, Oklahoma.

52. Carolyn Foreman, "History of Park Hill," typescript, in Foreman Papers, Gilcrease Institute, Tulsa, Oklahoma. The published version is *Park Hill* (Muskogee, Okla., 1948).

53. For the best information on Fort Gibson, see Grant Foreman, *The Advancing Frontier* (Norman: University of Oklahoma Press, 1933), pp. 35–48, 124–38.

CHAPTER FOUR

1. Grant Foreman, *The Five Civilized Tribes* (Norman: University of Oklahoma Press, 1934), p. 371.

2. A good discussion of the early public school system (including the law of 1841) can be found in Emmet Starr, *History of the Cherokee Indians* (New York: Kraus Reprint, 1969), pp. 225–42.

3. Ibid., pp. 225–46.

4. S. A. Worcester to David Greene, May 30, 1842, in Papers of the American Board of Commissioners for Foreign Missions, Houghton Library, Harvard University, Cambridge (hereafter cited as ABCFM).

5. Charles Pulsifer to David Greene, February 2, 1844, in ABCFM.

6. William G. McLoughlin, *Champions of the Cherokees: Evan and John B. Jones* (Princeton: Princeton University Press, 1990), p. 223.

7. John Ross, *The Papers of Chief John Ross*, introduction by Gary E. Moulton, 2 vols. (Norman: University of Oklahoma Press, 1985), 2:265–66.

8. James Payne to James McKissick, September 7, 1847, in William G. McLoughlin, *Cherokee Ghost Dance* (Macon, Ga.: Mercer University Press, 1984), pp. 499–500.

9. Ibid., p. 501. In 1847 there were 121 Cherokee orphans boarded at the nation's

expense in Cherokee homes and sent to the public schools. Ross, *Papers of Chief John Ross*, 2:266.

10. McLoughlin, *Cherokee Ghost Dance*, pp. 476–78.

11. Ibid., p. 478.

12. Elizur Butler to S. B. Treat, February 13, 1851, in ABCFM.

13. McLoughlin, *Cherokee Ghost Dance*, pp. 483–84.

14. S. A. Worcester to David Greene, June 27, 1856, and July 13, 1857, in ABCFM.

15. Edwin Teele to David Greene, June 1854, in ABCFM.

16. Elizur Butler to S. B. Treat, July 21 and November 22, 1852, in ABCFM.

17. Asa Hitchcock to David Greene, October 16, 1845, in ABCFM.

18. Marcus Palmer's report, April 18, 1854, in ABCFM.

19. S. A. Worcester to S. B. Treat, June 5, 1854, in ABCFM.

20. S. A. Worcester to S. B. Treat, November 16, 1858, in ABCFM.

21. Ibid.

22. Ibid.

23. Ibid.

24. Ross, *Papers of Chief John Ross*, 2:404.

25. McLoughlin, *Cherokee Ghost Dance*, p. 495.

26. Pierce M. Butler to T. H. Crawford, Government Microfilm Series, Bureau of Indian Affairs, Record Group 75, M-234, Letters Received by the Office of Indian Affairs, 1824–1881, reel 86, 0186–89; Morris Wardell, *A Political History of the Cherokee Nation, 1838–1907* (Norman: University of Oklahoma Press, 1938), pp. 92–93.

27. John Ross to Commissioner of Indian Affairs, November 27, 1849, M-234, reel 93, 0238, reel 94, 0161.

28. John Drew et al. to A. H. Stuart, September 30, 1850, M-234, reel 94, 0380–82.

29. W. G. Belknap to Commissioner of Indian Affairs, November 19, 1850, M-234, reel 94, 0139.

30. John Drennen to Commissioner of Indian Affairs, March 20, 1851, M-234, reel 95, 0146.

31. Ibid.

32. George Butler to Joseph H. Head, September 6, 1851, M-234, reel 95, 0214.

33. These inventories provide a good indication of what the Cherokee wanted in the way of manufactured goods in this decade. For example, see M-234, reel 95, 0214.

34. Wardell, *Political History*, p. 82.

35. Elijah Hicks et al. to Commissioner of Indian Affairs, May 10, 1853, M-234, reel 96, 0306.

36. W. P. Ross to Commissioner of Indian Affairs, June 17, 1850, M-234, reel 94, 0233.

37. George Butler to Commissioner of Indian Affairs, April 26, 1856, M-234, reel 98, 0060.

38. C. W. Dean and George Butler to George Manypenny, May 3, 1856, M-234, reel 98, 0058.

39. Grant Foreman, *The Advancing Frontier* (Norman: University of Oklahoma Press, 1933), p. 35.

40. See, for example, the letters of the Ross council to Arbuckle, April 22 and November 6, 1840, M-234, reel 84, 0179, and reel 85, 0036.

41. John Drennen to Commissioner of Indian Affairs, March 6, 1862, M-234, reel 95, 1001.

42. Ross, *Papers of Chief John Ross*, 2:369.

43. Foreman, *Advancing Frontier*, pp. 66–67. See also M-234, reel 86, 0176, 0183, 0420, 0434, and 0447, for other problems with the soldiers' behavior.

44. Pierce Butler to Commissioner of Indian Affairs, March 17, 1843, M-234, reel 87, 0049. See also Butler's complaint against a soldier, August 10, 1843, M-234, reel 87, 0330.

45. Pierce Butler to Commissioner of Indian Affairs, September 30, 1844, M-234, reel 88, 0225.

46. R. C. S. Brown to William Medill, June 18, 1847, M-234, reel 93, 0170.

47. John Ross to George Manypenny, September 8, 1854, M-234, reel 96, 0581.

48. Ross, *Papers of Chief John Ross*, 2:402.

49. John Ross to Secretary of the Interior, January 28, 1858, M-234, reel 98, 0808; Gary E. Moulton, *John Ross: Cherokee Chief* (Athens: University of Georgia Press, 1978), p. 161.

50. Moulton, *John Ross*, p. 161.

51. C. W. Dean to George Butler, August 15, 1856, M-234, reel 98, 0073.

52. Ibid. See also M-234, reel 98, 0598, 0600, 0760, and reel 99, 0224.

53. The Cherokees first requested that the headquarters of the federal agent should be situated at the nation's capital in 1850. John Ross et al. to Commissioner of Indian Affairs, March 4, 1850, M-234, reel 94, 0161.

54. See below for the 1846 U.S. Supreme Court decision in *Rogers v. Cherokee Nation*, in which this claim was gravely undercut. Wardell, *Political History*, p. 101.

55. Ibid., p. 100; Arthur Lee Beckett, *Know Your Oklahoma* (Oklahoma City: Harlow Publishing Company, 1930), p. 12; William P. Thompson, "Courts of the Cherokee Nation," *Chronicles of Oklahoma* 2 (March 1924): 63–74.

56. Ross, *Papers of Chief John Ross*, 2:113–14. Ross said, "I know not whether Fisher was really a white man or a citizen of the United States—rumor seems to deny to him both—but be this as it may, as I have already remarked, the Principal Chief cannot alter the case nor exercise any legal power over it. . . . It is certain, however, that Fisher was not in the Nation in accordance with the provision of the intercourse act or the treaty stipulations with the United States."

57. Ibid., 2:114.

58. Ibid., 2:134.

59. John Ross to William Medill, July 8, 1846, M-234, reel 90, 0237.

60. See Government Microfilm Series, Bureau of Indian Affairs, Record Group 75, M-348, Report Books of the Office of Indian Affairs, 1838–1885, reel 5, 0071–79, and M-234, reel 90, 0294.

61. For Taney's decision, see M-234, reel 90, 0294.

62. William Medill to John Ross, July 21, 1846, M-348, reel 5, 0071ff.

63. Foreman, *Five Civilized Tribes*, p. 413.

64. James McKissick to Commissioner of Indian Affairs, April 19, 1847, M-234, reel 91, 0335.

65. Unsigned, undated portion of a letter to James McKissick, probably from the commissioner of Indian affairs, M-234, reel 91, 0338.

66. James McKissick to Commissioner of Indian Affairs, July 7, 1847, M-234, reel 91, 0372.

67. Complaint of the Cherokee delegation to Commissioner of Indian Affairs, June 8, 1853, M-234, reel 96, 0308. See also the complaints of April 29, 1853, M-234, reel 96, 0293, 0299, and April 14, 1853, M-234, reel 98, 0149. For similar efforts of the Creeks to prevent federal marshals from arresting prisoners to stand trial in Arkansas, see M-234, reel 98, 0142 (September 15, 1853).

68. George Butler to C. W. Dean, April 9, 1856, M-234, reel 98, 0048.

69. C. W. Dean to Commissioner of Indian Affairs, April 16, 1856, M-234, reel 98, 0046.

70. Starr, *History*, p. 138.

71. C. W. Dean to John Ross, September 2, 1856, M-234, reel 98, 0076.

72. A. W. Wilson to C. W. Dean, August 16, 1856, M-234, reel 98, 0088.

73. George Butler to A. B. Greenwood, August 11, 1859, M-234, reel 99, 0058.

74. Wardell, *Political History*, pp. 101–2. See also George Butler's report, in *Annual Report of the Commissioner of Indian Affairs* (Washington, D.C., 1858).

75. Wardell, *Political History*, p. 102.

76. Ibid., p. 103.

77. Ibid., p. 109; Ross, *Papers of Chief John Ross*, 2:409.

78. Wardell, *Political History*, pp. 109–10.

79. Ross, *Papers of Chief John Ross*, 2:408–9.

80. C. W. Dean to George Butler, August 15, 1856, M-234, reel 98, 0073.

81. C. W. Dean to George Butler, January 17, 1857, M-234, reel 98, 0420, and George Butler to C. W. Dean, January 9, 1857, M-234, reel 98, 0422.

82. George Butler to C. W. Dean, October 12, 1857, M-234, reel 98, 0598.

83. Elias Rector to George Butler, November 29, 1857, M-234, reel 98, 0600.

84. George Butler to C. W. Dean, January 24, 1858, M-234, reel 98, 0760.

85. Annual report of the superintendents of Indian affairs, 1860, M-348, reel 12, 0031. See also George Butler to Commissioner of Indian Affairs, March 24, 1860, M-234, reel 99, 0224.

86. Wardell, *Political History*, p. 91; Moulton, *John Ross*, pp. 157–59.

87. George Manypenny to Robert McClelland, October 31, 1854, M-348, reel 8, 0081.

88. Thomas Drew to George Manypenny, February 22, 1854, M-234, reel 96, 0576.

89. George Butler to George Manypenny, April 5, 1854, M-234, reel 96, 0461.

90. Thomas Drew to George Butler, April 5, 1854, M-234, reel 97, 0160.

91. Ibid.

92. J. Sullivan Cowden to Commissioner of Indian Affairs, 1853, M-234, reel 97, 0085–94, 0098, 0115.

93. George Butler's report, September 8, 1857, in *Annual Report* (1858), p. 212. Butler spoke of "the superior advantages this country offers for a continuance of the southwestern branch of the Pacific railroad from St. Louis . . . to connect with the southern Pacific road at some point in New Mexico." See also Wardell, *Political History*, p. 108.

94. George Butler to Charles Mix, March 15, 1858, M-234, reel 98, 0769.

95. Wardell, *Political History*, p. 109.

96. Ibid., p. 105.

97. Ibid.

98. Ibid., pp. 105–8.

99. Ross, *Papers of Chief John Ross*, 2:443. Ross noted on May 23, 1860, that even before Kansas was made a territory by Congress in 1854, the Cherokees had protested to President Millard Fillmore, but they never received a response. He reminded Congress again that the Treaty of 1835 contained a clause "that the United States hereby covenant and agree that the lands ceded to the Cherokee nation . . . shall in no future time, without their consent, be included within the territorial limits or jurisdiction of any State or Territory." It appeared that Congress had broken this agreement while at the same time the United States was refusing to buy the Neutral Lands in Kansas at a fair price.

100. Wardell, *Political History*, p. 107.

101. Ibid.

102. George Butler's report, September 27, 1854, *Annual Report* (1855). "The bill now before Congress for organizing into Territories this and some of the adjoining nations, meets with considerable opposition from the Cherokees." Butler noted at this time that the Cherokee government "must inevitably cease to exist unless there is some permanent provision made for supplying their now empty treasury," which explained their desire to sell the Neutral Lands. Butler favored the purchase of these lands. Ibid., pp. 114, 115.

103. Ross, *Papers of Chief John Ross*, 2:389.

104. Ibid.

105. *The Standard* (Clarksville, Texas), March 10, 1855. This was signed by Joseph Vann, D. H. Ross, et al. for the Cherokees and by Benjamin Marshall, Teo W. Stidham, Hopolith-yar-ho-la, Motey Kenard, et al. for the Creeks.

106. Wardell, *Political History*, p. 108.

107. Ross, *Papers of Chief John Ross*, 2:409.

108. Letter, January 1, 1860, in ibid., 2:404.

109. Ibid., 2:429.

110. Starr, *History*, p. 89. In *Political History*, p. 111, Morris Wardell notes that in 1859 Sam Houston ran for governor of Texas on a platform that advocated federal territorial status for the Indian Territory.

CHAPTER FIVE

1. See Theda Perdue, *Slavery and the Evolution of Cherokee Society, 1540–1866* (Knoxville: University of Tennessee Press, 1979); Rudi Halliburton, Jr., *Red Over Black* (Westport, Conn.: Greenwood Press, 1977); and Michael Roethler, "Negro Slavery among the Cherokee Indians, 1540–1866" (Ph.D. diss., Fordham University, 1964).

2. See Daniel S. Butrick, January 7, 1845, and Jacob Hitchcock, April 10, 1845, both in Papers of the American Board of Commissioners for Foreign Missions, Houghton Library, Harvard University, Cambridge (hereafter cited as ABCFM), and Halliburton, *Red Over Black*, pp. 10–11.

3. James Mooney, *Myths of the Cherokees*, Smithsonian Institution, Bureau of American Ethnology, *19th Annual Report, 1897–98*, part 1 (Washington, D.C.: Government Printing Office, 1900), pp. 242–48.

4. William G. McLoughlin, *Cherokee Ghost Dance* (Macon, Ga.: Mercer University Press, 1984), p. 257.

5. Roethler, "Negro Slavery," p. 187.

6. Edwin Teele, November 17, 1853, in ABCFM.

7. Charles Torrey, "Notes of a Missionary among the Cherokees," ed. Grant Foreman, *Chronicles of Oklahoma* 16 (June 1938): 179.

8. Hannah Moore, September 10, 1844, in ABCFM.

9. For a statistical analysis of slavery and its growth, see McLoughlin, *Cherokee Ghost Dance*, pp. 215–51. See also Daniel S. Butrick on the "natural increase" of slaves, January 7, 1845, in ABCFM.

10. See George Butler's report, September 10, 1859, in *Annual Report of the Commissioner of Indian Affairs* (Washington, D.C., 1859), p. 173. There was no official Cherokee census after 1846, so the figures after that date are only estimates.

11. Perdue, *Evolution of Cherokee Society*, pp. 129–30; Kenny A. Franks, *Stand Watie* (Memphis: Memphis State University Press, 1979), chap. 7.

12. *American State Papers, Indian Affairs*, vols. 1 and 2, ed. Walter Lowrie et al. (Washington, D.C.: Gales and Seaton, 1832, 1834), 2:651.

13. Perdue, *Evolution of Cherokee Society*, p. 93.

14. Elizur Butler, March 5, 1845, in ABCFM.

15. The development of a "black code" of laws in the Cherokee Nation is amply discussed in Halliburton, *Red Over Black*, pp. 34, 68–69, 88, 142, and Perdue, *Evolution of Cherokee Society*, pp. 84–89. See also *Laws of the Cherokee Nation* (Tahlequah, 1852) for the laws themselves. For this particular law, see ibid., pp. 24–25.

16. *Laws of the Cherokee Nation*, p. 38.

17. Ibid., p. 39.

18. Ibid., p. 37.

19. The Cherokee constitution is printed in ibid., pp. 118–29, and in Emmet Starr, *History of the Cherokee Indians* (New York: Kraus Reprint, 1969), pp. 122–33.

20. December 3, 1833, and October 2, 1835, in Ross Papers, Gilcrease Institute, Tulsa, Oklahoma.

21. *Laws of the Cherokee Nation*, p. 19.

22. Perdue, *Evolution of Cherokee Society*, p. 85.

23. *Laws of the Cherokee Nation*, pp. 55–56.

24. Perdue, *Evolution of Cherokee Society*, p. 87.

25. Halliburton, *Red Over Black*, p. 87.

26. Ibid., p. 88.

27. Perdue, *Evolution of Cherokee Society*, p. 89.

28. Ross Papers, box 39, folder 115, Gilcrease Institute, Tulsa, Oklahoma.

29. Cephas Washburn, *Reminiscences of the Indians* (Richmond, Va., 1869), p. 192.

30. Francis Barker to Solomon Peck, January 12, 1850, in American Baptist Mission Union Papers, American Baptist Historical Society, Rochester, New York (hereafter cited as ABMU).

31. Elizur Butler, April 11, 1849, in ABCFM.

32. R. C. S. Brown, federal agent, to Commissioner of Indian Affairs, August 24, 1848, Government Microfilm Series, Bureau of Indian Affairs, Record Group 75, M-234, Letters Received by the Office of Indian Affairs, 1824–1881, reel 93, 0366.

33. Perdue, *Evolution of Cherokee Society*, p. 105.

34. Halliburton, *Red Over Black*, p. 74.

35. Ibid., p. 85.

36. George Butler to Commissioner of Indian Affairs, September 10, 1859, M-234, reel 99, 0126.

37. Halliburton, *Red Over Black*, pp. 65, 85, 86; Perdue, *Evolution of Cherokee Society*, p. 108.

38. See, for example, M-234, reel 90, 0554, 0563, reel 91, 0249, reel 93, 0097, and reel 96, 0204. See also Ross Papers for the 1850s, Gilcrease Institute, Tulsa, Oklahoma, and Perdue, *Evolution of Cherokee Society*, pp. 76–77.

39. Samuel Worcester to Jefferson Davis, September 6, 1854, in ABCFM. For other efforts of slave traders to kidnap blacks from the Cherokee Nation in the 1840s, see Perdue, *Evolution of Cherokee Society*, pp. 76–78.

40. There are many letters from Worcester to his board about this effort to save the Beam family from being returned to slavery; see, for example, August 29 and October 23, 1854, and January 25, 1855, in ABCFM. See also Elizur Butler, August 29, 1854, in ABCFM.

41. See the effort of Evan Jones to help one such slave in McLoughlin, *Cherokee Ghost Dance*, pp. 465–66.

42. Elizur Butler, December 1, 1853, in ABCFM.

43. The law passed in 1828 regarding free blacks stated that "all free negroes coming into the Cherokee Nation . . . shall be viewed and treated in every respect as intruders." They could reside in the nation only after obtaining a permit from the council. *Laws of the Cherokee Nation*, p. 37.

44. See, for example, the case of a slave named Tom who, in 1842, after his master died, claimed to have purchased his freedom but lost his plea. M-234, reel 86, 0334, 1741, 1746.

45. Daniel S. Butrick, November 7, 1837, in ABCFM.

46. S. A. Worcester, December 28, 1842, in ABCFM.

47. S. A. Worcester, October 26, 1842, in ABCFM.

48. S. A. Worcester, July 21, 1853, in ABCFM.

49. S. A. Worcester, May 4, 1853, in ABCFM.

50. See, for example, the letters of Jacob Hitchcock, April 10, 1845, and Daniel S. Butrick, January 1, 1845, both in ABCFM. Scholars have disagreed over this assumption. Roethler and Perdue seem to agree with Hitchcock and Butrick; Halliburton does not. In my view, Cherokee masters and overseers could be as cruel as southern whites in the treatment of their slaves, and so could Choctaw, Chickasaw, and Creek slave masters. Only the Seminoles appear to have treated them as equals, but after 1850, even they changed dramatically in this regard. See Daniel F. Littlefield, Jr., *Africans and Seminoles* (Westport, Conn.: Greenwood Press, 1977), chap. 8.

51. Elizur Butler, March 5, 1845, in ABCFM.

52. Daniel S. Butrick, January 1, 1845, in ABCFM.

53. McLoughlin, *Cherokee Ghost Dance*, p. 55.

54. Charles Torrey, October 9, 1860, in ABCFM.

55. Halliburton, *Red Over Black*, p. 88. For examples of experiences written by slaves of Cherokees, see Grant Foreman, "Pioneer Interviews," in Foreman Papers, Gilcrease Institute, Tulsa, Oklahoma, and George P. Rawick, ed., *The American Slave*, 19 vols. (Westport, Conn.: Greenwood Press, 1972), which contain accounts by former slaves of Cherokees that describe separations of families and sales "down the river" to New Orleans to pay off debts. See also Perdue, *Evolution of Cherokee Society*, pp. 81, 83.

56. *Cherokee Advocate*, March 2, 1852.

57. *Cherokee Advocate*, August 3, 1853.

58. Ibid.

59. For accounts of slave revolts, see Halliburton, *Red Over Black*, pp. 82–84; Perdue, *Evolution of Cherokee Society*, pp. 79–84; M-234, reel 88, 0125, 1061; John Ross, *The Papers of Chief John Ross*, introduction by Gary E. Moulton, 2 vols. (Norman: University of Oklahoma Press, 1985), 2:154, 157; Gary E. Moulton, *John Ross: Cherokee Chief* (Athens: University of Georgia Press, 1978), p. 134; Roethler, "Negro Slavery," p. 184; and *Fort Smith Elevator*, February 5, 1897.

60. Ross, *Papers of Chief John Ross*, 2:154; M-234, reel 86, 0476, reel 87, 0832, 0836, 0125, 1061.

61. Ross, *Papers of Chief John Ross*, 2:157; M-234, reel 87, 0122; *Laws of the Cherokee Nation*, p. 62. Reports of this slave revolt of 1842 seem to indicate that there were two separate incidents: first an escape on October 13, 1842, and then a larger escape of other slaves on November 15, 1842. John Drew reported capturing one group and returning them to Webber's Falls on December 8, 1842. He captured and returned the second group on January 15, 1843. However, the reports in the materials cited above do not clearly distinguish the two incidents. Slave revolts were always given as little publicity as possible. In most cases when a small group of slaves escaped, the slave owners simply constituted themselves into a posse, recaptured their slaves, and made no reports to anyone. For the report of an earlier escape in 1841, which may have been only a rumor, see Perdue, *Evolution of Cherokee Society*, pp. 163–64.

62. *Laws of the Cherokee Nation* p. 62, quoted in Halliburton, *Red Over Black*, p. 84.

63. See H. L. Smith to Stand Watie, April 4, 1846, in Edward E. Dale and Gaston Litton, *Cherokee Cavaliers* (Norman: University of Oklahoma Press, 1939), pp. 29–31. The "questioning" probably involved whipping.

64. Edwin C. McReynolds, *The Seminoles* (Norman: University of Oklahoma Press, 1964), p. 263; Littlefield, *Africans and Seminoles*, pp. 147–48, 164.

65. William Drew's letter is in the Foreman Papers, box 36, vol. 75, pp. 72–73, Gilcrease Institute, Tulsa, Oklahoma.

66. R. C. S. Brown to Commissioner of Indian Affairs, June 18, 1847, M-234, reel 93, 0170.

67. For the American Missionary Association, see Charles K. Whipple, *Relations of the American Board of Commissioners for Foreign Missions to Slavery* (Boston, 1861); for the Baptist Free Mission Society, see John R. McKivigan, "The American Baptist Free Mission Society," *Foundations* 21 (October–December 1978): 340–55.

68. See Robert Lewit, "Indian Missions and Anti-Slavery Sentiment," *Mississippi Valley Historical Review* 50 (June 1963): 39–55; McLoughlin, *Cherokee Ghost Dance*, pp. 337–42; and S. A. Worcester, December 28, 1842, in ABCFM.

69. Daniel S. Butrick, January 1, 1845, in ABCFM.

70. Elizur Butler, April 11, 1849, in ABCFM.

71. Elizur Butler, July 26, 1852, in ABCFM. Butler added, "He went on to speak in high terms of the colonization society and wishing that the United States Government would do something to remove the whole of the black population to Africa."

72. Elizur Butler, April 11, 1849, in ABCFM.

73. Elizur Butler, March 5, 1845, in ABCFM.

74. Daniel S. Butrick, January 1, 1845, in ABCFM.

75. S. A. Worcester to Solomon Peck, February 21, 1856, in ABMU. See also S. A. Worcester to David Greene, September 1844, in ABCFM. There are many letters from Worcester to his mission board in the years 1844–59 in which he discusses his refusal to preach against slavery, to discipline members for slaveholding, or to deny church membership to slave owners. See, for example, his letters of March 28 and August 17, 1848, and April 26 and May 4, 1853, in ABCFM.

76. Quoted in Althea Bass, *Cherokee Messenger: A Life of Samuel Austin Worcester* (Norman: University of Oklahoma Press, 1936), p. 237.

77. Halliburton, *Red Over Black*, p. 97.

78. *Cherokee Advocate*, October 23, 1848. See also Perdue, *Evolution of Cherokee Society*, pp. 121–22.

79. *Cherokee Advocate*, October 30, 1848.

80. For a detailed discussion of Jones's position on slavery, see William G. McLoughlin, *Champions of the Cherokees: Evan and John B. Jones* (Princeton: Princeton University Press, 1990), chaps. 11 and 13.

81. McLoughlin, *Cherokee Ghost Dance*, pp. 454–55.

82. Ibid.

83. Ibid., p. 459.

84. Ibid.

85. McLoughlin, *Evan and John B. Jones*, p. 295.

86. McLoughlin, *Cherokee Ghost Dance*, p. 461.

87. S. A. Worcester, April 6, 1853, in ABCFM.

88. Halliburton, *Red Over Black*, p. 99.

89. George M. Butler to Commissioner of Indian Affairs, October 23, 1855, M-234, reel 97, 0111.

90. Halliburton, *Red Over Black*, p. 100.

91. S. A. Worcester, October 16, 1854, in ABCFM.

92. McLoughlin, *Cherokee Ghost Dance*, pp. 460–64. See also M-234, reel 97, 0075–87, and reel 98, 0789–0800.

93. See Robert G. Gardner, *Cherokee Baptists in Georgia* (Atlanta: Georgia Baptist Historical Society, 1989), p. 188.

94. S. A. Worcester, December 12, 1851, and April 5 and June 11, 1852, in ABCFM. See also Halliburton, *Red Over Black*, p. 98.

95. S. A. Worcester, June 11, 1852, in ABCFM.

96. Affidavit of Stephen Foreman, June 11, 1852, M-234, reel 97, 0084–87.

97. George Butler to Commissioner of Indian Affairs, June 22, 1855, M-234, reel 97, 0080.

98. S. A. Worcester, August 27, 1855, in ABCFM.

99. Ibid.

100. George Butler sent a copy of this bill to the commissioner of Indian affairs, stating that "by which you can see that the Abolition Missionaries have been interfering with slavery." November 30, 1855, M-234, reel 97, 0110–12.

101. Ibid. It seems that the full-bloods in the lower house supported Ross on this.

102. Charles Torrey, June 16, 1865, in ABCFM; Halliburton, *Red Over Black*, p. 101.

103. Halliburton, *Red Over Black*, p. 100. Butler had written to his board a month earlier, on September 13, 1856, that "the sympathies of this people are not with the missionaries of the Board." See also Torrey, "Notes of a Missionary," p. 179.

104. George Butler to Commissioner of Indian Affairs, November 23, 1856, M-234, reel 98, 0005.

105. Charles Torrey, July 6, 1857, in ABCFM.

106. S. A. Worcester, July 13, 1857, in ABCFM. Worcester said here that the only way the Indian Territory could ever abolish slavery would be if Congress transformed it into a territory of the United States preparatory to statehood. It was highly unlikely that it would ever have been filled with antislavery whites, however.

107. Elizur Butler, July 13, 1857, in ABCFM.

108. The part the Joneses played in creating the full-blood Keetoowah Society is discussed more fully in chapter 8.

109. Halliburton, *Red Over Black*, p. 102.

110. Mary E. Wright, *The Missionary Work of the Southern Baptist Convention* (Philadelphia: American Baptist Publication Society, 1902), pp. 340–41; Norman W. Cox, ed., *Encyclopedia of Southern Baptists*, 2 vols. (Nashville: Broadman Press, 1969), 1:683.

111. John B. Jones, September 18, 1856, in ABMU.

112. *Mississippi Baptist*, September 17, 1857.

113. John B. Jones, May 5, 1858, in ABMU.

114. Ibid.

115. Ibid.

116. *Western Recorder and Baptist Banner* (Louisville, Kentucky), July 11, 1859.

117. *Mississippi Baptist*, May 27, 1858.

118. *Mississippi Baptist*, February 6, 1860.

119. George Butler to Commissioner of Indian Affairs, June 30, 1858, M-234, reel 98, 0774.

120. Bass, *Cherokee Messenger*, p. 340.

121. W. P. Adair to George Butler, August 21, 1858, M-234, reel 98, 0781. See also McLoughlin, *Cherokee Ghost Dance*, pp. 465–66, and *Evan and John B. Jones*, p. 366. The case involved a slave who had been fired by her mistress, but after the mistress's death, the attorney for the estate, Adair, wished to sell the slave because she was claimed by one of the heirs. The slave gave her "free papers" to Jones, who refused to release them to Adair.

122. W. P. Adair to George Butler, August 21, 1858, M-234, reel 98, 0781; Evan

Jones to W. P. Adair, July 24, 1858, M-234, reel 98, 0798; Evan Jones to George Butler, September 3, 1858, M-234, reel 98, 0789.

123. George Butler to Charles Mix, October 12, 1858, M-234, reel 98, 0778.

124. Charles Torrey, October 11, 1858, in ABCFM. Torrey said in this letter, "I received a note from the agent a short time ago charging me with being an abolitionist and demanding either a confession or a denial of the charge."

125. Annie H. Abel, *Slaveholding Indians*, 3 vols. (Cleveland: Arthur H. Clark, 1915), 1:47, 56.

126. S. A. Worcester, October 18, 1858, in ABCFM.

127. S. A. Worcester, November 16, 1858, in ABCFM.

128. *Southwest Independent* (Fayetteville, Arkansas), February 25, 1854, clipping with S. A. Worcester, June 22, 1854, in ABCFM.

129. George Butler's report, September 10, 1859, in *Annual Report* (1859), p. 172.

130. This letter was enclosed with a letter of Timothy Ranney to his board, October 21, 1860, in ABCFM.

CHAPTER SIX

1. John Ross to Evan Jones, May 5, 1855, in American Baptist Mission Union Papers, American Baptist Historical Society, Rochester, New York (hereafter cited as ABMU). See also Rudi Halliburton, Jr., *Red Over Black* (Westport, Conn.: Greenwood Press, 1977), pp. 119–20, 125, 144, 196.

2. While there has been some controversy over whether the first lodges of the Knights of the Golden Circle were organized before or after the Keetoowah Society, there is little doubt that the Blue Lodges preceded the Keetoowahs, and the Knights were clearly the successors to the Blue Lodges, probably with most of the same members. The most significant documents of the early Keetoowah movement are in the Shleppey Collection, University of Tulsa Library. See also Emmet Starr, *History of the Cherokee Indians* (New York: Kraus Reprint, 1969), pp. 143, 258, 479–80, and Halliburton, *Red Over Black*, pp. 118, 120, 125, 144.

3. James Mooney, *Myths of the Cherokees*, Smithsonian Institution, Bureau of American Ethnology, *19th Annual Report, 1897–98*, part 1 (Washington, D.C.: Government Printing Office, 1900), p. 525.

4. As previously noted, the name "Keetoowah" was also given to Fort Gibson after 1857 and later was used to name a town in the Going Snake District. The Northern Baptists and the members of the Keetoowah Society were numerous in Going Snake District.

5. See the letter of D. H. Ross, July 7, 1864, claiming that by that date the Keetoowah Society constituted "seven-tenths of the male population." John Ross, *The Papers of Chief John Ross*, introduction by Gary E. Moulton, 2 vols. (Norman: University of Oklahoma Press, 1985), 2:596.

6. This statement of John Ross to the Congress in 1866 is quoted in *Reply of the Southern Delegates . . . to the President, Senate and House* (Washington, D.C.: McGill and Witherow, 1866), p. 5.

7. E. C. Boudinot and William P. Adair, *Reply of the Southern Cherokees* (Washington, D.C., 1866), p. 5.

8. Howard Q. Tyner, "The Keetoowah Society in Cherokee History" (Master's thesis, University of Tulsa, 1949), appendix A, p. 102. Gritts probably wrote this in 1864. See also T. L. Ballenger, "The Keetoowahs," typescript, in Ballenger Papers, Newberry Library, Chicago. On October 20, 1864, Gritts wrote a letter to Abraham Lincoln saying that the opponents of the Keetoowah Society were "a very few wealthy half breeds who had for many years been . . . ultraproslavery." A copy of this letter is in the Western History Collection, University of Oklahoma, Norman.

9. Tyner, "Keetoowah Society," appendix A, p. 102.

10. The pins were crossed as an "X," not as a Christian cross or a plus sign. Janey Hendrix states that "the Pins were a separate organization of activists. . . . While most of them were Keetoowahs, it was not a requirement and there were many Keetoowahs who were not Pins." Apparently, no evidence has been located for the fact that they were separate organizations, but no doubt the less militant Keetoowahs may not have worn the pins during those turbulent years. See Janey B. Hendrix, "Redbird Smith and the Nighthawk Keetoowahs," *Journal of Cherokee Studies* 8 (Fall 1983): 24.

11. Boudinot and Adair, *Reply of the Southern Cherokees*, p. 5.

12. See William P. Adair to Stand Watie, August 29, 1861, in Edward E. Dale and Gaston Litton, *Cherokee Cavaliers* (Norman: University of Oklahoma Press, 1939), p. 108.

13. Halliburton, *Red Over Black*, p. 119.

14. A copy of the constitution of the Knights of the Golden Circle and its bylaws is in the Cherokee Collection, Northeastern Oklahoma State University, Tahlequah. See also Kenny A. Franks, *Stand Watie* (Memphis: Memphis State University Press, 1979), pp. 114–15.

15. Halliburton, *Red Over Black*, pp. 119–20.

16. Quoted in Annie H. Abel, *Slaveholding Indians*, 3 vols. (Cleveland: Arthur H. Clark, 1915), 1:85.

17. This incident is described in William G. McLoughlin, *Cherokee Ghost Dance* (Macon, Ga.: Mercer University Press, 1984), pp. 343–64. For the position of the Congregational missionaries among the Choctaws with respect to slavery, see Robert Lewit, "Indian Missions and Anti-Slavery Sentiment," *Mississippi Valley Historical Review* 50 (June 1963): 39–55.

18. See American Board of Commissioners for Foreign Missions, *Fifty-first Annual Report* (Boston, 1860), p. 138; Lewit, "Indian Missions," pp. 53–54; and Charles K. Whipple, *Relations of the American Board of Commissioners for Foreign Missions to Slavery* (Boston, 1861), pp. 3–4.

19. Charles Torrey, April 10, 1860, in Papers of the American Board of Commissioners for Foreign Missions, Houghton Library, Harvard University, Cambridge (hereafter cited as ABCFM).

20. Timothy Ranney, June 16, 1860, in ABCFM.

21. Letter of Cherokee converts at Lee's Creek, Cherokee Nation, October 21, 1860, forwarded by Timothy Ranney, in ABCFM.

22. Timothy Ranney, April 23, 1861, in ABCFM.

23. Charles Torrey, October 11, 1860, in ABCFM.

24. Charles Torrey, October 9, 1860, in ABCFM; "Notes from Autobiography of C. C. Torrey," Oklahoma Historical Society, Oklahoma City.

25. Willard Upham, February 7, 1860, in ABMU.

26. John B. Jones, November 17, 1859, ABMU. The legislator may well have been William Penn Adair. See also McLoughlin, *Cherokee Ghost Dance*, p. 469.

27. Abel, *Slaveholding Indians*, 1:290–92. In 1859, after George Butler sent a sheriff to arrest Evan Jones for "abolition activities," the sheriff "was deterred from executing the order by fear of the common people." Apparently the Pins had massed before Jones's home and frightened off the sheriff. John B. Jones, November 17, 1859, in ABMU.

28. Robert Cowart to John B. Jones, September 7, 1860, in ABMU.

29. Robert Cowart to A. B. Greenwood, September 8, 1860, Government Microfilm Series, Bureau of Indian Affairs, Record Group 75, M-234, Letters Received by the Office of Indian Affairs, 1824–1881, reel 99, 0248.

30. See William G. McLoughlin, *Champions of the Cherokees: Evan and John B. Jones* (Princeton: Princeton University Press, 1990), pp. 372–75.

31. See letter of Willard Upham, April 15, 1861, in ABMU.

32. Abel, *Slaveholding Indians*, 1:125, 229–33, 242, 294–97; Robert Cowart to A. B. Greenwood, September 8, 1860, M-234, reel 99, 0248.

33. Robert Cowart to A. B. Greenwood, November 6, 1860, M-234, reel 99, 0255; Abel, *Slaveholding Indians*, 1:292–93.

34. Robert Cowart to A. B. Greenwood, February 15, 1861, M-234, reel 99, 0416.

35. John Ross to John Ogden, February 26, 1861, in Ross, *Papers of Chief John Ross*, 2:466; Abel, *Slaveholding Indians*, 1:89.

36. George Butler to Commissioner of Indian Affairs, November 23, 1856, M-234, reel 98, 0005.

37. Ross, *Papers of Chief John Ross*, 2:429.

38. Butler's report, September 10, 1858, in *Annual Report of the Commissioner of Indian Affairs* (Washington, D.C., 1858), p. 141; Elias Rector's report, September 20, 1859, in *Annual Report* (1859), p. 159; and Robert Cowart to A. B. Greenwood, November 6, 1860, M-234, reel 99, 0255, and February 15, 1861, M-234, reel 99, 0416.

39. Abel, *Slaveholding Indians*, 1:41.

40. Ibid., 1:41–42.

41. *Arkansas Gazette*, June 2, 1860.

42. *Arkansas Gazette*, June 9, 1860.

43. *Arkansas Gazette*, June 23, 1860.

44. Ross, *Papers of Chief John Ross*, 2:442.

45. Abel, *Slaveholding Indians*, 1:58.

46. J. W. Washbourne to Stand Watie, May 18, 1861, in Dale and Litton, *Cherokee Cavaliers*, p. 106.

47. Ibid., p. 107.

48. Ross, *Papers of Chief John Ross*, 2:428.

49. Ibid., 2:450.

50. A. B. Greenwood's annual report to Commissioner of Indian Affairs, 1860, Government Microfilm Series, Bureau of Indian Affairs, Record Group 75, M-348, Report Books of the Office of Indian Affairs, 1838–1885, reel 12, 0031.

51. Ross, *Papers of Chief John Ross*, 2:458.

52. Ibid., 2:458, 464.

53. Ibid., 2:459–63.

54. Ibid., 2:463.

55. Ibid., 2:464.

56. Abel, *Slaveholding Indians*, 1:115.

57. Ibid.

58. Ross, *Papers of Chief John Ross*, 2:466.

59. Abel, *Slaveholding Indians*, 1:116.

60. Ibid., 1:91–92.

61. Ibid., 1:90–94.

62. Ibid.

63. Abel, *Slaveholding Indians*, 1:111–12.

64. Ross, *Papers of Chief John Ross*, 2:470–71.

65. Ibid., 2:469.

66. Ibid., 2:470.

67. Abel, *Slaveholding Indians*, 1:129–34.

68. Ibid., 1:135. This was written in 1866.

69. Ibid.

70. Ibid., 1:144–45.

71. Ross, *Papers of Chief John Ross*, 2:473.

72. Ibid., 2:475–76.

CHAPTER SEVEN

1. Annie H. Abel, *Slaveholding Indians*, 3 vols. (Cleveland: Arthur H. Clark, 1915), 1:157.

2. Edward E. Dale and Gaston Litton, *Cherokee Cavaliers* (Norman: University of Oklahoma Press, 1939), pp. 104–5.

3. Ibid., pp. 106–7.

4. Kenny A. Franks, *Stand Watie* (Memphis: Memphis State University Press, 1979), pp. 117–18.

5. William G. McLoughlin, *Champions of the Cherokees: Evan and John B. Jones* (Princeton: Princeton University Press, 1990), pp. 392–93.

6. Abel, *Slaveholding Indians*, 1:184.

7. John Crawford to William P. Dole, June 15, 1861, Government Microfilm Series, Bureau of Indian Affairs, Record Group 75, M-234, Letters Received by the Office of Indian Affairs, 1824–1881, reel 99, 0456. See also his letter of May 21, 1861, to Dole describing the "strife and discord" throughout the nation, M-234, reel 99, 0448, and Abel, *Slaveholding Indians*, 1:185.

8. Abel, *Slaveholding Indians*, 1:53, 75, 88.

9. Ibid., 1:80.

10. John Ross, *The Papers of Chief John Ross*, introduction by Gary E. Moulton, 2 vols. (Norman: University of Oklahoma Press, 1985), 2:478.

11. Ibid., 2:479.

12. James G. Slover to E. L. Compere, June 26, 1861, in Compere Papers, Dargan-Carver Library, Nashville, Tennessee.

13. Ross, *Papers of Chief John Ross*, 2:477.

14. Ibid., 2:478.

15. Ibid., 2:479.

16. Ross's desperation at this time is indicated by a reported remark he made in August 1861: "I felt like a man standing on the bank of a swollen stream and looking at the raging waters rapidly rising, higher and higher, until the grounds around him are all overflown; and, in that trying hour, expecting every moment to be swept away by the swift current . . . perchance a floating log comes within his reach and he jumps upon and seizes it—and in floating down the stream, he may drift to shore and be saved." Ibid., 2:666.

17. Franks, *Watie*, p. 118; Abel, *Slaveholding Indians*, 1:125. The Union defeats at Bull Run and Wilson's Creek seemed to Ross to indicate that the Union might not defeat the Confederacy.

18. Ross, *Papers of Chief John Ross*, 2:482; Abel, *Slaveholding Indians*, 1:217. See also W. S. Robertson's letter to his Presbyterian mission board, October 20, 1861, Presbyterian Historical Society, Philadelphia.

19. Abel, *Slaveholding Indians*, 1:217, citing Evan Jones to William P. Dole, November 2, 1861. Watie said he and his men came armed "to protect themselves from assassination." W. Craig Gaines, *The Confederate Cherokees* (Baton Rouge: Louisiana State University Press, 1989), p. 11.

20. W. S. Robertson to the Presbyterian mission board, October 20, 1861, Presbyterian Historical Society, Philadelphia.

21. Dale and Litton, *Cherokee Cavaliers*, pp. 108–10.

22. Ross, *Papers of Chief John Ross*, 2:430–31.

23. Abel, *Slaveholding Indians*, 1:223.

24. Wardell, *Political History*, p. 131; Gaines, *Confederate Cherokees*, p. 12.

25. Abel, *Slaveholding Indians*, 1:224.

26. W. S. Robertson to the Presbyterian mission board, October 20, 1861, Presbyterian Historical Society, Philadelphia.

27. Dale and Litton, *Cherokee Cavaliers*, p. 110.

28. Ross, *Papers of Chief John Ross*, 2:483.

29. Ibid., 2:482–83; Abel, *Slaveholding Indians*, 1:227.

30. Ross, *Papers of Chief John Ross*, 2:485–86; Wardell, *Political History*, p. 132.

31. Gaines, *Confederate Cherokees*, p. 15–21.

32. Abel, *Slaveholding Indians*, 1:158–77. Ross was forced to concede, however, that Confederate railroad companies would have the right to build tracks through his nation.

33. Ross, *Papers of Chief John Ross*, 2:492–95; Wardell, *Political History*, pp. 139–41; Franks, *Stand Watie*, p. 119.

34. Ross, *Papers of Chief John Ross*, 2:494–95; Abel, *Slaveholding Indians*, 1:137.

35. A copy of this "Declaration of Independence" is included in E. C. Boudinot and William P. Adair, *Reply of the Southern Cherokees* (Washington, D.C., 1866), pp. 15–19. Though signed by Ross and other council members, Albert Pike claimed to have written it. Abel, *Slaveholding Indians*, 1:84, 297. See also Emmet Starr, *History of the Cherokee Indians* (New York: Kraus Reprint, 1969), pp. 153–58.

36. Ross, *Papers of Chief John Ross*, 2:488–89; Gaines, *Confederate Cherokees*, pp. 26–27.

37. Abel, *Slaveholding Indians*, 1:137. Watie's regiment, however, continued to function as a unit of the Confederate army.

38. Ross, *Papers of Chief John Ross*, 2:492–95.

39. Abel, *Slaveholding Indians*, 1:137.

40. Ross, *Papers of Chief John Ross*, 2:492–95.

41. Ibid., 2:495.

42. A copy of this bill of November 6, 1861, is among the Ross Papers, Gilcrease Institute, Tulsa, Oklahoma. Until the promised annuity funds arrived from the Confederate treasury, the nation remained deeply in debt.

43. Ross, *Papers of Chief John Ross*, 2:501. This antimissionary bill may have been introduced by members of the Southern Rights party to embarrass Ross and to split those full-bloods who were antimissionary traditionalists from those who were Christians.

44. For Ross's futile and unwelcome effort to persuade Opothleyoholo to agree to support the Creek treaty with the Confederacy, see his letter of August 24, 1861, in Ross, *Papers of Chief John Ross*, 2:487.

45. David McIntosh to John Drew, September 11, 1861, in Drew Papers, Gilcrease Institute, Tulsa, Oklahoma.

46. Ross, *Papers of Chief John Ross*, 2:489.

47. Ibid., 2:490.

48. Ibid., 2:496.

49. Abel, *Slaveholding Indians*, 1:253.

50. Ross, *Papers of Chief John Ross*, 2:496.

51. The most detailed descriptions of John Drew's Cherokee regiment in this encounter with Opothleyoholo can be found in Gaines, *Confederate Cherokees*, pp. 34–74; Abel, *Slaveholding Indians*, 1:254–61; and Franks, *Stand Watie*, pp. 120–23.

52. Franks, *Stand Watie*, p. 120. Many free blacks joined Opothleyoholo because the Creek council had voted on March 1, 1861, that all free blacks had ten days to choose a master or face sale to the highest Creek bidder. Gaines, *Confederate Cherokees*, pp. 24, 34.

53. Ross, *Papers of Chief John Ross*, 2:505.

54. Ibid. See also Gaines, *Confederate Cherokees*, p. 39.

55. Ross, *Papers of Chief John Ross*, 2:507; Gaines, *Confederate Cherokees*, pp. 42–48.

56. Franks, *Stand Watie*, p. 121; Gaines, *Confederate Cherokees*, pp. 56–58. For a map showing Opothleyoholo's line of retreat and the various battle sites, see Abel, *Slaveholding Indians*, 1:263.

57. Franks, *Stand Watie*, p. 121.

58. Ibid., pp. 121–22.

59. For a contemporary estimate of Ross's actions by a Southern Cherokee, see Stephen Foreman, Diary, in Western History Collection, University of Oklahoma, Norman. Ross's own self-serving version of this was contained in a statement to President Andrew Johnson in 1866, in which he tried to explain away his apparent desertion of the Union cause at this time. As soon as he heard of the desertions from Drew's regiment, the statement claimed, "John Ross did with all possible speed, hasten to Col.

Cooper's headquarters at Fort Gibson, and there, by his tact and indomitable perseverance, prevailed with the rebel officers to waive the whole matter, and that very day had the satisfaction of warding off from the loyal [pro-Union] Cherokees the penalty that threatened for this act of devotion to the Union cause." *Communication of the Delegation of the Cherokee Nation to the President of the United States* (Washington, D.C.: Gibson Brothers, 1866), p. 11.

60. Abel, *Slaveholding Indians*, 1:257; Gaines, *Confederate Cherokees*, p. 57.

61. Ross, *Papers of Chief John Ross*, 2:508; Wardell, *Political History*, p. 132; Gaines, *Confederate Cherokees*, p. 61.

62. Ross, *Papers of Chief John Ross*, 2:508; Dale and Litton, *Cherokee Cavaliers*, p. 112.

63. Dale and Litton, *Cherokee Cavaliers*, p. 113.

64. Foreman, Diary, January 11, 1862, in Western History Collection, University of Oklahoma, Norman.

65. Ross, *Papers of Chief John Ross*, 2:509.

66. For descriptions of this defeat, see Gaines, *Confederate Cherokees*, pp. 76–93, and Alvin M. Josephy, Jr., *The Civil War in the American West* (New York: Knopf, 1991), pp. 324–48. See also Franks, *Stand Watie*, pp. 124–26, and Abel, *Slaveholding Indians*, 1:138. Some of the Indians (including Cherokees) on the Confederate side were accused of scalping and mutilating Union soldiers.

67. Ross, *Papers of Chief John Ross*, 2:510.

68. Abel, *Slaveholding Indians*, 1:138; Gaines, *Confederate Cherokees*, pp. 77–92.

69. Ross, *Papers of Chief John Ross*, 2:511.

70. Ibid., 2:512–13.

71. Ibid.; Gaines, *Confederate Cherokees*, p. 91.

72. Abel, *Slaveholding Indians*, 1:138, 165.

73. Ross, *Papers of Chief John Ross*, 2:513–15.

74. Foreman, Diary, January 11, 1862, in Western History Collection, University of Oklahoma, Norman.

75. See Evan Jones's letter of October 16, 1861, in American Baptist Mission Union Papers, American Baptist Historical Society, Rochester, New York, describing his meeting with Dole. For Jones's role in seeking Dole's assistance for Ross in 1861–62, see McLoughlin, *Evan and John B. Jones*, pp. 396–406. For Carruth's statement, see Abel, *Slaveholding Indians*, 1:85.

76. Evan Jones to William P. Dole, January 21, 1862, M-234, reel 99, 0586.

CHAPTER EIGHT

1. See, for example, W. Craig Gaines, *The Confederate Cherokees* (Baton Rouge: Louisiana State University Press, 1989), pp. 34–35, 39.

2. Annie H. Abel, *Slaveholding Indians*, 3 vols. (Cleveland: Arthur H. Clark, 1915), 1:229, 2:57–59; David A. Nichols, *Lincoln and the Indians* (Columbia: University of Missouri Press, 1978), p. 49.

3. Abel, *Slaveholding Indians*, 2:75.

4. See Alvin M. Josephy, Jr., *The Civil War in the American West* (New York: Knopf, 1991), p. 324; Gaines, *Confederate Cherokees*, pp. 80–81, 83, 88–89; and Abel, *Slaveholding Indians*, 2:148.

5. Nichols, *Lincoln and the Indians*, p. 49; Abel, *Slaveholding Indians*, 2:100–109.

6. John Ross, *The Papers of Chief John Ross*, introduction by Gary E. Moulton, 2 vols. (Norman: University of Oklahoma Press, 1985), 2:521; Abel, *Slaveholding Indians*, 2:114; Gaines, *Confederate Cherokees*, p. 96.

7. See letter of David E. Corwin describing the formation of these home guard regiments in *Communication of the Delegation of the Cherokee Nation to the President of the United States* (Washington, D.C.: Gibson Brothers, 1866), pp. 6–7, at the Gilcrease Institute, Tulsa, Oklahoma.

8. Gaines, *Confederate Cherokees*, pp. 96–102; Kenny A. Franks, *Stand Watie* (Memphis: Memphis State University Press, 1979), p. 128.

9. Gary E. Moulton, *John Ross: Cherokee Chief* (Athens: University of Georgia Press, 1978), pp. 174–75. Carruth shared Dole's view of Ross's loyalty, saying, "Many of the [refugee] Indians regard him as Secesh, but I will not credit it." See his letter to Walter Lowrie, February 20, 1862, in the Presbyterian Historical Society, Philadelphia. See also Wardell, *Political History*, p. 152, and Abel, *Slaveholding Indians*, 2:122.

10. Moulton, *John Ross*, p. 174.

11. Ibid., pp. 173–74.

12. Josephy, *Civil War in the American West*, p. 356; Abel, *Slaveholding Indians*, 2:130; Gaines, *Confederate Cherokees*, p. 102; Franks, *Stand Watie*, p. 129.

13. Abel, *Slaveholding Indians*, 2:130; Gaines, *Confederate Cherokees*, p. 102.

14. See David E. Corwin's letter in *Communication of the Delegation*, p. 7.

15. Abel, *Slaveholding Indians*, 2:135–37; Ross, *Papers of Chief John Ross*, 2:515–16; Gaines, *Confederate Cherokees*, pp. 105–9.

16. Salomon (or Solomon) later told General James G. Blunt, the head of the Union forces in the Southwest, that Weer "was either insane, premeditated treachery to his troops, or perhaps that his grossly intemperate habits, long continued, have produced idiocy or monomania." Blunt, however, brought no charges against either Weer or Salomon. See Josephy, *Civil War in the American West*, p. 357; Abel, *Slaveholding Indians*, 2:139–55; Gaines, *Confederate Cherokees*, pp. 112–16.

17. Abel, *Slaveholding Indians*, 2:142–45.

18. Moulton, *John Ross*, p. 175; Abel, *Slaveholding Indians*, 2:193.

19. Ross, *Papers of Chief John Ross*, 2:516–18.

20. Moulton, *John Ross*, p. 176.

21. Ibid., p. 178; Gaines, *Confederate Cherokees*, p. 11.

22. Hannah Hicks, Diary, August 24, 1862, at the Gilcrease Institute, Tulsa, Oklahoma.

23. Franks, *Stand Watie*, p. 131.

24. Hannah Hicks, Diary, August 31, 1862, at the Gilcrease Institute, Tulsa, Oklahoma.

25. See Josephy, *Civil War in the American West*, pp. 362–67, and Grant Foreman, *A History of Oklahoma* (Norman: University of Oklahoma Press, 1942), pp. 114–18.

26. The original documents of the Loyal or Ross council from 1863 to 1866 are at the Oklahoma Historical Society, Oklahoma City. See also William G. McLoughlin,

Champions of the Cherokees: Evan and John B. Jones (Princeton: Princeton University Press, 1990), pp. 408–9.

27. See the records of the Loyal councils, 1863–66, Oklahoma Historical Society, Oklahoma City. See also Abel, *Slaveholding Indians*, 2:256; Ross, *Papers of Chief John Ross*, 2:534–35; and Wardell, *Political History*, pp. 172–74. Between the emancipation acts of February 17 and February 19, 1863, a bill was voted on, but evidently never enacted, that asked the federal government to compensate Cherokee slave owners for slaves that were freed. The act of February 19 was not signed into law until February 21. See Cherokee Nation Records, reel 8, 0009–19, Oklahoma Historical Society, Oklahoma City.

28. Daniel F. Littlefield, Jr., *The Cherokee Freedmen* (Westport, Conn.: Greenwood Press, 1978), pp. 16–17. John Ross took several of his house slaves with him to Washington in 1862, but at the time of his death in August 1866, they were still unaware of the Cherokee emancipation act.

29. See the records of the Loyal councils, 1863–66, Oklahoma Historical Society, Oklahoma City. This delegation did not reach Washington until June 1863. Ross, *Papers of Chief John Ross*, 2:536–37. The instructions to the delegates are contained in the Cherokee Nation Records, reel 8, 0019ff., Oklahoma Historical Society, Oklahoma City.

30. See Josephy, *Civil War in the American West*, pp. 370–71; Abel, *Slaveholding Indians*, 2:258–61; Franks, *Stand Watie*, pp. 136–37; and Foreman, *Oklahoma*, pp. 115–17.

31. Justin Harlin to W. G. Coffin, September 2, 1863, in *Annual Report of the Commissioner of Indian Affairs* (Washington, D.C., 1863), p. 179. See also the other letters of Harlin (or Harlan) for 1863 contained in ibid., pp. 203, 211.

32. See Josephy, *Civil War in the American West*, pp. 371–72; Foreman, *Oklahoma*, pp. 120–24; Abel, *Slaveholding Indians*, 2:288–90; and Franks, *Stand Watie*, pp. 141, 147–48.

33. The confiscation act is contained in the Cherokee Nation Records, 1863, Oklahoma Historical Society, Oklahoma City. See also Wardell, *Political History*, p. 174.

34. Justin Harlin to W. G. Coffin, September 2, 1863, in *Annual Report* (1863), pp. 179–81. See also the letter of A. G. Proctor, November 28, 1863, in ibid., p. 223. Harlin laid the blame for all of these problems directly on the U.S. government: "The Cherokees have not received the protection stipulated in the treaty with them. . . . The government should send a sufficient force into the Territory to overawe the rebels . . . and that force should be continued as long as the war lasts."

35. William P. Ross to "Willie" [Ross], December 27, 1864, in Ross Papers, Gilcrease Institute, Tulsa, Oklahoma.

36. Justin Harlin to W. G. Coffin, September 2, 1863, in *Annual Report* (1863), p. 179.

37. Stephen Foreman, Diary, July 8 and 28, 1862, in Western History Collection, University of Oklahoma, Norman. Whenever the Pins "stole" slaves, they claimed to be liberating them, but they may have sold some to slave traders from the southern states, and some slaves, loyal to their masters or fearful of what the Pins might do, refused to be "liberated" and were shot.

38. Hannah Hicks, Diary, September 7, 1862, at the Gilcrease Institute, Tulsa, Okla-

homa. There are many similar entries. Hicks's husband was a mixed-blood Cherokee mistakenly shot by a Pin who thought he was one of the Watie faction.

39. Abel, *Slaveholding Indians*, 2:260, 263–64.

40. Justin Harlin to W. G. Coffin, September 2, 1863, in *Annual Report* (1863), p. 179.

41. Edward E. Dale and Gaston Litton, *Cherokee Cavaliers* (Norman: University of Oklahoma Press, 1939), pp. 143, 150; Abel, *Slaveholding Indians*, 2:279, 299, 317.

42. Dale and Litton, *Cherokee Cavaliers*, p. 137.

43. Ibid., p. 141.

44. Wardell, *Political History*, pp. 166–67; Dale and Litton, *Cherokee Cavaliers*, p. 126; Franks, *Stand Watie*, p. 136. This idea was first discussed on March 13.

45. Dale and Litton, *Cherokee Cavaliers*, p. 126.

46. Abel, *Slaveholding Indians*, 2:281; Franks, *Stand Watie*, p. 136; Wardell, *Political History*, p. 167. Eventually Watie's council did arrive at a compromise on this measure, because the regiment desperately needed men. The compromise limited the granting of bounties to a total of 1,000 white volunteers and to 160 acres each. These bounty lands were to be located in the Cherokee Outlet, not in the national homeland, and bounty land did not carry with it the right to Cherokee citizenship. It is not known whether any whites ever took advantage of this, and the defeat of the Confederacy mooted any benefits.

47. Dale and Litton, *Cherokee Cavaliers*, p. 128.

48. Ibid.

49. Ibid., pp. 144–45.

50. Ibid., pp. 188–89.

51. Ibid., pp. 156–57.

52. Ross, *Papers of Chief John Ross*, 2:649.

53. Moulton, *John Ross*, p. 178; Abel, *Slaveholding Indians*, 2:99; Wardell, *Political History*, p. 186.

54. Abel, *Slaveholding Indians*, 2:230, 233; Wardell, *Political History*, pp. 184, 186.

55. Wardell, *Political History*, pp. 160, 183. Pope's proposal was adopted by Congress in 1871. For Pope's view of the Indians, see Richard N. Ellis, *General Pope and U.S. Indian Policy* (Albuquerque: University of New Mexico Press, 1970).

56. Wardell, *Political History*, p. 183.

57. Moulton, *John Ross*, pp. 179–80.

58. Ibid., p. 177.

59. Ross, *Papers of Chief John Ross*, 2:560–68. They also asked President Lincoln's help on February 18, 1864. Ibid., 2:564.

60. Ibid., 2:596–97.

61. Ibid., 2:596. For other complaints about the robbing of Cherokees under this order, see Justin Harlin to W. G. Coffin, July 30, 1864, Government Microfilm Series, Bureau of Indian Affairs, Record Group 75, M-234, Letters Received by the Office of Indian Affairs, 1824–1881, reel 99, 0778; Smith Christie to W. G. Coffin, September 7, 1864, M-234, reel 99, 0789; and the protest by the Cherokee Loyal council, n.d., folder 64, item 5, in Ross Papers, Gilcrease Institute, Tulsa, Oklahoma. Agent Justin Harlin wrote to Colonel William G. Coffin on September 30, 1864, that the whites on the frontier caused as much devastation among the Cherokees as Watie's soldiers: "The

rebel army, bushwhackers and guerillas are not the worst enemies the Indians have. While the rebels, bushwhackers and guerillas have taken horses, cattle, hogs, corn and other crops—all they wanted—white men, loyal or pretending to be so, have taken five times as much and all kinds of stock has been driven north and west and sold" to enrich these unscrupulous frontier whites. *Annual Report* (1864), p. 309.

62. John P. Usher to W. P. Dole, April 6, 1865, M-234, reel 100, 0058.

63. Wardell, *Political History*, p. 178. Franks, *Stand Watie*, p. 181, states that Watie formally resigned his commission on June 25, 1865.

64. Franks, *Stand Watie*, pp. 182–83.

65. Charles G. Royce, *The Cherokee Nation of Indians* (Chicago: Aldine, 1975), p. 210; Wardell, *Political History*, p. 187.

66. Abel, *Slaveholding Indians*, 2:203–4. Ross said, "I defy any person to come forward and prove these charges against me. . . . I had three sons in your army, also three grandsons and three nephews. . . . If we have rights, we ought to be permitted to express them. . . . I have never been charged with being an enemy of the United States."

67. Royce, *Cherokee Nation*, p. 222; Wardell, *Political History*, p. 192. The treaty commissioners saw no validity in Ross's election (in absentia in 1862) by a couple of home guard regiments. They seemed to believe that Stand Watie truly represented the Cherokees, because he was elected in Tahlequah, he was on the ground (more or less) throughout the war, and the nation was still (in the commissioners' view) allied with the Confederacy in 1863–65. However, Watie too had been elected essentially by the men in his own troops, not by a regular national election.

68. Wardell, *Political History*, pp. 191–92; Royce, *Cherokee Nation*, p. 222.

CHAPTER NINE

1. Cherokee Nation Records, November 2 and 3, 1863, vol. 248, pp. 80–81, Oklahoma Historical Society, Oklahoma City.

2. *Reply of the Southern Delegates . . . to the President, Senate and House* (Washington, D.C.: McGill and Witherow, 1866), p. 8. This was probably written by E. C. Boudinot.

3. Russell Thornton cites an estimate of 14,000 by James Mooney and an estimate by Donald Englund of over 17,000; "Englund's figure includes, however, all Cherokee citizens—that is, Cherokees, freedmen, white, Shawnees, and Delawares. Considering only Cherokees by blood lowers the figure considerably. They probably numbered not more than 15,000." Russell Thornton, *The Cherokees: A Population History* (Lincoln: University of Nebraska Press, 1990), p. 94.

4. *Reply of the Delegates of the Cherokee Nation to the Demands of the Commissioner of Indian Affairs, May 12, 1866* (Washington, D.C.: Gibson Brothers, 1866), p. 10; John Ross, *The Papers of Chief John Ross*, introduction by Gary E. Moulton, 2 vols. (Norman: University of Oklahoma Press, 1985), 2:596.

5. Morris Wardell, *A Political History of the Cherokee Nation, 1838–1907* (Norman: University of Oklahoma Press, 1938), p. 199; Gary E. Moulton, *John Ross: Cherokee Chief* (Athens: University of Georgia Press, 1978), p. 192.

6. This letter by Washbourne (or Washburn) is in Edward E. Dale and Gaston Litton, *Cherokee Cavaliers* (Norman: University of Oklahoma Press, 1939), pp. 243–44.

7. Charles G. Royce, *The Cherokee Nation of Indians* (Chicago: Aldine, 1975), pp. 224–25; Wardell, *Political History*, pp. 196–201.

8. Dale and Litton, *Cherokee Cavaliers*, pp. 243–46; Wardell, *Political History*, p. 201.

9. Dale and Litton, *Cherokee Cavaliers*, p. 246.

10. *Reply of the Delegates*, p. 4.

11. This treaty is reprinted in Emmet Starr, *History of the Cherokee Indians* (New York: Kraus Reprint, 1969), pp. 167–77. Senator James Harlan of Kansas had proposed the territorialization bill to which Ross expressed opposition here. Harlan had since been appointed secretary of the interior, in charge of all Indian affairs. See Wardell, *Political History*, p. 198.

12. Starr, *History*, p. 167.

13. Wardell, *Political History*, p. 203. The Senate suggested a few minor amendments in the wording of the treaty, which the delegates agreed to on July 31, and the treaty was officially "proclaimed" on August 11, 1866.

14. Some would argue that he was not completely honest in some of the ways in which he tried to stall removal of the Cherokees from 1836 to 1838, and of course, the Southern Cherokees always considered him devious at best.

15. Wardell, *Political History*, p. 206.

16. Ibid., p. 205.

17. Dale and Litton, *Cherokee Cavaliers*, p. 247.

18. Daniel F. Littlefield, *The Cherokee Freedmen* (Westport, Conn.: Greenwood Press, 1978), pp. 25–29.

19. John Ross believed this arrangement would be temporary. It permitted a referendum to be conducted in the Canadian District, with the permission of the president of the United States, whenever Ross felt that the old animosities had subsided and the Canadian District wished to return to a position similar to those of the other eight districts.

20. Wardell, *Political History*, pp. 206–7.

21. Ibid., p. 209; John P. Humphreys to Commissioner of Indian Affairs, December 31, 1866, and January 18, 1867, Government Microfilm Series, Bureau of Indian Affairs, Record Group 75, M-234, Letters Received by the Office of Indian Affairs, 1824–1881, reel 101, 0054, 0063.

22. Wardell, *Political History*, pp. 212, 255.

23. See M-234, reel 101, 0285 (November 2, 1866), and "Act of Agreement with the Union Pacific Railroad," October 31, 1866, in "Railroads," Box 1, Western History Collection, University of Oklahoma, Norman. This railroad later became the Missouri, Kansas, and Texas Railroad.

24. Wardell, *Political History*, p. 213.

25. Royce, *Cherokee Nation*, p. 228; Wardell, *Political History*, p. 213.

26. Grant Foreman, *A History of Oklahoma* (Norman: University of Oklahoma Press, 1942), pp. 173–74. See also V. V. Masterson, *The Katy Railroad and the Last Frontier* (Norman: University of Oklahoma Press, 1952).

27. Royce, *Cherokee Nation*, p. 227. Dennis Cooley's report, in *Annual Report of*

the Commissioner of Indian Affairs (Washington, D.C., 1866), p. 13, said that the requirement that the Neutral Lands be paid for in cash resulted from the fear of receiving payment in Cherokee scrip: "The language referring to a sale 'for cash' [was] well understood by both parties to the treaty, being to exclude the receipt of a large amount of depreciated Cherokee scrip in payment for these lands."

28. Royce, *Cherokee Nation*, pp. 227–28; Wardell, *Political History*, pp. 213–14; M-234, reel 101, 1135. This required an amendment to the Treaty of 1866, to which the Cherokees agreed. There were only nineteen Cherokee families and a handful of blacks living on the Neutral Lands out of a total of 20,000 squatters. The squatters claimed and got 154,395 acres of the 800,000 for one dollar an acre—and many defaulted on their payments. See Cherokee Nation Records, reel 100, 1576, and reel 101, 1285 and 1135, Oklahoma Historical Society, Oklahoma City.

29. Harlan's report is in *Condition of the Indian Tribes: Report of the Special Joint Committee* (Washington, D.C.: Government Printing Office, 1867), pp. 442–50.

30. Ibid., pp. 446, 449. Agent Harlin said Senator Harlan's bill to consolidate all of the tribes under one government in a federal territory would be folly. "Two-fifths of the Cherokees, one-half or more of the Creeks and Seminoles, nine-tenths of the Choctaws and Chickasaws were rebels. . . . They are rebels still," and under a consolidated territorial government, they would elect rebels to office. Ibid., p. 446.

31. For the decision of the Cherokee council to publish bilingual textbooks for use in the public schools, see Cherokee Nation Records, November 29, 1866, vol. 248, reel 8, 0108, and November 23, 1867, vol. 253, reel 8, 0148, Oklahoma Historical Society, Oklahoma City.

32. William G. McLoughlin, *Champions of the Cherokees: Evan and John B. Jones* (Princeton: Princeton University Press, 1990), pp. 470–71. Justin Harlin said in August 11, 1866, "I am of opinion there are not less than twelve and perhaps fifteen hundred orphans in the nation." *Condition of the Indian Tribes*, p. 449.

33. McLoughlin, *Evan and John B. Jones*, pp. 468–69.

34. Ibid., pp. 459–62.

35. William B. Davis's report, October 1, 1868, in *Annual Report* (1868), p. 280.

36. John P. Humphreys to Commissioner of Indian Affairs, January 18, 1867, M-234, reel 101, 0063.

37. Kenny A. Franks, *Stand Watie* (Memphis: Memphis State University Press, 1979), p. 157.

38. Dale and Litton, *Cherokee Cavaliers*, p. 249.

39. Ibid., pp. 252–53.

40. Wardell, *Political History*, p. 211.

41. Dale and Litton, *Cherokee Cavaliers*, p. 246.

42. W. L. G. Miller to Nathaniel G. Taylor, October 2, 1867, M-234, reel 101, 0455. See also William G. McLoughlin, "Ghost Dance Movements," *Ethnohistory* 37 (Winter 1990): 25–44.

43. See the obituary of Miller in the *New York Herald*, September 16, 1872, clipping in Foreman Papers, box 57, folder 6, p. 66, Gilcrease Institute, Tulsa, Oklahoma.

44. Franks, *Stand Watie*, p. 195. Shortly after Downing's election, Watie was approached by his brother-in-law, John Candy, with a proposal to continue the division between the Loyal and Southern parties and to work for the overthrow of Downing.

Watie rejected the idea. At various times over the next three years, E. C. Boudinot and others urged Watie to run for a seat in the National Council to assist them in their various anti-Downing schemes, but he steadfastly refused. Watie was sixty-two years old in 1867, worn out by his military efforts and saddened by the deaths of his two sons, Saladin and Watica, whom he dearly loved. The strength of the Southern party waned steadily after 1867 with Watie's retirement from politics. By 1870 the federal agent reported that, as a party, it had disappeared. See ibid., p. 196, and Agent John M. Craig's report, September 30, 1870, in *Annual Report* (1870), p. 289.

45. Dale and Litton, *Cherokee Cavaliers*, p. 261. Saladin Watie died on February 13, 1868.

46. Nathaniel G. Taylor's report, in *Annual Report* (1868), p. 17.

47. Royce, *Cherokee Nation*, pp. 230–32.

48. Wardell, *Political History*, pp. 215–16.

49. William B. Davis's report, October 1, 1868, in *Annual Report* (1868), p. 280.

50. Wardell, *Political History*, p. 224; Littlefield, *Cherokee Freedmen*, pp. 21–24. The southern superintendent of Indian affairs tried to establish a colony of former slaves in the Indian Territory in 1867 but failed. Ibid., p. 47. The Cherokee council considered, but rejected, several bills put forward to grant former slaves tracts of their own for a separate colony within the nation, in 1866 and 1868, but these failed to pass. Wardell, *Political History*, p. 224.

51. For a thorough discussion of the problems of the former Cherokee slaves in these years, see Littlefield, *Cherokee Freedmen*.

52. Ibid., p. 28.

53. Wardell, *Political History*, pp. 226–27. The division within the nation was reflected in a statement by the agent explaining the difficulties the former slaves were experiencing: "Chief Downing and Colonel W. P. Ross agree in urging their adoption as citizens. The Editor of the *Cherokee Advocate* [W. P. Boudinot] and Chief Justice Vann on the other hand represent those who are opposed . . . as it involved the granting of lands and monies to them and diminishes the amount thus granted, the land and money remaining as the common heritage of the Cherokees." John B. Jones to F. A. Walker, February 21, 1872, M-234, reel 105, 0283.

54. Littlefield, *Cherokee Freedmen*, pp. 77–79.

55. John B. Jones to Commissioner of Indian Affairs, February 10, 1873, M-234, reel 106, 0183; Littlefield, *Cherokee Freedmen*, pp. 52–55, 252–53.

56. Wardell, *Political History*, p. 227. These bills were hotly debated from 1870 to 1877.

57. Louis Rough to President U. S. Grant, February 8, 1872, M-234, reel 105, 0903.

CHAPTER TEN

1. The agents were Justin Harlin, 1863–66; John P. Humphreys, 1867; E. C. Cleaveland, 1867; William Touples, 1867; J. J. Henderson, 1867; William B. Davis, 1868; and John Craig, 1869–70.

2. John B. Jones's report, September 1871, in *Annual Report of the Commissioner of Indian Affairs* (Washington, D.C., 1871), pp. 563–69.

3. Ibid.

4. Ibid.

5. Ibid.

6. Morris Wardell, *A Political History of the Cherokee Nation, 1838–1907* (Norman: University of Oklahoma Press, 1938), p. 217; Charles G. Royce, *The Cherokee Nation of Indians* (Chicago: Aldine, 1975), pp. 235–36.

7. Wardell, *Political History*, p. 217; Royce, *Cherokee Nation*, pp. 235–36.

8. Much later, the Pawnees, Tankawas, Poncas, Otoes, and Missouris moved into the Cherokee Outlet. Royce, *Cherokee Nation*, p. 242.

9. Royce, *Cherokee Nation*, p. 247.

10. John B. Jones to Commissioner of Indian Affairs, April 6, 1871, Government Microfilm Series, Bureau of Indian Affairs, Record Group 75, M-234, Letters Received by the Office of Indian Affairs, 1824–1881, reel 104, 0734.

11. Wardell, *Political History*, p. 275; Royce, *Cherokee Nation*, pp. 237–41.

12. John B. Jones's report, September 1871, in *Annual Report* (1871), p. 563; Royce, *Cherokee Nation*, pp. 234–38.

13. John B. Jones, September 21, [1873], in *Annual Report* (1873), p. 202.

14. For the Eastern Band in the Civil War, see John R. Finger, *The Eastern Band of Cherokees, 1819–1900* (Knoxville: University of Tennessee Press, 1984), chap. 5 and p. 109.

15. For the controversies over moving members of the eastern Cherokees to join those in the West, see ibid., pp. 103–5, 115; John Craig to Commissioner of Indian Affairs, October 30, 1869, M-234, reel 102, 0186–89; Gilbert Falls to Commissioner of Indian Affairs, March 15, 1867, M-234, reel 101, 0198; and George W. Bushyhead to Commissioner of Indian Affairs, March 15, 1867, M-234, reel 101, 0630.

16. For a list of expenses of every delegation from 1871 to 1878, see the speech of Chief Dennis W. Bushyhead in the *Indian Journal* (Muskogee, Oklahoma), July 31, 1879, clipping in Litton Transcripts, Oklahoma Historical Society, Oklahoma City. For evidence that the delegation bribed congressmen to vote against territorial bills, see C. H. Taylor to James M. Bell, January 9, 1878, in Bell Papers, Western History Collection, University of Oklahoma, Norman. Taylor, a member of the council, mentioned that W. P. Adair, when requesting a large sum of money for the delegation to Washington, "tryes to maik the impression that money will buy such men as Senator Ingalls and Gen. Alf Scales, Chairman of the Indian Committy of the house [of Representatives]." Taylor, being one who opposed sending delegations to Washington, chose not to believe Adair's allegation that money was needed for bribes.

17. The speech of Chief Dennis W. Bushyhead in the *Indian Journal* (Muskogee, Oklahoma), July 31, 1879, clipping in Litton Transcripts, Oklahoma Historical Society, Oklahoma City, notes that the delegations to Congress in 1873 and 1874 spent a total of $59,000 in lawyers' fees.

18. Emmet Starr, *History of the Cherokee Indians* (New York: Kraus Reprint, 1969), p. 170.

19. Edward E. Dale and Gaston Litton, *Cherokee Cavaliers* (Norman: University of Oklahoma Press, 1939), p. 259; Kenny A. Franks, *Stand Watie* (Memphis: Memphis State University Press, 1979), pp. 196–97, 201–2; Lois Forde, "Elias Cornelius Boudinot" (Ph.D. diss., Columbia University, 1951), chap. 15.

20. Franks, *Stand Watie*, p. 197.

21. Ibid., p. 205. See also E. C. Boudinot's printed memorial to George S. Boutwell, 1870, Western History Collection, University of Oklahoma, Norman, and *Cherokee Advocate*, March 18, July 8, and October 21, 1871.

22. Francis P. Prucha, *The Great Father*, 2 vols. (Lincoln: University of Nebraska Press, 1984), 1:531; Wardell, *Political History*, p. 256. This law contained another clause that stated, "Nothing herein contained shall be construed to invalidate or impair the obligation of any treaty heretofore lawfully made and ratified with any such Indian nation or tribe." It was this clause that made the Cherokees so determined to preserve their treaty rights. It was not their only bulwark of sovereignty.

23. See *Cherokee Advocate*, July 8, 1871.

24. E. C. Boudinot, claiming innocence, pursued his problem through appeals to Congress and President Grant and eventually won remuneration of $3,000 for claims for damages. For some reason the criminal charge against Boudinot was never pressed, but he was left with a large debt for legal fees. See Forde, "Boudinot," p. 140.

25. *Cherokee Advocate*, July 8, 1871.

26. *Cherokee Advocate*, October 21, 1871.

27. Ibid.

28. See E. C. Boudinot's printed memorial to George S. Boutwell, 1870, in Western History Collection, University of Oklahoma, Norman.

29. Royce, *Cherokee Nation*, p. 227; Wardell, *Political History*, p. 277.

30. Wardell, *Political History*, p. 277; Royce, *Cherokee Nation*, p. 227. See George Rainey, *The Cherokee Strip* (Guthrie, Okla.: Co-operative Publishing Company, 1933). The total payment came to $560,302.

31. Dale and Litton, *Cherokee Cavaliers*, p. 259. E. C. Boudinot wrote his bill in December 1867; his letter to Watie was dated January 9, 1868. See H. Craig Miner, *The Corporation and the Indian* (Columbia: University of Missouri Press, 1976), pp. 21–27.

32. See Foreman Papers, box 1, folder 16, Gilcrease Institute, Tulsa, Oklahoma.

33. Petition of the Cherokee Delegates to Congress, 1869, in *Annual Report* (1869), appendix F, p. 99.

34. See Cherokee Delegation to Commissioner of Indian Affairs, April 14 and January 18, 1870, M-234, reel 103, 0537, 0730. The council instructed its delegates to Washington in 1870 to tell the secretary of the interior that constructing their own railroad was of "vital importance" to their future. At the same time, the delegates also expressed to him their fear that white railroad builders posed a serious threat to their sovereignty: "They are assured that the possession and ownership of a most valuable tract or belt of land through the heart of their country by a corporation of citizens of the United States or foreign countries—capitalists and strangers who have no sympathy for Indians or their peculiarities . . . could only result in the disruption of their Nationality and the ruin of their people." Miner, *Corporation*, p. 26.

35. John Craig's report, September 20, 1870, in *Annual Report* (1870), pp. 285–87.

36. John B. Jones's report, September 1871, in *Annual Report* (1871), p. 566.

37. Dale and Litton, *Cherokee Cavaliers*, p. 301.

38. V. V. Masterson, *The Katy Railroad and the Last Frontier* (Norman: University of Oklahoma Press, 1952), pp. 74–75.

39. Miner, *Corporation*, p. 26. For maps showing the routes of the early railroads through the Cherokee Nation, see Masterson, *Katy Railroad*, pp. 6, 12, 75, 97, 270.

40. Wardell, *Political History*, pp. 255–65; Masterson, *Katy Railroad*, pp. 58–104. Masterson describes in detail how the railroads competing to be the first to reach the Cherokee border cheated in the way they laid their tracks and in their claims for having completed them.

41. Masterson, *Katy Railroad*, pp. 104–12. While Masterson's book provides a journalistic overview of the early railroads through the Cherokee Nation, the day-to-day details can be found in reports of the Cherokee agent and the southern superintendency. See, for example, John Craig to Commissioner of Indian Affairs, June 14, 1870, M-234, reel 103, 0257; John Craig to Commissioner of Indian Affairs, April 29, 1871, M-234, reel 104, 0055; and H. R. Clem to Secretary of the Interior, M-348, reel 20, 0012. For E. C. Boudinot's fraudulent effort to profit from advance knowledge of the railroad junction at Vinita, see Miner, *Corporation*, p. 44.

42. Wardell, *Political History*, p. 259. See also Grant Foreman, *A History of Oklahoma* (Norman: University of Oklahoma Press, 1942), pp. 169–81.

43. Wardell, *Political History*, p. 260; Foreman, *Oklahoma*, pp. 209–12.

44. Wardell, *Political History*, pp. 260–61.

45. John Craig to Commissioner of Indian Affairs, November 30, 1870, M-234, reel 103, 0485–97.

46. John B. Jones's report, September 1871, in *Annual Report* (1871), p. 566. See also the protest of Agent John Craig to the commissioner of Indian affairs that the railroad was illegally cutting Cherokee timber, September 15, 1870, M-234, reel 103, 0379. When the Cherokees tried to prevent the timber cutting, the railroads were able to get the U.S. Army to protect them against what they considered a threat to the safety of their workers. M-234, reel 103, 0396. The Bureau of Indian Affairs said it lacked sufficient evidence that the timber cutting was illegal. M-234, reel 103, 0807. Many other examples of railroad depredations are contained in the reports of the federal agents in these years. See William G. McLoughlin, *Champions of the Cherokees: Evan and John B. Jones* (Princeton: Princeton University Press, 1990), pp. 459–60.

47. John B. Jones to Commissioner of Indian Affairs, December 16, 1871, M-234, reel 104, 1105.

48. The Audrain case continued for over a year. See John B. Jones to Commissioner of Indian Affairs, December 16, 1871, M-234, reel 104, 1105, and reel 105, 0140, 0368, 0379, 0577, 0580, 0669. Jones's correspondence contains claims for railroad damages by many other Cherokees in these years. Miner mentions another incident in which the Atlantic and Pacific Railroad offered only $2.50 in damages for a track passing through Audrain's cornfield, which he valued at $400. Miner notes, however, that many claims were fraudulent, resulting from land staked out by shrewd Cherokees just days before the railroad was constructed across it. Miner, *Corporation*, p. 47.

49. Dale and Litton, *Cherokee Cavaliers*, p. 289; Franks, *Stand Watie*, 202–4; Wardell, *Political History*, pp. 293–96.

50. John B. Jones's report, September 1871, in *Annual Report* (1871), p. 568.

51. *Cherokee Advocate*, October 22, 1870.

52. Ibid.

53. Lewis Downing et al., *Protest of the Cherokee Nation Against a Territorial Gov-*

ernment (Washington, D.C., 1871), p. 7, in Western History Collection, University of Oklahoma, Norman.

54. W. P. Adair to James M. Bell, April 8, 1870, in Bell Papers, Western History Collection, University of Oklahoma, Norman.

55. The logical outcome of this outlook among the most acculturated Cherokee mixed-bloods was a continuing contempt for those they considered misguided, backward, "retrograde" members of the nation who still clung to "the ineradicable spirit of communism." Spencer S. Stevens (or Stephens), one of the leading members of the nation, wrote a tract in 1882 called *The Indian Question*, in which he said, "This communistic idea of holding land is now being discussed by the best minds of the age." Stevens took the view that "land held by a community is not the best plan for any tribe of nation. It is madness and folly to entertain any theory for the settlement of this question [the Indian question] that does not include as its final object, the incorporation of the Indian into the civil body politic" of the United States. However, even in 1882 this remained the view of a decided minority. Spencer S. Stevens, *The Indian Question* (1882), in Unprocessed papers, Western History Collection, University of Oklahoma, Norman.

56. There is no clear indication that the former slaves voted consistently for the Downing party in these years, but the fact that Downing himself strongly supported admitting the "too-late Negroes" to citizenship must have appealed to many of them.

57. One of the last official statements urging a separate, segregated black colony for the former Cherokee slaves was made by the southern superintendent, L. N. Robinson, in 1867. Daniel F. Littlefield, *The Cherokee Freedmen* (Westport, Conn.: Greenwood Press, 1978), p. 45.

58. William B. Davis's report, October 1, 1868, in *Annual Report* (1868), p. 281.

59. Littlefield, *Cherokee Freedmen*, pp. 75–76.

60. See Craig's census report for 1870, M-234, reel 103, 0452.

61. John Craig's report, September 30, 1870, in *Annual Report* (1870), p. 289. Littlefield says the Cherokee Supreme Court admitted 5 former slaves' families to citizenship in July 1871 and rejected 131. *Cherokee Freedmen*, p. 72. Wardell says that in 1871 the Cherokee Supreme Court admitted 77 former slaves to citizenship in June 1871 and rejected 131. *Political History*, p. 226.

62. John B. Jones's report, September 1871, *Annual Report* (1871), p. 568. Jones was in effect advocating federal interference in Cherokee national affairs, which contradicted his defense of Cherokee sovereignty.

63. *Cherokee Advocate*, December 9, 1871.

64. Littlefield, *Cherokee Freedmen*, p. 70. The most thorough analysis of the problem of intruders and citizenship among the Cherokees in these years is Nancy Hope Sober, *The Intruders: The Illegal Residents of the Cherokee Nation, 1866–1907* (Ponca City, Okla.: Cherokee Books, 1991).

65. John B. Jones to Commissioner of Indian Affairs, February 21, 1872, M-234, reel 105, 0283.

66. Jones mentioned this order in ibid.

67. John B. Jones's report, September 1871, in *Annual Report* (1871), pp. 566–68.

68. See McLoughlin, *Evan and John B. Jones*, pp. 454–56.

69. Ibid.

70. John Pope to R. C. Drum, January 30, 1875, M-234, reel 109, 2355. See also Sober, *Intruders*, p. 91. For Pope's general position on "the Indian question," see Richard N. Ellis, *General Pope and U.S. Indian Policy* (Albuquerque: University of New Mexico Press, 1970).

71. See McLoughlin, *Evan and John B. Jones*, pp. 454–56.

72. Ibid.

73. Ibid.

74. Ibid. See also Sober, *Intruders*, pp. 43, 90–91, 94.

75. McLoughlin, *Evan and John B. Jones*, p. 458.

76. Ibid. See also Sober, *Intruders*, pp. 43, 90–91, 94.

77. Ibid.

78. Ibid.

CHAPTER ELEVEN

1. Statement of W. P. Ross to the House Committee on Territories, February 8, 1874, in Litton Transcripts, Oklahoma Historical Society, Oklahoma City. See also Mrs. W. P. Ross, ed., *The Life and Times of Hon. William P. Ross* (Fort Smith, Ark., 1893), p. 120.

2. Ibid.

3. Daniel F. Littlefield, *The Cherokee Freedmen* (Westport, Conn.: Greenwood Press, 1978), p. 81. In 1874 the United States altered its system of appointing a separate resident agent for each major Indian nation without consulting the tribes. George W. Ingalls became the agent for all five of the major tribes in the Indian Territory and established his headquarters at Muskogee in the Creek Nation. This greatly weakened the power of the agent to effectively administer to the needs of these five tribes, whose total population was close to 50,000.

4. Littlefield, *Cherokee Freedmen*, p. 82. For an excellent discussion of white intruders, see Nancy Hope Sober, *The Intruders: The Illegal Residents of the Cherokee Nation, 1866–1907* (Ponca City, Okla.: Cherokee Books, 1991), pp. 44–82.

5. Littlefield, *Cherokee Freedmen*, pp. 82–84. Congress had agreed to a request of the Cherokee delegation that the money paid by the Osages for land in the nation could be used for "bread money." When distributed per capita (and "by blood"), it amounted to about $20 per person.

6. The Osages, being settled in the Outlet, were not officially residents of the nation and made no protest. Ingalls published notices in the *Cherokee Advocate* telling former slaves who wished to challenge their being omitted from the per capita payments or the Cherokee Supreme Court's rulings against their entitlement to citizenship that they could apply to his office for assistance. Littlefield, *Cherokee Freedmen*, pp. 82–87.

7. Littlefield, *Cherokee Freedmen*, pp. 82–83.

8. Ibid., p. 83; Sober, *Intruders*, pp. 92–94.

9. Morris Wardell, *A Political History of the Cherokee Nation, 1838–1907* (Norman: University of Oklahoma Press, 1938), pp. 277–78. See Sober, *Intruders*, pp. 64–82, for the prolonged controversy over the Watts family.

10. William H. Clayton to James Bell, September 23, 1879, in Bell Papers, Western

History Collection, University of Oklahoma, Norman. Larkin's case dragged on into the 1880s, and his appeal to the Bureau of Indian Affairs for payment for the cattle taken for the taxes was upheld. The bureau required the Cherokee Nation to pay him $4,875 for his lost cattle. See Wardell, *Political History*, pp. 279–80.

11. John B. Jones to Commissioner of Indian Affairs, June 1, 1872, Government Microfilm Series, Bureau of Indian Affairs, Record Group 75, M-234, Letters Received by the Office of Indian Affairs, 1824–1881, reel 105, 0493.

12. J. R. Trott to James M. Bell, December 1, 1872, in Bell Papers, Western History Collection, University of Oklahoma, Norman. For a good summary of the Cherokee laws governing white labor permits from 1843 to 1879, see Sober, *Intruders*, pp. 28–30.

13. E. C. Boudinot et al. to John B. Jones, February 4, 1873, M-234, reel 106, 0070.

14. John B. Jones to Commissioner of Indian Affairs, February 11, 1863, M-234, reel 106, 0187.

15. Ibid.

16. John B. Jones to Commissioner of Indian Affairs, May 6, 1873, M-234, reel 106, 0378.

17. John B. Jones to Commissioner of Indian Affairs, August 25, 1874, M-234, reel 107, 0446.

18. John B. Jones's report, September 1, 1872, *Annual Report of the Commissioner of Indian Affairs* (Washington, D.C., 1872), p. 234. Similar complaints about the district court in Van Buren were made by Jones's predecessor, John Craig (September 1869, *Annual Report* [1870], p. 405).

19. John B. Jones to Commissioner of Indian Affairs, July 28, 1872, M-234, reel 105, 0606. Jones states that "this court, with its officers, has become an outrageous machine for oppressing the Cherokee people."

20. See John B. Jones's report, September 1, 1872, in *Annual Report* (1872), p. 235. See also Grant Foreman, "The Tragedy at Going Snake Courthouse," *Daily Oklahoman*, October 7, 1934; William G. McLoughlin, *Champions of the Cherokees: Evan and John B. Jones* (Princeton: Princeton University Press, 1990), pp. 463–64; Wardell, *Political History*, pp. 307–8; Theda Perdue, *Nations Remembered* (Westport, Conn.: Greenwood Press, 1980), pp. 23–25; and Janey B. Hendrix, "Redbird Smith and the Nighthawk Keetoowahs," *Journal of Cherokee Studies* 8 (Spring 1983): 22–40.

21. Enoch Hoag to Commissioner of Indian Affairs, April 27, 1872, M-234, reel 105, 0183.

22. *Cherokee Advocate*, October 4, 1873; Foreman, "Tragedy at Going Snake Courthouse."

23. Enoch Hoag to Commissioner of Indian Affairs, April 29, 1872, M-234, reel 105, 0185.

24. *Cherokee Advocate*, October 4, 1873. An act of Congress transferred the federal district court from Van Buren to Fort Smith, Arkansas. Wardell, *Political History*, p. 308.

25. See Rennard Strickland, *Fire and the Spirits: Cherokee Law from Clan to Court* (Norman: University of Oklahoma Press, 1975), p. 175, and Wardell, *Political History*, p. 309.

26. See the report of Agent George W. Ingalls on this case, November 26, 1874, in Executive Documents, Western History Collection, University of Oklahoma, Norman.

27. Ibid.

28. John B. Jones to Commissioner of Indian Affairs, December 31, 1872, M-234, reel 106, 0140.

29. See the message of Oochalata (Charles Thompson) to the Cherokee council, November 6, 1878, in Executive Documents, Western History Collection, University of Oklahoma, Norman. Thompson in this message vetoed a bill to pay for the attorneys that the council had passed because "the Bill under consideration seems to admit that Murphy was a citizen of our nation . . . and not a citizen of the United States. . . . This legislative admission is too broad and dangerous to our Nation," because "all the rest of the said North Carolina Cherokees, who are now citizens of the United States, could force themselves upon us without the admission of our Nation Council."

30. John B. Jones's report, September 20, [1873], in *Annual Report* (1873), pp. 206–7.

31. Ibid.

32. John Q. Tufts's report, October 10, 1880, in *Annual Report* (1881), p. 94.

33. John B. Jones's report, September 20, [1873], in *Annual Report* (1874), p. 206.

34. John Craig's report, October 20, 1869, in *Annual Report* (1870), p. 405.

35. See, for example, M-234, reel 106, 0140, reel 107, 0507, and reel 105, 0345. The reports of the agent for the years 1872 to 1875 contain other references as well to the general increase in criminal activities during these years.

36. John B. Jones's report, September 20, [1873], in *Annual Report* (1874), p. 206.

37. The records of the Cherokee district and circuit courts for these years are in the microfilm records of the Cherokee Nation Records, reels 49–50, Oklahoma Historical Society, Oklahoma City.

38. John Craig's report, October 20, 1869, in *Annual Report* (1870), p. 405.

39. *Cherokee Advocate*, October 11, 1873.

40. *Cherokee Advocate*, October 21, 1871.

41. John B. Jones's report, September 20, [1873], in *Annual Report* (1874), p. 206.

42. For James M. Bell's views, see Bell Papers, Western History Collection, University of Oklahoma, Norman.

43. William N. West to James M. Bell, [March 1873], in Bell Papers, Western History Collection, University of Oklahoma, Norman.

44. William Stephens to Ulysses S. Grant, March 23, 1873, M-234, reel 106, 0777.

45. E. C. Boudinot to James M. Bell, March 8, 1873, in Bell Papers, Western History Collection, University of Oklahoma, Norman. Ross and the council also opposed Bell's efforts in February 1873 to protest to Congress against the council's action.

46. J. M. Lynch to James M. Bell, February 28, 1873, in Bell Papers, Western History Collection, University of Oklahoma, Norman.

47. S. H. Payne to James M. Bell, June 10, 1873, in Bell Papers, Western History Collection, University of Oklahoma, Norman.

48. George Harkins to James M. Bell, August 22, 1873, in Bell Papers, Western History Collection, University of Oklahoma, Norman.

49. James M. Bell and Sut Beck, "Address to the Citizens of the Cherokee Nation," [May or June 1873], in Undated papers, Ross Papers, Gilcrease Institute, Tulsa, Oklahoma. They state, "We have also presented a memorial to the Secretary of the Interior upon the subject of the late infamous permit law. We know we represent nineteen-

twentieths of the industrious and intelligent class of our people." The purpose of the address was to ask Ross to "call the National Council together without delay" in order to "wipe such disgraceful legislation from the statute book." They concluded, "We invite every Cherokee citizen who wants to own his property in his own right . . . to join us."

50. Spencer S. Stephens to James M. Bell, June 11, 1874, in Bell Papers, Western History Collection, University of Oklahoma, Norman.

51. These remarks are from an undated manuscript written by Bell in Bell Papers, Western History Collection, University of Oklahoma, Norman. The four-page manuscript appears to have been a draft for a letter to the *Cherokee Advocate* in response to a letter printed in the paper. However, a search of the *Advocate* has not disclosed which letter this manuscript refers to or that Bell's manuscript was ever submitted or printed. Evidence suggests that it was written in 1875 or 1876.

CHAPTER TWELVE

1. Daniel F. Littlefield, *The Cherokee Freedmen* (Westport, Conn.: Greenwood Press, 1978), pp. 78–80; William G. McLoughlin, *Champions of the Cherokees: Evan and John B. Jones* (Princeton: Princeton University Press, 1990), p. 425.

2. John B. Jones's report, September 1, 1872, in *Annual Report of the Commissioner of Indian Affairs* (Washington, D.C., 1873), p. 236; McLoughlin, *Evan and John B. Jones*, pp. 435–36. Throughout the 1870s, the Cherokees were spending from $50,000 to $60,000 annually on their public schools. See the report of John Tufts, October 10, 1880, in *Annual Report* (1881), p. 95. Tufts states that in 1880 the Cherokees spent $60,800 for their public schools.

3. *Cherokee Advocate*, May 9 and June 6, 1874.

4. John B. Jones's report, September 20, [1873], in *Annual Report* (1874), p. 204.

5. John B. Jones to Commissioner of Indian Affairs, February 10, 1873, Government Microfilm Series, Bureau of Indian Affairs, Record Group 75, M-234, Letters Received by the Office of Indian Affairs, 1824–1881, reel 106, 0183.

6. William P. Ross to Commissioner of Indian Affairs, March 8, 1873, M-234, reel 106, 0932.

7. For articles dealing with these problems regarding the orphan asylum, see *Cherokee Advocate*, May 9, 16, and 23, 1874.

8. *Cherokee Advocate*, December 26, 1874.

9. *Cherokee Advocate*, May 23, 1874. The last item probably refers to the desire of blacks for a share of the orphan funds and for a separate tract of land.

10. Emmeline Jones to John B. Jones, March 3, 1874, in Foreman Papers, Oklahoma Historical Society, Oklahoma City.

11. John B. Jones to Ely Parker, February 14, 1871, M-234, reel 104, 0671.

12. "To the Cherokee People," August 11, 1874, in Unprocessed papers, Western History Collection, University of Oklahoma, Norman. For the children's "sleeper claims," see *Cherokee Advocate*, March 28, 1874.

13. *Cherokee Advocate*, February 28, 1874, clipping in Litton Transcripts, Oklahoma Historical Society, Oklahoma City. For example, H. Craig Miner notes, "The

MK & T charged twelve cents a mile for passengers in the Cherokee Nation (vs. three to four cents in Missouri and Kansas) and similarly high freight rates, dashing forever the Indian hope that they were trading their privacy for the 'conveniences, privileges and profit' the railroad would provide." H. Craig Miner, *The Corporation and the Indian* (Columbia: University of Missouri Press, 1976), p. 52.

14. Emmet Starr, *History of the Cherokee Indians* (New York: Kraus Reprint, 1969), p. 263. Jack Kilpatrick and Anna Kilpatrick, *The Shadow of Sequoyah* (Norman: University of Oklahoma Press, 1965), gives Charles Thompson's Cherokee name as "Lichen" and his year of birth as around 1821 (p. 26, n. 4). He died in 1891.

15. John B. Jones to Commissioner of Indian Affairs, September 26, 1874, in Foreman Papers, Oklahoma Historical Society, Oklahoma City.

16. Ibid. See also Nancy Hope Sober, *The Intruders: The Illegal Residents of the Cherokee Nation, 1866–1907* (Ponca City, Okla.: Cherokee Books, 1991), pp. 42–63, 91–94.

17. The actual report submitted by Jones in 1874 was not printed verbatim in the *Annual Report* (1875) but is summarized there (pp. 48–49).

18. Markham was the lawyer hired by the Cherokees to conduct the case involving the Tahlequah Riot. He put in a claim for a large fee that, after some debate, the council agreed to pay.

19. Lipe·was a member of the Bell-Boudinot faction.

20. C. J. Hanks to John L. McCorkle, October 24, 1874, in Drew Papers, Gilcrease Institute, Tulsa, Oklahoma.

21. Morris Wardell, *A Political History of the Cherokee Nation, 1838–1907* (Norman: University of Oklahoma Press, 1938), p. 274.

22. Ibid., pp. 273–74. The Southern party, of course, gave no support to the bill. Joseph M. Lynch, a leader of the party, wrote to James M. Bell on February 18, 1875, "Everything is at a standstill in this country. The late white man [permit] law is a death blow to the [large] farmers and a great many farms will go to destruction for the want of labor." In Bell Papers, Western History Collection, University of Oklahoma, Norman.

23. "Platform of the National Party of the Cherokee Nation," November 23, 1874, in Unprocessed papers, Western History Collection, University of Oklahoma, Norman.

24. George W. Ingalls to Commissioner of Indian Affairs, December 16, 1874, M-234, reel 64, 0390. See also Ingalls's letter of November 27, 1874, M-234, reel 106, 0507.

25. This petition, dated September 7, 1874, is in Executive Documents, Western History Collection, University of Oklahoma, Norman.

26. Quoted in Grant Foreman, *A History of Oklahoma* (Norman: University of Oklahoma Press, 1942), p. 203; W. P. Adair et al. to G. W. Ingalls, February 1, 1875, M-234, reel 865, 0028. This was a request to the Cherokee delegation in Washington. The delegation claimed that $500,000 was needed. Adair's letter noted that the famine was increased by an extremely cold winter that killed many of the hogs and cattle. In a private letter written at this time, Adair, one of the wealthiest men in the Cherokee Nation, wrote that, in accordance with the traditional hospitality ethic, he felt obliged to feed any starving Cherokees who came to his door: "Our people are starving for bread. I feed great droves of them every day, and what little I have [left] will soon be gone."

27. E. R. Roberts to George W. Ingalls, April 9, 1875, M-234, reel 865, 0063.

28. G. W. Ingalls to E. P. Smith, January 2, 1875, M-234, reel 108, 0472. Ingalls evidently was not familiar with the name of the Downing party and occasionally referred to it in this letter as "the National Party." However, it is clear from the context that he was referring to the Downing party.

29. Ibid.

30. E. R. Roberts to G. W. Ingalls, January 7, 1875, M-234, reel 108, 0487.

31. E. R. Roberts to E. P. Smith, January 8, 1875, M-234, reel 108, 0488. See also E. R. Roberts to E. P. Smith, January 5, 1875, M-234, reel 108, 0492.

32. E. C. Boudinot to James M. Bell, January 6, 1875, in Bell Papers, Western History Collection, University of Oklahoma, Norman.

33. E. R. Roberts to E. P. Smith, January 8, 1875, M-234, reel 108, 0492.

34. E. R. Roberts to E. P. Smith, January 5 and 8, 1875, M-234, reel 108, 0488, 0492.

35. That Roberts did not have the whole story is evident from his own later corrections, particularly with regard to the alleged shooting of Alex Colston by "Wash" Mayes. He reported later that Mayes was killed outright by Cox and that Cox had admitted this just before he died of gunshot wounds. Roberts himself admitted, "It is very difficult to get at the exact facts as both parties tell entirely different stories and *swear to it.*" G. W. Ingalls to E. P. Smith, January 8, 1875, M-234, reel 108, 0478.

36. Dennis W. Bushyhead to G. W. Ingalls, January 13, 1875, M-234, reel 108, 0275.

37. W. P. Ross to G. W. Ingalls, January 13, 1875, M-234, reel 109, 2375.

38. *Cherokee Advocate*, January 16, 1875.

39. General John Pope to Columbus Delano, January 30, 1875, M-234, reel 108, 2355.

40. G. W. Ingalls to Zechariah Chandler, January 12, 1876, M-234, reel 865, 0552. This was written at the time Ingalls was in Washington to answer charges that he had meddled in Cherokee political affairs in early 1875.

41. G. W. Ingalls to E. P. Smith, July 16, 1875, M-234, reel 108, 0676.

42. The troops were sent to guard against unruly behavior at the time of the distribution of $500,000 in "bread money" to the Cherokees but left soon afterward. E. R. Roberts to G. W. Ingalls, April 21, 1875, M-234, reel 108, 0575.

43. D. H. Ross to D. W. Bushyhead, July 24, 1875, in Bell Papers, Western History Collection, University of Oklahoma, Norman.

44. G. W. Ingalls to Commissioner of Indian Affairs, July 22, 1875, M-234, reel 108, 0687.

45. G. W. Ingalls to Commissioner of Indian Affairs, July 27, 1875, M-234, reel 108, 0721.

46. Sarah C. Watie to James M. Bell, July 4, 1875, in Bell Papers, Western History Collection, University of Oklahoma, Norman.

47. G. W. Ingalls to E. P. Smith, July 30, 1875, M-234, reel 108, 0748. There is some doubt that Fields was a Downing man.

48. Ibid.

49. G. W. Ingalls to Zechariah Chandler, January 12, 1876, M-234, reel 865, 0552, 0561.

50. G. W. Ingalls to E. P. Smith, October 11, 1875, M-234, reel 108, 0813. Ingalls wrote, "Both sides claim to have carried the election."

51. B. R. Cowen to G. W. Ingalls, M-234, reel 108, 0822. Cowen was responding to the letter from Ingalls to E. P. Smith, October 11, 1875, M-234, reel 108, 0813. For Ross's response to Cowen, see his letter of October 19, 1875, M-234, reel 108, 0829. Ross seems to have found General G. P. C. Shanks at Fort Gibson very sympathetic to his position in this affair.

52. W. P. Ross to B. R. [Cowen], October 19, 1875, M-234, reel 108, 0829.

53. G. W. Ingalls to Zechariah Chandler, January 12, 1876, 0552–61.

54. Ibid.

55. See Cherokee Nation Records, reel 10, 0055–0277, Oklahoma Historical Society, Oklahoma City, for the tabulations and the challenges to the voting results in several districts. The council finally ruled that Oochalata received 1,789 votes and Ross received 1,778 votes. Oochalata was officially installed on November 26, 1875.

56. For the charges against Ingalls and his defense, see M-234, reel 865, 0552–87 (January 12, 1876).

CHAPTER THIRTEEN

1. Cherokee Nation Records, November 1876, reel 11, 0044, Oklahoma Historical Society, Oklahoma City. Oochalata's messages and other reports were translated into English by W. L. G. Miller, who acted, as he had for Lewis Downing, as executive secretary to the chief.

2. Ibid. Only one-third of the Cherokee Nation was considered fit for agriculture. Nancy Hope Sober, *The Intruders: The Illegal Residents of the Cherokee Nation, 1866–1907* (Ponca City, Okla.: Cherokee Books, 1991), p. 62.

3. Cherokee Nation Records, November 1878, reel 12, 0819, Oklahoma Historical Society, Oklahoma City.

4. Ibid.

5. Ibid.

6. This letter appeared in the *Cherokee Advocate*, October 1878, typescript in the T. L. Ballenger Collection, Northeastern Oklahoma State University, Tahlequah.

7. Howard Q. Tyner, "The Keetoowah Society in Cherokee History" (Master's thesis, University of Tulsa, 1949), p. 115. Katja May states that upon this reorganization, the Keetoowahs resolved that "the intention is . . . we should not become citizens of the United States." Katja May, "The Cherokee Nation's Political and Cultural Struggle for Independence," *Journal of Cherokee Studies* 11 (Spring 1886): 31.

8. This unsigned letter written on [November] 24, 1876, is in Bell Papers, Western History Collection, University of Oklahoma, Norman.

9. *Cherokee Advocate*, March 11, 1876, clipping in Litton Transcripts, Oklahoma Historical Society, Oklahoma City. E. C. Boudinot did not share this view. He wrote that "the two Adairs, elected to represent the Thompson or Downing party [as delegates,] are striving to have [W. P. Ross,] the plunderer of his people and the cause of bloodshed among the Cherokees[,] appointed U.S. Agent for the five tribes." Boudinot was convinced "that Col. Ross is answerable for the large number of murders in the country" over the past three years. *Cherokee Advocate*, March 1, 1876, clipping in Litton Transcripts, Oklahoma Historical Society, Oklahoma City.

10. *Cherokee Advocate*, March 11, 1876. Some have said Ross was not appointed because he was not a citizen of the United States, but that fact surely was known when Grant suggested him.

11. Journals of the legislature for 1875, Cherokee Nation Records, vol. 268, pp. 11, 63–65, Oklahoma Historical Society, Oklahoma City.

12. *Cherokee Advocate*, April 8, 1876.

13. *Star Vindicator*, November 17, 1877, clipping in Litton Transcripts, Oklahoma Historical Society, Oklahoma City.

14. *Star Vindicator*, November 22 and December 1, 1877, clippings in Litton Transcripts, Oklahoma Historical Society, Oklahoma City.

15. Ibid.

16. J. Q. Smith's report, in *Annual Report of the Commissioner of Indian Affairs* (Washington, D.C., 1876), p. xii.

17. Morris Wardell, *A Political History of the Cherokee Nation, 1838–1907* (Norman: University of Oklahoma Press, 1938), p. 296.

18. Minutes of the Executive Council Meeting, July 3, 1877, Cherokee Nation Records, reel 9, 0181, Oklahoma Historical Society, Oklahoma City. The use of the words "race and country" indicates a new terminology in Cherokee nationalism and points up the growing sense of "race" awareness and ethnic nationalism among minorities in the United States in these years.

19. Pan-Indian councils among the major tribes did continue to meet sporadically in these years to express opposition to territorial bills.

20. *Cherokee Advocate*, January 16, 1875. This bill also set fines of $500 to $1,000 for infringements of the law. For a summary of the various permit laws, see Sober, *Intruders*, pp. 28–30.

21. Wardell, *Political History*, p. 275. This law was modeled on one passed by the Chickasaw Nation on October 17, 1876. See *Star Vindicator*, March 3, 1887, clipping in Ballenger Transcripts, Oklahoma Historical Society, Oklahoma City.

22. Cherokee Nation Records, December 1, 1877, vol. 270, reel 11, Oklahoma Historical Society, Oklahoma City.

23. The bill is printed in the *Cherokee Advocate*, December 23, 1878.

24. Wardell, *Political History*, p. 275. See also E. A. Hayt to W. G. Robinson, January 20, 1879, in which he notes that at this time anyone seeking a white labor permit "must furnish satisfactory testimonials of unexceptionable character and fitness to be in the Indian Country," in Unprocessed papers, Western History Collection, University of Oklahoma, Norman.

25. Wardell, *Political History*, p. 275.

26. Cherokee Nation Records, November 1876, reel 11, 0044, Oklahoma Historical Society, Oklahoma City.

27. Ibid.

28. Cherokee Nation Records, November 13, 1877, reel 12, 0784–90, Oklahoma Historical Society, Oklahoma City.

29. Wardell, *Political History*, p. 300; *Cherokee Advocate*, November 23, 1878.

30. Cherokee Nation Records, reel 12, 0819–49, Oklahoma Historical Society, Oklahoma City.

31. Bushyhead's speech was printed in *Indian Journal* (Muskogee, Oklahoma),

July 31, 1879, clipping in Litton Transcripts, Oklahoma Historical Society, Oklahoma City.

32. Cherokee Nation Records, November 1878, reel 12, 0819, Oklahoma Historical Society, Oklahoma City.

33. Daniel F. Littlefield, *The Cherokee Freedmen* (Westport, Conn.: Greenwood Press, 1978), p. 85; Sober, *Intruders*, pp. 44, 92–93.

34. Littlefield, *Cherokee Freedmen*, pp. 86–89; Sober, *Intruders*, p. 45.

35. Littlefield, *Cherokee Freedmen*, p. 86.

36. Sober, *Intruders*, p. 94; Littlefield, *Cherokee Freedmen*, p. 89.

37. Sober, *Intruders*, p. 94; Littlefield, *Cherokee Freedmen*, pp. 87–88.

38. Sober, *Intruders*, pp. 95–96.

39. Littlefield, *Cherokee Freedmen*, p. 77. For the various inconsistencies in the approach of the Cherokee courts to the admission of former slaves and intermarried whites to citizenship in the years 1866 to 1879, see ibid., pp. 75–102. See also Sober, *Intruders*, chap. 5.

40. Littlefield, *Cherokee Freedmen*, p. 89.

41. Ibid.; Sober, *Intruders*, p. 95.

42. Littlefield, *Cherokee Freedmen*, p. 90.

43. Cherokee Nation Records, November 13, 1877, reel 12, 0784–90, Oklahoma Historical Society, Oklahoma City.

44. Littlefield, *Cherokee Freedmen*, pp. 90–91; Sober, *Intruders*, pp. 33–34, 48.

45. Littlefield, *Cherokee Freedmen*, p. 92. This statement was made by C. W. Holcomb, commissioner of Indian affairs, on February 28, 1878.

46. Ibid., p. 94.

47. Ibid.

48. Ibid., pp. 95–96.

49. Sober, *Intruders*, p. 49.

50. See E. A. Hayt to Secretary of the Interior, April 4, 1879, in Unprocessed papers, Western History Collection, University of Oklahoma, Norman, and Sober, *Intruders*, p. 49.

51. See Charles Devens to Carl Schurz, December 12, 1879, in Unprocessed papers, Western History Collection, University of Oklahoma, Norman.

52. Ibid. See also Sober, *Intruders*, pp. 49, 97.

53. Wardell, *Political History*, p. 300.

54. Ibid., p. 303.

55. *Cherokee Advocate*, March 11, 1876.

56. Wardell, *Political History*, pp. 297–98.

57. Lois Forde, "Elias Cornelius Boudinot" (Ph.D. diss., Columbia University, 1951), pp. 175–77; *Oklahoma Star*, April 18, 1876; Wardell, *Political History*, pp. 298–99; *Cherokee Advocate*, April 18, 1877.

58. Jeff J. Hibbetts to James M. Bell, July 23, 1874, in Bell Papers, Western History Collection, University of Oklahoma, Norman.

59. See Wardell, *Political History*, pp. 302–4, and W. M. Leeds to Charles Thompson (Oochalata), in Executive Documents, Western History Collection, University of Oklahoma, Norman.

60. Wardell, *Political History*, p. 304.

61. Committee of Safety to James Bell, Esq., September 12, 1881, in Bell Papers, Western History Collection, University of Oklahoma, Norman.

62. See Francis P. Prucha, *The Great Father*, 2 vols. (Lincoln: University of Nebraska Press, 1984), 2:659–86.

EPILOGUE

1. Morris Wardell, *A Political History of the Cherokee Nation, 1838–1907* (Norman: University of Oklahoma Press, 1938), p. 311. For a summary of the final days of Cherokee sovereignty, see Francis P. Prucha, *The Great Father*, 2 vols. (Lincoln: University of Nebraska Press, 1984), 2:661–79, 746–54.

2. Wardell, *Political History*, p. 317.

3. See ibid., p. 313.

4. Charles G. Royce, *The Cherokee Nation of Indians* (Chicago: Aldine, 1975), p. 90.

5. Wardell, *Political History*, p. 314.

6. Clyde A. Milner II and Floyd A. O'Neil, eds., *Churchmen and the Western Indian, 1820–1920* (Norman: University of Oklahoma Press, 1985), p. 154. See also Robert W. Mardock, *The Reformers and the American Indian* (Columbia: University of Missouri Press, 1971), and Francis P. Prucha, *American Indian Policy in Crisis* (Norman: University of Oklahoma Press, 1976).

7. Milner and O'Neil, *Churchmen*, p. 161.

8. All of the quotations from Francis Wayland that follow are taken from his *The Elements of Political Economy* (Boston: Gould and Lincoln, 1852).

9. *Appeal of the Delegates of the Chickasaw, Creek and Cherokee Nations to the President of the United States* [1887], in Unprocessed papers, Western History Collection, University of Oklahoma, Norman.

10. For the Keetoowah resistance to allotment, see Emmet Starr, *History of the Cherokee Indians* (New York: Kraus Reprint, 1969), pp. 480–82; Howard Q. Tyner, "The Keetoowah Society in Cherokee History" (Master's thesis, University of Tulsa, 1949); and Janey B. Hendrix, "Redbird Smith and the Nighthawk Keetoowahs," *Journal of Cherokee Studies* 8 (Spring 1983): 22–40.

11. John B. Jones's report, September 1, 1872, in *Annual Report of the Commissioner of Indian Affairs* (Washington, D.C., 1873), p. 237.

12. For the complex details of the negotiations with the thirty different tribes in the Indian Territory for the sale of their land, its surveying, its allocation to tribal members, and the settlement of whites on the "surplus" lands in each of the former Indian nations between 1885 and 1906, see Grant Foreman, *A History of Oklahoma* (Norman: University of Oklahoma Press, 1942), pp. 238–317.

13. Ibid., p. 251. The Cherokees had claimed they had title to the land and could lease it because the government had required that tribes settling on these lands pay the Cherokee Nation for the privilege, but the attorney general said Cherokee title did not apply to leasing land to whites, only selling to resettled tribes. The fact that the government had permitted the leases for a decade indicates clearly that the decision

was an effort to force the sale of the Outlet by denying the Cherokees the right to profit from its use.

14. The Outlet contained 6,574,486.55 acres, of which 230,014.44 had been assigned to the Pawnees, 129,113.20 to the Otoes and Missouris, 101,894.31 to the Poncas, and 90,710.89 to the Nez Perce, later given to the Tonkawas. The government negotiated cessions from all these tribes, allotted their land in severalty, and opened the remainder to whites. Ibid., p. 252.

15. Prucha, *American Indian Policy*, p. 399; Wardell, *Political History*, pp. 316–20; Foreman, *Oklahoma*, pp. 295–303.

16. Wardell, *Political History*, p. 320; Foreman, *Oklahoma*, p. 295; Prucha, *American Indian Policy*, pp. 399–400. The Choctaws and Chickasaws received 320 acres apiece; the Seminoles, 120. For details of the final days of the Cherokee Nation, see Wardell, *Political History*, pp. 320–49; Foreman, *Oklahoma*, pp. 295–317; Nancy Hope Sober, *The Intruders: The Illegal Residents of the Cherokee Nation, 1866–1907* (Ponca City, Okla.: Cherokee Books, 1991), pp. 127–34; and Prucha, *American Indian Policy*, pp. 382–401. For the resistance of the Keetoowah full-bloods, see Starr, *History*, pp. 479–82. The census compiled for allotment of land to the Cherokee Nation by the Dawes Commission contained the names of 41,798 Cherokees, of whom 8,698 were considered full-bloods (based on biology, not on the Cherokee definition of a full-blood as one who speaks only Cherokee). In this group was included 197 Delawares, 286 intermarried whites, and 4,305 former slaves or their descendants. Wardell, *Political History*, p. 333. When Oklahoma became a state in 1907, there were 71,000 Indian citizens and over 400,000 whites. In no area were the Indians sufficiently numerous to elect Indians to sit in the state legislature without white support, which was almost never given. Black citizens (former slaves of Indians or their descendants) were quickly subject to Jim Crow laws and lost the right to vote. In 1892 and again in 1908, hundreds of blacks left Oklahoma for Africa. For a detailed study of the back-to-Africa movement among former slaves of Indians, see William Bittle and Gilbert Geis, *The Longest Way Home* (Detroit: Wayne State University Press, 1964).

17. See Starr, *History*, p. 480; Grace Woodward, *The Cherokees* (Norman: University of Oklahoma Press, 1963), p. 322; and Angie Debo, *And Still the Waters Run* (Princeton: Princeton University Press, 1972), pp. 45–46.

18. E. P. Smith's report, November 1, 1873, in *Annual Report* (1874), p. 3. Smith said that even the most "civilized" Indians were reluctant to receive the "qualified citizenship" that he thought they could have, while "pride of nationality, dread of competition with the enterprise of the white man . . . cause this hesitation among the mass of the less educated. . . . Both classes appeal most strenuously to the letter of their treaties which requires the United States to protect them as sovereignties forever." This he found preposterous. Ibid., p. 6.

19. Spencer S. Stephens, *The Indian Question* (1882), pp. 32–33, in Unprocessed papers, Western History Collection, University of Oklahoma, Norman.

20. Ganenulisgi to Oochalata (Utsaledv), March 9, 1877, translation in Jack Kilpatrick and Anna Kilpatrick, *The Shadow of Sequoyah* (Norman: University of Oklahoma Press, 1965), pp. 26–28.

21. Anne Bell Shelton to Sarah Watie, October 6, 1873, in Watie Papers, Western History Collection, University of Oklahoma, Norman.

22. Anne Bell Shelton to Sarah Watie, February 19, 1877, in Watie Papers, Western History Collection, University of Oklahoma, Norman.

23. Anne Bell Shelton to Sarah Watie, August 27, 1876, in Watie Papers, Western History Collection, University of Oklahoma, Norman. Shelton's hope that somehow the Indians "could be cut off in a moment" from all contact with whites reflected the same hope for divine intervention to save their people that inspired the tremendous explosion of the Ghost Dance religion among the Plains Indians from 1872 to 1890.

24. Russell Thornton, *The Cherokees: A Population History* (Lincoln: University of Nebraska Press, 1990), p. 163. There are about 300 federally recognized tribes in the United States today.

Index

101–2; and education policy, 87–88, 94–95; and Methodists, 137, 144; supports neutrality, 168–75, 177–81; treaty with Confederacy, 182–91; criticized by Stephen Foreman, 196; captured by Union troops, 206; talks with Lincoln, 206; in Washington, D.C., 216–21; death of, 227–28

Ross, Lewis, 21, 78, 130, 135, 138, 152

Ross, William P., 144, 181, 211, 221, 229–30, 245–48, 274–75, 289, 313, 315, 319, 333, 335, 339, 344, 365

Ross party. *See* Patriot party

Round Mountain, battle of, 194

Schermerhorn, John, 15

Schurz, Carl, 357, 359, 360

Sequoyah, 7, 14, 18, 19, 20

Shoal Creek (or Chustenalah), battle of, 194

Slavery: among the Cherokees, 39, 71, 77, 81, 112, 121–52, 166–68; slave codes, 127–28; slave revolts, 134–36; emancipation, 208–9

Slover, James G., 148–49, 179–80

Smith, J. Q., 346–47, 355–56

Social Darwinism, 370, 380

Southern party (after Civil War), 223–26, 228–29, 245–48

Southern Rights party (before Civil War), 125, 145, 159, 164, 172–74, 178–80, 185–86, 192

Spencer, John C., 32, 40–41, 106

Starr, James, 16, 41

Starr gang, 42, 44–45, 49–55, 57

Stokes, Montfort, 13–20, 26–29, 97

Tahlequah, 81, 256

Tahlequah Council (1861), 182–83

Tahlequah Riot (1874), 301–2

Takatoka Council (1839), 10–14

Taney, Roger B., 106–7

Taylor, Nathaniel G., 249

Taylor, Richard, 14–15, 132

Taylor, Zachary, 45

Teele, Edwin, 93, 121, 124

Territorialization problems, 87, 96–97, 117–20, 217, 227, 274–80, 290, 292, 344, 346–47, 355, 360–64

Tobacco manufacturing, 265–66

Toostoo (Spring Frog), 208, 323

Torrey, Charles C., 72, 124, 133, 145–47, 150, 161

Trade and Intercourse Act, 67, 104, 108, 113, 284, 354, 357, 360

Trading licenses, 97–100, 227

Trail of Tears, 2–3, 7–9, 22, 35, 39, 46

Treaty of 1846, 57–58, 59–61, 78

Treaty of 1861, 189–90, 198

Treaty of 1866, 226–27, 258, 265, 266, 268, 299, 358

Treaty of New Echota (1835), 2, 4, 10–11, 20, 25, 56–57, 60

Treaty party. *See* Removal party

Tyler, John, 30–32, 40, 46–48

Underground railroad: among Cherokees, 136

Union army: Indian regiments, 203, 208

Upham, Willard, 90, 94, 162

Van Buren, Martin, 2, 20

Vann, Joseph, 21, 23, 26, 29–30, 44, 181, 207

Walker, Robert J., 111, 112, 119

Washbourne, J. Woodward, 155, 167, 177, 224–25

Watie, Stand, 13, 16, 19, 20, 42, 50, 53–55, 145, 155, 159, 221, 223, 231, 246–48, 265, 274, 307; serves in Confederate army, 175, 181–82, 187, 204, 207, 210–16

Watie party, 155, 159–61, 167, 180, 185, 189, 214, 231

Wayland, Francis, 369–70, 376

Webber's Falls, 180–81

Weer, William, 203–5

Western Cherokees. *See* Old Settlers

This powerful narrative

traces the social, cultural, and political history of the Cherokee Nation during the forty-year period after its members were forcibly removed from the southern Appalachians and resettled in what is now Oklahoma. In this master work, completed just before his death, William McLoughlin not only explains how the Cherokees rebuilt their lives and society, but also recounts their fight to govern themselves as a separate nation within the borders of the United States.

Long regarded by whites as one of the "civilized" tribes, the Cherokees had their own constitution (modeled after that of the United States), elected officials, and legal system. Once resettled, they attempted to reestablish these institutions and continued their long struggle for self-government under their own laws—an idea that met with bitter opposition from frontier politicians, settlers, ranchers, and business leaders.

From 1846 to 1861 the nation enjoyed a rebirth of its economic and political stability. But with the coming of the Civil War, the nation split over the issue of slavery, which the Cherokees and other southeastern tribes had adopted in the late eighteenth century as part of the acculturation process. When the war broke out, Lincoln failed to support the majority faction favoring the Union, and the